Taste of Home · Reader's Digest

EDITORIAL

Editor-in-Chief: Catherine Cassidy
Creative Director: Howard Greenberg
Editorial Operations Director: Kerri Balliet

Managing Editor, Print and Digital Books: Mark Hagen
Associate Creative Director: Edwin Robles Jr.

Editor: Janet Briggs
Associate Editor: Ellie Martin Cliffe
Contributing Art Director: Jessie Sharon
Layout Designer: Catherine Fletcher
Contributing Layout Designer: Holly Patch
Editorial Production Manager: Dena Ahlers
Copy Chief: Deb Warlaumont Mulvey
Copy Editors: Mary C. Hanson, Alysse Gear
Content Operations Manager: Colleen King
Executive Assistant: Marie Brannon

Chief Food Editor: Karen Berner
Food Editors: James Schend; Peggy Woodward, RD
Associate Food Editor: Krista Lanphier
Associate Editor/Food Content: Annie Rundle
Recipe Editors: Mary King; Jenni Sharp, RD; Irene Yeh

Test Kitchen and Food Styling Manager: Sarah Thompson
Test Kitchen Cooks: Alicia Rooker, RD (lead); Holly Johnson; Jimmy Cababa
Prep Cooks: Matthew Hass (lead); Nicole Spohrleder, Lauren Knoelke
Food Stylists: Kathryn Conrad (senior), Shannon Roum, Leah Rekau

Photographers: Dan Roberts, Jim Wieland
Photographer/Set Stylist: Grace Natoli Sheldon
Set Styling Manager: Stephanie Marchese
Set Stylists: Melissa Haberman, Dee Dee Jacq

BUSINESS

Vice President, Publisher: Jan Studin, jan_studin@rd.com

General Manager, Taste of Home Cooking Schools: Erin Puariea

Vice President, Brand Marketing: Jennifer Smith
Vice President, Circulation and Continuity Marketing: Dave Fiegel

READER'S DIGEST NORTH AMERICA

Vice President, Business Development: Jonathan Bigham
President, Books and Home Entertaining: Harold Clarke
Chief Financial Officer: Howard Halligan
VP, General Manager, Reader's Digest Media: Marilynn Jacobs
Chief Marketing Officer: Renee Jordan
Vice President, Chief Sales Officer: Mark Josephson
Vice President, General Manager, Milwaukee: Frank Quigley
Vice President, Chief Content Officer: Liz Vaccariello

THE READER'S DIGEST ASSOCIATION, INC.

President and Chief Executive Officer: Robert E. Guth

For other Taste of Home books and products, visit us at **tasteofhome.com**.

For more Reader's Digest products and information, visit **rd.com** (in the United States) or see **rd.ca** (in Canada).

International Standard Book Number: 978-1-61765-152-6
Library of Congress Control Number: 2013931309

Pictured on front cover (clockwise from left):
Southern Fried Chicken, page 144; Mexican Carnitas, page 338; Country Fish Chowder, page 54; and Oregon's Best Marionberry Pie, page 462.

Pictured on spine: German Black Forest Cake, page 271

Pictured on back cover (top to bottom): Hungarian Hot Dogs, page 224; Crunchy-Coated Walleye, page 207; and It's It Ice Cream Sandwiches, page 464.

Printed in China.
1 3 5 7 9 10 8 6 4 2

Contents

f **LIKE US**
facebook.com/tasteofhome

VISIT OUR BLOG
loveandhomemaderecipes.com

E-MAIL US
bookeditors@tasteofhome.com

TWEET US
@tasteofhome

SHOP WITH US
shoptasteofhome.com

FOLLOW US
pinterest.com/taste_of_home

SHARE A RECIPE
tasteofhome.com/submit

VISIT
tasteofhome.com
FOR
MORE!

Chicago Deep-Dish Pizza,
page 210

CHICAGO, IL

'As *American* as Apple Pie'

We've all heard those words and have probably enjoyed juicy slices of that **delectable dessert**, but **apple pie** is just the tip of the **American culinary** "iceberg."

Whether sinking your teeth into crispy Southern Fried Chicken, enjoying a Philly Cheese Steak or sampling a slice of Ozark Mountain Berry Pie, you simply can't beat the comfort of iconic American foods. Now, it's easier than ever to relish the flavors of our country with **Taste of Home Recipes Across America.** This keepsake collection is packed with **more than 730 recipes...dishes shared by family cooks in all 50 states**!

You'll take an armchair tour of the country with all-time classics such as Chicago Deep-Dish Pizza, Creole Jambalaya and Chocolate Texas Sheet Cake. In addition, this colorful collection offers dozens of little-known regional gems, including Mom's Dynamite Sandwiches, Brooklyn Blackout

STURBRIDGE, MA

BLACK HILLS, SD

Cake, Horseshoe Sandwiches and even Kool-Aid Pickles.

America's home cooks have always been clever. They borrowed their mother's recipes, substituted a few local ingredients and created tasty dishes that became **ingrained in the local culture**. The five regions (Northeast, South, Midwest, Southwest and West) showcased in Recipes Across America offer a delectable variety of foods from each area. You'll find everything from **quick supper ideas to impressive desserts**...each of which left a delicious mark on its part of the USA!

In addition, this more-than-a-cookbook treasury is also peppered with **hundreds of food facts, culinary trivia and snapshots of popular landmarks and food festivals** throughout the country.

With Recipes Across America it's a snap to **savor all the tastes** the USA has to offer without ever leaving your home!

" This fruit pie brimming with apples and pears really says fall. What a yummy way to use your backyard bounty or the pickings from local orchards! I've made plenty of pies over the years, and this is a real standout. "

—GRACE CAMP
OWINGSVILLE, KENTUCKY

Apple Pear Pie, page 179

Northeast

Get ready for a tour of flavor! From Maine lobsters to New Jersey hot dogs, the Northeast offers a wealth of tastes that will satisfy everyone in your home. Enjoy blue crab from Maryland, pizza from New York and all of the blueberry and cranberry delights this region has to offer. Whether you like to sink your teeth into a sub sandwich or treat friends to a clambake, the foods in this part of the country offer a little something for everyone!

The Portuguese-American Club holds its annual Feast of the Holy Ghost on Martha's Vineyard on the third weekend in July. A local custom since 1942, it honors the original celebration started by Portugal's Queen Isabel in the 13th century. The event features traditional dances, music and food. Cacoila is a popular mainstay at the festival.

MARTHA'S VINEYARD, MA

The Gay Head, or Aquinnah, Lighthouse shines in the fog.

Spicy Slow-Cooked Portuguese Cacoila

You're probably used to pulled pork coated with barbecue sauce and made into sandwiches. Portuguese pulled pork is a spicy dish often served at our large family functions. Each cook generally adds his or her own touches that reflect their taste and Portuguese heritage. A mixture of beef roast and pork can be used.

—**MICHELE MERLINO** EXETER, RHODE ISLAND

PREP: 20 MIN. **COOK:** 6 HOURS **MAKES:** 12 SERVINGS

4 **pounds boneless pork shoulder butt roast, cut into 2-inch pieces**
1½ **cups dry red wine or reduced-sodium chicken broth**
4 **garlic cloves, minced**
4 **bay leaves**
1 **tablespoon salt**
1 **tablespoon paprika**
2 **to 3 teaspoons crushed red pepper flakes**
1 **teaspoon ground cinnamon**
1 **large onion, chopped**
½ **cup water**
12 **bolillos or hoagie buns, split, optional**

1. Place pork in a large resealable bag; add wine, garlic and seasonings. Seal bag and turn to coat. Refrigerate overnight.

2. Transfer pork mixture to a 5- or 6-qt. slow cooker; add onion and water. Cook, covered, on low 6-8 hours or until meat is tender.

3. Skim fat. Remove bay leaves. Shred meat with two forks. If desired, serve with a slotted spoon on bolillos.

Coquilles St. Jacques

Buttery scallops in rich, creamy sauce would be tough to share...but if you must share, just double the recipe.

—BETSY ESLEY LAKE ALFRED, FLORIDA

PREP/TOTAL TIME: 30 MIN. **MAKES:** 1 SERVING

- 6 **ounces bay scallops**
- 3 **tablespoons white wine or chicken broth**
- 2 **teaspoons butter**
- ¼ **teaspoon dried minced onion**
- 1½ **teaspoons all-purpose flour**
- ¼ **cup heavy whipping cream**
- 3 **tablespoons shredded cheddar cheese**

TOPPING
- 4 **teaspoons dry bread crumbs**
- 1 **teaspoon butter, melted**
  Paprika

1. In a small skillet, combine scallops, wine, butter and onion. Bring to a boil. Reduce heat; cover and simmer for 1-2 minutes or until scallops are firm and opaque. Using a slotted spoon, remove scallops and keep warm.

2. Bring poaching liquid to a boil; cook until liquid is reduced to about 2 tablespoons, about 3 minutes. Stir in flour until smooth; gradually add cream. Bring to a boil; cook and stir for 1 minute or until thickened. Remove from the heat. Add cheese, stirring until melted. Return scallops to skillet. Pour into a greased 6-oz. ramekin or custard cup.

3. In a small bowl, combine bread crumbs and butter; sprinkle over top. Sprinkle with the paprika. Bake, uncovered, at 400° for 4-5 minutes or until golden brown.

Burgundy Lamb Shanks

For those who love fall-from-the-bone lamb, this recipe fills the bill. Burgundy wine adds a special touch to the sauce that's served alongside the meat.

—F. W. CREUTZ SOUTHOLD, NEW YORK

PREP: 10 MIN. **COOK:** 8¼ HOURS **MAKES:** 4 SERVINGS

- 4 **lamb shanks (about 20 ounces each)**
  Salt and pepper to taste
- 2 **tablespoons dried parsley flakes**
- 2 **teaspoons minced garlic**
- ½ **teaspoon dried oregano**
- ½ **teaspoon grated lemon peel**
- ½ **cup chopped onion**
- 1 **medium carrot, chopped**
- 1 **teaspoon olive oil**
- 1 **cup Burgundy wine or beef broth**
- 1 **teaspoon beef bouillon granules**

1. Sprinkle lamb with salt and pepper. Place in a 5-qt. slow cooker. Sprinkle with the parsley, garlic, oregano and lemon peel.

2. In a small saucepan, saute onion and carrot in oil for 3-4 minutes or until tender. Stir in wine and bouillon. Bring to a boil, stirring occasionally. Pour over lamb. Cover and cook on low for 8 hours or until meat is tender.

3. Remove lamb and keep warm. Strain cooking juices and skim fat. In a small saucepan, bring juices to a boil; cook until liquid is reduced by half. Serve with lamb.

NEW YORK, NY

For more than 20 million immigrants between 1892 and 1924, the Port of New York at Ellis Island was the first American soil they'd touch. The museum opened its doors in 1990, and more than 20 million people have visited since.

THE PALISADES

With stark cliffs rising above the west bank of the Hudson River, the Palisades are a sight to behold. Palisades Interstate Park was formed in 1900 and runs from Fort Lee, New Jersey, to Palisades, New York.

Jersey-Style Hot Dogs

I grew up in northern New Jersey, where this way of eating hot dogs was created. My husband never had them as a kid but has come to love them even more than me. The combination of ingredients and flavors is simple, but just right!

—SUZANNE BANFIELD BASKING RIDGE, NEW JERSEY

PREP: 20 MIN. **GRILL:** 40 MIN.
MAKES: 12 SERVINGS (10 CUPS POTATO MIXTURE)

- 6 medium Yukon Gold potatoes (about 3 pounds), halved and thinly sliced
- 3 large sweet red peppers, thinly sliced
- 3 large onions, peeled, halved and thinly sliced
- ⅓ cup olive oil
- 2 tablespoons minced garlic
- 3 teaspoons salt
- 1½ teaspoons pepper
- 12 bun-length beef hot dogs
- 12 hot dog buns, split

1. In a large bowl, combine potatoes, red peppers and onions. In a small bowl, combine oil, garlic, salt and pepper; add to the potato mixture and toss to coat. Transfer to a 13x9-in. disposable foil pan; cover with foil. Place pan on grill rack over medium heat; cook, covered, 30-35 minutes or until potatoes are tender. Remove from heat.

2. Grill hot dogs, covered, over medium heat 7-9 minutes or until heated through, turning occasionally. Place buns on grill, cut side down; grill until lightly toasted. Serve hot dogs with buns, topping each with ½ cup potato mixture. Serve with remaining potato mixture.

Antipasto Sub

One night instead of setting out sandwiches with antipasto on the side, I combined the two. A zesty sandwich piled high with flavor, it was a big hit with my friends.

—JEANETTE HIOS BROOKLYN, NEW YORK

PREP: 15 MIN. + CHILLING **MAKES:** 10-12 SERVINGS

- 1 loaf (1 pound) unsliced Italian bread
- 3 cans (2½ ounces each) sliced ripe olives, drained
- 3 jars (6½ ounces each) marinated artichoke hearts, drained
- 1 jar (16 ounces) roasted sweet red pepper strips, drained
- 8 ounces provolone cheese, thinly sliced
- ¾ pound thickly sliced salami
- 3 tablespoons olive oil
- 3 tablespoons cider vinegar
- ½ teaspoon garlic powder
- ½ teaspoon Italian seasoning
- ¼ teaspoon salt
- ¼ teaspoon pepper

1. Cut bread in half lengthwise; hollow out top, leaving a 1½-in. shell. (Discard removed bread or save for another use.) Invert bread top; layer with olives, artichokes, red pepper, cheese and salami. Replace bread bottom. Wrap tightly in plastic wrap; refrigerate.

2. In a jar with a tight-fitting lid, combine the remaining ingredients; shake well. Refrigerate. Cut sub into slices; serve with the dressing.

Editor's Note: *This recipe was tested with Vlasic roasted red pepper strips.*

Beef Stew with Sesame Seed Biscuits

PREP: 20 MIN. + SIMMERING **BAKE:** 30 MIN. **MAKES:** 5 SERVINGS

1 pound beef stew meat, cut into 1-inch cubes
2 tablespoons olive oil
1½ cups chopped onions
1 cup chopped celery
1 garlic clove, minced
1 tablespoon all-purpose flour
1½ cups water
1 cup diced tomatoes
½ cup Burgundy wine or beef broth
⅓ cup tomato paste
1 tablespoon sugar
¾ teaspoon salt
½ teaspoon Worcestershire sauce
¼ teaspoon pepper
2 cups cubed peeled potatoes
2 cups sliced fresh carrots
1 can (4 ounces) mushroom stems and pieces, drained
¼ cup sour cream

SESAME SEED BISCUITS

1¼ cups all-purpose flour
2 teaspoons baking powder
½ teaspoon salt
¼ cup shortening
¾ cup sour cream
2 tablespoons 2% milk
1 tablespoon sesame seeds

1. In a Dutch oven, brown the beef in oil in batches. Remove and keep warm. In the same pan, saute onions and celery until tender. Add garlic; cook 1 minute longer.

2. Stir in flour until blended. Gradually add the water; stir in the tomatoes, wine, tomato paste, sugar, salt, Worcestershire sauce, pepper and beef. Bring to a boil. Reduce heat; cover and simmer for 1¼ hours.

3. Add potatoes and carrots; cook for 30-45 minutes longer or until the beef and vegetables are tender. Stir in mushrooms and sour cream. Transfer to a greased 13x9-in. baking dish.

4. For biscuits, in a bowl, combine the flour, baking powder and salt. Cut in shortening until mixture resembles coarse crumbs. Stir in sour cream just until moistened.

5. Turn onto a lightly floured surface; knead 8-10 times. Roll out to ½-in. thickness; cut with a floured 2-in. biscuit cutter. Brush with milk; sprinkle with sesame seeds. Arrange over stew.

6. Bake at 400° for 30-35 minutes or until biscuits are golden brown.

> " Comfort food, warm and hearty, is what this dinner is all about. It has it all... homemade biscuits, tender meat and an assortment of veggies. "

—LINDA BACCI
LIVONIA, NEW YORK

Pat Olivieri of Pat's King of Steaks and his brother Harry are the inventors of the sandwich known as the Philly Cheese Steak. However, it was one of their restaurant managers who added a slice of provolone to make it a cheese sandwich. It can now be ordered with processed cheese sauce, provolone or American cheese.

PHILADELPHIA, PA

Find Pat's King of Steaks where 9th and Wharton Streets meet.

Pat's King of Steaks Philly Cheese Steak

This ultimate cheese steak, an iconic sandwich in Philly, is a best-seller at Pat's King of Steaks Restaurant. Patrons praise its thinly cut beef and crusty Italian rolls.

—FRANK OLIVIERI PHILADELPHIA, PENNSYLVANIA

PREP: 15 MIN. **COOK:** 5 MIN./BATCH **MAKES:** 4 SERVINGS

1	**large onion, sliced**
½	**pound sliced fresh mushrooms, optional**
1	**small green pepper, sliced, optional**
1	**small sweet red pepper, sliced, optional**
6	**tablespoons canola oil, divided**
1½	**pounds beef ribeye steaks, thinly sliced**
4	**crusty Italian rolls, split**
	Process cheese sauce
	Ketchup, optional

1. In a large skillet, saute onion and, if desired, mushrooms and peppers in 3 tablespoons oil until tender. Remove and keep warm. In the same pan, saute the beef in remaining oil for 45-60 seconds or until the meat reaches desired doneness.

2. On each roll bottom, layer the beef, onion mixture, cheese and ketchup if desired. Replace tops.

Broiled Cod

This is the easiest and tastiest fish you'll serve. Even finicky eaters who think they don't like fish will love it because it lacks a fishy taste and is beautiful and flaky.

—KIM RUSSELL NORTH WALES, PENNSYLVANIA

PREP: 10 MIN. + MARINATING **BROIL:** 10 MIN.
MAKES: 2 SERVINGS

- ¼ cup fat-free Italian salad dressing
- ½ teaspoon sugar
- ⅛ teaspoon each salt, garlic powder, curry powder, paprika and pepper
- 2 cod fillets (6 ounces each)
- 2 teaspoons butter

1. In a large resealable plastic bag, combine the dressing, sugar and seasonings. Add the fish; seal bag and turn to coat. Refrigerate for 10-30 minutes.

2. Drain and discard marinade; place fillets on a broiler pan coated with cooking spray. Broil 3-4 in. from the heat for 10-12 minutes or until fish flakes easily with a fork. Place 1 teaspoon butter on each fillet; let stand until melted.

Pesto Scallops Vermicelli

Quick and easy with a gourmet flavor, tender bay scallops shine in a simple sauce made with pesto and white wine.

—MARILYN LUSTGARTEN WENTZVILLE, MISSOURI

PREP/TOTAL TIME: 15 MIN. **MAKES:** 2 SERVINGS

- 4 ounces uncooked vermicelli
- 2 tablespoons butter
- ½ teaspoon garlic powder
- ¼ teaspoon dried oregano
- ⅛ teaspoon pepper
- ½ pound bay scallops
- 2 tablespoons white wine or chicken broth
- 3 tablespoons prepared pesto

1. Cook vermicelli according to the package directions. Meanwhile, in a large skillet, melt butter. Stir in the garlic powder, oregano and pepper. Add scallops and wine; cook and stir over medium heat for 5-6 minutes or until the scallops are firm and opaque.

2. Reduce heat to low. Stir in the pesto; heat through. Drain the vermicelli; toss with the scallop mixture.

CAPE COD, MA

Cape Cod got its name in the 1600s, when the surrounding waters teemed with this fish.

The first shelf-stable marshmallow cream product, Snowflake Marshmallow Creme, was introduced in 1913 by the brother and sister team of Avery and Emma Curtis. From their factory in Melrose, Massachusetts, Emma devised all types of uses for the new product, including the classic Fluffernutter sandwich—peanut butter and marshmallow creme on white bread, which is still very popular in New England. Variations over the years have included wheat bread and added ingredients, such as the chocolate syrup used in our recipe.

Chocolate Fluffernutter Sandwiches

These fun sandwiches are sure to be greeted with smiles when served with sliced bananas and a glass of milk for lunch.

—TASTE OF HOME TEST KITCHEN

PREP/TOTAL TIME: 5 MIN. **MAKES:** 2 SERVINGS

- ¼ **cup chunky peanut butter**
- 4 **thick slices white bread**
- 1 **tablespoon chocolate syrup**
- ¼ **cup marshmallow creme**

1. Spread the peanut butter on two slices of bread. Drizzle with chocolate syrup; spread with the marshmallow creme. Top with the remaining bread.

Prosciutto-Stuffed Meat Loaf

Ingredients like prosciutto, sun-dried tomatoes, fresh basil and cheese blend together to make this delectable rolled loaf extraordinary.

—CAROLE HERMENAU OVIEDO, FLORIDA

PREP: 45 MIN. **BAKE:** 1¼ HOURS
MAKES: 6-8 SERVINGS

- 1 **cup finely chopped red onion**
- 1 **tablespoon olive oil**
- 1 **tablespoon butter**
- 2 **garlic cloves, minced**
- ½ **pound whole fresh mushrooms, coarsely chopped**
- ¾ **teaspoon salt**
- ½ **teaspoon pepper**
- 2 **eggs, lightly beaten**
- 1¾ **cups soft sourdough bread crumbs**
- ¾ **cup grated Parmesan cheese**
- ⅓ **cup minced fresh parsley**
- 1 **teaspoon minced fresh thyme**
- 1½ **pounds lean ground beef**
- ¾ **pound bulk Italian sausage**

FILLING
- 3 **ounces thinly sliced prosciutto**
- 5 **ounces thinly sliced Havarti cheese**
- 1¼ **cups loosely packed basil leaves, cut into thin strips**
- ⅓ **cup oil-packed sun-dried tomatoes, drained and cut into strips**

1. In a large skillet, saute the onion in oil and butter for 2 minutes. Add garlic; cook 1 minute longer. Add mushrooms; cook 6-8 minutes longer or until mushrooms are tender and no liquid remains. Stir in salt and pepper.

2. In a large bowl, combine the eggs, bread crumbs, Parmesan cheese, parsley, thyme and mushroom mixture. Crumble beef and sausage over mixture; mix well.

3. On a large piece of heavy-duty foil, pat the beef mixture into a 15x10x1-in. rectangle. Layer the prosciutto, Havarti, basil and tomatoes to within 1 in. of edges. Roll up jelly-roll style, starting with a short side and peeling foil away while rolling. Seal seams and ends.

4. Place loaf seam side down in a greased 13x9-in. baking dish. Bake, uncovered, at 350° for 75-85 minutes or until no pink remains and a thermometer reads 160°. Let stand for 5 minutes. Using two large spatulas, carefully transfer meat loaf to a serving platter.

Grilled Lobster Tail

I had never made lobster at home until I tried this convenient and deliciously different grilled recipe. It turned out to be amazing, and now I'm not sure I'll ever order lobster at a restaurant again.

—**KATIE RUSH** KANSAS CITY, MISSOURI

PREP: 15 MIN. + MARINATING **GRILL:** 10 MIN.
MAKES: 6 SERVINGS

- 6 **frozen lobster tails (8 to 10 ounces each), thawed**
- ¾ **cup olive oil**
- 3 **tablespoons minced fresh chives**
- 3 **garlic cloves, minced**
- ½ **teaspoon salt**
- ½ **teaspoon pepper**

1. Using scissors, cut top of the lobster shell lengthwise down the center, leaving tail fin intact. Loosen meat from shell, keeping the fin end attached; lift meat and lay over shell. With a knife, cut a slit, ½ inch deep, down center of meat.

2. In a small bowl, combine the remaining ingredients; spoon over lobster meat. Cover and refrigerate for 20 minutes.

3. Place lobster tails, meat side up, on grill rack. Grill, covered, over medium heat for 10-12 minutes or until meat is opaque.

Classic Fried Chicken

Back when we used farm-fresh ingredients, our foods didn't need much embellishment to make them look and taste wonderful. This traditional chicken dish is a perfect example.

—**SANDRA ANDERSON** NEW YORK, NEW YORK

PREP: 10 MIN. **COOK:** 45 MIN. **MAKES:** 6 SERVINGS

- 1½ **cups all-purpose flour**
- 1½ **teaspoons salt**
- ½ **teaspoon garlic powder**
- ½ **teaspoon pepper**
- 1 **broiler/fryer chicken (3 to 4 pounds), cut up**
    Oil for frying

1. In a large resealable plastic bag, combine first four ingredients. With paper towels, pat chicken dry; add to bag, a few pieces at a time. Seal bag and shake to coat.

2. In a large skillet over medium-high heat, heat ½ in. of oil; fry chicken until browned on all sides. Reduce heat; cover and cook for 30-35 minutes or until juices run clear, turning occasionally. Uncover chicken and cook 5 minutes longer. Drain on paper towels.

COASTAL MAINE

Lobster buoys aren't painted bright hues just so they're more handsome. Each lobsterman uses a different color scheme so he can tell his apart from others nearby.

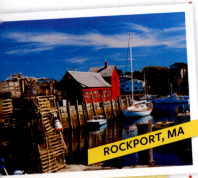
ROCKPORT, MA

Ebenezer Thorndike invented the lobster trap, or pot, in 1808.

Irish Stew

My satisfying stew is full of potatoes, turnips, carrots and lamb. I like to serve it with Irish soda bread, which makes a hearty St. Patrick's Day meal.

—**LOIS GELZER** STANDISH, MAINE

PREP: 20 MIN. **COOK:** 1¾ HOURS **MAKES:** 6 SERVINGS

  1½ **pounds lamb stew meat**
  2 **teaspoons olive oil**
  4 **cups water**
  2 **cups sliced peeled potatoes**
  1 **medium onion, sliced**
  ½ **cup sliced carrot**
  ½ **cup cubed turnip**
  1 **teaspoon salt**
  ½ **teaspoon each dried marjoram, thyme and rosemary, crushed**
  ⅛ **teaspoon pepper**
  2 **tablespoons all-purpose flour**
  3 **tablespoons fat-free milk**
  ½ **teaspoon browning sauce, optional**
  3 **tablespoons minced fresh parsley**

1. In a Dutch oven, brown the lamb in oil over medium-high heat. Add water; bring to a boil. Reduce heat; cover and simmer for 1 hour.

2. Add the potatoes, onion, carrot, turnip and seasonings. Bring to a boil. Reduce heat; cover and simmer for 30 minutes or until the vegetables are tender.

3. In a small bowl, combine the flour, milk and browning sauce if desired until smooth; stir into stew. Add parsley. Bring to a boil; cook and stir for 2 minutes or until thickened.

Lobster Newburg

We live in Maine, so we like to use fresh lobster in this time-honored recipe. However, it can also be made with frozen, canned or imitation lobster. No matter how you prepare it, your guests will be impressed when you treat them to these rich individual seafood casseroles.

—**WENDY CORNELL** HUDSON, MAINE

PREP/TOTAL TIME: 25 MIN. **MAKES:** 4 SERVINGS

  3 **cups cooked lobster meat or canned flaked lobster meat or imitation lobster chunks**
  3 **tablespoons butter**
  ¼ **teaspoon paprika**
  3 **cups heavy whipping cream**
  ½ **teaspoon Worcestershire sauce**
  3 **egg yolks, lightly beaten**
  1 **tablespoon sherry, optional**
  ¼ **teaspoon salt**
  ⅓ **cup crushed butter-flavored crackers (about 8 crackers)**

1. In a large skillet, saute the lobster in butter and paprika for 3-4 minutes; set aside. In a large saucepan, bring cream and Worcestershire sauce to a gentle boil. Meanwhile, in a bowl, combine egg yolks, sherry if desired and salt.

2. Remove cream from the heat; stir a small amount into egg yolk mixture. Return all to the pan, stirring constantly. Bring to a gentle boil; cook and stir for 5-7 minutes or until slightly thickened. Stir in the lobster.

3. Divide lobster mixture among four 10-oz. baking dishes. Sprinkle with cracker crumbs. Broil 6 in. from the heat for 2-3 minutes or until golden brown.

Penne alla Vodka Sauce

This was the first Italian dish I made for my husband and the kids. Not being Italian like them, I was a little nervous. I passed the test! This is now a family-favorite recipe that I usually double for entertaining.

—**KATHY KOCHISS MONGILLO**
TRUMBULL, CONNECTICUT

PREP: 10 MIN. **COOK:** 45 MIN. **MAKES:** 7½ CUPS

- ½ **cup butter, cubed**
- 4 **ounces sliced pancetta, chopped**
- 8 **cans (8 ounces each) no-salt-added tomato sauce**
- ⅓ **cup vodka**
- 1 **cup heavy whipping cream**
  Hot cooked penne pasta
  Shredded Parmesan cheese

1. In a large skillet, melt butter over medium heat. Add pancetta; cook and stir until slightly crisp. Stir in tomato sauce and vodka.

2. Bring to a boil. Reduce heat; simmer, uncovered, for 30-40 minutes or until slightly thickened, stirring occasionally. Add cream and heat through. Serve sauce with pasta; sprinkle with Parmesan cheese.

Maple Pancakes

Our family looks forward to tapping the maple trees in March...and then enjoying the pure maple syrup year-round. This is just one of the recipes I like to make that has maple syrup as an ingredient.

—**MARY COLBATH** CONCORD, NEW HAMPSHIRE

PREP/TOTAL TIME: 15 MIN. **MAKES:** 6 PANCAKES

- 1 **cup all-purpose flour**
- 1½ **teaspoons baking powder**
- ½ **teaspoon salt**
- 1 **egg**
- 1 **cup 2% milk**
- 2 **tablespoons canola oil**
- 1 **tablespoon maple syrup**
  Additional maple syrup

1. In a small bowl, combine the flour, baking powder and salt. In another bowl, combine the egg, milk, oil and syrup; stir into dry ingredients just until blended.

2. Pour batter by ¼ cupfuls onto a lightly greased hot griddle; turn when bubbles form on top of pancakes. Cook until second side is golden brown (pancakes will be thin). Serve with additional syrup.

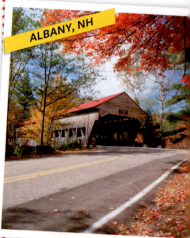

ALBANY, NH

Built in 1858, the Albany Bridge crosses the Swift River in White Mountain National Forest.

> " This peerless pastrami sandwich was adapted from a menu favorite at Primanti Bros. Restaurant in Philadelphia. Their marketing office shared the basic ingredients with us. From there, we created this spot-on copy, including our version of the secret coleslaw topping. "
>
> **—TASTE OF HOME TEST KITCHEN**

Ultimate Pastrami Sandwiches

PREP: 25 MIN. + STANDING   **BAKE:** 5 MIN.   **MAKES:** 4 SERVINGS

½ cup sugar, divided
½ cup cider vinegar, divided
4 cups shredded cabbage
3½ cups frozen waffle-cut fries
¼ teaspoon salt
¼ teaspoon celery seed
¼ teaspoon pepper
1 pound sliced deli pastrami
4 slices provolone cheese
2 medium tomatoes, thinly sliced
8 slices Italian bread (¾ inch thick), toasted

1. In a large bowl, combine ¼ cup each sugar and vinegar; add cabbage and toss to coat. Cover and let stand for 30 minutes. Meanwhile, bake fries according to package directions.

2. Drain cabbage. In a bowl, combine salt, celery seed, pepper and remaining sugar and vinegar; pour over cabbage and toss to coat.

3. On an ungreased baking sheet, divide pastrami into four stacks; top each with cheese. Bake at 450° for 2-3 minutes or until cheese is melted. Place pastrami on four toast slices. Layer with fries, coleslaw, tomato slices and remaining toast. Serve immediately.

Yankee Pot Roast

Here's a traditional main dish that's tested and true. We've been enjoying it for years.

—VERA BURKE WEST PITTSTON, PENNSYLVANIA

PREP: 20 MIN. **COOK:** 2¾ HOURS **MAKES:** 12-14 SERVINGS

- 1 **boneless beef chuck roast (4 to 5 pounds)**
- 1 **tablespoon canola oil**
- 2 **large onions, coarsely chopped**
- 2 **cups sliced carrots**
- 2 **celery ribs, sliced**
- 2 **cans (14½ ounces each) Italian stewed tomatoes**
- 1¾ **cups water**
- 1 **teaspoon salt**
- ½ **teaspoon dried thyme**
- ¼ **teaspoon pepper**
- 4 **medium potatoes, peeled and cut into eighths**

1. In a Dutch oven, brown roast on all sides over medium-high heat in oil. Remove roast and keep warm. In the same pan, add the onions, carrots, celery, tomatoes, water, salt, thyme and pepper. Bring to a boil. Return the roast to pan. Reduce heat; cover and simmer for 2 hours.

2. Add the potatoes. Cover; cook 40 minutes longer or until meat and vegetables are tender.

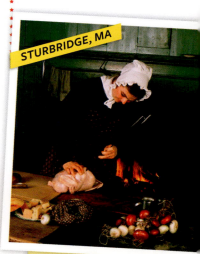

STURBRIDGE, MA

At Old Sturbridge Village, historians show visitors what daily life was like in early New England. Here, you can watch a home cook prepare "receipts" 1830s-style.

LANCASTER, PA

Observe living history of the Pennsylvania Dutch at the Landis Valley Village & Farm Museum. It's open year-round.

Pennsylvania Dutch Pork Chops

Recipes of Pennsylvania Dutch heritage, like this one, are popular in our area. We like to serve these sweet-and-sour pork chops with dumplings or spaetzle, red cabbage coleslaw and applesauce. Dutch apple pie makes the perfect dessert for this entree.

—JOYCE BROTZMAN MCVEYTOWN, PENNSYLVANIA

PREP: 25 MIN. **BAKE:** 1 HOUR **MAKES:** 6 SERVINGS

- 6 bone-in pork loin chops (¾ inch thick and 8 ounces each)
- 2 tablespoons butter
- ½ cup unsweetened pineapple juice
- ½ cup ketchup
- 2 tablespoons white vinegar
- 2 tablespoons honey
- 1½ teaspoons ground mustard
- ¼ teaspoon salt
- 4 teaspoons cornstarch
- 2 tablespoons water

1. In a large skillet, brown the pork chops in butter. Using a slotted spoon, transfer to an ungreased 13x9-in. baking dish.

2. Combine the pineapple juice, ketchup, vinegar, honey, mustard and salt; add to the drippings. Cook and stir until mixture comes to a boil. Pour over chops.

3. Cover and bake at 350° for 45 minutes. Uncover; bake 15 minutes longer or until a thermometer reads 160°. Remove chops and keep warm.

4. In a small saucepan, combine cornstarch and water; stir in pan juices. Bring to a boil; cook and stir for 1-2 minutes or until thickened. Serve with pork chops.

Red Flannel Hash

This is an old-fashioned meal that satisfies big appetites with its hearty mix of ingredients. It's named for the rosy color the dish picks up from the beets.

—JESSE & ANNE FOUST BLUEFIELD, WEST VIRGINIA

PREP/TOTAL TIME: 30 MIN. **MAKES:** 4 SERVINGS

- 3 tablespoons canola oil
- 1 can (14½ ounces) sliced beets, drained and chopped
- 2 cups chopped cooked corned beef
- 2½ cups diced cooked potatoes
- 1 medium onion, chopped
- ¼ cup half-and-half cream
- 2 tablespoons butter, melted
- 2 teaspoons dried parsley flakes
- 1 teaspoon Worcestershire sauce
- ¼ teaspoon salt
- ⅛ teaspoon pepper

1. Heat the oil in a 12-in. skillet. Add all the remaining ingredients. Cook and stir over low heat for 20 minutes or until lightly browned and heated through.

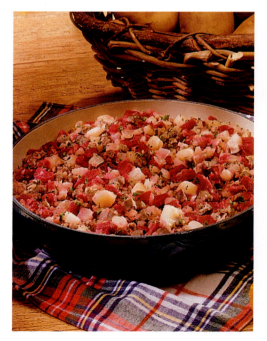

◄● **dishing about food**

Clam shacks dot the coastline of New England, and fried clams are a staple menu item. Lawrence "Chubby" Woodman served the first fried clams at his roadside stand in Essex, Massachusetts, on July 3, 1916, after a local fisherman, who had tried some of Woodman's homemade potato chips, joked that the cook should fry clams to increase business. Woodman and his wife, Bessie, experimented with different batters until they found the perfect coating. Howard Johnson of the restaurant chain learned to fry clams from Chubby and soon introduced even more New Englanders to the taste sensation.

Fried Clams

The crunchy golden coating on these clams will truly melt in your mouth. One bite and you'll understand why these are considered a delicacy!

—**TIM CONNOLLY** FREEPORT, MAINE

PREP/TOTAL TIME: 30 MIN. **MAKES:** 1 DOZEN

- 1½ cups yellow cornmeal, divided
- ½ cup cake flour, divided
- ⅔ cup water
- 12 fresh cherrystone clams, shucked
  Oil for deep-fat frying
- ½ teaspoon salt
  Tartar sauce or seafood cocktail sauce, optional

1. In a shallow bowl, combine ¾ cup cornmeal and ¼ cup flour with the water, forming a batter. In another bowl, combine the remaining cornmeal and flour.

2. Dip clams in batter; shake off excess. Coat with cornmeal mixture.

3. In an electric skillet or deep-fat fryer, heat oil to 375°. Fry the clams, a few at a time, for 4-5 minutes or until golden brown. Drain on paper towels; sprinkle with salt.

4. Serve immediately with sauce if desired.

Boiled dinners can be found in the cuisine of many countries. The appeal of this one-pot meal is the simplicity of preparation and the wonderfully warm and filling meal it produces. New England recipes use a variety of root vegetables and potatoes.

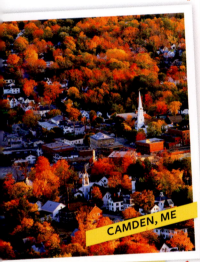

CAMDEN, ME

Don't miss New England's breathtaking fall foliage! Leaves in the northern areas of the region peak in mid-October. Farther south, the color often lasts into November.

New England Boiled Dinner

This has been a popular dinner with our family for a long time. When we moved to California in 1960, I'd make it often to remind us of New England. We're back home now and continue to enjoy this comforting dish.

—**NATALIE COOK** SCARBOROUGH, MAINE

PREP: 10 MIN.   **COOK:** 2 HOURS   **MAKES:** 8-10 SERVINGS

1   **smoked boneless pork shoulder butt roast (2 to 2½ pounds)**
1   **pound fresh carrots, sliced lengthwise and halved**
8   **medium red potatoes. peeled and halved**
2   **medium onions, cut into quarters**
1   **large head cabbage, cut into quarters**
1   **large turnip, peeled and cut into quarters**
1   **large rutabaga, peeled, halved and sliced**

1. Place pork roast in a large Dutch oven; cover with water. Bring to a boil. Reduce heat; cover and simmer for 1 hour.

2. Add the remaining ingredients; return to a boil. Reduce the heat. Cover and simmer for 1 hour or until the vegetables are tender; drain.

Lobster-Stuffed Beef Wellington

PREP: 45 MIN. + CHILLING **BAKE:** 40 MIN. + STANDING **MAKES:** 14 SERVINGS

- 3 lobster tails (8 to 10 ounces each)
- ½ cup heavy whipping cream
- 2 fresh thyme sprigs
- 1¼ teaspoons salt, divided
- 1⅛ teaspoons pepper, divided
- ⅔ cup dry bread crumbs
- 1 beef tenderloin roast (4 to 5 pounds)
- 1 package (17.3 ounces) frozen puff pastry, thawed
- 1 egg white
- 3 tablespoons butter, melted

1. Using kitchen scissors, cut through lobster shells; carefully remove lobster and chop. In a small skillet, combine the lobster, cream, thyme, ¼ teaspoon salt and ⅛ teaspoon pepper. Bring to a boil over medium heat; cook 3-5 minutes or until lobster is firm and opaque. Discard thyme sprigs. Stir in bread crumbs; set aside to cool.

2. Make a lengthwise slit down the center of tenderloin to within ½ in. of bottom. Open meat so it lies flat. Place lobster mixture down the center. Close tenderloin; tie several times with kitchen string. Sprinkle with remaining salt and pepper.

3. Place the tenderloin in a greased 15x10x1-in. baking pan; fold ends under tenderloin.

Bake, uncovered, at 475° for 20-25 minutes or until browned. Cool to room temperature; refrigerate until chilled.

4. On a lightly floured surface, unfold one puff pastry sheet; cut lengthwise along one fold line, forming two rectangles. Cut smaller rectangle into a 6x3-in. rectangle; use remaining piece for decorations if desired. Moisten a 6-in. edge of large rectangle with water. Attach smaller rectangle along that edge, pressing lightly to seal. Roll out 2 in. longer than the tenderloin on each side. Transfer to an ungreased baking sheet. Brush with egg white.

5. Remove and discard kitchen string from tenderloin; place onto the pastry. Roll out remaining puff pastry into a rectangle 8 in. wide and 5 in. longer than the tenderloin; place over the meat. Brush pastry edges with water; fold edges under meat. With a sharp knife, make four slashes across top of pastry. Brush with butter.

6. Bake, uncovered, at 425° for 40 minutes (meat will be cooked to medium doneness); cover loosely with foil to prevent overbrowning if necessary. Transfer to a serving platter. Let stand for 15 minutes before slicing.

> "Instead of stuffing a tenderloin with the typical mushrooms, I use lobster for a more elegant feel. A side of potatoes and salad completes the festive meal."
>
> **—TERRY SMIGIELSKI**
> BOOTHBAY HARBOR, MAINE

Mock chicken legs were popular during the Depression, when chicken and eggs were in short supply and expensive. Ground pork and/or veal, which cost less than chicken during that time, was shaped into a drumstick around a skewer. Sometimes known as city chicken, this simple dish was popular in many parts of the country, including upstate New York.

Mock Chicken Legs

When I was young, my mother made this recipe for us. I was recently going through her cookbook collection and found it. Now I make this tasty, fun dish for my own family and enjoy mixing the old memories with new ones.

—JEANNE HERDA BURNSVILLE, MINNESOTA

PREP: 20 MIN. **COOK:** 25 MIN. **MAKES:** 1 DOZEN

- 1 egg, lightly beaten
- ½ cup cornflake crumbs
- ¼ cup milk
- 2 tablespoons finely chopped green pepper
- 1 teaspoon salt
- ¾ pound ground pork
- ¾ pound ground veal
- 12 Popsicle sticks

COATING
- 1 egg
- ¼ cup milk
- 2 cups cornflake crumbs
  Oil for frying

1. In a large bowl, combine the first five ingredients. Crumble ground meat over mixture and mix well. Shape ¼ cupful of meat mixture around each Popsicle stick to resemble a 3-in. log.

2. In a shallow bowl, whisk egg and milk. Place cornflake crumbs in another shallow bowl. Coat each leg in crumbs, then dip in egg mixture and recoat in crumbs. Let stand for 5 minutes.

3. In an electric skillet, heat ¼ in. oil to 375°. Fry legs, a few at a time, for 1 minute on each side or until golden brown. Drain the legs on paper towels.

4. Arrange on an ungreased baking sheet. Bake at 350° for 15-20 minutes or until no pink remains and a thermometer reads 160°.

Salisbury Steak with Onion Gravy

These moist meat patties are simmered in a delicious gravy that starts with French onion soup. Let the egg noodles cook while you prepare the rest of the recipe, and dinner will be done in 30 minutes.

—**KIM KIDD** NEW FREEDOM, PENNSYLVANIA

PREP: 10 MIN. **COOK:** 25 MIN. **MAKES:** 6 SERVINGS

- 1 **egg**
- 1 **can (10½ ounces) condensed French onion soup, undiluted, divided**
- ½ **cup dry bread crumbs**
- ¼ **teaspoon salt**
   Dash pepper
- 1½ **pounds ground beef**
- ¼ **cup water**
- ¼ **cup ketchup**
- 1 **teaspoon Worcestershire sauce**
- ½ **teaspoon prepared mustard**
- 1 **tablespoon all-purpose flour**
- 2 **tablespoons cold water**
- 6 **cups hot cooked egg noodles**
   Chopped fresh parsley, optional

1. In a large bowl, beat egg. Stir in ⅓ cup of soup, bread crumbs, salt and pepper. Crumble beef over mixture and mix well. Shape into six oval patties.

2. In a large skillet, brown the patties over medium heat for 3-4 minutes on each side or until a thermometer reads 160° and juices run clear. Remove and set aside; drain. Add the water, ketchup, Worcestershire sauce, mustard and remaining soup to skillet. Bring to a boil.

3. Return patties to the skillet. Reduce heat; cover and simmer for 15 minutes or until heated through.

4. Combine flour and cold water until smooth. Stir into pan. Bring to a boil; cook and stir for 2 minutes or until thickened. Serve the patties and gravy with noodles. Garnish with parsley if desired.

Lobster Rolls

Mayonnaise infused with dill and lemon lend refreshing flavor to these super sandwiches. Try toasting the buns for something special.

—**TASTE OF HOME TEST KITCHEN**

PREP/TOTAL: 30 MIN. **MAKES:** 8 SERVINGS

- 1 **cup chopped celery**
- ⅓ **cup mayonnaise**
- 2 **tablespoons lemon juice**
- ½ **teaspoon dill weed**
- 5 **cups cubed cooked lobster meat (about 4 small lobsters)**
- 8 **hoagie rolls, split and toasted**

1. In a large bowl, combine the celery, mayonnaise, lemon juice and dill weed. Gently stir in lobster. Serve on rolls.

◄● dishing about food

Did you know that James H. Salisbury, a 19th-century American physician, invented the Salisbury steak and promoted it as a health food? He believed that a diet very high in meat (three steaks a day) and low in vegetables and starchy foods would cure many ailments. What a difference a century can make!

◄● dishing about food

In many parts of the country, a lobster dinner is a special treat. But in Maine and other New England states with commercial lobster fishing, it turns up in meals more frequently. One of the region's many staples is the lobster roll, which consists of fresh lobster salad on a hot dog bun.

dishing about food ➡️

Spiedis are a specialty of Binghamton in Broome County, New York.

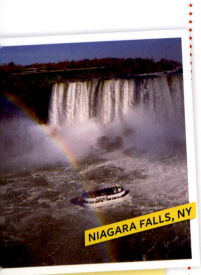

NIAGARA FALLS, NY

Picturesque Niagara Falls has been dubbed the Honeymoon Capital of the World since the early 19th century, when wealthy newlyweds began spending their first days of married life there.

1. In a large resealable plastic bag, combine the oil, vinegar, Worcestershire sauce, onion and seasonings; add meat. Seal bag and turn to coat; refrigerate for 24 hours, turning occasionally.

2. Drain and discard marinade. Thread meat on metal or soaked wooden skewers. Using long-handled tongs, moisten a paper towel with cooking oil and lightly coat the grill rack.

3. Grill meat, covered, over medium heat or broil 4 in. from the heat for 10-15 minutes or until meat reaches desired doneness, turning occasionally. Remove meat from skewers and serve on long Italian rolls or hot dog buns.

Chicken with Blueberry Sauce

This is one of my best recipes. Blueberries are mixed with apricot jam and mustard to create a sweet, tangy sauce for tender chicken.

—**THOMAS JEWELL SR.** AVENEL, NEW JERSEY

PREP: 10 MIN. **COOK:** 35 MIN. **MAKES:** 4 SERVINGS

- 4 **boneless skinless chicken breast halves (1 pound)**
- 1 **tablespoon canola oil**
- ½ **cup apricot preserves or spreadable fruit**
- 3 **tablespoons Dijon mustard**
- ⅓ **cup white wine vinegar**
- ½ **cup fresh or frozen blueberries**
  Hot cooked rice, optional

1. In a large skillet over medium heat, cook chicken in oil for about 4 minutes on each side or until lightly browned. Combine preserves and mustard; spoon over chicken. Reduce heat; cover and simmer for 15 minutes or until chicken juices run clear.

2. With a slotted spoon, remove chicken and keep warm. Add vinegar to skillet; bring to a boil. Reduce heat; simmer, uncovered, for 3 minutes or until sauce is reduced by one-third, stirring occasionally. Stir in blueberries. Serve over chicken and rice if desired.

Spiedis

This traditional Italian dish features skewered meat grilled like kabobs, then wrapped in Italian bread and eaten like a sandwich. The seasonings in this recipe work well with pork, beef, lamb and poultry.

—**GERTRUDE SKINNER** BINGHAMTON, NEW YORK

PREP: 10 MIN. + MARINATING **GRILL:** 10 MIN. **MAKES:** 8 SERVINGS

- 1 **cup canola oil**
- ⅔ **cup cider vinegar**
- 2 **tablespoons Worcestershire sauce**
- ½ **medium onion, finely chopped**
- ½ **teaspoon salt**
- ½ **teaspoon sugar**
- ½ **teaspoon dried basil**
- ½ **teaspoon dried marjoram**
- ½ **teaspoon dried rosemary, crushed**
- 2½ **pounds boneless lean pork, beef, lamb, venison, chicken or turkey, cut into 1½-to 2-inch cubes**
  Italian rolls or hot dog buns

Double-Cheese Eggs Benedict

Making breakfast is my favorite part of running a bed-and-breakfast. Returning guests often request this poached egg dish. I serve it over English muffins and Canadian bacon, then I top the eggs with cheese sauce.

—**MEGAN HAKES** WELLSVILLE, PENNSYLVANIA

PREP: 15 MIN. **COOK:** 20 MIN. **MAKES:** 8 SERVINGS

- 2 tablespoons butter
- 2 tablespoons plus 1½ teaspoons all-purpose flour
- 1½ cups 2% milk
- ¼ cup shredded cheddar cheese
- 2 tablespoons shredded Parmesan cheese
- ½ teaspoon Dijon mustard
- ⅛ teaspoon salt
- ⅛ teaspoon white pepper

POACHED EGGS
- 1 tablespoon white vinegar
- 8 eggs
- 4 English muffins, split and toasted
- 8 slices Canadian bacon, warmed
- 8 bacon strips, cooked and crumbled

1. For cheese sauce, in a large saucepan, melt butter. Stir in flour until smooth; gradually add the milk. Bring to a boil; cook and stir for 2 minutes or until thickened. Reduce heat to medium-low. Add the cheese, mustard, salt and pepper, stirring until cheese is melted. Cover and keep warm.

2. Place 2-3 in. of water in a large skillet with high sides; add vinegar. Bring to a boil; reduce heat and simmer gently. Break cold eggs, one at a time, into a custard cup or saucer; holding the cup close to the surface of the water, slip egg into water.

3. Cook 4 eggs, uncovered, until whites are completely set, about 4 minutes. With a slotted spoon, lift each egg out of the water. Repeat with remaining eggs.

4. To assemble, top each muffin half with one slice Canadian bacon, one egg, cheese sauce and bacon.

Fish Fillets with Stuffing

Here is a perfect weeknight meal. Fish cooks up so moist in the microwave, it takes just minutes to cook and the dish is easy to clean!

—**DONNA SMITH** VICTOR, NEW YORK

PREP/TOTAL TIME: 25 MIN. **MAKES:** 6-8 SERVINGS

- 2 tablespoons butter, melted
- ⅓ cup chicken broth
- ½ cup finely chopped onion
- ½ cup finely grated carrots
- ½ cup chopped fresh mushrooms
- ¼ cup minced fresh parsley
- ½ cup dry bread crumbs
- 1 egg, beaten
- 1 tablespoon lemon juice
- 1 teaspoon salt
- ⅛ teaspoon pepper
- 2½ to 3 pounds fish fillets (cod, whitefish, haddock, etc.)
  Paprika

1. In a large bowl, combine the first 11 ingredients and mix well. In a greased 13x9-in. microwave-safe dish, arrange the fillets with stuffing between them. Moisten paper towels with water; place over fish. Cook 9-11 minutes or until the fish flakes easily with a fork, rotating dish occasionally. Sprinkle with paprika.

Editor's Note: *This recipe was tested in a 1,100-watt microwave.*

◄◆► dishing about food

There are different accounts of the origins of Eggs Benedict, but two are connected to restaurants in New York City—Delmonico's and the Waldorf. In both versions of the story, the patron who suggested the concoction was named Benedict.

NEW YORK, NY

Wall Street itself is nothing to marvel at. It's the financial giants in the area that give the industry its cachet. The New York Stock Exchange (above) happens to be just a few blocks from Delmonico's.

Cranberry Pork Medallions

This juicy pork with its festive cranberry glaze is so simple to prepare. It tastes so special and looks so good, people will think you spent hours making it. Serve with refrigerated mashed potatoes and frozen green beans for a super easy meal.

—**MARIA BRENNAN** WATERBURY, CONNECTICUT

PREP/TOTAL TIME: 20 MIN. **MAKES:** 3 SERVINGS

- 1   pork tenderloin (about 1 pound), cut into ½-inch slices
- 3   tablespoons olive oil
- 1   medium onion, finely chopped
- 1   garlic clove, minced
- 3   tablespoons sugar
- ¾   cup apple juice
- ½   cup cranberry juice
- ½   cup fresh or frozen cranberries, thawed
- 2   teaspoons Dijon mustard
- ½   teaspoon minced fresh rosemary or ⅛ teaspoon dried rosemary, crushed
      Additional cranberries and fresh rosemary, optional

1. In a large nonstick skillet, brown the pork in oil for 3-4 minutes on each side. Remove and set aside.

2. In the same skillet, saute the onion, garlic and sugar until onion is caramelized and tender. Stir in the apple juice, cranberry juice, cranberries, mustard and rosemary. Bring to a boil. Reduce heat; simmer , uncovered, for 5-6 minutes or until sauce is reduced by half.

3. Return the pork to pan; heat through. Sprinkle with additional cranberries and rosemary if desired.

Creamed Beef on Toast

World War II vets may have gotten their first taste of this old-time recipe when they were in the Army. It is easy to make and I find it a comforting dish.

—**MARGE ROSSELIT** OTTAWA, OHIO

PREP/TOTAL TIME: 25 MIN. **MAKES:** 4 SERVINGS

- 2   tablespoons plus 1½ teaspoons all-purpose flour
- 1   teaspoon minced fresh parsley
- ¼   teaspoon celery seed
- ¼   teaspoon pepper
- ⅛   teaspoon onion powder
- ¾   cup 2% milk
- ½   cup water
- 1   package (2½ ounces) thinly sliced dried beef, coarsely chopped
- 3   hard-cooked eggs, chopped
- 4   slices white bread, toasted

1. In a small saucepan, combine the first five ingredients. Whisk in milk and water. Bring to a boil; cook and stir for 2 minutes or until thickened. Add beef and eggs; heat through. Serve over toast.

Toasted Reubens

When New Yorkers taste my Reuben, they say it's like those served by delis in the Big Apple. For a little less kick, omit the horseradish from the mayonnaise mixture.

—**PATRICIA KILE** ELIZABETHTOWN, PENNSYLVANIA

PREP/TOTAL TIME: 15 MIN. **MAKES:** 4 SERVINGS

- ½ cup mayonnaise
- 3 tablespoons ketchup
- 2 tablespoons sweet pickle relish
- 1 tablespoon prepared horseradish
- 4 teaspoons prepared mustard
- 8 slices rye bread
- 1 pound thinly sliced deli corned beef
- 4 slices Swiss cheese
- 1 can (8 ounces) sauerkraut, rinsed and well drained
- 2 tablespoons butter

1. In a small bowl, combine the mayonnaise, ketchup, pickle relish and horseradish; set aside. Spread mustard on one side of four slices of bread, then layer with corned beef, cheese, sauerkraut and mayonnaise mixture; top with remaining bread.

2. In a large skillet, melt butter over medium heat. Add sandwiches; cover and toast on both sides until bread is lightly browned and cheese is melted.

New England Salmon Pie

My mom always made salmon pie on Christmas Eve. Now I bake this dish for the holidays and other get-togethers during the year. It takes little time to prepare, and with a salad on the side, it makes a satisfying meal.

—**JEANNE UTTLEY** SALEM, NEW HAMPSHIRE

PREP: 15 MIN. **BAKE:** 40 MIN. **MAKES:** 6-8 SERVINGS

- 3½ cups warm mashed potatoes (without added milk and butter)
- 1 medium onion, finely chopped
- ⅓ cup milk
- ½ teaspoon celery seed
- ½ teaspoon garlic powder
- ½ teaspoon salt
- ¼ teaspoon white pepper
- 1 can (14¾ ounces) salmon, drained, bones and skin removed
- 2 tablespoons minced fresh parsley
  Pastry for double-crust pie (9 inches)
- 1 egg
- 1 tablespoon water

1. In a bowl, combine the potatoes, onion, milk, celery seed, garlic powder, salt and pepper. Stir in salmon and parsley. Line a 9-in. pie plate with bottom pastry; trim even with edges. Spread salmon mixture into crust.

2. Roll out remaining pastry to fit top of pie; place over filling. Trim, seal and flute edges. Cut slits in top. Beat egg and water; brush over pastry. Bake at 350° for 40-45 minutes or until crust is golden. Refrigerate leftovers.

MAINE & NEW HAMPSHIRE

The Androscoggin River is a favorite spot for Maine and New Hampshire anglers. It's a hot spot for different types of salmon, trout and bass.

> **Dill-seasoned dumplings top this homey stew featuring tender venison, carrots and potatoes.**

—ELIZABETH SMITH
MIDDLEBURY, VERMONT

Venison Dumpling Stew

PREP: 20 MIN. **COOK:** 45 MIN. **MAKES:** 4 SERVINGS

¼ cup all-purpose flour
1 pound venison stew meat, cut into 1-inch cubes
3 tablespoons butter
4 to 5 cups water
2 bay leaves
2 teaspoons beef bouillon granules
3 tablespoons Worcestershire sauce
1 teaspoon salt
½ to ¾ teaspoon pepper
5 medium potatoes, peeled and cubed
5 medium carrots, peeled and cut into ¾-inch slices
1 medium onion, chopped

DILLED DUMPLINGS
1 cup all-purpose flour
1 teaspoon baking powder
½ teaspoon salt
½ teaspoon dill weed
1 egg
½ cup milk

1. In a large resealable plastic bag, combine flour and venison; shake to coat. In a Dutch oven, brown meat in butter. Add water; stir to loosen browned bits from pan. Add the bay leaves, bouillon, Worcestershire sauce, salt and pepper. Bring to a boil. Reduce heat; cover and simmer for 1 hour or until meat is tender.

2. Discard bay leaves. Add potatoes, carrots and onion. Cover and simmer for 25 minutes.

3. For dumplings, in a large bowl, combine the flour, baking powder, salt and dill. Stir in the egg and milk just until moistened. Drop by tablespoonfuls onto simmering stew. Cover and simmer for 15 minutes (do not lift cover) or until a toothpick inserted near the center comes out clean.

Homemade Pizza

This recipe is a hearty, zesty main dish with a crisp golden crust. Feel free to use whatever toppings your family enjoys.

—MARIANNE EDWARDS LAKE STEVENS, WASHINGTON

PREP: 25 MIN. + RISING **BAKE:** 25 MIN. **MAKES:** 2 PIZZAS (3 SERVINGS EACH)

- 1 **package (¼ ounce) active dry yeast**
- 1 **teaspoon sugar**
- 1¼ **cups warm water (110° to 115°)**
- ¼ **cup canola oil**
- 1 **teaspoon salt**
- 3½ **cups all-purpose flour**
- ½ **pound ground beef**
- 1 **small onion, chopped**
- 1 **can (15 ounces) tomato sauce**
- 3 **teaspoons dried oregano**
- 1 **teaspoon dried basil**
- 1 **medium green pepper, diced**
- 2 **cups (8 ounces) shredded part-skim mozzarella cheese**

1. In large bowl, dissolve yeast and sugar in water; let stand for 5 minutes. Add the oil and salt. Stir in the flour, a cup at a time, until a soft dough forms.

2. Turn onto floured surface; knead until smooth and elastic, about 2-3 minutes. Place in a greased bowl, turning once to grease the top. Cover and let rise in a warm place until doubled, about 45 minutes. Meanwhile, cook beef and onion over medium heat until meat is no longer pink; drain.

3. Punch down dough; divide in half. Press each into a greased 12-in. pizza pan. Combine the tomato sauce, oregano and basil; spread over each crust. Top with beef mixture, green pepper and cheese.

4. Bake at 400° for 25-30 minutes or until crust is lightly browned.

◀◉ dishing about food

Pizzerias in New York often have red pepper flakes, oregano and Parmesan available for their customers to add to their pie, which is often sold by the slice. To eat the pizza like a New Yorker, fold the wedge in half to enjoy like a sandwich.

NEW YORK, NY

The top of the Empire State Building is lit in a rainbow of colors to observe holidays and special events throughout the year, like Christmas and the Super Bowl.

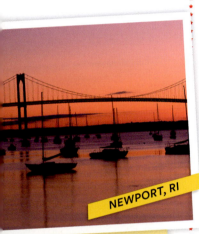

NEWPORT, RI

The beautiful Claiborne Pell Bridge, known to many simply as the Newport Bridge, spans part of the Narragansett Bay to connect Jamestown and Newport. It's pictured on the Rhode Island state quarter.

Chorizo Sausage Corn Chowder

The spiciness of the sausage is a wonderful counterpoint to the sweetness of the corn.

—**ROBIN HAAS** CRANSTON, RHODE ISLAND

PREP: 25 MIN. **COOK:** 20 MIN.
MAKES: 6 SERVINGS (2½ QUARTS)

- 3 cups frozen corn, thawed
- 1 large onion, chopped
- 1 celery rib, chopped
- 1 teaspoon olive oil
- 2 garlic cloves, minced
- 3 cans (14½ ounces each) reduced-sodium chicken broth
- 1 tablespoon sherry or additional reduced-sodium chicken broth
- 2 bay leaves
- 1 teaspoon dried thyme
- ½ teaspoon pepper
- 1 package (12 ounces) fully cooked chorizo chicken sausage or flavor of your choice, chopped
- 1 cup half-and-half cream
- 1 cup (4 ounces) shredded smoked Gouda cheese
- 1 medium sweet red pepper, chopped
- 2 green onions, chopped

1. In a nonstick Dutch oven coated with cooking spray, saute corn, onion and celery in oil until tender. Add garlic; cook 1 minute longer. Stir in broth, sherry, bay leaves, thyme and pepper. Bring to a boil. Reduce heat; simmer, uncovered, for 8-10 minutes. Discard bay leaves.

2. Cool slightly. In a food processor, process soup in batches until blended. Return to pan. Stir in sausage and cream; heat through. Top with cheese, red pepper and green onions.

Lamb Kabobs with Bulgur Pilaf

I love to make this old family recipe that shows my Armenian heritage. The tender, slightly sweet lamb is complemented perfectly by the savory bulgur pilaf.

—**RUTH HARTUNIAN ALUMBAUGH**
WILLIMANTIC, CONNECTICUT

PREP: 15 MIN. + MARINATING **COOK:** 35 MIN.
MAKES: 6 SERVINGS

- 30 garlic cloves, crushed (1½ to 2 bulbs)
- ½ cup balsamic vinegar
- ¾ cup chopped fresh mint or
  ¼ cup dried mint
- ¼ cup olive oil
- 2 pounds lean boneless lamb, cut into 1½-inch cubes

PILAF
- ½ cup butter, cubed
- 1 large onion, chopped
- 1 cup uncooked mini spiral pasta
- 2 cups bulgur
- 3 cups beef broth

1. In a large resealable plastic bag, combine the garlic, vinegar, mint and oil; add lamb. Seal bag and turn to coat; refrigerate for several hours or overnight.

2. For pilaf, in a large skillet, melt butter. Add onion and pasta; saute until pasta is lightly browned. Add bulgur and stir to coat. Stir in broth. Bring to a boil. Reduce heat; cover and simmer for 25-30 minutes or until tender. Remove from the heat; let stand for 5 minutes. Fluff with a fork.

3. Drain and discard marinade. Thread onto six metal or soaked wooden skewers.

4. Grill kabobs, covered, over medium heat for 8-10 minutes or until meat reaches desired doneness, turning frequently. Serve with pilaf.

Editor's Note: *This recipe was tested with Barilla brand mini fusilli pasta.*

Baked Blueberry & Peach Oatmeal

Baked oatmeal is a staple in our home. It's very easy to prepare the night before; just keep the dry and wet ingredients separate until ready to bake. I've tried a variety of fruits in this dish, but the blueberry and peach combination is our favorite.

—ROSEMARIE WELESKI NATRONA HEIGHTS, PENNSYLVANIA

PREP: 20 MIN. **BAKE:** 35 MIN. **MAKES:** 9 SERVINGS

3 cups old-fashioned oats
½ cup packed brown sugar
2 teaspoons baking powder
½ teaspoon salt
2 egg whites
1 egg
1¼ cups fat-free milk
¼ cup canola oil
1 teaspoon vanilla extract
1 can (15 ounces) sliced peaches in juice, drained and chopped
1 cup fresh or frozen blueberries
⅓ cup chopped walnuts
   Additional fat-free milk, optional

1. In a large bowl, combine the oats, brown sugar, baking powder and salt. Whisk the egg whites, egg, milk, oil and vanilla; add to dry ingredients and stir until blended. Let stand for 5 minutes. Stir in peaches and blueberries.

2. Transfer to an 11x7-in. baking dish coated with cooking spray. Sprinkle with the walnuts. Bake, uncovered, at 350° for 35-40 minutes or until top is lightly browned and a thermometer reads 160°. Serve oatmeal with additional milk if desired.

PHILADELPHIA, PA

You can't visit the City of Brotherly Love without stopping at Robert Indiana's LOVE sculpture. It's located in John F. Kennedy Plaza in Center City.

Toasty Deli Hoagie

My deluxe sub sandwich is stacked with yummy ingredients, then broiled, so it's perfect for a backyard picnic. For an even fresher taste, whip up your own guacamole.

—**STACI HOARD** BRONSTON, KENTUCKY

PREP: 35 MIN. **BROIL:** 5 MIN. **MAKES:** 6 SERVINGS

- 1 loaf (1 pound) French bread
- 2 tablespoons mayonnaise
- 1 tablespoon lemon juice
- 2 garlic cloves, minced
- ½ pound thinly sliced deli smoked turkey
- ½ pound thinly sliced deli ham
- 6 slices hard salami
- 1 medium sweet yellow pepper, julienned
- 1 small red onion, thinly sliced
- ½ pound sliced provolone cheese
- 1½ cups guacamole

1. Cut French bread in half lengthwise; place cut side up on a baking sheet. Bake at 350° for 4-5 minutes or until toasted.

2. In a small bowl, combine the mayonnaise, lemon juice and garlic; spread over bread bottom. Layer with turkey, ham, salami, pepper, onion and cheese. Bake for 7-8 minutes or until meat is heated through; broil 3-4 in. from the heat for 3 minutes or until cheese is lightly browned.

3. Spread guacamole over bread top; place over cheese. Cut into six slices.

Simple Pan-Fried Trout

One summer when my husband and I were enjoying our first getaway in years, we found ourselves stranded in our cabin cruiser with a dead battery. When hunger set in, he rigged up a fishing line, and soon there were two trout sizzling on the portable grill. We eventually made it home all right—and kept the recipe we'd devised.

—**FELICIA CUMMINGS** RAYMOND, MAINE

PREP/TOTAL TIME: 20 MIN. **MAKES:** 4 SERVINGS

- 4 lake trout fillets (about 8 ounces each)
- ½ cup grated Parmesan cheese
- ½ cup bacon-flavored crackers, crushed
- ½ cup cornmeal
- ¼ to ½ teaspoon garlic salt
    Dash pepper
- 2 eggs
- ½ cup milk
- ½ cup canola oil
    Lemon wedges and/or minced chives or parsley, optional

1. Rinse fish in cold water; pat dry. In a shallow bowl, combine the cheese, cracker crumbs, cornmeal, garlic salt and pepper. In another bowl, beat eggs and milk. Dip fish in the egg mixture, then gently roll in the crumb mixture.

2. In a large skillet, fry the fillets in oil for 3-4 minutes on each side or until the fish flakes easily with a fork. Garnish with lemon, chives and/or parsley if desired.

Corned Beef and Cabbage

St. Patrick's Day is one of my favorite holidays. I'm not Irish, but as they say, everyone's Irish on March 17! Everything about St. Pat's is so festive, especially the food.

—CONNIE LOU BLOMMERS PELLA, IOWA

PREP: 20 MIN. **COOK:** 3 HOURS **MAKES:** 8 SERVINGS

- ¼ cup packed brown sugar
- 2 teaspoons finely grated orange peel
- 2 teaspoons yellow mustard
- ¼ teaspoon ground cloves
- 1 corned beef brisket with spice packet (2 to 3 pounds)
- 2 medium onions, sliced
- 2 quarts water
- 1 cup apple juice
- 8 carrots, cut into 3-inch pieces
- 1 small head cabbage

1. In a small bowl, combine the first four ingredients; set aside. In a Dutch oven, place corned beef and seasoning packet. Add onions, water and apple juice; bring to a boil. Reduce heat; cover and simmer for 2 to 2½ hours or until meat is tender.

2. Remove brisket from cooking liquid; place in a greased roasting pan. Rub sugar mixture over warm meat. Bake at 350° for 15 minutes.

3. Add carrots to cooking liquid. Cover and simmer for 10 minutes. Cut cabbage into eight wedges, leaving a portion of the core on each wedge; add to carrots. Cover and simmer for 15-20 minutes or until vegetables are tender. Thinly slice meat; serve with vegetables.

Tourtieres

Some time ago, a co-worker brought a meat pie to lunch. The aroma was familiar—and after one taste, I was amazed to discover it was the same pie my grandmother used to serve when I was a youngster! She shared the recipe, and I have been enjoying it ever since.

—RITA WINTERBERGER HUSON, MONTANA

PREP: 20 MIN. **BAKE:** 30 MIN.
MAKES: 2 PIES (8 SERVINGS EACH)

- 2 large onions, thinly sliced
- ¼ cup canola oil
- 2 pounds ground beef
- 2 pounds ground pork
- 3 cups frozen mixed vegetables
- 2 cups mashed potatoes
- 1 tablespoon ground allspice
- 2 teaspoons salt
- ½ teaspoon pepper
  Pastry for two double-crust pies (9 inches)
- 1 egg, lightly beaten

1. In a Dutch oven, saute onions in oil until tender. Remove and set aside. In the same pan, cook beef and pork over medium heat until no longer pink; drain. Remove from the heat. Add the onions, vegetables, potatoes and seasonings.

2. Line two 9-in. pie plates with bottom crusts; trim pastry even with edge of plate. Fill each with about 5 cups filling. Roll out remaining pastry to fit tops of pies; place over filling. Trim, seal and flute edges. Cut slits in pastry and brush tops with egg.

3. Bake pis at 375° for 30-35 minutes or until golden brown.

BOSTON, MA

The city of Boston and its suburbs boast a higher percentage of folks with Irish heritage than any other place in the U.S.—nearly 20 percent!

> **Maple lends a sweet touch to blackberry salsa. This easy recipe is also great made with fish.**
>
> **—TAMMY THOMAS**
> MORRISVILLE, VERMONT

Crumb-Coated Chicken & Blackberry Salsa

PREP/TOTAL TIME: 25 MIN.   **MAKES:** 2 SERVINGS

- ½ cup fresh blackberries
- 1 jalapeno pepper, seeded and minced
- 2 tablespoons minced fresh cilantro
- 2 tablespoons chopped red onion
- 2 tablespoons maple syrup
- 2 tablespoons balsamic vinegar
- 2 boneless skinless chicken breast halves (5 ounces each)
- ⅛ teaspoon salt
- ⅛ teaspoon pepper
- ¼ cup all-purpose flour
- 1 egg, beaten
- ½ cup panko (Japanese) bread crumbs
- 1 tablespoon olive oil

1. In a bowl, combine the first six ingredients. Cover and refrigerate until serving.

2. Flatten the chicken to ¼-in. thickness; sprinkle with salt and pepper. Place flour, egg and bread crumbs in separate shallow bowls. Coat chicken with flour, dip in egg, then coat with crumbs.

3. In a large skillet, cook chicken in oil over medium heat for 4-6 minutes on each side or until no longer pink. Serve with salsa.

Editor's Note: *Wear disposable gloves when cutting hot peppers; the oils can burn skin. Avoid touching your face.*

Portuguese Pork Tenderloin

I won a contest to attend a cooking school in Portugal, where the chef laughed at all ideas of cooking light. This is my version of one of his recipes. I cut back on the olive oil and heavy cream. It reminds me of the flavors of Miguel's roast, but I don't feel guilty about eating it.

—JESSIE GREARSON-SAPAT FALMOUTH, MAINE

PREP: 20 MIN. **COOK:** 40 MIN. **MAKES:** 4 SERVINGS

- 2 large potatoes, peeled and cut into 1-inch cubes
- 3 tablespoons olive oil, divided
- ¾ teaspoon pepper, divided
- ½ teaspoon salt, divided
- 2 cups dry red wine or chicken broth
- ¼ cup tawny port wine or grape juice
- 1 cup pitted dried plums
- 2 fresh rosemary sprigs
- 2 pounds pork tenderloin, cut into 1-inch cubes
- 1 cup reduced-sodium chicken broth
- 2 tablespoons reduced-fat cream cheese
- 2 tablespoons heavy whipping cream
  Additional fresh rosemary sprigs, optional

1. Place potatoes in a large bowl; drizzle with 1 tablespoon oil. Sprinkle with ½ teaspoon pepper and ¼ teaspoon salt; toss to coat.

2. Transfer to a greased 15x10-in. baking pan. Bake at 400° for 40-45 minutes or until tender, stirring occasionally.

3. Meanwhile, in a small saucepan, combine the red wine, port wine, plums and rosemary. Bring to a boil; cook until liquid is reduced to about 1 cup, about 25-30 minutes. Remove rosemary and discard. Transfer to a blender; cover and process until smooth. Set aside.

4. Sprinkle pork with remaining pepper and salt. In a large skillet, brown pork in remaining oil; remove and keep warm.

5. Add the broth, cream cheese, cream and plum mixture to skillet; cook over medium-low heat until blended. Return the pork to the pan; cook and stir for 8-10 minutes or until meat is no longer pink. Serve the pork and sauce with potatoes. Garnish with additional rosemary if desired.

Shredded Venison Sandwiches

My husband hunts for deer every November, so I'm always looking for new recipes for venison. The whole family loves these slow cooker sandwiches seasoned with soy sauce, brown sugar, ketchup and hot pepper sauce.

—RUTH SETTERLUND FREYBURG, MAINE

PREP: 15 MIN. **COOK:** 8 HOURS
MAKES: 14-18 SERVINGS

- 1 boneless venison roast (4 pounds)
- 1½ cups ketchup
- 3 tablespoons brown sugar
- 1 tablespoon ground mustard
- 1 tablespoon lemon juice
- 1 tablespoon soy sauce
- 1 tablespoon liquid smoke, optional
- 2 teaspoons celery salt
- 2 teaspoons pepper
- 2 teaspoons Worcestershire sauce
- 1 teaspoon onion powder
- 1 teaspoon garlic powder
- ⅛ teaspoon ground nutmeg
- 3 drops hot pepper sauce
- 14 to 18 hamburger buns, split

1. Cut venison roast in half; place in a 5-qt. slow cooker. In a large bowl, combine the ketchup, brown sugar, mustard, lemon juice, soy sauce, liquid smoke if desired and seasonings. Pour over venison. Cover and cook on low for 8-10 hours or until meat is tender.

2. Remove the roast; set aside to cool. Shred meat with two forks; return to the slow cooker and heat through. Using a slotted spoon, place meat mixture on bun bottoms. Replace tops.

dishing about food

There are large populations of people with Portuguese heritage in the New England area, particularly in Rhode Island and Massachusetts.

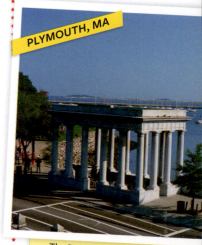

PLYMOUTH, MA

The Roman Doric portico marks the spot where the *Mayflower* landed at Plymouth Rock in 1620.

Native Americans introduced early settlers to the concept of steaming seafood on the beach. East Coast residents still enjoy doing this today. Those of us who don't live along the coast can enjoy succulent seafood with this grilled variation, along with extras like corn on the cob, onions and potatoes.

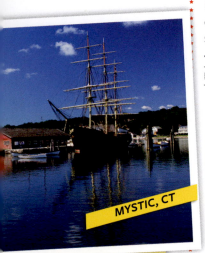

MYSTIC, CT

Get a hearty dose of maritime history at the Mystic Seaport, the Museum of America and the Sea. In 2000, workers at the shipyard built a replica of the *Amistad*, the famed schooner seized by slaves to commemorate the 200th anniversary of the end of the Atlantic slave trade.

Grilled Clam Bake

With clams and crab legs, this grilled entree looks impressive but is quite easy to prepare on the grill. Add corn and potatoes, and it's a satisfying meal.

—TASTE OF HOME TEST KITCHEN

PREP: 20 MIN. **GRILL:** 25 MIN. **MAKES:** 6 SERVINGS

- 18 fresh littleneck clams
- 4 medium ears sweet corn, husks removed and cut into thirds
- 8 medium red potatoes, cut into ½-inch cubes
- 2 medium onions, cut into 2-inch pieces
- 1 cup white wine or chicken broth
- 1 cup minced fresh parsley
- ¼ cup minced fresh basil
- ½ cup olive oil
- 2 garlic cloves, minced
- 1 teaspoon coarsely ground pepper
- 1 teaspoon hot pepper sauce
- ½ teaspoon salt
- 3 bay leaves
- 3 pounds uncooked snow crab legs
- ¼ cup butter, cubed
  French bread, optional

1. Tap clams; discard any that do not close.

2. In a large disposable roasting pan, layer the clams, corn, potatoes, onions, wine, herbs, oil, garlic, pepper, pepper sauce, salt and bay leaves. Grill, covered, over medium heat for 15 minutes.

3. Add crab; cook until potatoes are tender, about 25-30 minutes. Discard bay leaves; stir in butter. Serve with bread if desired.

New England Fish Bake

I've lived in Rhode Island for 36 years and love the fresh seafood dishes served here. This is a favorite of mine. My mother-in-law gave me the recipe.

—NORMA DESROCHES WARWICK, RHODE ISLAND

PREP: 25 MIN. **BAKE:** 20 MIN. **MAKES:** 3-4 SERVINGS

- 4 medium potatoes, peeled
- 1 teaspoon all-purpose flour
- 1 small onion, sliced into rings
- ½ teaspoon salt
- ¼ teaspoon pepper
- ¾ cup milk, divided
- 1½ pounds cod fillets or freshwater fish (trout, catfish or pike)
- 3 tablespoons grated Parmesan cheese, optional
- 2 tablespoons minced fresh parsley or 2 teaspoons dried parsley flakes
- ¼ teaspoon paprika

1. Place potatoes in a saucepan and cover with water. Bring to a boil. Reduce heat; cover and simmer for 15-20 minutes or until tender. Drain; cool slightly.

2. Slice potatoes ⅛ in. thick; place in a greased shallow 2-qt. baking dish. Sprinkle with flour. Top with onion; sprinkle with salt and pepper. Pour half of the milk over potatoes. Place fish on top; pour remaining milk over fish. Sprinkle with Parmesan cheese if desired.

3. Cover and bake at 375° for 20-30 minutes or until fish flakes easily with a fork. Sprinkle with parsley and paprika.

Moroccan Vegetable Chicken Tagine

PREP: 45 MIN.   **COOK:** 7½ HOURS   **MAKES:** 6 SERVINGS

- 1 medium butternut squash (about 3 pounds), peeled and cut into 1-inch cubes
- 2 medium red potatoes, cut into 1-inch cubes
- 1 medium sweet potato, peeled and cut into 1-inch cubes
- 1 large onion, halved and sliced
- 2 garlic cloves, minced
- 6 chicken leg quarters, skin removed
- ½ teaspoon salt
- ¼ teaspoon pepper
- ½ cup dried apricots, chopped
- ½ cup dried cranberries, chopped
- 2 tablespoons all-purpose flour
- 1 can (14¾ ounces) reduced-sodium chicken broth
- ¼ cup chili sauce
- 1 tablespoon minced fresh gingerroot
- 1 teaspoon curry powder
- ½ teaspoon ground cinnamon
- ½ teaspoon ground cumin
- 1 can (15 ounces) garbanzo beans or chickpeas, rinsed and drained
   Hot cooked couscous, optional

1. In a 6-qt. slow cooker, combine the squash, potatoes, onion and garlic. Sprinkle chicken with salt and pepper; place over vegetables. Top with apricots and cranberries.

2. In a small bowl, combine flour and broth until smooth. Stir in the chili sauce, ginger, curry, cinnamon and cumin. Pour over the chicken. Cover and cook on low for 7-8 hours or until chicken and vegetables are tender.

3. Stir in garbanzo beans; cover and cook for 30 minutes or until heated through. Serve with couscous if desired.

"I grew up in a German-Dutch community and this dish was a favorite there. I like to eat scrapple in the wintertime, but my husband thinks it's perfect anytime. As he always says, 'It really sticks to your ribs.'"

—MRS. MERLIN BRUBAKER
BETTENDORF, IOWA

Cornmeal Scrapple

PREP: 20 MIN. + CHILLING **BAKE:** 10 MIN. **MAKES:** 6 SERVINGS

- 1 cup white or yellow cornmeal
- 1 cup milk
- 1 teaspoon sugar
- 1 teaspoon salt
- 2¾ cups boiling water
- 8 ounces bulk pork sausage, cooked, drained and crumbled
  All-purpose flour
- 2 tablespoons butter
  Maple syrup, optional

1. In a saucepan, combine the cornmeal, milk, sugar and salt; gradually stir in water. Cook and stir until thickened and bubbly. Reduce heat; cook, covered, 10 minutes longer or until very thick, stirring occasionally.

2. Remove from the heat and stir in sausage. Pour into a greased 7½ x 3½-in. loaf pan (the pan will be very full). Cover with plastic wrap and refrigerate.

3. To serve, unmold and cut into ⅓-in. slices. Dip both sides in flour. In a skillet, melt butter over medium heat; brown scrapple on both sides. Serve with maple syrup if desired.

Chicken with Slippery Dumplings

These dumplings are cooked in a mild broth and are served with chicken and gravy at church dinners. The old-fashioned dish reminds many of us of simpler days growing up on the farm.

—**BETTY JEAN BOYD** WILMINGTON, DELAWARE

PREP: 30 MIN. + RESTING **COOK:** 20 MIN.
MAKES: 8 SERVINGS

- 1 **stewing chicken (about 5 pounds), cut up**
- 4 **celery ribs, chopped**
- 1 **medium onion, chopped**
- 4 **medium carrots, coarsely chopped**
- 1 **tablespoon chicken bouillon granules**

DUMPLINGS
- 3 **cups all-purpose flour**
- 1 **teaspoon salt, optional**
- ½ **teaspoon baking powder**
  Minced fresh parsley, optional

1. Place chicken, celery and onion in a Dutch oven. Cover with water; bring to a boil. Reduce heat; cover and simmer until chicken is tender. Remove chicken and keep warm. Skim fat from the pan juices; add water to measure 3 qts. Set aside 1½ cups for dumplings; cool. Return the remaining broth to the Dutch oven; add carrots and bouillon.

2. For dumplings, combine flour, salt if desired and baking powder. Add enough reserved broth to form a stiff dough. Divide dough into thirds; cover and let rest for 10-15 minutes.

3. Meanwhile, bring broth to a simmer. Roll each portion of dough to ⅛-in. thickness; cut into 2-in. squares. Drop one at a time into simmering broth. Cover Dutch oven and cook for 5-7 minutes, stirring occasionally.

4. Serve immediately with the chicken. Sprinkle with parsley if desired.

Fiddlehead Shrimp Salad

Fiddleheads are tightly curled fronds from bracken, ostrich and cinnamon ferns that sprout in moist fields and open wooded areas. Each spring, fiddleheads are prepared in dozens of ways, in everything from soups to cakes, at the Fiddlehead Festival in my home state.

—**WILMA JOHNSON** THORNDIKE, MAINE

PREP/TOTAL TIME: 15 MIN. **MAKES:** 4 SERVINGS

- 3 **cups fiddlehead ferns**
- 1 **cup cooked shell macaroni**
- ½ **cup diced unpeeled apple**
- ¼ **cup chopped celery**
- 1 **cup diced cooked shrimp**
- ¼ **to ½ cup mayonnaise**
- 1 **tablespoon lemon juice**
- 1 **teaspoon grated lemon peel**
  Salt and pepper to taste

1. Cook ferns in a small amount of water until tender. Drain. Toss with all remaining ingredients. Cover and refrigerate until mixture is chilled.

◄● dishing about food

In downstate (southern) Delaware, slippery dumplings are a comforting treat. Slippery dumplings are a cross between a noodle and a dumpling. Unlike the classic round dumpling, the dough is rolled out and cut into squares. The squares are then cooked in simmering broth. Recipes for these dumplings may or may not use baking powder.

LEWES, DE

Hailed as the first town in the first state, Lewes is the site of the Zwaanendael Museum, which honors the history and culture of the area. Its distinctive facade was modeled after the Hoorn town hall in the Netherlands. Lewes was settled by the Dutch in 1631.

dishing about food ◆➔

More than 20 states have Amish communities, but the largest is in Lancaster County, Pennsylvania. These descendants of Swiss-German settlers prepare simple fare made mostly from unprocessed ingredients. Their recipes tend to be high in calories, but the Amish easily burn those off working their farms.

Amish Breakfast Casserole

We enjoyed a hearty breakfast bake during a visit to an Amish inn. When I asked for the recipe, one of the ladies told me the ingredients right off the top of her head. I modified it to create this version my family loves. Try breakfast sausage in place of bacon.

—**BETH NOTARO** KOKOMO, INDIANA

PREP: 15 MIN. **BAKE:** 35 MIN. + STANDING **MAKES:** 12 SERVINGS

- 1 **pound sliced bacon, diced**
- 1 **medium sweet onion, chopped**
- 6 **eggs, lightly beaten**
- 4 **cups frozen shredded hash brown potatoes, thawed**
- 2 **cups (8 ounces) shredded cheddar cheese**
- 1½ **cups (12 ounces) 4% cottage cheese**
- 1¼ **cups shredded Swiss cheese**

1. In a large skillet, cook bacon and onion over medium heat until bacon is crisp; drain. In a large bowl, combine the remaining ingredients; stir in bacon mixture. Transfer to a greased 13 x9-in. baking dish.

2. Bake, uncovered, at 350° for 35-40 minutes or until a knife inserted near the center comes out clean. Let casserole stand for 10 minutes before cutting.

LANCASTER COUNTY, PA

Travel to Lancaster County, Pennsylvania, and you'll have many opportunities to experience Amish Country, from touring the Amish Village to taking a buggy ride.

Fish with Fennel

PREP: 30 MIN. **COOK:** 10 MIN. **MAKES:** 4 SERVINGS

- 1   medium lime
- 1   teaspoon fennel seeds
- 1   large fennel bulb, sliced
- ¼   teaspoon salt
- 4   teaspoons olive oil, divided
- 2   garlic cloves, minced
- 4   striped bass or barramundi fillets (8 ounces each)
- 1   tablespoon chopped fennel fronds

1. Cut lime in half; cut four slices from one half for garnish. Finely grate enough peel from remaining half to measure ¾ teaspoon; squeeze juice from lime half. Set aside.

2. In a small dry skillet over medium heat, toast the fennel seeds until aromatic, about 1-2 minutes. Cool. Crush seeds in a spice grinder or with a mortar and pestle.

3. In a large saucepan, bring 1 in. of water to a boil. Add sliced fennel and salt; cover and boil for 6-10 minutes or until crisp-tender. Drain and pat dry.

4. In a large nonstick skillet, saute fennel in 2 teaspoons oil for 3 minutes or until fennel is lightly browned. Add garlic; cook 1 minute longer. Remove from the pan and set aside.

5. In the same skillet over medium-high heat, cook fillets in remaining oil for 3-4 minutes on each side or until fish flakes easily with a fork.

6. Drizzle with lime juice; sprinkle with lime peel and crushed fennel seeds. Serve with sauteed fennel. Garnish with fennel fronds and lime slices.

The New Haven clam pizza, or white clam pie, was created by Connecticut pizzeria owner Frank Pepe in the 1960s. It was so popular that other area pizzerias began serving it, too. It's traditionally served with just a sprinkling of Romano cheese and no mozzarella.

New Haven Clam Pizza

This appetizer is the perfect start to any meal. It's always a big hit with our family and friends.

—**SUSAN SEYMOUR** VALATIE, NEW YORK

PREP: 20 MIN. + RISING   **BAKE:** 20 MIN.   **MAKES:** 8 SERVINGS

- 1 **package (¼ ounce) active dry yeast**
- 1 **cup warm water (110° to 115°)**
- 1 **teaspoon sugar**
- 2½ **cups all-purpose flour**
- 1 **teaspoon salt**
- 2 **tablespoons canola oil**
- 2 **cans (6½ ounces each) chopped clams, drained**
- 4 **bacon strips, cooked and crumbled**
- 3 **garlic cloves, minced**
- 2 **tablespoons grated Parmesan cheese**
- 1 **teaspoon dried oregano**
- 1 **cup (4 ounces) shredded mozzarella cheese**

1. In a large bowl, dissolve yeast in water. Add sugar; let stand for 5 minutes. Add the flour, salt and oil; beat until smooth. Cover and let dough rise in a warm place until doubled, about 15-20 minutes.

2. Punch dough down. Press onto the bottom and up the sides of a greased 14-in. pizza pan; build up edges slightly. Prick dough several times with a fork.

3. Bake at 425° for 6-8 minutes. Sprinkle remaining ingredients over crust in order listed. Bake for 13-15 minutes or until crust is golden and cheese is melted. Cut into wedges.

Mom's Dynamite Sandwiches

Whenever we had a family get-together and my mom had a lot of people to feed, she'd make her delicious dynamite sandwiches. I am from Woonsocket, Rhode Island, and this is a staple in this area. Dynamites are to Woonsocket what cheese steaks are to Philadelphia.

—KATHY HEWITT CRANSTON, RHODE ISLAND

PREP: 15 MIN.   **COOK:** 1 HOUR 20 MIN.
MAKES: 16 SERVINGS

- 2½ pounds ground beef
- 5 medium green peppers, finely chopped
- 4 large onions, chopped (6 cups)
- 1 can (28 ounces) crushed tomatoes in puree
- 1 can (16 ounces) tomato sauce
- 1 can (12 ounces) tomato paste
- 1 cup water
- 2 tablespoons sugar
- 2 tablespoons garlic powder
- 1 tablespoon Italian seasoning
- 1 tablespoon dried oregano
- 2¼ teaspoons salt
- 2 teaspoons hot pepper sauce
- 1½ teaspoons pepper
- ½ teaspoon crushed red pepper flakes, optional
- 12 hoagie buns or other sandwich rolls, split

1. In a Dutch oven, cook beef over medium-high heat 8-10 minutes or until no longer pink, breaking into crumbles; drain.

2. Stir in all remaining ingredients except buns. Bring to a boil. Reduce heat; simmer, uncovered, 1 hour or until desired consistency and flavors are blended, stirring occasionally. Serve on buns.

Breaded Eggplant Sandwiches

Eggplant Parmesan is one of my family's favorite comfort foods. We love this version served open-faced with a salad.

—HOLLY GOMEZ SEABROOK, NEW HAMPSHIRE

PREP: 30 MIN.   **BAKE:** 25 MIN.   **MAKES:** 6 SERVINGS

- ¼ cup minced fresh basil
- 2 teaspoons olive oil
- ¼ teaspoon dried oregano
- ¼ teaspoon pepper
- ⅛ teaspoon salt
- 2 egg whites, lightly beaten
- 1 cup seasoned bread crumbs
- 1 medium eggplant
- 2 large tomatoes
- 1½ cups (6 ounces) shredded part-skim mozzarella cheese
- 2 tablespoons grated Parmesan cheese
- 1 garlic clove, peeled
- 12 slices Italian bread (½ inch thick), toasted

1. Combine the basil, oil, oregano, pepper and salt; set aside. Place egg whites and bread crumbs in separate shallow bowls. Cut eggplant lengthwise into six slices. Dip slices in egg whites, then coat in crumbs.

2. Place on a baking sheet coated with cooking spray. Bake at 37° for 20-25 minutes or until tender and golden brown, turning once.

3. Cut each tomato into six slices; place two slices on each eggplant slice. Spoon reserved basil mixture over tomatoes and sprinkle with cheeses. Bake for 3-5 minutes or until cheese is melted.

4. Meanwhile, rub garlic over one side of each slice of bread; discard garlic. Place each eggplant stack on a slice of bread, garlic side up. Top with remaining bread, garlic side down.

◀▶ dishing about food

Iowa has its loose meat sandwiches and Rhode Island has its spicy tomato-sauced dynamites. Dynamites are a Woonsocket specialty, although their origin remains a mystery. Local cooks like to add their own special touches. Some versions are made with loose meat, like a sloppy joe with a kick. In another variation, the filling is formed into meatballs and served like a meatball hero.

Potato pancakes have a place in the cuisine of many Eastern European countries such as Poland, Lithuania, Germany and the Czech Republic, with each country adding its own unique touch. Latkes, the Yiddish word for pancakes, is one of the foods traditionally served for Hanukkah.

Latkes with Lox

Lox, a salty smoked salmon, is a year-round delicacy. This recipe, inspired by one from the *Jewish Journal*, uses lox as a topping.

—TASTE OF HOME TEST KITCHEN

PREP: 20 MIN. **COOK:** 5 MIN./BATCH **MAKES:** 3 DOZEN

- 2 **cups finely chopped onion**
- ¼ **cup all-purpose flour**
- 6 **garlic cloves, minced**
- 2 **teaspoons salt**
- 1 **teaspoon coarsely ground pepper**
- 4 **eggs, lightly beaten**
- 4 **pounds russet potatoes, peeled and shredded**
- ¾ **cup canola oil**

TOPPINGS
- 4 **ounces lox**
  Sour cream and minced fresh chives, optional

1. In a large bowl, combine the first five ingredients. Stir in eggs until blended. Add potatoes; toss to coat.

2. Heat 2 tablespoons oil in a large nonstick skillet over medium heat. Drop batter by ¼ cupfuls into oil; press lightly to flatten. Fry in batches until golden brown on both sides, using remaining oil as needed. Drain on paper towels.

3. Serve with lox; top with sour cream and chives if desired.

Cream of Mussel Soup

Every New England cook has his or her own personal version of mussel soup, depending on the favored regional herbs and cooking customs they prefer. Feel free to start with my recipe, and develop your own luscious variation.

—DONNA NOEL GRAY, MAINE

PREP: 35 MIN.   **COOK:** 10 MIN.   **MAKES:** 5 SERVINGS

- 3 **pounds fresh mussels (about 5 dozen), scrubbed and beards removed**
- 2 **medium onions, finely chopped**
- 2 **celery ribs, finely chopped**
- 1 **cup water**
- 1 **cup white wine or chicken broth**
- 1 **bottle (8 ounces) clam juice**
- ¼ **cup minced fresh parsley**
- 2 **garlic cloves, minced**
- ¼ **teaspoon salt**
- ¼ **teaspoon pepper**
- 1 **cup half-and-half cream**

1. Tap mussels; discard any that do not close. Set aside. In a stockpot, combine the onions, celery, water, wine, clam juice, parsley, garlic, salt and pepper.

2. Bring to a boil. Reduce heat; add mussels. Cover and simmer for 5-6 minutes or until mussels have opened. Remove mussels with a slotted spoon, discarding any unopened ones; set aside opened mussels and keep warm.

3. Cool cooking liquid slightly. In a blender, cover and process cooking liquid in batches until blended. Return all to pan. Add the cream and reserved mussels; heat through (do not boil).

COASTAL MAINE

Blue mussels live in colonies called mussel beds. They grow wild but are also farmed.

Long Island Iced Tea

"Smooth but potent" describes this cooling drink. Adjust the tequila to suit your taste: If you like a bolder flavor, use one ounce; for a more mellow drink, try half an ounce.

—**TASTE OF HOME TEST KITCHEN**

PREP/TOTAL TIME: 5 MIN. **MAKES:** 1 SERVING

    1   to 1¼ cups ice cubes
    1   ounce vodka
    ½   to 1 ounce tequila
    1   ounce light rum
    1   ounce sour mix
    1   ounce Triple Sec
    ½   ounce cola

1. Place ice in a Collins or highball glass. Pour the remaining ingredients into the glass; stir.

Watergate Salad

This fluffy salad is a real treat, creamy but not overly sweet. Easy to mix up, the flavor gets better the longer it stands. It's perfect for St. Patrick's Day, served in a green bowl.

—**PATTIE ANN FORSSBERG** LOGAN, KANSAS

PREP: 5 MIN. + CHILLING **MAKES:** 12 SERVINGS

    1   carton (16 ounces) frozen whipped
         topping, thawed
    1   package (3.4 ounces) instant pistachio
         pudding mix
    6   to 7 drops green food coloring, optional
    3   cups miniature marshmallows
    1   can (20 ounces) crushed pineapple,
         undrained
    ½   cup chopped pistachios or walnuts

1. In a large bowl, combine whipped topping, pudding mix and food coloring if desired. Fold in the marshmallows and pineapple. Cover and refrigerate for at least 2 hours. Just before serving, sprinkle with nuts.

Soft Pretzels

Big soft pretzels are all the rage in shopping malls across the country. I think it's worth the time to make them from scratch to get the incomparable homemade taste.

—**LUCINDA WALKER** SOMERSET, PENNSYLVANIA

PREP: 20 MIN. + RISING **BAKE:** 15 MIN.
MAKES: 32 PRETZELS

    2   packages (¼ ounce each) active dry yeast
    2   cups warm water (110° to 115°)
    ½   cup sugar
    ¼   cup butter, softened
    2   teaspoons salt
    1   egg
    6½   to 7½ cups all-purpose flour
    1   egg yolk
    2   tablespoons cold water
         Coarse salt

1. In a large bowl, dissolve yeast in warm water. Add the sugar, butter, salt, egg and 2 cups flour. Beat until smooth. Stir in enough remaining flour to form a stiff dough. Place in a greased bowl, turning once to grease top. Cover and refrigerate for 2-24 hours.

2. Punch dough down. Turn onto a lightly floured surface; divide in half. Cut each half into 16 pieces. Roll each piece into a 20-in. rope. Shape into a pretzel.

3. Place on greased baking sheets. Beat egg yolk and cold water; brush over pretzels. Sprinkle with coarse salt. Cover and let rise in a warm place until doubled, about 25 minutes.

4. Bake at 400° for 15-20 minutes or until golden brown. Remove from pans to wire racks to cool.

Chicken Corn Soup with Rivels

Traditional chicken soup gets an interesting twist from a dumplinglike broth-stretcher called rivels. This low-fat recipe is brimming with chicken, vegetables and herbs. You won't be able to resist it!

—ELISSA ARMBRUSTER MEDFORD, NEW JERSEY

PREP/TOTAL TIME: 25 MIN. **MAKES:** 7 SERVINGS

- 1 cup chopped carrots
- 1 celery rib, chopped
- 1 medium onion, chopped
- 2 teaspoons canola oil
- 2 cans (14½ ounces each) reduced-sodium chicken broth
- 2 cups fresh or frozen corn
- 2 cups cubed cooked chicken breast
- ½ teaspoon minced fresh parsley
- ¼ teaspoon salt
- ¼ teaspoon dried tarragon
- ¼ teaspoon pepper
- ¾ cup all-purpose flour
- 1 egg, beaten

1. In a large saucepan, saute the carrots, celery and onion in oil until tender. Add the broth, corn, chicken, parsley, salt, tarragon and pepper. Bring to a boil.

2. Meanwhile, for rivels, place the flour in a bowl; mix in egg with a fork just until blended. Drop dough by teaspoonfuls into boiling soup, stirring constantly. Cook and stir for 1-2 minutes or until rivels are cooked through.

Crab Puffs

If you're looking for a scrumptious way to get a party started, bring out a tray of these cheesy crab puffs. They bake up golden brown and taste wonderful right out of the oven. Try serving them with soup instead of bread or crackers.

—NADIA MIHEYEV RICHMOND HILL, NEW YORK

PREP: 25 MIN. **BAKE:** 25 MIN.
MAKES: ABOUT 4 DOZEN

- 1 cup plus 1 tablespoon water
- ½ cup butter
- 1 tablespoon ground mustard
- 1 teaspoon salt
- 1 teaspoon ground cumin
- ⅛ teaspoon hot pepper sauce
- 1 cup all-purpose flour
- 4 eggs
- 2 cups (8 ounces) shredded Swiss cheese
- 1 can (6 ounces) crabmeat, drained, flaked and cartilage removed

1. In a large saucepan, bring the water, butter, mustard, salt, cumin and hot pepper sauce to a boil. Add flour all at once and stir until a smooth ball forms. Remove from the heat; let stand for 5 minutes.

2. Add eggs, one at a time, beating well after each addition. Continue beating until smooth and shiny. Stir in the cheese and crab.

3. Drop by rounded teaspoonfuls 2 in. apart onto greased baking sheets. Bake at 400° for 23-26 minutes or until golden brown. Remove to wire racks. Serve warm.

◄◆ dishing about food

Rivels, also known as rivelets, are small dumplings popular with the Pennsylvania Dutch. They can be made as this recipe directs, with just flour and egg, but other variations may include salt and milk or water.

BALTIMORE, MD

The Chesapeake Bay area is famous for its cuisine starring blue crab, Maryland's state crustacean.

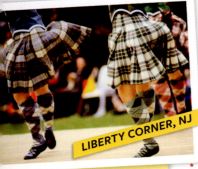

LIBERTY CORNER, NJ

Scotch Broth

Add a side of bread to this luscious concoction of lamb, vegetables and barley, and you'll have all a hungry body needs. I like to skim the fat to fit our lighter way of eating.

—**KELSEY HAMILTON** HIGHLAND PARK, NEW JERSEY

PREP: 2¼ HOURS **COOK:** 1¼ HOURS **MAKES:** 4 SERVINGS

- 1 **lamb shank (about 1 pound)**
- 2 **teaspoons canola oil**
- 4 **cups water**
- 2 **cans (14½ ounces each) reduced-sodium beef broth**
- 2 **whole cloves**
- 1 **medium onion, halved**
- 1 **medium carrot, halved**
- 1 **celery rib, halved**
- 1 **bay leaf**
- ¼ **cup minced fresh parsley**
- ¼ **teaspoon dried rosemary, crushed**
- ¼ **teaspoon dried thyme**
- ¼ **teaspoon whole peppercorns**

SOUP
- ⅓ **cup medium pearl barley**
- 1½ **cups julienned peeled turnips (1-inch pieces)**
- 1 **cup coarsely chopped carrots**
- 1 **medium leek (white portion only), thinly sliced**
- ¼ **teaspoon salt**
- ¼ **teaspoon pepper**

1. In a Dutch oven, brown lamb shank in oil on all sides; drain. Stir in water and broth. Insert cloves into onion. Add the onion, carrot, celery and seasonings to the pan. Bring to a boil. Reduce heat; cover and simmer for 2 hours or until meat is very tender.

2. Remove shank from broth; cool slightly. Remove meat from the bone; cut into small pieces. Discard bone. Strain broth, discarding vegetables and seasonings.

3. Skim fat from broth. In a large saucepan, bring broth to a boil. Stir in barley. Reduce heat; cover and simmer for 40 minutes.

4. Add turnips, carrots, leek, salt and pepper. Return to a boil. Reduce heat; cover and simmer for 15 minutes or until vegetables are tender. Add lamb; heat through.

U.S. Senate Bean Soup

Chock-full of ham, beans and celery, this hearty soup makes a wonderful meal at any time of year. Freeze the bone from a holiday ham until you're ready to make the soup. Once prepared, it freezes well for a great make-ahead supper!

—ROSEMARIE FORCUM HEATHSVILLE, VIRGINIA

PREP: 30 MIN. + STANDING
COOK: 3¾ HOURS + COOLING
MAKES: 8-10 SERVINGS (2½ QUARTS)

- **1 pound dried great northern beans**
- **1 meaty ham bone or 2 smoked ham hocks**
- **3 medium onions, chopped**
- **3 garlic cloves, minced**
- **3 celery ribs, chopped**
- **¼ cup minced fresh parsley**
- **1 cup mashed potatoes or ⅓ cup instant potato flakes**
- **Salt and pepper to taste**
- **Minced parsley or chives**

1. Rinse and sort beans. Place the beans in a Dutch oven or stockpot; add water to cover by 2 in. Bring to a boil; boil for 2 minutes. Remove from the heat; cover and let stand for 1 to 4 hours or until beans are softened.

2. Drain and rinse, discarding liquid. In a large Dutch oven or stockpot, place the beans, ham bone or hocks and 3 quarts water. Bring to boil. Reduce heat; cover and simmer for 2 hours.

3. Skim fat if necessary. Add onions, garlic, celery, parsley, potatoes, salt and pepper; simmer 1 hour longer.

4. Set aside ham bones until cool enough to handle. Remove meat from bones; discard bones. Cut the meat into bite-size pieces and return to Dutch oven. Heat through. Sprinkle with parsley or chives.

Cranberry Apple Cider

I love to start this soothing cider in the slow cooker on nights before my husband goes hunting. Then he can fill his thermos and take it with him out into the cold. The cider has a terrific fruit flavor we both enjoy.

—JENNIFER NABOKA
NORTH PLAINFIELD, NEW JERSEY

PREP: 10 MIN. **COOK:** 2 HOURS
MAKES: 10 SERVINGS (ABOUT 2½ QUARTS)

- **4 cups water**
- **4 cups apple juice**
- **1 can (12 ounces) frozen apple juice concentrate, thawed**
- **1 medium apple, peeled and sliced**
- **1 cup fresh or frozen cranberries**
- **1 medium orange, peeled and sectioned**
- **1 cinnamon stick**

1. In a 5-qt. slow cooker, combine all ingredients. Cover and cook on low for 2 hours or until cider reaches desired temperature. Discard cinnamon stick. If desired, remove fruit with a slotted spoon before serving.

WASHINGTON, DC

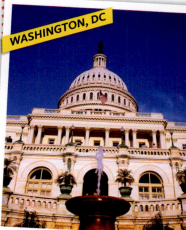

Visit the U.S. Capitol, and you may be able to watch senators or representatives in action! Tours are free, but you need to reserve your spot in advance.

Gnocchi—Italian for dumplings—are usually served as a side dish.

NEW YORK, NY

Each September, Little Italy's Mulberry Street is decked out for the Feast of San Gennaro, the city's longest-running alfresco religious festival. Parades, street games and lots of food honor Naples' patron saint.

Gnocchi with Thyme Butter

If you've never attempted homemade gnocchi, this recipe is the one to try. The gnocchi are tender with a delicate butter and thyme flavor. They're absolutely delicious as a side dish with your favorite meat or seafood.

—**ANNETTE LEAR** SANBORNVILLE, NEW HAMPSHIRE

PREP: 70 MIN. **COOK:** 10 MIN. **MAKES:** 5 SERVINGS

- 1½ **pounds russet potatoes, peeled and quartered**
- 1 **cup all-purpose flour**
- 1 **egg**
- 1 **teaspoon salt**
- ½ **teaspoon pepper**
- 4 **quarts water**
- ½ **cup butter, cubed**
- 4 **teaspoons fresh thyme leaves**
  Grated Parmesan cheese, optional

1. Place potatoes in a large saucepan and cover with water. Bring to a boil. Reduce heat; cover and simmer for 15-20 minutes or until tender. Drain; return potatoes to the pan.

2. Over very low heat, stir the potatoes for 1-2 minutes or until steam has evaporated. Press through a potato ricer or strainer into a small bowl; cool slightly.

3. Using a fork, make a well in the potatoes; sprinkle with flour. Whisk the egg, salt and pepper; pour into well. Stir until blended. On a lightly floured surface, knead 10-12 times, forming a soft dough.

4. Divide dough into four portions. On a floured surface, roll each portion into ½-in.-thick ropes; cut into ¾-in. pieces. Press and roll each piece with a lightly floured fork.

5. In a Dutch oven, bring water to a boil. Cook the gnocchi in batches for 30-60 seconds or until they float. Remove with a slotted spoon; keep warm.

6. In a large heavy saucepan, melt butter over medium heat. Add thyme and gnocchi; stir gently to coat. Sprinkle with cheese if desired.

Maple Syrup Corn Bread

Here's a good old New England recipe. Flavored with a hint of maple syrup, the corn bread makes a perfect companion to spicy chili or stew.

—**ROGER HICKUM** PLYMOUTH, NEW HAMPSHIRE

PREP/TOTAL TIME: 30 MIN. **MAKES:** 12 SERVINGS

- 1¼ **cups all-purpose flour**
- 1 **cup cornmeal**
- 2 **teaspoons baking powder**
- 1 **teaspoon salt**
- 1 **egg**
- ¾ **cup fat-free milk**
- ½ **cup maple syrup**
- 3 **tablespoons butter, melted**

1. In a large bowl, combine the flour, cornmeal, baking powder and salt. In a small bowl, whisk together the egg, milk, syrup and butter; stir into dry ingredients just until moistened.

2. Pour into a 9-in. square baking pan coated with cooking spray. Bake at 400° for 15-20 minutes or until a toothpick inserted near the center comes out clean. Serve warm.

Orange Julius

I serve this in the morning when we have overnight guests. It's easy to make and requires only a few basic ingredients. Guests always rave about its "wake-up" taste!

—**JOYCE MUMMAU** MT. AIRY, MARYLAND

PREP/TOTAL TIME: 10 MIN. **MAKES:** 4-6 SERVINGS

- 1 **can (6 ounces) frozen orange juice concentrate**
- 1 **cup cold water**
- 1 **cup milk**
- ⅓ **cup sugar**
- 1 **teaspoon vanilla extract**
- 10 **ice cubes**

1. Combine the first five ingredients in a blender; process at high speed. Add ice cubes, a few at a time, blending until smooth. Serve immediately.

Chickpea Fritters with Sweet-Spicy Sauce

Chickpeas are a common ingredient in Pakistan, where I grew up. In my home I try to combine the light spice of Pakistani foods with the love of deep-fried foods that many Americans, including my daughters, enjoy.

—**SHAHRIN HASAN** YORK, PENNSYLVANIA

PREP: 15 MIN. **COOK:** 5 MIN./BATCH
MAKES: 2 DOZEN (1 CUP SAUCE)

- 1 **cup plain yogurt**
- 2 **tablespoons sugar**
- 1 **tablespoon honey**

- ½ **teaspoon salt**
- ½ **teaspoon pepper**
- ½ **teaspoon crushed red pepper flakes**

FRITTERS
- 1 **can (15 ounces) chickpeas or garbanzo beans, rinsed and drained**
- 1 **teaspoon ground cumin**
- ½ **teaspoon salt**
- ½ **teaspoon garlic powder**
- ½ **teaspoon ground ginger**
- 1 **egg**
- ½ **teaspoon baking soda**
- ½ **cup chopped fresh cilantro**
- 2 **green onions, thinly sliced**
  Oil for deep-fat frying

1. In a small bowl, combine the first six ingredients; refrigerate until serving.

2. Place chickpeas and seasonings in a food processor; process until finely ground. Add egg and baking soda; pulse until blended. Transfer to a bowl; stir in cilantro and green onions.

3. In an electric skillet or deep fryer, heat oil to 375°. Shape rounded tablespoonfuls of bean mixture into balls. Drop a few at a time into hot oil. Fry 2-3 minutes or until golden brown, turning frequently. Drain on paper towels. Serve with sauce.

QUEENS, NY

Some of the structures built for the 1964 World's Fair still stand in Flushing Meadows Park, including the Unisphere, the world's largest global sculpture.

❝ You'll think you're on Cape Cod when you taste this thick wholesome chowder made from a recipe I've treasured for many years. It's one of my husband's favorites. He likes it more and more, because over the years I've "customized" the basic recipe by including ingredients he enjoys. ❞

—LINDA LAZAROFF
HEBRON, CONNECTICUT

Country Fish Chowder

PREP: 15 MIN. **COOK:** 25 MIN. **MAKES:** 8-10 SERVINGS (2½ QUARTS)

- 1 cup chopped onion
- 4 bacon strips, chopped
- 3 cans (12 ounces each) evaporated milk
- 1 can (15¼ ounces) whole kernel corn, undrained
- 1 can (6½ ounces) chopped clams, undrained
- 3 medium potatoes, peeled and cubed
- 3 tablespoons butter
- 1 teaspoon salt
- ¾ teaspoon pepper
- 1 pound fish fillets (haddock, cod or flounder), cooked and broken into pieces

Crumbled cooked bacon, optional
Minced chives, optional

1. In a large saucepan, cook onion and bacon over medium heat until onion is tender; drain. Add milk, corn, clams, potatoes, butter, salt and pepper. Cover and cook over medium heat, stirring occasionally, until potatoes are tender, about 20 minutes.

2. Stir in fish and heat through. Ladle into bowls. If desired, top with bacon and chives.

Colcannon Potatoes

Every Irish family has its own version of this classic dish...my recipe comes from my father's family in Ireland. It's part of my St. Pat's menu, along with lamb chops, carrots and soda bread.

—MARILOU ROBINSON PORTLAND, OREGON

PREP: 10 MIN.   **COOK:** 35 MIN.   **MAKES:** 12-16 SERVINGS

- 2 **pounds cabbage, shredded**
- 2 **cups water**
- 4 **pounds potatoes, peeled and quartered**
- 2 **cups milk**
- 1 **cup chopped green onions**
  Salt and coarsely ground pepper to taste
- ¼ **cup butter, melted**
  Crumbled cooked bacon and minced fresh parsley

1. In a large saucepan, bring cabbage and water to a boil. Reduce heat; cover and simmer for 10-12 minutes or until tender. Drain, reserving cooking liquid. Keep cabbage warm.

2. Place cooking liquid and potatoes in a large saucepan; add enough additional water to cover the potatoes. Bring to a boil. Reduce heat; cover and cook for 15-17 minutes or until tender. Drain and keep warm.

3. In a small saucepan, bring the milk and onions to a boil; remove from the heat. In a large bowl, mash potatoes. Add milk mixture; beat until blended. Beat in the cabbage, salt and pepper. Drizzle with the melted butter, bacon and parsley.

A roll with a hole in the middle is nothing new. Even in ancient Egypt, some breads had holes in the middle. Versions of bagels can be found in a variety of cultures. Israelis don't boil bagels before baking, as Americans do; that technique is considered a Polish custom. When Jewish immigrants settled in Manhattan's Lower East Side, they wanted a taste of home, which included bagels. By 1900, those neighborhoods had 70 Jewish bakeries. In 1907, the International Beigel Bakers' Union was founded to keep a tight rein on bagel production. Harry Lender started one of the first bagel factories outside New York City, in New Haven, Connecticut, in 1927. He and his son, Murray, were the first to freeze bagels, which allowed them to be shipped to supermarkets across the country.

From-Scratch Bagels

Instead of going to a bakery, head to the kitchen and surprise your family with homemade bagels. For variation and flavor, sprinkle the tops with cinnamon-sugar instead of sesame and poppy seeds.

—REBECCA PHILLIPS BURLINGTON, CONNECTICUT

PREP: 30 MIN. + RISING **BAKE:** 20 MIN. + COOLING
MAKES: 1 DOZEN

- 1 teaspoon active dry yeast
- 1¼ cups warm milk (110° to 115°)
- ½ cup butter, softened
- 2 tablespoons sugar
- 1 teaspoon salt
- 1 egg yolk
- 3¾ to 4¼ cups all-purpose flour
  Sesame or poppy seeds, optional

1. In a large bowl, dissolve yeast in warm milk. Add the butter, sugar, salt and egg yolk; mix well. Stir in enough flour to form a soft dough.

2. Turn onto a floured surface; knead until smooth and elastic, about 6-8 minutes. Place in a greased bowl, turning once to grease top. Cover and let rise in a warm place until doubled, about 1 hour.

3. Punch dough down. Shape into 12 balls. Push thumb through centers to form a 1½-in. hole. Stretch and shape dough to form an even

ring. Place on a floured surface. Cover and let rest for 10 minutes; flatten bagels slightly.

4. Fill a Dutch oven two-thirds full with water; bring to a boil. Drop bagels, two at a time, into boiling water. Cook for 45 seconds; turn and cook 45 seconds longer. Remove with a slotted spoon; drain well on paper towels.

5. Sprinkle with sesame or poppy seeds if desired. Place 2 in. apart on greased baking sheets. Bake at 400° for 20-25 minutes or until golden brown. Remove from pans to wire racks to cool.

Anadama Bread

This Early American recipe from New England features an interesting combination of cornmeal and molasses.

—TASTE OF HOME TEST KITCHEN

PREP: 40 MIN. + RISING **BAKE:** 25 MIN.
MAKES: 1 LOAF (12 SLICES)

- ½ cup water
- ¼ cup cornmeal
- ½ cup molasses
- 2 tablespoons butter
- 1 package (¼ ounce) active dry yeast
- ½ cup warm water (110° to 115°)
- 1 teaspoon salt
- 3 to 3½ cups all-purpose flour

1. In a small saucepan, bring water and cornmeal to a boil. Reduce heat; cook for 2 minutes or until mixture thickens, stirring constantly. Remove from the heat; stir in molasses and butter. Cool to 110°-115°.

2. In a large bowl, dissolve yeast in warm water. Add the cornmeal mixture, salt and 2 cups flour; beat until smooth. Stir in enough remaining flour to form a soft dough.

3. Turn onto a floured surface; knead until smooth and elastic, about 6-8 minutes. Place in a greased bowl, turning once to grease top. Cover and let rise in a warm place until doubled, about 1 hour.

4. Punch dough down. Turn onto a lightly floured surface; shape into a loaf. Place in a greased 9-in. x 5-in. loaf pan. Cover and let rise until doubled, about 1 hour.

5. Bake at 375° for 25-30 minutes or until browned (cover loosely with foil if top browns too quickly). Remove from pan to a wire rack to cool.

Chestnut Dressing

I enjoyed this stuffing when I spent my first Thanksgiving with my husband, Mike. It's a family recipe his mother has been making for years. Italian seasoning and chestnuts add flavor and texture.

—**SHARON BRUNNER** MOHNTON, PENNSYLVANIA

PREP: 25 MIN. **BAKE:** 20 MIN.
MAKES: 18 SERVINGS (½ CUP EACH)

- 4 **celery ribs, chopped**
- 1 **large onion, chopped**
- 1½ **cups butter, cubed**
- 3 **cups chestnuts, shelled and coarsely chopped**
- 3 **tablespoons Italian seasoning**
- 10 **slices Italian bread (¾ inch thick), cubed**

1. In a large skillet, cook and stir celery and onion in butter until tender. Add chestnuts and Italian seasoning. Bring to a boil. Reduce heat; simmer, uncovered, for 10 minutes. Add bread cubes and stir to coat.

2. Transfer to an ungreased 13x9-in. baking dish. Bake, uncovered, at 350° for 20-25 minutes until golden brown.

Smoked Salmon Appetizer

I often spoon my salmon spread onto endive leaves for an easy and pretty presentation. It's a healthful addition to any celebration.

—**PATRICIA NIEH**
PORTOLA VALLEY, CALIFORNIA

PREP: 15 MIN. **MAKES:** 16 SERVINGS

- 12 **ounces reduced-fat cream cheese, cubed**
- ⅓ **cup fat-free sour cream**
- 4 **ounces smoked salmon or lox**
- 2 **tablespoons capers, drained**
- 3 **green onions, chopped (white parts only)**
- 1 **tablespoon dried thyme**
- 1 **tablespoon lemon juice**
- ¼ **teaspoon hot pepper sauce**
- ⅛ **teaspoon pepper**
- 1 **tablespoon minced chives**
  Assorted fresh vegetables or assorted crackers

1. Place the first nine ingredients in a food processor; cover and process until smooth. Chill until serving. Sprinkle with chives; serve with vegetables.

◄● dishing about food

The Northeast was known for its large chestnut harvests until the early 20th century, when a blight wiped out most of the American chestnut trees. Roasting chestnuts on the streets of Manhattan was a time-honored winter tradition, but it is less common today with rising prices and changing American tastes.

◄● dishing about food

Smoking has been a food-preservation technique for centuries. In America, West Coast anglers first did this to store bountiful catches of wild salmon. In the early 1900s, the smoking industry took off in Brooklyn, New York, with Acme Smoked Fish. Today, this family-run business is one of the largest smoked fish processors in the U.S.

Poutine is an indulgent Canadian comfort food that first was served in the 1950s in rural Quebec. It has since crossed the border into many of the neighboring states, especially in New England. You'll find poutine sold as mixed fries or mix fry in Maine, disco or Elvis fries in New Jersey and gravy-cheddar fries in Connecticut. There are endless variations, and hearty steak fries may be used instead of shoestrings. The super-fresh cheese curds can be replaced with mozzarella, cheddar, feta, American cheese or cheese sauce. The thin gravy might be omitted or another sauce, such as spaghetti sauce, used.

SHELBURNE, VT

The Shelburne Museum, located in northern Vermont, features several restored buildings, as well as a diverse offering of art and Americana.

Poutine

The ultimate in French-Canadian junk food, poutine commonly features warm fries topped with cheese curds and gravy. This side dish is quick to fix with frozen potatoes and packaged gravy but has all the traditional greasy-spoon comfort.

—**SHELISA TERRY** HENDERSON, NEVADA

PREP/TOTAL TIME: 30 MIN. **MAKES:** 4 SERVINGS

- 4 **cups frozen French-fried potatoes**
- 1 **envelope brown gravy mix**
- ¼ **teaspoon pepper**
- ½ **cup white cheddar cheese curds or cubed white cheddar cheese**

1. Prepare fries according to package directions.

2. Meanwhile, prepare gravy mix according to package directions. Stir in pepper. Place fries on a serving plate; top with cheese curds and gravy.

Buffalo Chicken Wings

Hot wings got their start in Buffalo, New York. Although there was no sporting event on at the time, today spicy wings and cool sauces are traditional game-day fare. Cayenne, hot sauce and spices keep these tangy wings good and hot, just like the originals.

—NANCY CHAPMAN CENTER HARBOR, NEW HAMPSHIRE

PREP: 10 MIN. **COOK:** 10 MIN./BATCH **MAKES:** ABOUT 4 DOZEN

- 25 **whole chicken wings (5 pounds)**
  Oil for frying
- 1 **cup butter, cubed**
- ¼ **cup Louisiana-style hot sauce**
- ¾ **teaspoon cayenne pepper**
- ¾ **teaspoon celery salt**
- ½ **teaspoon onion powder**
- ½ **teaspoon garlic powder**
  Celery ribs and ranch salad dressing, optional

1. Cut chicken wings into three sections; discard wing tip sections. In an electric skillet, heat 1 in. of oil to 375°. Fry wings in oil, a few at a time, for 3-4 minutes on each side or until chicken juices run clear. Drain on paper towels.

2. Meanwhile, in a small saucepan, melt butter. Stir in the hot sauce and spices. Place chicken in a large bowl; add sauce and toss to coat. Remove to a serving plate with a slotted spoon. Serve with celery and ranch dressing if desired.

Editor's Note: *Uncooked chicken wing sections (wingettes) may be substituted for whole chicken wings.*

BUFFALO, NY

The Anchor Bar isn't the only stop you should make in Buffalo. Try to include Shea's Performing Arts Center on Main Street, where you could take in a touring Broadway production.

Pickled Eggs with Beets

Ever since I can remember, my mother has served pickled eggs at Easter. It was a tradition that my family expected. I made them for my granddaughter the last time she visited, and they were all gone before she left!

—**MARY BANKER** FORT WORTH, TEXAS

PREP: 10 MIN. + CHILLING   **MAKES:** 12 SERVINGS

 2 **cans (15 ounces each) whole beets**
12 **hard-cooked eggs, peeled**
 1 **cup sugar**
 1 **cup water**
 1 **cup cider vinegar**

1. Drain the beets, reserving 1 cup juice (discard remaining juice or save for another use). Place beets and eggs in a 2-qt. glass jar.

2. In a small saucepan, bring the sugar, water, vinegar and reserved beet juice to a boil. Pour over beets and eggs; cool.

3. Cover tightly and refrigerate for at least 24 hours before serving.

Korean Wontons

Korean wontons (called mandoo) are not hot and spicy like many of the traditional Korean dishes. Filled with inexpensive vegetables and beef, the fried dumplings are very easy to prepare.

—**CHRISTY LEE** HORSHAM, PENNSYLVANIA

PREP: 35 MIN.   **COOK:** 30 MIN.   **MAKES:** 5 DOZEN

 2 **cups shredded cabbage**
 1 **cup canned bean sprouts**
 ½ **cup shredded carrots**
1½ **teaspoons plus 2 tablespoons canola oil, divided**
 ⅓ **pound ground beef**
 ⅓ **cup sliced green onions**
1½ **teaspoons sesame seeds, toasted**
1½ **teaspoons minced fresh gingerroot**
 3 **garlic cloves, minced**
1½ **teaspoons sesame oil**
 ½ **teaspoon salt**
 ½ **teaspoon pepper**
 1 **package (12 ounces) wonton wrappers**
 1 **egg, lightly beaten**
 3 **tablespoons water**

1. In a wok or large skillet, stir-fry cabbage, bean sprouts and carrots in 1½ teaspoons canola oil until tender; set aside.

2. In a small skillet, cook beef over medium heat until no longer pink; drain. Add to the vegetable mixture. Stir in the onions, sesame seeds, ginger, garlic, sesame oil, salt and pepper.

3. Place about 1 tablespoon of filling in the center of each wonton wrapper. Combine egg and water. Moisten wonton edges with egg mixture; fold opposite corners over filling and press to seal.

4. Heat the remaining canola oil in a large skillet. Cook wontons in batches for 1-2 minutes on each side or until golden brown, adding additional oil if needed.

Matzo Ball Soup

My mother is of Russian descent and would make this for Friday night dinner when I was growing up. It's a very comforting soup that brings back so many happy memories.

—BERNICE POLAK NEW SMYRNA BEACH, FLORIDA

PREP: 10 MIN. **COOK:** 2¾ HOURS
MAKES: 18 SERVINGS (4½ QUARTS)

- 1 **broiler/fryer chicken (3½ to 4 pounds), cut up**
- 8 **cups water**
- 6 **carrots, cut in half lengthwise, then into 2-inch pieces**
- 1 **large onion, peeled**
- 2 **celery ribs, cut in half**
- 2 **sprigs fresh dill (3-inch pieces)**
- 1 **can (49½ ounces) chicken broth**
- 2 **teaspoons salt**
- ½ **teaspoon pepper**
- 2 **cups cooked noodles**

MATZO BALLS
- 2 **eggs**
- 1 **cup matzo meal**
- 2 **tablespoons rendered chicken fat or canola oil**
- 2 **tablespoons minced fresh parsley**
- 2 **teaspoons salt**
  Dash pepper
- ½ **to 1 cup cold water**

1. Place chicken and water in an 8-qt. stockpot. Cover and bring to a boil; skim fat. Add carrots, onion and celery. Fold dill in half and wrap many times with thread or kitchen string; add to soup. Bring to a boil. Reduce heat to medium-low; cover but keep lid ajar and simmer for 2½ hours.

2. Meanwhile, combine first six matzo ball ingredients in a medium bowl. Add enough water to make a thick pancakelike batter. Refrigerate for 2 hours (mixture thickens as it stands).

3. Remove and discard onion, celery and dill from broth. Remove chicken and allow to cool; debone and cut into chunks. Skim fat from broth. Return chicken to stockpot. Add the broth, salt and pepper; bring to a boil. Reduce heat; cover and simmer.

4. To complete matzo balls, bring 4 quarts water to a boil in a 5-qt. Dutch oven. With very wet hands, form heaping teaspoonfuls of batter

into balls. If mixture is too thin, stir in 1-2 tablespoons of matzo meal.

5. Drop balls into boiling water. They will sink when dropped but will rise in a few minutes. Cook for 10 minutes. Remove with slotted spoon and add to simmering soup. Add noodles; heat through.

Glazed Cinnamon Apples

If you are seeking comfort food on the sweet side, this warm and yummy apple dish, made with cinnamon and nutmeg, fits the bill.

—MEGAN MAZE OAK CREEK, WISCONSIN

PREP: 20 MIN. **COOK:** 3 HOURS **MAKES:** 7 SERVINGS

- 6 **large tart apples**
- 2 **tablespoons lemon juice**
- ½ **cup packed brown sugar**
- ½ **cup sugar**
- 2 **tablespoons all-purpose flour**
- 1 **teaspoon ground cinnamon**
- ¼ **teaspoon ground nutmeg**
- 6 **tablespoons butter, melted**
  Vanilla ice cream

1. Peel, core and cut each apple into eight wedges; transfer to a 3-qt. slow cooker. Drizzle with lemon juice. Combine the sugars, flour, cinnamon and nutmeg; sprinkle over apples. Drizzle with butter.

2. Cover and cook on low for 3-4 hours or until apples are tender. Serve as a side or as a dessert with ice cream.

NEW YORK, NY

A household name across America, the Waldorf-Astoria Hotel has been famous for its Art Deco grandeur, as well as delicious cuisine, for more than 100 years.

Waldorf Salad

Lemon juice gives this easy salad a tangy zip, and the apples and nuts offer a nice crunch. It's light, refreshing and effortless to assemble. What's not to love?

—CHUCK HINZ PARMA, OHIO

PREP/TOTAL TIME: 30 MIN. **MAKES:** 9 SERVINGS

- 2 **medium Red Delicious apples, chopped**
- 2 **medium Golden Delicious apples, chopped**
- 2 **tablespoons lemon juice**
- 2 **celery ribs, chopped**
- ¾ **cup chopped walnuts**
- ½ **cup raisins**
- 1 **cup mayonnaise**

Ground cinnamon and ground nutmeg, optional

1. In a large bowl, toss apples with lemon juice. Gently stir in the celery, walnuts, raisins and mayonnaise. Sprinkle with cinnamon and nutmeg if desired. Refrigerate until serving.

Daiquiris

This daiquiri blends sweet and tart to perfection! For a party, make it in chilled pitchers, then pour over ice before serving.

—TASTE OF HOME TEST KITCHEN

PREP/TOTAL TIME: 10 MIN. **MAKES:** 4 SERVINGS

- 5 to 5½ cups ice cubes, divided
- ¾ cup light rum
- 2½ ounces lime juice
- 2 ounces simple syrup

GARNISH

- Lime slices

1. Fill a shaker three-fourths full with ice. Divide remaining ice among four hurricane or cocktail glasses; set aside.

2. Add the rum, lime juice and simple syrup to shaker; cover and shake for 10-15 seconds or until condensation forms on outside of shaker. Strain into prepared glasses. Garnish with lime slices as desired.

Crumb-Topped Clams

In my family, it wouldn't be Christmas Eve without baked clams. They're simple to make and always a hit.

—ANNMARIE LUCENTE MONROE, NEW YORK

PREP: 35 MIN. **BROIL:** 10 MIN. **MAKES:** 2 DOZEN

- 2 pounds kosher salt
- 2 dozen fresh littleneck clams
- ½ cup dry bread crumbs
- ¼ cup chicken broth
- 1 tablespoon minced fresh parsley
- 2 tablespoons olive oil
- 2 garlic cloves, minced
- ¼ teaspoon dried oregano
  Dash pepper
- 1 tablespoon panko (Japanese) bread crumbs
  Lemon wedges

1. Spread salt into an ovenproof metal serving platter or a 15x10x1-in. baking pan. Shuck clams, leaving clams and juices in bottom shells. Arrange on prepared platter; divide juices among shells.

2. In a small bowl, mix dry bread crumbs, chicken broth, parsley, oil, garlic, oregano and pepper; spoon over clams. Sprinkle with bread crumbs.

3. Broil 4-6 in. from heat for 6-8 minutes or until the clams are firm and crumb mixture is crisp and golden brown. Serve immediately with lemon wedges.

The most popular theory about this dressing's origin is that it was named for the Thousand Islands region in New York, between the St. Lawrence Seaway and Lake Ontario. One of the guides who took fishing parties to the Thousand Islands always served his wife's special salad dressing as part of their shore dinners. New York actress and cookbook author Mary Irwin is said to have named the recipe after one such meal. Another version of the story, however, claims a chef at the Drake Hotel in Chicago came up with the recipe.

NEW YORK, NY

The first fine dining restaurant in the U.S., Delmonico's opened in 1837 on Beaver Street in the city's Financial District.

Thousand Island Dressing

This creamy dressing has a fresh taste that complements any tossed salad.

—ELIZABETH HUNTER PROSPERITY, SOUTH CAROLINA

PREP/TOTAL TIME: 10 MIN. MAKES: 1 CUP

- ¾ cup fat-free plain yogurt
- 3 tablespoons chili sauce
- 1 tablespoon sweet pickle relish
  Sugar substitute equivalent to ¾ teaspoon sugar

1. In a small bowl, whisk together all ingredients. Refrigerate until serving.

Wild Blueberry Muffins

Nothing is better then a warm blueberry muffin in the morning. The flavor of wild blueberries makes these extra-special!

—DEWEY GRINDLE BLUE HILL, MAINE

PREP: 15 MIN. BAKE: 20 MIN. MAKES: 1 DOZEN

- ¼ cup butter, softened
- ⅓ cup sugar
- 1 egg
- 2⅓ cups all-purpose flour
- 4 teaspoons baking powder
- ½ teaspoon salt
- 1 cup milk
- 1 teaspoon vanilla extract
- 1½ cups fresh or frozen wild blueberries or 1 can (15 ounces) water-packed wild blueberries, well drained

STREUSEL TOPPING
- ½ cup sugar
- ⅓ cup all-purpose flour
- ½ teaspoon ground cinnamon
- ¼ cup cold butter, cubed

1. In a bowl, cream butter and sugar. Add egg; mix well. Combine dry ingredients; add to creamed mixture alternately with milk. Stir in vanilla. Gently fold in blueberries.

2. Fill greased or paper-lined muffin cups two-thirds full. In a small bowl, combine the sugar, flour and cinnamon; cut in the butter until crumbly. Sprinkle over muffins. Bake at 375° for 20-25 minutes or until a toothpick comes out clean. Cool for 5 minutes before removing from pan to wire rack.

Delmonico Potatoes

These rich, cheesy potatoes are perfect for a large family gathering or a potluck supper.

—ARNOLD SONNENBERG BROOKVILLE, OHIO

PREP: 55 MIN. + CHILLING BAKE: 50 MIN.
MAKES: 12-16 SERVINGS

- 9 medium potatoes, unpeeled
- 1 cup milk
- 1 cup heavy whipping cream
- 1½ teaspoons salt
- 1 teaspoon ground mustard
- ¼ teaspoon pepper
- ¼ teaspoon ground nutmeg
- 1½ pounds shredded sharp cheddar cheese

1. Place potatoes in a large saucepan and cover with water. Bring to a boil. Reduce heat; cover and cook for 30-40 minutes or until tender. Drain and refrigerate several hours or overnight.

2. Peel potatoes and coarsely shred. In a saucepan, heat the milk, cream, salt, mustard, pepper and nutmeg over medium heat until bubbles form around side of pan. Reduce heat; add cheese, stirring until melted.

3. Place potatoes in a greased 13x9-in. baking dish. Pour cheese sauce over potatoes. Bake at 325° for 50-55 minutes or until heated through.

Amish Potato Bread

A tasty mix of whole wheat and all-purpose flour, plus a small amount of mashed potatoes, give this golden bread its wonderful texture. The loaf is very moist and stays that way even days after making it.

—**SUE VIOLETTE** NEILLSVILLE, WISCONSIN

PREP: 30 MIN. + RISING **BAKE:** 40 MIN. + COOLING
MAKES: 1 LOAF (16 SLICES)

1 package (¼ ounce) active dry yeast
¼ cup warm water (110° to 115°)
1¾ cups warm fat-free milk (110° to 115°)
⅓ cup butter, softened
¼ cup mashed potatoes (without added milk and butter)
3 tablespoons sugar
1½ teaspoons salt
1½ cups whole wheat flour
3½ to 4 cups all-purpose flour

1. In a large bowl, dissolve yeast in warm water. Add the milk, butter, potatoes, sugar, salt, whole wheat flour and ½ cup all-purpose flour. Beat until smooth. Stir in enough remaining flour to form a firm dough.

2. Turn onto a lightly floured surface; knead until smooth and elastic, about 6-8 minutes. Place in a bowl coated with cooking spray, turning once to coat the top. Cover and let rise in a warm place until doubled, about 1 hour.

3. Punch dough down and turn onto a floured surface; shape into a loaf. Place in a 9x5-in. loaf pan coated with cooking spay. Cover and let rise until doubled, about 30 minutes.

4. Bake at 350° for 40-45 minutes or until golden brown. Remove from pan to wire rack to cool.

Wilted Greens Over Potatoes

Here's a homespun recipe representative of my Pennsylvania Dutch heritage. I can remember not liking this dish as a child, but I've become fond of it over the years.

—**BONNIE BLACK** SLIGO, PENNSYLVANIA

PREP/TOTAL TIME: 30 MIN. **MAKES:** 4 SERVINGS

4 cups packed fresh spinach, dandelion, collard, mustard, beet or turnip greens
2 cups plus 2 tablespoons water, divided
5 thick-sliced bacon strips, diced
4 teaspoons all-purpose flour
1 tablespoon sugar
1 cup 2% milk
½ teaspoon salt
1 egg yolk, lightly beaten
⅓ cup cider vinegar
Hot mashed potatoes

1. In a large saucepan, bring greens and 2 cups water to a boil. Reduce heat; cover and simmer for 4-8 minutes or until tender. Drain and set aside.

2. In a large skillet, cook bacon over medium heat until crisp. Using a slotted spoon, remove to paper towels; drain, discarding drippings.

3. In a small bowl, combine flour and sugar; stir in the milk, salt and remaining water until smooth. Pour into skillet and bring to a boil; cook and stir for 2 minutes or until thickened.

4. Stir a small amount of the hot mixture into the egg yolk; return all to the pan, stirring constantly. Bring to a gentle boil; cook and stir 2 minutes longer. Add the vinegar, greens and bacon; heat through. Serve over the mashed potatoes.

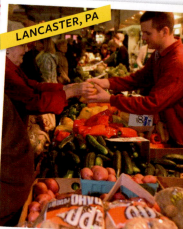

LANCASTER, PA

America's oldest continually running farmers market—more than 275 years!—the Lancaster Central Market is the place to go for fresh produce, dairy and baked goods.

Soda bread was a quick bread baked by cooks in many countries. Native Americans used potash from wood ashes to leaven their bread. When yeast bread made with hard flour became more popular in England and the U.S., the Irish continued to use their soft flour, which rises better with baking soda. True Irish soda bread does not contain raisins. Bread with raisins is called railway cake or spotted dog.

BOSTON, MA

The South Boston St. Patrick's Day parade was first marched in 1737, making it the world's oldest parade of its kind.

Irish Soda Bread

This bread is prepared much like a biscuit. Mix the dough just until moistened to keep it tender.

—**GLORIA WARCZAK** CEDARBURG, WISCONSIN

PREP: 15 MIN. **BAKE:** 30 MIN. **MAKES:** 6-8 SERVINGS

- 2 **cups all-purpose flour**
- 2 **tablespoons brown sugar**
- 1 **teaspoon baking powder**
- 1 **teaspoon baking soda**
- ½ **teaspoon salt**
- 3 **tablespoons butter**
- 2 **eggs**
- ¾ **cup buttermilk**
- ⅓ **cup raisins**

1. In a large bowl, combine flour, brown sugar, baking powder, baking soda and salt. Cut in butter until crumbly. In a small bowl, whisk 1 egg and buttermilk. Stir into flour mixture just until moistened. Fold in raisins.

2. Knead on a floured surface for 1 minute. Shape into a round loaf; place on a greased baking sheet. Cut a ¼-in.-deep cross in top of loaf. Beat remaining egg; brush over loaf.

3. Bake at 375° for 30-35 minutes or until golden brown.

Caraway Irish Soda Bread: *Add 1 to 2 tablespoons caraway seeds to the dry ingredients.*

Cape Codder

Here's a delicious cranberry-flavored drink that is not only refreshing in the summertime, but would be great any time of the year.

—TASTE OF HOME TEST KITCHEN

PREP/TOTAL TIME: 5 MIN. **MAKES:** 1 SERVING

- ½ to ¾ cup ice cubes
- 1½ ounces vodka
- 3 ounces cranberry juice

GARNISH
    Lime twist

1. Place ice in a highball glass. Pour the vodka and cranberry juice into the glass. Garnish as desired.

Crispy Oven-Fried Oysters

These flavorful breaded and baked oysters, served with a zippy jalapeno mayonnaise, are just divine! I entered this recipe in a seafood contest and took first place in the hors d'oeuvres category. Oysters make an interesting party finger food.

—MARIE RIZZIO INTERLOCHEN, MICHIGAN

PREP/TOTAL TIME: 30 MIN.
MAKES: ABOUT 2½ DOZEN
(ABOUT ⅔ CUP JALAPENO MAYONNAISE)

- ¾ cup all-purpose flour
- ⅛ teaspoon salt
- ⅛ teaspoon pepper
- 2 eggs

- 1 cup dry bread crumbs
- ⅔ cup grated Romano cheese
- ¼ cup minced fresh parsley
- ½ teaspoon garlic salt
- 1 pint shucked oysters or 2 cans (8 ounces each) whole oysters, drained
- 2 tablespoons olive oil

JALAPENO MAYONNAISE
- ¼ cup mayonnaise
- ¼ cup sour cream
- 2 medium jalapeno peppers, seeded and finely chopped
- 2 tablespoons milk
- 1 teaspoon lemon juice
- ¼ teaspoon grated lemon peel
- ⅛ teaspoon salt
- ⅛ teaspoon pepper

1. In a shallow bowl, combine the flour, salt and pepper. In another shallow bowl, whisk eggs. In a third bowl, combine the bread crumbs, cheese, parsley and garlic salt.

2. Coat oysters with flour mixture, then dip in eggs, and coat with crumb mixture. Place in a greased 15x10x1-in. baking pan; drizzle with oil.

3. Bake at 400° for 15 minutes or until golden brown. Meanwhile, in a small bowl, whisk the jalapeno mayonnaise ingredients. Serve with oysters.

Editor's Note: *Wear disposable gloves when cutting hot peppers; the oils can burn skin. Avoid touching your face.*

MASSACHUSETTS

The Bay State's largest food crop, cranberries garner lots of attention. Not only are they the official state berry, they're the official color and beverage.

Both New York and San Francisco lay claim to inventing the martini. However, their versions before Prohibition are not what we think of as today's martini; both coasts used bitters and gin in the original drink. The martini has waxed and waned in popularity. The movie *Goldfinger* brought the martini back to the American consciousness when James Bond asked for "a vodka martini, shaken, not stirred." The drink had another resurgence in the 1980s and '90s. With all the flavored variations available today, it seems the martini will be remain in the forefront for a while.

Martini

Martinis can be made with either vodka or gin. Our taste panel's preference was for gin, but try them both and decide for yourself. Be warned, this is a strong and serious drink.

—TASTE OF HOME TEST KITCHEN

PREP/TOTAL TIME: 5 MIN. **MAKES:** 1 SERVING

Ice cubes
3 ounces gin or vodka
½ ounce dry vermouth
GARNISH
Pimiento-stuffed olives

1. Fill a mixing glass or tumbler three-fourths full with ice. Add gin and vermouth; stir until condensation forms on outside of glass. Strain into a chilled cocktail glass. Garnish as desired.

Editor's Note: *This recipe makes a dry martini. Use less vermouth for an extra-dry martini; use more for a "wet" martini. You may also serve the martini over ice in a rocks glass.*

Apple Martini: *Omit vermouth and olives. Reduce vodka to 2 ounces and use 1½ ounces sour apple liqueur and 1½ teaspoons lemon juice. Garnish with a green apple slice.*

Chocolate Martini: *Omit vermouth and olives. Reduce vodka to 2 ounces and use 2 ounces creme de cacao or chocolate liqueur. Garnish with chocolate shavings.*

Butternut Squash Risotto

Change up the flavor of risotto any time by using in-season vegetables like butternut squash, spices and broths for a consistency that's both creamy and comforting.

—KATIE FERRIER WASHINGTON, WASHINGTON DC

PREP: 35 MIN. **COOK:** 30 MIN. **MAKES:** 6 SERVINGS

8 cups cubed peeled butternut squash
¼ cup olive oil, divided
½ teaspoon salt
¼ teaspoon pepper
4 to 4½ cups vegetable broth
1 cup water
1 small onion, chopped
2 garlic cloves, minced
2 cups uncooked arborio rice
1 cup lager
2 tablespoons butter
1 teaspoon ground ancho chile pepper
½ teaspoon ground nutmeg
1 cup grated Parmesan cheese

1. In a bowl, combine squash, 2 tablespoons oil, salt and pepper; toss to coat. Transfer to a greased 15x10x1-in. baking pan. Bake, uncovered, at 450° for 20-25 minutes or until tender, stirring once.

2. In a large saucepan, heat broth and water; keep warm. In a large skillet, saute onion and garlic in remaining oil until tender. Add rice; cook and stir for 2-3 minutes. Reduce heat; stir in lager. Cook and stir until all of the liquid is absorbed.

3. Add heated broth mixture, ½ cup at a time, stirring constantly. Allow the liquid to absorb between additions. Cook just until risotto is creamy and rice is almost tender. (Cooking time is about 20 minutes.) Add the butter, chili pepper, nutmeg and squash; cook and stir until heated through. Remove from the heat; stir in cheese. Serve immediately.

Chesapeake Crab Dip

Our school is a Maryland Green School, and many of our students work to improve the health of our local treasure, the Chesapeake Bay. This recipe, starring crab in a rich creamy dip, reminds me of the importance of that.

—CAROL BRZEZINSKI MARRIOTTSVILLE, MARYLAND

PREP: 20 MIN. **BAKE:** 20 MIN. **MAKES:** 2¼ CUPS

- 1 package (8 ounces) cream cheese, softened
- 1 cup (8 ounces) sour cream
- 1 tablespoon lemon juice
- 1 teaspoon ground mustard
- 1 teaspoon seafood seasoning
- ⅛ teaspoon garlic salt
- 3 cans (6 ounces each) lump crabmeat, drained
- ½ cup shredded cheddar cheese
- ⅛ teaspoon paprika
  Assorted crackers

1. In a large bowl, combine the cream cheese, sour cream, lemon juice, mustard, seafood seasoning and garlic salt. Fold in crab. Transfer to a greased 9-in. pie plate. Sprinkle with cheese and paprika.

2. Bake at 325° for 20-25 minutes or until bubbly. Serve warm with crackers. Refrigerate leftovers.

Turnip Casserole

I think turnips are great alone or with other vegetables. Try chopping them to add texture and flavor to soups and stews, and enjoy them in this change-of-pace hot dish.

—DORIS HUBERT EAST KILLINGLY, CONNECTICUT

PREP: 25 MIN. **BAKE:** 20 MIN. **MAKES:** 4 SERVINGS

- 4 medium turnips, peeled and cubed
- 1 egg, lightly beaten
- ⅓ cup sugar
- 3 tablespoons butter
- ½ teaspoon salt
- ¼ teaspoon ground cinnamon

1. Place turnips in a large saucepan and cover with water. Bring to a boil. Reduce heat; cover and cook for 15 minutes or until tender and drain. Transfer turnips to a bowl and mash. Add the egg, sugar, butter and salt.

2. Transfer to a greased 1-qt. baking dish; sprinkle with cinnamon. Cover and bake at 350° for 20-25 minutes or until a thermometer reads 160°.

Classic Corn Chowder

PREP/TOTAL TIME: 30 MIN. **MAKES:** 4-6 SERVINGS

- 6 potatoes, peeled and diced
  Water
- 1 can (16 ounces) whole kernel corn, drained
- 4 cups whole milk
- 1 large onion, diced
- 4 bacon strips, cooked and crumbled
- 1 teaspoon salt
- ¼ teaspoon pepper
- ¼ teaspoon dried thyme

1. Place potatoes in a Dutch oven and cover with water. Bring to a boil. Reduce heat; cover and cook for 10-15 minutes or until tender. Drain. Add remaining ingredients; bring to a boil. Reduce heat and simmer for 15 minutes or until onion is soft.

"My grandmother and mother made this dish to warm their families during the cold winter months. Nothing chased away a chill like this chowder! Now when it's cold and damp outside, I make this and think of those days. Everyone in my household enjoys the delicious warmth of a steaming bowl of corn chowder."

—PHYLLIS WATSON
HAVELOCK, NORTH CAROLINA

dishing about food ◆➤

New England settlers originally had apple orchards on their farms so they could produce hard cider, which the entire family drank. Once beer became readily available and people moved to the cities, the demand for hard cider declined.

NEW ENGLAND

New England's orchards grow more than 40 varieties of apples, from Akane to Zestar!, some of which are still used for cider.

Apple Cider Cinnamon Rolls

Feeling creative, I put an apple spin on a traditional cinnamon roll recipe. The results were yummy! A panful is perfect for a weekend morning.

—**KIM FORNI** CLAREMONT, NEW HAMPSHIRE

PREP: 1 HOUR + RISING **BAKE:** 30 MIN. **MAKES:** 1 DOZEN

3¼ cups all-purpose flour
¼ cup sugar
1 package (¼ ounce) quick-rise yeast
½ teaspoon salt
¾ cup 2% milk
¼ cup apple cider or juice
¼ cup plus ⅓ cup butter, softened, divided
1 egg
2 cups finely chopped peeled tart apples
1¼ cups packed brown sugar

¾ cup finely chopped walnuts
3 teaspoons ground cinnamon

APPLE CIDER CREAM CHEESE FROSTING
2 cups apple cider or juice
1 cinnamon stick (3 inches)
1 package (8 ounces) cream cheese, softened
¼ cup butter, softened
1 cup confectioners' sugar

1. In a large bowl, combine 2¼ cups flour, sugar, yeast and salt. In a small saucepan, heat the milk, cider and ¼ cup butter to 120°-130°. Add to dry ingredients; beat just until moistened. Add egg; beat until smooth. Stir in enough remaining flour to form a soft dough (dough will be sticky).

2. Turn onto a floured surface; knead until smooth and elastic, about 6-8 minutes. Cover and let rest for 10 minutes. Roll into a 15x10-in. rectangle. Spread remaining butter to within ½ in. of edges. Combine the apples, brown sugar, walnuts and cinnamon; sprinkle over butter.

3. Roll up jelly-roll style, starting with a long side; pinch seam to seal. Cut into 12 slices. Place cut side down in a greased 13x9-in. baking dish. Cover and let rise in a warm place for 30 minutes.

4. Bake at 325° for 30-35 minutes or until golden brown. For frosting, place cider and cinnamon stick in a small saucepan. Bring to a boil; cook until liquid is reduced to ¼ cup, about 20 minutes. Discard cinnamon stick; cool cider.

5. In a large bowl, beat cream cheese and butter until fluffy. Add confectioners' sugar and reduced cider; beat until smooth. Spread over warm rolls.

Bloody Mary

Horseradish makes this Bloody Mary special. Without the horseradish, you'll have a more traditional drink, and without the alcohol, you'll have a Virgin Mary. Serve it with a stalk of celery, dill pickle spear or green olives.

—TASTE OF HOME TEST KITCHEN

PREP/TOTAL TIME: 10 MIN. **MAKES:** 1 SERVING

1½ to 2 cups ice cubes, divided
2 ounces vodka
1 cup tomato juice, chilled
1 tablespoon lemon juice
1½ teaspoons lime juice
¾ teaspoon Worcestershire sauce
½ teaspoon prepared horseradish, optional
⅛ teaspoon celery salt
⅛ teaspoon pepper
⅛ teaspoon hot pepper sauce

GARNISHES
  Celery rib, pickle spear, green and ripe olives, cucumber slice and/or cocktail shrimp

1. Fill a shaker three-fourths full with ice. Place remaining ice in a highball glass; set aside.

2. Add the vodka, juices, Worcestershire sauce, horseradish if desired, celery salt, pepper and pepper sauce to shaker; cover and shake for 10-15 seconds or until condensation forms on outside of shaker. Strain into prepared glass. Garnish as desired.

Editor's Note: *To make a batch of Bloody Marys (4 servings), place 1 cup ice in a 2-qt. pitcher. Add 1 cup vodka, 4 cups tomato juice, ¼ cup lemon juice, 2 tablespoons lime juice, 1 tablespoon Worcestershire sauce, 2 teaspoons prepared horseradish if desired, ½ teaspoon celery salt, ½ teaspoon pepper and ½ teaspoon hot pepper sauce; stir to combine. Serve over ice.*

◆◆ dishing about food

French bartender Fernand Petiot is credited with creating the Bloody Mary at the famous Harry's New York Bar in Paris. After Prohibition, Petiot crossed the Atlantic to work at the King Cole Bar in the St. Regis Hotel in New York, and brought the drink with him. It was first called the Red Snapper, but later, the name Bloody Mary stuck. It is usually considered a morning drink or a hangover cure.

Coffee Milk

After one sip, you'll see why this is the official drink of Rhode Island…it's just delectable!

—TASTE OF HOME TEST KITCHEN

PREP: 10 MIN. **COOK:** 35 MIN. + CHILLING
MAKES: 4 SERVINGS (1 CUP SYRUP)

- ½ **cup finely ground coffee**
- 2 **cups cold water**
- 1 **cup sugar**

EACH SERVING
- 1 **cup cold 2% milk**

1. Place ground coffee in filter basket of a drip coffeemaker. Add 2 cups cold water to water reservoir and brew according to manufacturer's directions.

2. In a small saucepan, combine coffee and sugar; bring to a boil. Reduce heat; simmer until reduced by half, about 30 minutes. Remove from heat; transfer to a small bowl or covered container. Refrigerate, covered, 30 minutes or until cold. Store in the refrigerator, covered, up to 2 weeks.

To prepare coffee milk: *In a tall glass, mix 1 cup milk and 2-4 tablespoons coffee milk syrup.*

Manhattan Clam Chowder

I typically serve this chowder with a tossed salad and hot rolls. It's easy to make and tastes wonderful on cold winter evenings. My family's enjoyed it for more than 30 years.

—JOAN HOPEWELL COLUMBUS, NEW JERSEY

PREP: 10 MIN. **COOK:** 40 MIN.
MAKES: 6-8 SERVINGS (ABOUT 2 QUARTS)

- 1 **cup chopped onion**
- ⅔ **cup chopped celery**
- 2 **teaspoons minced green pepper**
- 1 **garlic clove, minced**
- 2 **tablespoons butter**
- 2 **cups hot water**
- 1 **cup cubed peeled potatoes**
- 1 **can (28 ounces) diced tomatoes, undrained**
- 2 **cans (6½ ounces each) minced clams, undrained**
- 1 **teaspoon salt**
- ½ **teaspoon dried thyme**
- ¼ **teaspoon pepper**
     Dash cayenne pepper
- 2 **teaspoons minced fresh parsley**

1. In a 3-qt. saucepan, cook the onion, celery, green pepper and garlic in butter over low heat for 20 minutes, stirring frequently. Add the water and potatoes; bring to a boil. Reduce heat; cover and simmer for 15 minutes or until the potatoes are tender.

2. Add the tomatoes, clams, salt, thyme, pepper and cayenne; heat through. Stir in parsley. Serve immediately.

Cinnamon Apples

Teenagers will have fun melting the red cinnamon candies that give bright color to these tender apples. Serve as a salad or a side dish to accompany pork.

—ALMA DINSMORE LEBANON, INDIANA

PREP: 20 MIN. + CHILLING **MAKES:** 6 SERVINGS

- 2 **cups water**
- ¾ **cup red-hot candies**
- ⅓ **cup sugar**
- 6 **medium tart apples, peeled and quartered**

1. In a large saucepan, bring the water, candies and sugar to a boil over medium heat; boil and stir until candies and sugar are dissolved.

2. Reduce heat; carefully add apples. Cook, uncovered, until apples are tender. Cool slightly. With a slotted spoon, transfer apples to a serving dish; pour sugar syrup over apples. Cool slightly. Cover and refrigerate for at least 3 hours.

Parker House Dinner Rolls

It's impossible to eat just one of my mom's famous yeast rolls. They're light and fluffy with a wonderful flavor...and even more delicious served warm with a little butter!

—**SUSAN HANSEN** AUBURN, ALABAMA

PREP: 1 HOUR + RISING **BAKE:** 10 MIN.
MAKES: 3 DOZEN

- ½ **cup shortening**
- ¼ **cup sugar**
- 2 **teaspoons salt**
- 1½ **cups boiling water**
- 2 **tablespoons active dry yeast**
- ½ **cup warm water (110° to 115°)**
- 3 **eggs**
- 6¾ to 7¼ **cups all-purpose flour**
- ¼ **cup butter, melted**

1. In a large bowl, combine the shortening, sugar and salt. Stir in boiling water. Cool to 110°-115°. Dissolve yeast in warm water. Add yeast mixture, eggs and 3 cups flour to shortening mixture. Beat until smooth. Stir in enough remaining flour to form a soft dough.

2. Turn onto a floured surface; knead until smooth and elastic, about 6-8 minutes. Place in a greased bowl, turning once to grease the top. Cover and let rise in a warm place until doubled, about 45 minutes.

3. Punch dough down; turn onto a lightly floured surface. Roll dough to ½-in. thickness. Cut with a 2½-in. biscuit cutter. Fold circles in half; press edges to seal. Place 2 in. apart on baking sheets coated with cooking spray. Cover and let rise until doubled, about 30 minutes.

4. Bake at 400° for 10-12 minutes or until golden brown. Remove to wire racks. Brush with butter. Serve warm.

Calico Clams Casino

A few years ago, I came across this recipe in the back of my files when I was looking for a special appetizer. Everyone raved about it. Now it's an often-requested dish.

—**PAULA SULLIVAN** BARKER, NEW YORK

PREP/TOTAL TIME: 20 MIN. **MAKES:** 8 SERVINGS

- 3 **cans (6½ ounces each) minced clams**
- 1 **cup (4 ounces) shredded part-skim mozzarella cheese**
- 1 **cup (4 ounces) shredded cheddar cheese**
- 4 **bacon strips, cooked and crumbled**
- 3 **tablespoons seasoned bread crumbs**
- 3 **tablespoons butter, melted**
- 2 **tablespoons each finely chopped onion, celery and sweet red, yellow and green peppers**
- 1 **garlic clove, minced**
   Dash dried parsley flakes

1. Drain the clams, reserving 2 tablespoons juice. In a large bowl, combine the clams and remaining ingredients; stir in the reserved clam juice. Spoon mixture into greased 6-oz. custard cups or clamshell dishes; place on baking sheets.

2. Bake at 350° for 10-15 minutes or until heated through and lightly browned.

BOSTON, MA

Patriot Paul Revere was a metalsmith by trade, crafting everything from silverware to ship siding. His statue stands in Paul Revere Mall; you can visit his restored home nearby, on 19 North Square.

Authentic Boston Brown Bread

The rustic, old-fashioned flavor of this hearty bread is out of this world!

—SHARON DELANEY-CHRONIS
SOUTH MILWAUKEE, WISCONSIN

PREP: 20 MIN. **COOK:** 50 MIN. + STANDING
MAKES: 1 LOAF (12 SLICES)

- ½ cup cornmeal
- ½ cup whole wheat flour
- ½ cup rye flour
- ½ teaspoon baking powder
- ½ teaspoon baking soda
- ¼ teaspoon salt
- 1 cup buttermilk
- ⅓ cup molasses
- 2 tablespoons brown sugar
- 1 tablespoon canola oil
- 3 tablespoons chopped walnuts, toasted
- 3 tablespoons raisins
  Cream cheese, softened, optional

1. In a large bowl, combine the first six ingredients. In another bowl, whisk the buttermilk, molasses, brown sugar and oil. Stir into dry ingredients just until moistened. Fold in walnuts and raisins. Transfer to a greased 8x4-in. loaf pan; cover with foil.

2. Place pan on a rack in a boiling-water canner or other large, deep pot; add 1 in. of hot water to pot. Bring to a gentle boil; cover and steam for 45-50 minutes or until a toothpick inserted near the center comes out clean, adding more water to the pot as needed.

3. Remove pan from the pot; let stand for 10 minutes before removing bread from pan to a wire rack. Serve with cream cheese if desired.

Cinnamon Blueberry Jam

Watching my grandmother can hundreds of jars of tomatoes, peaches and pears inspired me to first try making jams and jellies myself. I can remember, as a girl, going down into her cellar—all those jars on the shelves gave me such a warm, homey feeling! My family enjoys this jam on warm corn or blueberry muffins. The cinnamon's a bit of a surprise.

—BARBARA BURNS PHILLIPSBURG, NEW JERSEY

PREP: 15 MIN. **PROCESS:** 10 MIN.
MAKES: 4 HALF-PINTS

- 1 pound fresh or frozen blueberries (about 1 quart)
- 3½ cups sugar
- 1 tablespoon bottled lemon juice
- ¼ teaspoon ground cinnamon
- ⅛ teaspoon ground cloves
- 1 pouch (3 ounces) liquid fruit pectin

1. Crush the blueberries; measure 2½ cups and place in a large saucepan. Add the sugar, lemon juice, cinnamon and cloves; bring to a rolling boil over high heat, stirring constantly. Quickly stir in pectin. Return to a full rolling boil; boil for 1 minute, stirring constantly.

2. Remove from the heat; skim off foam. Carefully ladle hot mixture into hot half-pint jars, leaving ¼-in. headspace. Remove air bubbles; wipe rims and adjust lids. Process for 10 minutes in a boiling-water canner.

Editor's Note: *The processing time listed is for altitudes of 1,000 feet or less. Add 1 minute to the processing time for each 1,000 feet of additional altitude.*

◀●▶ **dishing about food**

Baked beans can be made with an array of ingredients from ketchup to molasses or corn syrup. In 2012, Vermont led the country in the production of maple syrup with 750,000 gallons. So it's no surprise that Vermont-style baked beans use maple syrup!

Vermont Baked Beans

These baked beans are nothing like the canned variety you may be used to. The rich sauce has a wonderful smokiness from chopped bacon and a subtle sweetness from maple syrup.

—ELIZABETH HORTON BRATTLEBORO, VERMONT

PREP: 15 MIN. + SOAKING **BAKE:** 3 HOURS **MAKES:** 8 SERVINGS

- 1 **pound dried navy beans**
- 4 **cups water**
- ½ **pound thick-sliced bacon strips, chopped**
- 1 **large onion, chopped**
- ⅔ **cup maple syrup**
- 2 **teaspoons salt**
- 1 **teaspoon ground mustard**
- ½ **teaspoon coarsely ground pepper**

1. Soak beans according to package directions. Drain and rinse beans, discarding the liquid. Place beans in a Dutch oven; add water. Bring to a boil.

2. Meanwhile, in a large skillet, cook bacon over medium heat until crisp; drain. Stir the onion, syrup, salt, mustard, pepper and bacon into the beans.

3. Cover and bake at 300° for 3 to 3½ hours or until beans are tender and reach desired consistency, stirring every 30 minutes.

KENNETT SQUARE, PA

One weekend each September, State Street in Kennett Square becomes Mushroom Boulevard for the Mushroom Festival. Fungus fans come from near and far to celebrate (and eat!) the area's prize crop.

Mushroom-Swiss Mac & Cheese

Portobello mushrooms and three kinds of cheese give an upscale spin to a classic casserole. To make this more of an entree, I add 2 cups of cubed cooked chicken.

—**DAWN MOORE** WARREN, PENNSYLVANIA

PREP: 40 MIN. **BAKE:** 25 MIN. **MAKES:** 8 SERVINGS

- 1 package (16 ounces) mini penne pasta
- ½ pound baby portobello mushrooms, chopped
- 1 small onion, finely chopped
- 2 tablespoons butter
- 1 tablespoon olive oil
- 1 garlic clove, minced

SAUCE
- 5 tablespoons butter
- 1 package (8 ounces) cream cheese, cubed
- 1¼ cups whole milk
- 1¼ cups half-and-half cream
- 2½ cups (10 ounces) shredded Swiss cheese
- 1¼ cups grated Parmesan and Romano cheese blend
- ¼ teaspoon salt
- ¼ teaspoon pepper
- 6 bacon strips, cooked and crumbled

TOPPING
- ⅓ cup panko (Japanese) bread crumbs
- 2 tablespoons minced fresh parsley
- 2 tablespoons butter, melted

1. Cook pasta according to package directions. Meanwhile, in a large skillet, saute mushrooms and onion in butter and oil until tender. Add garlic; cook 1 minute longer. Set aside.

2. For sauce, in a large saucepan, melt butter. Stir in cream cheese until smooth. Gradually add milk and cream; heat through. Stir in the cheeses, salt and pepper until blended. Stir in bacon.

3. Drain pasta; toss with mushroom mixture and sauce. Transfer to a greased 13x9-in. baking dish. Combine the bread crumbs, parsley and melted butter; sprinkle over mixture. Bake, uncovered, at 375° for 25-30 minutes or until golden brown.

Turtle Soup

This hearty soup has a real "snappy" flavor from the cayenne pepper and lemon juice. It's a treat and makes good use of turtle meat. Serve up a steaming bowlful with a salad and fresh bread for a satisfying meal.

—DAVE WOOD ELMWOOD PARK, NEW JERSEY

PREP: 25 MIN. **COOK:** 2¼ HOURS
MAKES: 4-6 SERVINGS

- 1⅓ **pounds turtle meat**
- 4½ **cups water**
- 2 **medium onions**
- 1 **bay leaf**
- ¼ **teaspoon cayenne pepper**
- 1¼ **teaspoons salt**
- 5 **tablespoons butter, cubed**
- ⅓ **cup all-purpose flour**
- 3 **tablespoons tomato puree**
- 3 **tablespoons Worcestershire sauce**
- ⅓ **cup chicken broth**
- 2 **hard-cooked eggs, chopped**
- ¼ **cup lemon juice**
  Chopped fresh parsley, optional

1. In a heavy 4-qt. saucepan, bring turtle meat and water to a boil. Skim off foam. Chop 1 onion and set aside. Quarter the other onion; add to saucepan along with bay leaf, cayenne pepper and salt. Cover and simmer for 2 hours or until the meat is tender.

2. Remove meat with a slotted spoon and cut into ½-in. cubes; set aside. Strain broth and set aside.

3. Rinse and dry saucepan; melt butter over medium-high heat. Cook chopped onion until tender. Add flour; cook and stir until bubbly

and lightly browned. Whisk in reserved broth; cook and stir until thickened. Reduce heat; stir in tomato puree and Worcestershire sauce. Simmer, uncovered, for 10 minutes.

4. Add chicken broth, eggs, lemon juice and meat. Simmer for 5 minutes or until heated through. Garnish with parsley if desired.

Blueberry Tea Bread

When you're looking for a "berry" impressive treat, turn to this recipe.

—DOROTHY SIMPSON BLACKWOOD, NEW JERSEY

PREP: 15 MIN. **BAKE:** 1 HOUR + COOLING
MAKES: 1 LOAF

- 2 **cups all-purpose flour**
- 1 **cup sugar**
- 1 **tablespoon baking powder**
- ¼ **teaspoon salt**
- 1½ **cups fresh or frozen blueberries**
- 1 **teaspoon grated orange peel**
- 2 **eggs**
- 1 **cup milk**
- 3 **tablespoons canola oil**
  Whipped cream cheese, optional

1. In a bowl, combine flour, sugar, baking powder and salt. Stir in blueberries and orange peel. In another bowl, beat eggs; add milk and oil. Stir into dry ingredients just until moistened.

2. Pour into a greased 9x5-in. loaf pan. Bake at 350° for 1 hour or until a toothpick inserted near the center comes out clean. Cool in pan for 10 minutes; remove to a wire rack to cool completely. Serve with cream cheese if desired.

◀◆ dishing about food

Turtle soup was once a delicacy served only by the wealthy at special occasions. The middle class dined on mock turtle soup, which used calves' heads for the turtle meat. When the English came to America, they found an abundance of turtles and the soup became commonplace.

◀◆ dishing about food

Wild or low-bush blueberries grow in many parts of our country, but Maine has the honor of being the largest blueberry producer.

Buckle is an old-fashioned cakelike dessert. It's typically made with blueberries, but other fresh berries can be used. The streusel topping gives the dessert a crumbled (buckled) look.

Blueberry Buckle

This recipe came from my grandmother. As children, my sister and I remember going to Pennsylvania for blueberry picking. Mother taught us to pick only perfect berries, and those gems went into this wonderful recipe.

—**CAROL DOLAN** MT. LAUREL, NEW JERSEY

PREP: 20 MIN. **BAKE:** 30 MIN. **MAKES:** 4-6 SERVINGS

¼ cup butter, softened
¾ cup sugar
1 egg
2 cups all-purpose flour
2 teaspoons baking powder
¼ teaspoon salt
½ cup milk
2 cups fresh blueberries

TOPPING
⅔ cup sugar
½ cup all-purpose flour
½ teaspoon ground cinnamon
⅓ cup cold butter, cubed

1. In a small bowl, cream butter and sugar until light and fluffy. Beat in egg. Combine the flour, baking powder and salt; add to creamed mixture alternately with milk, beating well after each addition. Fold in blueberries. Pour into greased 9-in. square baking pan.

2. For topping, in a small bowl, combine the sugar, flour and cinnamon; cut in butter until crumbly. Sprinkle over blueberry mixture.

3. Bake at 375° for 40-45 minutes or until a toothpick inserted near the center comes out clean. Cool on a wire rack.

Special Raisin Pie

When I first made this pie, I thought it was great. Then I entered it at the county fair and I guess the judges thought it was great, too, because it won first place!

—**LAURA FALL-SUTTON** BUHL, IDAHO

PREP: 40 MIN. **BAKE:** 35 MIN. + COOLING
MAKES: 8 SERVINGS

- 2½ **cups raisins**
- 2 **cups water**
- ⅓ **cup packed brown sugar**
- ⅓ **cup sugar**
- ⅛ **teaspoon salt**
- 2 **tablespoons plus 1½ teaspoons cornstarch**
- ¼ **cup cold water**
- 2 **tablespoons lemon juice**
- 1 **tablespoon orange juice**
- 2 **teaspoons grated orange peel**
- 1 **teaspoon grated lemon peel**
- ½ **teaspoon rum extract**
  Pastry for double-crust pie (9 inches)
- 2 **tablespoons butter**

1. In a small saucepan, combine raisins and water. Bring to a boil; cook 2 minutes. Add sugars and salt; cook until sugars are dissolved. Combine cornstarch and cold water until smooth; gradually stir into the pan. Cook and stir for 2 minutes or until thickened and bubbly. Remove from the heat; stir in the juices, peels and extract.

2. Roll out half of the pastry to fit a 9-in. pie plate; transfer pastry to pie plate. Fill with raisin mixture. Dot with butter.

3. Roll out remaining pastry; make a lattice crust. Trim, seal and flute edges. Bake at 375° for 35-40 minutes or until crust is golden brown and filling is bubbly, covering edges with foil during the last 10 minutes. Cool on a wire rack. Refrigerate leftovers.

Amish Sugar Cookies

These easy-to-make cookies simply melt in your mouth! I've passed the recipe around to many friends. After I gave the recipe to my sister, she entered the cookies in a local fair and won the "best of show" prize.

—**SYLVIA FORD** KENNETT, MISSOURI

PREP: 10 MIN. **BAKE:** 10 MIN./BATCH
MAKES: ABOUT 5 DOZEN

- 1 **cup butter, softened**
- 1 **cup canola oil**
- 1 **cup sugar**
- 1 **cup confectioners' sugar**
- 2 **eggs**
- 1 **teaspoon vanilla extract**
- 4½ **cups all-purpose flour**
- 1 **teaspoon baking soda**
- 1 **teaspoon cream of tartar**

1. In large bowl, beat the butter, oil and sugars. Beat in the eggs until well blended. Beat in the vanilla. Combine the flour, baking soda and cream of tartar; gradually add to the creamed mixture.

2. Drop dough by small teaspoonfuls onto ungreased baking sheets. Bake at 375° for 8-10 minutes or until lightly browned. Remove to wire racks to cool.

Grapes once grew wild throughout New England. Ephraim Bulls took the seeds from these plants and created the Concord grape in 1849. He named it after the town he lived near—Concord, Massachusetts. The hearty Concord grape ripens earlier than European varieties and can be picked before the weather turns cold. It's a key component of the mainstay PB&J sandwich, and is grown primarily in New York, Pennsylvania, Ohio, Michigan, Missouri and Washington.

Concord was home to several literary greats, including Ralph Waldo Emerson, Henry David Thoreau and Louisa May Alcott.

Concord Grape Pie

Instead of featuring typical fruits like cherries, blueberries, apples or peaches, this pie spotlights Concord grapes. Why not surprise your family with this delightfully different dessert tonight?

—LINDA ERICKSON HARBORCREEK, PENNSYLVANIA

PREP: 30 MIN. **BAKE:** 35 MIN. + COOLING
MAKES: 8 SERVINGS

- 4½ cups Concord grapes (about 2 pounds)
- 1 cup sugar
- ¼ cup all-purpose flour
- 2 teaspoons lemon juice
- ⅛ teaspoon salt
- 1 unbaked pastry shell (9 inches)

TOPPING
- ½ cup quick-cooking oats
- ½ cup packed brown sugar
- ¼ cup all-purpose flour
- ¼ cup butter, cubed

1. Squeeze the end of each grape opposite the stem to separate skins from pulp. Set skins aside. Place pulp in a medium saucepan; bring to a boil. Boil and stir for 1 minute. Press through a strainer or food mill to remove seeds.

2. In a large bowl, combine the pulp, skins, sugar, flour, lemon juice and salt; pour into pastry shell. In a small bowl, combine the oats, brown sugar and flour; cut in butter until crumbly. Sprinkle over filling.

3. Cover edges of pastry with foil. Bake at 425° for 15 minutes. Remove foil; bake 20 minutes longer or until golden brown. Cool the pie on a wire rack.

Five-Fruit Pie

This recipe gets compliments galore. I've given it to new neighbors or anyone who needs a pick-me-up. They all love it!

—JEAN ROSS OIL CITY, PENNSYLVANIA

PREP: 40 MIN. **BAKE:** 45 MIN. + COOLING
MAKES: 8 SERVINGS

- 1½ cups sugar
- 3 tablespoons cornstarch
- 2 tablespoons quick-cooking tapioca
- 1 cup chopped peeled tart apples
- 1 cup chopped fresh or frozen rhubarb
- 1 cup each fresh or frozen raspberries, blueberries and sliced strawberries

CRUST
- 2 cups all-purpose flour
- ½ teaspoon salt
- ½ cup shortening
- 1 egg
- ¼ cup cold water
- 2 teaspoons white vinegar
- 2 tablespoons half-and-half cream
- 2 tablespoons coarse sugar

1. In a large bowl, combine sugar, cornstarch, tapioca and fruit; let stand for 15 minutes. In another bowl, combine flour and salt; cut in shortening until mixture resembles coarse crumbs. Combine the egg, water and vinegar; stir into flour mixture just until moistened.

2. Divide dough in half so that one portion is slightly larger than the other. On a lightly floured surface, roll out larger portion to fit a 9-in. pie plate. Transfer pastry to pie plate; trim pastry to ½ in. beyond edge of plate. Spoon fruit mixture into crust.

3. Roll out remaining pastry to fit top of pie; make a lattice crust. Trim, seal and flute edges. Brush with cream; sprinkle with coarse sugar.

4. Bake at 375° for 45-55 minutes or until crust is golden brown and filling is bubbly. Cool completely on a wire rack.

Editor's Note: *If using frozen fruit, measure fruit while still frozen, then thaw completely. Drain in a colander, but do not press liquid out.*

Funnel cakes are a tradition at amusement parks, church festivals and state fairs. The name comes from the cooking method—pouring the batter through a funnel into hot oil. Many cultures have a variation of this treat, but the Pennsylvania Dutch are said to have made it popular in the United States.

BROOKLYN, NY

Past and present home to some of the world's most famous amusement parks, Coney Island has been a destination for funseekers since the 1830s.

Funnel Cakes

These are much simpler to make than doughnuts but taste just as good. They have been a regular treat of ours since we came across them when we lived in the Ozarks.

—MARY FAITH YODER UNITY, WISCONSIN

PREP: 15 MIN. **COOK:** 5 MIN./BATCH **MAKES:** 8 CAKES

- 2 **eggs**
- 1 **cup milk**
- 1 **cup water**
- ½ **teaspoon vanilla extract**
- 3 **cups all-purpose flour**
- ¼ **cup sugar**
- 1 **tablespoon baking powder**
- ¼ **teaspoon salt**
  Oil for deep-fat frying
  Confectioners' sugar

1. In a large bowl, beat eggs. Add milk, water and vanilla until well blended. Combine flour, sugar, baking powder and salt; beat into egg mixture until smooth. In an electric skillet or deep-fat fryer, heat oil to 375°.

2. Cover the bottom of a funnel spout with your finger; ladle ½ cup of batter into the funnel. Holding the funnel several inches above the oil, release your finger and move the funnel in a spiral motion until all the batter is released (scraping with a rubber spatula if needed).

3. Fry for 2 minutes on each side or until golden brown. Drain on paper towels. Dust with confectioners' sugar and serve warm.

Editor's Note: *The batter also can be poured from a liquid measuring cup instead of a funnel.*

Snickerdoodles

The history of this whimsically named treat is widely disputed, but the popularity of the classic cinnamon-sugar-coated cookie is undeniable! Add this version to your holiday cookie collection.

—**TASTE OF HOME TEST KITCHEN**

PREP/TOTAL TIME: 25 MIN. **MAKES:** 2½ DOZEN

- ½ **cup butter, softened**
- 1 **cup plus 2 tablespoons sugar, divided**
- 1 **egg**
- ½ **teaspoon vanilla extract**
- 1½ **cups all-purpose flour**
- ¼ **teaspoon baking soda**
- ¼ **teaspoon cream of tartar**
- 1 **teaspoon ground cinnamon**

1. In a large bowl, cream butter and 1 cup sugar until light and fluffy. Beat in egg and vanilla. Combine the flour, baking soda and cream of tartar; gradually add to the creamed mixture and mix well. In a small bowl, combine cinnamon and remaining sugar.

2. Shape dough into 1-in. balls; roll in cinnamon-sugar. Place 2 in. apart on ungreased baking sheets. Bake at 375° for 10-12 minutes or until lightly browned. Remove to wire racks to cool.

New York State Apple Muffins

I used to work at an apple orchard before retiring. We would give out this recipe to our customers, and so many of them came back telling us how good the muffins were. My family agrees! I think the cream cheese makes these stand out from other apple muffins.

—**LILLIAN DAVIS** BERKSHIRE, NEW YORK

PREP: 20 MIN. **BAKE:** 20 MIN. **MAKES:** 2 DOZEN

- 2 **cups all-purpose flour**
- ¾ **cup packed brown sugar**
- ½ **cup sugar**
- 2 **teaspoons baking soda**
- 1½ **teaspoons ground cinnamon**
- ½ **teaspoon salt**
- ¼ **to ½ teaspoon ground cloves**
- ⅛ **teaspoon ground nutmeg**
- 3 **eggs**
- ½ **cup butter, melted**
- 1 **package (3 ounces) cream cheese, cut into ¼-inch cubes and softened**
- ½ **teaspoon vanilla extract**
- 2 **cups chopped peeled apples**
- ½ **cup raisins**
- ½ **cup chopped walnuts**

TOPPING
- ½ **cup packed brown sugar**
- ½ **cup finely chopped walnuts**
- ¼ **cup all-purpose flour**
- 2 **tablespoons butter, melted**
- 1 **teaspoon ground cinnamon**
- 1 **teaspoon grated lemon peel**

1. In a large bowl, combine the first eight ingredients. Combine the eggs, butter, cream cheese and vanilla; stir into dry ingredients just until moistened (batter will be stiff). Fold in the apples, raisins and walnuts. Fill greased or paper-lined muffin cups two-thirds full. Combine the topping ingredients; sprinkle over batter.

2. Bake at 375° for 20-25 minutes or until a toothpick comes out clean. Cool for 5 minutes before removing from pans to wire racks.

Maine Potato Candy

Years ago, folks in Maine ate potatoes daily and used leftovers in bread, doughnuts and candies like this one.

—**BARBARA ALLEN** CHELMSFORD, MASSACHUSETTS

PREP: 30 MIN. + CHILLING **MAKES:** 2 POUNDS

- 4 **cups confectioners' sugar**
- 4 **cups flaked coconut**
- ¾ **cup cold mashed potatoes (without added milk and butter)**
- 1½ **teaspoons vanilla extract**
- ½ **teaspoon salt**
- 1 **pound dark chocolate candy coating, coarsely chopped**

1. In a large bowl, combine the first five ingredients. Line a 9-in. square pan with foil; butter the foil. Spread coconut mixture into pan. Cover and chill overnight. Cut into 2-in. x 1-in. rectangles. Cover and freeze.

2. In a microwave, melt candy coating; stir until smooth. Dip bars in coating; allow excess to drip off. Place on waxed paper to set. Store in an airtight container.

Big & Buttery Chocolate Chip Cookies

We love that the classic American cookie accidentally got its start when Ruth Wakefield used a Nestle chocolate bar as a substitute for baker's chocolate. The chocolate didn't melt, and the chocolate chip cookie was born. Our version—it's big, thick and soft—is based on a recipe from a bakery in California called Hungry Bear.

—**TASTE OF HOME TEST KITCHEN**

PREP: 35 MIN. + CHILLING **BAKE:** 10 MIN.
MAKES: 2 DOZEN

- 1 **cup butter, softened**
- 1 **cup packed brown sugar**
- ¾ **cup sugar**
- 2 **eggs**
- 1½ **teaspoons vanilla extract**
- 2⅔ **cups all-purpose flour**
- 1¼ **teaspoons baking soda**
- 1 **teaspoon salt**
- 1 **package (12 ounces) semisweet chocolate chips**
- 2 **cups coarsely chopped walnuts, toasted**

1. In a large bowl, cream the butter, brown sugar and sugar until light and fluffy. Beat in eggs and vanilla. Combine the flour, baking soda and salt; gradually add to creamed mixture and mix well. Stir in chocolate chips and walnuts.

2. Shape quarter cupfuls of dough into balls. Place in an airtight container, separating layers with waxed or parchment paper; cover and refrigerate overnight.

3. To bake, place dough balls 3 in. apart on parchment paper-lined baking sheets. Press a shallow indentation in the center of each with your thumb, reshaping sides to smooth any cracks. Let stand at room temperature for 30 minutes.

4. Bake at 400° for 10-12 minutes or until edges are golden brown. Cool for 2 minutes before removing from pans to wire racks; cool.

These cookies, similar to macaroons, are a treat in southern Italy and Sicily. The outside is covered with pine nuts and the inside is soft and chewy.

Italian Pignoli Cookies

Cookies are the crown jewels of Italian confections. I can't let a holiday go by without baking these traditional almond cookies rolled in mild pine nuts.

—MARIA REGAKIS SOMERVILLE, MASSACHUSETTS

PREP: 30 MIN. **BAKE:** 15 MIN./BATCH **MAKES:** 2½ DOZEN

1¼ cups (12 ounces) almond paste
½ cup sugar
4 egg whites, divided
1 cup confectioners' sugar
1½ cups pine nuts

1. In a small bowl, beat almond paste and sugar until crumbly. Beat in 2 egg whites. Gradually add confectioners' sugar; mix well.

2. Whisk remaining egg whites in a shallow bowl. Place pine nuts in another shallow bowl. Shape dough into 1-in. balls. Roll in the egg whites and coat with pine nuts. Place 2 in. apart on parchment paper-lined baking sheets. Flatten slightly.

3. Bake at 325° for 15-18 minutes or until lightly browned. Cool for 1 minute before removing from pans to wire racks. Store in an airtight container.

Grandma's Tandy Kake

My grandmother made this for all our family gatherings. Everyone loves it, and now I make it for every party we attend or host.

—JOHN MORGAN III LEBANON, PENNSYLVANIA

PREP: 20 MIN. **BAKE:** 20 MIN.+ CHILLING **MAKES:** 24 SERVINGS

- 4 eggs
- 2 cups sugar
- 1 cup 2% milk
- 1 teaspoon vanilla extract
- 2 cups all-purpose flour
- 1 teaspoon baking powder
- ¼ teaspoon salt
- 1¾ cups creamy peanut butter
- 5 milk chocolate candy bars (1.55 ounces each), chopped
- 2 tablespoons butter

1. Preheat oven to 350°. In a large bowl, beat eggs and sugar until thick and lemon-colored. Beat in milk and vanilla. In another bowl, combine flour, baking powder and salt; gradually add to egg mixture and mix well.

2. Spread into a greased 15x10x1-in. baking pan. Bake 20-25 minutes or until lightly browned. Cool 15 minutes on a wire rack. Spread peanut butter over top; cool completely.

3. In a double boiler or metal bowl over simmering water, melt chocolate and butter; stir until smooth. Gently spread over peanut butter. Refrigerate 30 minutes or until firm.

◀◆ dishing about food

Tandy Kakes, also known as Kandy Kakes, were first sold in 1931 by the Tastykake Baking Co. in the Philadelphia area and have been a Philly favorite ever since. The top seller is the peanut butter flavor, which is a sponge cake topped with peanut butter, then covered in milk chocolate.

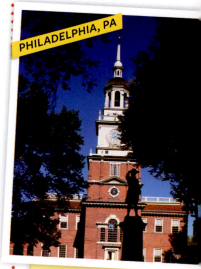

PHILADELPHIA, PA

Independence Hall, the province's state house at the time, was finished in 1756; 74 years after Philadelphia was founded.

New York-Style Cheesecake

My mother-in-law got this recipe from an Italian friend many years ago. I added the chocolate-nut crust. It is our very favorite dessert.

—**GLORIA WARCZAK** CEDARBURG, WISCONSIN

PREP: 20 MIN. **BAKE:** 45 MIN. + CHILLING
MAKES: 12 SERVINGS

- 1¼ cups crushed chocolate wafers
- ½ cup chopped walnuts
- ⅓ cup sugar
- ½ cup butter, melted

FILLING
- 2 packages (8 ounces each) cream cheese, softened
- 3 tablespoons sour cream
- ⅓ cup sugar
- ½ cup evaporated milk
- 1 teaspoon lemon juice
- 2 eggs, lightly beaten

TOPPING
- 2 cups (16 ounces each) sour cream
- 5 tablespoons sugar
- 1 teaspoon vanilla extract
  Cherry pie filling

1. In a small bowl, combine the wafer crumbs, walnuts and sugar; stir in butter. Press onto the bottom and halfway up the sides of an ungreased 10-in. springform pan. Freeze for 15 minutes.

2. In a large bowl, beat the cream cheese, sour cream and sugar until smooth. Combine milk and lemon juice; add to cream cheese mixture just until blended. Add eggs; beat on low speed just until combined.

3. Pour into crust. Place pan on a baking sheet. Bake at 350° for 35-40 minutes or until center is almost set.

4. Combine the sour cream, sugar and vanilla; carefully spread over cheesecake. Bake 10 minutes longer. Cool on a wire rack for 10 minutes. Carefully run a knife around edge of pan to loosen; cool 1 hour longer. Refrigerate overnight. Top with cherry pie filling. Refrigerate leftovers.

Maple Syrup Pudding

If you make this pudding just before eating, it will still be warm at dessert time, which makes it a comforting addition to a winter supper.

—**JEANETTE CAKOUROS** BRUNSWICK, MAINE

PREP/TOTAL TIME: 10 MIN. **MAKES:** 4 SERVINGS

- 1¾ cups milk
- 1 package (3 ounces) cook-and-serve vanilla pudding mix
- ¼ cup maple syrup
  Whipped topping, optional

1. In a microwave-safe bowl, whisk the milk, pudding mix and syrup until combined. Cover and microwave on high for 5-6 minutes or until mixture comes to a full boil, stirring every 2 minutes.

2. Pour into dessert dishes; cool slightly. Garnish with whipped topping if desired. Refrigerate leftovers.

Editor's Note: *This recipe was tested in a 1,100-watt microwave.*

First-Prize Doughnuts

One year I entered 18 different baked goods in the county fair, and all of them won ribbons. Here's my favorite prizewinning doughnut recipe. I've been making doughnuts since I was a bride—quite some time ago!

—**BETTY CLAYCOMB** ALVERTON, PENNSYLVANIA

PREP: 25 MIN. + RISING **COOK:** 5 MIN./BATCH
MAKES: 20 DOUGHNUTS

- 2 packages (¼ ounce each) active dry yeast
- ½ cup warm water (110° to 115°)
- ½ cup warm 2% milk (110° to 115°)
- ½ cup sugar
- ½ cup shortening
- 2 eggs
- 1 teaspoon salt
- 4½ to 5 cups all-purpose flour
  - Oil for deep-fat frying

TOPPINGS

- 1¼ cups confectioners' sugar
- 4 to 6 tablespoons water
  - Colored sprinkles and/or assorted breakfast cereals

1. In a large bowl, dissolve the yeast in warm water. Add the milk, sugar, shortening, eggs, salt and 2 cups flour; beat until smooth. Stir in enough remaining flour to form a soft dough.

2. Turn onto a floured surface; knead until smooth and elastic, about 6-8 minutes. Place in a greased bowl, turning once to grease the top. Cover and let rise in a warm place until doubled, about 1 hour.

3. Punch dough down. Turn onto a floured surface; roll out to ½-in. thickness. Cut with a floured 2½-in. doughnut cutter. Place on greased baking sheets. Cover and let rise until doubled, about 1 hour.

4. In an electric skillet or deep fryer, heat oil to 375°. Fry doughnuts, a few at a time, until golden brown on both sides. Drain on paper towels.

5. In a shallow bowl, combine confectioners' sugar and water until smooth. Dip the warm doughnuts in glaze; decorate as desired with sprinkles and/or cereals.

Pizzelle

This recipe was adapted from one used by my Italian-born mother and grandmother. They used old irons on a gas stove, but now we have the convenience of electric pizzelle irons. The cookies are so delectable and beautiful, they're worth the cost!

—**ELIZABETH SCHWARTZ**
TREVORTON, PENNSYLVANIA

PREP: 10 MIN. **COOK:** 5 MIN./BATCH **MAKES:** 7 DOZEN

- 18 eggs
- 3½ cups sugar
- 1¼ cups canola oil
- 1 tablespoon anise oil
- 6½ cups all-purpose flour

1. In a large bowl, beat the eggs, sugar and oils until smooth. Gradually add flour and mix well.

2. Bake in a preheated pizzelle iron according to manufacturer's directions until golden brown. Remove to wire racks to cool. Store in an airtight container.

"Dress up a cookie plate with these old-fashioned spice bars full of raisins, molasses, cinnamon, ginger and nuts. The chewy treats are great with coffee or hot cocoa on frosty days. These cookies are said to be called "hermits" because they keep well—they're even better when hidden away like a hermit for several days!"

—JERI TIRMENSTEIN
APACHE JUNCTION, ARIZONA

Hermits

PREP: 25 MIN.   **BAKE:** 10 MIN. + COOLING   **MAKES:** 16 COOKIES

- ⅓ cup raisins
- 1 cup all-purpose flour
- ⅓ cup packed brown sugar
- ½ teaspoon baking powder
- ½ teaspoon ground ginger
- ½ teaspoon ground cinnamon
- ¼ teaspoon salt
- ¼ cup molasses
- 3 tablespoons butter, melted
- 1 egg white or 2 tablespoons egg substitute
- 1 teaspoon vanilla extract
- ⅓ cup chopped walnuts

1. Place raisins in a small bowl; cover with boiling water. Let stand for 5 minutes; drain and set aside.

2. In a large bowl, combine the flour, brown sugar, baking powder, ginger, cinnamon and salt. Combine the molasses, butter, egg white and vanilla; stir into dry ingredients just until moistened. Fold in walnuts and raisins.

3. Divide batter in half; shape each half into a 12-in. x 2-in. rectangle 2 in. apart on an ungreased baking sheet. Bake at 375° for 10-15 minutes or until edges are lightly browned and edges are set.

4. Transfer to a cutting board; cut with a serrated knife into 1½-in. rectangles. Remove to wire racks to cool. Store in an airtight container.

Chocolate Guinness Cake

One bite and everyone will propose a toast to this moist, chocolaty cake. The cream cheese frosting resembles the foamy head on a pint of dark ale.

—MARJORIE HENNIG SEYMOUR, INDIANA

PREP: 25 **BAKE:** 45 MIN. + COOLING **MAKES:** 12 SERVINGS

- 1 cup Guinness (dark beer)
- ½ cup butter, cubed
- 2 cups sugar
- ¾ cup baking cocoa
- 2 eggs, beaten
- ⅔ cup sour cream
- 3 teaspoons vanilla extract
- 2 cups all-purpose flour
- 1½ teaspoons baking soda

TOPPING

- 1 package (8 ounces) cream cheese, softened
- 1½ cups confectioners' sugar
- ½ cup heavy whipping cream

1. Grease a 9-in. springform pan and line the bottom with parchment paper; set aside.

2. In a small saucepan, heat beer and butter until butter is melted. Remove from the heat; whisk in sugar and cocoa until blended. Combine the eggs, sour cream and vanilla; whisk into beer mixture. Combine flour and baking soda; whisk into beer mixture until smooth. Pour batter into prepared pan.

3. Bake at 350° for 45-50 minutes or until a toothpick inserted near the center comes out clean. Cool completely in pan on a wire rack. Remove sides of pan.

4. In a large bowl, beat cream cheese until fluffy. Add confectioners' sugar and cream; beat until smooth (do not overbeat). Remove cake from the pan and place on a platter or cake stand. Ice top of cake so that it resembles a frothy pint of beer. Refrigerate leftovers.

POTTSVILLE, PA

Orange-Glazed Crullers

I enjoy preparing these lovely treats with my grandchildren. The make-ahead dough is great when planning a gathering.

—**MURIEL LERDAL** HUMBOLDT, IOWA

PREP: 25 MIN. + RISING
COOK: 20 MIN. + CHILLING **MAKES:** ABOUT 3 DOZEN

- 1 package (¼ ounce) active dry yeast
- ¼ cup warm water (110° to 115°)
- ¾ cup warm 2% milk (110° to 115°)
- ½ cup butter, softened
- 2 eggs, lightly beaten
- ¼ cup sugar
- 1 teaspoon salt
- 4 cups all-purpose flour
  Oil for deep-fat frying

GLAZE
- 2 cups confectioners' sugar
- 3 tablespoons orange juice
- 1 teaspoon grated orange peel

1. In a large bowl, dissolve yeast in water. Beat in the milk, butter, eggs, sugar, salt and 2 cups of flour. Beat until smooth. Stir in enough remaining flour to form a soft dough. Place in a greased bowl, turning once to grease top. Cover and refrigerate overnight.

2. Punch dough down; divide in half. Return one portion to the refrigerator. On a floured surface, roll out second portion into an 18x9-in. rectangle; cut widthwise into ¾-in. strips. Fold each strip in half lengthwise and twist several times. Pinch the ends to seal.

3. Place on greased baking sheets. Repeat with remaining dough. Cover and let rise until almost doubled, about 35-45 minutes.

4. In an electric skillet or deep-fat fryer, heat oil to 375°. Fry crullers, a few at a time, about 1 minute on each side or until golden brown, turning with a slotted spoon. Drain on paper towels. In a small bowl, combine glaze ingredients; brush over warm crullers.

Shoofly Pie

Shoofly pie is to the Pennsylvania Dutch as pecan pie is to Southerners. And my grandmother's recipe makes the very best traditional Shoofly Pie!

—**MARK MORGAN** WATERFORD, WISCONSIN

PREP: 30 MIN. **BAKE:** 45 MIN. **MAKES:** 6-8 SERVINGS

- 1 unbaked pastry shell (9 inches)
- 1 egg yolk, lightly beaten

FILLING
- ½ cup packed brown sugar
- ½ cup molasses
- 1 egg
- 1½ teaspoons all-purpose flour
- ½ teaspoon baking soda
- 1 cup boiling water

TOPPING
- 1½ cups all-purpose flour
- ¾ cup packed brown sugar
- ¾ teaspoon baking soda
  Dash salt
- 6 tablespoons cold butter

1. Line pastry with a double thickness of heavy-duty foil. Bake at 350° for 10 minutes. Remove foil; brush crust with egg yolk. Bake 5 minutes longer; cool on a wire rack.

2. For filling, in a small bowl, combine the brown sugar, molasses, egg, flour and baking soda; gradually add boiling water. Cool to room temperature; pour into prepared crust.

3. For topping, in a large bowl, combine the flour, brown sugar, baking soda and salt. Cut in butter until crumbly. Sprinkle over filling.

4. Bake at 350° for 45-50 minutes or until golden brown and filling is set. Cool on a wire rack. Store in the refrigerator.

Mamie Eisenhower's Fudge

My mother came across this effortless recipe in a newspaper some 40 years ago. One taste and you'll see why it doesn't take long for a big batch to disappear.

—**LINDA FIRST** HINSDALE, ILLINOIS

PREP: 20 MIN. + CHILLING **MAKES:** ABOUT 6 POUNDS

- 1 tablespoon plus ½ cup butter, divided
- 3 milk chocolate candy bars (two 7 ounces, one 1.55 ounces), broken into pieces
- 4 cups (24 ounces) semisweet chocolate chips
- 1 jar (7 ounces) marshmallow creme
- 1 can (12 ounces) evaporated milk
- 4½ cups sugar
- 2 cups chopped walnuts

1. Line a 13x9-in. pan with foil and butter the foil with 1 tablespoon butter; set aside. In a large heat-proof bowl, combine the candy bars, chocolate chips and marshmallow creme; set aside.

2. In a large heavy saucepan over medium-low heat, combine the milk, sugar and remaining butter. Bring to a boil, stirring constantly. Boil and stir for 4½ minutes. Pour over chocolate mixture; stir until chocolate is melted and mixture is smooth and creamy. Stir in walnuts. Pour into prepared pan. Cover and refrigerate until firm.

3. Using foil, lift fudge out of pan; cut into 1-in. squares. Store in an airtight container in the refrigerator.

Pumpkin Patch Pie

If you'd like to make pumpkin pie from a fresh pumpkin, here's an easy recipe that eliminates the guesswork. Use a pie pumpkin for maximum flavor.

—**JANE VAN DEUSEN** ONEONTA, NEW YORK

PREP: 1 HOUR 55 MIN. **BAKE:** 1¼ HOURS
MAKES: 6-8 SERVINGS

- 1 medium pie pumpkin (about 3 pounds)
- ⅔ cup sugar, divided
- 1½ teaspoons ground cinnamon, divided
- ⅛ teaspoon salt
- ½ teaspoon ground ginger
- ½ teaspoon ground nutmeg
- 3 eggs, lightly beaten
- 1 can (5 ounces) evaporated milk
- ½ cup milk
  Pastry for single-crust pie (9 inches)

1. Wash pumpkin; cut a 6-in. circle around stem. Remove top and set aside. Remove loose fibers and seeds from the inside and discard or save seeds for toasting. In a small bowl, combine ⅓ cup sugar, ½ teaspoon cinnamon and salt; sprinkle around inside of pumpkin.

2. Replace the top. Place in a greased 15x10x 1-in. baking pan. Bake at 325° for 1½ hours or until very tender. Cool.

3. Scoop out pumpkin; puree in a blender until smooth. Place 2 cups pureed pumpkin in a large bowl. Add the ginger, nutmeg and the remaining sugar and cinnamon. Stir in the eggs, evaporated milk and milk.

4. Line a 9-in. pie plate with pastry; trim pastry to ½ in. beyond edge of plate. Flute edges or decorate with pastry leaves. Pour filling into crust.

5. Cover edges with foil. Bake at 375° for 75-80 minutes or until a knife inserted near the center comes out clean. Cool on a wire rack.

Editor's Note: *Additional pastry will be needed to decorate pie with pastry leaves.*

WASHINGTON, DC

The White House kitchen staff is equipped to prepare full meals for 140 and hors d'oeuvres for more than 1,000!

Both Maine and Pennsylvania lay claim to whoopie pies, also known as gobs in western Pennsylvania. Two cakelike cookies hold a fluffy white filling, like a soft version of a sandwich cookie. In Maine, the cookies may be as large as a hamburger bun. In fact, Labadie's Bakery in Lewiston first sold the treat in 1925 and sells 5-, 12- and 16-inch pies today. The Amish whoopie pie recipe is thought to have originated in Germany and emigrated with them. In the coalfields of western Pennsylvania, gobs were included in miners' lunch buckets. The dark cakes may have reminded miners of the coal lumps in the refuse pile, which were called gobs. Today, whoopie pies are made in a variety of flavors.

Chocolate Dream Whoopie Pies

Chocolate lovers will simply adore these cute triple-chocolate irresistible goodies. Two luscious cookies, a yummy mousselike filling and mini semisweet chips—mmm!

—JILL PAPKE OCONOMOWOC, WISCONSIN

PREP: 40 MIN.   **BAKE:** 15 MIN./BATCH + COOLING   **MAKES:** ABOUT 1 DOZEN

1 package chocolate cake mix (regular size)	1 cup 2% milk
3 eggs	½ cup milk chocolate chips
½ cup canola oil	⅔ cup shortening
1 teaspoon vanilla extract	⅓ cup butter, softened
FILLING	¾ teaspoon vanilla extract
⅔ cup sugar	**GARNISH**
2 tablespoons all-purpose flour	1 cup miniature semisweet chocolate chips
⅛ teaspoon salt	

1. In a large bowl, combine the cake mix, eggs, oil and vanilla; beat on low speed for 30 seconds. Beat on medium for 2 minutes (mixture will be sticky).

2. Drop by 2 tablespoonfuls 2 in. apart onto greased baking sheets. Bake at 350° for 9-11 minutes or until edges are set. Cool for 2 minutes before removing to wire racks to cool completely.

3. For filling, in a small saucepan, combine the sugar, flour and salt. Gradually add milk. Bring to a boil; cook and stir for 1-2 minutes or until thickened. Stir in chocolate chips until melted. Transfer to a small bowl; cover and refrigerate until chilled, about 1 hour.

4. In a large bowl, beat the shortening and butter until fluffy. Beat in chocolate mixture and vanilla.

5. Spread chocolate filling on the bottoms of half of the cookies, about 2 tablespoons on each; top with remaining cookies. Roll sides in miniature chocolate chips for garnish. Store in the refrigerator.

Watergate Cake

This cake was a huge hit the very first time I made it. I hadn't been sure I'd like it, but I was hooked immediately! It has a nice, light flavor if you like to avoid super-sweet desserts.

—STEPHANIE CURVELO
NEW BEDFORD, MASSACHUSETTS

PREP: 10 MIN. **BAKE:** 30 MIN. + COOLING
MAKES: 15 SERVINGS

- 1 package yellow cake mix (regular size)
- 1 package (3.4 ounces) instant pistachio pudding mix
- 1 cup club soda
- ½ cup canola oil
- 3 eggs
- ¾ cup pistachios

FROSTING
- 2 packages (3.4 ounces each) instant pistachio pudding mix
- 2 cups heavy whipping cream
- 1 cup 2% milk

1. Preheat oven to 350°. In a large bowl, combine cake mix, pudding mix, club soda, oil and eggs; beat on low speed for 30 seconds. Beat on medium for 2 minutes. Stir in pistachios. Transfer to a greased 13x9-in. baking pan. Bake 30-35 minutes or until a toothpick inserted in center comes out clean. Cool on a wire rack.

2. For frosting, in a small bowl, combine pudding mix, whipping cream and milk; beat until soft peaks form. Spread over cake.

Maine Mud Cookies

Every year as winter makes way for spring, we here in Maine experience a fifth season we call "mud season." I made this special treat just to get through that period. These cookies bring a smile to every face.

—KATHLEEN WINSLOW SWANVILLE, MAINE

PREP: 15 MIN. **BAKE:** 10 MIN./BATCH
MAKES: 4 DOZEN

- 2⅓ cups all-purpose flour
- ⅔ cup baking cocoa
- ⅔ cup sugar
- ⅓ cup packed brown sugar
- ¾ teaspoon baking soda
- ¼ teaspoon salt
- 1 cup buttermilk
- ⅓ cup unsweetened applesauce

1. In a large bowl, combine the flour, cocoa, sugars, baking soda and salt. Stir in the buttermilk and applesauce (dough will be thick and moist).

2. Drop by tablespoonfuls 2 in. apart on baking sheets coated with cooking spray. Spread with a fork to make irregular shapes.

3. Bake at 350° for 8-10 minutes or until firm. Remove to wire racks.

◆◆ dishing about food

Pistachio cake was rechristened after the Watergate scandal in 1972, when members of President Nixon's re-election committee ordered a break-in at Democratic National Committee headquarters in the Watergate office complex. The ensuing cover-up and scandal resulted in Nixon's resignation. No one really knows why the name of the dessert changed, but some say it's because the cake, like the scandal, had nuts and was covered with fluff.

WASHINGTON, DC

Located in Washington's Foggy Bottom neighborhood, the Watergate complex was designed by Italian architect Luigi Moretti.

VERMONT

Native Americans have been sweetening their meals with maple syrup for ages. Now, making syrup is a full-fledged industry in the Northeast and Midwest, especially in Vermont. Many sugarmakers invite visitors to watch the process firsthand, from collecting the sap to boiling it down to syrup in sugarhouses.

Mock Apple Pie

My mother made this dessert often during the Depression, and our guests were always astounded that soda crackers could double as such convincing "apples."

—SHIRLEY HUNTER ST. PAUL, MINNESOTA

PREP: 15 MIN. + COOLING **BAKE:** 25 MIN.
MAKES: 8 SERVINGS

Pastry for double-crust pie
18 saltines, halved
1½ cups sugar
1¼ cups water
2 tablespoons lemon juice
1 teaspoon cream of tartar
½ to 1 teaspoon ground cinnamon
½ to 1 teaspoon ground nutmeg

1. Place bottom pastry in a 9-in. pie plate. Layer crackers in shell; set aside. In a small saucepan, combine remaining ingredients; bring to a boil. Carefully pour over crackers (filling will be very thin). Cool for 10 minutes.

2. Cut lattice strips from remaining pastry; place over filling. Seal and flute edges. Bake at 400° for 25-20 minutes or until golden brown. Cool on a wire rack.

Maple Sugar Cake

Old-fashioned maple sugar frosting tops my spice cake. Its homemade goodness was just what judges were looking for at our local fair, where it won a blue ribbon.

—ELIN LEE LANCASTER, MASSACHUSETTS

PREP: 20 MIN. **BAKE:** 20 MIN. + COOLING
MAKES: 12-14 SERVINGS

½ cup butter, softened
1¼ cups packed brown sugar
3 eggs
½ cup maple syrup
¼ cup 2% milk
¼ cup sour cream
1 teaspoon maple flavoring
2½ cups cake flour
1 teaspoon baking powder
½ teaspoon baking soda
½ teaspoon salt
½ teaspoon ground cloves
¼ teaspoon each ground allspice, nutmeg and mace

MAPLE SUGAR FROSTING
6 tablespoons butter, softened
1½ teaspoons maple flavoring
4½ cups confectioners' sugar
½ to ¾ cup sour cream
Chopped walnuts, optional

1. In a large bowl, cream butter and brown sugar until light and fluffy. Add eggs, one at a time, beating well after each addition. In a small bowl, combine the syrup, milk, sour cream and maple flavoring. In another bowl, combine the flour, baking powder, baking soda, salt, cloves, allspice, nutmeg and mace; gradually add to creamed mixture alternately with syrup mixture, beating well after each addition.

2. Pour into two greased and floured 9-in. round baking pans. Bake at 350° for 20-25 minutes or until a toothpick inserted near the center comes out clean. Cool for 10 minutes before removing from pans to a wire rack to cool.

3. For frosting, in a large bowl, cream butter and maple flavoring until fluffy. Gradually beat in the confectioners' sugar until smooth. Add enough sour cream to achieve spreading consistency.

4. Spread frosting between layers and over top and sides of cake. Sprinkle with walnuts if desired. Store in the refrigerator.

Kettle Corn

If one of the reasons you go to fairs is to satisfy your craving for kettle corn, you'll get the same wonderful salty-sweet taste at home with my recipe. Now you can indulge whenever the mood strikes you!

—**JENN MARTIN** SEBAGO, MAINE

PREP/TOTAL TIME: 15 MIN. **MAKES:** 3 QUARTS

- ½ **cup popcorn kernels**
- ¼ **cup sugar**
- 3 **tablespoons canola oil**
- 2 **to 3 tablespoons butter, melted**
- ½ **teaspoon salt**

1. In a Dutch oven over medium heat, cook the popcorn, sugar and oil until oil begins to sizzle. Cover and shake for 3-4 minutes or until popcorn stops popping.

2. Transfer to a large bowl. Drizzle with butter. Add salt; toss to coat.

Grandma's Red Velvet Cake

It's just not Christmas at our house without this cake. I baked the first one for the holidays in 1963, when I found the recipe in our newspaper. It's different from other red velvet cakes I've tasted over the years and has a mild chocolate taste, with icing is as light as snow.

—**KATHRYN DAVISON**
CHARLOTTE, NORTH CAROLINA

PREP: 30 MIN. **BAKE:** 20 MIN. + COOLING
MAKES: 14 SERVINGS

- ½ **cup butter, softened**
- 1½ **cups sugar**
- 2 **eggs**
- 2 **bottles (1 ounce each) red food coloring**
- 1 **tablespoon white vinegar**
- 1 **teaspoon vanilla extract**
- 2¼ **cups cake flour**
- 2 **tablespoons baking cocoa**
- 1 **teaspoon baking soda**
- 1 **teaspoon salt**
- 1 **cup buttermilk**

FROSTING
- 1 **tablespoon cornstarch**
- ½ **cup water**
- 2 **cups butter, softened**
- 2 **teaspoons vanilla extract**
- 3½ **cups confectioners' sugar**

1. In a large bowl, cream butter and sugar until light and fluffy. Add eggs, one at a time, beating well after each addition. Beat in the food coloring, vinegar and vanilla. Combine the flour, cocoa, baking soda and salt; add to creamed mixture alternately with buttermilk, beating well after each addition.

2. Pour into two greased and floured 9-in. round baking pans. Bake at 350° for 20-25 minutes or until a toothpick inserted near the center comes out clean. Cool for 10 minutes before removing from pans to wire racks to cool completely.

3. For frosting, in a small saucepan, combine cornstarch and water until smooth. Cook and stir over medium heat for 2-3 minutes or until thickened and opaque. Cool to room temperature.

4. In a large bowl, beat butter and vanilla until light and fluffy. Beat in cornstarch mixture. Gradually add confectioners' sugar; beat until frosting is light and fluffy. Spread frosting between layers and over top and sides of cake.

Almond Frosting: *Decrease vanilla extract to 1 teaspoon; add ½ teaspoon almond extract. Proceed as directed.*

Chocolate Frosting: *Decrease confectioners' sugar to 3¼ cups; add ¼ cup baking cocoa. Sift ingredients together before adding to butter mixture. Proceed as directed.*

◄● dishing about food

The first references to kettle corn were found in papers from Dutch settlers in Pennsylvania in the 18th century. The slightly sweet-salty combo was a favorite through the 19th century as an evening snack for farmers. Originally, it was sweetened with honey or molasses, but later, sugar became the sweetener of choice because it was easier to work with and did not make the corn soggy. Eventually, kettle corn took a backseat to other snack items and lost its appeal. But it's made a comeback in recent years and can be found at fairs and flea markets, where you can watch it being made in cast-iron cauldrons.

Cannoli (cannolo is the singular) are Sicilian pastries from Palermo and date back to 1000 AD. Cannoli were originally made for Carnival (then called Carnivale), a festival where the faithful could enjoy one last indulgence before Lent's restrictive diet. The traditional filling is ricotta or mascarpone cheese. When Sicilians emigrated here, however, it was hard to find ricotta and almost impossible to find mascarpone, so they improvised and started filling cannoli with custard.

Brandy Snap Cannoli

This recipe combines two classic recipes...brandy snaps and cannoli. You can assemble and chill the treats up to an hour before serving.

—TASTE OF HOME TEST KITCHEN

PREP: 1½ HOURS **BAKE:** 5 MIN./BATCH + COOLING **MAKES:** ABOUT 2 DOZEN

½ cup butter, cubed
½ cup sugar
3 tablespoons molasses
1 teaspoon ground ginger
¼ teaspoon salt
1 cup all-purpose flour
2 tablespoons brandy

FILLING
1½ cups ricotta cheese
3 tablespoons grated orange peel
3 tablespoons sugar, divided
1½ cups miniature semisweet chocolate chips, divided
1½ cups heavy whipping cream

1. In a small saucepan, combine the first five ingredients. Cook and stir over medium heat until butter is melted. Remove from the heat. Stir in flour and brandy; keep warm.

2. Drop tablespoonfuls of batter onto a parchment paper-lined or well-greased baking sheet; spread each into a 4-in. circle. Bake at 350° for 5-6 minutes or until edges begin to brown. Cool for about 1 minute or just until cookies start to firm.

3. Working quickly, loosen each cookie and curl around a metal cannoli tube to shape. Remove cookies from tubes; cool on wire racks.

4. For filling, in a large bowl, combine the ricotta, orange peel and 1 tablespoon sugar; stir in ½ cup chocolate chips. In a small bowl, beat cream on medium speed until soft peaks form. Gradually add remaining sugar, beating on high until stiff peaks form. Fold into ricotta mixture. Chill until serving.

5. Just before serving, pipe filling into cannoli shells. Dip ends in remaining chocolate chips.

Apple Betty with Almond Cream

I love making this treat for friends during the peak of apple season. I plan a quick soup-and-bread meal, so we can get right to the dessert!

—**LIBBY WALP** CHICAGO, ILLINOIS

PREP: 15 MIN. **COOK:** 3 HOURS **MAKES:** 8 SERVINGS

 3 **pounds tart apples, peeled and sliced**
10 **slices cinnamon-raisin bread, cubed**
 ¾ **cup packed brown sugar**
 ½ **cup butter, melted**
 1 **teaspoon almond extract**
 ½ **teaspoon ground cinnamon**
 ¼ **teaspoon ground cardamom**
 ⅛ **teaspoon salt**
WHIPPED CREAM
 1 **cup heavy whipping cream**
 2 **tablespoons sugar**
 1 **teaspoon grated lemon peel**
 ½ **teaspoon almond extract**

1. Place apples in an ungreased 4- or 5-qt. slow cooker. In a large bowl, combine the bread, brown sugar, butter, extract, cinnamon, cardamom and salt; spoon over apples. Cover and cook on low for 3-4 hours or until apples are tender.

2. In a small bowl, beat cream until it begins to thicken. Add the sugar, lemon peel and extract; beat until soft peaks form. Serve with apple mixture.

Chef George Crum is said to have created the potato chip while working at Moon's Lake House, a resort in Saratoga Springs, New York, after a difficult customer complained about his fried potatoes. First known as Saratoga chips, they quickly became popular along the East Coast. And a chip manufacturer is believed to have created the first potato chip cookies—to encourage increased consumption of his product.

SARATOGA SPRINGS, NY

A few hours' drive from New York City, Saratoga Springs remains a hot spot for horse enthusiasts who come for the racing, dressage, polo and more.

Potato Chip Cookies

Give this cookie a try the next time you're looking for a sweet-and-salty treat! They quickly bake to a crispy, golden brown...and disappear even faster!

—**MONNA LU BAUER** LEXINGTON, KENTUCKY

PREP: 15 MIN. **BAKE:** 10 MIN./BATCH **MAKES:** 4 DOZEN

1	cup butter-flavored shortening
¾	cup sugar
¾	cup packed brown sugar
2	eggs
2	cups all-purpose flour
1	teaspoon baking soda
2	cups crushed potato chips
1	cup butterscotch chips

1. In a large bowl, cream shortening and sugars until light and fluffy. Beat in eggs. Combine flour and baking soda; gradually add to creamed mixture and mix well. Stir in potato chips and butterscotch chips.

2. Drop by tablespoonfuls 2 in. apart onto ungreased baking sheets. Bake at 375° for 10-12 minutes or until golden brown. Cool for 1 minute before removing to wire racks.

Indian Pudding

This recipe comes from a 1900 cookbook, although I've made some adjustments to better fit today's ingredients and cooking methods. Everyone seems to love this timeless, comforting, baked pudding!

—JENNIFER MUSGROVE WHEATLAND, IOWA

PREP: 30 MIN. + COOLING
BAKE: 1 HOUR + STANDING MAKES: 8 SERVINGS

- 4 cups cold milk, divided
- 1 cup cornmeal
- ¾ cup molasses
- ¼ cup butter, softened
- 3 tablespoons sugar
- ½ teaspoon salt
- ¼ teaspoon each ground ginger, cinnamon and nutmeg
- 2 eggs, beaten
  Whipped topping or vanilla ice cream, optional

1. In a saucepan, heat 3 cups milk over medium heat until bubbles form around sides of pan. In a small bowl, combine cornmeal and remaining cold milk; gradually add to heated milk. Cook over medium-low heat for 10 minutes, stirring occasionally. Remove from the heat. Stir in the molasses, butter, sugar, salt, ginger, cinnamon and nutmeg. Cool for 10 minutes. Whisk in the eggs.

2. Pour into a greased 11x7-in. baking dish. Bake at 325° for 1 hour or until center is almost set. Let stand for 30 minutes. Serve warm with whipped topping or ice cream if desired.

Maple-Cream Apple Pie

Here's a pleasing pie that features a rich, maple cream filling topped with cinnamony apples and a crunchy streusel topping. It's heavenly!

—SUE SMITH NORWALK, CONNECTICUT

PREP: 25 MIN. + CHILLING
BAKE: 20 MIN. + COOLING MAKES: 6-8 SERVINGS

- 4 cups thinly sliced peeled tart apples
- ¼ cup sugar
- 1 teaspoon ground cinnamon
- ¼ cup butter, cubed
- 1 pastry shell (9 inches), baked

FILLING
- 1 package (8 ounces) cream cheese, softened
- 1½ cups cold milk
- 1 package (3.4 ounces) instant vanilla pudding mix
- 1 teaspoon maple extract

TOPPING
- ¼ cup sugar
- 3 tablespoons quick-cooking oats
- 3 tablespoons all-purpose flour
- ½ teaspoon ground cinnamon
- 2 tablespoons butter, melted

1. In a large bowl, toss apples, sugar and cinnamon. In a large skillet, cook apple mixture in butter for 10-12 minutes or until tender; cool. Spoon into pastry shell; set aside.

2. In a small bowl, beat cream cheese until fluffy. In another bowl, whisk milk and pudding mix for 2 minutes. Let stand for 2 minutes or until soft-set. Gradually beat into cream cheese. Stir in extract. Spoon over apple layer. Cover and refrigerate for 2 hours or until set.

3. Meanwhile, in a small bowl, combine topping ingredients. Spread onto an ungreased baking sheet. Bake at 350° for 20-25 minutes or until crisp and golden brown, stirring three or four times. Cool. Just before serving, sprinkle topping over pie.

PLYMOUTH, MA

Built in 1957, the *Mayflower II* is a full-scale replica of the ship that brought Pilgrims to the New World. Visit Plimoth Plantation to learn about 17th century life and to tour the ship.

DOVER, DE

The architecture of Delaware's capitol, called the Legislative Hall, may look centuries old, but it was built in 1933!

Crumble-Top Coffee Cake

Thinly sliced apples are baked right in this cake, providing delicious flavor and moisture. The golden crumb topping only adds to the dessert's popularity.

—JANICE HOSE HAGERSTOWN, MARYLAND

PREP: 25 MIN. **BAKE:** 55 MIN. **MAKES:** 12 SERVINGS

- ⅓ cup butter, softened
- ⅓ cup shortening
- 2 cups sugar
- 2 eggs
- 3 cups all-purpose flour
- 2 teaspoons baking powder
- 1 teaspoon ground cinnamon
- ½ teaspoon baking soda
- ¼ teaspoon salt
- 1¾ cups buttermilk
- 2 medium apples, peeled and sliced

TOPPING

- ½ cup all-purpose flour
- ½ cup packed brown sugar
- 1½ teaspoons ground cinnamon
- 3 tablespoons cold butter
- ½ cup chopped walnuts

1. In a large bowl, cream the butter, shortening and sugar until light and fluffy. Add eggs one at a time, beating well after each addition. Combine the flour, baking powder, cinnamon, baking soda and salt; add to the creamed mixture alternately with buttermilk, beating well after each addition.

2. Spoon half of the batter into a greased 13x9-in. baking dish. Top with apple slices; spread with remaining batter.

3. In a small bowl, combine the flour, brown sugar and cinnamon; cut in the butter until crumbly. Stir in walnuts. Sprinkle over batter.

4. Bake at 350° for 55-60 minutes or until a toothpick inserted near the center comes out clean.

Apple Rhubarb Crumble

In Vermont, we enjoy a bounty of rhubarb, apples and maple syrup. These ingredients inspired me to create this dessert.

—LIZ BACHILAS SHELBURNE, VERMONT

PREP: 10 MIN. **BAKE:** 45 MIN. **MAKES:** 4-6 SERVINGS

- 3 cups chopped fresh or frozen rhubarb
- 2 medium tart apples, peeled and chopped
- 1 egg

- ¾ cup sugar
- ¼ cup maple syrup
- ¼ to ½ teaspoon ground nutmeg
- ¼ teaspoon ground cinnamon
- 1 cup all-purpose flour
- ½ cup packed brown sugar
  Dash salt
- ½ cup cold butter, cubed

1. In a bowl, combine the rhubarb, apples, egg, sugar, syrup, nutmeg and cinnamon. Pour into a greased 2-qt. baking dish.

2. In another bowl, combine the flour, brown sugar and salt. Cut in butter until the mixture resembles coarse crumbs; sprinkle over fruit mixture. Bake at 350° for 45-55 minutes or until bubbly.

Sacher Torte

Guests will be surprised to hear this dessert starts with a convenient cake mix. Each bite features chocolate, almonds and apricots.

—TASTE OF HOME TEST KITCHEN

PREP: 30 MIN. **BAKE:** 25 MIN. + CHILLING
MAKES: 12-16 SERVINGS

- ½ cup chopped dried apricots
- ½ cup amaretto
- 1 package devil's food cake mix (regular size)
- ¾ cup water
- ⅓ cup canola oil
- 3 eggs

APRICOT FILLING

- ⅔ cup apricot preserves
- 1 tablespoon amaretto

FROSTING

- ½ cup butter, softened
- 4½ cups confectioners' sugar
- ¾ cup baking cocoa

⅓ cup boiling water
1 tablespoon amaretto
1 cup sliced almonds, toasted

1. In a small bowl, combine apricots and amaretto; let stand for 15 minutes. In a large bowl, combine the cake mix, water, oil, eggs and apricot mixture. Beat on low speed for 30 seconds; beat on medium for 2 minutes.

2. Pour into two greased and floured 9-in. round baking pans. Bake at 350° for 25-30 minutes or until a toothpick inserted near the center comes out clean. Cool for 10 minutes before removing from pans to wire racks to cool completely.

3. For filling, in a small saucepan, heat apricot preserves and amaretto on low until preserves are melted, stirring occasionally; set aside.

4. For frosting, in a large bowl, cream the butter, confectioners' sugar and cocoa until light and fluffy. Add water and amaretto. Beat on low speed until combined. Beat on medium for 1 minute or until frosting achieves spreading consistency.

5. Cut each cake horizontally into two layers. Place a bottom layer on a serving plate; spread with half of the filling. Top with another cake layer; spread with ⅔ cup frosting. Top with third layer and remaining filling. Top with remaining cake layer.

6. Frost top and sides of cake with remaining frosting. Gently press almonds into the sides. Refrigerate for several hours before slicing.

↔● dishing about food

A young apprentice cook named Franz Sacher developed his classic torte in 1832, after his employer, Prince Metternich, asked him to create an extraordinary dessert for his guests. Franz created a rich chocolate cake layered with apricot jam and topped with a silky icing, which is customarily served with unsweetened whipped cream on the side. Austrian immigrants brought the recipe along when they settled in urban areas of the Northeast. The dessert is still widely available at restaurants in New York City, as well as the Sacher Hotel in Vienna, which was opened by Franz's son Eduard in 1876.

This rich chocolate cake, created by Ebinger Baking Co. in Brooklyn, New York, is so dark it's almost black— like the blackout curtains people used during World War II. New Yorkers had blackout drills, when all lights were turned off and windows covered. This was intended to prevent the city lights from silhouetting U.S. ships offshore, in case German bombers or submarines appeared.

BROOKLYN, NY

Settled by the Dutch in 1624, Brooklyn didn't become part of New York City until 1898. Now it's the most populous borough with more than 2.5 million people. That's a lot of light!

Brooklyn Blackout Cake

If you like chocolate, you will LOVE this cake. I found the recipe when looking for a special cake to make for my chocolate-loving daughter-in-law's birthday. Be sure to give the pudding and the cake enough time to cool or the end results might be disappointing.

—DONNA BARDOCZ HOWELL, MICHIGAN

PREP: 1¼ HOURS + CHILLING **BAKE:** 35 MIN. + COOLING **MAKES:** 8 SERVINGS

PUDDING
- ½ cup sugar
- 2 tablespoons cornstarch
- ¼ teaspoon salt
- 1½ cups whole milk
- 3 ounces semisweet chocolate, chopped
- 1 teaspoon vanilla extract

CAKE
- 1½ cups all-purpose flour
- 2 teaspoons baking powder
- ½ teaspoon baking soda
- ½ teaspoon salt
- ½ cup unsalted butter, cubed
- ¾ cup Dutch-processed cocoa

1 cup sugar
1 cup packed brown sugar
1 cup buttermilk
1 cup strong brewed coffee
1 teaspoon vanilla extract
2 eggs

FROSTING
8 ounces semisweet chocolate, chopped
½ cup unsalted butter, cubed
⅓ cup hot water
2 teaspoons light corn syrup
2 teaspoons vanilla extract

1. In a small heavy saucepan, mix sugar, cornstarch and salt. Whisk in milk. Cook and stir over medium heat until thickened and bubbly. Reduce heat to low; cook and stir 2 minutes longer. Stir in chocolate until melted. Transfer to a bowl; stir in vanilla. Cool slightly, stirring occasionally. Press plastic wrap onto surface of pudding. Refrigerate, covered, for 2 hours or until cold.

2. Preheat oven to 325°. Line bottoms of two greased 8-in. round baking pans with parchment paper; grease paper. In a small bowl, whisk flour, baking powder, baking soda and salt. In a large saucepan, melt butter over medium heat. Add cocoa; cook and stir until blended. Stir in sugars. Remove from heat; stir in buttermilk, coffee and vanilla. Whisk in eggs, one at a time, until blended. Stir in flour mixture just until combined.

3. Transfer batter to prepared pans. Bake 35-40 minutes or until toothpick inserted in center comes out clean. Cool in pans 10 minutes before removing to wire racks; remove paper. Cool completely.

4. For frosting, in the top of a double boiler or a metal bowl over hot water, melt chocolate and butter; stir until smooth. Remove from heat. Whisk in hot water, all at once. Whisk in corn syrup and vanilla. Refrigerate 25-30 minutes or just until spreadable.

5. Using a long serrated knife, cut each cake horizontally in half. Place a cake layer on a serving plate. Spread with half of the pudding. Repeat layers. Top with a third cake layer. Spread frosting over top and sides of cake.

6. Crumble remaining cake layer; sprinkle over top and sides of cake, pressing lightly to adhere. Refrigerate leftovers.

Joe Froggers

Large, soft and chewy, these cookies make a great snack. The classic recipe has a warm blend of spices that seem to be more pronounced the second day. Your family is sure to ask you to make these again.

—**TASTE OF HOME TEST KITCHEN**

PREP: 15 MIN. + CHILLING
BAKE: 15 MIN./BATCH **MAKES:** 1½ DOZEN

½ cup shortening
1 cup packed brown sugar
1 cup molasses
⅓ cup hot water
2 tablespoons rum or 1 teaspoon rum extract
3½ cups all-purpose flour
1½ teaspoons salt
1½ teaspoons ground ginger
1 teaspoon baking soda
½ teaspoon ground cloves
½ teaspoon ground nutmeg
¼ teaspoon ground allspice
Sugar

1. In a large bowl, cream shortening and brown sugar until light and fluffy. In a small bowl, whisk molasses, hot water and rum. In another bowl, whisk the flour, salt and spices; add to creamed mixture alternately with molasses mixture, beating after each addition. Refrigerate, covered, 4 hours or until easy to handle.

2. Preheat oven to 375°. Shape dough into 1½-in. balls and place 3 in. apart on greased baking sheets. Flatten to ½-in. thickness with bottom of a custard cup dipped in sugar.

3. Bake 12-14 minutes or until lightly browned. Cool on pans 2 minutes. Remove to wire racks to cool completely. Store in airtight containers.

BOSTON, MA

There's a hidden and historic gem in the heart of Boston: Faneuil Hall Marketplace, where folks can find entertainment, shops and good eats indoors and out.

Boston Cream Pie

Yellow cake mix and vanilla pudding mix help create this classic dessert in no time. A rich chocolate glaze provides a fast finishing touch.

—EDWINA OLSON ENID, OKLAHOMA

PREP: 10 MIN. + COOLING **BAKE:** 30 MIN.
MAKES: 6-8 SERVINGS

 1 **package yellow cake mix (regular size)**
1½ **cups cold milk**
 1 **package (3.4 ounces) instant vanilla pudding mix**
 2 **ounces unsweetened chocolate**
 2 **tablespoons butter**
 1 **cup confectioners' sugar**
½ **teaspoon vanilla extract**
 2 **to 3 tablespoons hot water**

1. Prepare cake mix batter according to package directions. Pour into two greased and floured 9-in. round baking pans.

2. Bake at 350° for 28-33 minutes or until a toothpick inserted near the center comes out clean. Cool for 10 minutes before removing the cake from pans to wire racks to cool completely.

3. In a small bowl, whisk milk and pudding mix for 2 minutes. Let stand for 2 minutes or until soft-set. Cover and refrigerate.

4. In a microwave, melt chocolate and butter; stir until smooth. Stir in confectioners' sugar, vanilla and enough water to achieve a thick glaze; set aside.

5. Place one cake layer on a serving plate; spread with pudding. Top with the second cake layer. Spoon chocolate glaze over the top, allowing it to drip down sides of cake. Refrigerate until serving.

Raspberry Ice Cream

When our garden produces an abundance of raspberries, we know it's time to make this fruity frozen dessert. It's super in the summertime...and a treat throughout the year made with frozen raspberries.

—DIANA LESKAUSKAS CHATHAM, NEW JERSEY

PREP: 15 MIN. + CHILLING
PROCESS: 20 MIN./BATCH+ FREEZING
MAKES: ABOUT 1½ QUARTS

 2 **cups fresh or frozen raspberries**
 2 **cups heavy whipping cream**
 1 **cup half-and-half cream**
 1 **cup sugar**
 2 **teaspoons vanilla extract**

1. Place the raspberries in a blender; cover and process on medium-high speed until chopped; set aside. In a large saucepan, heat milk to 175°; stir in sugar until dissolved. Remove from the heat. Stir in whipping cream and vanilla. Fold in raspberries. Refrigerate until chilled.

2. Fill cylinder of ice cream freezer two-thirds full; freeze according to the manufacturer's directions. Refrigerate remaining mixture until ready to freeze. When ice cream is frozen, transfer to a freezer container; freeze for 2-4 hours before serving.

Walnut Mincemeat Pie

Here's a tasty twist on the more traditional mincemeat pie. This one's sweeter, creamier, easier to make and so yummy!

—**MARY REAGAN** WARSAW, NEW YORK

PREP: 15 MIN. **BAKE:** 40 MIN. + COOLING **MAKES:** 6-8 SERVINGS

Pastry for single-crust pie (9 inches)
1 **cup sugar**
2 **tablespoons all-purpose flour**
⅛ **teaspoon salt**
3 **eggs, lightly beaten**
¼ **cup butter, melted**
1 **cup prepared mincemeat**
½ **cup chopped walnuts**

1. Line a 9-in. pie plate with pastry; flute edges. Line pastry shell with a double thickness of heavy-duty foil. Bake at 450° for 5 minutes. Remove foil; bake 5 minutes longer. Cool on a wire rack. Reduce heat to 350°.

2. In a large bowl, combine the sugar, flour and salt. Stir in the eggs, butter, mincemeat and walnuts until blended. Pour into crust.

3. Bake for 40-45 minutes or until a knife inserted near the center comes out clean. Cover edges with foil during the last 15 minutes to prevent overbrowning if necessary. Cool on a wire rack.

South

Hey, y'all! Who's ready to eat? Nothing whets appetites like the promise of Southern cooking. Fried chicken, pulled pork and barbecue are just a few of the savory staples this region has to offer...but there's so much more! Don't forget about Cajun cooking, spicy Creole favorites and Cuban specialties that are sure to mix up your dinnertime routine. Desserts? The South is famous for them! Pecan pies, Key lime treats, beignets, hummingbird cakes and fruit cobblers conclude a truly Southern menu you'll never forget!

Chicken and Okra Gumbo

We used to live in New Orleans and learned to love the cuisine there. Even though we've since moved, I still make many Creole dishes, and this gumbo is one of our favorites.

—**CATHERINE BOUIS** PALM HARBOR, FLORIDA

PREP: 40 MIN. **COOK:** 2 HOURS **MAKES:** 8-10 SERVINGS

- 1 broiler/fryer chicken (2½ to 3 pounds), cut up
- 2 quarts water
- ¼ cup canola oil or bacon drippings
- 2 tablespoons all-purpose flour
- 2 medium onions, chopped
- 2 celery ribs, chopped
- 1 medium green pepper, chopped
- 3 garlic cloves, minced
- 1 can (28 ounces) tomatoes, drained
- 2 cups fresh or frozen sliced okra
- 2 bay leaves
- 1 teaspoon dried basil
- 1 teaspoon salt
- ½ teaspoon pepper
- 1 to 2 teaspoons hot pepper sauce
- 2 tablespoons sliced green onions
  Minced fresh parsley
  Hot cooked rice

1. Place chicken and water in a stockpot. Cover and bring to a boil. Reduce heat; cover and simmer for 30-45 minutes or until chicken is tender.

2. Remove chicken; reserve broth. Set chicken aside until cool enough to handle. Remove the chicken from bones; discard bones and cut meat into cubes; set aside.

3. In a stockpot, combine oil or drippings and flour until smooth. Cook over medium-high heat for 5 minutes, stirring constantly. Reduce heat to medium. Cook and stir about 5 minutes more or until mixture is reddish-brown (the color of a penny). Turn the heat to high. Stir in 2 cups reserved broth. Bring to a boil; cook and stir for 2 minutes or until thickened.

4. Add the onions, celery, green pepper and garlic; cook and stir for 5 minutes. Add the tomatoes, okra, bay leaves, basil, salt, pepper and pepper sauce. Cover and simmer for 1½ to 2 hours.

5. Discard bay leaves. Garnish with green onions and parsley. Serve with rice.

Toasted PB & Banana Sandwiches

A sandwich worthy of Elvis himself, this grilled, finger-licking treat may surprise you with its flavor. I saw the recipe and wasn't expecting much...but it's delicious!

—**MARIAN PICKETT** ARGYLE, WISCONSIN

PREP/TOTAL TIME: 20 MIN. **MAKES:** 4 SERVINGS

    2 **large ripe bananas**
    6 **tablespoons reduced-fat peanut butter**
    8 **slices whole wheat bread**
    2 **tablespoons honey**
       Refrigerated butter-flavored spray

1. Cut each banana in half widthwise, then cut each half lengthwise into four pieces. Spread peanut butter on bread. Place banana slices on four slices of bread; drizzle with honey. Top with remaining bread.

2. Spritz the outsides of sandwiches with butter-flavored spray. In a large nonstick skillet, toast sandwiches over medium heat until golden brown.

◄●► **dishing about food**

Peanut-butter-and-banana sandwiches are still associated with the singer who made them famous, Elvis Presley. There are a few acceptable variations to this sandwich: the honey may be omitted or bacon can be added. If you're in a hurry, you can even skip toasting it.

MEMPHIS, TN

Few homes are as well known as Graceland. Elvis fans make pilgrimages there to tour the king of rock and roll's 14-acre estate, now a museum with restaurants, shops, a wedding chapel and the Heartbreak Hotel!

DALLAS, TX

Whether a tour of Southfork Ranch, Dealey Plaza or the arboretum is more your speed, there's plenty to see and do (and eat!) in this east Texas cultural hub.

Southern Barbecued Chicken

Nothing says Texas like outdoor grilling. And summer is a prime time for patio picnics featuring my barbecued chicken. Guests are surprised to find the basis for my "mystery marinade" is simply vinegar and oil.

—**REVONDA STROUD** FORT WORTH, TEXAS

PREP: 25 MIN. + MARINATING **GRILL:** 40 MIN.
MAKES: 4 SERVINGS

- 2 **cups cider vinegar**
- 1 **cup canola oil**
- 1 **egg, lightly beaten**
- 2 **tablespoons hot pepper sauce**
- 1 **tablespoon garlic powder**
- 1 **tablespoon poultry seasoning**
- 2 **teaspoons salt**
- 1 **teaspoon pepper**
- 1 **broiler/fryer chicken (3 to 4 pounds), cut up**

1. In a large saucepan, combine the first eight ingredients. Bring to a boil, stirring constantly. Reduce heat; simmer, uncovered, for 10 minutes, stirring often. Cool.

2. Pour 1⅔ cups of the marinade into a large resealable plastic bag; add the chicken. Seal bag and turn to coat; refrigerate overnight, turning occasionally. Cover and refrigerate remaining marinade for basting.

3. Prepare grill for indirect heat, using a drip pan. Drain and discard marinade from chicken. Place skin side down over pan. Grill, covered, over indirect medium heat for 20 -25 minutes on each side or until juices run clear, basting occasionally with reserved marinade.

Cuban Pork Roast

A citrus and spice marinade seasons this moist, tender roast. The pork is flavorful but mild, so everyone likes it. You can serve it Cuban-style with black beans and rice, or make a traditional Cuban sandwich of pork, ham, Swiss cheese, tomatoes, lettuce, mustard, mayonnaise and dill pickle.

—**VIRGINIA CRONK** LITTLE TORCH KEY, FLORIDA

PREP: 10 MIN. + MARINATING
BAKE: 1 HOUR + STANDING **MAKES:** 12 SERVINGS

- 1 **cup lime juice**
- 1 **cup orange juice**
- 10 **garlic cloves, minced**
- 4 **teaspoons ground cumin**
- 2 **tablespoons minced fresh thyme or 2 teaspoons dried thyme**
- 2 **tablespoons minced fresh cilantro**
- 4 **bay leaves**
- 1 **boneless pork top loin roast (3 pounds)**
- ½ **teaspoon salt**
- ¼ **teaspoon pepper**

1. In a large bowl, combine the first seven ingredients. Pour half of the marinade into a large resealable plastic bag; add the pork roast. Seal bag and turn to coat; refrigerate the pork for 2 hours. Refrigerate remaining marinade.

2. Drain and discard marinade from pork. Place roast in an ungreased 13x9-in. baking dish. Pour reserved marinade over the roast. Sprinkle with salt and pepper.

3. Cover and bake at 350° for 45 minutes. Uncover; baste with pan drippings. Bake 15 minutes longer or until a thermometer reads 145°. Discard bay leaves. Let roast stand for 10 minutes before slicing.

Deluxe Muffuletta

I first made this hearty sandwich for my husband, friends and family who were helping to build our deck. They enjoyed it so much, I have made it several times since. It also makes a quick and impressive summer party entree!

—DANA SCHMITT AMES, IOWA

PREP/TOTAL TIME: 25 MIN. **MAKES:** 6 SERVINGS

- ⅔ cup pimiento-stuffed olives, chopped
- 1 can (4¼ ounces) chopped ripe olives
- 6 tablespoons shredded Parmesan cheese
- ¼ cup Italian salad dressing
- 2 teaspoons minced garlic
- 1 loaf (1 pound) Italian bread
- ½ pound sliced deli turkey
- ¼ pound sliced Swiss cheese
- ¼ pound thinly sliced hard salami
- ¼ pound sliced provolone cheese
- ¼ pound thinly sliced bologna

1. In a small bowl, combine the first five ingredients; set aside.

2. Cut the bread in half horizontally; carefully hollow out the top and bottom, leaving a 1-in. shell (discard removed bread or save for another use).

3. Spoon half of olive mixture over bottom half of bread. Layer with turkey, Swiss cheese, salami, provolone cheese, bologna and remaining olive mixture. Replace bread top. Cut into six wedges.

Bourbon Baked Ham

Because of its simple ingredient list, easy preparation and unbeatable flavor, this baked ham is one you'll come to rely on often. The honey-bourbon glaze not only looks lovely, but also helps to seal in the meat's juices.

—JEAN ADAMS WAYCROSS, GEORGIA

PREP: 15 MIN. **BAKE:** 2½ HOURS
MAKES: 15 SERVINGS

- 1 bone-in fully cooked spiral-sliced ham (7 to 9 pounds)
- 1 cup honey
- ½ cup bourbon
- ½ cup molasses
- ¼ cup orange juice
- 2 tablespoons Dijon mustard

1. Place ham on a rack in a shallow roasting pan. Score the surface of the ham, making diamond shapes ½ in. deep. Bake at 325° for 2 hours.

2. In a small saucepan, combine remaining ingredients; cook and stir until smooth.

3. Brush the ham with some of the glaze; bake 20-25 minutes longer or until a thermometer reads 140°, brushing occasionally with remaining glaze.

◀● dishing about food

Sicilian Lupo Salvatore, owner of the Central Grocery in New Orleans, is credited with creating the first muffuletta. Italian farmers coming into the city would eat lunch at his store. They would eat their meat, cheese and olive salad on plates while sitting on crates or barrels. Salvatore experimented until, in 1906, he came up with a sandwich that had all the ingredients and was easy to eat—the muffuletta.

NEW ORLEANS, LA

Among the most famous streets in the U.S., Bourbon Street is full of historic spots, from Galatoire's Restaurant, one of the city's oldest, to Jean Lafitte's Blacksmith Shop, the front for an 18th century privateering outfit.

Blackening is a cooking technique in which meat or fish is rubbed with a mixture of Cajun spices like paprika, garlic powder and peppers. It's then cooked in hot butter in a cast-iron skillet over high heat. The result is a dark, crisp coating on the food. The cooking fumes from this technique can be strong, so be ready with a powerful exhaust fan. Try to do your blackening on the grill outside. Then you don't need to worry about it.

Blackened Chicken

This spicy standout packs a one-two punch of flavor. The grilled chicken is basted with a peppery white sauce, and there's always plenty extra left over for dipping.

—STEPHANIE KENNEY FALKVILLE, ALABAMA

PREP/TOTAL TIME: 25 MIN. **MAKES:** 4 SERVINGS

1	tablespoon paprika
4	teaspoons sugar, divided
1½	teaspoons salt, divided
1	teaspoon garlic powder
1	teaspoon dried thyme
1	teaspoon lemon-pepper seasoning
1	teaspoon cayenne pepper
1½ to 2	teaspoons pepper, divided
4	boneless skinless chicken breast halves (4 ounces each)
1⅓	cups mayonnaise
2	tablespoons water
2	tablespoons cider vinegar

1. In a small bowl, combine the paprika, 1 teaspoon sugar, 1 teaspoon salt, garlic powder, thyme, lemon-pepper, cayenne and ½ to 1 teaspoon pepper; sprinkle over both sides of chicken. Set aside.

2. In another bowl, combine the mayonnaise, water, vinegar and remaining sugar, salt and pepper; cover and refrigerate 1 cup for serving. Save remaining sauce for basting.

3. Grill chicken, covered, over indirect medium heat for 4-6 minutes on each side or until a thermometer reads 165°, basting frequently with remaining sauce. Serve with reserved sauce.

Hot Brown Sandwiches

This is a fabulous open-faced sandwich to make when you have leftover turkey. If you're craving one and don't have any leftovers, try sliced, cooked turkey from the deli counter.

—TASTE OF HOME TEST KITCHEN

PREP/TOTAL TIME: 25 MIN. **MAKES:** 8 SERVINGS

- ¼ cup butter
- ¼ cup all-purpose flour
- 1 cup milk
- 1 cup chicken broth
- ½ teaspoon Worcestershire sauce
- ¾ cup shredded cheddar cheese
- ¼ teaspoon salt
- ⅛ teaspoon white pepper
- 8 slices Italian bread (½ inch thick), toasted
- 1½ pounds sliced cooked turkey
- 8 cooked bacon strips, halved
- 2 medium tomatoes, sliced
- 1 cup (4 ounces) shredded Parmesan cheese

1. In a large saucepan, melt butter over low heat. Stir in flour until smooth; gradually add milk, broth and Worcestershire sauce. Bring to a boil; cook and stir for 2 minutes or until thickened. Stir in the cheese, salt and white pepper until cheese is melted. Remove from the heat.

2. Place slices of toast on a baking sheet. Layer each with turkey, cheese sauce, bacon, tomatoes and Parmesan cheese. Broil 3-4 in. from the heat for 3-4 minutes or until cheese is melted.

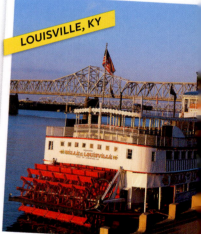

LOUISVILLE, KY

Built in 1914, the Belle of Louisville is the oldest riverboat in the U.S. Take in views of the Ohio River while you enjoy a lunch, dinner or sightseeing cruise aboard this floating National Historic Landmark.

Frogmore Stew

Enjoy a relaxing dinner with this simple but hearty Southern fare. If you like a little spice in your food, definitely use the hot links.

—TASTE OF HOME TEST KITCHEN

PREP: 10 MIN. **COOK:** 35 MIN. **MAKES:** 8 SERVINGS

- 16 **cups water**
- 1 **large sweet onion, quartered**
- 3 **tablespoons seafood seasoning**
- 2 **medium lemons, halved, optional**
- 1 **pound small red potatoes**
- 1 **pound smoked kielbasa or fully cooked hot links, cut into 1-inch pieces**
- 4 **medium ears sweet corn, cut into thirds**
- 2 **pounds uncooked medium shrimp, peeled and deveined**
   Seafood cocktail sauce
   Melted butter
   Additional seafood seasoning

1. In a stockpot, combine the water, onion, seafood seasoning and, if desired, lemons; bring to a boil. Add potatoes; cook, uncovered, 10 minutes. Add kielbasa and corn; return to a boil. Reduce heat; simmer 10-12 minutes or until potatoes are tender. Add shrimp; cook 2-3 minutes longer or until shrimp turn pink.

2. Drain; transfer to a large serving bowl. Serve with cocktail sauce, butter and additional seasoning.

Black-and-Blue Pizzas

Gooey with cheese and loaded with flavorful toppings, these pizzas are rich and filling. Add a green salad to make your meal complete.

—MICHELLE HUELSKAMP
MARION, NORTH CAROLINA

PREP: 40 MIN. **BAKE:** 15 MIN.
MAKES: 2 PIZZAS (12 PIECES EACH)

- 2 **loaves (1 pound each) frozen bread dough, thawed**
- 8 **bacon strips, chopped**
- 1 **pound boneless skinless chicken breasts, cut into strips**
- 5 **teaspoons blackened seasoning**
- 3 **shallots, finely chopped**
- 2 **garlic cloves, minced**
- 1 **jar (15 ounces) Alfredo sauce**
- 2½ **cups sliced fresh shiitake mushrooms**
- 1 **can (3.8 ounces) sliced ripe olives, drained**
- ½ **cup finely chopped sun-dried tomatoes (not packed in oil)**
- 1¼ **cups (5 ounces) crumbled blue cheese**
- 3 **tablespoons minced fresh basil or 3 teaspoons dried basil**
- 2 **tablespoons minced fresh thyme or 2 teaspoons dried thyme**
- 12 **slices provolone cheese**
- 3 **ounces Parmesan cheese, shaved into strips or ¾ cup grated Parmesan cheese**

1. Roll dough into two 16x10-in. rectangles; transfer to ungreased baking sheets and build up edges slightly.

2. In a large skillet, cook bacon over medium heat until crisp. Remove to paper towels with a slotted spoon; drain, reserving 2 tablespoons drippings. Sprinkle chicken with blackened seasoning; cook chicken in the drippings until no longer pink. Add shallots and garlic; cook 1 minute longer. Set aside.

3. Spread sauce over crusts; top with chicken mixture, bacon, mushrooms, olives and tomatoes. Sprinkle with blue cheese, basil and thyme; top with provolone and Parmesan cheeses.

4. Bake at 450° for 14-18 minutes or until bubbly and cheese is melted.

Southern Pan-Fried Quail with Cream Cheese Grits

Growing up in Tennessee, Southern- or Country-Fried Chicken was a staple in our home. It wasn't until I moved to South Carolina that I was introduced to quail and discovered different ways to prepare it.

—**ATHENA RUSSELL** FLORENCE, SOUTH CAROLINA

PREP: 40 MIN. + MARINATING **COOK:** 25 MIN.
MAKES: 8 SERVINGS

- 1½ cups buttermilk
- 1½ teaspoons salt, divided
- 1 teaspoon pepper, divided
- 8 split and flattened quail (4 ounces each), thawed
- 1 cup all-purpose flour
- ½ teaspoon onion powder
- ½ teaspoon garlic powder
- ¼ teaspoon cayenne pepper
- ⅔ cup canola oil

GRAVY
- 3 tablespoons all-purpose flour
- 1½ cups heavy whipping cream
- 1 cup chicken broth
- ¼ teaspoon salt
- ¼ teaspoon pepper

GRITS
- 1 cup uncooked old-fashioned grits
- ½ cup cream cheese, softened
- ½ cup heavy whipping cream
- ¼ teaspoon salt
- ¼ teaspoon pepper
- 4 bacon strips, cooked and crumbled, optional
- 2 green onions, thinly sliced, optional

1. In a large resealable plastic bag, combine the buttermilk, ½ teaspoon each salt and pepper. Add the quail; seal bag and turn to coat. Refrigerate for 1 hour. Drain and discard marinade.

2. In a shallow bowl, combine the flour, onion powder, garlic powder, cayenne and remaining salt and pepper. Coat quail with flour mixture.

3. In a large skillet, cook quail in oil in batches over medium heat for 4-6 minutes on each side or until a thermometer reads 165°. Drain on paper towels. Remove to a serving platter and keep warm.

4. For gravy, stir flour into pan drippings until blended; cook and stir for 4 minutes or until golden brown. Gradually add the cream, broth, salt and pepper. Bring to a boil; cook and stir for 2 minutes or until thickened.

5. Meanwhile, prepare grits according to package directions. Add the cream cheese, cream, salt and pepper. Cook and stir until cream cheese is melted and grits are heated through. Serve with quail and gravy; sprinkle with bacon and green onions if desired.

Country Ham Sandwiches

PREP/TOTAL TIME: 5 MIN. **MAKES:** 2 SERVINGS

- 2 tablespoons mayonnaise
- 2 tablespoons sour cream
- ⅛ teaspoon garlic powder
- 4 slices whole wheat bread
- 2 ounces smoked cheddar cheese, sliced
- 4 slices tomato
- 4 ounces thinly sliced deli ham
- 2 lettuce leaves

1. In a bowl, combine the mayonnaise, sour cream and garlic powder. Spread over two slices of bread. Layer each with cheese, tomato, ham and lettuce. Top with remaining bread.

> "This yummy sandwich is perfect for lunches or a quick weeknight dinner when there's no time for a big meal. Smoked cheddar and a creamy garlic-infused spread lend special appeal to this easy hand-held sandwich."

—**JENNIFER PARHAM**
BROWNS SUMMIT,
NORTH CAROLINA

> **" Growing up in South Florida, my culinary taste buds were influenced by the Cuban culture so prominent in that area. If 'the way to a man's heart is through his stomach,' this Cuban twist on pulled pork will knock the socks off of any man! Make it into a sandwich with Cuban bread or tortillas. "**
>
> **—KRISTINA WILEY**
> JUPITER, FLORIDA

Slow-Cooked Lechon with Cuban Mojito Sauce

PREP: 15 MIN. + MARINATING **COOK:** 9 HOURS
MAKES: 12 SERVINGS (1½ CUPS SAUCE)

- 2 large onions, quartered
- 12 garlic cloves
- 1 bottle (18 ounces) Cuban-style mojo sauce and marinade
- ½ cup lime juice
- ½ teaspoon salt
- ¼ teaspoon pepper
- 1 bone-in pork shoulder butt roast (5 to 5¼ pounds)

MOJITO SAUCE
- ¾ cup canola oil
- 1 medium onion, finely chopped
- 6 garlic cloves, finely chopped
- ⅓ cup lime juice
- ½ teaspoon salt
- ¼ teaspoon pepper
  Lime wedges, optional
  Chopped onions, optional

1. Place onions and garlic in a food processor; cover and process until finely chopped. Add mojo sauce, lime juice, salt and pepper; cover and process until blended. Pour half of the marinade into a large resealable plastic bag. Cut roast into quarters; add to bag. Seal the bag and turn to coat. Refrigerate for 8 hours or overnight. Cover and refrigerate the remaining marinade.

2. Drain pork, discarding marinade. Place pork roast in a 5-qt. slow cooker coated with cooking spray. Top with remaining marinade. Cook, covered, on low 8-10 hours or until pork is tender.

3. For sauce, in a small saucepan, heat oil over medium heat 2½ to 3 minutes or until a thermometer reads 200°. Carefully add onion, cook 2 minutes, stirring occasionally. Stir in garlic; remove from heat. Stir in lime juice, salt and pepper.

4. Remove roast from slow cooker; cool slightly. Skim fat from cooking juices. Remove meat from bone; discard bone. Shred pork with two forks. Return pork to slow cooker; heat through.

5. Using tongs, remove meat to a platter. Serve with chopped onion, lime wedges and mojito sauce, stirring just before serving.

Country Captain Chicken

The Southern side of my family originally came from Columbus, Georgia, and the recipe for Country Captain has been passed down for generations. It is said to have originated in India and has been served since the earliest American colonies were founded.

—**SARAH MCKENNEY** TAYLORS, SOUTH CAROLINA

PREP: 40 MIN. **BAKE:** 35 MIN. **MAKES:** 4 SERVINGS

- 2 **pounds bone-in chicken thighs**
- 1 **pound bone-in chicken breast halves**
- ¼ **cup all-purpose flour**
- 1¼ **teaspoons salt, divided**
- ½ **teaspoon pepper**
- 3 **tablespoons canola oil**
- 2 **medium onions, finely chopped**
- 2 **medium green peppers, finely chopped**
- 1 **garlic clove, minced**
- 2 **teaspoons curry powder**
- 1 **can (28 ounces) diced tomatoes, undrained**
- ¼ **cup dried currants or raisins**
- 2 **tablespoons minced fresh parsley**
- ½ **teaspoon dried thyme**
  Hot cooked rice
- ¼ **cup slivered almonds, toasted**
  Additional minced fresh parsley, optional

1. Preheat oven to 350°. Place chicken in a large bowl. Mix flour, 1 teaspoon salt and pepper; sprinkle over chicken and toss to coat. In a Dutch oven, heat oil over medium-high heat. Brown chicken in batches on all sides; remove from pan.

2. Add onions, peppers and garlic to drippings; cook and stir over low heat until tender. Increase heat to medium-high. Add curry powder; cook and stir 1 minute longer. Stir in tomatoes, currants, parsley, thyme and remaining salt. Bring to a boil. Return chicken to pan.

3. Bake, covered, 35-45 minutes or until the chicken is tender. Skim fat. Serve chicken and sauce over rice; sprinkle with almonds and additional parsley, if desired.

dishing about food

Curry-spiced Country Captain is said to have originated in India. It's likely that the dish arrived in the South centuries ago, via a ship carrying spices to a port city. General George S. Patton enjoyed it so much that for a few years, it was one of the ready-to-eat meal packs for the U.S. Army.

CALABASH, NC

The Myrtle Beach area is a top destination for fun in the sun in the Carolinas. Golfers flock here to play at the many courses, including the Meadowlands Golf Club.

Popular since colonial times and inspired by recipes much more ancient, crab cakes combine crabmeat with bread and spices and are then fried or sauteed.

CHESAPEAKE BAY

Although blue crab is often called Maryland crab, many of those we eat were actually caught in Chesapeake Bay's Virginian waters!

Crab Cakes with Chesapeake Bay Mayo

I placed my personal stamp on my Aunt Ellie's crab cake recipe by changing up some of her ingredients. I like to serve mine with a tart and tangy creamy sauce.

—**MICHELLE CRITCHELL** MOON, VIRGINIA

PREP: 20 MIN. + CHILLING   **COOK:** 10 MIN./BATCH   **MAKES:** 16 CRAB CAKES

- ½ cup sour cream
- ½ cup mayonnaise
- 2 tablespoons sweet pickle relish
- 1 tablespoon spicy brown mustard
- ¼ teaspoon seafood seasoning

CRAB CAKES
- 1 egg, beaten
- ¼ cup grated Parmesan cheese
- ¼ cup seasoned bread crumbs
- ¼ cup mayonnaise
- 2 tablespoons finely chopped onion
- 1 tablespoon minced fresh parsley
- 1 tablespoon spicy brown mustard
- ½ teaspoon seafood seasoning
- ⅛ teaspoon pepper
- 3 cans (6 ounces each) lump crabmeat, drained
- ¼ cup canola oil

1. In a large bowl, combine the first five ingredients. Cover and chill until serving. For crab cakes, in a large bowl, combine the egg, cheese, bread crumbs, mayonnaise, onion, parsley, mustard, seafood seasoning and pepper. Fold in crab. Refrigerate for at least 30 minutes.

2. With floured hands, shape the mixture by 2 tablespoonfuls into ½-in.-thick patties. In a large skillet over medium heat, cook crab cakes in oil in batches for 3-4 minutes on each side or until golden brown. Serve with the sauce.

Pepperoni Rolls

When I was growing up, I loved pepperoni and would walk around the house munching on sticks of it. One day my mother made these pepperoni rolls for me—and I fell in love with them. If you like, add some chopped-up veggies to the rolls and use as a meal.

—**WENDY STEINER** SUWANEE, GEORGIA

PREP: 45 MIN. **BAKE:** 15 MIN. **MAKES:** 32 APPETIZERS

- 2 loaves (1 pound each) frozen bread dough, thawed
- 1 stick (6½ ounces) pepperoni, cut into 32 slices
- 6 ounces fresh mozzarella cheese, cut into 32 cubes
- 1 jar (14 ounces) pizza sauce, warmed

1. Divide one loaf of dough into 16 pieces; roll each into a 3-in. circle. Place a piece of pepperoni and cheese in the center of each circle. Fold all edges together; press to seal. Place rolls, seam side down, on a parchment paper-lined baking sheet.

2. Preheat oven to 350°. Repeat with the remaining ingredients. Bake 15-20 minutes or until the rolls are golden brown. Serve warm with pizza sauce.

Sweet Potato Pancakes with Caramel Sauce

Sometimes sweet potatoes end up as leftovers. By happy chance, they can really dress up pancake batter. Topped with butter, caramel sauce and toasted cashews, they look nothing like yesterday's forgotten dish. No leftovers? Use canned sweet potatoes!

—**SHERYL LITTLE** SHERWOOD, ARKANSAS

PREP: 25 MIN. **COOK:** 10 MIN./BATCH
MAKES: 7 SERVINGS

- 2 cups all-purpose flour
- 2 tablespoons packed brown sugar
- 3 teaspoons baking powder
- ½ teaspoon salt
- ½ teaspoon ground ginger
- ¼ teaspoon ground allspice
- ¼ teaspoon ground cinnamon
- ¼ teaspoon ground nutmeg
- 1 egg

- 1¾ cups 2% milk
- ½ cup canned sweet potatoes, mashed
- 2 tablespoons butter, melted
- 1 jar (12 ounces) hot caramel ice cream topping, warmed
- ¾ cup coarsely chopped unsalted cashews, toasted
  Whipped butter, optional

1. In a small bowl, combine the first eight ingredients. In another bowl, whisk the egg, milk, sweet potatoes and melted butter. Stir into dry ingredients just until moistened.

2. Pour batter by ¼ cupfuls onto a greased hot griddle; turn when bubbles form on top. Cook until the second side is golden brown.

3. Drizzle with caramel topping; sprinkle with nuts. Serve with whipped butter if desired.

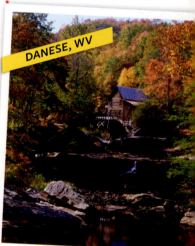

DANESE, WV

Tucked inside Babcock State Park, the Glade Creek Grist Mill makes a lovely rustic photo op. Mills like it were once the lifeblood of the surrounding communities.

CHALMETTE, LA

Each year, scores of seafood lovers kick off the trapping season at the Louisiana Crawfish Festival. There's always plenty of music, fun and, of course, crawfish to go around.

Crawfish Fettuccine

I have lived in this close-knit community all my life and enjoy cooking Cajun dishes, especially those with seafood. Along with a green salad and garlic bread, this dish is great for family gatherings. The recipe can easily be doubled to serve a larger group, and if you'd like it less spicy, just remove the seeds from the jalapeno before chopping it.

—**CAROLYN LEJEUNE** WELSH, LOUISIANA

PREP: 30 MIN. **COOK:** 30 MIN. **MAKES:** 8 SERVINGS

- 1 large onion, chopped
- 1 medium sweet red pepper, chopped
- ⅔ cup sliced green onions
- 1 celery rib, chopped
- 1¼ cups butter, cubed
- 1 garlic clove, minced
- ¼ cup all-purpose flour
- 8 ounces process cheese (Velveeta), cubed
- 1 cup half-and-half cream
- 1 tablespoon chopped jalapeno pepper
- ½ teaspoon salt
- 8 ounces uncooked fettuccine
- 1½ pounds frozen cooked crawfish tails, thawed, or cooked medium shrimp, peeled and deveined

1. In a Dutch oven, saute the onion, red pepper, green onions and celery in butter for 5 minutes or until vegetables are crisp-tender. Add garlic; cook 1 minute longer. Stir in flour until blended; cook and stir for 2 minutes. Add the cheese, cream, jalapeno and salt; cook and stir for 10 minutes or until mixture is thickened and cheese is melted.

2. Meanwhile, cook fettuccine according to package directions; drain. Stir fettuccine and crawfish into the vegetable mixture. Cook, uncovered, over medium heat for 10 minutes or until heated through, stirring occasionally.

Editor's Note: *Wear disposable gloves when cutting hot peppers; the oils can burn skin. Avoid touching your face.*

Creole Jambalaya

Creole jambalaya, also known as red jambalaya, is a traditional Louisiana dish with deep roots in French and Spanish cuisines. Tomatoes, seafood, rice and the holy trinity of onions, green peppers and celery are the key ingredients in this Southern favorite. Most recipes also call for chicken or sausage, but mine uses ham for a unique taste twist.

—**RUBY WILLIAMS** BOGALUSA, LOUISIANA

PREP: 20 MIN. **COOK:** 35 MIN. **MAKES:** 8 SERVINGS

- ¾ cup chopped onion
- ½ cup chopped celery
- ¼ cup chopped green pepper
- 2 tablespoons butter
- 2 garlic cloves, minced
- 2 cups cubed fully cooked ham
- 1 can (28 ounces) diced tomatoes, undrained
- 1 can (10½ ounces) condensed beef broth, undiluted
- 1 cup uncooked long grain white rice
- 1 cup water
- 1 teaspoon sugar
- 1 teaspoon dried thyme
- ½ teaspoon chili powder
- ¼ teaspoon pepper
- 1½ pounds fresh or frozen uncooked shrimp, peeled and deveined
- 1 tablespoon minced fresh parsley

1. In a Dutch oven, saute the onion, celery and green pepper in butter until tender. Add the garlic; cook 1 minute longer. Add the next nine ingredients; bring to a boil. Reduce heat; cover and simmer until rice is tender, about 25 minutes.

2. Add shrimp and parsley; simmer, uncovered, for 7-10 minutes or until shrimp turn pink.

Cool-Kitchen Meat Loaf

Juicy slices of this tender meat loaf are wonderful served with a homemade sweet-and-sour sauce. It's such an easy supper to fix!

—**SUSAN TAUL** BIRMINGHAM, ALABAMA

PREP: 10 MIN. **GRILL:** 30 MIN.
MAKES: 2 LOAVES (3 SERVINGS EACH)

- 1 cup soft bread crumbs
- 1 medium onion, chopped
- ½ cup tomato sauce
- 1 egg
- 1½ teaspoons salt
- ¼ teaspoon pepper
- 1½ pounds lean ground beef

SAUCE
- ½ cup ketchup
- 3 tablespoons brown sugar
- 3 tablespoons Worcestershire sauce
- 2 tablespoons white vinegar
- 2 tablespoons prepared mustard

1. In a large bowl, combine the first six ingredients. Crumble the beef over mixture and mix well. Shape into two loaves; place each loaf in a disposable 8x4-in. loaf pan. Cover with foil.

2. Prepare the grill for indirect heat. Grill, covered, over medium heat for 30 minutes or until meat is no longer pink and a thermometer reads 160°.

3. Meanwhile, in a small saucepan, combine sauce ingredients. Cook and stir over low heat until sugar is dissolved. Spoon over meat loaves before serving.

Hot Chicken Salad

I know you'll enjoy this rich and creamy chicken dish. Topped with crunchy potato chips and almonds, the delicious casserole is a fabulous way to use up leftover chicken.

—**DORIS HEATH** FRANKLIN, NORTH CAROLINA

PREP: 10 MIN. **BAKE:** 30 MIN. **MAKES:** 4 SERVINGS

- 2 cups diced cooked chicken
- 1 can (10¾ ounces) condensed cream of chicken soup, undiluted
- 2 celery ribs, finely chopped
- ½ cup mayonnaise
- 1 can (4 ounces) mushroom stems and pieces, drained
- 2 tablespoons finely chopped onion
- ½ cup crushed butter-flavored crackers (about 12 crackers)
- ½ cup crushed potato chips
- ½ cup sliced almonds, toasted

1. In a large bowl, combine the chicken, soup, celery, mayonnaise, mushrooms and onion. Stir in cracker crumbs. Spoon into a greased 1½-qt. baking dish.

2. Bake, uncovered, at 375° for 15 minutes. Sprinkle with the potato chips and almonds. Bake 15 minutes longer or until bubbly and lightly browned.

Picadillo is enjoyed in many Latin American countries. The Cuban version of this hashlike dish contains ground beef and raisins. It's served with rice and sometimes with beans.

MIAMI, FL

With Cuban-Americans comprising about 25 percent of Miami's population, Cuban cuisine is prevalent, and Havanan flavors are popular with people of many ethnic backgrounds.

Easy Cuban Picadillo

My girlfriend gave me this delicious recipe years ago. I've made it ever since for family and friends, and they all love it. My daughter says it's the best dish I make and she loves to take leftovers to school for lunch the next day.

—**MARIE WIELGUS** WAYNE, NEW JERSEY

PREP/TOTAL TIME: 30 MIN. **MAKES:** 4 SERVINGS

- 1 **pound lean ground beef (90% lean)**
- 1 **small green pepper, chopped**
- ¼ **cup chopped onion**
- 1 **can (8 ounces) tomato sauce**
- ½ **cup sliced pimiento-stuffed olives**
- ¼ **cup raisins**
- 1 **tablespoon cider vinegar**
- 2 **cups hot cooked rice**

1. In a large nonstick skillet, cook the beef, pepper and onion over medium heat until the meat is no longer pink; drain. Stir in the tomato sauce, olives, raisins and vinegar. Cook for 5-6 minutes or until raisins are plumped. Serve with rice.

Lakes Burgoo

While I was visiting a friend in Kentucky, I was treated to this delicious local dish. It's both hearty and healthy , and I simply love it!

—DONNA REAVIS CROFTON, KENTUCKY

PREP: 20 MIN. **COOK:** 1 HOUR
MAKES: 8 SERVINGS (3 QUARTS)

- 1½ pounds ground beef
- 2 cups diced potatoes
- 1 large onion, chopped
- ¾ cup chopped green pepper
- 1 can (14½ ounces) diced tomatoes, undrained
- 1 can (14½ ounces) peas, drained
- 1 can (14½ ounces) cut green beans, drained
- 1 can (14½ ounces) whole kernel corn, drained
- 1 bottle (18 ounces) barbecue sauce
- 2 cups water
- 1 can (14½ ounces) tomato puree
- ½ cup ketchup
- ½ teaspoon salt
- ½ teaspoon pepper

1. In a large skillet, cook beef over medium heat until no longer pink; drain. Transfer to a Dutch oven. Add remaining ingredients. Bring to a boil. Reduce heat; simmer for 1 to 1¼ hours or until potatoes are tender.

Southern Barbecued Brisket

Ever since a former neighbor shared this recipe with me, it has been a family favorite. Since it makes a lot, it's good for a company dinner or buffet. The meat gets nice and tender from baking slowly for several hours.

—LORRAINE HODGE MCLEAN, VIRGINIA

PREP: 10 MIN. **BAKE:** 3 HOURS + STANDING
MAKES: 12 SERVINGS

- 1 fresh beef brisket (5 pounds)
- 1 large onion, chopped
- 1 cup ketchup
- ¼ cup water
- 3 tablespoons brown sugar
- 1 tablespoon Liquid Smoke, optional
- 2 teaspoons celery seed
- 1 teaspoon salt
- 1 teaspoon ground mustard
- ⅛ teaspoon cayenne pepper

1. Place brisket on a large sheet of heavy-duty foil; seal tightly. Place in a greased shallow roasting pan. Bake at 325° for 2 to 2½ hours or until meat is tender.

2. Meanwhile, in a small saucepan, combine the remaining ingredients. Bring to a boil. Reduce heat; cover and simmer for 20 minutes, stirring occasionally. Remove from the heat.

3. Carefully open foil to allow steam to escape. Remove brisket from foil; let stand for 20 minutes. Thinly slice meat across the grain. Place in an ungreased 13x9-in. baking dish. Spoon sauce over meat. Cover and bake for 1 hour or until heated through.

Editor's Note: *This is a fresh beef brisket, not corned beef.*

◀● dishing about food

Kentuckians are fond of their burgoo, a thick stew. Burgoo, like most dishes of its type, consists of meat and vegetables. Originally, squirrel and wild game starred in the stew. Now mutton, beef, pork and chicken often take their place. Variations on this versatile dish are as numerous as the cooks who make it.

HODGENVILLE, KY

Abraham Lincoln was born in rural Kentucky in 1809. To honor the centennial of his birth, a monument was built at Lincoln's birthplace—Theodore Roosevelt laid the cornerstone and William Howard Taft dedicated the building two years later.

A comforting dish, biscuits and gravy are not only a Southern breakfast favorite, but also enjoyed in many parts of the country. It's said that this economical specialty came from the logging camps in Appalachia. It is also known as "poor-do" since the entree feeds several people with just a little bit of meat.

As many as 3 million people visit the Appalachian Trail each year, with up to 2,000 hiking the whole thing—that's about 2,180 miles! The Trail crosses through 14 states, from Springer Mountain, Georgia, to Katahdin, Maine.

Home-Style Sausage Gravy and Biscuits

My mother-in-law introduced me to her hamburger gravy, and I modified it slightly. We enjoy this dish every weekend.

—MICHELE BAPST JACKSONVILLE, NORTH CAROLINA

PREP/TOTAL TIME: 30 MIN. **MAKES:** 8 SERVINGS

- 1 tube (16.3 ounces) large refrigerated flaky biscuits
- 1 pound bulk pork sausage
- 1 cup chopped sweet onion
- 2 tablespoons butter
- 1 envelope country gravy mix
- 1 tablespoon all-purpose flour
  Dash each garlic powder, Italian seasoning, onion powder and pepper
- 1½ cups 2% milk
- 1 cup reduced-sodium chicken broth

1. Bake the biscuits according to the package directions.

2. Meanwhile, in a large skillet, cook sausage and onion over medium heat until sausage is no longer pink; drain. Add butter, cook until melted. Stir in the gravy mix, flour and seasonings until blended. Gradually add milk and broth. Bring to a boil; cook and stir for 1 minute or until thickened. Serve with biscuits.

Nutty Oven-Fried Chicken

The pecans that give this dish its unique nutty flavor are plentiful in the South, and so is chicken. I love to prepare and serve this easy favorite because the chicken comes out moist, tasty and crispy.

—DIANE HIXON NICEVILLE, FLORIDA

PREP: 10 MIN. **BAKE:** 1 HOUR **MAKES:** 6 SERVINGS

- ½ cup evaporated milk
- 1 cup biscuit/baking mix
- ⅓ cup finely chopped pecans
- 2 teaspoons paprika
- ½ teaspoon salt
- ½ teaspoon poultry seasoning
- ½ teaspoon rubbed sage
- 1 broiler/fryer chicken (3 to 4 pounds), cut up
- ⅓ cup butter, melted

1. Place milk in a shallow bowl. In another shallow bowl, combine the baking mix, pecans and seasonings. Dip chicken pieces in milk, then coat generously with pecan mixture.

2. Place in a lightly greased 13x9-in. baking dish. Drizzle with butter. Bake, uncovered, at 350° for 1 hour or until chicken is golden brown and crispy and juices run clear.

Pork Chops with Mushroom Bourbon Sauce

These golden-crusted pork chops are accompanied with a rich mushroom sauce. The scrumptious entree is loved by my family and makes a terrific company dish. It's wonderful served with mashed potatoes.

—**NADINE MESCH** MOUNT HEALTHY, OHIO

PREP: 20 MIN.   **COOK:** 30 MIN.   **MAKES:** 2 SERVINGS

- ½ **pound sliced fresh mushrooms**
- 2 **tablespoons chopped onion**
- 2 **tablespoons olive oil, divided**
- 1 **tablespoon butter**
- 1 **garlic clove, minced**
- ¼ **cup white wine or reduced-sodium chicken broth**
- 2 **tablespoons bourbon**
- ½ **cup reduced-sodium chicken broth**
- ¼ **cup heavy whipping cream**
- 2 **boneless pork loin chops (6 ounces each)**
- ¼ **teaspoon salt**
- ¼ **teaspoon paprika**
- ⅛ **teaspoon pepper**
- 1 **egg**
- 2 **tablespoons water**
- 3 **tablespoons all-purpose flour**
- ½ **cup panko (Japanese) bread crumbs**
- 4 **teaspoons minced fresh basil**

1. In a large skillet, saute mushrooms and onion in 1 tablespoon oil and butter until tender. Add the garlic; cook 1 minute longer. Remove from the heat.

2. Add the wine and bourbon; cook over medium heat until liquid is evaporated. Add chicken broth and cream; bring to a boil. Reduce heat and simmer until sauce is thickened, stirring occasionally; keep warm.

3. Sprinkle chops with salt, paprika and pepper. In a shallow bowl, whisk egg and water. Place flour and bread crumbs in separate shallow bowls. Dip pork in the flour, egg mixture, then bread crumbs.

4. In a large skillet, cook chops over medium heat in remaining oil for 4-5 minutes on each side or until crisp and a thermometer reads 165°. Stir basil into mushroom sauce; serve over the pork.

Ham on Biscuits

I like entertaining friends with a luncheon. They always compliment me on these special little ham sandwiches made on cheesy homemade biscuits. Usually, I use Smithfield ham, but if salty ham is not your preference, any thin-sliced ham works well.

—**BETSY HEDEMAN** TIMONIUM, MARYLAND

PREP/TOTAL TIME: 30 MIN.   **MAKES:** 8 SANDWICHES

- 1 **cup all-purpose flour**
- 2 **teaspoons sugar**
- 1⅛ **teaspoons baking powder**
- ¼ **teaspoon baking soda**
- ⅛ **teaspoon salt**
- 2 **tablespoons cold butter**
- ½ **cup 4% cottage cheese**
- 1 **egg**
- 3 **tablespoons milk**
- 8 **teaspoons butter, softened**
- ½ **pound sliced deli ham**

1. In a small bowl, combine the flour, sugar, baking powder, baking soda and salt; cut in cold butter until mixture resembles coarse crumbs. In a small bowl, beat cottage cheese for 2 minutes. Beat in egg and milk until blended. Stir into crumb mixture just until moistened.

2. Turn onto a lightly floured surface; knead 8-10 times. Pat or roll out to ½-in. thickness; cut out eight biscuits with a floured 2½-in. biscuit cutter.

3. Place 1 in. apart on an ungreased baking sheet. Bake at 450° for 8-12 minutes or until golden brown. Split biscuits in half; spread with softened butter. Place ham on biscuit bottoms; replace tops.

Shrimp and grits is a popular and timeless combination in the Charleston area of South Carolina—with some claiming it's actually essential to life! It's even on menus for breakfast during shrimping season. A 1985 article by Craig Claiborne in *The New York Times* helped spread a new awareness of this Southern favorite to the entire country.

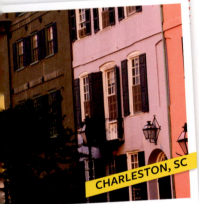

CHARLESTON, SC

In an effort to help revive Charleston decades after the Civil War, Dorothy Pocher Legge bought a few row houses on East Bay Street. She painted them candy pink. Other homeowners followed suit, and eventually Rainbow Row was born.

Southern Shrimp & Grits

This is just a classic old, Southern, stick-to-your-ribs dinner combining fresh shrimp, a medley of peppers, onion and creamy cheese grits. It's great served with corn bread and sliced tomatoes.

—**MELISSA HASS** GILBERT, SOUTH CAROLINA

PREP/TOTAL TIME: 30 MIN. **MAKES:** 4 SERVINGS

- 2½ **cups chicken broth**
- 1 **cup quick-cooking grits**
- 1 **medium onion, sliced**
- 1 **package (14 ounces) frozen pepper strips, thawed**
- 4 **teaspoons olive oil**
- 12 **uncooked jumbo shrimp, peeled and deveined**
- ¼ **cup minced fresh parsley**
- 1 **teaspoon lemon juice**
- 1 **cup (4 ounces) shredded sharp cheddar cheese**
- ½ **cup sour cream**

1. In a large saucepan, bring broth to a boil. Slowly stir in grits. Reduce heat; cook and stir for 5-7 minutes or until thickened.

2. Meanwhile, in a large skillet, saute onion and pepper strips in oil until crisp-tender. Add the shrimp, parsley and lemon juice; saute 3-4 minutes longer or until shrimp turn pink.

3. Stir cheese and sour cream into grits; serve with shrimp mixture.

Carolina Marinated Pork Tenderloin

PREP: 10 MIN. + MARINATING **GRILL:** 20 MIN. **MAKES:** 4 SERVINGS

- ¼ cup molasses
- 2 tablespoons spicy brown mustard
- 1 tablespoon cider vinegar
- 1 pork tenderloin (1 pound)

1. In a large resealable plastic bag, combine the molasses, mustard and vinegar; add the pork. Seal bag and turn to coat; refrigerate for 8 hours or overnight.

2. Prepare grill for indirect heat, using a drip pan. Drain and discard marinade. Moisten a paper towel with cooking oil; using long-handled tongs, lightly coat grill rack.

3. Place pork over drip pan and grill, covered, over indirect medium-hot heat for 20-27 minutes or until a thermometer reads 145°, turning occasionally. Let stand for 5 minutes before slicing.

> "You'll need just three ingredients to make a melt-in-your-mouth marinade that friends, family and neighbors will rave about."
>
> —SHARISSE DUNN
>
> ROCKY POINT, NORTH CAROLINA

New Orleans cooks are proud of their etouffees! Meaning "to smother" in French, an etouffee is similar to gumbo in that it uses the same seasonings and also, a roux. But while gumbo uses a rich and reddish-brown roux, an etouffee uses a blond one.

LOUISIANA

The bayou is a unique and diverse ecosystem. The swampy terrain is home to crawfish, alligators, catfish and shrimp—all popular eats in Cajun cuisine.

Crawfish Etouffee

I like to serve this Cajun sensation when I entertain. Etouffee is typically served with shellfish over rice and is similar to gumbo.

—**TAMRA DUNCAN** LINCOLN, ARKANSAS

PREP: 15 MIN.   **COOK:** 50 MIN.   **MAKES:** 6-8 SERVINGS

  ½ **cup butter, cubed**
  ½ **cup plus 2 tablespoons all-purpose flour**
 1¼ **cups chopped celery**
  1 **cup chopped green pepper**
  ½ **cup chopped green onions**
  1 **can (14½ ounces) chicken broth**
  1 **cup water**
  ¼ **cup minced fresh parsley**
  1 **tablespoon tomato paste**
  1 **bay leaf**
  ½ **teaspoon salt**
  ¼ **teaspoon pepper**
  ¼ **teaspoon cayenne pepper**
  2 **pounds frozen cooked crawfish tail meat, thawed**
     Hot cooked rice

1. In a large heavy skillet, melt butter; stir in the flour. Cook and stir over low heat for about 20 minutes until mixture is a caramel-colored paste. Add the celery, pepper and onions; stir until coated. Add the broth, water, parsley, tomato paste, bay leaf, salt, pepper and cayenne pepper. Bring to a boil.

2. Reduce the heat; cover and simmer for 30 minutes, stirring occasionally. Discard bay leaf. Add crawfish and heat through. Serve with rice.

Test Kitchen Tip: *Sometimes Tamra serves this with cooked penne pasta instead of rice. You can mix it all together or just serve it over the pasta. Also, you can add a bit more tomato paste for a deeper color and more cayenne pepper to raise the heat level.*

Peanutty Chicken

We use peanuts in a variety of dishes. This tender chicken, covered in a tasty gravy and sprinkled with peanuts, has a zip that perks up the taste buds!

—**MARY KAY DIXSON** DECATUR, ALABAMA

PREP: 10 MIN.   **COOK:** 45 MIN.   **MAKES:** 4 SERVINGS

  1 **teaspoon chili powder**
  1 **teaspoon salt**
  ¼ **teaspoon pepper**
  1 **broiler/fryer chicken (3½ to 4 pounds), cut up**
  5 **tablespoons butter**
  1 **cup orange juice**
  ⅔ **to 1 cup salted peanuts**
     Orange slices or minced fresh cilantro, optional

1. In a small bowl, combine the chili powder, salt and pepper; rub over chicken. In a large skillet, saute chicken in butter until golden brown. Reduce heat; cover and cook for 30 minutes or until juices run clear.

2. Transfer chicken to a serving platter and keep warm. Add orange juice to skillet, stirring to loosen browned bits from pan; simmer for 5 minutes. Pour over chicken. Sprinkle with peanuts. Garnish with orange slices and cilantro if desired.

Tomato Sandwiches

Use garden-fresh tomatoes for this sandwich. It's simple, but what a refreshing way to savor your tomato crop!

—TASTE OF HOME TEST KITCHEN

PREP/TOTAL TIME: 5 MIN MAKES: 4 SERVINGS

- 8 slices white bread, toasted if desired
- ½ cup mayonnaise, divided
- 2 large ripe tomatoes, sliced ½ inch thick
- ¼ teaspoon salt
- ¼ teaspoon pepper

1. Spread four slices of bread with half of the mayonnaise. Top with tomatoes; season with salt and pepper. Spread remaining mayonnaise over remaining bread; close sandwiches.

Cajun Shrimp Lasagna Roll-Ups

If you enjoy Creole and Cajun dishes, you'll love this one. The seasoning and andouille sausage give it a nice kick, and seafood fans will appreciate the shrimp.

—MARY BETH HARRIS-MURPHREE TYLER, TEXAS

PREP: 30 MIN. BAKE: 25 MIN. + STANDING
MAKES: 6 SERVINGS

- 1¼ pounds uncooked medium shrimp, peeled and deveined
- 1 medium onion, chopped
- 2 tablespoons olive oil
- 4 medium tomatoes, seeded and chopped
- 2 tablespoons Cajun seasoning
- 3 garlic cloves, minced
- ¼ cup butter, cubed
- ¼ cup all-purpose flour
- 2 cups milk
- 1½ cups (6 ounces) shredded cheddar cheese
- 1 cup diced fully cooked andouille sausage
- 12 lasagna noodles, cooked and drained
- 4 ounces pepper jack cheese, shredded
- 1 teaspoon paprika

1. In a large skillet, saute shrimp and onion in oil until shrimp turn pink. Stir in tomatoes and Cajun seasoning; set aside.

2. In a large saucepan, saute garlic in butter for 1 minute. Stir in flour until blended. Gradually add milk. Bring to a boil over medium heat; cook and stir for 2 minutes or until thickened.

Remove from the heat; stir in cheddar cheese until smooth. Add sausage; set aside.

3. Spread ⅓ cup shrimp mixture over each noodle. Carefully roll up; place seam side down in a greased 13x9-in. baking dish. Top with cheese sauce. Sprinkle with pepper jack cheese and paprika.

4. Cover and bake at 350° for 15 minutes. Uncover; bake 10-15 minutes longer or until bubbly. Let stand 15 minutes before serving.

◆◀● dishing about food

Southerners can agree on the simple delights of a homegrown, vine-ripened tomato sandwich. However, exactly how to make that sandwich is another matter. Are the tomatoes peeled or unpeeled, thin-sliced or thick-sliced? Is the white bread plain or toasted? Most everyone does agree, however, that the sandwich *must* be made with regular mayonnaise (no substitutions!), salt, pepper and classic white bread. It's a summertime tradition and treat.

Kentucky Grilled Chicken

This chicken is perfect for an outdoor summer meal. It takes about an hour on the grill. I use a new paintbrush to "mop" on the basting sauce.

—**JILL EVELY** WILMORE, KENTUCKY

PREP: 5 MIN. + MARINATING **GRILL:** 40 MIN.
MAKES: 10 SERVINGS

- 1 cup cider vinegar
- ½ cup canola oil
- 5 teaspoons Worcestershire sauce
- 4 teaspoons hot pepper sauce
- 2 teaspoons salt
- 10 bone-in chicken breast halves (10 ounces each)

1. In a small bowl, combine the first five ingredients. Pour 1 cup marinade into a large resealable plastic bag; add the chicken. Seal bag and turn to coat; refrigerate for at least 4 hours. Cover and refrigerate the remaining marinade for basting.

2. Drain and discard marinade from chicken. Using long-handled tongs, moisten a paper towel with cooking oil and lightly coat the grill rack. Prepare the grill for indirect heat, using a drip pan.

3. Place chicken breast bone side down and grill, covered, over indirect medium heat for 20 minutes on each side or until a thermometer reads 170°, basting occasionally with reserved marinade.

Cajun Catfish Sandwiches

You won't miss the fat and calories in this lightened-up version of a restaurant-style sandwich. Serve alongside your favorite vegetable side dish and enjoy.

—**SHAUNIECE FRAZIER** LOS ANGELES, CALIFORNIA

PREP/TOTAL TIME: 25 MIN. **MAKES:** 4 SERVINGS

- ¾ teaspoon seasoned pepper
- ½ teaspoon chili powder
- ½ teaspoon cayenne pepper
- ¼ teaspoon seasoned salt
- 4 catfish fillets (4 ounces each)
- 2 teaspoons olive oil, divided
- 2 green onions, chopped
- 3 garlic cloves, minced
- ½ cup fat-free mayonnaise
- 4 French or kaiser rolls, split and toasted
- 4 romaine leaves

1. Combine the seasoned pepper, chili powder, cayenne and seasoned salt; sprinkle over fillets.

2. In a large skillet, cook fillets in 1 teaspoon oil for 4-6 minutes on each side or until fish flakes easily with a fork. Remove; keep warm.

3. In the same skillet, saute the onions in the remaining oil until the onions are tender. Add the garlic; cook 1 minute longer. Remove from the heat; stir in the mayonnaise. Spread over rolls; top each with a romaine leaf and fillet. Replace tops.

Salmon Croquettes

Mom frequently served salmon when I was a girl. Learning the ropes in the kitchen as I grew up, I got the chore of deboning the salmon. I didn't mind, because these light crisp croquettes are absolutely delicious.

—MARY MCGUIRE GRAHAM, NORTH CAROLINA

PREP/TOTAL TIME: 30 MIN. **MAKES:** 4-6 SERVINGS

- 1 can (14¾ ounces) pink salmon, drained, deboned and flaked
- 1 cup evaporated milk, divided
- 1½ cups cornflake crumbs, divided
- ¼ cup dill pickle relish
- ¼ cup finely chopped celery
- 2 tablespoons finely chopped onion
  Oil for deep-fat frying

TARTAR SAUCE
- ⅔ cup evaporated milk
- ¼ cup mayonnaise
- 2 tablespoons dill pickle relish
- 1 tablespoon finely chopped onion

1. In a large bowl, combine the salmon, ½ cup milk, ½ cup crumbs, relish, celery and onion. With wet hands, shape ¼ cupfuls into cones. Dip into remaining milk, then into remaining crumbs. Heat oil in a deep-fat fryer to 365°. Fry croquettes, a few at a time, for 2 to 2½ minutes or until golden brown, Drain on paper towels; keep warm.

2. In a small saucepan, combine tartar sauce ingredients; cook over medium-low heat until heated through and slightly thickened. Serve warm with croquettes.

Shredded Barbecue Chicken over Grits

There's nothing like juicy meat sitting atop a pile of steaming grits. And the pumpkin in these grits makes them taste like a spicy, comforting bowl of fall flavors. Your family will come running to the table for this one!

—ERIN RENOUF MYLROIE SANTA CLARA, UTAH

PREP: 20 MIN. **COOK:** 25 MIN. **MAKES:** 6 SERVINGS

- 1 pound boneless skinless chicken breasts
- ¼ teaspoon pepper
- 1 can (14½ ounces) reduced-sodium chicken broth, divided
- 1 cup hickory smoke-flavored barbecue sauce
- ¼ cup molasses
- 1 tablespoon ground ancho chili pepper
- ½ teaspoon ground cinnamon
- 2¼ cups water
- 1 cup quick-cooking grits
- 1 cup canned pumpkin
- ¾ cup shredded pepper jack cheese
- 1 medium tomato, seeded and chopped
- 6 tablespoons reduced-fat sour cream
- 2 green onions, chopped
- 2 tablespoons minced fresh cilantro

1. Sprinkle chicken with pepper; place in a nonstick skillet coated with cooking spray.

2. In a large bowl, combine 1 cup broth, barbecue sauce, molasses, chili pepper and cinnamon; pour over the chicken. Bring to a boil. Reduce the heat; cover and simmer for 20-25 minutes or until a thermometer reads 165°. Shred meat with two forks and return to the skillet.

3. Meanwhile, in a large saucepan, bring water and remaining broth to a boil. Slowly stir in grits and pumpkin. Reduce heat; cook and stir for 5-7 minutes or until thickened. Stir in cheese until melted.

4. Divide grits among six serving bowls; top each with ½ cup chicken mixture. Serve with tomato, sour cream, green onions and cilantro.

MIAMI BEACH, FL

From 1923 to 1943, Art Deco architecture was all the rage— especially in Miami Beach. Today, the hotels, apartments and other buildings in this district are on the National Register of Historic Places.

Cuban Roasted Pork Sandwiches

For an incredible hot sandwich, slowly roast pork in a seasoned citrus marinade, then layer slices with pickles, zippy mustard, ham and cheese.

—TASTE OF HOME TEST KITCHEN

PREP: 10 MIN. +MARINATING **BAKE:** 2¾ HOURS + STANDING **MAKES:** 24 SERVINGS

- 1 boneless pork shoulder butt roast (5 to 6 pounds)
- 4 garlic cloves, sliced
- 2 large onions, sliced
- 1 cup orange juice
- 1 cup lime juice
- 2 tablespoons dried oregano
- 2 teaspoons ground cumin
- 1 teaspoon salt
- 1 teaspoon pepper

SANDWICHES
- 4 loaves (1 pound each) French bread
- ¾ cup butter, softened
  Yellow mustard, optional
- 24 thin sandwich pickle slices
- 2¼ pounds sliced deli ham
- 2¼ pounds Swiss cheese, sliced

1. Cut sixteen 1-in. slits in roast; insert garlic slices. In a large bowl, combine the onions, orange juice, lime juice and seasonings. Pour 1½ cups marinade into a large resealable plastic bag; add pork. Seal bag and turn to coat; refrigerate for at least 8 hours or overnight. Cover and refrigerate remaining marinade.

2. Drain and discard marinade. Place roast and reserved marinade in a shallow roasting pan. Bake at 350° for 2¾ to 3¼ hours or until a thermometer reads 160°, basting occasionally. Let stand for 15 minutes before slicing.

3. Meanwhile, cut each loaf of bread in half lengthwise. Spread butter and mustard if desired over cut sides of bread. Cut pork into thin slices. Layer bottom halves of bread with pickles, pork, ham and cheese. Replace tops. Cut each loaf into sixths.

4. Cook in batches on a panini maker or indoor grill for 4-5 minutes or until bread is browned and cheese is melted.

> **"** The addition of hot sauce zips up this cut of meat. It takes me back to spicy dinners I enjoyed as a child in the Southwest. I like to use the leftovers in different dishes—including BBQ beef sandwiches, quesadillas and spicy burritos. **"**
>
> **—CAROL STEVENS**
> BASYE, VIRGINIA

Red-Eye Beef Roast

PREP: 25 MIN. **BAKE:** 2 HOURS + STANDING **MAKES:** 10-12 SERVINGS

- 1 boneless beef eye of round roast (about 3 pounds)
- 1 tablespoon canola oil
- 2½ cups water, divided
- 1 envelope onion soup mix
- 3 tablespoons cider vinegar
- 2 tablespoons Louisiana hot sauce
- 2 tablespoons all-purpose flour

1. In a Dutch oven, brown roast on all sides in oil over medium-high heat; drain. Combine ¾ cup water, soup mix, vinegar and hot sauce; pour over roast.

2. Cover and bake at 325° for 2-3 hours or until the beef is tender. Transfer to a serving platter and keep warm. Let stand for 10-15 minutes before slicing.

3. For gravy, combine flour and remaining water until smooth; stir into meat juices. Bring to a boil; cook and stir for 2 minutes or until thickened. Serve with meat.

"Moist, tender and slightly sweet from the marinade, this juicy steak boasts wonderful flavor and oh-so-easy preparation. Serve with potatoes and a green vegetable for a complete meal."

—TASTE OF HOME
TEST KITCHEN

Whiskey Sirloin Steak

PREP: 10 MIN. + MARINATING **BROIL:** 15 MIN. **MAKES:** 4 SERVINGS

¼ cup whiskey or apple cider
¼ cup reduced-sodium soy sauce
1 tablespoon sugar
1 garlic clove, thinly sliced
½ teaspoon ground ginger
1 beef top sirloin steak (1 inch thick and 1 pound)

1. In a large resealable plastic bag, combine the first five ingredients; add the beef. Seal bag and turn to coat; refrigerate for 8 hours or overnight.

2. Drain and discard marinade. Place beef on a broiler pan coated with cooking spray. Broil 4-6 in. from the heat for 7-8 minutes on each side or until meat reaches desired doneness (for medium-rare, a thermometer should read 145°; medium, 160°; well-done, 170°).

Louisiana Red Beans and Rice

Smoked turkey sausage and red pepper flakes punch up the flavor of this saucy, slow-cooked version of the New Orleans classic. For extra heat, add red pepper sauce at the table.

—**JULIA BUSHREE** GEORGETOWN, TEXAS

PREP: 20 MIN. **COOK:** 8 HOURS **MAKES:** 9 SERVINGS

- 4 cans (16 ounces each) kidney beans, rinsed and drained
- 1 can (14½ ounces) diced tomatoes, undrained
- 1 package (14 ounces) smoked turkey sausage, sliced
- 1 cup chicken broth
- 3 celery ribs, chopped
- 1 large onion, chopped
- 1 medium green pepper, chopped
- 1 small sweet red pepper, chopped
- 6 garlic cloves, minced
- 1 bay leaf
- ½ teaspoon crushed red pepper flakes
- 2 green onions, chopped
  Hot cooked rice

1. In a 4-qt. slow cooker, combine the first 11 ingredients. Cover and cook on low for 8-10 hours or until vegetables are tender. Stir before serving. Discard bay leaf.

2. Sprinkle each serving with onions. Serve with rice.

❝ This brisket roasts in a sauce that adds great flavor. When one of our sons lived in the South, I learned that "mop sauce" is traditionally prepared for Texas ranch-style barbecues in batches so large that it's brushed on the meat with a mop! You won't need that much for my recipe but will get the big-time taste. **❞**

—DARLIS WILFER
WEST BEND, WISCONSIN

Beef Brisket with Mop Sauce

PREP: 20 MIN. **BAKE:** 2 HOURS
MAKES: 10-12 SERVINGS

- ½ cup water
- ¼ cup cider vinegar
- ¼ cup Worcestershire sauce
- ¼ cup ketchup
- ¼ cup dark corn syrup
- 2 tablespoons canola oil
- 2 tablespoons prepared mustard
- 1 fresh beef brisket (3 pounds)

1. In a large saucepan, combine the first seven ingredients. Bring to a boil, stirring constantly. Reduce the heat; simmer for 5 minutes, stirring occasionally. Remove from the heat.

2. Place the brisket in a shallow roasting pan; pour sauce over the top. Cover and bake at 350° for 2 to 2½ hours or until meat is tender. Let stand for 5 minutes. Thinly slice meat across the grain.

Tangy Beef Brisket: *Omit sauce. In a large saucepan, saute ½ cup diced onion in ¼ cup butter until tender. Add 1¾ cups ketchup, ¾ cup packed brown sugar, ¼ cup Worcestershire sauce, 3 tablespoons lemon juice, 1 tablespoon chili powder, ¾ teaspoon hot pepper sauce, ½ teaspoon each salt and prepared horseradish and ¼ teaspoon garlic powder. Bring to a boil. Reduce heat; simmer, uncovered, for 30-40 minutes. Proceed as directed in step 2.*

Editor's Note: *This is a fresh beef brisket, not corned beef.*

Bayou Burgers with Spicy Remoulade

I like to serve these Southern, slightly spicy and flavorful burgers with sweet potato fries.

—MICHELE CLAYBROOK-LUCAS
MEDIA, PENNSYLVANIA

PREP/TOTAL TIME: 30 MIN. **MAKES:** 4 SERVINGS

- 1 small onion, chopped
- 2 tablespoons olive oil
- ¼ pound fully cooked andouille sausage link, casing removed, finely chopped
- 1 teaspoon Creole seasoning
- ¾ teaspoon garlic powder, divided
- ¼ teaspoon salt
- ¼ teaspoon pepper
- 1 pound ground turkey
- ¼ pound Italian turkey sausage link, casing removed
- 4 slices cheddar cheese
- ½ cup Miracle Whip
- 2 tablespoons lemon juice
- 1 tablespoon hot pepper sauce
- 2 teaspoons sweet pickle relish
- 1 teaspoon capers, drained
- 4 kaiser rolls, split
- 1 tablespoon butter

1. In a large skillet, saute onion in oil until tender. Add andouille sausage; cook 1 minute longer. Transfer to a large bowl. Stir in the Creole seasoning, ¼ teaspoon garlic powder, salt and pepper. Crumble turkey and turkey sausage over mixture and mix well. Shape into four patties.

2. In a large skillet over medium heat, cook burgers for 5-7 minutes on each side or until a thermometer reads 165° and juices run clear. Top with cheese; cover and cook for 1-2 minutes or until cheese is melted.

3. For remoulade, in a small bowl, combine the Miracle Whip, lemon juice, pepper sauce, relish and capers. Spread rolls with butter and sprinkle with remaining garlic powder. Broil 4 in. from the heat for 2-3 minutes or until lightly browned. Serve burgers on rolls with the remoulade.

Editor's Note: *The following spices may be substituted for 1 teaspoon Creole seasoning: ¼ teaspoon each salt, garlic powder and paprika; and a pinch each of dried thyme, ground cumin and cayenne pepper.*

Whiskey Barbecue Pork

The list of ingredients seems long for my saucy pork, but most items are common things you already have in your kitchen. I think the liquid smoke gives it the authentic taste!

—REBECCA HORVATH JOHNSON CITY, TENNESSEE

PREP: 15 MIN. **COOK:** 6 HOURS **MAKES:** 8 SERVINGS

- ½ to ¾ cup packed brown sugar
- 1 can (6 ounces) tomato paste
- ⅓ cup barbecue sauce
- ¼ cup whiskey
- 2 tablespoons liquid smoke
- 2 tablespoons Worcestershire sauce
- 3 garlic cloves, minced
- ½ teaspoon chili powder
- ½ teaspoon salt
- ½ teaspoon pepper
- ½ teaspoon hot pepper sauce
- ¼ teaspoon ground cumin
- 1 boneless pork shoulder butt roast (3 to 4 pounds)
- 1 medium onion, quartered
- 8 hamburger buns, split

1. In a small bowl, mix the first 12 ingredients. Place the pork roast and onion in a 5-qt. slow cooker. Add sauce mixture. Cook, covered, on low for 6-8 hours or until pork is tender.

2. Remove roast and onion. Cool pork slightly; discard onion. Meanwhile, skim fat from sauce. If desired, transfer sauce to a small saucepan; bring to a boil and thicken slightly.

3. Shred the pork with two forks. Return pork and sauce to slow cooker; heat through. Serve on buns.

Molasses-Glazed Baby Back Ribs

My husband sizzles up his luscious ribs recipe for our family of five at *least* once a month in the summer. The sweet-and-sour barbecue sauce is the perfect condiment for the moist tender meat.

—KIM BRALEY DUNEDIN, FLORIDA

PREP: 20 MIN. + MARINATING **GRILL:** 70 MIN.
MAKES: 4 SERVINGS

- 4½ pounds pork baby back ribs
- 1 bottle (2 liters) cola
- ½ teaspoon salt
- ½ teaspoon pepper
- ¼ teaspoon garlic salt
- ¼ teaspoon dried oregano
- ¼ teaspoon onion powder
- ⅛ teaspoon cayenne pepper

BARBECUE SAUCE
- ¼ cup ketchup
- ¼ cup honey
- ¼ cup molasses
- 1 tablespoon prepared mustard
- ½ teaspoon cayenne pepper
- ½ teaspoon salt

1. Place the ribs in large resealable plastic bags; add cola. Seal bags and turn to coat; refrigerate for 8 hours or overnight.

2. Drain and discard cola. Pat ribs dry with paper towels. Combine the seasonings; rub over the ribs.

3. Prepare grill for indirect heat, using a drip pan. Place ribs over pan; grill, covered, over indirect medium heat for 1 hour, or until tender, turning occasionally.

4. In a small bowl, combine the barbecue sauce ingredients. Brush over the ribs; grill, covered, over medium heat 10-20 minutes longer or until ribs are browned, turning and basting occasionally.

◄● dishing about food

Tennessee is known for its whiskey, especially Jack Daniel's. So it's no surprise that Tennessee barbecue sauce often has a splash or more of whiskey in it.

LYNCHBURG, TN

Sights on the Jack Daniel's tour offer an indoors-and-out view of the famous distiller's world, including a cave spring, which still provides water for the whiskey.

According to popular theory, the Po-Boy sandwich came about during the 1929 streetcar strike in New Orleans. Former streetcar conductors Clovis and Bennie Martin operated a small coffee stand and restaurant at the time, and during the strike, they vowed to feed the strikers until the strike was over. When one of the strikers came by, the Martins would call out, "Here comes another poor boy." The name eventually stuck—to the sandwiches they handed out.

NEW ORLEANS, LA

Cruise historic New Orleans in a streetcar! The three lines, St. Charles, Canal Street and Riverfront, offer access to many must-see spots in the French Quarter and beyond.

Shrimp Po-Boys

You don't have to feel poor after you pay in for your taxes. These sandwiches will star on the table and add a Louisiana flair. You can adjust the cayenne pepper to suit your tastes.

—**BETTY JEAN JORDAN** MONTICELLO, GEORGIA

PREP: 30 MIN. **COOK:** 15 MIN. **MAKES:** 8 SERVINGS

- ½ cup mayonnaise
- ½ cup finely chopped onion
- ½ cup chopped dill pickles
- 1⅓ cups all-purpose flour
- 1 teaspoon salt
- 4 eggs, separated
- 1⅓ cups 2% milk
- 2 tablespoons canola oil
- 8 French sandwich rolls, split
  - Additional oil for deep-fat frying
- 2 pounds uncooked large shrimp, peeled and deveined
  - Cayenne pepper to taste
- 4 cups shredded lettuce
- 16 tomato slices

1. In a small bowl, combine the mayonnaise, onion and pickles; set aside. For the batter, combine flour and salt in a bowl. Add the egg yolks, milk and oil; beat until smooth.

2. In a small bowl, beat egg whites until stiff peaks form; fold in batter.

3. Wrap sandwich rolls in foil. Bake at 350° for 10 minutes or until warmed. Meanwhile, in a large skillet or deep-fat fryer, heat ½ in. of oil to 375°. Dip shrimp in batter; fry for 2-3 minutes on each side or until golden brown. Drain on paper towels; sprinkle with cayenne

4. Spread mayonnaise mixture over rolls; top with lettuce, tomato slices and shrimp.

Creole Chicken

Chili powder lends just a hint of heat to this full-flavored and oh-so-easy chicken entree.

—**SUSAN SHIELDS** ENGLEWOOD, FLORIDA

PREP: 15 MIN. **COOK:** 25 MIN. **MAKES:** 2 SERVINGS

- 2 boneless skinless chicken breast halves (4 ounces each)
- 1 teaspoon canola oil
- 1 can (14½ ounces) stewed tomatoes, cut up
- ⅓ cup julienned green pepper
- ¼ cup chopped celery
- ¼ cup sliced onion
- ½ to 1 teaspoon chili powder
- ½ teaspoon dried thyme
- ⅛ teaspoon pepper
- 1 cup hot cooked rice

1. In a small nonstick skillet coated with cooking spray, cook the chicken in oil over medium heat for 5-6 minutes on each side or a thermometer reads 165° Remove; keep warm.

2. In the same skillet, combine the tomatoes, green pepper, celery, onion, chili powder, thyme and pepper. Bring to a boil. Reduce heat; cover and simmer for 10 minutes or until vegetables are crisp-tender. Return chicken to pan; heat through. Serve with rice.

BATON ROUGE, LA

A towering 34 stories high, the Louisiana State Capitol is the tallest in the country. It was built in the early '30s and is surrounded by lush gardens.

South Carolina barbecue sauce reflects a German influence. During the 1730s through the 1750s, the English who had settled in the area encouraged Germans to immigrate to South Carolina by paying their passage and giving them land grants. The Germans brought their tradition of family farming—along with their love of mustard, demonstrated in the area's mustard-based barbecue sauce.

CHARLESTON, SC

Since its founding in 1738, Drayton Hall has survived the Revolution, the Civil War and several natural disasters. Visit and you'll see the oldest surviving example of Georgian-Palladian architecture.

South Carolina-Style Ribs

This recipe makes some of the very best country-style pork ribs you'll ever eat. We use the same delicious sauce on barbecued chicken, too.

—**KAREN CONKLIN** SUPPLY, NORTH CAROLINA

PREP: 15 MIN. **BAKE:** 2¼ HOURS
MAKES: 6-8 SERVINGS

- 4 **pounds pork baby back ribs**
- ½ **cup red wine vinegar**
- ½ **cup honey**
- ½ **cup prepared mustard**
- 2 **tablespoons canola oil**
- 4 **teaspoons Worcestershire sauce**
- 2 **teaspoons butter**
- 2 **teaspoons coarsely ground pepper**
- 1 **teaspoon salt**
- 1 **teaspoon hot pepper sauce**

1. Cut ribs into serving-size pieces. Place ribs meat side up in a roasting pan. Cover and bake at 325° for 1½ to 2 hours or until tender; drain.

2. Meanwhile, combine the remaining ingredients in a saucepan. Bring to a boil over medium heat. Reduce the heat; simmer, uncovered, for about 30 minutes or until slightly reduced.

3. Brush sauce over ribs. Bake, uncovered, for 30-44 minutes or until the ribs are glazed, basting occasionally.

Cajun Beef Burgers

Flavor abounds in these hefty and juicy Cajun burgers, spiked with bits of veggies and Cajun seasoning. A creamy mayonnaise-and-Creole-mustard spread adds even more Louisiana-style flair.

—**REBECCA BAIRD** SALT LAKE CITY, UTAH

PREP: 30 MIN. **GRILL:** 10 MIN. **MAKES:** 4 SERVINGS

- ¼ **cup mayonnaise**
- 1 **green onion, thinly sliced**
- 1½ **teaspoons Creole mustard**
- ½ **teaspoon minced garlic**
- ½ **teaspoon grated lime peel**
- ½ **teaspoon lime juice**
- ¼ **teaspoon pepper**
- ⅛ **teaspoon salt**
  Dash hot pepper sauce
  Dash Worcestershire sauce

BURGERS
- ¼ **cup each finely chopped onion, celery and carrot**
- 2 **tablespoons minced fresh parsley**
- 1 **tablespoon butter**
- 1 **tablespoon Cajun seasoning**
- ¼ **teaspoon salt**
- ¼ **teaspoon hot pepper sauce**
- 1 **pound lean ground beef (90% lean)**
- 4 **onion rolls, split**

1. In a small bowl, combine the first 10 ingredients until blended; chill until serving.

2. In a large skillet, saute the onion, celery, carrot and parsley in butter for 6-8 minutes or until tender; cool slightly.

3. In a large bowl, combine the vegetable mixture, Cajun seasoning, salt and pepper sauce. Crumble beef over mixture and mix well. Shape into four patties.

4. Grill burgers, covered, over medium heat or broil 4 in. from the heat for 5-7 minutes on each side or until a thermometer reads 160° and juices run clear. Grill rolls, cut side down, over medium heat for 30-60 seconds or until toasted. Serve burgers on rolls with sauce.

Arkansas Travelers

I came across this club-style sandwich in a tearoom in Arkansas. I brought the "secret" recipe back home, much to the delight of my husband and our two sons.

—**ROBI KASTNER** SPRINGFIELD, MISSOURI

PREP/TOTAL TIME: 15 MIN. **MAKES:** 5 SERVINGS

- 1 **pound turkey breast**
- 1 **block (5 ounces) Swiss cheese**
- 1 **avocado, peeled and pitted**
- 1 **large tomato**
- 10 **bacon strips, cooked and crumbled**
- ⅓ to ½ **cup ranch salad dressing**
- 10 **slices whole wheat bread, toasted**

1. Chop turkey, cheese, avocado and tomato into ¼-in. cubes; place in a large bowl. Add bacon and dressing. Spoon ½ cup between two slices of toast.

Soda Pop Chops with Smashed Potatoes

Root beer gives this family-friendly recipe a tangy taste kids will love. Served alongside the smashed potatoes, this recipe makes a stick-to-the-ribs meal any weeknight.

—**TASTE OF HOME TEST KITCHEN**

PREP: 25 MIN. **COOK:** 15 MIN. **MAKES:** 4 SERVINGS

- 1½ **pounds small red potatoes, halved**
- 1 **cup root beer**
- 1 **cup ketchup**
- 1 **tablespoon brown sugar**
- 2 **teaspoons chili powder**
- 2 **teaspoons Worcestershire sauce**
- ¼ **teaspoon garlic powder**
- 2 **tablespoons all-purpose flour**
- ¾ **teaspoon pepper, divided**
- ½ **teaspoon salt, divided**
- 4 **bone-in pork loin chops (7 ounces each)**
- 2 **tablespoons olive oil**
- 2 **tablespoons butter**
- ¼ **teaspoon garlic powder**

1. Place potatoes in a large saucepan and cover with water. Bring to a boil. Reduce heat; cover and cook for 15-20 minutes or until tender.

2. Meanwhile, in a small bowl, combine the root beer, ketchup, brown sugar, chili powder, Worcestershire sauce and garlic powder;

set aside. In a large resealable plastic bag, combine the flour, ½ teaspoon pepper and ¼ teaspoon salt. Add pork chops, one at a time, and shake to coat.

3. In a large skillet, cook the chops in oil over medium heat for 2-3 minutes on each side or until chops are lightly browned; drain. Add root beer mixture. Bring to a boil. Reduce heat; cover and simmer 6-8 minutes or until a thermometer reads 145°. Remove the pork and keep warm. Let stand for 5 minutes before serving.

4. Bring sauce to a boil; cook until liquid is reduced by half. Meanwhile, drain potatoes; mash with the butter, garlic powder and remaining salt and pepper. Serve with pork chops and sauce.

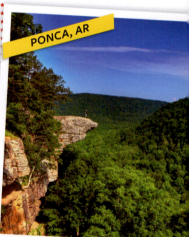

PONCA, AR

Adventurous travelers in Arkansas won't want to miss hiking to famous Hawksbill Crag in the Ozark National Forest. Bring your camera—the natural vistas can't be beat!

BRUNSWICK, GA

Drive along Georgia's coast, and you may cross the Sidney Lanier Bridge, the longest one in the state. Built in 2003, the bridge features special lighting designed to protect turtles nesting nearby.

Brunswick Stew

When this stick-to-your-ribs recipe is on the menu, no one leaves the table hungry. The tomato-based stew has chicken and ham in addition to the beef and is thickened with mashed potatoes.

—**JUDI BRINEGAR** LIBERTY, NORTH CAROLINA

PREP: 45 MIN. **COOK:** 2 HOURS
MAKES: ABOUT 8 QUARTS (25-30 SERVINGS)

- 4 large onions, halved and thinly sliced
- ¼ cup butter, cubed
- 1 broiler/fryer chicken (3 to 4 pounds), cut up
- 8 cups water
- 2 cans (28 ounces each) crushed tomatoes
- 1¾ cups ketchup
- 1 can (6 ounces) tomato paste
- 1 can (10¾ ounces) condensed tomato soup, undiluted
- 2 medium jalapeno peppers, seeded and chopped
- 3 teaspoons salt
- 1 teaspoon Worcestershire sauce
- 1 teaspoon hot pepper sauce
- 1 teaspoon pepper
- 2 pounds ground beef, cooked and drained
- 1 pound cubed fully cooked ham
- 1 package (16 ounces) frozen cut green beans
- 1 package (16 ounces) frozen butter beans
- 1 package (16 ounces) frozen corn
- 6 cups hot mashed potatoes (without added milk and butter)

1. In a large stockpot, saute onions in butter until tender. Add chicken and water. Bring to a boil. Reduce heat; cover and simmer for 1 hour.

2. Remove chicken; when cool enough to handle, remove meat from bones. Discard bones and dice meat. Skim fat from broth; return chicken to broth.

3. Stir in the next 14 ingredients; bring to a boil. Reduce heat; cover and simmer for 1 hour or until vegetables are tender. Stir in potatoes; heat through.

Editor's Note: *Wear disposable gloves when cutting hot peppers; the oils can burn skin. Avoid touching your face.*

Southern Eggs and Biscuits

To me, nothing beats the flavor of Southern cooking, especially for breakfast! The rich flavor of these eggs served over homemade biscuits is a hearty way to start any day.

—**RUTH WARD** LEXINGTON, TENNESSEE

PREP: 30 MIN. **BAKE:** 25 MIN. **MAKES:** 6-8 SERVINGS

- 10 hard-cooked eggs, sliced
- 1 pound sliced bacon, diced
- ⅓ cup all-purpose flour
- ¼ teaspoon salt
- ⅛ teaspoon pepper
- 4 cups milk
- 2 cups cubed process cheese (Velveeta)

BISCUITS
- ½ cup shortening
- 3 cups self-rising flour
- 1¼ cups buttermilk

1. Place eggs in a greased 13x9-in. baking dish. In a large skillet, cook bacon over medium heat until crisp. Drain, reserving ¼ cup drippings. Sprinkle bacon over eggs.

2. Whisk the flour, salt and pepper into reserved drippings until smooth. Gradually add milk. Bring to a boil. Cook and stir for 2 minutes or until thickened and bubbly. Add cheese, stirring until melted; pour over eggs.

3. For biscuits, cut shortening into flour until mixture resembles coarse crumbs. Stir in buttermilk; gently knead six to eight times. Roll out on a lightly floured surface to ½-in. thickness. Cut with a 2½-in. biscuit cutter and place on a greased baking sheet.

4. Bake biscuits and eggs at 400° for 25 minutes or until biscuits are golden brown. Serve eggs over biscuits.

Creole Steaks

PREP: 15 MIN. **COOK:** 35 MIN. **MAKES:** 4 SERVINGS

- 1 **large onion, chopped**
- ¼ **cup chopped green pepper**
- ¼ **cup chopped celery**
- 4 **tablespoons canola oil, divided**
- 3 **garlic cloves, minced**
- 1 **tablespoon all-purpose flour**
- ½ **teaspoon salt**
- ½ **teaspoon dried thyme**
- ½ **teaspoon cayenne pepper**
- ½ **teaspoon pepper**
- 2 **cans (14½ ounces each) fire-roasted diced tomatoes, undrained**
- ¼ **teaspoon hot pepper sauce**
- 1 **tablespoon lemon juice**
- 4 **beef cubed steaks (4 ounces each)**
  Additional salt and pepper

1. In a large skillet, saute the onion, green pepper and celery in 2 tablespoons oil until crisp-tender. Add garlic; cook 1 minute longer. Stir in flour, salt, thyme, cayenne and pepper.

2. Add tomatoes and pepper sauce; bring to a boil. Reduce heat; simmer, uncovered, for 20-25 minutes or until thickened, stirring occasionally. Remove from the heat; stir in lemon juice and keep warm.

3. Sprinkle steaks with salt and pepper to taste. In another large skillet, cook steaks in remaining oil over medium heat for 3-4 minutes on each side or until no longer pink. Serve with sauce.

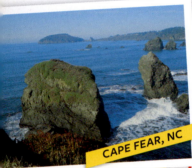

CAPE FEAR, NC

A large number of Highland Scots settled around Cape Fear in the 18th and 19th centuries, perhaps in part because the rugged terrain resembles their homeland.

Southern Fried Chicken

In the South, they often serve fried chicken with a creamy seasoned gravy.
—TASTE OF HOME TEST KITCHEN

PREP: 25 MIN. **COOK:** 45 MIN. **MAKES:** 6 SERVINGS

1 cup all-purpose flour
1 teaspoon onion powder
1 teaspoon paprika
¾ teaspoon salt
½ teaspoon rubbed sage
½ teaspoon pepper
¼ teaspoon dried thyme
1 egg
½ cup milk
1 broiler/fryer chicken (3 to 3½ pounds), cut up
  Oil for frying

CREAMY GRAVY
⅓ cup all-purpose flour
¼ teaspoon salt
¼ teaspoon dried thyme
¼ to ½ teaspoon pepper
2½ cups milk
½ cup heavy whipping cream

1. In a large resealable plastic bag, combine the first seven ingredients. In a shallow bowl, beat egg and milk. Dip chicken pieces into egg mixture, then add to flour mixture, a few pieces at a time, and shake to coat.

2. In a large skillet, heat ¼ in. of oil; fry chicken until browned on all sides. Cover and simmer for 35-40 minutes or until juices run clear and chicken is tender, turning occasionally. Uncover and cook 5 minutes longer. Drain on paper towels and keep warm. Drain skillet, reserving 3 tablespoons of the drippings.

3. For gravy, in a small bowl, combine the flour, salt, thyme and pepper. Gradually whisk in milk and cream until smooth; add to skillet. Bring to a boil over medium heat; cook and stir for 2 minutes or until thickened. Serve with the chicken.

Low Country Boil

Ideal for camping and relaxing trips to the beach, this crowd-pleasing recipe includes a combination of shrimp, crab, sausage, corn and potatoes.

—MAGESWARI ELAGUPILLAI VICTORVILLE, CALIFORNIA

PREP: 20 MIN. **COOK:** 40 MIN. **MAKES:** 4 SERVINGS

- 2 quarts water
- 1 bottle (12 ounces) beer
- 2 tablespoons seafood seasoning
- 1½ teaspoons salt
- 4 medium red potatoes, cut into wedges
- 1 medium sweet onion, cut into wedges
- 4 medium ears sweet corn, cut in half
- ⅓ pound smoked chorizo or kielbasa, cut into 1-inch slices
- 3 tablespoons olive oil
- 6 large garlic cloves, minced
- 1 tablespoon ground cumin
- 1 tablespoon minced fresh cilantro
- ½ teaspoon paprika
- ½ teaspoon pepper
- 1 pound uncooked large shrimp, deveined
- 1 pound uncooked snow crab legs

Optional condiments: seafood cocktail sauce, lemon wedges and melted butter

1. In a stockpot, combine the water, beer, seafood seasoning and salt; add potatoes and onion. Bring to a boil. Reduce heat; simmer, uncovered, for 10 minutes. Add corn and chorizo; simmer 10-12 minutes longer or until potatoes and corn are tender.

2. Meanwhile, in a small skillet, heat oil. Add the garlic, cumin, cilantro, paprika and pepper. Cook and stir over medium heat for 1 minute.

3. Stir the shrimp, crab legs and garlic mixture into the stockpot; cook for 4-6 minutes or until shrimp and crab turn pink. Drain; transfer seafood mixture to a large serving bowl. Serve with condiments of your choice.

◀● dishing about food

Low Country Boil is also known as Beaufort Stew. "Low Country" refers to the area around Charleston, South Carolina, to Savannah and the coast of southern Georgia. It's rich with waterways and seafood.

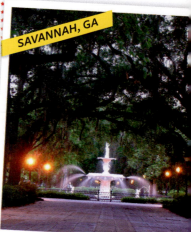

SAVANNAH, GA

Wander the streets of Savannah's historic district and you're sure to find Forsyth Park. The ornate Forsyth Fountain was unveiled in 1858.

North Carolina is the No. 1 producer of sweet potatoes in the United States. As sweet potato fries become more popular, consumption of this nutritional powerhouse continues to grow.

NORTH CAROLINA

Sweet potatoes are known for containing lots of vitamins A and C and offering good doses of fiber, potassium and other important minerals. But did you know they increase blood sugar more slowly than regular potatoes, so they are a good option for diabetics?

Sweet Potato Fries

Nutritious sweet potatoes lend a distinctive flavor to these extra-crunchy fries. With the tasty mayo-chutney dip, this super side could double as a party appetizer!

—**KELLY MCWHERTER** HOUSTON, TEXAS

PREP: 15 MIN. **BAKE:** 25 MIN. **MAKES:** 2 SERVINGS

- 2 **tablespoons beaten egg**
- 1 **tablespoon water**
- ⅓ **cup dry bread crumbs**
- 2 **tablespoons grated Parmesan cheese**
- ¼ **teaspoon cayenne pepper**
- ¼ **teaspoon pepper**
- 1 **large sweet potato (14 ounces), peeled**
- 2 **teaspoons olive oil**

MANGO CHUTNEY MAYONNAISE
- ¼ **cup mayonnaise**
- 2 **tablespoons mango chutney**
- ¼ **teaspoon curry powder**
  Dash salt
- 2 **teaspoons minced fresh parsley, optional**

1. In a shallow bowl, whisk egg and water. In a resealable plastic bag, combine the bread crumbs, cheese, cayenne and pepper. Cut sweet potato into ¼-in. strips. Add to egg mixture, a few at a time, and toss to coat. Add to the crumb mixture, a few at a time; seal bag and shake to coat.

2. Arrange potato strips in a single layer on a baking sheet coated with cooking spray; drizzle with oil. Bake at 450° for 25-30 minutes or until golden brown and crisp, turning occasionally.

3. In a small bowl, combine the mayonnaise, chutney, curry powder and salt. If desired, sprinkle parsley over fries. Serve with mango chutney mayonnaise.

Watermelon Rind Pickles

"Waste not, want not" has always been smart advice—especially when it produces results as delicious and refreshing as this recipe.

—TASTE OF HOME TEST KITCHEN

PREP: 45 MIN. + CHILLING **PROCESS:** 10 MIN. **MAKES:** 4 PINTS

- 8 **cups sliced peeled watermelon rind (2x1-inch pieces)**
- 6 **cups water**
- 1 **cup canning salt**
- 4 **cups sugar**
- 2 **cups white vinegar**
- 6 **cinnamon sticks (3 inches), divided**
- 1 **teaspoon whole cloves**
- 1 **teaspoon whole peppercorns**

1. Place rind in a large nonreactive bowl; stir in water and salt. Refrigerate for several hours or overnight. Rinse and drain well.

2. In a Dutch oven, mix sugar, vinegar, 2 cinnamon sticks, cloves and peppercorns. Bring to a boil. Add rinds; return to a boil. Reduce heat; simmer, uncovered, 10 minutes or until tender. Discard cinnamon sticks.

3. Carefully ladle hot mixture into four hot 1-pint jars, leaving ½-in. headspace. Add a remaining cinnamon stick to each jar. Remove air bubbles and adjust headspace, if necessary, by adding hot liquid. Wipe rims. Center lids on jars; screw on bands until fingertip tight.

4. Place jars into canner, ensuring that they are completely covered with water. Bring to a boil; process for 10 minutes. Remove jars and cool.

Editor's Note: *To prepare watermelon rind, remove dark green peel from watermelon rind and discard. The processing time listed is for altitudes of 1,000 feet or less. For altitudes up to 3,000 feet, add 5 minutes; 6,000 feet, add 10 minutes; 8,000 feet, add 15 minutes; 10,000 feet, add 20 minutes.*

◄● dishing about food

Anyone who's sliced watermelon for a fruit salad or served it at a picnic knows there's a lot of rind left behind. Instead of tossing it out, create a sweet-sour pickle with it as Southerners have done for generations.

CAVE CITY, AR

For decades, citizens of one north Arkansas town have been hosting an annual celebration of their juiciest crop at the Cave City Watermelon Festival.

Potlikker, also known as pot or collard liquor, is the greenish broth that's left over after boiling collard, turnip or mustard greens. This savory liquid is used as a base for soups and stews, poured over rice or grits, or soaked up directly on the plate with corn bread or rolls. Some people even drink it by the glass!

Bacon Collard Greens

Collard greens are a staple vegetable of Southern cuisine. This side dish is often made with smoked or salt-cured meats, such as ham hocks, pork or fatback.

—MARSHA ANKENEY NICEVILLE, FLORIDA

PREP: 25 MIN. **COOK:** 55 MIN. **MAKES:** 9 SERVINGS

- 2 **pounds collard greens**
- 4 **thick-sliced bacon strips, chopped**
- 1 **cup chopped sweet onion**
- 5 **cups reduced-sodium chicken broth**
- 1 **cup sun-dried tomatoes (not packed in oil), chopped**
- ½ **teaspoon garlic powder**
- ¼ **teaspoon salt**
- ¼ **teaspoon crushed red pepper flakes**

1. Trim thick stems from collard greens; coarsely chop leaves. In a Dutch oven, saute bacon for 3 minutes. Add onion; cook and stir 8-9 minutes longer or until onion is tender and bacon is crisp. Add the greens; cook just until wilted.

2. Stir in remaining ingredients. Bring to a boil. Reduce heat; cover and simmer for 45-50 minutes or until greens are tender.

Georgia Peanut Salsa

Former President Jimmy Carter gave First Place to this zippy salsa at the Plains Peanut Festival in his Georgia hometown. My daughter and I came up with the recipe just days before the competition. Although we weren't allowed in the judging room, we later saw a tape of President Carter tasting our salsa and saying, "M-m-m, that's good." Elizabeth was only 9 at the time, but it's a day she'll never forget.

—LANE MCCLOUD SILOAM SPRINGS, ARKANSAS

PREP: 25 MIN. + CHILLING **MAKES:** ABOUT 6½ CUPS

- 3 **plum tomatoes, seeded and chopped**
- 1 **jar (8 ounces) picante sauce**
- 1 **can (7 ounces) white or shoepeg corn, drained**
- ⅓ **cup Italian salad dressing**
- 1 **medium green pepper, chopped**
- 1 **medium sweet red pepper, chopped**
- 4 **green onions, thinly sliced**
- ½ **cup minced fresh cilantro**
- 2 **garlic cloves, minced**
- 2½ **cups salted roasted peanuts or boiled peanuts**
  Hot pepper sauce, optional
  Tortilla chips

1. In a large bowl, combine the first nine ingredients. Cover and refrigerate for at least 8 hours.

2. Just before serving, stir in peanuts and pepper sauce if desired. Serve with tortilla chips.

Editor's Note: *This recipe was tested with salted peanuts, but the original recipe used boiled peanuts, which are often available in the South.*

Mixed Citrus Marmalade

I often have an abundance of grapefruit and oranges, which I love to use in this orange-colored marmalade. It makes a great gift, too.

—CORKY HUFFSMITH INDIO, CALIFORNIA

PREP: 1½ HOURS **PROCESS:** 5 MIN.
MAKES: 10 HALF-PINTS

- 1 **pound lemons, thinly sliced and seeds removed**
- 1 **pound grapefruit, thinly sliced and seeds removed**
- 1 **pound oranges, thinly sliced and seeds removed**
- 2 **quarts water**
- 8 **cups sugar**

1. In a large bowl, combine the lemons, grapefruit, oranges and water. Cover and refrigerate overnight.

2. Transfer to a Dutch oven. Bring to a boil. Reduce heat; simmer, uncovered, for 10-15 minutes or until fruit is tender. Stir in the sugar. Bring to a boil. Cook and stir for 45-55 minutes or until thickened, stirring frequently.

3. Remove from the heat; skim off the foam. Carefully ladle the hot mixture into hot sterilized half-pint jars, leaving ¼-in. headspace. Remove air bubbles; wipe rims and adjust lids. Process for 5 minutes in a boiling-water canner.

Editor's Note: *The processing time listed is for altitudes of 1,000 feet or less. Add 1 minute to the processing time for each 1,000 feet of additional altitude.*

Homey Mac & Cheese

I also call this "My Grandson's Mac and Cheese." Zachary has been to Iraq and Afghanistan with both the Marines and Navy, and I've been privileged to make his favorite casserole for him for more than 20 years.

—ALICE BEARDSELL OSPREY, FLORIDA

PREP: 20 MIN. **BAKE:** 25 MIN. **MAKES:** 8 SERVINGS

- 2½ **cups uncooked elbow macaroni**
- ¼ **cup butter, cubed**
- ¼ **cup all-purpose flour**
- ½ **teaspoon salt**
- ¼ **teaspoon pepper**
- 3 **cups 2% milk**
- 5 **cups (20 ounces) shredded sharp cheddar cheese, divided**
- 2 **tablespoons Worcestershire sauce**
- ½ **teaspoon paprika**

1. Preheat oven to 350°. Cook macaroni according to package directions for al dente.

2. Meanwhile, in a large saucepan, heat butter over medium heat. Stir in flour, salt and pepper until smooth; gradually whisk in milk. Bring to a boil, stirring constantly; cook and stir for 2-3 minutes or until thickened. Reduce heat. Stir in 3 cups cheese and Worcestershire sauce until cheese is melted.

3. Drain macaroni; stir into sauce. Transfer to a greased 11x7-in. baking dish. Bake, uncovered, 20 minutes. Top with remaining cheese; sprinkle with paprika. Bake 5-10 minutes longer or until cheese is melted.

FLORIDA

Love OJ? Find out how it gets from grove to carton by visiting one of the many Florida orange juice producers that are open for tours across the state.

Sally Lunn bread has a texture like sponge cake. One story claims the French Protestant refugees who brought it to England called it *soleil et lune* (sun and moon) because of its brown crust and light, airy interior. The English accent turned that into Sally Lunn. Another story claims Sally Lunn was a French refugee who settled in Bath, England, and became famous for her baked goods. The English brought the recipe to the States, and it's been a Southern favorite since Colonial times. It's traditionally baked in a tube pan but can also be made as loaves or buns.

Sally Lunn Batter Bread

The tantalizing aroma of this golden loaf as it's baking always draws people into my mother's kitchen. With its circular shape, it's as pretty as it is delicious. I've never seen it last more than 2 days once it's out of the oven!

—JEANNE VOSS ANAHEIM HILLS, CALIFORNIA

PREP: 15 MIN. + RISING **BAKE:** 25 MIN. **MAKES:** 12-16 SERVINGS

- 1 **package (¼ ounce) active dry yeast**
- ½ **cup warm water (110° to 115°)**
- 1 **cup warm milk (110° to 115°)**
- ½ **cup butter, softened**
- ¼ **cup sugar**
- 2 **teaspoons salt**
- 3 **eggs**
- 5½ **to 6 cups all-purpose flour**

HONEY BUTTER
- ½ **cup butter, softened**
- ½ **cup honey**

1. In a large bowl, dissolve yeast in warm water. Add the milk, butter, sugar, salt, eggs and 3 cups flour; beat until smooth. Stir in enough remaining flour to form a soft dough.

2. Do not knead. Place in a greased bowl, turning once to grease the top. Cover and let rise in a warm place until doubled, about 1 hour.

3. Stir the dough down. Spoon into a greased and floured 10-in. tube pan. Cover and let rise until doubled, about 1 hour.

4. Bake at 400° for 25-30 minutes or until golden brown. Remove from pan to a wire rack to cool.

5. Combine the honey butter ingredients until smooth. Serve with bread.

Creamy Succotash

This is a creation from my sister Jenny. When I first saw her making it, I didn't think the ingredients would be very tasty together, but I changed my mind immediately upon tasting it!

—**SHANNON KOENE** BLACKSBURG, VIRGINIA

PREP: 10 MIN. **COOK:** 20 MIN. + COOLING
MAKES: 10 SERVINGS

- 4 **cups frozen lima beans**
- 1 **cup water**
- 4 **cups frozen corn**
- ⅔ **cup reduced-fat mayonnaise**
- 2 **teaspoons Dijon mustard**
- ½ **teaspoon onion powder**
- ½ **teaspoon garlic powder**
- ¼ **teaspoon salt**
- ¼ **teaspoon pepper**
- 2 **medium tomatoes, finely chopped**
- 1 **small onion, finely chopped**

1. In a large saucepan, bring the lima beans and water to a boil. Reduce heat; cover and simmer for 10 minutes. Add the corn; return to a boil. Reduce heat; cover and simmer 5-6 minutes longer or until vegetables are tender. Drain; cool for 10-15 minutes.

2. Meanwhile, in a large bowl, combine the mayonnaise, mustard, onion powder, garlic powder, salt and pepper. Stir in the bean mixture, tomatoes and onion. Serve immediately or refrigerate.

Sweet Tea Concentrate

Sweet iced tea is a Southern classic, and this is a fabulous recipe for a party of tea lovers. The concentrate will make 20 servings.

—**NATALIE BREMSON** PLANTATION, FLORIDA

PREP: 30 MIN. + COOLING
MAKES: 20 SERVINGS (5 CUPS CONCENTRATE)

- 2 **medium lemons**
- 4 **cups sugar**
- 4 **cups water**
- 1½ **cups English breakfast tea leaves or 20 black tea bags**
- ⅓ **cup lemon juice**

EACH SERVING
- 1 **cup cold water**
  Ice cubes

1. Remove peels from lemons; save fruit for another use.

2. In a large saucepan, combine the sugar and water. Bring to a boil over medium heat. Reduce heat; simmer, uncovered, for 3-5 minutes or until the sugar is dissolved, stirring occasionally. Remove from the heat; add the tea leaves and lemon peels. Cover and steep for 15 minutes. Strain tea, discarding tea leaves and lemon peels; stir in lemon juice. Cool to room temperature.

3. Transfer to a container with a tight-fitting lid. Store in the refrigerator for up to 2 weeks.

To prepare tea: *In a tall glass, combine water with ¼ cup concentrate; add ice.*

ALEXANDRIA, VA

Once home to President George Washington and his family, Mount Vernon not only has spectacular buildings, but abundant gardens as well. There, caretakers still grow flowers, nuts, fruits and veggies, including many of the ingredients used in succotash.

Black-eyed peas were consumed on many continents, including Africa and Asia, before hopping over to the United States. History shows that African slaves brought the peas with them, and the peas are still popular in the South to this day. Eating Hoppin' John on New Year's Day is believed to bring good luck and prosperity.

Hoppin' John

A New Year's tradition, this mildly flavored rice dish is a great accompaniment to almost any meat entree.

—**BETH WALL** INMAN, SOUTH CAROLINA

PREP/TOTAL TIME: 15 MIN. **MAKES:** 2 SERVINGS

- ¼ cup chopped sweet red pepper
- ¼ cup chopped green pepper
- 2 tablespoons chopped onion
- ¼ teaspoon garlic powder
- ⅛ teaspoon salt
- 1 tablespoon butter
- ⅔ cup canned black-eyed peas, rinsed and drained
- ⅔ cup cooked rice

1. In a small skillet, saute the peppers, onion, garlic powder and salt in butter for 4-5 minutes or until vegetables are tender. Stir in the peas and rice; heat through, stirring occasionally.

Peach Chutney

Here's my take on several different chutney recipes combined. The sweet and spicy condiment pairs well with meat or poultry.

—**JOANNE SURFUS** STURGEON BAY, WISCONSIN

PREP: 1 HOUR **PROCESS:** 15 MIN.
MAKES: 7 HALF-PINTS

- 2½ cups white vinegar
- 1 cup packed brown sugar
- ¾ cup sugar
- 1 medium sweet red pepper, finely chopped
- 1 small onion, finely chopped
- 1 banana pepper, seeded and finely chopped
- ⅔ cup golden raisins
- 1 tablespoon minced fresh gingerroot
- 1 teaspoon canning salt
- 6 whole cloves
- 1 cinnamon stick (3 inches), cut in half
- 3 pounds fresh peaches, peeled and chopped

1. In a Dutch oven, bring the vinegar, brown sugar and sugar to a boil. Add the red pepper, onion, banana pepper, raisins, ginger and salt. Place cloves and cinnamon stick on a double thickness of cheesecloth; bring up corners of cloth and tie with string to form a bag. Add to the pan. Return to a boil. Reduce heat; simmer, uncovered, for 10 minutes.

2. Add peaches and return to a boil. Reduce heat; simmer, uncovered, for 25-30 minutes or until thickened. Discard spice bag.

3. Carefully ladle hot chutney into hot half-pint jars, leaving ½-in. headspace. Remove air bubbles; wipe rims and adjust lids. Process for 15 minutes in a boiling-water canner.

Editor's Note: *The processing time listed is for altitudes of 1,000 feet or less. For altitudes up to 3,000 feet, add 5 minutes; 6,000 feet, add 10 minutes; 8,000 feet, add 15 minutes; 10,000 feet, add 20 minutes.*

▶◀● dishing about food

During World War II, whiskey was in short supply. It was said that liquor salesmen forced bar owners to buy several cases of rum (which was abundant at the time) in order to get one case of whiskey. A bartender at Pat O'Brien's in New Orleans created this fruity cocktail to use up the bar's abundance of rum.

NEW ORLEANS, LA

The Big Easy boasts a thriving restaurant business. That's good news for hungry tourists—who number about 7.5 million a year.

Passion Fruit Hurricanes

This is our version of the famous beverage that's so popular in New Orleans. As tropical as a hurricane and with just as much punch, this is the perfect summer cooler!

—TASTE OF HOME TEST KITCHEN

PREP/TOTAL TIME: 10 MIN. **MAKES:** 6 SERVINGS

- 2 **cups passion fruit juice**
- 1 **cup plus 2 tablespoons sugar**
- ¾ **cup lime juice**
- ¾ **cup light rum**
- ¾ **cup dark rum**
- 3 **tablespoons grenadine syrup**
- 6 **to 8 cups ice cubes**
  Orange slices and maraschino cherries

1. In a pitcher, combine the fruit juice, sugar, lime juice, rum and grenadine; stir until sugar is dissolved.

2. Pour into hurricane or highball glasses filled with ice. Garnish with orange slices and cherries.

BILOXI, MS

If you're on the Gulf Coast and see a boat decorated this way, chances are it has recently been blessed! Shrimping communities, including Biloxi, have an annual Blessing of the Fleet to safeguard their boats.

South Coast Hominy

The first time I tasted this hominy dish, I just couldn't get enough. It's something my stepmother has prepared for a long time. And now, whenever I fix it for friends or family, there are never any leftovers.

—LESLIE HAMPEL PALMER, TEXAS

PREP: 25 MIN. **BAKE:** 30 MIN. **MAKES:** 6-8 SERVINGS

- ½ cup chopped onion
- ½ cup chopped green pepper
- 5 tablespoons butter, divided
- 3 tablespoons all-purpose flour
- 1 teaspoon salt
- ½ teaspoon ground mustard
  Dash cayenne pepper
- 1½ cups milk
- 1 cup (4 ounces) shredded cheddar cheese
- 1 can (15½ ounces) white hominy, drained
- ½ cup sliced ripe olives, optional
- ½ cup dry bread crumbs

1. In a skillet, saute onion and green pepper in 3 tablespoons butter until tender. Add the flour, salt, mustard and cayenne; cook and stir until smooth and bubbly, about 2 minutes. Gradually add milk; bring to a boil. Boil for 2 minutes, stirring constantly. Stir in cheese until melted.

2. Remove from the heat; add the hominy and olives if desired. Pour into a greased 1½-qt. baking dish. Melt remaining butter and toss with bread crumbs; sprinkle over hominy mixture. Bake, uncovered, at 375° for 30 minutes or until golden.

Texas Tea

Why not try making a pitcher of this "tea" for a get-together on a hot summer day? It's a potent drink, so limit yourself to one or two!

—TASTE OF HOME TEST KITCHEN

PREP/TOTAL TIME: 10 MIN. **MAKES:** 8 SERVINGS

- 1 cup cola
- 1 cup sour mix
- ½ cup vodka
- ½ cup gin
- ½ cup Triple Sec
- ½ cup golden or light rum
- ½ cup tequila
  Lemon or lime slices

1. In a pitcher, combine the first seven ingredients; serve over ice. Garnish with lemon or lime slices.

Watermelon Spritzer

Beverages don't get much easier than this bright spritzer! Watermelon blended with limeade is so cool and refreshing— a wonderful thirst quencher on those steamy summer afternoons.

—GERALDINE SAUCIER ALBUQUERQUE, NEW MEXICO

PREP: 5 MIN. + CHILLING **MAKES:** 5 SERVINGS

- 4 cups cubed seedless watermelon
- ¾ cup frozen limeade concentrate, thawed
- 2½ cups carbonated water
  Lime slices

1. Place the watermelon in a blender. Cover and process until blended. Strain and discard the pulp; transfer juice to a pitcher. Stir in the limeade concentrate. Refrigerate for 6 hours or overnight.

2. Just before serving, stir in carbonated water. Garnish servings with lime slices.

Rice Dressing

This yummy rice mixture is a delightful change from our traditional corn bread dressing. To make it a meal in itself, I sometimes add finely chopped cooked chicken.

—LINDA EMERY BEARDEN, ARKANSAS

PREP: 35 MIN. **BAKE:** 30 MIN.
MAKES: 10-12 SERVINGS

- 4 cups chicken broth, divided
- 1½ cups uncooked long grain rice
- 2 cups chopped onion
- 2 cups chopped celery
- ½ cup butter, cubed
- 2 cans (4 ounces each) mushroom stems and pieces, drained
- 3 tablespoons minced fresh parsley
- 1½ to 2 teaspoons poultry seasoning
- ¾ teaspoon salt
- ½ teaspoon pepper
  Fresh sage and thyme, optional

1. In a saucepan, bring 3½ cups broth and rice to a boil. Reduce heat; cover and simmer for 20 minutes or until tender.

2. Meanwhile, in a skillet, saute onion and celery in butter until tender. Stir in the rice, mushrooms, parsley, poultry seasoning, salt, pepper and the remaining broth. Pour into a greased 13x9-in. baking dish. Bake, uncovered, at 350° for 30 minutes. Garnish with sage and thyme if desired.

Baked Oysters with Tasso Cream

I love nothing more than a cold beer and a shucked oyster, so when my partners and I opened Saw's Juke Joint in Birmingham, we wanted to add oysters to the menu. We love making them, we love serving them and our guests love eating them. We take a lot of pride in our food, particularly this item. Apalachicola oysters are the best! We wouldn't make this dish without them.

—TAYLOR HICKS BIRMINGHAM, ALABAMA

PREP: 1 HOUR **BAKE:** 10 MIN.
MAKES: 1 DOZEN (1½ CUPS SAUCE).

- 4 slices white bread
- ¼ cup butter, melted
- ⅛ teaspoon salt
- ⅛ teaspoon pepper
- 3 ounces tasso ham or fully cooked chorizo, finely chopped (about ½ cup)
- 2 tablespoons chopped sweet onion
- 1 garlic clove, minced
- 2 cups heavy whipping cream
- 1 to 2 dashes Louisiana-style hot sauce
  Salt and pepper to taste
- 1 dozen fresh oysters in the shell, scrubbed

1. Preheat oven to 300°. Place bread on an ungreased baking sheet; bake 8-10 minutes on each side or until lightly browned. Break bread into smaller pieces; place in a food processor. Pulse until coarse crumbs form. Transfer to a small bowl. Add melted butter, salt and pepper; toss to combine.

2. In a large skillet, cook ham over medium heat until lightly browned, stirring occasionally. Add onion and garlic; cook and stir 1-2 minutes or until tender. Stir in cream. Bring to a boil; cook until liquid is reduced by half, stirring occasionally. Add hot sauce; season with salt and pepper to taste. Keep warm.

3. Increase oven setting to 350°. Shuck oysters, leaving oysters in the half-shell. Arrange on a rack in a shallow baking pan; sprinkle with bread crumbs. Bake 8-10 minutes or until topping is golden brown and oysters are plump. Top with sauce just before serving.

◄● dishing about food

Rice plantations in Georgia and South Carolina died out after the Civil War. Today, Arkansas devotes more acreage to rice production than any other state.

BIRMINGHAM, AL

Looking for some unbeatable barbecue? Stop by Saw's Juke Joint in Birmingham. Guests are encouraged to write on the chalkboard walls of this hot spot, which offers live music regularly. You might even catch the owner, *American Idol* winner Taylor Hicks, onstage entertaining the crowd!

> **If you own a barbecue joint like I do, you pretty much dream about barbecue all the time. And jalapeno poppers are one of my favorite appetizers, so this recipe is a great way to combine those foods. They're very popular on the menu at my place. Try your own variation by using cooked chicken or beef for the stuffing.**
>
> —**TAYLOR HICKS**
> BIRMINGHAM, ALABAMA

Taylor's Jalapeno Poppers

PREP: 35 MIN. **COOK:** 5 MIN./BATCH
MAKES: 6 SERVINGS.

- 6 large jalapeno peppers
  Oil for deep-fat frying
- 1 cup refrigerated fully cooked barbecued shredded pork (about 8 ounces)
- 1 cup (4 ounces) shredded mild cheddar cheese
- ¼ cup barbecue sauce
- 1 cup all-purpose flour
- 1 cup cornstarch
- 3 teaspoons salt
- 3 teaspoons paprika
- 12 ounces beer
  White barbecue sauce, optional

1. Cut off stem end of jalapenos. Using the tip of a small knife, remove seeds and membrane. In a large saucepan, bring 8 cups water to a boil. Add the jalapenos; cook, uncovered, 2-3 minutes or just until crisp-tender. Remove and immediately drop into ice water. Drain and pat completely dry.

2. In an electric skillet or deep fryer, heat oil to 375°. In a small bowl, mix pork, cheese and barbecue sauce; spoon into jalapenos. In another bowl, whisk flour, cornstarch, salt and paprika; stir in beer just until moistened.

3. Using tongs, dip stuffed jalapenos into batter; fry in batches 3-4 minutes or until golden brown. Drain on paper towels. If desired, serve with white barbecue sauce.

Cheese 'n' Grits Casserole

Grits are a staple in Southern cooking. Serve this flavorful casserole as a brunch item with bacon or as a side dish for dinner. For a little extra tang, use sharp cheddar cheese and sprinkle a bit on top before baking.

—**JENNIFER WALLIS**
GOLDSBORO, NORTH CAROLINA

PREP: 10 MIN. **BAKE:** 30 MIN. + STANDING
MAKES: 8 SERVINGS

- 4 cups water
- 1 cup uncooked old-fashioned grits
- ½ teaspoon salt
- ½ cup 2% milk
- ¼ cup butter, melted
- 2 eggs, lightly beaten
- 1 cup (4 ounces) shredded cheddar cheese
- 1 tablespoon Worcestershire sauce
- ⅛ teaspoon cayenne pepper
- ⅛ teaspoon paprika

1. In a large saucepan, bring water to a boil. Slowly stir in grits and salt. Reduce heat; cover and simmer for 5-7 minutes or until thickened. Cool slightly. Gradually whisk in the milk, butter and eggs. Stir in the cheese, Worcestershire sauce and cayenne.

2. Transfer to a greased 2-qt. baking dish. Sprinkle with paprika. Bake, uncovered, at 350° for 30-35 minutes or until bubbly. Let stand for 10 minutes before serving.

Southern Fried Okra

Nothing beats a batch of okra right from the garden! Golden brown, with a little fresh green color showing through, these okra nuggets are crispy and flavorful. My sons like to dip theirs in ketchup.

—PAM DUNCAN SUMMERS, ARKANSAS

PREP/TOTAL TIME: 30 MIN. **MAKES:** 2 SERVINGS

- 1½ cups sliced fresh or frozen okra, thawed
- 3 tablespoons buttermilk
- 2 tablespoons all-purpose flour
- 2 tablespoons cornmeal
- ¼ teaspoon salt
- ¼ teaspoon garlic herb seasoning blend
- ⅛ teaspoon pepper
  Oil for deep-fat frying
  Additional salt and pepper, optional

1. Pat okra dry with paper towels. Place the buttermilk in a shallow bowl. In another shallow bowl, combine the flour, cornmeal, salt, seasoning blend and pepper. Dip okra in buttermilk, then roll in cornmeal mixture.

2. In an electric skillet or deep-fat fryer, heat 1 in. of oil to 375°. Fry the okra, a few pieces at a time, for 1½ to 2½ minutes on each side or until golden brown. Drain the okra on paper towels. Season with additional salt and pepper if desired.

Yellow Summer Squash Relish

My friends can barely wait for the growing season to arrive so I can make this incredible relish. The color really dresses up a hot dog!

—RUTH HAWKINS JACKSON, MISSISSIPPI

PREP: 1 HOUR + MARINATING
PROCESS: 15 MIN. **MAKES:** 6 PINTS

- 10 cups shredded yellow summer squash (about 4 pounds)
- 2 large onions, chopped
- 1 large green pepper, chopped
- 6 tablespoons canning salt
- 4 cups sugar
- 3 cups cider vinegar
- 1 tablespoon each celery seed, ground mustard and ground turmeric
- ½ teaspoon ground nutmeg
- ½ teaspoon pepper

1. In a large container, combine the squash, onions, green pepper and salt. Cover and refrigerate overnight. Drain; rinse and drain again.

2. In a Dutch oven, combine sugar, vinegar and seasonings; bring to a boil. Add the squash mixture; return to a boil. Reduce heat; simmer for 15 minutes. Remove from the heat.

3. Carefully ladle hot mixture into six hot pint jars, leaving ½-in. headspace. Remove air bubbles; wipe rims and adjust lids. Process for 15 minutes in a boiling-water canner. Refrigerate remaining relish for up to 1 week.

Editor's Note: *The processing time listed is for altitudes of 1,000 feet or less. For altitudes up to 3,000 feet, add 5 minutes; 6,000 feet, add 10 minutes; 8,000 feet, add 15 minutes; 10,000 feet, add 20 minutes.*

◄● dishing about food

Fried okra is one of 12 foods featured in Oklahoma's Official State Meal. Other menu items include chicken-fried steak, biscuits and gravy, black-eyed peas and pecan pie. The state legislature approved the meal in 1988.

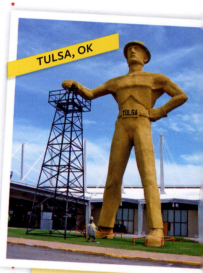

TULSA, OK

Pass the Tulsa County Fairgrounds and you're sure to notice the Golden Driller standing guard. Built for the 1953 International Petroleum Expo, he was named Oklahoma's official state monument in 1979.

Kool-Aid Pickles

Everyone will love getting into these pickles. They owe their color and sweet-sour taste to a long marinating in a fruity drink mix.

—TASTE OF HOME TEST KITCHEN

PREP: 10 MIN. + CHILLING **MAKES:** 3 CUPS

- 1 jar (32 ounces) whole dill pickles, undrained
- ⅔ cup sugar
- 1 envelope unsweetened Kool-Aid mix, flavor of your choice

1. Drain pickles, reserving juice. In a bowl, combine the reserved juice, sugar and Kool-Aid, stirring until sugar is dissolved. Set aside.

2. Slice the pickles and return to jar. Pour the juice mixture over pickles. Discard any remaining juice. Cover and refrigerate for one week before serving.

Kentucky Spoon Bread

Here's a traditional Kentucky recipe that's a popular side dish and served all year long. If you've never tried spoon bread before, I think you might enjoy this one.

—CAROLINE BROWN LEXINGTON, KENTUCKY

PREP: 20 MIN. **BAKE:** 40 MIN. **MAKES:** 8 SERVINGS

- 4 cups 2% milk
- 1 cup cornmeal
- 3 teaspoons sugar
- 1 teaspoon salt
- ½ teaspoon baking powder

- 2 tablespoons butter
- 3 eggs, separated

1. In a saucepan, heat 3 cups milk over medium heat until bubbles form around sides of pan.

2. Meanwhile, in a small bowl, combine the cornmeal, sugar, salt and remaining milk until smooth. Slowly whisk cornmeal mixture into hot milk. Cook and stir until mixture comes to a boil. Reduce heat; simmer for 5 minutes, stirring constantly.

3. Remove from the heat. Sprinkle baking powder over the cornmeal mixture, then stir it in with the butter. In a small bowl, beat egg yolks; stir in a small amount of hot cornmeal mixture. Return all to the pan and mix well.

4. In a small bowl, beat egg whites until stiff peaks form. Fold a fourth of the egg whites into the cornmeal mixture. Fold in remaining egg whites until blended.

5. Transfer to a greased 2½-qt. baking dish. Bake, uncovered, at 350° for 40-45 minutes or until puffed and golden brown. Serve immediately.

Louisiana Shrimp

This is a Lenten favorite at our house. I serve it right out of the roaster with corn on the cob and boiled potatoes or just serve by itself as an appetizer.

—SUNDRA HAUCK BOGALUSA, LOUISIANA

PREP: 40 MIN. **BAKE:** 20 MIN. **MAKES:** 10 SERVINGS

- 1 pound butter, cubed
- 3 medium lemons, sliced
- 2 tablespoons plus 1½ teaspoons coarsely ground pepper
- 2 tablespoons Worcestershire sauce
- 2 garlic cloves, minced
- ½ teaspoon salt
- ½ teaspoon hot pepper sauce
- 2½ pounds uncooked shell-on medium shrimp

1. In a large saucepan, combine the first seven ingredients. Bring to a boil. Reduce the heat; cover and simmer for 30 minutes, stirring occasionally.

2. Place shrimp in a large roasting pan; pour butter mixture over top. Bake, uncovered, at 375° for 20-25 minutes or until shrimp turn pink. Serve warm with a slotted spoon.

Buttermilk Corn Bread

My grandmother always referred to this recipe as "comfort food"—made from ingredients available on the farm or staples found in her pantry. She cooked the corn bread in her seasoned cast-iron skillet, and it turned out slick as butter every time!

—ELIZABETH COOPER MADISON, ALABAMA

PREP/TOTAL TIME: 30 MIN. **MAKES:** 2-4 SERVINGS

- 1 tablespoon canola oil
- 1 cup cornmeal
- ¼ cup all-purpose flour
- 1½ teaspoons baking powder
- ½ teaspoon salt
- ½ teaspoon baking soda
- 1 egg
- 1 cup buttermilk

1. Place oil in an 8-in. ovenproof skillet; tilt to coat bottom and sides. Place in a 425° oven for 10 minutes.

2. In a small bowl, combine cornmeal, flour, baking powder, salt and baking soda. Beat egg and buttermilk; add to the dry ingredients just until moistened.

3. Pour batter into the hot skillet. Bake for 15 minutes or until golden brown and a toothpick inserted in center comes out clean.

Marinated Tomatoes

A niece introduced me to this colorful, easy recipe some time ago. I especially like making it for buffets or large gatherings because it can be prepared hours ahead. It's one great way to use a bumper crop of tomatoes!

—MYRTLE MATTHEWS MARIETTA, GEORGIA

PREP: 10 MIN. + MARINATING **MAKES:** 8 SERVINGS

- 3 large fresh tomatoes, thickly sliced
- ⅓ cup olive oil
- ¼ cup red wine vinegar
- 1 teaspoon salt, optional
- ¼ teaspoon pepper
- ½ garlic clove, minced
- 2 tablespoons chopped onion
- 1 tablespoon minced fresh parsley
- 1 tablespoon minced fresh basil or
  1 teaspoon dried basil

1. Arrange the tomatoes in a large shallow dish. Combine the remaining ingredients in a jar; cover tightly and shake well. Pour over the tomato slices. Cover and refrigerate for several hours before serving.

◄● dishing about food

The early settlers were able to grow corn more easily than wheat or rye, so it became a grain that was used widely to make bread. The Northeast, South and Southwest all have corn bread recipes suited to their regional preferences. The Northeast likes theirs sweet, the South savory, and the Southwest with a little zip.

Fried Green Tomatoes gained new popularity after the 1991 movie of the same name became a hit. Before that, the recipe rarely appeared on menus in the South. In fact, according to Robert F. Moss, culinary historian, it seems that this dish emerged from farther north, coming from homemakers in states with colder climates.

DOUBLE SPRINGS, AL

Scores of waterfalls lend Alabama's Sipsey Wilderness a beautiful nickname: Land of a Thousand Waterfalls. The Wilderness is surrounded by the William B. Bankhead National Forest just northwest of Birmingham.

Fried Green Tomatoes

Panko bread crumbs have a coarser texture than ordinary bread crumbs, which can also be used to coat the tomatoes. But panko crumbs will give them a uniquely light and crispy texture.

—JACQUELYNNE STINE LAS VEGAS, NEVADA

PREP: 20 MIN. **COOK:** 25 MIN. **MAKES:** 10 SERVINGS

¾ cup all-purpose flour
3 eggs, lightly beaten
2 cups panko (Japanese) bread crumbs
5 medium green tomatoes, cut into ¼-inch slices
   Oil for deep-fat frying
   Salt

1. In three separate shallow bowls, place the flour, eggs and bread crumbs. Dip tomatoes in flour, then in eggs; coat with bread crumbs.

2. In an electric skillet or deep-fat fryer, heat oil to 375°. Fry the tomatoes, a few at a time, for 2-3 minutes on each side or until golden brown. Drain on paper towels. Sprinkle with the salt. Serve immediately.

Mint Juleps

This classic Kentucky Derby drink features the perfect blend of mint, bourbon and sugar. The refreshing beverage is as strongly associated with the South as sweet tea. Mint juleps were traditionally served in a silver or pewter mug, but today folks enjoy them in a cocktail or highball glass with a straw.

—TASTE OF HOME TEST KITCHEN

PREP: 30 MIN. + CHILLING
MAKES: 10 SERVINGS (2½ CUPS SYRUP)

MINT SYRUP
- 2 cups sugar
- 2 cups water
- 2 cups loosely packed chopped fresh mint

EACH SERVING
- ½ to ¾ cup crushed ice
- ½ to 1 ounce bourbon
- Mint sprig

1. For syrup, combine the sugar, water and chopped mint in a large saucepan. Bring to a boil over medium heat; cook until sugar is dissolved, stirring occasionally. Remove from the heat; cool to room temperature.

2. Line a mesh strainer with a double layer of cheesecloth or a coffee filter. Strain syrup; discard mint. Cover and refrigerate syrup for at least 2 hours or until chilled.

3. For each serving, place ice in a metal julep cup or rocks glass. Pour ¼ cup mint syrup and bourbon into the glass; stir until mixture is well chilled. Garnish with mint sprig.

Orange-Pecan Hot Wings

We have an orange tree in our backyard and like to use oranges and orange juice in lots of different ways. These chicken wings are a fun appetizer that our friends are very fond of.

—JUNE JONES HUDSON, FLORIDA

PREP: 25 MIN. **BAKE:** 55 MIN. **MAKES:** 8-10 SERVINGS

- 3 pounds whole chicken wings
- 3 eggs
- 1 can (6 ounces) frozen orange juice concentrate, thawed
- 2 tablespoons water
- 1 cup all-purpose flour
- ½ cup finely chopped pecans
- ½ cup butter, melted

RED HOT SAUCE
- 2 cups ketchup
- ¾ cup packed brown sugar
- 2 to 3 tablespoons hot pepper sauce

1. Cut chicken wings into three pieces; discard wing tips.

2. In a bowl, whisk the eggs, orange juice concentrate and water. In another bowl or a resealable plastic bag, combine flour and pecans. Dip wings in egg mixture, then roll or toss in flour mixture.

3. Pour butter into a 15x10x1-in. baking pan. Arrange wings in a single layer in pan. Bake, uncovered, at 375° for 25 minutes.

4. Meanwhile, combine sauce ingredients. Spoon half over the wings; turn. Top with remaining sauce. Bake 30 minutes longer or until meat juices run clear.

Editor's Note: *Uncooked chicken wing sections (wingettes) may be substituted for whole chicken wings.*

LOUISVILLE, KY

For more than 135 years, horse racing fans and people-watchers have gathered at Churchill Downs to witness one of the most prestigious races in the country. Here's I'll Have Another, winner of the 2012 contest.

Pimiento Cheese Spread

A classic Southern comfort food, this cheese spread is often served as an appetizer with crackers, corn chips or celery. It is also spread on white bread for sandwiches, or used as a topping for hamburgers and hot dogs.

—**EILEEN BALMER** SOUTH BEND, INDIANA

PREP: 10 MIN. + CHILLING **MAKES:** 1¼ CUPS

- 1½ cups (6 ounces) shredded cheddar cheese
- 1 jar (4 ounces) diced pimientos, drained and finely chopped
- ⅓ cup mayonnaise
  Assorted crackers

1. In a small bowl, combine the cheese, pimientos and mayonnaise. Refrigerate for at least 1 hour. Serve with crackers.

Oyster Stuffing

My mother made this special recipe every Thanksgiving for my father—who absolutely loves it!

—**AMY VOIGHTS** BRODHEAD, WISCONSIN

PREP: 30 MIN. **BAKE:** 30 MIN. **MAKES:** 4 SERVINGS

- 1 celery rib, chopped
- 1 small onion, chopped
- ¼ cup butter, cubed
- 2 tablespoons minced fresh parsley
- ¼ teaspoon poultry seasoning
- ⅛ teaspoon rubbed sage
- ⅛ teaspoon pepper
- 3 cups cubed day-old bread
- 1 egg, beaten
- ⅔ cup chicken broth
- 1 cup shucked oysters, drained and coarsely chopped

1. In a small skillet, saute celery and onion in butter until tender; transfer to a large bowl. Stir in the parsley, poultry seasoning, sage and pepper. Add bread cubes. Combine the egg, broth and oysters; add to bread mixture, stirring gently to combine.

2. Transfer to a greased 1-qt. baking dish. Cover and bake at 350° for 20 minutes. Uncover; bake 10-15 minutes longer or until a thermometer reads 160° and stuffing is lightly browned.

Barbecue Sauce with Mustard

Forget about ho-hum barbecue. Add some zing to chicken or pork with our sauce.

—**CHARLIE AND RUTHIE KNOTE** CAPE GIRARDEAU, MISSOURI

PREP/TOTAL TIME: 15 MIN. **MAKES:** 4 CUPS

- ½ cup sugar
- ¼ teaspoon ground oregano
- ½ teaspoon ground thyme
- 1 teaspoon salt
- ½ teaspoon pepper
- ⅛ teaspoon cayenne pepper
- ½ teaspoon cornstarch
- ½ cup vinegar
- 1 cup molasses
- 1 cup ketchup
- 1 cup prepared mustard
- 2 tablespoons canola oil

1. Combine first seven ingredients in a small saucepan. Stir in enough vinegar to make paste. Combine molasses, ketchup, mustard, oil and remaining vinegar; add to herb paste. Bring to a boil, stirring constantly. Reduce heat and simmer 10 minutes. Remove from heat; cool completely.

2. Pour into a glass jar; cover tightly. Store refrigerated for up to 3 months. Baste over smoked chicken, turkey, ham or hot dogs.

Andouille-Shrimp Cream Soup

This dish is a variation on a creamy southern Louisiana corn stew. The bold flavor of andouille sausage blends beautifully with the shrimp and subtle spices.

—JUDY ARMSTRONG PRAIRIEVILLE, LOUISIANA

PREP: 20 MIN. **COOK:** 30 MIN. **MAKES:** 7 SERVINGS

½   **pound fully cooked andouille sausage links, thinly sliced**
1   **medium onion, chopped**
2   **celery ribs, thinly sliced**
1   **medium sweet red pepper, chopped**
1   **medium green pepper, chopped**
1   **jalapeno pepper, seeded and chopped**
¼   **cup butter, cubed**
3   **garlic cloves, minced**
2   **cups fresh or frozen corn, thawed**
4   **medium plum tomatoes, chopped**
1   **cup vegetable broth**
2   **tablespoons minced fresh thyme or 2 teaspoons dried thyme**
1   **teaspoon chili powder**
½   **teaspoon salt**
½   **teaspoon pepper**
¼   **to ½ teaspoon cayenne pepper**

1   **pound uncooked medium shrimp, peeled and deveined**
1   **cup heavy whipping cream**

1. In a large skillet, saute the first six ingredients in butter until the vegetables are tender. Add the garlic; cook 1 minute longer. Add the corn, tomatoes, broth, thyme, chili powder, salt, pepper and cayenne. Bring to a boil. Reduce heat; simmer, uncovered, for 10 minutes.

2. Stir in shrimp and cream. Bring to a gentle boil. Simmer, uncovered, for 8-10 minutes or until shrimp turn pink.

Editor's Note: *Wear disposable gloves when cutting hot peppers; the oils can burn skin. Avoid touching your face.*

NEW ORLEANS, LA

Ornate ironwork, flat tile roofs and kaleidoscope of paint make French Quarter townhouses unmistakable. The signature architecture is actually influenced by French, Spanish and American styles.

MONTGOMERY, AL

Montgomery was not Alabama's first permanent capital city. Cahaba was the first, in 1820, and Tuscaloosa followed in 1826. Montgomery finally became the seat of state government in 1846.

Southern Buttermilk Biscuits

The recipe for these four-ingredient biscuits has been handed down for many generations.

—**FRAN THOMPSON** TARBORO, NORTH CAROLINA

PREP/TOTAL TIME: 30 MIN. **MAKES:** 9 BISCUITS

- ½ **cup cold butter, cubed**
- 2 **cups self-rising flour**
- ¾ **cup buttermilk**
  Melted butter

1. In a large bowl, cut butter into flour until mixture resembles coarse crumbs. Stir in buttermilk just until moistened. Turn onto a lightly floured surface; knead 3-4 times. Pat or lightly roll to ¾-in. thickness. Cut with a floured 2½-in. biscuit cutter.

2. Place on a greased baking sheet. Bake at 425° for 11-13 minutes or until golden brown. Brush tops with butter. Serve warm.

Editor's Note: *As a substitute for each cup of self-rising flour, place 1½ teaspoons baking powder and ½ teaspoon salt in a measuring cup. Add all-purpose flour to measure 1 cup.*

Dirty Rice

This is an old Louisiana recipe that I've had for longer than I can remember. It's a very popular Southern dish. To turn this into a main meal, simply add more sausage and chicken livers.

—**LUM DAY** BASTROP, LOUISIANA

PREP/TOTAL TIME: 30 MIN. **MAKES:** 10-12 SERVINGS

- ½ **pound bulk pork sausage**
- ½ **pound chicken livers, chopped**
- 1 **cup chopped onion**
- ½ **cup chopped celery**
- ⅓ **cup sliced green onions**
- 2 **tablespoons minced fresh parsley**
- 3 **tablespoons butter**
- 1 **garlic clove, minced**
- 1 **can (10½ ounces) chicken broth**
- ½ **teaspoon dried basil**
- ½ **teaspoon dried thyme**
- ½ **teaspoon salt**
- ¼ **teaspoon pepper**
- ¼ **teaspoon hot pepper sauce**
- 3 **cups cooked rice**

1. In a large skillet, cook the sausage for 2-3 minutes; stir in the chicken livers. Cook 5-7 minutes longer or until sausage and chicken livers are no longer pink; drain and set aside.

2. In the same skillet, saute the onion, celery, green onions and parsley in butter until the vegetables are tender. Add the garlic; cook 1 minute longer. Add the broth, basil, thyme, salt, pepper and hot pepper sauce. Stir in the rice, sausage and chicken livers. Heat through, stirring constantly.

Alabama White BBQ Sauce

My boys used to spend summers with their grandmother in Alabama. She would treat them to a meal at a restaurant that served white barbecue sauce over chicken, and my family thought it was wonderful. I started making the sauce at home and every time I do, it still brings back memories of those summers in Tuscaloosa. The white sauce should be applied only at the very end of your grilling or smoking because it will break down and separate if heated too long.

—**SABRINA EVERETT** THOMASVILLE, GEORGIA

PREP: 5 MIN. + CHILLING **MAKES:** 3 CUPS

- 2 **cups mayonnaise**
- 1 **cup cider vinegar**
- 2 **tablespoons pepper**
- 2 **tablespoons lemon juice**
- 1 **teaspoon salt**
- ½ **teaspoon cayenne pepper**

1. In a small bowl, whisk all ingredients. Refrigerate for at least 8 hours. Brush sauce over meats during the last few minutes of grilling. Serve remaining sauce on the side for dipping.

Corn Bread Layered Salad

My mother's corn bread salad is so complete, it could be a meal in itself! The recipe has been in our family for years and is great for potlucks.

—JODY MILLER OKLAHOMA CITY, OKLAHOMA

PREP: 20 MIN. **BAKE:** 20 MIN. + COOLING **MAKES:** 6-8 SERVINGS

- 1 package (8½ ounces) corn bread/muffin mix
- 6 green onions, chopped
- 1 medium green pepper, chopped
- 1 can (15¼ ounces) whole kernel corn, drained
- 1 can (15 ounces) pinto beans, rinsed and drained
- ¾ cup mayonnaise
- ¾ cup sour cream
- 2 medium tomatoes, seeded and chopped
- ½ cup shredded cheddar cheese

1. Prepare and bake corn bread according to package directions. Cool on a wire rack.

2. Crumble corn bread into a 2-qt. glass serving bowl. Layer with onions, green pepper, corn and beans.

3. In a small bowl, combine mayonnaise and sour cream; spread over the vegetables. Sprinkle with tomatoes and cheese. Refrigerate until serving.

Bernell Austin popularized the beloved fried dills. In 1963, he wanted a gimmick to draw more customers to his restaurant—Duchess Drive-In, in Atkins, Arkansas. The fried snacks took off, and other places in the South started serving them, too. His secret recipe, however, is still held by his immediate family.

ATKINS, AR

Everyone's crazy for cukes at Picklefest, which has been taking place in Atkins each May for decades. And yes, they're serving fried pickles, this town's culinary claim to fame.

Fried Pickle Coins

It took me several tries to create the ideal seasoning blend for my fried pickles, which are a hit with my family and friends. Serve them as a side or as an appetizer with dips.

—AMANDA THORNTON ALEXANDRIA, KENTUCKY

PREP: 20 MIN.   **COOK:** 5 MIN./BATCH
MAKES: 16 SERVINGS

    2 cups all-purpose flour
    1 teaspoon garlic powder
    1 teaspoon ground mustard
    1 teaspoon dill weed
    1 teaspoon paprika
    ½ teaspoon garlic salt
    ½ teaspoon cayenne pepper
    ¼ teaspoon pepper
    2 eggs
    3 tablespoons 2% milk
    1 garlic clove, minced
    3 cups dill pickle slices
       Oil for deep-fat frying
       Ranch salad dressing and prepared
          mustard, optional

1. In a shallow bowl, combine the first eight ingredients. In another shallow bowl, whisk the eggs, milk and garlic. Drain pickles and pat dry. Coat pickles with flour mixture, then dip in egg mixture; coat again with flour mixture.

2. In an electric skillet or deep-fat fryer, heat oil to 375°. Fry pickles, about 10 at a time, for 1-2 minutes or until golden brown, turning once. Drain on paper towels. Serve warm with ranch dressing and mustard if desired.

Ambrosia Fruit Salad

This fresh and creamy salad is a favorite around my house. I make it with plenty of fruit and yogurt for dressing, and I mix in just enough goodies (marshmallows and coconut) so that it tastes like the richer version I grew up with. Fuss-free!

—TRISHA KRUSE EAGLE, IDAHO

PREP/TOTAL TIME: 10 MIN.   **MAKES:** 6 SERVINGS

    1 can (8¼ ounces) fruit cocktail, drained
    1 can (8 ounces) unsweetened pineapple
          chunks, drained
    1 cup green grapes

    1 cup seedless red grapes
    1 cup miniature marshmallows
    1 medium banana, sliced
    ¾ cup vanilla yogurt
    ½ cup flaked coconut

1. In a large bowl, combine all the ingredients.

Candied Sweet Potatoes

My town is known as the Yam Capital of the United States. Here's a simple recipe that goes well with baked ham or roasted turkey.

ESSIE NEALEY TABOR CITY, NORTH CAROLINA

PREP: 40 MIN. + COOLING   **BAKE:** 15 MIN.
MAKES: 8-10 SERVINGS

    3 pounds sweet potatoes, peeled
    ½ cup packed brown sugar
    1 teaspoon ground cinnamon
    ¼ cup butter, cubed
    ¼ cup corn syrup

1. Place the sweet potatoes in a Dutch oven and cover with water. Cover and bring to a boil; boil gently for 30-45 minutes or until potatoes can be easily pierced with the tip of a sharp knife.

2. When cool enough to handle, peel potatoes and cut into wedges. Place in an ungreased 11x7-in. baking dish. Sprinkle with brown sugar and cinnamon. Dot with butter; drizzle with the corn syrup.

3. Bake, uncovered, at 375° for 15-20 minutes or until bubbly, basting with sauce occasionally.

Down-Home Hush Puppies

Hush puppies are a classic side dish served at many get-togethers in the South. This sweet-and-spicy recipe has delighted my friends and family for decades.

—**GENE PITTS** WILSONVILLE, ALABAMA

PREP: 15 MIN. + STANDING **COOK:** 20 MIN.
MAKES: 2½ DOZEN

- 1 cup cornmeal
- 1 cup self-rising flour
- 1½ teaspoons baking powder
- ½ teaspoon salt
- 1 large onion, chopped
- 2 jalapeno peppers, seeded and diced
- ¼ cup sugar
- 1 egg
- 1 cup buttermilk
  Canola oil

1. In a large bowl, combine first seven ingredients. Beat egg and buttermilk; stir into flour mixture until dry ingredients are moistened. Set aside at room temperature for 30 minutes. Do not stir again.

2. In an electric skillet or deep fryer, heat 2-3 in. of oil to 375°. Drop batter by rounded tablespoonfuls, a few at a time, into hot oil. Fry until golden brown, about 1½ minutes on each side. Drain on paper towels.

Editor's Note: *As a substitute for 1 cup of self-rising flour, place 1½ teaspoons baking powder and ½ teaspoon salt in a measuring cup. Add all-purpose flour to measure 1 cup.*

Cheddar Rice Casserole

With its blend of garlic, parsley and cheese, this casserole makes a savory side dish. It's one of my favorite ways to serve rice.

—**NANCY BAYLOR** HOLIDAY ISLAND, ARKANSAS

PREP: 10 MIN. **BAKE:** 40 MIN. **MAKES:** 6-8 SERVINGS

- ¼ cup chopped onion
- 2 garlic cloves, minced
- ¼ cup butter, cubed
- 3 cups cooked long grain rice
- 2 cups (8 ounces) shredded cheddar cheese
- 1 cup minced fresh parsley
- 1 cup milk

- 4 eggs, lightly beaten
- 2 teaspoons Worcestershire sauce
- 1 teaspoon salt

1. In a large saucepan, saute onion and garlic in butter until tender. Add remaining ingredients; mix well.

2. Transfer to a greased shallow 1-qt. baking dish. Bake, uncovered, at 350° for 40-45 minutes or until a knife inserted near the center comes out clean.

Pickled Beets

I grew up with my mother's pickled beets. They came from our garden, and she canned them for the winter months. Even as a child, I loved beets for the color they brought to our table. And their tangy flavor makes a great complement to so many meals.

—**SARA LINDLER** IRMO, SOUTH CAROLINA

PREP: 20 MIN. + CHILLING **MAKES:** 6-8 SERVINGS

- 8 medium fresh beets
- 1 cup vinegar
- ½ cup sugar
- 1½ teaspoons whole cloves
- 1½ teaspoons whole allspice
- ½ teaspoon salt

1. Remove and discard greens and all but ½ in. of the stems from beets. Cook beets in boiling water until tender; drain and cool. Peel and slice; place in a bowl and set aside.

2. In a small saucepan, combine vinegar, sugar, cloves, allspice and salt. Bring to a boil; boil for 5 minutes. Pour over beets. Refrigerate at least 1 hour. Drain before serving.

Sweet Potato Muffins

Minced gingerroot and dried orange peel enhance the taste of these spiced muffins. I especially love the whipped ginger butter served with these treats.

—SUSAN BRACKEN APEX, NORTH CAROLINA

PREP: 15 MIN. **BAKE:** 20 MIN. **MAKES:** 1 DOZEN

1½ cups all-purpose flour
1 cup plus 1 tablespoon sugar, divided
3 teaspoons grated orange peel
1½ teaspoons baking powder
1 teaspoon ground ginger
¼ teaspoon salt
¼ teaspoon baking soda
2 eggs, lightly beaten
1 cup cold mashed sweet potatoes (prepared without milk and butter)
¼ teaspoon ground cinnamon

GINGER BUTTER
½ cup butter, softened
2 tablespoons finely chopped crystallized ginger

1. In a large bowl, combine the flour, 1 cup sugar, orange peel, baking powder, ginger, salt and baking soda. In a small bowl, combine eggs and sweet potatoes; stir into dry ingredients just until moistened.

2. Fill greased or paper-lined muffin cups two-thirds full. Combine cinnamon and remaining sugar; sprinkle over batter.

3. Bake at 400° for 16-20 minutes or until a toothpick inserted in center comes out clean. Cool for 5 minutes before removing from pans to wire racks.

4. In a small bowl, combine the ginger butter ingredients. Serve with warm muffins.

Black-Eyed Pea Salad

PREP/TOTAL TIME: 10 MIN. **MAKES:** 4 SERVINGS

- 1 can (15½ ounces) black-eyed peas, rinsed and drained
- 1 large tomato, diced
- 1 medium ripe avocado, peeled and diced
- ⅓ cup chopped green pepper
- 2 green onions, chopped
- 1 tablespoon minced fresh cilantro
- 1 jalapeno pepper, seeded and chopped
- ⅓ cup Italian salad dressing

1. In a large serving bowl, combine all the ingredients; toss to coat. Serve with a slotted spoon.

Black-Eyed Pea Corn Salad: *Omit the tomato, avocado, green pepper and green onions. Add 2 cups corn and ¼ cup chopped red onion to the salad mixture.*

Editor's Note: *Wear disposable gloves when cutting hot peppers; the oils can burn skin. Avoid touching your face.*

> " I've had a lot of compliments and requests for this recipe over the years. My husband loves it, and it's especially great on hot days. The salad dressing keeps the avocado from turning dark, even if you have leftovers— which doesn't happen often! It's a fun alternative to pasta or potato salad. "

—NANCY CARIKER
BAKERSFIELD, CALIFORNIA

Catfish Spread

Whenever we have a fish fry, we begin the meal with this dip. My children and grandchildren love it, and it gets a positive response at picnics and potlucks. Someone always requests the recipe.

—EDNA CARTER WEST POINT, VIRGINIA

PREP: 20 MIN. + CHILLING **MAKES:** 5 CUPS

- 1 **pound catfish fillets**
- 2 **teaspoons water**
- 2 **packages (8 ounces each) cream cheese, softened**
- 2 **packages (6½ ounces each) garlic-herb spreadable cheese**
- 4 **green onions, thinly sliced**
- ½ **cup minced fresh parsley**
- 1 **tablespoon lemon juice**
- 2 **teaspoons Worcestershire sauce**
- ⅛ **teaspoon garlic powder**
- ⅛ **teaspoon cayenne pepper**
  Dash paprika
- 1 **can (6 ounces) crabmeat, drained, flaked and cartilage removed**
- 1 **can (6 ounces) small shrimp, rinsed and drained**
  Assorted fresh vegetables

1. Place the catfish in a 2-qt. microwave-safe dish; drizzle with water. Cover and microwave on high for 4-6 minutes or until fish flakes easily with a fork. Drain and discard cooking liquid. Using a fork, flake fish into small pieces; set aside.

2. In a large bowl, beat cream cheese and spreadable cheese until smooth. Add the onions, parsley, lemon juice, Worcestershire sauce and seasonings and mix well. Stir in the crab, shrimp and catfish. Cover and refrigerate for at least 2 hours. Serve with vegetables.

Editor's Note: *This recipe was tested in a 1,100-watt microwave.*

Fried Onion Rings

Here's a yummy snack that's also a great side dish. Try it as an accompaniment to hamburgers or fried fish, or with steaks on the grill. The recipe's from my mom, and it's one of her most popular. (As a newlywed years ago, I often found myself on the kitchen "hotline" to her!)

—MARSHA MOORE POPLAR BLUFF, MISSOURI

PREP: 15 MIN. + SOAKING **COOK:** 15 MIN.
MAKES: 4-6 SERVINGS

- 2 **large sweet onions**
- 1 **egg, lightly beaten**
- ⅔ **cup water**
- 1 **tablespoon canola oil**
- 1 **teaspoon lemon juice**
- 1 **cup all-purpose flour**
- 1½ **teaspoons baking powder**
- 1 **to 1¼ teaspoons salt**
- ⅛ **to ¼ teaspoon cayenne pepper**
- **Additional oil for deep-fat frying**

1. Cut onions into ½-in. slices; separate into rings. Place in a bowl; cover with ice water and soak for 30 minutes.

2. Meanwhile, combine the egg, water, oil and lemon juice in a bowl. Combine the flour, baking powder, salt and cayenne; stir into egg mixture until smooth.

3. Drain onion rings; dip into batter. In an electric skillet or deep-fat fryer, heat 1 in. of oil to 375°. Fry onion rings, a few at a time, for 1 to 1½ minutes on each side or until golden brown. Drain on paper towels.

Editor's Note: *Onion rings may be kept warm in a 200° oven while frying remainder of batch.*

Persimmon Salad with Honey Spiced Vinaigrette

The sweetness of the persimmons makes a delectable contrast to the bite of the arugula. And their pop of orange color gives a festive look to this winter salad.

—TASTE OF HOME TEST KITCHEN

PREP/TOTAL TIME: 20 MIN.
MAKES: 12 SERVINGS (1 CUP EACH)

- 12 **cups torn mixed salad greens**
- 4 **cups fresh arugula or baby spinach**
- 4 **persimmons, peeled and sliced**
- 1 **cup walnut halves, broken and toasted**
- 1 **cup dried cranberries**
- 1 **medium red onion, finely chopped**
- ¼ **cup lemon juice**
- ¼ **cup canola oil**
- 2 **tablespoons honey**
- ½ **teaspoon ground allspice**
- ¼ **teaspoon salt**
- 1 **cup crumbled feta cheese**

1. In a large bowl, combine salad greens, arugula, persimmons, walnuts, cranberries and onion. In a small bowl, whisk lemon juice, oil, honey, allspice and salt. Drizzle over salad; toss to coat. Sprinkle with cheese.

Vidalia Onion Bake

Mild tasting Vidalias make this casserole appealing to those who love onions—and even those who don't! It's great served with beef, pork or chicken.

KATRINA STITT ZEPHYRHILLS, FLORIDA

PREP: 25 MIN. **BAKE:** 20 MIN. **MAKES:** 4-6 SERVINGS

- 6 **large sweet onions, sliced (about 12 cups)**
- ½ **cup butter, cubed**
- 2 **cups crushed butter-flavored crackers**
- 1 **cup shredded Parmesan cheese**
- ½ **cup shredded cheddar cheese**
- ¼ **cup shredded Romano cheese**

1. In a large skillet, saute onions in butter until tender and liquid has evaporated. Place half of the onions in a greased 2-qt. baking dish; sprinkle with half of the cracker crumbs and cheeses. Repeat layers.

2. Bake, uncovered, at 325° for 20-25 minutes or until golden brown.

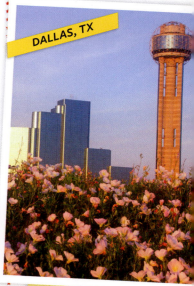

DALLAS, TX

Get a fresh look at downtown Dallas atop Reunion Tower, a distinctive silhouette in the city's skyline.

NASHVILLE, TN

Home of the Grand Ole Opry from 1943 until 1974, the Ryman Auditorium remains a major hub of country music.

Old-Fashioned Stack Cakes

My grandmother has always fixed these at Christmas and they are the first thing everyone asks about. "Where is the stack cake?" The super-thin layers are what make this recipe stand out...delicious!

—**STEPHANIE GILBERT** WHITESBURG, KENTUCKY

PREP: 35 MIN. **BAKE:** 5 MIN./BATCH
MAKES: 3 STACK CAKES (6 SLICES EACH)

- ½ cup butter, softened
- 1 cup sugar
- 2 eggs
- 2 teaspoons vanilla extract
- 4 cups all-purpose flour
- 4 teaspoons baking powder
- 1½ teaspoons ground ginger
- ½ teaspoon baking soda
- 1 teaspoon salt
- ½ cup molasses
- ½ cup buttermilk
- 2 cups apple butter
  Additional apple butter, optional

1. Preheat oven to 450°. In a large bowl, cream butter and sugar until light and fluffy. Beat in eggs and vanilla. In another bowl, whisk flour, baking powder, ginger, baking soda and salt; add to creamed mixture alternately with molasses and buttermilk, beating well after each addition.

2. Drop two scant ¼ cupfuls of batter 7 in. apart onto a parchment paper-lined baking sheet. With well-floured fingers, pat each into a 5- to 6-in. circle. Bake 2-3 minutes or until golden brown. Remove from pans to wire racks to cool. Repeat with remaining batter.

3. To assemble, place one cake layer on a serving plate; spread with 2 tablespoons apple butter. Repeat layers four times; top with a sixth layer. Repeat to make two more stack cakes. Refrigerate, covered, until serving. If desired, serve with additional apple butter.

Chocolate Pecan Torte

This impressive dessert looks lovely on a buffet table. It requires several steps but is worth the effort for special occasions.

—**LOIS SCHLICKAU** HAVEN, KANSAS

PREP: 1 HOUR **BAKE:** 20 MIN. + COOLING
MAKES: 12-16 SERVINGS

- 8 eggs, separated
- 1½ cups sugar, divided
- 1½ cups ground pecans
- ⅔ cup all-purpose flour
- ⅔ cup baking cocoa
- 1 teaspoon baking soda
- ½ teaspoon salt
- ½ cup water
- 2 teaspoons vanilla extract

CHOCOLATE FROSTING
- 3 cups heavy whipping cream
- 1 cup confectioners' sugar
- ½ cup baking cocoa
- 2 teaspoons vanilla extract

CHOCOLATE GLAZE
- 2 tablespoons baking cocoa
- 2 tablespoons water
- 1 tablespoon butter
- 1 cup confectioners' sugar
- ¼ teaspoon vanilla extract

1. Let eggs stand at room temperature for 30 minutes. In a large bowl, beat egg yolks. Gradually add 1 cup sugar, beating until thick and lemon-colored. Combine pecans, flour, cocoa, baking soda and salt; add to yolk mixture alternately with water. Stir in vanilla.

2. In another large bowl, beat egg whites until foamy. Gradually add remaining sugar, 1 tablespoon at a time, beating until stiff peaks form; fold into batter.

3. Spoon into two greased and floured 9-in. round baking pans. Bake at 375° for 20-22 minutes or until cake springs back when lightly touched. Cool for 10 minutes before removing from pans to wire racks to cool completely.

4. For frosting, in a large bowl, beat cream until soft peaks form. Beat in sugar, cocoa and vanilla until stiff peaks form. Cut each cake horizontally into two layers. Place bottom layer on a plate; top with about 1 cup frosting. Repeat layers twice. Top with remaining layer.

5. For glaze, in a small saucepan, combine cocoa, water and butter. Cook and stir over medium heat until butter is melted. Remove from the heat; stir in confectioners' sugar and vanilla until smooth. Spread over top cake layer. Spread remaining frosting over sides of cake. Store in the refrigerator.

Marshmallow-Almond Key Lime Pie

It's great to see that many grocers now carry Key limes, which give this pie its distinctive sweet-tart flavor.

—**JUDY CASTRANOVA** NEW BERN, NORTH CAROLINA

PREP: 40 MIN. **BAKE:** 15 MIN. + CHILLING **MAKES:** 8 SERVINGS

- 1 cup all-purpose flour
- 3 tablespoons brown sugar
- 1 cup slivered almonds, toasted, divided
- ¼ cup butter, melted
- 1 tablespoon honey
- 1 can (14 ounces) sweetened condensed milk
- 1 package (8 ounces) cream cheese, softened, divided
- ½ cup Key lime juice
- 1 tablespoon grated Key lime peel
  Dash salt
- 1 egg yolk
- 1¾ cups miniature marshmallows
- 4½ teaspoons butter
- ½ cup heavy whipping cream

1. Place the flour, brown sugar and ½ cup almonds in a food processor. Cover and process until blended. Add melted butter and honey; cover and process until crumbly. Press onto the bottom and up the sides of a greased 9-in. pie plate. Bake at 350° for 8-10 minutes or until crust is lightly browned. Cool on a wire rack.

2. In a large bowl, beat the milk, 5 ounces cream cheese, lime juice, peel and salt until blended. Add egg yolk; beat on low speed just until combined. Pour into crust. Bake for 15-20 minutes or until center is almost set. Cool on a wire rack.

3. In a saucepan, combine marshmallows and butter. Cook and stir over medium-low heat until melted. Remove from the heat and transfer to a bowl. Add cream and remaining cream cheese; beat until smooth. Cover and refrigerate until chilled.

4. Beat marshmallow mixture until light and fluffy. Spread over pie; sprinkle with remaining almonds.

 **dishing about food**

Key lime pie is a story of culinary ingenuity. With no grazing land for cows and no refrigeration, the Florida Keys relied on canned sweetened condensed milk for cooking, which businessman, William Curry brought there in the late 1850s. It was only natural that the milk would be paired with the local Key limes for a pie. Some say it was sponge divers who first put the two ingredients together. Others say it was William Curry's cook, Aunt Sally, who first created the pie.

Bourbon Chocolate Pecan Pie

When my fiance first made this for me, I declared it to be the best pie ever! Creamy chocolate combines with crunchy nuts in a great, gooey filling.

—**TANYA TAYLOR** CARY, NORTH CAROLINA

PREP: 25 MIN. + CHILLING **BAKE:** 55 MIN. + COOLING **MAKES:** 8 SERVINGS

- 1 **cup all-purpose flour**
- 1 **tablespoon sugar**
- ½ **teaspoon salt**
- 6 **tablespoons cold butter**
- 2 **to 3 tablespoons cold water**

FILLING

- 3 **eggs**
- 1 **cup packed dark brown sugar**
- ½ **cup light corn syrup**
- ½ **cup dark corn syrup**
- ¼ **cup bourbon**
- 2 **tablespoons butter, melted**
- ½ **teaspoon salt**
- 1½ **cups pecan halves, divided**
- ¾ **cup 60% cacao bittersweet chocolate baking chips, divided**

1. In a small bowl, combine the flour, sugar and salt. Cut in butter until mixture resembles coarse crumbs. Add water; toss with a fork until mixture forms a ball. Flatten into a disk. Wrap dough in plastic wrap and refrigerate for 30 minutes or until easy to handle.

2. On a floured surface, roll out dough to fit a 9-in. deep-dish pie plate. Transfer to pie plate; trim to ½ in. beyond edge of plate and flute edges.

3. In a large bowl, beat eggs, brown sugar, corn syrups, bourbon, butter and salt until blended. Stir in 1 cup pecans and ½ cup chocolate chips. Pour filling into crust; sprinkle with remaining pecans and chocolate chips.

4. Bake at 325° for 50-60 minutes or until the crust is golden brown and filling is puffed. Cool completely on a wire rack.

Bananas Foster

Guests are always impressed when I ignite the rum in this delicious dessert. Use perfectly ripe bananas for best results.

—MARY LOU WAYMAN SALT LAKE CITY, UTAH

PREP/TOTAL TIME: 25 MIN. **MAKES:** 4 SERVINGS

- ⅓ cup butter, cubed
- ¾ cup packed dark brown sugar
- ¼ teaspoon ground cinnamon
- 3 medium bananas
- 2 tablespoons creme de cacao or banana liqueur
- ¼ cup dark rum
- 2 cups vanilla ice cream

1. In a large skillet or flambé pan, melt butter over medium-low heat. Stir in brown sugar and cinnamon until combined. Cut each banana lengthwise and then widthwise into quarters; add to butter mixture. Cook, stirring gently, for 3-5 minutes or until glazed and slightly softened. Stir in creme de cacao; heat through.

2. In a small saucepan, heat rum over low heat until vapors form on surface. Carefully ignite the rum and slowly pour over the bananas, coating evenly.

3. Leaving skillet or pan on the cooking surface, gently shake pan back and forth until flames are completely extinguished.

4. Spoon ice cream into fluted glasses; top with bananas and sauce. Serve immediately.

Editor's Note: *Keep liquor bottles and other flammables at a safe distance when preparing this dessert. We do not recommend using a nonstick skillet.*

South Carolina Cobbler

With peach orchards just a couple of miles from home, it's easy to treat my family to this traditional dessert.

—MATTIE CARTER ROCK HILL, SOUTH CAROLINA

PREP: 10 MIN. **BAKE:** 50 MIN. **MAKES:** 8 SERVINGS

- 4 cups sliced peeled fresh or frozen peaches, thawed
- 1 cup sugar, divided
- ½ teaspoon almond extract
- ⅓ cup butter, melted
- ¾ cup all-purpose flour
- 2 teaspoons baking powder
  Dash salt
- ¾ cup milk
  Vanilla ice cream, optional

1. In a large bowl, gently toss peaches, ½ cup sugar and extract; set aside. Pour butter into a 2-qt. baking dish.

2. In a small bowl, combine the flour, baking powder, salt and remaining sugar; stir in milk until smooth. Pour evenly over butter (do not stir). Top with peach mixture.

3. Bake at 350° for 50-55 minutes or until golden brown and bubbly. Serve with ice cream if desired.

NEW ORLEANS, LA

Brennan's Restaurant is still hopping. You'll find it at 417 Royal St. in the French Quarter.

NATURAL BRIDGE, VA

The Blue Ridge Mountains run through much of Appalachia and boast some amazing formations. One is this natural bridge, a 215-foot limestone archway.

Chocolate Hazelnut Tassies

Your taste buds will be delighted to find these delicious tassies filled not with the standard pecans but with dark chocolate and hazelnuts.

—JOAN RANZINI WAYNESBORO, VIRGINIA

PREP: 25 MIN. **BAKE:** 20 MIN./BATCH + COOLING
MAKES: 3 DOZEN

- 1 cup butter, softened
- 2 packages (3 ounces each) cream cheese, softened
- 1 tablespoon sugar
- 2 teaspoons grated lemon peel
- 2 cups all-purpose flour

FILLING
- ¼ cup Nutella
- ½ cup packed brown sugar
- 1 egg
- 1 tablespoon butter, melted
- 1 teaspoon vanilla extract
- ½ cup finely chopped hazelnuts
- ¼ cup miniature semisweet chocolate chips

1. In a large bowl, cream the butter, cream cheese, sugar and lemon peel. Beat in flour. Shape into 36 balls. With floured fingers, press onto the bottom and up the sides of ungreased miniature muffin cups.

2. For filling, in a small bowl, beat the Nutella, brown sugar, egg, butter and vanilla until blended. Stir in hazelnuts and chocolate chips. Fill prepared cups three-fourths full.

3. Bake at 375° for 16-18 minutes or until set. Cool on wire racks for 10 minutes. Carefully remove from pans to wire racks. Store in an airtight container.

Old-Time Buttermilk Pie

This recipe is older than I am, and I was born in 1919! My mother and grandmother made this pie with buttermilk and eggs from our farm and took it to church meetings and social gatherings. I did the same and now our children make it, too!

—KATE MATHEWS SHREVEPORT, LOUISIANA

PREP: 15 MIN. **BAKE:** 45 MIN. + COOLING
MAKES: 8-10 SERVINGS

CRUST
- 1½ cups all-purpose flour
- 1 teaspoon salt
- ½ cup shortening
- ¼ cup cold milk
- 1 egg, lightly beaten

FILLING
- ½ cup butter, softened
- 2 cups sugar
- 3 tablespoons all-purpose flour
- 3 eggs
- 1 cup buttermilk
- 1 teaspoon vanilla extract
- 1 teaspoon ground cinnamon
- ¼ cup lemon juice

1. In a large bowl, mix flour and salt. Cut in shortening until smooth. Gradually add milk and egg and mix well. On a floured surface, roll dough out very thin. Place in a 10-in. pie pan; set aside.

2. For filling, cream butter and sugar in a bowl. Add flour. Add eggs, one at a time, beating well after each addition. Stir in remaining ingredients and mix well. Pour into crust.

3. Bake at 350° for 45 minutes. Cool completely before serving.

Strawberry Biscuit Shortcake

This is a perfect finish to any meal. I make the most of fresh berries with this dessert.

—**STEPHANIE MOON** BOISE, IDAHO

PREP/TOTAL TIME: 30 MIN. **MAKES:** 8 SERVINGS

- 2 **cups all-purpose flour**
- 3 **tablespoons sugar, divided**
- 1 **tablespoon baking powder**
- ½ **teaspoon salt**
- ¼ **cup cold butter**
- 1 **cup milk**
- 2 **pints strawberries, sliced**
- 1 **tablespoon orange juice**
- 1½ **cups whipped topping**

1. In a large bowl, combine flour, 2 tablespoons sugar, baking powder and salt. Cut in butter until the mixture resembles coarse crumbs. Gradually stir in milk until a soft dough forms.

2. Drop the dough by heaping tablespoonfuls into eight mounds on a lightly greased baking sheet. Bake at 425° for 12-15 minutes or until lightly browned. Cool on a wire rack.

3. Meanwhile, place the strawberries, orange juice and remaining sugar in a bowl; toss gently. Split the shortcakes in half horizontally. Place bottom halves on serving plates; top with the whipped topping and strawberries. Replace shortcake tops.

Berry Shortcake: *Replace 1 pint strawberries with 1 pint fresh blueberries.*

Mixed Fruit Shortcake: *Omit strawberries and orange juice. Combine 4 cups mixed fresh berries, 2 cups sliced fresh peaches and 2 teaspoons sugar.*

Golden Pound Cake

The surprise ingredient in this cake is a can of Mountain Dew. I sometimes substitute orange cake mix and a can of orange Crush soda for a flavorful variation.

—**VICKI BOYD** MECHANICSVILLE, VIRGINIA

PREP: 10 MIN. **BAKE:** 45 MIN. + COOLING
MAKES: 12 SERVINGS

- 1 **package lemon cake mix (regular size)**
- 1 **package (3.4 ounces) instant vanilla pudding mix**
- 4 **eggs**
- ¾ **cup canola oil**
- 1 **can (12 ounces) Mountain Dew**
  Confectioners' sugar, optional

1. In a large bowl, combine cake mix, pudding mix, eggs, oil and soda; beat on low speed for 30 seconds. Beat on medium for 2 minutes.

2. Pour into a greased and floured 10-in. fluted tube pan. Bake at 350° for 45-50 minutes or until a toothpick inserted near the center comes out clean. Cool for 10 minutes before removing from pan to a wire rack to cool completely. Dust with confectioners' sugar if desired.

LITTLE ROCK, AR

UNION STATION

Arrive at Little Rock's Union Station in style—aboard a passenger train! This depot, built in 1921, is one of many with the same name across the United States.

Simple chess pie has been enjoyed in the South for centuries. The name is perplexing, but two theories prevail. One is that the pie resembles English lemon cheese pie, and the name might have been Americanized, with the pronunciation changed to "chess." The other theory is based on the fact that the dessert contains enough sugar to safely store the pie at room temperature in a pie chest. The Southern accent may have turned "chest" into "chess."

Lemon Chess Pie

This creamy, lemony pie cuts beautifully and has a smooth texture. It's one of my favorites.

—HANNAH LARUE RIDER EAST POINT, KENTUCKY

PREP: 15 MIN. **BAKE:** 35 MIN. + CHILLING **MAKES:** 6 SERVINGS

1	**sheet refrigerated pie pastry**
4	**eggs**
1½	**cups sugar**
½	**cup lemon juice**
¼	**cup butter, melted**
1	**tablespoon cornmeal**
2	**teaspoons all-purpose flour**
⅛	**teaspoon salt**

1. Unroll pastry on a lightly floured surface. Transfer to a 9-in. pie plate. Trim pastry to ½ in. beyond edge of plate; flute edges.

2. In a large bowl, beat eggs for 3 minutes. Gradually add sugar; beat for 2 minutes or until mixture becomes thick and lemon-colored. Beat in the lemon juice, butter, cornmeal, flour and salt.

3. Pour into pastry shell. Bake at 350° for 35-40 minutes or until a knife inserted near the center comes out clean. Cool on a wire rack for 1 hour. Refrigerate for at least 3 hours before serving.

Grandma's Blackberry Cake

Here's a lightly seasoned spice cake that lets the wonderful flavor of blackberries shine through.

—DIANA MARTIN MOUNDSVILLE, WEST VIRGINIA

PREP: 15 MIN. **BAKE:** 45 MIN. + COOLING
MAKES: 9 SERVINGS

- 1 cup fresh blackberries
- 2 cups all-purpose flour, divided
- ½ cup butter, softened
- 1 cup sugar
- 2 eggs
- 1 teaspoon baking soda
- 1 teaspoon ground cinnamon
- 1 teaspoon ground nutmeg
- ½ teaspoon salt
- ¼ teaspoon ground cloves
- ¼ teaspoon ground allspice
- ¾ cup buttermilk
  Whipped cream, optional

1. Toss the blackberries with 2 tablespoons of flour; set aside. In a large bowl, cream the butter and sugar until light and fluffy. Beat in eggs. Combine the baking soda, cinnamon, nutmeg, salt, cloves, allspice and remaining flour; add to creamed mixture alternately with buttermilk, beating well after each addition. Fold in blackberries. Pour into a greased and floured 9-in. square baking pan.

2. Bake at 350° for 45-50 minutes or until a toothpick inserted in the center comes out clean. Cool on a wire rack. Serve with whipped cream if desired.

Apple Pear Pie

This fruit pie brimming with apples and pears really says fall. What a yummy way to use your backyard bounty or the pickings from local orchards! I've made plenty of pies over the years, and this is a real standout.

—GRACE CAMP OWINGSVILLE, KENTUCKY

PREP: 20 MIN. **BAKE:** 1 HOUR **MAKES:** 8 SERVINGS

- Pastry for double-crust pie (9 inches)
- 3 medium ripe pears, peeled and thinly sliced
- 3 medium tart apples, peeled and thinly sliced
- 1 cup plus 1 teaspoon sugar, divided
- 1 teaspoon lemon juice
- 1 teaspoon ground cinnamon
- ¼ teaspoon ground nutmeg
- 3 tablespoons butter
- 1 teaspoon whole milk

1. Line a 9-in. pie plate with bottom pastry; trim to 1 in. beyond edge of plate. In a large bowl, combine the pears, apples, 1 cup sugar, lemon juice, cinnamon and nutmeg. Transfer mixture to crust; dot with butter.

2. Roll out remaining pastry to fit top of pie; cut slits or decorative cutouts in pastry. Place over filling; trim, seal and flute edges. Add decorative cutouts if desired. Brush with milk; sprinkle with remaining sugar. Cover edges loosely with foil.

3. Bake at 350° for 30 minutes. Remove foil; bake 30-35 minutes longer or until crust is golden brown. Cool on a wire rack.

◀◆ dishing about food

Blackberries grow wild in the Ozarks and are very popular. Southern varieties of this juicy berry reach peak ripeness in June.

BRANSON, MO

No matter the season, fun times await the whole family in Branson. Watch a show, take a lake cruise—even explore the nearby caverns!

> "I receive a great response every time I serve this cake, and it seems like I'm forever sharing the recipe! People are always curious about the ingredients, and when I tell them the cake has cola in it, they are really surprised! The unusual combination makes it moist and delicious."

—ANNA BAKER
BLAINE, WASHINGTON

Coke Cake

PREP: 15 MIN. **BAKE:** 35 MIN. **MAKES:** 8-10 SERVINGS

- 2 **cups all-purpose flour**
- 2 **cups sugar**
- 1 **teaspoon baking soda**
- 1 **cup butter, cubed**
- 3 **tablespoons baking cocoa**
- 1 **cup cola**
- ½ **cup buttermilk**
- 2 **eggs, beaten**
- 1 **teaspoon vanilla extract**
- 1 **cup miniature marshmallows**

ICING
- ½ **cup butter, cubed**
- 2 **to 3 tablespoons baking cocoa**
- 6 **tablespoons cola**
- 3¼ **cups confectioners' sugar**
- 1 **cup coarsely chopped nuts**

1. In a bowl, combine the flour, sugar and baking soda; set aside.

2. In a saucepan, bring the butter, cocoa and cola to a boil; stir into dry ingredients. Stir in buttermilk, eggs, vanilla and marshmallows; mix well.

3. Pour into a greased 13x9-in. baking pan. Bake at 350° for 35 minutes or until a toothpick inserted in the center comes out clean.

4. For icing, combine the butter, cocoa and cola in a saucepan; bring to a boil and stir until smooth. Remove from the heat; stir in confectioners' sugar; mix well. Spread over hot cake. Sprinkle with nuts. Cool before cutting.

Georgia Peach Ice Cream

My state is well known for growing good peaches. This delightful recipe has been a family favorite for more than 50 years.

—MARGUERITE ETHRIDGE AMERICUS, GEORGIA

PREP: 45 MIN. + CHILLING **PROCESS:** 20 MIN./BATCH + FREEZING **MAKES:** 3¾ QUARTS

- 4 **eggs**
- 1¼ **cups sugar, divided**
- ½ **teaspoon salt**
- 4 **cups whole milk**
- 2 **cans (14 ounces each) sweetened condensed milk**
- 1¾ **pounds fresh peaches, peeled and sliced**

1. In a large heavy saucepan, whisk eggs, 1 cup sugar and salt until blended; stir in milk. Cook over low heat, stirring constantly, until mixture is just thick enough to coat a spoon and a thermometer reads at least 160°. Do not allow to boil. Remove from heat immediately.

2. Quickly transfer to a bowl; place bowl in a pan of ice water. Stir gently and occasionally for 2 minutes. Stir in sweetened condensed milk. Press plastic wrap onto surface of custard. Refrigerate several hours or overnight.

3. When ready to freeze, in a small bowl, mash peaches with remaining sugar; let stand 30 minutes. Pour custard into cylinder of ice cream freezer; stir in peaches. Freeze according to manufacturers' directions.

◀◆ dishing about food

For more than 150 years, Georgia farmers have been growing plump, golden peaches, the state's official fruit—and Americans have been happily wiping the sweet juice from their chins! The fact is, Georgia ranks third in peach production behind California and South Carolina.

GEORGIA

Franciscan monks brought peaches to Georgia's coastal islands in the late 16th century.

Some say Lady Baltimore Cake sprang from the imagination of author Owen Wister, who described the dessert in his 1906 novel, *Lady Baltimore*. Others maintain that socialite Alicia Rhett Mayberry baked the cake for Wister, who then described it in his novel. Still others believe sisters Florence and Nina Ottolengui, owners of Lady Baltimore Tea Room in Charleston, South Carolina, created it. One thing is certain: This classic is not from Baltimore!

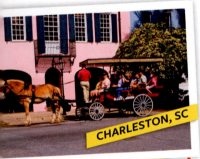

CHARLESTON, SC

A carriage ride is a quaint way to take in the sights of historic Charleston. Several companies offer guided tours.

Lady Baltimore Cake

I first made this cake for my father's birthday and now it is the only cake he requests. It has complex flavors with the raisin-fig filling and is very unique.

—CLEO GONSKE REDDING, CALIFORNIA

PREP: 30 MIN. + STANDING **BAKE:** 20 MIN. + COOLING
MAKES: 16 SERVINGS

- 1⅔ cups raisins, chopped
- 8 dried figs, finely chopped
- ½ cup brandy

CAKE
- 2½ cups all-purpose flour
- 2 cups sugar
- 2 teaspoons grated orange peel
- 1 teaspoon baking powder
- ½ teaspoon baking soda
- ⅛ teaspoon salt
- 1⅓ cups buttermilk
- ½ cup butter, softened
- 1 teaspoon vanilla extract
- 4 egg whites

FROSTING
- 2 cups butter, softened
- 6 cups confectioners' sugar, sifted
- 2 teaspoons vanilla extract
- ¼ to ⅓ cup heavy whipping cream
- 1 cup finely chopped pecans, toasted

1. In a small bowl, combine the raisins and figs. Add brandy; toss to combine. Let stand, covered, at room temperature about 2 hours or until brandy is absorbed, stirring occasionally.

2. Preheat oven to 350°. Line bottoms of three greased 8-in. round cake pans with parchment paper; grease paper.

3. In a large bowl, mix the flour, sugar, orange peel, baking powder, baking soda and salt until blended. Add the buttermilk, butter and vanilla; beat on low speed 30 seconds or just until the dry ingredients are moistened. Beat on medium for 2 minutes. Add the egg whites; beat 2 minutes longer.

4. Transfer batter to prepared pans. Bake 20-25 minutes or until a toothpick inserted in center comes out clean. Cool in pans for 10 minutes before removing from the pans to wire racks to cool completely.

5. In a large bowl, cream butter until fluffy. Gradually beat in confectioners' sugar. Beat in vanilla and enough cream to reach desired consistency. For filling, remove 1 cup frosting to a small bowl; stir in pecans and raisin mixture.

6. Place one cake layer on a serving plate; spread with half of the filling. Add another cake layer; top with remaining filling. Add remaining cake layer; spread remaining frosting over top and sides of cake.

Bourbon Pecan Pralines

Like authentic pralines found in New Orleans, these treats are sweet, crunchy and rich!

—TASTE OF HOME TEST KITCHEN

PREP: 15 MIN. **COOK:** 25 MIN. + STANDING
MAKES: 1 POUND

- ¼ cup butter, cubed
- ½ cup sugar
- ½ cup packed brown sugar
- ¾ cup heavy whipping cream
- 1 cup pecan halves, toasted
- ½ cup chopped pecans, toasted
- 1 tablespoon bourbon

1. Grease two baking sheets; set aside. In a large heavy saucepan over medium heat, melt butter. Stir in the sugars, then cream; cook and stir until mixture comes to a boil. Cook, stirring occasionally, until a candy thermometer reads 236° (soft-ball stage), about 20 minutes.

2. Remove from the heat; stir in pecan halves, chopped pecans and bourbon. Immediately drop by tablespoonfuls onto prepared baking sheets. Let stand until pralines are set and no longer glossy. Store in an airtight container.

Editor's Note: *We recommend that you test your candy thermometer before each use by bringing water to a boil; the thermometer should read 212°. Adjust your recipe temperature up or down based on your test.*

Shortbread Lemon Tart

For a change from ordinary lemon bars, we added orange peel to both the crust and filling and turned the recipe into a tart. It's a refreshing finish to heavy holiday meals.

—TASTE OF HOME TEST KITCHEN

PREP: 20 MIN. **BAKE:** 25 MIN. + COOLING
MAKES: 10-12 SERVINGS

- 3 eggs
- ¼ cup lemon juice
- 1¼ cups sugar
- 1 tablespoon grated orange peel
- ¼ cup butter, melted

CRUST
- 1 cup all-purpose flour
- ⅓ cup confectioners' sugar
- ½ cup ground almonds
- 1 teaspoon grated lemon peel
- 1 teaspoon grated orange peel
- ½ cup cold butter, cubed
  Additional confectioners' sugar

1. For filling, in a blender, combine the eggs, lemon juice, sugar and orange peel. Cover and blend on high until smooth. Add butter; cover and process on high just until smooth. Set aside.

2. In a food processor, combine the flour, confectioners' sugar, almonds, lemon peel, orange peel and butter; cover and process until mixture forms a ball. Press pastry onto the bottom and up the sides of an ungreased 9-in. tart pan with removable bottom.

3. Pour filling into crust. Bake at 350° for 25-30 minutes or until center is almost set. Cool on a wire rack. Just before serving, sprinkle with confectioners' sugar.

Devil's food cake is said to be a Southern creation that appeared on dining tables in the early 1900s. Some argue that it should be made with cocoa, while others say the original recipe used melted chocolate. There are many tales about how the cake was named, from its dark color or sinfully rich flavor to the idea that it was the antithesis of angel food cake.

Devil's Food Cake with Chocolate Fudge Frosting

This recipe won several blue ribbons at our state fair. The made-from-scratch chocolate layer cake topped with a fudgy homemade frosting is truly a can't-miss dessert.

—DONNA CARMAN TULSA, OKLAHOMA

PREP: 45 MIN. **BAKE:** 25 MIN. + COOLING **MAKES:** 12 SERVINGS

- 3 **ounces unsweetened chocolate, chopped**
- ½ **cup butter, softened**
- 2¼ **cups packed brown sugar**
- 3 **eggs**
- 1½ **teaspoons vanilla extract**
- 2¼ **cups cake flour**
- 1 **teaspoon baking soda**
- ½ **teaspoon baking powder**
- ½ **teaspoon salt**
- 1 **cup water**
- 1 **cup (8 ounces) sour cream**

FROSTING
- ½ **cup butter, cubed**
- 4 **ounces unsweetened chocolate, chopped**
- 3¾ **cups confectioners' sugar**
- ½ **cup milk**
- 2 **teaspoons vanilla extract**

1. In a microwave, melt the chocolate; stir until smooth. Set aside. In a large bowl, cream butter and brown sugar until light and fluffy.

Add eggs, one at a time, beating well after each addition. Beat in vanilla and melted chocolate.

2. Combine the flour, baking soda, baking powder and salt; add to the creamed mixture alternately with the water and sour cream. Transfer to two greased and floured 9-in. round baking pans.

3. Bake at 350° for 25-30 minutes or until a toothpick inserted in center comes out clean. Cool for 10 minutes before removing from pans to wire racks to cool completely.

4. For frosting, in a small heavy saucepan, melt butter and chocolate over low heat. Remove from the heat; cool for 5 minutes. In a large bowl, beat the confectioners' sugar, milk and vanilla until smooth. Gradually beat in chocolate mixture until frosting is light and fluffy. Spread between layers and over top and sides of cake. Refrigerate leftovers.

Southern Lane Cake

Guest will just love this impressive and festive cake. With the fruit filling and topping, it is reminiscent of a fruitcake, but it's so much more delicious!

—MABEL PARVI RIDGEFIELD, WASHINGTON

PREP: 40 MIN. **BAKE:** 20 MIN. + CHILLING
MAKES: 12 SERVINGS

- 6 **egg whites**
- ¾ **cup butter, softened**
- 1½ **cups sugar**
- 1 **teaspoon vanilla extract**
- 2¼ **cups all-purpose flour**
- 2½ **teaspoons baking powder**
- ½ **teaspoon salt**
- ¾ **cup 2% milk**

FILLING

- 6 **egg yolks**
- 1 **cup sugar**
- ½ **cup butter, cubed**
- ¼ **cup bourbon**
- 1 **tablespoon grated orange peel**
- ¼ **teaspoon salt**
- ¾ **cup raisins**
- ¾ **cup flaked coconut**
- ¾ **cup chopped pecans**
- ¾ **cup coarsely chopped red candied cherries**
- 1 **cup heavy whipping cream, whipped and sweetened**

1. Line bottoms of three greased 9-in. round baking pans with parchment paper; grease paper; set aside. Place egg whites in a large bowl; let stand at room temperature for 30 minutes.

2. In another large bowl, cream butter and sugar until light and fluffy. Beat in vanilla. In another bowl, whisk flour, baking powder and salt; add to creamed mixture alternately with milk, beating well after each addition. Beat egg whites until stiff peaks form; fold into batter. Transfer to prepared pans.

3. Bake at 325° for 20-25 minutes or until a toothpick inserted in center comes out clean. Cool for 10 minutes before removing from pans to wire racks; remove paper. Cool completely.

4. For filling, combine egg yolks and sugar in a large saucepan. Add butter; cook and stir over medium-low heat until sugar is dissolved and mixture thickens, but does not boil. Remove from the heat. Stir in bourbon, orange peel, and salt. Fold in the raisins, coconut, pecans and cherries. Cool.

5. Place one cake layer on a serving plate; spread with a third of the filling. Repeat for second cake layer. Top with third cake layer, then remaining filling. Frost sides of cake with whipped cream. Store in the refrigerator.

Louisiana's French settlers brought recipes for deep-frying pastries, and the beignet evolved from fruit-filled fritters to squares of fried sweet dough generously dusted with confectioners' sugar. Historic Cafe Du Monde is famous for its beignets. You can find its original location on New Orleans' famed Jackson Square.

NEW ORLEANS, LA

Jackson Square was named for Andrew Jackson, the general who led troops to defeat the British in the Battle of New Orleans during the War of 1812. He was later elected president. In the square, St. Louis Cathedral towers over Jackson's statue and the crowds that gather to enjoy the artists and musicians performing there.

New Orleans Beignets

These sweet French doughnuts are square instead of round and have no hole in the middle. They're a traditional part of breakfast in New Orleans.

—**BETH DAWSON** JACKSON, LOUISIANA

PREP: 15 MIN. **COOK:** 35 MIN. **MAKES:** 4 DOZEN

- 1 **package (¼ ounce) active dry yeast**
- ¼ **cup warm water (110° to 115°)**
- 1 **cup evaporated milk**
- ½ **cup canola oil**
- ¼ **cup sugar**
- 1 **egg**
- 4½ **cups self-rising flour**
   Oil for deep-fat frying
   Confectioners' sugar

1. In a large bowl, dissolve yeast in warm water. Add the milk, oil, sugar and egg and 2 cups flour. Beat until smooth. Stir in enough remaining flour to form a soft dough (dough will be sticky). Do not knead. Cover and refrigerate overnight.

2. Punch dough down. Turn onto a floured surface; roll into a 16-in. x 12-in. rectangle. Cut into 2-in. squares.

3. In an electric skillet or deep-fat fryer, heat oil to 375°. Fry the squares, a few at a time, until golden brown on both sides. Drain the beignets on paper towels. Roll the warm beignets in confectioners' sugar.

Editor's Note: *As a substitute for each cup of self-rising flour, place 1½ teaspoons baking powder and ½ teaspoon salt in a measuring cup. Add all-purpose flour to measure 1 cup.*

Old-Fashioned Jam Cake

I remember my Aunt Murna telling me she made this cake often when she was a young girl. Through the years, she made improvements to it, and her cake became a real family favorite. It has been a popular staple at our reunions.

—JANET ROBINSON LAWRENCEBURG, KENTUCKY

PREP: 25 MIN. + STANDING
BAKE: 40 MIN. + COOLING **MAKES:** 12-16 SERVINGS

- 1 **cup raisins**
- 1 **can (8 ounces) crushed pineapple, undrained**
- 1 **cup butter, softened**
- 1 **cup sugar**
- 4 **eggs**
- 3 **cups all-purpose flour**
- ⅓ **cup baking cocoa**
- 1 **teaspoon baking soda**
- 1 **teaspoon ground cinnamon**
- 1 **teaspoon ground nutmeg**
- ½ **teaspoon ground cloves**
- 1 **jar (12 ounces) or 1 cup blackberry jam**
- ⅔ **cup buttermilk**
- 1 **cup chopped pecans**

CARAMEL ICING
- 1 **cup butter, cubed**
- 2 **cups packed brown sugar**
- ½ **cup 2% milk**
- 3½ **to 4 cups confectioners' sugar**

1. In a small bowl, combine raisins and pineapple; let stand for at least 30 minutes.

2. In a large bowl, cream butter and sugar until light and fluffy. Add eggs, one at a time, beating well after each addition. Combine dry ingredients; gradually add to creamed mixture alternately with jam and buttermilk, beating well after each addition. Stir in raisin mixture and nuts.

3. Spread into two greased and floured 9-in. round baking pans. Bake at 350° for 40-45 minutes or until a toothpick inserted in center comes out clean. Cool the cake for 10 minutes before removing from pans to wire racks to cool completely.

4. For icing, in a large saucepan, melt butter over medium heat. Stir in sugar and milk. Bring to a boil. Remove from the heat; cool until just warm. Pour into a large bowl; beat in enough confectioners' sugar to achieve a spreading consistency. Spread the frosting between layers and over the top and sides of the cake.

Strawberry Rhubarb Pie

My niece tasted this pie at a family dinner and urged me to enter it in our hometown pie contest. She said it would win the Grand Prize, and it did! I cook at our local nursing home, and everyone enjoys this recipe.

—JANICE SCHMIDT BAXTER, IOWA

PREP: 25 MIN. + CHILLING **MAKES:** 8 SERVINGS

- 2 **tablespoons cornstarch**
- 1 **cup sugar**
- 1 **cup water**
- 1 **cup sliced rhubarb**
- 3 **tablespoons strawberry gelatin powder**
- 1 **pastry shell (9 inches), baked**
- 2 **pints fresh strawberries, halved**

1. In a large saucepan, mix cornstarch and sugar. Stir in water until smooth. Add rhubarb; cook and stir until clear and thickened. Add gelatin and stir until dissolved. Cool.

2. Pour about half of the rhubarb sauce into the pastry shell. Arrange berries over sauce; top with remaining sauce. Refrigerate for 3-4 hours before serving. Store in the refrigerator.

PADUCAH, KY

Now among the most popular tourist destinations in Kentucky, the National Quilt Museum opened in 1991. On-site and traveling exhibits display the fine work of quilters and fiber artists from around the world.

Featuring vanilla pudding, bananas and vanilla wafers, banana pudding can be served plain, with whipped cream or crowned with meringue. Love banana pudding? Head to the annual National Banana Pudding Festival in Centerville, Tennessee.

Banana Pudding

I didn't see my son, Lance Cpl. Eric Harris, for more than two years after he enlisted in the Marines following high school. When I saw him for the first time at the airport last fall, I just grabbed hold of him and busted out crying. The first thing he ate when we got home was two bowls of my banana pudding. He's a true Southern boy!

—**STEPHANIE HARRIS** MONTPELIER, VIRGINIA

PREP: 15 MIN. + COOLING
COOK: 20 MIN. + CHILLING **MAKES:** 9 SERVINGS

- ¾ cup sugar
- ¼ cup all-purpose flour
- ¼ teaspoon salt
- 3 cups 2% milk
- 3 eggs
- 1½ teaspoons vanilla extract
- 58 vanilla wafers, divided
- 4 large ripe bananas, cut into ¼-inch slices

1. In a large saucepan, mix sugar, flour and salt. Whisk in milk. Cook and stir over medium heat until thickened and bubbly. Reduce heat to low; cook and stir 2 minutes longer. Remove from heat.

2. In a small bowl, whisk eggs. Whisk a small amount of hot mixture into eggs; return all to pan, whisking constantly. Bring to a gentle boil; cook and stir 2 minutes. Remove from heat. Stir in vanilla. Cool 15 minutes, stirring occasionally.

3. In an ungreased 8-in.-square baking dish, layer 25 vanilla wafers, half the banana slices and half of the pudding. Repeat layers.

4. Press plastic wrap onto surface of pudding. Refrigerate at least 4 hours. Just before serving, crush remaining wafers; sprinkle over top.

Old-Fashioned Coconut Pie

My husband says it's not good cooking unless it's made from scratch. This is an old-fashioned way of making coconut pie.

—**BARBARA SMITH** FRANKLIN, GEORGIA

PREP: 20 MIN. **BAKE:** 15 MIN. + COOLING
MAKES: 6-8 SERVINGS

- 1 cup sugar
- ¼ cup all-purpose flour
  Dash salt
- 3 eggs, lightly beaten
- 2 cups milk
- 1½ teaspoons vanilla extract
- 1¼ cups flaked coconut, divided
- 1 pie shell (9 inches), baked

MERINGUE
- 3 egg whites
- 6 tablespoons sugar

1. In a saucepan, combine sugar, flour and salt. Combine egg yolks and milk; stir into dry ingredients until smooth. Cook and stir over medium heat until thickened and bubbly. Reduce heat to low; cook and stir 2 minutes longer. Remove from heat; stir in vanilla and 1 cup coconut. Pour hot filling into pie shell.

2. For meringue, beat egg whites in a bowl until soft peaks form. Gradually beat in sugar until mixture forms stiff glossy peaks and sugar is dissolved. Spread meringue over hot filling. Sprinkle with remaining coconut. Bake at 350° for 12-15 minutes or until golden. Cool. Store in the refrigerator.

Deep-Fried Cherry Pies

These stuffed cherry pies with a wonderful flaky crust make a quick dessert. My family also loves them for snacks, and they're a handy and delicious addition to my husband's take-along lunches.

—MONICA LARKIN SHINNSTON, WEST VIRGINIA

PREP/TOTAL TIME: 30 MIN. **MAKES:** 4 SERVINGS

- 1 cup all-purpose flour
- ¼ teaspoon baking powder
- ¼ teaspoon salt
- 2 tablespoons shortening
- ⅓ cup boiling water
- 1 cup cherry pie filling
  - Oil for deep-fat frying
- ¼ cup maple syrup
- ¼ cup whipped topping

1. In a small bowl, combine the flour, baking powder and salt. Cut in the shortening until mixture resembles coarse crumbs. Stir in the water just until moistened. Turn onto a lightly floured surface; knead 8-10 times.

2. Divide dough into four portions; roll each into an 8-in. circle. Place ¼ cup of pie filling in the center of each circle. Fold dough over filling; secure with toothpicks.

3. In an electric skillet or deep fat-fryer, heat 1 in. of oil to 375°. Fry pies, folded side down, in oil for 2-3 minutes or until lightly browned. Turn and fry 2-3 minutes longer. Drain on paper towels. Remove toothpicks. Serve with syrup and whipped topping.

Candied Pecans

I packed these crispy pecans in jars tied with pretty ribbon for family and friends. My granddaughter gave some to a doctor at the hospital where she works, and he said they were "too good to be true!"

—OPAL TURNER HUGHES SPRINGS, TEXAS

PREP: 20 MIN. **BAKE:** 40 MIN.
MAKES: ABOUT 1 POUND

- 2¾ cups pecan halves
- 2 tablespoons butter, softened, divided
- 1 cup sugar
- ½ cup water
- ½ teaspoon salt
- ½ teaspoon ground cinnamon
- 1 teaspoon vanilla extract

1. Place the pecans in a shallow baking pan in a 250° oven for 10 minutes or until pecans are warmed. Grease a 15x10x1-in. baking pan with 1 tablespoon butter; set aside.

2. Grease the sides of a large heavy saucepan with remaining butter; add sugar, water, salt and cinnamon. Cook and stir over low heat until sugar is dissolved. Cook and stir over medium heat until mixture comes to a boil. Cover and cook for 2 minutes to dissolve the sugar crystals.

3. Cook, without stirring, until a candy thermometer reads 236° (soft-ball stage). Remove from the heat; add vanilla. Stir in warm pecans until evenly coated.

4. Spread onto prepared baking pan. Bake at 250° for 30 minutes, stirring every 10 minutes. Spread on a waxed paper-lined baking sheet to cool.

Editor's Note: *We recommend that you test your candy thermometer before each use by bringing water to a boil; the thermometer should read 212°. Adjust your recipe temperature up or down based on your test.*

◄● dishing about food

Fried pies were originally cooked in cast-iron skillets throughout the South and the Northeast. Now the pastries are deep-fried and have become an iconic Southern treat. Apple and peach are the most popular flavors, but cherries and berries make scrumptious fillings, too.

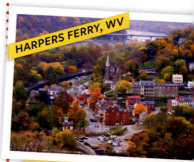
HARPERS FERRY, WV

Many famous Americans have ties to Harpers Ferry, including George Washington, Lewis and Clark, John Brown, Stonewall Jackson and Frederick Douglass.

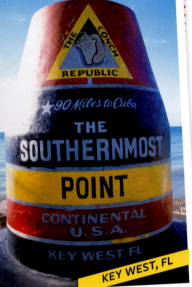

The southernmost spot in the U.S., Key West is only 90 miles from Cuba! The laid-back island has been frequented by many famous folks over the years, including Ernest Hemingway, Lou Gehrig and Tennessee Williams.

Orange Natilla Custard Pie

I tasted this custard at a small Cuban restaurant in Key West and knew that I had to make it into a pie.

—**AMY MILLS** SEBRING, FLORIDA

PREP: 30 MIN. + CHILLING **BAKE:** 35 MIN. + CHILLING
MAKES: 8 SERVINGS

- 1   cup whole milk
- 1   orange peel strip
- 1   lemon peel strip
- 1   whole star anise

CRUST
- 1¼ cups all-purpose flour
- ⅛   teaspoon salt
- 7   tablespoons cold butter, cubed
- 5   to 6 tablespoons cold water

FILLING
- 4   eggs
- 1   can (14 ounces) sweetened condensed milk
- ½   cup sugar
- ¼   cup orange juice
- 1   teaspoon ground cinnamon
- 1   teaspoon vanilla extract

FINISHING
- 1   egg
- 2   tablespoons water
- 2   tablespoons sugar
- ¼   teaspoon ground cinnamon
       Orange peel curls, optional

1. In a small saucepan, heat the milk, orange peel, lemon peel and star anise until bubbles form around sides of pan, stirring occasionally. Remove from the heat. Cool. Cover and steep overnight in the refrigerator.

2. In a large bowl, combine flour and salt; cut in butter until crumbly. Gradually add water, tossing with a fork until dough forms a ball. Wrap in plastic wrap. Refrigerate for 1 hour or until easy to handle.

3. Roll out pastry to ⅛-in. thickness; transfer to a 9-in. pie plate. Trim pastry to ½ in. beyond edge of plate; flute edges.

4. Line unpricked pastry with a double thickness of heavy-duty foil. Fill with dried beans, uncooked rice or pie weights. Bake at 450° for 12 minutes. Remove foil and weights; bake 5 minutes longer or until golden brown. Cool on a wire rack.

5. Strain milk mixture, discarding peels and star anise. In a blender, combine the eggs, condensed milk, strained milk, sugar, orange juice, cinnamon and vanilla; cover and process until smooth. Pour into crust.

6. In a small bowl, whisk egg and water; brush over pastry edges. Bake at 400° for 15 minutes. Reduce heat to 350°; sprinkle with sugar. Bake for 18-22 minutes or until center is almost set. (Pie surface will still jiggle. Custard will set upon cooling.) Cool on a wire rack for 1 hour.

7. Cover and refrigerate until chilled. Sprinkle with cinnamon just before serving. Garnish with orange peel curls if desired. Refrigerate leftovers.

Editor's Note: *Let pie weights cool before storing. Beans and rice may be reused as pie weights, but not for cooking.*

Sad Cake

Sad is such a misnomer for this dessert. It's so simple to make—it takes only 10 minutes to mix up—is sweet, chewy and yummy!

—LORI HANLEY HARTSVILLE, SOUTH CAROLINA

PREP: 10 MIN. **BAKE:** 30 MIN. **MAKES:** 15 SERVINGS

- 2¼ cups packed brown sugar
- 2 cups biscuit/baking mix
- 4 eggs
- ½ cup canola oil
- 1 teaspoon vanilla extract
- 1 cup chopped pecans
- 1 cup flaked coconut

1. Preheat oven to 350°. In a large bowl, mix brown sugar and baking mix. In another bowl, whisk eggs, oil and vanilla until blended. Add to sugar mixture; stir just until moistened. Fold in pecans and coconut.

2. Transfer to a greased 13x9-in. baking pan. Bake 30-35 minutes or until browned and a toothpick inserted in center comes out with moist crumbs. Cool the cake completely in pan on a wire rack.

Butterscotch Peach Pie

When peach season arrives, this great old-fashioned pie is sure to be on the table. The recipe has been in our family for more than 60 years, and I still make it every summer. Butterscotch buffs love it.

—BARBARA MOYER TIFFIN, OHIO

PREP: 30 MIN. + CHILLING **BAKE:** 45 MIN. + COOLING
MAKES: 8 SERVINGS

- 2 cups all-purpose flour
- 1 teaspoon salt
- ¾ cup shortening
- 4 to 5 tablespoons cold water

FILLING

- ¾ cup packed brown sugar
- 2 tablespoons all-purpose flour
- ⅓ cup light corn syrup
- 3 tablespoons butter, melted
- 2 tablespoons lemon juice
- ¼ teaspoon almond extract
- 8 medium peaches, peeled and sliced

1. In a large bowl, combine flour and salt; cut in shortening until crumbly. Gradually add water, tossing with a fork until dough forms a ball. Cover and refrigerate for 30 minutes or until easy to handle.

2. For filling, in a small saucepan, combine brown sugar and flour. Stir in corn syrup and butter until blended. Bring to a boil; cook and stir for 2 minutes or until thickened. Remove from the heat; stir in lemon juice and extract. Place peaches in a large bowl; add syrup mixture and toss to coat.

3. Divide dough in half so one ball is slightly larger than the other. Roll out larger ball to fit a 9-in. pie plate. Transfer to pie plate; trim pastry to ½ in. beyond rim of plate. Add filling. Roll out remaining pastry; make a lattice crust. Trim, seal and flute edges. Cover edges loosely with foil.

4. Bake at 375° for 25 minutes. Uncover; bake 20-25 minutes longer or until crust is golden brown and filling is bubbly. Cool on a wire rack.

When Mrs. L.H. Wiggins of Greensboro, North Carolina, published her hummingbird cake recipe in 1978, Southern baking was changed forever. Nobody knows exactly how the cake got its fanciful name, but according to local lore, when you take a bite of the cake, you'll hum with pleasure.

ASHEVILLE, NC

If you enjoy learning about the lifestyles of the rich and famous, pay a visit to the largest home in America: the Biltmore, which was built for George Vanderbilt in 1895. These days, you can even stay the night!

Hummingbird Cake

What an impressive cake! It's my dad's favorite, so I always make it for his birthday. It also makes a great Easter dessert and is lovely with a summer meal.

—NANCY ZIMMERMAN CAPE MAY COURT HOUSE, NEW JERSEY

PREP: 40 MIN. **BAKE:** 25 MIN. + COOLING
MAKES: 12-14 SERVINGS

- 2 cups mashed ripe bananas
- 1½ cups canola oil
- 3 eggs
- 1 can (8 ounces) unsweetened crushed pineapple, undrained
- 1½ teaspoons vanilla extract
- 3 cups all-purpose flour
- 2 cups sugar
- 1 teaspoon baking soda
- 1 teaspoon salt
- 1 teaspoon ground cinnamon
- 1 cup chopped walnuts

PINEAPPLE FROSTING
- ¼ cup shortening
- 2 tablespoons butter, softened
- 1 teaspoon grated lemon peel
- ¼ teaspoon salt
- 6 cups confectioners' sugar
- ½ cup unsweetened pineapple juice
- 2 teaspoons half-and-half cream
  Chopped walnuts, optional

1. In a large bowl, beat the bananas, oil, eggs, pineapple and vanilla until well blended. In another bowl, combine the flour, sugar, baking soda, salt and cinnamon; gradually beat into banana mixture until blended. Stir in walnuts.

2. Pour into three greased and floured 9-in. round baking pans. Bake at 350° for 25-30 minutes or until a toothpick inserted in center comes out clean. Cool the layers for 10 minutes before removing from pans to wire racks to cool completely.

3. For frosting, in a large bowl, beat the shortening, butter, lemon peel and salt until fluffy. Add confectioners' sugar alternately with pineapple juice. Beat in cream. Spread between layers and over top and sides of cake. Sprinkle with walnuts if desired.

Chunky Fresh Mango Cake

This delicious cake originated years ago with a great-aunt who lived in Florida and had her own mango tree. It's a sweet, moist cake with slightly crisp edges.

—ALLENE BARY-COOPER WICHITA FALLS, TEXAS

PREP: 20 MIN. **BAKE:** 30 MIN. + COOLING
MAKES: 4 SERVINGS

- ½ cup sugar
- ⅓ cup canola oil
- 1 egg
- ½ cup plus 2 tablespoons all-purpose flour
- ¾ teaspoon baking powder
- ¼ teaspoon salt
- ¼ teaspoon ground cinnamon
- ⅛ teaspoon ground nutmeg
- ¾ cup chopped peeled mango
- ¼ cup chopped pecans
  Confectioners' sugar and whipped topping, optional

1. In a small bowl, beat the sugar, oil and egg until well blended. In another bowl, combine the flour, baking powder, salt, cinnamon and nutmeg; gradually beat into sugar mixture and mix well. Fold in mango and pecans.

2. Transfer to a greased 6-in. round baking pan. Bake at 375° for 25-30 minutes or until a toothpick inserted near the center comes out clean. Cool for 10 minutes before removing from pan to a wire rack to cool completely. Garnish with confectioners' sugar and whipped topping if desired.

Buttermilk Pound Cake

PREP: 10 MIN. **BAKE:** 70 MIN. + COOLING **MAKES:** 16-20 SERVINGS

- 1 **cup butter, softened**
- 2½ **cups sugar**
- 4 **eggs**
- 3 **cups all-purpose flour**
- ¼ **teaspoon baking soda**
- 1 **cup buttermilk**
- 1 **teaspoon vanilla extract**
  Confectioners' sugar, optional

1. In a large bowl, cream butter and sugar until light and fluffy. Add eggs, one at a time, beating well after each addition. Combine flour and baking soda; add alternately with buttermilk and beat well. Stir in vanilla.

2. Pour into a greased and floured 10-in. fluted tube pan. Bake at 325° for 70 minutes or until a toothpick inserted near the center comes out clean. Cool in pan for 15 minutes before removing to a wire rack to cool completely. Dust with confectioners' sugar if desired.

Lemon-Filled Coconut Cake

PREP: 35 MIN. **BAKE:** 25 MIN. + COOLING **MAKES:** 16 SERVINGS

- 1 cup butter, softened
- 2 cups sugar
- 3 eggs
- 2 teaspoons vanilla extract
- 3¼ cups all-purpose flour
- 3¼ teaspoons baking powder
- ¾ teaspoon salt
- 1½ cups 2% milk

FILLING
- 1 cup sugar
- ¼ cup cornstarch
- 1 cup water
- 4 egg yolks, lightly beaten
- ⅓ cup lemon juice
- 2 tablespoons butter

FROSTING
- 1½ cups sugar
- 2 egg whites
- ⅓ cup water
- ¼ teaspoon cream of tartar
- 1 teaspoon vanilla extract
- 3 cups flaked coconut

1. In a large bowl, cream butter and sugar until light and fluffy. Add eggs, one at a time, beating well after each addition. Beat in vanilla. Combine the flour, baking powder and salt; add to creamed mixture alternately with milk, beating well after each addition.

2. Transfer to three greased and floured 9-in. round baking pans. Bake at 350° for 25-30 minutes or until a toothpick inserted in the center comes out clean. Cool for 10 minutes before removing from pans to wire racks to cool completely.

3. For filling, in a small saucepan, combine the sugar, cornstarch and water until smooth. Bring to a boil; cook and stir 2 minutes longer or until thickened and bubbly. Remove from the heat.

4. Stir a small amount of hot mixture into egg yolks; return all to the pan, stirring constantly. Bring to a gentle boil; cook and stir 2 minutes longer. Remove from the heat; gently stir in lemon juice and butter. Cool to room temperature without stirring.

5. Place one cake on serving plate; spread with half of the filling. Repeat layers. Top with remaining cake.

6. For frosting, in a large heavy saucepan, combine the sugar, egg whites, water and cream of tartar. With a portable mixer, beat on low speed for 1 minute. Continue beating on low over low heat until frosting reaches 160°, about 10 minutes.

7. Transfer to a large bowl; add vanilla. Beat on high until stiff peaks form, about 7 minutes. Frost top and sides of cake. Sprinkle with coconut. Store in the refrigerator.

Ozark Pudding Cake

The homey dessert uses kitchen staples to create a comforting but simple treat, with a meringue cookie-like topping and an apple-nut base. There are different versions of the recipe, but one of the most famous is this one from Bess Truman, the wife of President Harry Truman.

—TASTE OF HOME TEST KITCHEN

PREP: 15 MIN. **BAKE:** 20 MIN. **MAKES:** 6 SERVINGS

- 2 tablespoons all-purpose flour
- 1¼ teaspoons baking powder
- ⅛ teaspoon salt
- 1 egg
- ¾ cup sugar
- 1 teaspoon vanilla extract
- 1 cup chopped peeled apple
- ½ cup chopped walnuts or pecans
  Whipped cream or vanilla ice cream, optional

1. Preheat oven to 350°. Grease a 9-in. deep-dish pie plate.

2. In a small bowl, mix flour, baking powder and salt. In another bowl, beat egg and sugar until thick and lemon-colored. Stir in vanilla, then flour mixture. Fold in apple and walnuts.

3. Transfer to prepared pie plate. Bake for 20-25 minutes or until golden brown. (Cake will puff up, then fall when removed from oven.) With a knife, loosen sides from pie plate while still warm.

4. Serve the cake warm. If desired, top with whipped cream.

Southern Sweet Potato Pie

Sweet potato pie is very popular in the South. It's a particular favorite at our house because we always have plenty of sweet potatoes in our garden. Top it with whipped cream.

—BONNIE HOLCOMB FULTON, MISSISSIPPI

PREP: 15 MIN. **BAKE:** 55 MIN. + CHILLING **MAKES:** 8 SERVINGS

- 3 tablespoons all-purpose flour
- 1⅔ cups sugar
- ¼ teaspoon ground nutmeg
  Dash salt
- 1 cup mashed sweet potatoes
- 2 eggs
- ¼ cup light corn syrup
- ½ cup butter, softened
- ¾ cup evaporated milk
- 1 unbaked pastry shell (9 inches)

1. In a small bowl, combine the flour, sugar, nutmeg and salt. In a large bowl, beat the potatoes, eggs, corn syrup, butter and sugar mixture. Gradually stir in milk. Pour into pastry shell.

2. Bake at 350° for 55-60 minutes. Cool on a wire rack for 1 hour. Refrigerate pie for at least 3 hours before serving. Refrigerate leftovers.

THE OZARKS

The enormous hills that roll across the south-central U.S. lend a beauty to this region that makes it unlike anyplace else.

In New Orleans, Mardi Gras season begins on Jan. 6—Epiphany, when the wise men brought their gifts to the baby Jesus—and ends on Fat Tuesday, the day before Ash Wednesday. During this season, king cake parties are held all over the region. A small plastic baby is traditionally hidden in the king cake. The person who finds this good-luck charm gets to host the party the following year.

NEW ORLEANS, LA

During Mardi Gras, you'll likely notice a color scheme. The hues have special meaning: gold for power, green for faith and purple for justice.

Traditional New Orleans King Cake

Get in on the fun of the king cake. Hide a little toy baby in the cake and whoever finds it has one year of good luck!

—**REBECCA BAIRD** SALT LAKE CITY, UTAH

PREP: 40 MIN. + RISING **BAKE:** 25 MIN. + COOLING **MAKES:** 1 CAKE (12 SLICES)

2 packages (¼ ounce each) active dry yeast
½ cup warm water (110° to 115°)
¾ cup sugar, divided
½ cup butter, softened
½ cup warm 2% milk (110° to 115°)
2 egg yolks
1¼ teaspoons salt
1 teaspoon grated lemon peel
¼ teaspoon ground nutmeg
3¼ to 3¾ cups all-purpose flour
1 teaspoon ground cinnamon
1 egg, beaten

GLAZE
1½ cups confectioners' sugar
2 teaspoons lemon juice
2 to 3 tablespoons water
Green, purple and yellow sugars

1. In a large bowl, dissolve yeast in warm water. Add ½ cup sugar, butter, milk, egg yolks, salt, lemon peel, nutmeg and 2 cups flour. Beat until smooth. Stir in enough remaining flour to form a soft dough (dough will be sticky).

2. Turn onto a floured surface; knead until smooth and elastic, about 6-8 minutes. Place in a greased bowl, turning once to grease the top. Cover and let rise in a warm place until doubled, about 1 hour.

3. Punch dough down. Turn onto a lightly floured surface. Roll into a 16x10-in. rectangle. Combine cinnamon and remaining sugar; sprinkle over dough to within ½ in. of edges. Roll up jelly-roll style, starting with a long side; pinch seam to seal. Place seam side down on a greased baking sheet; pinch ends together to form a ring. Cover and let rise until doubled, about 1 hour. Brush with egg.

4. Bake at 375° for 25-30 minutes or until golden brown. Cool completely on a wire rack. For glaze, combine the confectioners' sugar, lemon juice and enough water to achieve desired consistency. Spread over cake. Sprinkle with colored sugars.

Mississippi Mud Cake

This rich cake is ideal for special occasions. It's a smaller cake, so if you're watching your weight, you won't have to worry about being tempted with leftovers.

—PRISCILLA PRESCOTT FOREST CITY, NORTH CAROLINA

PREP: 30 MIN. **BAKE:** 30 MIN. + COOLING **MAKES:** 6 SERVINGS

- ¼ cup butter, softened
- ½ cup sugar
- 1 egg
- ½ teaspoon vanilla extract
- ¼ cup all-purpose flour
- 3 tablespoons baking cocoa
- ¼ teaspoon salt
- 2 tablespoons chopped pecans

FROSTING
- 3 tablespoons butter
- 1 tablespoon plus 2 teaspoons 2% milk
- 2 teaspoons baking cocoa
- 1 cup confectioners' sugar
- ⅛ teaspoon vanilla extract
- ⅓ cup marshmallow creme
- 2 tablespoons coarsely chopped pecans

1. Coat a 6-in. springform pan with cooking spray and dust with flour; set aside. In a small bowl, cream butter and sugar until light and fluffy. Beat in egg and vanilla. Combine the flour, cocoa and salt; stir into creamed mixture just until blended. Stir in pecans.

2. Transfer to prepared pan. Bake at 350° for 30-35 minutes or until a toothpick inserted in center comes out clean.

3. For frosting, in a small saucepan, combine the butter, milk and cocoa; bring to a boil. Remove from the heat; beat in confectioners' sugar and vanilla.

4. Place the springform pan on a wire rack. Immediately spread marshmallow creme over hot cake. Drop 2 tablespoons of frosting over creme; cut through with a knife to swirl. Cool completely.

5. Carefully run a knife around edge of pan to loosen; remove sides of pan. Spread remaining frosting over top and sides of cake. Sprinkle with pecans.

MISSISSIPPI

Mississippi's other big river, the Pascagoula, is mighty in its own right. Flowing through the southeast part of the state, it's the largest undammed river in the continental U.S. and offers plenty of opportunities for outdoor recreation.

Sorghum, a grass native to East Africa, may have been introduced to U.S. agriculture by Benjamin Franklin. By the mid-1800s, sorghum was being boiled down into molasses-like syrup. Today, sorghum has a wide variety of other uses, from a gluten-free grain substitute for flour and livestock feed to building materials and fencing.

TEXAS

The Lone Star State is the second-largest producer of sorghum in the U.S., after Kansas. Oklahoma comes in third.

Sorghum Cookies

Sorghum syrup, a natural sweetener that was a 19th century staple, is making a comeback these days. My family makes syrup from our homegrown sorghum cane. I use it for baking treats, like these delicious, soft, old-fashioned cookies.

—**JENNIFER KRAMER** LYNNVILLE, IOWA

PREP: 30 MIN. **BAKE:** 10 MIN./BATCH
MAKES: ABOUT 2½ DOZEN

- 1 **cup butter, softened**
- 1⅓ **cups sugar**
- 2 **eggs**
- ¼ **cup sorghum syrup**
- 1 **teaspoon grated orange peel**
- 3 **cups all-purpose flour**
- 1 **teaspoon baking soda**
- 1 **teaspoon baking powder**
- 1 **teaspoon ground cinnamon**
- ¼ **teaspoon salt**
- ¼ **teaspoon each ground cloves, cardamom and nutmeg**

1. In a large bowl, cream butter and sugar until light and fluffy. Beat in the eggs, syrup and orange peel. Combine the flour, baking soda, baking powder, cinnamon, salt, cloves, cardamom and nutmeg; gradually add to creamed mixture and mix well.

2. Drop the dough by tablespoonfuls 2 in. apart onto ungreased baking sheets. Bake at 375° for 10-12 minutes or until set. Remove to wire racks.

New Orleans Bread Pudding

For an extra-special dessert, try this sweet and buttery bread pudding. The cowboys we serve it to say it tastes like home.

—**LINDA WIESE** PAYETTE, IDAHO

PREP: 35 MIN. **BAKE:** 35 MIN. **MAKES:** 12 SERVINGS

- ½ **cup raisins**
- ¼ **cup brandy or unsweetened apple juice**
- ½ **cup butter, melted, divided**
- 1 **tablespoon sugar**
- 4 **eggs, lightly beaten**
- 2 **cups half-and-half cream**
- 1 **cup packed brown sugar**
- 2 **teaspoons vanilla extract**
- ½ **teaspoon salt**
- ½ **teaspoon freshly ground nutmeg**
- 10 **slices day-old French bread (1 inch thick), cubed**

SAUCE
- ½ **cup packed brown sugar**
- 2 **tablespoons cornstarch**
  Dash salt
- 1 **cup cold water**
- 1 **tablespoon butter**
- 2 **teaspoons vanilla extract**

1. In a small saucepan, combine raisins and brandy. Bring to a boil. Remove from the heat; cover and set aside. Brush a shallow 2½-qt. baking dish with 1 tablespoon butter; sprinkle with sugar and set aside.

2. In a large bowl, combine the eggs, cream, brown sugar, vanilla, salt and nutmeg. Stir in remaining butter and reserved raisin mixture. Gently stir in bread; let stand for 15 minutes or until bread is softened.

3. Transfer to prepared dish. Bake, uncovered, at 350° for 35-40 minutes or until a knife inserted near the center comes out clean.

4. For sauce, in a small saucepan, combine the brown sugar, cornstarch and salt; gradually add water. Bring to a boil; cook and stir for 1-2 minutes or until thickened. Remove from the heat; stir in butter and vanilla. Serve with bread pudding.

Chocolate Moon Pies

I love chocolate and this recipes always satisfies my craving for chocolate. A rich, buttery filling is sandwiched between moist chocolate cookies.

—ROZ KEIMIG GUYMON, OKLAHOMA

PREP: 20 MIN. **BAKE:** 10 MIN./BATCH + COOLING
MAKES: 2 DOZEN

- ⅔ cup dark chocolate chips
- ½ cup butter, cubed
- 2 cups all-purpose flour
- ⅔ cup sugar
- ⅓ cup packed brown sugar
- ¼ cup baking cocoa
- ½ teaspoon baking soda
- ¼ teaspoon salt
- 1 egg, beaten
- ½ cup buttermilk
- 1 teaspoon vanilla extract
- ¼ teaspoon almond extract

FILLING
- ⅔ cup dark chocolate chips
- ¼ cup butter, cubed
- 4 ounces cream cheese, softened
- 1 jar (7 ounces) marshmallow creme
- ¼ teaspoon almond extract
- 1 cup miniature semisweet chocolate chips

1. In a microwave, melt chocolate chips and butter; stir until smooth. Cool.

2. In a large bowl, combine the flour, sugars, cocoa, baking soda and salt. Combine the egg, buttermilk, extracts and cooled chocolate mixture; add to dry ingredients and beat just until moistened (batter will be very thick).

3. Drop by tablespoonfuls or with a small scoop 2 in. apart onto parchment paper-lined baking sheets.

4. Bake at 350° for 8-10 minutes or until edges are set. Cool for 2 minutes before removing from pans to wire racks to cool completely.

5. For filling, melt chocolate chips and butter; stir until smooth. Cool. In a small bowl, beat the cream cheese, marshmallow creme and almond extract until smooth. Beat in cooled chocolate mixture. Spread 1 heaping teaspoon of filling on the bottoms of half of the cookies; top with remaining cookies.

6. Roll sides of cookies in miniature chocolate chips. Store in the refrigerator.

Orange Meringue Pie

If you love lemon meringue pie, you're sure to be delighted with my citrus twist on the traditional favorite. Try this pie the next time you have company, and you're sure to be asked for the recipe.

—KARYN LEE WEST COLUMBIA, SOUTH CAROLINA

PREP: 30 MIN. + CHILLING **BAKE:** 15 MIN. + COOLING
MAKES: 6-8 SERVINGS

- ¾ cup sugar
- ¼ cup cornstarch
- 1½ cups orange juice
- 3 egg yolks, lightly beaten
- 1 tablespoon butter

MERINGUE
- 3 egg whites
- 6 tablespoons sugar
- 1 pastry shell (9 inches), baked
  Orange peel strips, optional

1. In a large saucepan, combine sugar and cornstarch. Stir in orange juice until smooth. Cook and stir over medium-high heat until thickened and bubbly. Reduce heat; cook and stir 2 minutes longer. Remove from the heat. Stir ½ cup hot mixture into egg yolks; return all to the pan, stirring constantly. Bring to a gentle boil; cook and stir 2 minutes longer. Stir in butter; keep warm.

2. In a small bowl, beat the egg whites on medium speed until foamy. Gradually beat in sugar, 1 tablespoon at a time, on high just until stiff peaks form and sugar is dissolved. Pour hot filling into pastry shell. Spread meringue over filling, sealing edges to crust.

3. Bake at 375° for 15 minutes or until the meringue is golden brown. Cool on a wire rack for 1 hour.

4. Refrigerate for at least 3 hours before serving. Garnish with orange peel if desired. Refrigerate leftovers.

◀● dishing about food

Chattanooga Bakery in Chattanooga, Tennessee, invented Moon Pies in 1917. The shop had opened 15 years earlier to use excess flour from the Mountain City Milling Co. The town of Bell Buckle, about 90 miles away, honors the iconic regional treat every year at the RC Cola-Moon Pie Festival, which also gives a nod to the soda so popular in the South.

BELL BUCKLE, TN

It has just over 500 year-round residents, but Bell Buckle's population swells in June during the RC Cola-Moon Pie Festival.

" These muffins are one of the first things my husband, U.S. Army Major John Duda Jr., gets hungry for when he's home from deployment. I make sure to have my overripe bananas ready. These are a family tradition.**"**

—KIMBERLY DUDA
SANFORD, NORTH CAROLINA

Favorite Banana Chip Muffins

PREP: 20 MIN. **BAKE:** 20 MIN. **MAKES:** ABOUT 1 DOZEN

1½ cups all-purpose flour
⅔ cup sugar
1 teaspoon baking soda
¼ teaspoon ground cinnamon
⅛ teaspoon salt
1 egg
1⅓ cups mashed ripe bananas (about 3 medium)
⅓ cup butter, melted
1 teaspoon vanilla extract
½ cup semisweet chocolate chips

1. Preheat oven to 375°. In a large bowl, whisk flour, sugar, baking soda, cinnamon and salt. In another bowl, whisk egg, bananas, melted butter and vanilla until blended. Add to flour mixture; stir just until moistened. Fold in chocolate chips.

2. Fill greased or paper-lined muffin cups three-fourths full. Bake 17-20 minutes or until a toothpick inserted in center comes out clean. Cool 5 minutes before removing from pan to a wire rack. Serve warm.

Benne Wafers

These are very special cookies served often in the South. They're perfect with tea or coffee. My whole family loves them.

—**MAXINE TRIVELY** HIGHLANDS, NORTH CAROLINA

PREP: 10 MIN. **BAKE:** 10 MIN./BATCH + COOLING **MAKES:** ABOUT 9 DOZEN

1¼ **cups butter, softened**
2 **cups packed brown sugar**
1 **egg**
1 **teaspoon vanilla extract**
1 **cup all-purpose flour**
½ **teaspoon baking powder**
¼ **teaspoon salt**
1 **cup sesame seeds, toasted and cooled**

1. In a bowl, cream the butter and brown sugar; add egg and vanilla. Combine remaining ingredients; add to the creamed mixture.

2. Drop by teaspoonfuls 2 in. apart onto greased baking sheets. Bake at 350° for 7-9 minutes or until golden brown. Cool on pan for 30 seconds before removing to a wire rack to cool completely.

◀● **dishing about food**

The word benne, meaning sesame, is derived from an African dialect. Sesame was one of the many African crops introduced to Southern agriculture. Sesame seeds have a nutty aroma and buttery taste. Benne wafers are a specialty of Charleston, South Carolina.

MOUNT PLEASANT, SC

It's said that people take more photos of Boone Hall Plantation, a Charleston-area gem, than any other in the country. Visit for cultural festivals, history lessons and tours of the verdant grounds.

Lemonade Icebox Pie

You will detect a definite lemonade flavor in this refreshing pie. High and fluffy, the dessert has a creamy, smooth consistency that we really appreciate.

—**CHERYL WILT** EGLON, WEST VIRGINIA

PREP: 15 MIN. + CHILLING **MAKES:** 8 SERVINGS

1 package (8 ounces) cream cheese, softened
1 can (14 ounces) sweetened condensed milk
¾ cup thawed lemonade concentrate
1 carton (8 ounces) frozen whipped topping, thawed
  Yellow food coloring, optional
1 graham cracker crust (9 inches)

1. In a large bowl, beat cream cheese and milk until smooth. Beat in lemonade concentrate. Fold in whipped topping and food coloring if desired. Pour into crust. Cover and refrigerate until set. Store in the refrigerator.

Blackberry Cobbler

PREP: 25 MIN. **BAKE:** 30 MIN. **MAKES:** 9 SERVINGS

- 3 cups fresh or frozen blackberries
- 1 cup sugar
- ¼ teaspoon ground cinnamon
- 3 tablespoons cornstarch
- 1 cup cold water
- 1 tablespoon butter

BISCUIT TOPPING
- 1½ cups all-purpose flour
- 1 tablespoon sugar
- 1½ teaspoons baking powder
- ½ teaspoon salt
- ½ cup cold butter, cubed
- ½ cup 2% milk
  - Whipped topping or vanilla ice cream, optional

1. In a large saucepan, combine blackberries, sugar and cinnamon. Cook and stir until mixture comes to a boil. Combine cornstarch and water until smooth; stir into fruit mixture. Bring to a boil; cook and stir for 2 minutes or until thickened. Pour into a greased 8-in. square baking dish. Dot with butter.

2. For topping, in a small bowl, combine the flour, sugar, baking powder and salt. Cut in butter until mixture resembles coarse crumbs. Stir in the milk just until moistened. Drop by tablespoonfuls onto hot berry mixture.

3. Bake, uncovered, at 350° for 30-35 minutes or until filling is bubbly and topping is golden brown. Serve warm with whipped topping or ice cream.

> " I love to pull our homegrown blackberries out of the freezer in winter and make this warm cobbler to enjoy summer's sweetness. "

—LORI DANIELS
BEVERLY, WEST VIRGINIA

Midwest

Welcome to the area known as the breadbasket of the country! Featuring hearty breads, rolls and biscuits among its many comfort foods, the Midwest delivers all of the stick-to-your-ribs favorites that today's families crave. This area's rich farmland attracted settlers from Sweden, Norway, Germany, Poland and Greece—and they brought with them the beer, sausages, roasts, meatballs and cheeses everyone loves! You'll also discover tasty rice and veggie side dishes as well as desserts you'll turn to time and again.

Coffee Beef Pot Roast

PREP: 5 MIN. **COOK:** 9½ HOURS **MAKES:** 10-12 SERVINGS

- 2 **medium onions, thinly sliced**
- 2 **garlic cloves, minced**
- 1 **boneless beef chuck roast (3½ to 4 pounds), quartered**
- 1 **cup brewed coffee**
- ¼ **cup soy sauce**
- ¼ **cup cornstarch**
- 6 **tablespoons cold water**

1. Place half of the onions in a 5-qt. slow cooker. Top with garlic and half of the beef. Top with remaining onion and beef. Combine coffee and soy sauce; pour over beef. Cover and cook on low for 9-10 hours or until the meat is tender.

2. Combine cornstarch and water until smooth; stir into cooking juices. Cover and cook on high for 30 minutes or until the gravy is thickened.

◄● dishing about food

In 1965, Minnesota declared walleye the state fish. Many towns, including five in Minnesota, claim to be the Walleye Capital of the World. Interestingly, two towns named Garrison, one in Minnesota and the other in North Dakota, also make that claim.

GARRISON, ND

GARRISON

If you're at Garrison's City Park, you sure won't miss the tribute to this central North Dakota town's claim to fame: Wally the Walleye is 26 feet long!

Crunchy-Coated Walleye

Potato flakes make a golden coating for these fish fillets, which are a breeze to fry on the stovetop. It's a fabulous way to cook up the catch of the day!

—SONDRA OSTHEIMER BOSCOBEL, WISCONSIN

PREP/TOTAL TIME: 20 MIN. **MAKES:** 4 SERVINGS

⅓ cup all-purpose flour
1 teaspoon paprika
½ teaspoon salt
¼ teaspoon pepper
¼ teaspoon onion powder
¼ teaspoon garlic powder
2 eggs
2¼ pounds walleye, perch or pike fillets
1½ cups mashed potato flakes
⅓ cup canola oil
  Tartar sauce and lemon wedges, optional

1. In a shallow bowl, combine flour, paprika, salt, pepper, onion powder and garlic powder. In another bowl, beat the eggs. Dip both sides of fillets in flour mixture and eggs, then coat with potato flakes.

2. In a large skillet, fry the fillets in oil for 5 minutes on each side or until fish flakes easily with a fork. Serve with tartar sauce and lemon if desired.

SOUTH HAVEN, MI

It's only natural that the Highbush Blueberry Capital of the World would host the National Blueberry Festival! For five decades, residents of South Haven and beyond have looked forward to its pie-eating contests, pageants, concerts, bake-offs and more.

Blueberry French Toast Cobbler

Every summer I pick fresh blueberries and freeze them with this family favorite in mind. It's a great way to recapture the warmth of past summer days on chilly Midwestern mornings.

—MARIE HERR BEREA, OHIO

PREP: 20 MIN. + CHILLING   **BAKE:** 30 MIN.   **MAKES:** 6-8 SERVINGS

  4   eggs
  ½   cup milk
  1   teaspoon vanilla extract
  ¼   teaspoon baking powder
 10   slices day-old French bread (¾ inch thick)
 4½   cups unsweetened frozen blueberries
  ½   cup sugar
  2   tablespoons butter, melted
  1   teaspoon cornstarch
  1   teaspoon ground cinnamon
  1   tablespoon butter, softened

1. In a large bowl, beat the eggs, milk, vanilla and baking powder until smooth. Pour into a large shallow baking dish. Add bread slices, turning once to coat. Cover and chill for 8 hours or overnight.

2. In a large bowl, combine the blueberries, sugar, melted butter, cornstarch and cinnamon. Pour into a greased 13x9-in. baking dish. Cover and chill 8 hours or overnight.

3. Remove both pans from the refrigerator 30 minutes before baking. Place prepared bread on top of blueberry mixture. Spread softened butter on top.

4. Bake, uncovered, at 400° for 30-35 minutes or until toast is golden brown and blueberries are bubbly.

Pizza Tot Casserole

For a new spin on a classic casserole, try my easy version. You can also add your own family's favorite pizza toppings!

—SHARON SKILDUM MAPLE GROVE, MINNESOTA

PREP: 10 MIN. **BAKE:** 35 MIN. **MAKES:** 8 SERVINGS

- 1½ pounds ground beef
- 1 medium green pepper, chopped, optional
- 1 medium onion, chopped
- ½ pound sliced fresh mushrooms
- 1 can (15 ounces) pizza sauce
- 1 teaspoon dried basil
- 3 cups (12 ounces) shredded part-skim mozzarella cheese
- 1 package (32 ounces) frozen Tater Tots
- 1 cup (4 ounces) shredded cheddar cheese

1. In a large skillet, cook the beef, green pepper, onion and mushrooms over medium heat until meat is no longer pink; drain. Add pizza sauce and basil.

2. Transfer to a greased 3-qt. baking dish. Top with mozzarella cheese and potatoes. Bake, uncovered, at 400° for 30-35 minutes or until potatoes are lightly browned.

3. Sprinkle with the cheddar cheese; bake 5 minutes longer or until cheese is melted.

Cashew Chicken

I love to cook and bake for my family and friends. I season this chicken-and-rice casserole with ground ginger, then stir in some crunchy cashews.

—BONNIE DEVRIES BRAINERD, MINNESOTA

PREP: 10 MIN. **BAKE:** 45 MIN. **MAKES:** 4 SERVINGS

- 1 pound boneless skinless chicken breasts, cut into 1-inch cubes
- 1 medium onion, chopped
- 2 cups frozen broccoli cuts
- 1¾ cups boiling water
- 1 cup uncooked long grain rice
- 1 jar (6 ounces) sliced mushrooms, drained
- 1 tablespoon chicken bouillon granules
- ½ to 1 teaspoon ground ginger
  Pepper to taste
- ¾ cup salted cashews, divided

1. In a large bowl, combine the first nine ingredients. Transfer to a greased shallow 1½-qt. baking dish.

2. Cover and bake at 375° for 45-55 minutes or until rice is tender and chicken is no longer pink. Stir in ½ cup of cashews. Sprinkle with remaining cashews.

TWO HARBORS, MN

From forests and lakes to bluffs and prairieland, breathtaking Minnesota terrain beckons nature lovers. Here's the Gooseberry River in Gooseberry Falls State Park.

The first deep-dish pizza was served in 1943, at Pizzeria Uno on the corner of Wabash and Ohio in Chicago. There have been several takes on the style since then from other restaurants. This knife-and-fork pizza is now a hit around the world.

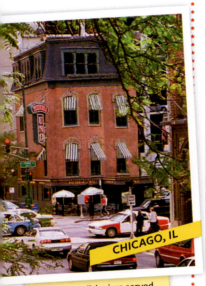

CHICAGO, IL

The deep-dish pizza served by Pizzeria Uno is so popular, it's generated a national chain: Uno Chicago Grill!

Chicago Deep-Dish Pizza

Since I live near Chicago, I've managed to sample more than my share of deep-dish pizzas. This recipe lets you re-create the best my town offers—right there in your town!
—**LYNN HAMILTON** NAPERVILLE, ILLINOIS

PREP: 40 MIN. + RISING **BAKE:** 40 MIN.
MAKES: 12 SERVINGS

- 2 to 2½ cups all-purpose flour
- ¼ cup cornmeal
- 1 package (¼ ounce) quick-rise yeast
- 1½ teaspoons sugar
- ½ teaspoon salt
- 1 cup water
- ⅓ cup olive oil

TOPPINGS

- ½ pound sliced fresh mushrooms
- 4 teaspoons olive oil, divided
- 1 can (28 ounces) diced tomatoes, well drained
- 1 can (8 ounces) tomato sauce
- 1 can (6 ounces) tomato paste
- 2 to 3 garlic cloves, minced
- ½ teaspoon salt
- ¼ teaspoon dried basil
- ¼ teaspoon dried oregano
- ¼ teaspoon pepper
- 3 cups (12 ounces) shredded part-skim mozzarella cheese, divided
- 1 pound bulk Italian sausage, cooked and crumbled
- 24 slices pepperoni, optional
- ½ cup grated Parmesan cheese
  Thinly sliced fresh basil leaves, optional

1. In a large bowl, combine 1½ cups flour, cornmeal, yeast, sugar and salt. In a small saucepan, heat water and oil to 120°-130°. Add to dry ingredients; beat just until moistened. Stir in enough of the remaining flour to form a soft dough.

2. Turn onto a floured surface; knead until smooth and elastic, about 6-8 minutes. Place in a greased bowl, turning once to grease the top. Cover and let rise in warm place until doubled, about 30 minutes.

3. In a large skillet, cook and stir mushrooms in 2 teaspoons oil over medium-high heat until tender. In a small bowl, mix tomatoes, tomato sauce, tomato paste, garlic and seasonings.

4. Generously grease a 13x9-in. baking pan or dish with the remaining 2 teaspoons oil. Punch dough down. Roll out into a 15x11-in. rectangle. Transfer to prepared pan, pressing onto the bottom and halfway up the sides of the pan. Sprinkle with 2 cups mozzarella cheese.

5. Spoon half of the sauce over the cheese (save remaining sauce for other use or use for dipping). Layer with the sausage, sauteed mushrooms and, if desired, pepperoni; top with the remaining mozzarella cheese and Parmesan cheese.

6. Cover and bake at 450° for 35 minutes. Uncover; bake about 5 minutes longer or until lightly browned. Sprinkle with basil if desired.

Hungarian Goulash

My son shared this recipe with me many years ago. You will love how easily this slow-cooked version of a beloved ethnic dish comes together.

—JACKIE KOHN DULUTH, MINNESOTA

PREP: 15 MIN. **COOK:** 8 HOURS **MAKES:** 6-8 SERVINGS

- 2 pounds beef top round steak, cut into 1-inch cubes
- 1 cup chopped onion
- 2 tablespoons all-purpose flour
- 1½ teaspoons paprika
- 1 teaspoon garlic salt
- ½ teaspoon pepper
- 1 can (14½ ounces) diced tomatoes, undrained
- 1 bay leaf
- 1 cup (8 ounces) sour cream
  Hot cooked egg noodles

1. Place beef and onion in a 3-qt. slow cooker. Combine the flour, paprika, garlic salt and pepper; sprinkle over beef and stir to coat. Stir in tomatoes; add bay leaf. Cover and cook on low for 8-10 hours or until meat is tender.

2. Discard bay leaf. Just before serving, stir in sour cream; heat through. Serve with noodles.

Salisbury Steak with Gravy

Here's a lightened-up twist on classic comfort food. The recipe was shared at a weight-management meeting I attended, and my whole family really enjoys it. I like that it's so tasty and quick to prepare.

—DANELLE WEIHER VERNDALE, MINNESOTA

PREP: 15 MIN. **BAKE:** 50 MIN. **MAKES:** 4 SERVINGS

- ½ cup fat-free milk
- 14 fat-free saltines, crushed
- 2 tablespoons dried minced onion
- 2 teaspoons dried parsley flakes
- 1 pound lean ground beef (90% lean)
- 1 jar (12 ounces) fat-free beef gravy
- 2 tablespoons ketchup
- 2 teaspoons Worcestershire sauce
- ¼ teaspoon pepper

1. In a large bowl, combine the milk, saltines, onion and parsley. Crumble beef over mixture and mix well. Shape into four patties. Place in an 8-in. square baking dish coated with cooking spray.

2. In a small bowl, combine gravy, ketchup, Worcestershire and pepper; pour over patties. Bake, uncovered, at 350° for 50-55 minutes or until a thermometer reads 160°.

CLEVELAND, OH

For a period in the 20th century, this Ohio city had the second-largest Hungarian population in the world! The first, of course, was Hungary.

Marinated Ribeyes

We have these tempting steaks weekly. If neighbors happen to drop by when I'm preparing them, I cube the meat and grill it on skewers with onions and mushrooms.

—ROSALIE USRY FLAXTON, NORTH DAKOTA

PREP: 10 MIN. + MARINATING **GRILL:** 10 MIN.
MAKES: 2 SERVINGS

- 2 beef ribeye steaks (about 1 inch thick and 12 ounces each)
- ⅓ cup hot water
- 3 tablespoons finely chopped onion
- 2 tablespoons red wine vinegar
- 2 tablespoons olive oil
- 2 tablespoons soy sauce
- 1 teaspoon beef bouillon granules
- 1 garlic clove, minced
- ½ teaspoon paprika
- ½ teaspoon coarsely ground pepper

1. Pierce both sides of steaks several times with a fork. In a small bowl, combine remaining ingredients. Remove ½ cup marinade to another bowl; cover and refrigerate until serving. Pour remaining marinade into a large resealable plastic bag; add steaks. Seal bag and turn to coat; cover and refrigerate overnight.

2. Drain and discard marinade. Grill steaks, covered, over medium heat for 5-7 minutes on each side or until meat reaches desired doneness (for medium-rare, a thermometer should read 145°; medium, 160°; well-done, 170°). Warm reserved marinade; serve with the steaks.

Bacon-Wrapped Meat Loaf

Our family and friends love this no-fail recipe. It's a staple in our home. A topping of bacon adds wonderful flavor to the moist meat loaf. And the brown sugar-ketchup glaze takes it to a whole new level. Yum!

—ZAC FREEMAN AND PAIGE PONDER CHICAGO, ILLINOIS

PREP: 40 MIN. **BAKE:** 50 MIN. **MAKES:** 8 SERVINGS

- 1 medium onion, chopped
- 2 garlic cloves, minced
- 2 teaspoons canola oil
- ½ cup 2% milk
- 2 eggs, lightly beaten
- 2 teaspoons Worcestershire sauce
- 2 teaspoons Dijon mustard
- ¼ teaspoon hot pepper sauce
- ⅔ cup crushed saltines
- ⅓ cup minced fresh parsley
- 1 teaspoon salt
- ½ teaspoon pepper
- ½ teaspoon dried thyme
- 1 pound ground beef
- ½ pound ground pork
- ½ pound ground veal
- 9 slices bacon strips

SAUCE
- ½ cup ketchup
- ¼ cup packed brown sugar
- ¼ cup cider vinegar

1. In a small skillet, saute onion and garlic in oil for 4-5 minutes or until tender.

2. Meanwhile, in a large bowl, combine milk, eggs, Worcestershire sauce, Dijon, pepper sauce, saltines, parsley and seasonings; stir in onion mixture. Crumble meats over mixture and mix well. With wet hands, shape into a loaf and place in a greased foil-lined 13x9-in. baking dish.

3. In a small saucepan, combine the sauce ingredients; cook and stir until the sugar is dissolved and sauce has thickened. Spoon some sauce over loaf; place bacon over top.

4. Bake, uncovered, at 350° for 50-55 minutes or until no pink remains and a thermometer reads 160°.

Sauerkraut Meatballs

This zesty recipe is a great way to pep up a party! The hot pork sausage and sauerkraut make terrific-tasting meatballs, and the mustard dipping sauce is a nice complement.

—**CHRISTINE BATTS** MURRAY, KENTUCKY

PREP/TOTAL TIME: 30 MIN. **MAKES:** ABOUT 2 DOZEN

- ½ **pound bulk spicy pork sausage**
- ¼ **cup finely chopped onion**
- 1 **can (14 ounces) sauerkraut, rinsed, drained and finely chopped**
- 2 **tablespoons plus ¾ cup dry bread crumbs, divided**
- 1 **package (3 ounces) cream cheese, softened**
- 2 **tablespoons minced fresh parsley**
- ½ **teaspoon ground mustard**
- ¼ **teaspoon garlic salt**
- ⅛ **teaspoon pepper**
- ¼ **cup all-purpose flour**
- 2 **eggs**
- ¼ **cup milk**
-    **Oil for deep-fat frying**
- ½ **cup mayonnaise**
- 2 **tablespoons spicy brown mustard**

1. In a skillet, cook sausage and onion over medium heat until meat is no longer pink and onion is tender; drain. Stir in sauerkraut and 2 tablespoons bread crumbs; set aside. In a small bowl, combine the cream cheese, parsley, mustard, garlic salt and pepper; stir into the sauerkraut mixture. Cover and refrigerate for at least 1 hour or overnight.

2. Shape into ¾-in. balls; roll in the flour. In a small bowl, beat eggs and milk. Dip meatballs into the egg mixture, then roll in remaining bread crumbs.

3. In an electric skillet, heat 2 in. of oil to 375°. Fry meatballs until golden brown; drain. Combine mayonnaise and mustard; serve with meatballs. Refrigerate leftovers.

Sausage and Pumpkin Pasta

PREP: 20 MIN. **COOK:** 15 MIN. **MAKES:** 4 SERVINGS

- 2 **cups uncooked multigrain bow tie pasta**
- ½ **pound Italian turkey sausage links, casings removed**
- ½ **pound sliced fresh mushrooms**
- 1 **medium onion, chopped**
- 4 **garlic cloves, minced**
- 1 **cup reduced-sodium chicken broth**
- 1 **cup canned pumpkin**
- ½ **cup white wine or additional reduced-sodium chicken broth**
- ½ **teaspoon rubbed sage**
- ¼ **teaspoon salt**
- ¼ **teaspoon garlic powder**
- ¼ **teaspoon pepper**
- ¼ **cup grated Parmesan cheese**
- 1 **tablespoon dried parsley flakes**

1. Cook the pasta according to the package directions.

2. Meanwhile, in a large nonstick skillet coated with cooking spray, cook the sausage, mushrooms and onion over medium heat until meat is no longer pink. Add the garlic; cook 1 minute longer. Stir in broth, pumpkin, wine, sage, salt, garlic powder and pepper. Bring to a boil. Reduce heat; simmer, uncovered, for 5-6 minutes or until slightly thickened.

3. Drain pasta; add to the skillet and heat through. Just before serving, sprinkle with cheese and parsley.

" Pumpkin and white wine flavor this delightful pasta with Italian turkey sausage. It makes an easy weekday meal that's nice enough to serve to company. "

—**KATIE WOLLGAST**
FLORISSANT, MISSOURI

DAKOTAS & MINNESOTA

Once a crop cultivated in many states, beautiful blue flax now comes primarily from the Dakotas and Minnesota. You can grow it in your backyard, too!

Flaxseed Oatmeal Pancakes

I came up with this healthy and really tasty recipe because my husband loves pancakes. They have a great texture and cinnamon taste.

—**SHARON HANSEN** PONTIAC, ILLINOIS

PREP/TOTAL TIME: 20 MIN. **MAKES:** 4 PANCAKES

- ⅓ cup whole wheat flour
- 3 tablespoons quick-cooking oats
- 1 tablespoon flaxseed
- ½ teaspoon baking powder
- ¼ teaspoon ground cinnamon
- ⅛ teaspoon baking soda
   Dash salt
- 1 egg, separated
- ½ cup buttermilk
- 1 tablespoon brown sugar
- 1 tablespoon canola oil
- ½ teaspoon vanilla extract

1. In a large bowl, combine the first seven ingredients. In a small bowl, whisk the egg yolk, buttermilk, brown sugar, oil and vanilla; stir into dry ingredients just until moistened.

2. In a small bowl, beat egg white on medium speed until stiff peaks form. Fold into batter.

3. Pour batter by ¼ cupfuls onto a hot griddle coated with cooking spray; turn when bubbles form on top. Cook until the second side is golden brown.

Swedish Meatballs

Nutmeg, allspice and cardamom lend a little something extra to the traditional taste of these moist meatballs. The creamy sauce has a rich beefy flavor with a touch of dill.

—TASTE OF HOME TEST KITCHEN

PREP/TOTAL TIME: 30 MIN. **MAKES:** 4 SERVINGS

- ½ cup soft bread crumbs
- 1 medium onion, chopped
- 1 egg, lightly beaten
- 2 tablespoons heavy whipping cream
- ½ teaspoon salt
- ⅛ teaspoon ground nutmeg
- ⅛ teaspoon ground allspice
- ⅛ teaspoon ground cardamom
- ¾ pound lean ground beef (90% lean)
- ½ pound ground pork

GRAVY
- 2 tablespoons butter
- 2 tablespoons all-purpose flour
- 1 cup beef broth
- ½ cup heavy whipping cream
- ¼ teaspoon dill weed
- ¼ cup minced fresh parsley, optional

1. In a large bowl, combine the first eight ingredients. Crumble the beef and pork over mixture and mix well. Shape into 1½-in. meatballs. Place the meatballs on a greased rack in a shallow baking pan. Bake at 400° for 11-12 minutes or until a thermometer reads 160°; drain.

2. Meanwhile, in a large saucepan, melt butter. Stir in flour until smooth; gradually add broth. Bring to a boil; cook and stir for 1-2 minutes or until thickened. Stir in cream and dill; simmer for 1 minute. Place meatballs in a serving dish; pour gravy over top. Garnish with parsley if desired.

Schreiner's Baked Lamb Shanks

This recipe has been on the menu at Bernard Schreiner's restaurant for decades. I started working there as a busboy more than 29 years ago, and baked lamb shanks were a favorite then, too. The recipe was passed down from his mother. It's a comfort food you'll want to share with your own family.

—DALE GRANTMAN DES MOINES, IOWA

PREP: 10 MIN. **BAKE:** 3 HOURS **MAKES:** 4 SERVINGS

- 4 lamb shanks (14 to 16 ounces each)
- ½ teaspoon salt
- ⅛ teaspoon pepper
- 4 cups beef broth
- ½ cup finely chopped onion
- 2 teaspoons dried rosemary, crushed
- 1 teaspoon garlic powder
- 1 teaspoon ground mustard
  Mint jelly, optional

1. Place the lamb shanks in an ungreased 13x9-in. baking pan. Sprinkle with salt and pepper. Bake, uncovered, at 400° for 30 minutes.

2. Remove from the oven and reduce heat to 350°. Add broth to the pan. Combine onion, rosemary, garlic powder and mustard; sprinkle over lamb. Cover tightly and bake for 2½ to 3 hours or until very tender. If desired, make gravy from pan drippings. Serve lamb with gravy and mint jelly if desired.

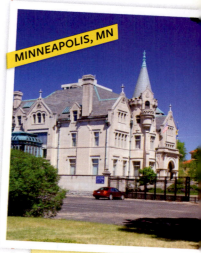

MINNEAPOLIS, MN

Since Minnesota has the highest population of residents of Swedish descent, it makes sense that the American Swedish Institute is there. Visit the museum, housed primarily in Turnblad Mansion, to learn more about Swedish arts and culture—or even to learn the language.

"Rubbed with garden-fresh herbs, this turkey has such a wonderful aroma when it's roasting that it lures everyone into the kitchen. Guests often comment on how moist and flavorful this elegant entree is."

—BECKY GOLDSMITH
EDEN PRAIRE, MINNESOTA

Herb-Roasted Turkey

PREP: 10 MIN. **BAKE:** 4 HOURS **MAKES:** 12-14 SERVINGS

- 1 turkey (14 pounds)
- 1 tablespoon salt
- 1 teaspoon pepper
- 18 sprigs fresh thyme, divided
- 4 medium onions, sliced
- 4 celery ribs, sliced
- 2 medium carrots, sliced
- 3 bay leaves
- 1 tablespoon peppercorns
- ½ cup butter, melted
- 1 teaspoon minced fresh sage or ½ teaspoon rubbed sage
- 1 teaspoon minced fresh thyme or ½ teaspoon dried thyme
- 1 teaspoon minced chives

1. Rub the surface of the turkey and sprinkle cavity with salt and pepper. Place 12 sprigs of thyme in cavity.

2. In a large heavy roasting pan, place onions, celery, carrots, bay leaves, peppercorns and remaining thyme sprigs. Place the turkey, breast side up, over vegetables. Drizzle butter over turkey and sprinkle with minced herbs.

3. Cover loosely with foil. Bake at 325° for 2½ hours. Remove foil; bake 1½ to 2 hours longer or until a meat thermometer reads 180°, basting every 20 minutes.

4. Cover and let stand for 20 minutes before carving. Discard bay leaves and peppercorns; thicken pan drippings for gravy if desired.

Crown Roast with Plum-Apple Stuffing

All eyes will be on this impressive roast when you place it on your dinner table. The fruity combination of golden raisins, dried plums and apples is a nice complement to the pork.

—**MARIE RIZZIO** INTERLOCHEN, MICHIGAN

PREP: 30 MIN. **BAKE:** 3 HOURS + STANDING **MAKES:** 14 SERVINGS

- 1 pork crown roast (14 ribs and about 9 pounds)
- 2 tablespoons all-purpose flour
- 1½ teaspoons kosher salt
- ¼ teaspoon coarsely ground pepper
- ½ cup chopped pitted dried plums
- 1 cup boiling water
- 2½ cups cubed whole wheat bread, toasted
- 1 cup chopped peeled tart apple
- ¼ cup golden raisins
- ¼ cup unsweetened apple juice
- ¼ cup butter, melted
- 2 tablespoons brown sugar
- 1 teaspoon grated lemon peel
- ¼ teaspoon paprika
- ¼ teaspoon ground cinnamon

1. Place roast, rib ends up, in a large shallow roasting pan. Combine the flour, salt and pepper; rub over roast. Cover rib ends with foil. Bake, uncovered, at 350° for 1 hour.

2. Meanwhile, place plums in a large bowl. Cover with boiling water; let stand for 5 minutes. Drain. Stir in the bread cubes, apple, raisins, apple juice, butter, brown sugar, lemon peel, paprika and cinnamon.

3. Carefully spoon stuffing into center of the roast. Bake 45 to 75 minutes longer or until a thermometer reads 145°. Transfer to a warm serving platter. Remove foil. Let roast stand for 10-15 minutes. Cut between ribs to serve.

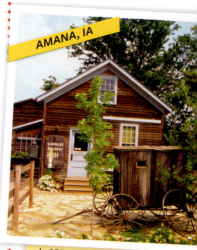

AMANA, IA

In 1855, a group of Germans arrived in Iowa seeking a better life and refuge from religious persecution. There, they set up a communal society. Today, their colonies are a National Historic Landmark.

Cincinnati considers itself the chili capital of the country with chili parlors all over the city! In Cincinnati, chili is served various ways: Two-Way is spaghetti topped with chili; Three-Way adds shredded cheddar cheese; Four-Way, chopped onions; and Five-Way uses kidney or chili beans smothered with spaghetti, chili, cheese and onions. The chili's typically served with oyster crackers. Tom Kiradjieff made Cincinnati-style chili in 1922 for his diner by blending traditional chili ingredients with Greek seasonings.

CINCINNATI, OH

Located on the banks of the Ohio River, the Cincinnati metro area includes northern Kentucky, too. In all, nearly 2 million people live there.

Cincinnati Chili

Cinnamon and cocoa give a rich brown color to this hearty chili.

—**EDITH JOYCE** PARKMAN, OHIO

PREP: 20 MIN. **COOK:** 1¾ HOURS **MAKES:** 8 SERVINGS

- 1 **pound ground beef**
- 1 **pound ground pork**
- 4 **medium onions, chopped**
- 6 **garlic cloves, minced**
- 2 **cans (16 ounces each) kidney beans, rinsed and drained**
- 1 **can (28 ounces) crushed tomatoes**
- ¼ **cup white vinegar**
- ¼ **cup baking cocoa**
- 2 **tablespoons chili powder**
- 2 **tablespoons Worcestershire sauce**
- 4 **teaspoons ground cinnamon**
- 3 **teaspoons dried oregano**
- 2 **teaspoons ground cumin**
- 2 **teaspoons ground allspice**
- 2 **teaspoons hot pepper sauce**
- 3 **bay leaves**
- 1 **teaspoon sugar**
  Salt and pepper to taste
  Hot cooked spaghetti
  Shredded cheddar cheese, sour cream, chopped tomatoes and green onions

1. In a Dutch oven, cook beef, pork and onions over medium heat until meat is no longer pink. Add garlic; cook 1 minute longer. Drain.

2. Add the beans, tomatoes, vinegar, cocoa and seasonings; bring to a boil. Reduce heat; cover and simmer for 1½ hours or until heated through.

3. Discard bay leaves. Serve with spaghetti. Garnish with cheese, sour cream, tomatoes and onions.

Beef Gyros

Going out to restaurants for gyros can be expensive, so I came up with this homemade version. Usually, I set out the fixings so everyone can assemble their own.

—**SHERI SCHEERHORN** HILLS, MINNESOTA

PREP/TOTAL TIME: 30 MIN. **MAKES:** 5 SERVINGS

- 1 **cup ranch salad dressing**
- ½ **cup chopped seeded peeled cucumber**
- 1 **pound beef top sirloin steak, cut into thin strips**
- 2 **tablespoons olive oil**
- 5 **whole pita breads, warmed**
- 1 **medium tomato, chopped**
- 1 **can (2¼ ounces) sliced ripe olives, drained**
- ½ **small onion, thinly sliced**
- 1 **cup (4 ounces) crumbled feta cheese**
- 2½ **cups shredded lettuce**

1. In a small bowl, combine salad dressing and cucumber; set aside. In a large skillet, cook beef in oil over medium heat until no longer pink.

2. Layer half of each pita with steak, tomato, olives, onion, cheese, lettuce and dressing mixture. Fold each pita over filling; secure with toothpicks.

Slow Cooker Goetta

My husband's grandfather, who is of German heritage, introduced me to goetta when I was a newlywed. I loved hearing his stories of how this recipe started and all his memories of cooking it all day long during the Depression, anticipating that first bite when it was finished! I found a slow cooker recipe and changed some ingredients to make this the best goetta around, and many people have requested the recipe. When you can take 2 pounds of meat and turn it into 6 pounds of goetta to feed your family, that's truly "a very good thing!"

—SHARON GEERS WILMINGTON, OHIO

PREP: 45 MIN. **COOK:** 4 HOURS
MAKES: 2 LOAVES (16 SLICES EACH)

- 6 **cups water**
- 2½ **cups steel-cut oats**
- 6 **bay leaves**
- 3 **tablespoons beef bouillon granules**
- ¾ **teaspoon salt**
- 1 **teaspoon each garlic powder, rubbed sage and pepper**
- ½ **teaspoon ground allspice**
- ½ **teaspoon crushed red pepper flakes**
- 2 **pounds bulk pork sausage**
- 2 **medium onions, chopped**

1. In a 5-qt. slow cooker, combine water, oats and seasonings. Cook, covered, on high 2 hours. Remove bay leaves.

2. In a large skillet, cook sausage and onions over medium heat 8-10 minutes or until no longer pink, breaking up sausage into crumbles. Drain, reserving 2 tablespoons drippings. Stir sausage mixture and reserved drippings into oats. Cook, covered, on low for 2 hours.

3. Transfer mixture to two plastic wrap-lined 9x5-in. loaf pans. Refrigerate, covered, overnight.

4. To serve, slice each loaf into 16 slices. In a large skillet, cook goetta in batches, over medium heat 3-4 minutes on each side or until lightly browned and heated through.

Freeze option: *After shaping goetta in loaf pans, cool and freeze, covered, until firm. Transfer goetta to resealable plastic freezer bags or wrap securely in foil. To use, partially thaw in refrigerator overnight; slice and cook as directed*

Pork Chops with Cherry Sauce

Enjoy the rich flavor of this dish. The spice rub also works well on lamb or beef.

—KENDRA DOSS KANSAS CITY, MISSOURI

PREP/TOTAL TIME: 25 MIN. **MAKES:** 2 SERVINGS

- 1 **tablespoon finely chopped shallot**
- 1 **teaspoon olive oil**
- 1 **cup fresh or frozen pitted dark sweet cherries, halved**
- ⅓ **cup ruby port wine**
- 1 **teaspoon balsamic vinegar**
- ⅛ **teaspoon salt**

PORK CHOPS
- 1 **teaspoon coriander seeds, crushed**
- ¾ **teaspoon ground mustard**
- ¼ **teaspoon salt**
- ¼ **teaspoon pepper**
- 2 **bone-in pork loin chops (7 ounces each)**
- 2 **teaspoons olive oil**

1. In a small saucepan, saute shallot in oil until tender. Stir in the cherries, wine, vinegar and salt. Bring to a boil; cook until liquid is reduced by half, about 10 minutes.

2. Meanwhile, in a small bowl, combine the coriander, mustard, salt and pepper; rub over chops. In a large skillet, cook chops in oil over medium heat for 4-5 minutes on each side or until a thermometer reads 145°. Serve with the sauce.

Horseshoe Sandwiches

Meat-and-potato lovers in your family will be happy to indulge in the Horseshoe Sandwich. Our recipe uses the classic ham steak, but hamburger patties are a popular alternative. Even though the sandwich is topped with a homemade cheese sauce, the blue-plate special only takes 30 minutes to make.

—TASTE OF HOME TEST KITCHEN

PREP/TOTAL TIME: 30 MIN. **MAKES:** 2 SERVINGS

- 3 cups frozen French-fried potatoes

CHEESE SAUCE
- 2 tablespoons butter
- 2 tablespoons all-purpose flour
- ¼ teaspoon salt
- ⅛ teaspoon ground mustard
- ⅛ teaspoon pepper
- ¾ cup 2% milk
- 1 cup (4 ounces) shredded white cheddar cheese
- ¼ cup beer, room temperature
- ¾ teaspoon Worcestershire sauce

ASSEMBLY
- 1 fully cooked boneless ham steak (1 pound), cut into 4 pieces
- 4 slices Texas toast or other white bread, toasted
  Paprika

1. Cook potatoes according to the package directions. Meanwhile, in a small saucepan, melt butter over medium heat. Stir in the flour, salt, mustard and pepper until smooth; gradually whisk in the milk. Bring to a boil, stirring constantly; cook and stir 2 minutes or until thickened.

2. Reduce heat to medium-low. Stir in cheese until blended. Stir in beer and Worcestershire sauce; heat through.

3. Heat a large skillet over medium-high heat. Cook ham 1-2 minutes on each side or until lightly browned and heated through.

4. To serve, place two toasts on each of two serving plates; top with ham, fries and cheese sauce. Sprinkle with paprika.

Chicago-Style Beef Sandwiches

I'm originally from the Windy City, so I love Chicago-style beef. These tender sandwiches lend an authentic flavor, and they're so simple to prepare using a slow cooker.

—LOIS SZYDLOWSKI TAMPA, FLORIDA

PREP: 30 MIN. **COOK:** 8 HOURS **MAKES:** 12 SERVINGS

- 1 boneless beef chuck roast (4 pounds)
- 1 teaspoon salt
- ¾ teaspoon pepper
- 2 tablespoons olive oil
- ½ pound fresh mushrooms
- 2 medium carrots, cut into chunks
- 1 medium onion, cut into wedges
- 6 garlic cloves, halved
- 2 teaspoons dried oregano
- 1 carton (32 ounces) beef broth
- 1 tablespoon beef base
- 12 Italian rolls, split
- 1 jar (16 ounces) giardiniera, drained

1. Cut the roast in half; sprinkle with salt and pepper. In a large skillet, brown meat in oil on all sides; drain. Transfer to a 5-qt. slow cooker.

2. In a food processor, combine mushrooms, carrots, onion, garlic and oregano. Cover and process until finely chopped. Transfer to slow cooker. Combine beef broth and base; pour over top. Cover and cook on low for 8-10 hours or until tender.

3. Remove meat and shred with two forks. Skim fat from cooking juices. Return meat to slow cooker; heat through. Using a slotted spoon, serve beef on buns; top with giardiniera.

Editor's Note: *Look for beef base near the broth and bouillon.*

Brats in Beer

The flavor of this recipe's marinade really comes through in the grilled onions.

—JILL HAZELTON HAMLET, INDIANA

PREP: 10 MIN. + MARINATING **GRILL:** 15 MIN.
MAKES: 8 SERVINGS

- 1 can (12 ounces) beer or nonalcoholic beer
- 2 tablespoons brown sugar
- 2 tablespoons soy sauce
- 1 tablespoon chili powder
- 1 tablespoon prepared mustard
- ⅛ teaspoon garlic powder
- 8 uncooked bratwurst links
- 1 large onion, thinly sliced
- 8 brat or hot dog buns, split

1. In a small bowl, combine the first six ingredients. Pour 1¾ cups into a large resealable plastic bag; add bratwurst. Seal bag and turn to coat; refrigerate for 4 hours or overnight. Cover and refrigerate remaining marinade.

2. Add onion to remaining marinade; toss to coat. Place on a double thickness of heavy-duty foil (about 18 in. square). Fold foil around onion mixture and seal tightly. Drain and discard marinade from bratwurst.

3. Grill bratwurst and onion, covered, over medium heat or broil 4 in. from the heat for 15-20 minutes or until meat is no longer pink and onion is tender, turning frequently. Open foil carefully to allow steam to escape. Serve brats in buns with onion mixture.

German Potato Salad with Sausage

Hearty and saucy, this potato salad is an old family recipe that was updated using cream of potato soup to ease preparation. The sausage and sauerkraut give it a special zip.

—TERESA MCGILL TROTWOOD, OHIO

PREP: 30 MIN. **COOK:** 6 HOURS **MAKES:** 5 SERVINGS

- 8 bacon strips, finely chopped
- 1 large onion, chopped
- 1 pound smoked kielbasa or Polish sausage, halved and cut into ½-inch slices
- 2 pounds medium red potatoes, cut into chunks
- 1 can (10¾ ounces) condensed cream of potato soup, undiluted
- 1 cup sauerkraut, rinsed and well drained
- ½ cup water
- ¼ cup cider vinegar
- 1 tablespoon sugar
- ½ teaspoon salt
- ½ teaspoon coarsely ground pepper

1. In a large skillet, cook bacon over medium heat until crisp. Remove to paper towels with a slotted spoon to drain. Saute onion in drippings for 1 minute. Add the sausage; cook until lightly browned. Add the potatoes; cook 2 minutes longer. Drain.

2. Transfer sausage mixture to a 3-qt. slow cooker. In a small bowl, combine the soup, sauerkraut, water, vinegar, sugar, salt and pepper. Pour over sausage mixture. Sprinkle with bacon. Cover and cook on low for 6-7 hours or until potatoes are tender.

JOHNSONVILLE, WI

With its headquarters located just outside Sheboygan, Johnsonville Sausage is doing its part to spread the word about bratwurst. The 65-foot-long, fully loaded Big Taste Grill can cook 750 brats at a time. It travels to festivals, benefits and other special occasions all over the country.

> **"** While looking for an alternative to pan frying our venison steak, we decided to give it a little Italian flair. The recipe turned out to be a big hit! **"**
>
> **—PHIL ZIPP**
> TOMAHAWK, WISCONSIN

Venison Parmigiana

PREP: 25 MIN. **BAKE:** 1 HOUR **MAKES:** 6 SERVINGS

- 2 **pounds boneless venison steaks**
- 1 **egg**
- 1 **tablespoon milk**
- ⅔ **cup seasoned bread crumbs**
- ⅓ **cup grated Parmesan cheese**
- 5 **tablespoons olive oil**
- 1 **small onion, finely chopped**
- 2 **cups hot water**
- 1 **can (6 ounces) tomato paste**
- 1 **teaspoon pepper**
- ½ **teaspoon salt**
- ½ **teaspoon sugar**
- ½ **teaspoon dried marjoram**
- 2 **cups (8 ounces) shredded part-skim mozzarella cheese**

1. Pound steaks to ¼-in. thickness; cut into serving-size pieces. In a shallow bowl, beat egg and milk. In another bowl, combine bread crumbs and Parmesan cheese. Dip venison in egg mixture, then coat with crumb mixture.

2. In a large skillet, brown meat in oil on both sides. Place in a greased 13x9-in. baking dish. In the drippings, saute onion for 2-3 minutes or until tender. Stir in the water, tomato paste, pepper, salt, sugar and marjoram. Bring to a boil. Reduce the heat; simmer, uncovered, for 5 minutes. Pour over venison.

3. Cover and bake at 350° for 50 minutes or until meat is tender. Uncover; sprinkle with cheese. Bake 10-15 minutes longer or until cheese is melted.

Sweet 'n' Smoky Kansas City Ribs

Tender and juicy, these ribs are packed with a big smoky punch. You won't believe how quickly they move from grill to plate!

—GLORIA WARCZAK CEDARBURG, WISCONSIN

PREP: 35 MIN. + STANDING **GRILL:** 70 MIN. **MAKES:** 5 SERVINGS

⅓ cup packed brown sugar
2 teaspoons chicken bouillon granules
2 teaspoons paprika
2 teaspoons chili powder
1 teaspoon ground cumin
¾ teaspoon garlic powder
½ teaspoon each minced fresh basil, rosemary and sage
½ teaspoon ground celery seed
¼ teaspoon ground coriander
⅛ teaspoon fennel seed, crushed
2 pork baby back ribs (about 5 pounds)
2 cups soaked wood chips (mesquite, hickory or alder), optional

SAUCE
1 large onion, chopped
2 tablespoons olive oil
1 tablespoon butter
2 tablespoons brown sugar
1 tablespoon Worcestershire sauce
1 teaspoon each minced fresh basil, marjoram and rosemary, crushed
1 teaspoon each minced fresh dill, sage and cilantro
1 teaspoon minced chives
1 bottle (18 ounces) barbecue sauce

1. In a small bowl, combine the brown sugar, bouillon, seasonings and herbs; rub over ribs. Let stand for 15 minutes.

2. Prepare grill for indirect heat, using a drip pan. Add 1 cup of soaked wood chips if desired. Place ribs in a disposable foil pan. Grill, covered, over indirect medium heat for 30 minutes. Remove ribs from pan and place on grill rack over drip pan. Add remaining wood chips. Grill 30 minutes longer, turning occasionally.

3. Meanwhile, in a small saucepan, saute onion in oil and butter until tender. Stir in the brown sugar, Worcestershire sauce and herbs; cook and stir for 1 minute. Add barbecue sauce. Bring to a boil. Reduce heat; simmer, uncovered, for 5 minutes. Baste ribs with sauce; grill for 10-15 minutes or until meat is tender, turning and basting occasionally.

KANSAS CITY, MO

Kansas City is widely known for its good eats: It has more restaurants per capita than any other American city!

If you grew up on the TV show *M*A*S*H*, you might remember Toledo, Ohio, native Cpl. Max Klinger talking fondly of Tony Packo's Hungarian hot dogs. In real life, Packo and his wife, Rose, opened their first Hungarian restaurant in East Toledo in 1932. It was there that Tony invented the Hungarian hot dog and it's been a neighborhood favorite ever since.

Hungarian Hot Dogs

When you travel around the country, you'll discover that different cities dish up their hot dogs with their own unique combination of toppings. Toledo is no exception...Tony Packo's Hungarian hot dog is a citywide favorite.

—**TASTE OF HOME TEST KITCHEN**

PREP: 10 MIN. **COOK:** 40 MIN. **MAKES:** 6 SERVINGS (2 CUPS CHILI)

CHILI
- 1 **pound ground beef**
- 1 **garlic clove, minced**
- 1½ **teaspoons brown sugar**
- 1 **tablespoon chili powder**
- 1½ **teaspoons Hungarian paprika**
- ¾ **teaspoon pepper**
- ¾ **teaspoon ground cumin**
- ¾ **teaspoon dried thyme**
- ½ **teaspoon salt**
   Dash cayenne pepper
- 1½ **cups water**

HOT DOGS
- 1 **package (14 ounces) smoked kielbasa links**
- 6 **hot dog buns, split**
   Optional toppings: shredded cheddar cheese, yellow mustard and chopped onion

1. In a large skillet, cook beef and garlic over medium heat 6-8 minutes or until beef is no longer pink, breaking up beef into crumbles; drain. Stir in brown sugar and seasonings. Add water; bring to a boil. Reduce heat; simmer 25-30 minutes or liquid is almost evaporated.

2. Cook kielbasa according to the package directions. Serve in buns with chili and toppings, if desired.

Bachelor Chili

As a single male, I prepare my own meals night after night. This prize-winning chili that I concocted years ago recently appeared in a local cookbook.

—DAN ELLISON HERMAN, MINNESOTA

PREP: 25 MIN. **COOK:** 20 MIN. + SIMMERING
MAKES: 10-12 SERVINGS (3 QUARTS)

- 1 boneless venison, elk, moose or beef chuck roast (3 to 3½ pounds)
- 1 tablespoon canola oil
- 2 medium onions, chopped
- 1 medium green pepper, chopped
- 2 garlic cloves, minced
- ¼ to ½ teaspoon crushed red pepper flakes
- 4 cans (14½ ounces each) diced tomatoes, undrained
- 1 cup water
- 1 can (12 ounces) tomato paste
- 1 tablespoon sugar
- ½ teaspoon ground cumin
- ½ teaspoon dried oregano
- ¼ teaspoon pepper

1. Cut meat into ¼-in. pieces. In a 4-qt. Dutch oven, brown meat in oil; remove with a slotted spoon and set aside.

2. In the same pan, saute onions, green pepper, garlic and pepper flakes until vegetables are tender. Return meat to pan. Add remaining ingredients; bring to a boil. Reduce heat; cover and simmer for 3 hours or until the meat is tender.

German Meatballs and Gravy

These meatballs are a celebration of my heritage. I love making them for my family, especially because they're such a quick meal!

—MARSHELLE GREENMYER-BITTNER LISBON, NORTH DAKOTA

PREP: 30 MIN. **COOK:** 35 MIN. **MAKES:** 8 SERVINGS

- 1 egg
- 3½ cups milk, divided
- ½ teaspoon Worcestershire sauce
- 1 cup finely shredded uncooked peeled potatoes
- 2 tablespoons finely chopped onion
- 2 teaspoons salt
- ½ teaspoon ground nutmeg
- ¼ teaspoon ground ginger
- ¼ teaspoon ground allspice
- ⅛ teaspoon pepper
- 2 pounds ground beef
- ¼ cup butter, cubed
- ¼ cup all-purpose flour
  Hot mashed potatoes, optional

1. In a large bowl, combine egg, ½ cup milk, Worcestershire sauce, shredded potatoes, onion, salt, nutmeg, ginger, allspice and pepper. Crumble beef over mixture and mix well. Shape into 48 balls.

2. In a large skillet over medium heat, cook meatballs in butter in batches until no longer pink; remove and keep warm.

3. Stir flour into drippings until blended; gradually add remaining milk. Bring to a boil; cook and stir for 2 minutes or until thickened. Return meatballs to the pan; heat through. Serve with mashed potatoes if desired.

BUFFALO COUNTY, WI

Located on the Mississippi River in western Wisconsin, Buffalo County is known for its trophy whitetail bucks.

Onion Loose Meat Sandwiches

With French onion soup, these sandwiches don't have the typical flavor of most sloppy joes. My sisters and I rely on this recipe from Mom on days when there's little time to cook.

—KATHY PETORSKY
BELLE VERNON, PENNSYLVANIA

PREP/TOTAL TIME: 25 MIN. **MAKES:** 6-8 SERVINGS

- 1½ pounds ground beef
- 2 tablespoons all-purpose flour
  Salt and pepper to taste
- 1 can (10½ ounces) condensed French onion soup, undiluted
- 6 to 8 hamburger buns, split
  Sliced cheddar cheese and dill pickles, optional

1. In a large skillet, cook beef over medium heat until no longer pink; drain. Stir in the flour, salt and pepper until blended. Gradually add the soup. Bring to a boil; cook and stir for 2 minutes or until thickened.

2. Spoon onto buns; top with cheese and pickles if desired.

Editor's Note: *For even more onion flavor, add ½ cup chopped onion to the filling of Onion Loose Meat Sandwiches.*

Pecan Chicken with Blue Cheese Sauce

Special in every way, this moist chicken is coated with pecans and drizzled with a rich, blue cheese sauce. It's easy and delicious...a real winner in my book. You can also use turkey breast and adjust the cooking time.

—MAGGIE RUDDY ALTOONA, IOWA

PREP: 15 MIN. **BAKE:** 20 MIN. **MAKES:** 4 SERVINGS

- 4 boneless skinless chicken breast halves (5 ounces each)
- ¼ teaspoon salt
- ⅛ teaspoon pepper
- ¼ cup all-purpose flour
- 1 tablespoon minced fresh rosemary or 1 teaspoon dried rosemary, crushed
- ¼ cup butter, melted
- 1 tablespoon brown sugar
- ¾ cup finely chopped pecans

SAUCE

- 1 cup heavy whipping cream
- ⅓ cup crumbled blue cheese
- 1 tablespoon finely chopped green onion
- ¼ teaspoon salt
- ¼ teaspoon pepper

1. Sprinkle chicken with salt and pepper. In a shallow bowl, combine flour and rosemary; in a separate shallow bowl, combine butter and brown sugar. Place pecans in another shallow bowl. Coat chicken with flour mixture, then dip in butter mixture and coat with pecans.

2. Transfer to a greased baking sheet. Bake at 375° for 20-25 minutes or until a thermometer reads 165°.

3. Meanwhile, place cream in a small saucepan. Bring to a boil; cook and stir for 8-10 minutes or until thickened. Stir in the cheese, onion, salt and pepper. Serve with the chicken.

Lori's Marzetti Bake

With a family of 8 kids, a meal for us has to be delicious, appealing—and make enough to feed us all. We also like leftovers for lunch the next day. Now when grandkids come to visit during the holidays, we sometimes serve this casserole. I also take it to other big family functions and potlucks, and I always come home with an empty dish.

—LORI SMITH NEWARK, OHIO

PREP: 30 MIN. **BAKE:** 35 MIN.
MAKES: 2 CASSEROLES (12 SERVINGS EACH)

- 2 **pounds ground beef**
- 1 **cup sliced fresh mushrooms**
- 1 **medium onion, finely chopped**
- ⅓ **cup chopped green pepper**
- 2 **garlic cloves, minced**
- 1 **teaspoon salt**
- ½ **teaspoon pepper**
- 3 **cans (15 ounces each) plus 1 can (8 ounces) tomato sauce**
- 1 **can (15 ounces) diced tomatoes, undrained**
- 2 **tablespoons brown sugar**
- 1 **package (16 ounces) egg noodles**
- 3 **cups (12 ounces) shredded cheddar cheese, divided**

1. Preheat oven to 400°. In a Dutch oven, cook the first seven ingredients over medium heat 8-10 minutes or until beef is no longer pink and vegetables are tender, breaking up beef into crumbles; drain. Stir in tomato sauce, tomatoes and brown sugar; bring to a boil. Reduce heat; simmer 10-15 minutes or until flavors are blended, stirring occasionally.

2. Meanwhile cook noodles according to the package directions. Drain; add to sauce. Stir in 2 cups cheese. Transfer to two greased 11x7-in. baking dishes.

3. Cover with greased foil and bake for 30-35 minutes or until heated through. Sprinkle with remaining cheese; bake, uncovered, 5 minutes longer or until cheese is melted.

Special Strip Steaks

I like to use my wonderful cast-iron skillet, inherited from my mother, whenever I'm preparing this delectable steak.

—JANICE MITCHELL AURORA, COLORADO

PREP/TOTAL TIME: 25 MIN. **MAKES:** 2 SERVINGS

- 2 **boneless beef top loin steaks (8 ounces each)**
- 1 **garlic clove, halved**
- ¼ **teaspoon salt**
- ¼ **teaspoon pepper**
- 1 **tablespoon butter**
- ¼ **cup sherry or beef broth**
- ¼ **teaspoon Worcestershire sauce**
- 2 **tablespoons chopped green onion**

1. Rub steaks with garlic and sprinkle with salt and pepper; set aside. Melt butter in a large skillet. Add the sherry or broth, Worcestershire sauce and onion. Bring to a boil. Reduce heat; simmer, uncovered, for 5 minutes.

2. Add the steaks and cook over medium heat for 3-7 minutes on each side or until the meat reaches desired doneness (for medium-rare, a meat thermometer should read 145°; medium, 160°; well-done, 170°).

Editor's Note: *Top loin steak may be labeled as strip steak, Kansas City steak, New York strip steak, ambassador steak or boneless club steak in your region.*

◄● dishing about food

Teresa Marzetti and her husband, Joseph, moved to Columbus, Ohio, from Italy in 1896. She ran restaurants in the city for 76 years and became known for her casserole, the Johnny Marzetti. Teresa created it in the 1920s and named it after her brother-in-law. (You might also know her for Marzetti salad dressings.) Like so many popular dishes, the Johnny Marzetti has had many reincarnations. It can feature noodles or pasta, various combinations of vegetables, and it may or may not include canned soup. Even the ways it's served can differ, depending on the cook. Some mix the pasta with the meat; others simply layer the ingredients in their dish.

Morels are plentiful in cooler areas of the United States, with the Great Lakes region being a particularly good hunting ground for these tasty bites. If you have never hunted for wild mushrooms, go with a seasoned mushroom hunter who can point out which ones are poisonous. And if you are unsure whether a variety is edible, remember the adage, "when in doubt, throw it out." This recipe calls for dried morels and fresh baby portabellos.

MESICK, MI

Every spring, mushroom enthusiasts gather in the U.S. Mushroom Capital for a festival. It features all types of fungi, including odd-looking but delicious-tasting morels.

Morel Mushroom Ravioli

My friend and I really enjoy mushroom hunting. The exercise and fresh air, along with the beauty of the outdoors, is so invigorating. I came up with this recipe to use up the bounty of our harvest. The dish is easy, yet elegant—and absolutely delicious!

—KELLY KNOBLOCK EMMETT, IDAHO

PREP: 35 MIN.   **COOK:** 5 MIN./BATCH   **MAKES:** 4 SERVINGS

- ⅔ **ounce dried morel mushrooms**
- ¼ **cup olive oil**
- ½ **cup finely chopped onion**
- 2 **cups coarsely chopped baby portobello mushrooms**
- 12 **garlic cloves, minced**
- 4 **ounces reduced-fat cream cheese**
- ⅓ **cup shredded Asiago cheese**
- ¼ **teaspoon salt**
- ¼ **teaspoon pepper**
- 48 **wonton wrappers**
- 2 **cups pasta sauce of your choice**
- 2 **tablespoons shredded Parmesan cheese**
- 1 **tablespoon minced fresh Italian parsley**

1. Place the mushrooms in a small bowl; add warm water to cover. Soak 30 minutes or until softened. Remove mushrooms with a slotted spoon; rinse and finely chop.

2. In a skillet, heat oil over medium-high heat. Add the onion; cook and stir 3-4 minutes or until tender. Add the fresh mushrooms, chopped morels and garlic; cook 3-4 minutes longer or until the mushrooms are tender and liquid is evaporated. Stir in the cream cheese, Asiago cheese, salt and pepper. Remove from the heat; cool.

3. Place 1 tablespoon filling in center of each of half of the wonton wrappers. Moisten wrapper edges with water; top with another wrapper. Press around filling to remove air pockets and seal edges. (Cover remaining wrappers with a damp paper towel until ready to use.)

4. In a Dutch oven, bring water to a boil. Add ravioli in batches. Reduce heat; simmer gently 1-2 minutes or until ravioli float and wrappers are translucent. Remove with a slotted spoon. Serve with sauce; sprinkle with Parmesan cheese and parsley.

Howard's Sauerbraten

Cooking for family and friends is one of my favorite pastimes. People always seem to look forward to this tender beef roast with traditional tangy gravy.

—HOWARD KOCH LIMA, OHIO

PREP: 20 MIN. + MARINATING **COOK:** 3 HOURS
MAKES: 8 SERVINGS

- 2½ cups water
- 1½ cups red wine vinegar
- 2 medium onions, sliced
- 1 carrot, finely chopped
- 1 celery rib, finely chopped
- 8 whole cloves
- 4 bay leaves
- ½ teaspoon whole peppercorns
- 1 beef rump roast or eye of round (about 3 pounds)
- ¼ cup butter, cubed

GINGERSNAP GRAVY
- ½ cup water
- 2 tablespoons sugar
- ½ cup gingersnap crumbs (about 12 cookies)

1. In a 4-cup measure, combine the water and vinegar; pour half into a suacepan. Divide each of the vegetables and seasonings between both mixtures. Bring mixture in saucepan to a boil; cool to room temperature. Cover and refrigerate mixture in glass measure.

2. Place beef in a large resealable plastic bag; add cooled vinegar mixture and turn to coat. Place in a baking dish. Refrigerate for 2 days, turning occasionally.

3. Drain beef, discarding marinade and vegetables in bag; pat roast dry. In a Dutch oven, brown roast in butter on all sides. Add reserved vinegar mixture; bring to a boil. Reduce heat; cover and simmer until meat is tender, about 3 hours.

4. For gravy, remove roast and keep warm. Strain cooking juices, discarding vegetables and seasonings. Measure 1½ cups of the cooking juices; add to saucepan. Add water and sugar. Bring to a boil, stirring to dissolve sugar. Reduce heat. Add gingersnap crumbs; simmer until gravy thickens. Serve with roast.

Ham 'n' Noodle Hot Dish

Frozen green peas add lovely color to this comforting meal-in-one dish. The easy, cheesy recipe is a terrific way to use up extra baked ham from a holiday feast or dinner party. No one feels like they're eating leftovers when I serve this tasty bake.

—RENEE SCHWEBACH DUMONT, MINNESOTA

PREP: 15 MIN. **BAKE:** 30 MIN. **MAKES:** 4 SERVINGS

- 3 tablespoons butter, divided
- 2 tablespoons all-purpose flour
- 1 cup milk
- 1 cup (4 ounces) shredded process cheese (Velveeta)
- ½ teaspoon salt
- 2 cups diced fully cooked ham
- 1½ cups elbow macaroni or medium noodles, cooked and drained
- 1 cup frozen peas, thawed
- ¼ cup dry bread crumbs
- ½ teaspoon dried parsley flakes

1. In a saucepan, melt 2 tablespoons butter; stir in flour until smooth. Gradually add milk. Bring to a boil over medium heat; cook and stir for 2 minutes. Remove from the heat; stir in cheese and salt until cheese is melted.

2. Add the ham, noodles and peas. Pour into a greased 1-qt. baking dish. Melt remaining butter; add bread crumbs and parsley. Sprinkle over casserole.

3. Bake, uncovered, at 350° for 30 minutes or until heated through.

> **"** I got this recipe from my sister and my family really likes it a lot. It makes the house smell so good! The amount of garlic might seem high, but it's just right. You get every bit of the flavor without it overpowering the other items. **"**
>
> —**TERRI CHRISTENSEN**
> MONTAGUE, MICHIGAN

Greek Chicken Dinner

PREP: 20 MIN. **COOK:** 5 HOURS **MAKES:** 6 SERVINGS

- 6   **medium Yukon Gold potatoes, quartered**
- 1   **broiler/fryer chicken (3½ pounds), cut up and skin removed**
- 2   **large onions, quartered**
- 1   **whole garlic bulb, separated and peeled**
- 3   **teaspoons dried oregano**
- 1   **teaspoon salt**
- ¾   **teaspoon pepper**
- ½   **cup plus 1 tablespoon water, divided**
- 1   **tablespoon olive oil**
- 4   **teaspoons cornstarch**

1. Place potatoes in a 5-qt. slow cooker. Add the chicken, onions and garlic. Combine the oregano, salt, pepper and ½ cup water; pour over chicken and vegetables. Drizzle with oil. Cover and cook on low for 5-6 hours or until the chicken juices run clear and vegetables are tender.

2. Remove chicken and vegetables to a serving platter; keep warm. Strain cooking juices and skim fat; transfer to a small saucepan. Bring liquid to a boil. Combine the cornstarch and remaining water until smooth. Gradually stir into the pan. Bring to a boil; cook and stir for 2 minutes or until thickened. Serve with the chicken and vegetables.

Pheasant in Mustard Sauce

Until I met my husband, an avid hunter, I'd never cooked or eaten pheasant. I tried several different recipes before creating this one using our favorite ingredients.

—**JOAN MIHALKO** ELKTON, SOUTH DAKOTA

PREP: 20 MIN. **COOK:** 15 MIN. **MAKES:** 2 SERVINGS

- 2   **boneless skinless pheasant breast halves**
- ¼   **teaspoon salt**
- ⅛   **teaspoon pepper**
- 1   **tablespoon canola oil**
- 1   **tablespoon butter**
- ¼   **cup chopped onion**
- 1   **garlic clove, minced**
- ½   **cup chicken broth**
- 2   **tablespoons lemon juice**
- 3   **tablespoons Dijon mustard**
- ¾   **teaspoon dried marjoram**
     Hot cooked rice

1. Sprinkle pheasant with salt and pepper. In a skillet over medium heat, brown pheasant in oil and butter on both sides, about 6-8 minutes.

2. In a small bowl, combine the onion, garlic, broth, lemon juice, mustard and marjoram; add to skillet. Bring to a boil. Reduce heat; cover and simmer for 15-20 minutes or until pheasant juices run clear. Serve with rice.

Pork Chops with Sauerkraut

I was a high school student when I received this recipe from my friend's mom, who is German. She often made these chops for us after church on Sunday. Forty years later, I still love them.

—**ROBERTA BYERS** CHAFFEE, MISSOURI

PREP: 15 MIN. **BAKE:** 45 MIN. **MAKES:** 6 SERVINGS

- 6 bone-in pork loin chops (1 inch thick and 8 ounces each)
- 3 tablespoons butter
- 1 can (14 ounces) sauerkraut, rinsed and well drained
- 1½ cups sweetened applesauce
- ⅓ cup chopped onion
- 1 garlic clove, minced
- 5 teaspoons brown sugar
- 1 teaspoon caraway seeds
- 1 teaspoon ground cinnamon

1. In a large skillet over medium-high heat, brown pork chops in butter on both sides. Transfer to a greased 13-in. x 9-in. baking dish.

2. In a bowl, combine the sauerkraut, applesauce, onion, garlic, brown sugar, caraway seeds and cinnamon. Spoon over chops.

3. Cover and bake at 375° for 45-50 minutes or until meat juices run clear.

Blue Cheese Clubs

These sandwiches look so elegant, but they're really easy to make. They're loaded with plenty of turkey, and the blue cheese spread offers a nice zip.

—**NANCY JO LEFFLER** DEPAUW, INDIANA

PREP/TOTAL TIME: 25 MIN. **MAKES:** 4 SERVINGS

- 1 package (3 ounces) cream cheese, softened
- ½ cup crumbled blue cheese
- 4 tablespoons mayonnaise, divided
- 1 teaspoon dried minced onion
   Dash salt and pepper
   Dash Worcestershire sauce
- 8 slices white bread, toasted
- 8 slices tomato
- 8 slices deli turkey
- 4 slices Swiss cheese
- 4 slices whole wheat bread, toasted
- 8 bacon strips, cooked
- 4 lettuce leaves

1. In a small bowl, beat cream cheese until smooth. Beat in the blue cheese, 1 tablespoon mayonnaise, onion, salt, pepper and Worcestershire sauce until blended.

2. Spread over four slices of white bread; layer with tomato, turkey, Swiss cheese, wheat bread, bacon and lettuce. Spread remaining mayonnaise over remaining white bread; place over lettuce. Secure with toothpicks; cut into triangles.

dishing about food

Most of us associate sauerkraut with German or Polish cuisine, but the first to enjoy the tangy cabbage dish were the Chinese. They preserved shredded cabbage in rice wine thousands of years ago when the Great Wall was being built. It's believed that Ghenghis Khan introduced fermented cabbage to Europe when his army invaded the area. In the 16th century, Germans switched from vinegar to salt, which draws out the excess water, and is still the custom today. German and Dutch settlers brought sauerkraut to the new world along with their tradition of eating pork and sauerkraut on New Year's Day for good luck in the New Year.

> **" A quick marinade gives these lamb chops subtle hints of peach along with the tang of balsamic vinegar. The mushrooms are very tender. "**
>
> **—DIANE BARR**
> LOUISVILLE, KENTUCKY

Portobello Lamb Chops

PREP: 10 MIN. + MARINATING **GRILL:** 20 MIN. **MAKES:** 4 SERVINGS

- ¾ cup peach preserves
- 1 tablespoon balsamic vinegar
- ¼ teaspoon pepper
- ⅛ teaspoon salt
- 4 lamb loin chops (2 inches thick and 5 ounces each)
- ¼ cup olive oil
- 1 teaspoon dried rosemary, crushed
- 4 large portobello mushrooms

1. In a small bowl, combine the first four ingredients. Pour ⅓ cup marinade into a large resealable plastic bag; add lamb chops. Seal bag and turn to coat; refrigerate for 1-4 hours. Cover and refrigerate remaining marinade.

2. In a small bowl, combine oil and rosemary; brush over mushrooms. Moisten a paper towel with cooking oil; using long-handled tongs, lightly coat the grill rack.

3. Grill the lamb chops and mushrooms, uncovered, over medium heat or broil 4 in. from heat for 8-10 minutes on each side or until meat reaches desired doneness (for medium-rare, a thermometer should read 145°; medium, 160°; well-done, 170°), basting frequently with reserved marinade. Slice mushrooms and serve with lamb chops.

Wild Rice Chicken Dinner

With chicken, green beans and the nice crunch of water chestnuts and almonds, this casserole has everything you need. Using ready-to-serve wild rice makes putting it together a breeze.

—LORRAINE HANSON INDEPENDENCE, IOWA

PREP/TOTAL TIME: 30 MIN. **MAKES:** 2 CASSEROLES (6-8 SERVINGS EACH)

- 2 packages (8.8 ounces each) ready-to-serve long grain and wild rice
- 2 packages (16 ounces each) frozen French-style green beans, thawed
- 2 cans (10¾ ounces each) condensed cream of celery soup, undiluted
- 2 cans (8 ounces each) sliced water chestnuts, drained
- ⅔ cup chopped onion
- 2 jars (4 ounces each) sliced pimientos, drained
- 1 cup mayonnaise
- ½ cup 2% milk
- 1 teaspoon pepper
- 6 cups cubed cooked chicken
- 1 cup slivered almonds, divided

1. Heat rice according to package directions. Meanwhile, in a Dutch oven, combine green beans, soup, water chestnuts, onion, pimientos, mayonnaise, milk and pepper. Bring to a boil. Reduce heat; cover and simmer for 5 minutes. Stir in chicken and rice; cook 3-4 minutes longer or until the chicken is heated through.

2. Transfer half of the mixture to a serving dish; sprinkle with ½ cup almonds. Serve immediately. Pour the remaining mixture into a greased 13x9-in. baking dish; cool. Sprinkle with remaining almonds. Cover and freeze for up to 3 months.

To use frozen casserole: *Thaw in the refrigerator overnight. Cover and bake at 350° for 40-45 minutes or until heated through.*

dishing about food ◆▶

The words Coney Island evoke images of amusement parks, the beach and New York. However, these hot dogs are native to Detroit! The sausages are topped with a beanless chili, some onions and yellow mustard. Cincinnati natives top theirs with shredded cheese and call them "cheesy Coneys."

DETROIT, MI

Together, the distinctive towers of the GM Renaissance Center make up the crowning jewel in the Motor City skyline. Inside, you'll find many companies (including General Motors' headquarters), restaurants, a hotel, shops and more.

Chili Coney Dogs

Everyone in our family, from smallest kids to oldest adults, loves these dogs. They're so easy to throw together and cook in the slow cooker. Your family will adore them, too!

—**MICHELE HARRIS** VICKSBURG, MICHIGAN

PREP: 20 MIN. **COOK:** 4 HOURS **MAKES:** 8 SERVINGS

- 1 pound lean ground beef (90% lean)
- 1 can (15 ounces) tomato sauce
- ½ cup water
- 2 tablespoons Worcestershire sauce
- 1 tablespoon dried minced onion
- ½ teaspoon garlic powder
- ½ teaspoon ground mustard
- ½ teaspoon chili powder
- ½ teaspoon pepper
  Dash cayenne pepper
- 8 hot dogs
- 8 hot dog buns, split
  Shredded cheddar cheese, relish and chopped onion, optional

1. In a large skillet, cook beef over medium heat until no longer pink; drain. Stir in the tomato sauce, water, Worcestershire sauce, onion and seasonings.

2. Place hot dogs in a 3-qt. slow cooker; top with beef mixture. Cover and cook on low for 4-5 hours or until heated through. Serve on buns with cheese, relish and onion if desired.

Black Bean 'n' Pumpkin Chili

My family relishes this chili, especially on cold days. It's a wonderful variation on standard chili and it also freezes well and tastes even better as leftovers!

—**DEBORAH VLIET** HOLLAND, MICHIGAN

PREP: 20 MIN. **COOK:** 4 HOURS
MAKES: 10 SERVINGS (2½ QUARTS)

- 1 medium onion, chopped
- 1 medium sweet yellow pepper, chopped
- 2 tablespoons olive oil
- 3 garlic cloves, minced
- 3 cups chicken broth
- 2 cans (15 ounces each) black beans, rinsed and drained
- 2½ cups cubed cooked turkey
- 1 can (15 ounces) solid-pack pumpkin
- 1 can (14½ ounces) diced tomatoes, undrained
- 2 teaspoons dried parsley flakes
- 2 teaspoons chili powder
- 1½ teaspoons dried oregano
- 1½ teaspoons ground cumin
- ½ teaspoon salt

1. In a large skillet, saute the onion and yellow pepper in oil until tender. Add the garlic; cook 1 minute longer. Transfer to a 5-qt. slow cooker; stir in the remaining ingredients. Cover and cook on low for 4-5 hours or until the chili is heated through.

Church Supper Hot Dish

PREP: 40 MIN. **BAKE:** 30 MIN. **MAKES:** 8 SERVINGS

- 1 **pound ground beef**
- 2 **cups sliced peeled potatoes**
- 2 **cups finely chopped celery**
- ¾ **cup finely chopped carrots**
- ¼ **cup finely chopped green pepper**
- ¼ **cup finely chopped onion**
- 2 **tablespoons butter**
- 1 **cup water**
- 2 **cans (10¾ ounces each) condensed cream of mushroom soup, undiluted**
- 1 **can (5 ounces) chow mein noodles, divided**
- 1 **cup (4 ounces) shredded cheddar cheese**

1. In a large skillet, cook beef over medium heat until no longer pink; drain and set aside.

2. In the same skillet, saute the potatoes, celery, carrots, green pepper and onion in butter for 5 minutes. Add water; cover and simmer for 10 minutes or until vegetables are tender. Stir in soup and cooked ground beef until blended.

3. Sprinkle half of the chow mein noodles into a greased shallow 2-qt. baking dish. Spoon meat mixture over noodles. Cover and bake at 350° for 20 minutes. Top with cheese and remaining noodles. Bake, uncovered, 10 minutes longer or until heated through.

The Midwest is the place for walleyes. From Minnesota and Wisconsin to Ohio and Kentucky, fishermen delight in catching this popular variety. Not only can you fish for them in large bodies of water such as Lake Michigan, Lake Erie and the Mississippi River, but they are also found in smaller lakes and streams, such as Millie Lacs and Fox Lake in Minnesota. In winter, take to the ice for some ice fishing, and fry up your catch with the recipe at right.

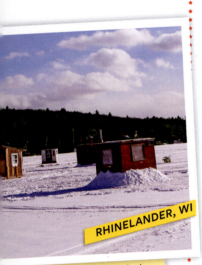

RHINELANDER, WI

Thanks to its spectacular ice fishing conditions, Rhinelander was named Ice Fishing Capital of the World in 2010. When local lakes freeze, shanties like these seem to pop up overnight.

Honey-Fried Walleye

We fish on most summer weekends, so we have lots of fresh fillets. Everyone who tries this crisp, golden fish loves it. It's my husband's favorite, and I never have leftovers. Honey gives the coating a deliciously different twist.

—**SHARON COLLIS** COLONA, ILLINOIS

PREP/TOTAL TIME: 15 MIN. **MAKES:** 4-6 SERVINGS

    1   egg
    1   teaspoon honey
    1   cup coarsely crushed saltines (about 22
        crackers)
    ⅓   cup all-purpose flour
    ¼   teaspoon salt
    ¼   teaspoon pepper
    4   to 6 walleye fillets (about 1½ pounds)
        Canola oil
        Additional honey

1. In a shallow bowl, beat egg and honey. In another bowl, combine the cracker crumbs, flour, salt and pepper. Dip fillets into egg mixture, then coat with crumb mixture.

2. In a large skillet, heat ¼ in. of oil; fry fish over medium-high heat for 3-4 minutes on each side or until fish flakes easily with a fork. Drizzle with honey.

Sunday Pot Roast

This recipe proves you don't have to slave over a hot stove to prepare a delicious down-home crowd-pleaser like Grandma used to make. Slices of this roast turn out tender and savory every time.

—**BRANDY SCHAEFER** GLEN CARBON, ILLINOIS

PREP: 10 MIN. + CHILLING   **COOK:** 8 HOURS
MAKES: 12-14 SERVINGS

    1   boneless whole pork loin roast
        (3½ to 4 pounds), trimmed
    1   teaspoon dried oregano
    ½   teaspoon onion salt
    ½   teaspoon pepper
    ½   teaspoon caraway seeds
    ¼   teaspoon garlic salt
    6   medium carrots, peeled and cut into
        1½-inch pieces
    3   large potatoes, peeled and quartered
    3   small onions, quartered
    1½ cups beef broth
    ⅓   cup all-purpose flour
    ⅓   cup cold water
    ¼   teaspoon browning sauce, optional

1. Cut roast in half. In a small bowl, combine the seasonings; rub over roast. Wrap in plastic wrap and refrigerate overnight.

2. Place the carrots, potatoes and onions in a 6-qt. slow cooker; add broth. Unwrap roast and place in the slow cooker. Cover and cook on high for 2 hours. Reduce heat to low and cook 6 hours longer or until meat is tender.

3. Transfer roast and vegetables to a serving platter; keep warm. Pour broth into a saucepan. Combine flour and water until smooth; stir into broth. Bring to a boil; cook and stir for 2 minutes or until thickened. Add browning sauce if desired. Serve with roast.

Hungarian Chicken Paprikash

My mom learned to make this tender chicken dish when she volunteered to help prepare the dinners served at her church. It's my favorite main dish, and the gravy, seasoned with paprika, sour cream and onions, is the best!

—**PAMELA EATON** MONCLOVA, OHIO

PREP: 20 MIN.   **BAKE:** 1½ HOURS   **MAKES:** 6 SERVINGS

- 1 **large onion, chopped**
- ¼ **cup butter, cubed**
- 4 **to 5 pounds broiler/fryer chicken pieces**
- 2 **tablespoons paprika**
- 1 **teaspoon salt**
- ½ **teaspoon pepper**
- 1½ **cups hot water**
- 2 **tablespoons cornstarch**
- 2 **tablespoons cold water**
- 1 **cup (8 ounces) sour cream**

1. In a large skillet, saute onion in butter until tender. Sprinkle chicken with paprika, salt and pepper; place in an ungreased roasting pan. Spoon onion mixture over chicken. Add hot water. Cover and bake at 350° for 1½ hours or until chicken juices run clear.

2. Remove chicken and keep warm. In a small bowl, combine cornstarch and cold water until smooth. Gradually add to pan juices and onion. Bring to a boil over medium heat; cook and stir for 2 minutes or until thickened. Remove from the heat. Stir in sour cream. Serve with chicken.

> "I love Reuben sandwiches, so this recipe was a dream come true! I think when I use my husband's homemade sauerkraut in this casserole it is just great."

—SUSAN STAHL

DULUTH, MINNESOTA

Corned Beef 'n' Sauerkraut Bake

PREP: 10 MIN. **BAKE:** 30 MIN. **MAKES:** 6 SERVINGS

- 1¾ cups sauerkraut, rinsed and well drained
- ½ pound thinly sliced deli corned beef, julienned
- 2 cups (8 ounces) shredded Swiss cheese
- ¼ cup Thousand Island salad dressing
- 2 medium tomatoes, thinly sliced
- 6 tablespoons butter, divided
- 1 cup coarsely crushed seasoned rye crackers

1. In a greased 1½-qt. baking dish, layer half of sauerkraut, corned beef and cheese. Repeat layers. Drop salad dressing by teaspoonfuls over the cheese. Arrange tomato slices over the top; dot with 2 tablespoons butter.

2. In a small saucepan, melt remaining butter. Stir in crumbs; sprinkle over top of casserole. Bake, uncovered, at 400° for 30-35 minutes or until heated through.

Runza

When I moved to Nebraska, I discovered many ethnic foods that I had never heard of before. A friend introduced me to this German-Russian beef sandwich, and it quickly became a family favorite.

—**DOLLY CROGHAN** MEAD, NEBRASKA

PREP: 35 MIN. + RISING **BAKE:** 20 MIN.
MAKES: 12 SERVINGS

- 4½ **cups all-purpose flour, divided**
- ¼ **cup sugar**
- 2 **packages (¼ ounce each) active dry yeast**
- 1 **teaspoon salt**
- ¾ **cup milk**
- ½ **cup water**
- ½ **cup shortening**
- 2 **eggs**

FILLING
- 2 **pounds lean ground beef (90% lean)**
- 2 **medium onions, chopped**
- 4 **cups chopped cabbage**
- 2 **teaspoons seasoned salt**
- 1 **teaspoon garlic powder**
- 1 **teaspoon pepper**

1. Place 1¾ cups flour, sugar, yeast and salt in a large bowl. Heat the milk, water and shortening to 120°-130°. Pour over flour mixture; add the eggs. Beat with an electric mixer on low speed until blended. Beat 3 additional minutes on high. Stir in the remaining flour; knead until smooth and elastic, about 6-8 minutes.

2. Place the dough in a greased bowl; cover and let rise in a warm place until doubled, about 1 hour.

3. Meanwhile, in a large skillet, cook beef and onions over medium heat until meat is no longer pink; drain. Add the cabbage, seasoned salt, garlic powder and pepper; cook until cabbage is wilted.

4. Punch dough down; divide into 12 portions and cover with plastic wrap. Working with one piece at a time, roll into a 6-in. square. Place ¾ cup meat mixture in the center of each square. Fold the dough over filling, forming a rectangle. Pinch edges tightly to seal and place on greased baking sheets.

5. Bake at 350° for 18-20 minutes or until golden brown. Serve hot.

Perfect Prime Rib Roast

If you've never made prime rib before, you can't go wrong with this recipe. It comes from a chef at a favorite local restaurant.

—**PAULINE WAASDORP** FERGUS FALLS, MINNESOTA

PREP: 5 MIN. + MARINATING
BAKE: 2½ HOURS + STANDING **MAKES:** 8-10 SERVINGS

- ½ **cup Worcestershire sauce**
- 3 **teaspoons garlic salt**
- 3 **teaspoons seasoned salt**
- 3 **teaspoons coarsely ground pepper**
- 1 **bone-in beef rib roast (5 to 6 pounds)**

1. In a small bowl, combine the first four ingredients; rub half over the roast. Place roast in a large resealable plastic bag; seal and refrigerate overnight, turning often. Cover and refrigerate remaining marinade.

2. Drain and discard marinade. Place roast fat side up in a large roasting pan; pour reserved marinade over roast. Tent with foil.

3. Bake at 350° for 1 hour. Uncover and bake 1½ hours longer or until meat reaches desired doneness (for medium-rare, a thermometer should read 145°; medium, 160°; well-done 170°). Let stand for 15 minutes before slicing.

LINCOLN, NE

Designed by architect Bertram G. Goodhue, Nebraska's stately capitol building was completed in 1932 at a cost of $9.8 million, which would be more than $160 million today!

Swedish pancakes are known as "pannkakor" in Sweden. Some think they are the same as crepes, but the batter is thinner and the pancakes are a little trickier to turn over. They are traditionally served with lingonberries, but kids sometimes eat them with ice cream.

Swedish Pancakes

Whenever we spend the night at my mother-in-law's house, our kids beg her to make these crepelike pancakes for breakfast. They're a little lighter than traditional pancakes, so my family can eat a lot!

—SUSAN JOHNSON LYONS, KANSAS

PREP/TOTAL TIME: 20 MIN. **MAKES:** 20 PANCAKES

 2 **cups milk**
 4 **eggs**
 1 **tablespoon canola oil**
1½ **cups all-purpose flour**
 3 **tablespoons sugar**
 ¼ **teaspoon salt**
    Lingonberries or raspberries
    Seedless raspberry jam or fruit spread, warmed
    Whipped topping

1. In a blender, combine first six ingredients. Cover and process until blended. Heat a lightly greased 8-in. nonstick skillet; pour ¼ cup batter into center of pan. Lift and tilt pan to evenly coat bottom. Cook until top appears dry; turn and cook 15-20 seconds longer.

2. Repeat with remaining batter, adding oil to skillet as needed. Stack pancakes with waxed paper or paper towels in between. Reheat in the microwave if desired.

3. Fold pancakes into quarters; serve with berries, raspberry jam and whipped topping.

Breakfast Mess

Whenever my family goes camping (which is often!), this filling breakfast really gets our day going. Everyone who's tried the "Anderson Family Special" agrees that it's the best!

—DEE ANDERSON KENT, WASHINGTON

PREP: 10 MIN. **COOK:** 35 MIN. **MAKES:** 6-8 SERVINGS

- 1 package (26 ounces) frozen shredded hash brown potatoes
- ¼ cup canola oil
- 1 large green pepper, chopped
- 1 large onion, chopped
- 2 garlic cloves, minced
- 2 cans (12 ounces each) Spam or 3 cups cubed fully cooked ham
- 6 eggs, lightly beaten
- ½ teaspoon salt
- ¼ teaspoon pepper
- 1½ cups (6 ounces) shredded cheddar cheese

1. In a large skillet, fry potatoes in oil for 10 minutes. Add green pepper, onion and garlic; cook for 25 minutes or until potatoes are browned and vegetables are tender.

2. Stir in Spam; heat through. Cover and remove from the heat. In another greased skillet, combine eggs, salt and pepper. Cook and stir gently until the eggs are set. Stir into potato mixture. Top with cheese; cover for 3-5 minutes or until cheese is melted.

AUSTIN, MN

Get your fill of Spam history at the 16,500-square-foot museum dedicated to this well-known luncheon meat.

BAILEYS HARBOR, WI

Dotted with lighthouses (including the one at Cana Island), orchards, forests and villages, Door Peninsula ranks among Wisconsin's most beloved vacation spots.

Cherry Wild Rice Salad

While in Door County, Wisconsin, I sampled this salad. As soon as I got home, I wrote the lady who'd made it, requesting the recipe. The mix of rice, vegetables and orchard-fresh fruit is a tasty way to remember our state's premier cherry-growing area.

—YVONNE GORGES NEW LONDON, WISCONSIN

PREP/TOTAL TIME: 25 MIN. **MAKES:** 6-8 SERVINGS

- 2 cups fresh snow peas, halved
- 2 cups cooked wild rice
- 1 cup cooked long grain rice
- 1 can (8 ounces) sliced water chestnuts, drained
- 1 cup dried cherries
- ½ cup thinly sliced celery
- ¼ cup chopped green onions

DRESSING
- 6 tablespoons sugar
- 6 tablespoons canola oil
- 3 tablespoons cider vinegar
- 4½ teaspoons soy sauce
- 1 to 2 garlic cloves, peeled
- ¾ teaspoon minced fresh gingerroot
- ¾ cup cashew halves, toasted

1. In a large bowl, combine the first seven ingredients. For dressing, in a blender, combine the sugar, oil, vinegar, soy sauce, garlic and ginger; cover and process until blended.

2. Pour over rice mixture and toss to coat. Cover and refrigerate until serving. Just before serving, stir in the cashews.

Grandma's Potato Dumplings

Don't be surprised if this recipe inspires you to make too many mashed potatoes on purpose. Day-old rolls and leftover spuds are scrumptious in buttery potato dumplings.

—WENDY STENMAN GERMANTOWN, WISCONSIN

PREP/TOTAL TIME: 25 MIN. **MAKES:** 4 SERVINGS

- 2 day-old hard rolls
- ½ cup water
- 2 teaspoons canola oil
- ½ cup leftover mashed potatoes
- 1 egg, lightly beaten
  Dash ground nutmeg
- 1 to 2 tablespoons all-purpose flour
- ¼ cup butter, cubed

1. Tear rolls into ½-in. pieces; place in a 15x10x1-in. baking pan. Drizzle with water and squeeze dry.

2. In a large skillet, heat the oil over medium-high. Add bread; cook and stir for 1-2 minutes or until lightly toasted.

3. In a small bowl, combine the potatoes, egg, nutmeg and bread. Add enough flour to achieve desired consistency to shape into balls. With floured hands, shape mixture into 3-in. balls.

4. Fill a Dutch oven two-thirds full with water; bring water to a boil. Carefully add the dumplings. Reduce heat; simmer, uncovered, for 8-10 minutes or until a toothpick inserted into a dumpling comes out clean. Meanwhile, in a heavy saucepan, heat butter over medium heat until golden brown. Serve dumplings warm with butter.

Spicy Peanut Soup

After enjoying a spicy peanut soup at a little cafe, I knew I had to try to duplicate it at home. I think my version comes pretty close. It's the best way I know to chase away winter's chill.

—**LISA MEREDITH** EAGAN, MINNESOTA

PREP: 35 MIN. **COOK:** 20 MIN. **MAKES:** 7 SERVINGS

- 2 medium carrots, chopped
- 1 small onion, chopped
- 2 tablespoons olive oil
- 2 garlic cloves, minced
- 1 large sweet potato, peeled and cubed
- ½ cup chunky peanut butter
- 2 tablespoons red curry paste
- 2 cans (14½ ounces each) vegetable broth
- 1 can (14½ ounces) fire-roasted diced tomatoes, undrained
- 1 bay leaf
- 1 fresh thyme sprig
- ½ teaspoon pepper
- ½ cup unsalted peanuts

1. In a large saucepan, cook carrots and onion in oil over medium heat for 2 minutes. Add the garlic; cook 1 minute longer.

2. Stir in sweet potato; cook 2 minutes longer. Stir in peanut butter and curry paste until blended. Add the broth, tomatoes, bay leaf, thyme and pepper.

3. Bring to a boil. Reduce heat; cover and simmer for 15-20 minutes or until sweet potatoes and carrots are tender. (Soup will appear curdled.) Discard bay leaf and thyme sprig. Stir soup until blended. Sprinkle with peanuts.

Chunky Blue Cheese Dressing

This flavorful full-bodied dressing is better than any bottled dressing I've ever tasted, and it's easy to prepare, too! I found the recipe in a church cookbook.

—**LEONA LUECKING** WEST BURLINGTON, IOWA

PREP/TOTAL TIME: 10 MIN. **MAKES:** ABOUT 4 CUPS

- ¼ cup milk
- 3 cups mayonnaise
- 1 cup (8 ounces) sour cream
- 4 ounces crumbled blue cheese
- 2 teaspoons garlic salt

1. Place milk, mayonnaise, sour cream, blue cheese and garlic salt in a blender. Cover and process until smooth. Refrigerate until serving.

Kansas Whole Wheat Bread

We harvested wheat for 36 years, and I was the chief cook for the crew. This lightly textured bread won an award at the Celebrate Kansas Wheat Bake-Off several years ago.

—LINDA PAULS BUHLER, KANSAS

PREP: 25 MIN. + RISING **BAKE:** 35 MIN.
MAKES: 2 LOAVES (12 SLICES EACH)

- 2½ cups whole wheat flour
- ½ cup quick-cooking oats
- ¼ cup toasted wheat germ
- 2 packages (¼ ounce each) active dry yeast
- 2 teaspoons salt
- 1 cup water
- 1 cup (8 ounces) 4% cottage cheese
- ½ cup mashed potatoes (without added milk and butter)
- ¼ cup butter, softened
- ¼ cup milk
- ¼ cup honey
- 2 tablespoons molasses
- 2 eggs
- 3 to 4 cups all-purpose flour

1. In a large bowl, combine the whole wheat flour, oats, wheat germ, yeast and salt. In a saucepan, heat the water, cottage cheese, potatoes, butter, milk, honey and molasses to 120°-130°. Add to dry ingredients; beat just until moistened. Add eggs; beat until smooth. Stir in enough of the all-purpose flour to form a soft dough.

2. Turn onto a floured surface; knead until smooth and elastic, about 8-10 minutes. Place in a greased bowl, turning once to grease the top. Cover and let rise in a warm place until doubled, about 1 hour.

3. Punch dough down. Turn onto a lightly floured surface; divide in half. Shape into two flattened balls. Place on two greased baking sheets. Cover and let rise until doubled, about 45 minutes.

4. With a sharp knife, make a shallow X-shaped cut in the top of each loaf. Bake at 350° for 35-40 minutes. Cover loosely with foil if top browns to quickly. Remove from pans to wire racks to cool.

Honey Whole Wheat Bread

Turn out two beautiful golden brown loaves that make the perfect bread for a week of healthy sandwiches.

—ROBYN LINDBERG KECHI, KANSAS

PREP: 25 MIN. + RISING
BAKE: 35 MIN. + COOLING
MAKES: 2 LOAVES (16 SLICES EACH)

- 2 packages (¼ ounce each) active dry yeast
- 3 cups warm water (110° to 115°)
- ½ cup nonfat dry milk powder
- ½ cup honey
- ⅓ cup wheat bran
- ⅓ cup toasted wheat germ
- ¼ cup ground flaxseed
- 2 tablespoons canola oil
- 2 teaspoons salt
- 4 cups whole wheat flour
- 3½ to 4 cups all-purpose flour

1. In a large bowl, dissolve yeast in warm water. Add the milk powder, honey, wheat bran, wheat germ, flax, oil, salt, whole wheat flour and 3 cups all-purpose flour. Beat until smooth. Stir in enough remaining flour to form a soft dough (dough will be sticky).

2. Turn onto a lightly floured surface; knead until smooth and elastic, about 6-8 minutes. Place in a bowl coated with cooking spray, turning once to coat the top. Cover and let rise in a warm place until doubled, about 1 hour.

3. Punch dough down and turn onto a floured surface; shape into two loaves. Place in two 9x5-in. loaf pans coated with cooking spay. Cover and let rise until doubled, about 30 minutes.

4. Bake at 350° for 35-40 minutes or until golden brown. Remove from pans to wire rack to cool.

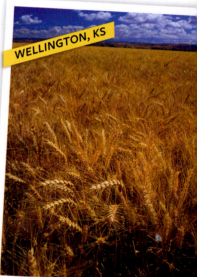

WELLINGTON, KS

The town of Wellington hosts the annual Kansas Wheat Festival, a community event for more than a century!

The United States is the top producer of corn in the world. The Corn Belt cuts a swath through the Midwest from Nebraska to Missouri. The top producers are Iowa, Illinois, Nebraska and Minnesota.

MITCHELL, SD

Though South Dakota isn't one of America's biggest corn producers, it's home to the Corn Palace! Each year, 12 new murals are made on the building, each using different colored corn kernels and other natural materials.

Creamed Corn

Five ingredients are all you'll need for my popular dinner accompaniment. It's wonderful no matter what the occasion is. Try it on a barbecue buffet or holiday menu.

—**BARBARA BRIZENDINE**
HARRISONVILLE, MISSOURI

PREP: 10 MIN. **COOK:** 3 HOURS **MAKES:** 5 SERVINGS

- 2 packages (one 16 ounces, one 10 ounces) frozen corn
- 1 package (8 ounces) cream cheese, softened and cubed
- ¼ cup butter, cubed
- 1 tablespoon sugar
- ½ teaspoon salt

1. In a 3-qt. slow cooker coated with cooking spray, combine all the ingredients. Cover and cook on low for 3 to 3½ hours or until cheese is melted and corn is tender. Stir just before serving.

Four-Cheese Macaroni

I adapted this recipe from one that a friend gave me. It has a distinctive blue cheese taste and is very filling. I like to serve it with chicken.

—**DARLENE MARTURANO**
WEST SUFFIELD, CONNECTICUT

PREP/TOTAL TIME: 20 MIN. **MAKES:** 12 SERVINGS

- 1 package (16 ounces) elbow macaroni
- ¼ cup butter, cubed
- ¼ cup all-purpose flour
- ½ teaspoon salt
- ⅛ teaspoon pepper

- 3 cups 2% milk
- 2 cups (8 ounces) shredded cheddar cheese
- 1½ cups (6 ounces) shredded Swiss cheese
- ½ cup crumbled blue cheese
- ½ cup grated Parmesan cheese

1. Cook macaroni according to the package directions. Meanwhile, in a Dutch oven over medium heat, melt butter. Stir in flour, salt and pepper until smooth; gradually whisk in milk. Bring to a boil, stirring constantly; cook and stir 2 minutes or until thickened.

2. Reduce heat to low; add cheeses and stir until melted. Drain macaroni; add to cheese sauce and stir until well coated.

Corn and Broccoli in Cheese Sauce

This dish is a standby. My daughter likes to add leftover ham to it. Save room in the oven by making this savory side in your slow cooker.

—**JOYCE JOHNSON** UNIONTOWN, OHIO

PREP: 10 MIN. **COOK:** 3 HOURS **MAKES:** 8 SERVINGS

- 1 package (16 ounces) frozen corn, thawed
- 1 package (16 ounces) frozen broccoli florets, thawed
- 4 ounces reduced-fat process cheese (Velveeta), cubed
- ½ cup shredded cheddar cheese
- 1 can (10¼ ounces) reduced-fat reduced-sodium condensed cream of chicken soup, undiluted
- ¼ cup fat-free milk

1. In a 4-qt. slow cooker, combine the corn, broccoli and cheeses. In a small bowl, combine soup and milk; pour over vegetable mixture. Cover and cook on low for 3-4 hours or until heated through. Stir before serving.

Latkes

These thin onion and potato pancakes make a tasty accompaniment to any meal. The key to their crispiness is draining all the liquid from the grated potatoes and onion before frying.

—TASTE OF HOME TEST KITCHEN

PREP: 20 MIN. **COOK:** 20 MIN. **MAKES:** 2 DOZEN

- 2 **pounds russet potatoes, peeled**
- 1 **medium onion**
- ½ **cup chopped green onions**
- 1 **egg, lightly beaten**
- 1 **teaspoon salt**
- ¼ **teaspoon pepper**
  Oil for deep-fat frying
  Applesauce

1. Coarsely grate potatoes and onion; drain any liquid. Place in a bowl; add green onions, egg, salt and pepper.

2. In an electric skillet, heat ⅛ in. of oil to 375°. Drop batter by heaping tablespoonfuls into hot oil. Flatten to form patties. Fry until golden brown; turn and cook the other side. Drain on paper towels. Serve with applesauce.

Three-Bean Salad

PREP: 20 MIN. + CHILLING **MAKES:** 8 SERVINGS

- 1 **can (15½ ounces) great northern beans, rinsed and drained**
- 1 **can (15 ounces) garbanzo beans or chickpeas, rinsed and drained**
- 1 **can (15 ounces) black beans, rinsed and drained**
- 1 **medium tomato, chopped**
- 1 **medium onion, chopped**
- 1 **celery rib, chopped**
- ⅓ **cup each chopped green, sweet red and yellow pepper**
- ½ **cup water**
- 3 **tablespoons minced fresh basil or 1 tablespoon dried basil**
- 2 **tablespoons minced fresh parsley**
- 2 **tablespoons lemon juice**
- 2 **tablespoons olive oil**
- 1½ **teaspoons minced fresh oregano or ½ teaspoon dried oregano**
- ½ **teaspoon salt**
- ½ **teaspoon pepper**
- ¼ **teaspoon cayenne pepper**

1. In a large bowl, combine the beans, tomato, onion, celery and peppers. In a small bowl, whisk the remaining ingredients; gently stir into bean mixture. Cover and refrigerate for 4 hours, stirring occasionally.

"Fresh herbs and cayenne pepper provide the fantastic flavor in this marinated salad featuring fresh veggies and canned beans."

—CAROL TUCKER
WOOSTER, OHIO

Fireside Glogg

Aromatic spices flavor this superb wine-based beverage. It is served warm, and its sweet, fruity taste will warm you to your toes. This traditional Scandinavian recipe is served during the holidays.

—SUE BROWN WEST BEND, WISCONSIN

PREP: 45 MIN. **COOK:** 20 MIN.
MAKES: 8 SERVINGS (¾ CUP EACH)

- 4 cups port wine or apple cider, divided
- 3 cups fresh or frozen cranberries, thawed
- ¼ cup packed brown sugar
- 4 orange peel strips (3 inches)
- 3 cinnamon sticks (3 inches)
- 5 slices fresh peeled gingerroot
- 5 cardamom pods
- 5 whole cloves
- 4 cups apple cider or juice
- ½ cup blanched almonds
- ½ cup raisins

1. In a large saucepan, combine 3 cups wine, cranberries, brown sugar, orange peel, cinnamon, ginger, cardamom and cloves. Cook over medium heat until cranberries pop, about 15 minutes. Mash slightly and cook 10 minutes longer.

2. Strain and discard pulp, orange peel and spices. Return mixture to pan; stir in the cider, almonds, raisins and remaining wine. Bring to a boil. Reduce heat; simmer, uncovered, for 15 minutes.

Hearty Chili Mac

Luckily, this recipe makes a lot, since everyone is apt to want another bowl. It freezes well and makes excellent leftovers— if there are any. Now that I'm a retired farmwife, I enjoy traveling and volunteering.

—FANNIE WEHMAS SAXON, WISCONSIN

PREP: 20 MIN. **COOK:** 1¼ HOURS
MAKES: 10-12 SERVINGS

- 2 pounds ground beef
- 1 medium onion, chopped
- 1 can (46 ounces) tomato juice
- 1 can (28 ounces) diced tomatoes, undrained
- 2 celery ribs, chopped
- 3 tablespoons brown sugar
- 2 tablespoons chili powder
- 1 teaspoon salt
- 1 teaspoon prepared mustard
- ¼ teaspoon pepper
- 2 cans (16 ounces each) kidney beans, rinsed and drained
- ½ cup uncooked elbow macaroni

1. In a Dutch oven, cook beef and onion over medium heat until meat is no longer pink; drain. Stir in tomato juice, tomatoes, celery, brown sugar, chili powder, salt, mustard and pepper. Bring to a boil. Reduce heat; simmer, uncovered, for 1 hour, stirring occasionally.

2. Add the beans and macaroni; simmer 15-20 minutes longer or until macaroni is tender.

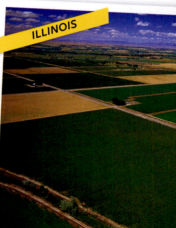
◀● dishing about food

Horseradish has been around since ancient times. Its use spread throughout Europe, and settlers brought it to North America. In the 1850s, horseradish farms were established in the Midwest, especially in Illinois.

When people think of Illinois, their minds may immediately jump to Chicago. But farmland covers more than 28 million acres—that's about 80 percent of the Land of Lincoln!

Mashed Potatoes with a Kick

A few basic ingredients, a pot and a bowl are all you need to quickly make a great side that goes with any meal. These are my favorite potatoes!

—**VALERIE BELLEY** ST. LOUIS, MISSOURI

PREP/TOTAL TIME: 30 MIN. **MAKES:** 8 SERVINGS

- 10 **medium potatoes (3 pounds), peeled and cubed**
- 1 **cup heavy whipping cream**
- ¼ **cup butter, cubed**
- 2 **tablespoons prepared horseradish**
- 1 **teaspoon salt**
- 1 **teaspoon pepper**

1. Place the potatoes in a Dutch oven and cover with water. Bring to a boil. Reduce heat; cover and cook for 10-15 minutes or until tender. Drain.

2. In a large bowl, mash potatoes with remaining ingredients.

CHICAGO, IL

Chicagoland has a thriving Polish community. In fact, since immigrants from Poland first arrived there in 1837, the population of those with Polish heritage has risen to more than 1 million.

Homemade Pierogies

Pierogies are dumplings or tiny pies stuffed with a filling—often potatoes and cheese—and boiled, then cooked in butter. Our friends always ask us to bring them to potlucks.

—**DIANE GAWRYS** MANCHESTER, TENNESSEE

PREP: 1 HOUR + FREEZING **COOK:** 5 MIN./BATCH **MAKES:** 1 SERVING

- 5 **cups all-purpose flour**
- 1 **teaspoon salt**
- 1 **cup water**
- 3 **eggs**
- ½ **cup butter, softened**

FILLING
- 4 **medium potatoes, peeled and cubed**
- 2 **medium onions, chopped**
- 2 **tablespoons butter**
- 5 **ounces cream cheese, softened**
- ½ **teaspoon salt**
- ½ **teaspoon pepper**

ADDITIONAL INGREDIENTS (FOR EACH SERVING)
- ¼ **cup chopped onion**
- 1 **tablespoon butter**
  Minced fresh parsley

1. In a food processor, combine flour and salt; cover and pulse to blend. Add water, eggs and butter; cover and pulse until dough forms a ball, adding an additional 1 to 2 tablespoons of water or flour if needed. Let rest, covered, for 15 to 30 minutes.

2. Place potatoes in a large saucepan and cover with water. Bring to a boil. Reduce heat; cover and simmer for 10-15 minutes or until tender. Meanwhile, in a large skillet, saute onions in butter until tender; set aside.

3. Drain potatoes. Over very low heat, stir potatoes for 1-2 minutes or until steam has evaporated. Press through a potato ricer or strainer into a large bowl. Stir in the cream cheese, salt, pepper and onion mixture; set aside.

4. Divide dough into four parts. On a lightly floured surface, roll one portion of dough to ⅛-in. thickness; cut with a floured 3-in. biscuit cutter. Place 2 teaspoons of filling in the center of each circle. Moisten edges with water; fold in half and press edges to seal. Repeat with remaining dough and filling.

5. Bring a Dutch oven of water to a boil; add pierogies in batches. Reduce heat to a gentle simmer; cook for 1-2 minutes or until pierogies float to the top and are tender. Remove with a slotted spoon; cool slightly.

6. Place on waxed paper-lined 15x10x1-in. baking pans; freeze until firm. Transfer to resealable plastic freezer bags. May be frozen for up to 3 months.

To Prepare Frozen Pierogies: *In a large skillet, saute four pierogies and onion in butter until pierogies are lightly browned and heated through; sprinkle with parsley.*

Navy Bean Soup

This soup has been on our restaurant's menu for about 25 years. Customers tell us they love its flavor. A clear chicken broth makes it different from other bean soups.

—**ROBERT DOUMAS** GAYLORD, MICHIGAN

PREP: 20 MIN. + STANDING
COOK: 1 HOUR 20 MIN. **MAKES:** 8-10 SERVINGS

- 1 **pound dried navy beans**
- 2 **quarts chicken broth**
- 2 **tablespoons minced fresh parsley**
- 2 **bay leaves**
- ¼ **teaspoon pepper**
- 1 **medium onion, chopped**
- 1 **medium carrot, chopped**
- 1 **celery rib, chopped**
- 6 **bacon strips, cooked and crumbled**

1. Place beans in a Dutch oven or stockpot; add water to cover by 2 in. Bring to a boil; boil for 2 minutes. Remove from the heat; cover and let soak for 1 to 4 hours. Drain and rinse beans; discard liquid.

2. In a large saucepan, combine broth, beans, parsley, bay leaves and pepper. Bring to a boil. Reduce heat; cover and simmer for 1 hour. Add the onion, carrot and celery. Cover and simmer for 20-25 minutes or until vegetables and beans are tender. Stir in bacon. Discard the bay leaves before serving.

Beer Margaritas

There's nothing more refreshing than this cool combination of two popular drinks, beer and lime margaritas.

—**TASTE OF HOME TEST KITCHEN**

PREP/TOTAL TIME: 10 MIN. **MAKES:** 4 SERVINGS

- ¾ **cup thawed limeade concentrate**
- 1 **bottle (12 ounces) beer**
- ¾ **cup vodka**
- ¾ **cup water**
   Ice cubes, optional

GARNISH
   Lime slices

1. In a pitcher, combine limeade concentrate, beer, vodka and water. Serve over ice if desired in pilsner or highball glasses. Garnish as desired.

Editor's Note: *This recipe was tested with Corona beer.*

MILWAUKEE, WI

Residents of Brew City have taken beermaking seriously since the 19th century. Miller Beer (ballpark sponsor of the Milwaukee Brewers) wasn't the only historic brewery founded there: Pabst, Blatz and Schlitz were, too. Today, several other breweries operate in the area, and many offer regular tours.

Cheese Soup

Here's a creative twist on cheese soup that uses veggies and chicken broth. It tastes a bit lighter and fresher than most cheese soups, and is great for entertaining.

—**SHARON DELANEY-CHRONIS**
SOUTH MILWAUKEE, WISCONSIN

PREP/TOTAL TIME: 30 MIN.
MAKES: 12 SERVINGS (3 QUARTS)

- 4 medium carrots, chopped
- 2 celery ribs, chopped
- 1 large onion, chopped
- 1 medium green pepper, chopped
- ½ cup butter
- ¾ cup all-purpose flour
- 1 teaspoon salt
- 3 quarts 2% milk
- 1⅓ cups reduced-sodium chicken broth
- 1 package (8 ounces) process cheese (Velveeta), cubed
- 1½ cups (6 ounces) shredded cheddar cheese

1. In a Dutch oven, saute the carrots, celery, onion and green pepper in butter until tender. Stir in flour and salt until blended; gradually add milk and broth. Bring to a boil; cook and stir for 2 minutes or until thickened. Reduce heat to low; stir in cheeses until melted.

Grandma's Dill Pickles

Treasured family recipes like this one are like old friends. The crispy spears have a slightly salty, tart flavor with a good balance of dill, garlic and peppers. They make a great accompaniment for sandwiches.

—**BETTY SITZMAN** WRAY, COLORADO

PREP: 50 MIN. **PROCESS:** 15 MIN. **MAKES:** 9 QUARTS

- 11 cups water
- 5 cups white vinegar
- 1 cup canning salt
- 12 pounds pickling cucumbers, quartered or halved lengthwise
- 9 dill sprigs or heads
- 18 garlic cloves
- 18 dried hot chilies

1. In a stockpot, bring the water, vinegar and salt to a boil; boil for 10 minutes. Pack cucumbers into hot quart jars within ½ in. of top. Place one dill head, two garlic cloves and two peppers in each jar.

2. Carefully ladle hot mixture into jars, leaving ½-in. headspace. Remove air bubbles, wipe rims and adjust lids. Process for 15 minutes in a boiling-water canner.

Editor's Note: *The processing time listed is for altitudes of 1,000 feet or less. For altitudes up to 3,000 feet, add 5 minutes; 6,000 feet, add 10 minutes; 8,000 feet, add 15 minutes; 10,000 feet, add 20 minutes.*

WEST BAYARD, NE

Pioneers of many ancestries passed by Chimney Rock on their journeys west. It was on the routes of the Oregon, Mormon and California trails.

Spaetzle Dumplings

These tender homemade noodles take only minutes to make and are a natural accompaniment to my mom's chicken. You can enjoy them with the chicken gravy or simply buttered and sprinkled with parsley.

—**PAMELA EATON** MONCLOVA, OHIO

PREP/TOTAL TIME: 15 MIN. **MAKES:** 6 SERVINGS

- 2 **cups all-purpose flour**
- 4 **eggs, lightly beaten**
- ⅓ **cup 2% milk**
- 2 **teaspoons salt**
- 8 **cups water**
- 1 **tablespoon butter**

1. In a large bowl, stir the flour, eggs, milk and salt until smooth (dough will be sticky). In a large saucepan, bring water to a boil.

2. Pour dough into a colander or spaetzle maker coated with cooking spray; place over boiling water. With a wooden spoon, press dough until small pieces drop into boiling water. Cook for 2 minutes or until dumplings are tender and float. Remove with a slotted spoon; toss with butter.

Elegant Scalloped Potatoes

PREP: 30 MIN. **BAKE:** 15 MIN. **MAKES:** 10-12 SERVINGS

- 8 large baking potatoes
- 6 tablespoons butter, cubed
- 6 tablespoons all-purpose flour
- 1 to 2 teaspoons garlic powder
- ½ teaspoon salt
- ½ teaspoon pepper
- 3½ cups milk
- 12 ounces process cheese (Velveeta), cubed
- ⅓ cup crumbled cooked bacon
- 1 cup (4 ounces) shredded cheddar cheese
- ¼ cup sliced green onions

1. Scrub and pierce the potatoes; place on a microwave-safe plate. Microwave on high for 15-20 minutes or until tender. Cool slightly.

2. In a saucepan, melt butter. Stir in the flour, garlic powder, salt and pepper until smooth; gradually whisk in milk. Bring to a boil; cook and stir for 2 minutes or until thickened. Add the process cheese and bacon; stir until cheese is melted. Remove from the heat; set aside.

3. Cut potatoes into ¼-in. slices. Place a third of the slices in a greased 13x9-in. baking dish; top with a third of the cheese sauce. Repeat layers twice. Sprinkle with cheddar cheese and onions.

4. Bake, uncovered, at 350° for 15 minutes or until cheese is melted.

Editor's Note: *This recipe was tested in a 1,100-watt microwave.*

Split Pea Soup with Meatballs

The addition of tender meatballs adds a flavorful twist to ordinary split pea soup. Whenever I prepare this for our church soup suppers, I come home with an empty pot!

—DONNA SMITH GREY CLIFF, MONTANA

PREP: 20 MIN. **COOK:** 2 HOURS
MAKES: 10-14 SERVINGS (3½ QUARTS)

- 1 pound dry green split peas
- 3 medium carrots, cut into ½-inch pieces
- ¾ cup diced celery
- 1 medium onion, diced
- 8 cups water
- 3 medium potatoes, cut into ½-inch cubes
- 2½ teaspoons salt
- ¼ teaspoon pepper

MEATBALLS
- ¾ cup finely chopped celery
- 1 medium onion, finely chopped
- 4 tablespoons canola oil, divided
- 1½ cups soft bread crumbs
- 2 tablespoons water
- 1 teaspoon salt
- ½ teaspoon dried sage, crushed
- 1 egg
- 1 pound ground pork

1. In a Dutch oven or stockpot, combine the peas, carrots, celery, onion and water; bring to a boil over medium heat. Reduce heat; cover and simmer for 1 hour.

2. Add potatoes, salt and pepper; cover and simmer for 30 minutes.

3. Meanwhile, in a large skillet, saute celery and onion in 2 tablespoons oil until tender; transfer to a large bowl. Add bread crumbs, water, salt, sage and egg; crumble pork over mixture and mix well. Form into ¾-in. balls.

4. In the same skillet, brown meatballs in remaining oil until a thermometer reads 160°. Add to soup; cover and simmer for 15 minutes.

Fried Squash Blossoms Snack

Savvy gardeners know that flowers from plants in the squash family make flavorful fare. Remove only the male blossoms—those with thin, trim stems—if you'd also like to harvest some squash. You'll find these to be a treat that's tender on the inside and crisp on the outside.

—LYNN BUXKEMPER SLATON, TEXAS

PREP/TOTAL TIME: 30 MIN. **MAKES:** 4 SERVINGS

- ½ cup all-purpose flour
- ½ teaspoon baking powder
- ¼ teaspoon garlic salt
- ¼ teaspoon ground cumin
- 1 egg
- ½ cup milk
- 1 tablespoon canola oil
  Additional oil for frying
- 12 large freshly picked squash blossoms

1. In a medium bowl, combine flour, baking powder, garlic salt and cumin. In another bowl, beat egg, milk and oil; add to dry ingredients and stir until smooth. In a skillet, heat 2 in. of oil to 375°. Dip blossoms into batter and fry in oil a few at a time until crisp. Drain on paper towels. Keep warm until serving.

Old-World Rye Bread

Rye and caraway lend this bread wonderful flavor, while the surprise ingredient of baking cocoa gives it a rich, dark color. For a variation, stir in a cup each of raisins and chopped walnuts.

—PERLENE HOEKEMA LYNDEN, WASHINGTON

PREP: 25 MIN. + RISING
BAKE: 35 MIN. + COOLING
MAKES: 2 LOAVES (12 SLICES EACH)

- 2 packages (¼ ounce each) active dry yeast
- 1½ cups warm water (110° to 115°)
- ½ cup molasses
- 6 tablespoons butter, softened
- 2 cups rye flour
- ¼ cup baking cocoa
- 2 tablespoons caraway seeds
- 2 teaspoons salt
- 3½ to 4 cups all-purpose flour
  Cornmeal

1. In a large bowl, dissolve yeast in warm water. Beat in the molasses, butter, rye flour, cocoa, caraway seeds, salt and 2 cups all-purpose flour until smooth. Stir in enough of the remaining all-purpose flour to form a stiff dough.

2. Turn onto a floured surface; knead until smooth and elastic, about 6-8 minutes. Place in a greased bowl, turning once to grease the top. Cover and let rise in a warm place until doubled, about 1½ hours.

3. Punch dough down. Turn onto a lightly floured surface; divide in half. Shape each piece into a loaf, about 10 in. long. Grease two baking sheets and sprinkle with cornmeal. Place loaves on prepared pans. Cover and let rise until doubled, about 1 hour.

4. Bake at 350° for 35-40 minutes or until bread sounds hollow when tapped. Remove from pans to wire racks to cool.

OBETZ, OH

Want to show your love for zucchini? Mark your calendar for the weekend before Labor Day. It's Zucchinifest, in Obetz, Ohio, a four-day party dedicated to honoring this prolific veggie.

66 The concept of an old-fashioned dates back to the early 1800s and includes whiskey, bitters, cherry juice, sugar and water. This version, which is extremely popular in Wisconsin, uses brandy in place of whiskey and lemon-lime soda instead of water for a milder cocktail. 99

—TASTE OF HOME
TEST KITCHEN

Brandy Old-Fashioned Sweet

PREP/TOTAL TIME: 10 MIN.   **MAKES:** 1 SERVING

1 orange slice	2 teaspoons water
1 maraschino cherry	1 teaspoon orange juice
1½ ounces maraschino cherry juice	3 ounces lemon-lime soda
1 teaspoon bitters	
¼ to ⅓ cup ice cubes	
1½ ounces brandy	

1. In a rocks glass, muddle the orange slice, cherry, cherry juice and bitters. Add ice. Pour in the brandy, water, orange juice and soda.

Khachapuri

While in Russia, where we adopted our two children, my husband and I discovered these marvelous cheese pies. The traditional pastries can be served with a salad for a celebratory supper or shaped into bite-sized hors d'oeuvres.

—RACHEL SAUDER TREMONT, ILLINOIS

PREP: 30 MIN. + RISING **BAKE:** 30 MIN. **MAKES:** 6 SERVINGS

- 3½ teaspoons active dry yeast
- ¾ cup warm milk (110° to 115°)
- 6 tablespoons butter, melted
- 2 tablespoons honey
- 2 to 2½ cups all-purpose flour
- 1 teaspoon salt
- ¼ teaspoon ground coriander

FILLING
- 1 egg, lightly beaten
- 12 ounces brick cheese, shredded

1. In a large bowl, dissolve the yeast in warm milk. Stir in butter and honey. In another bowl, combine 1¾ cups flour, salt and coriander; gradually add to yeast mixture, beating until smooth. Stir in enough remaining flour to form a soft dough.

2. Turn onto a lightly floured surface; knead until smooth and elastic, about 6-8 minutes. Place in a greased bowl, turning once to grease top. Cover and let rise in a warm place until doubled, about 1 hour.

3. Punch dough down. Let rise until doubled, about 30 minutes. Turn onto a lightly floured surface; divide into six balls. Roll each into a 6½-in. circle.

4. In a small bowl, combine egg and cheese. Mound about ½ cup cheese mixture in the center of each circle. Fold dough over filling, gathering and twisting into a knot to seal. Place on an ungreased baking sheet. Let stand for 10 minutes. Bake at 375° for 30-35 minutes or until lightly browned. Serve immediately.

In 1885, milkshakes were adults-only beverages because they were made with whiskey, milk and eggs. They didn't become non-alcoholic until around 1900, when they also turned sweet, thanks to a syrup flavoring. The treat we now know as a chocolate shake or malt appeared in 1922, when Ivar Coulson, an employee at Walgreens, added two scoops of ice cream to malted milk. It was an instant hit.

Thick Chocolate Shake

For a quick, chocolaty treat on a hot summer day, this recipe is perfect. Kids will absolutely love it.

—**BONNIE RUETER** ENGLEWOOD, FLORIDA

PREP/TOTAL TIME: 10 MIN. **MAKES:** 3-4 SERVINGS

- 1 cup milk
- ½ cup instant chocolate drink mix
- 3 cups vanilla ice cream

1. Place all ingredients in a blender container; cover and process on high until smooth. Pour into glasses. Refrigerate any leftovers.

Warm Blue Cheese, Bacon & Garlic Dip

This is a favorite snack of mine that I serve when hosting my husband's office parties. Crunchy smoked almonds complement the creamy cheese dip.

—**BARB WHATLEY** FREMONT, NEBRASKA

PREP: 15 MIN. **BAKE:** 30 MIN. **MAKES:** 2 CUPS

- 7 bacon strips, chopped
- 2 garlic cloves, minced
- 1 package (8 ounces) cream cheese, softened
- ¼ cup half-and-half cream
- 1 cup (4 ounces) crumbled blue cheese
- 2 tablespoons minced chives
- 3 tablespoons coarsely chopped smoked almonds
  Bagel chips

1. In a large skillet, cook bacon over medium heat until crisp. Using a slotted spoon, remove to paper towels; drain, reserving ½ teaspoon of the drippings.

2. Saute the garlic in reserved drippings for 1 minute; transfer to a small bowl. Add cream cheese and cream; beat until smooth. Stir in the blue cheese, chives and bacon.

3. Transfer to a 1-qt. baking dish; cover and bake at 350° for 25 minutes. Uncover and bake 5-10 minutes longer or until lightly browned. Sprinkle with almonds; serve with chips.

Over-the-Top Cherry Jam

We live in Door County, Wisconsin, an area known for its wonderful tart cherries. This beautiful sweet jam makes lovely gifts.

—**KAREN HAEN** STURGEON BAY, WISCONSIN

PREP: 35 MIN. **PROCESS:** 5 MIN. **MAKES:** 6 HALF-PINTS

- 2½ pounds fresh tart cherries, pitted
- 1 package (1¾ ounces) powdered fruit pectin
- ½ teaspoon butter
- 4¾ cups sugar

1. In a food processor, cover and process cherries in batches until finely chopped. Transfer to a Dutch oven; stir in the pectin and butter. Bring to a full rolling boil over high heat, stirring constantly. Stir in sugar; return to a full rolling boil. Boil for 1 minute, stirring constantly.

2. Remove from the heat; skim off the foam. Ladle hot mixture into hot sterilized half-pint jars, leaving ¼-in. headspace. Remove air bubbles; wipe rims and adjust lids. Process for 5 minutes in a boiling-water canner.

Editor's Note: *The processing time listed is for altitudes of 1,000 feet or less. Add 1 minute to the processing time for each 1,000 feet of additional altitude.*

Standish House Cranberry Relish

As a descendant of Myles Standish, I sponsored a dinner at my bed-and-breakfast a few years back to offer folks some holiday history and a taste of the foods offered at the first Thanksgiving. This relish was one of the menu items.

—NORMAN STANDISH LANARK, ILLINOIS

PREP: 20 MIN. + CHILLING **MAKES:** ABOUT 3 CUPS

- ¾ cup orange or apple juice
- ⅔ cup sugar
- ¼ teaspoon ground cinnamon
- ¼ teaspoon ground nutmeg
  Dash ground cloves
- 1 package (12 ounces) fresh or frozen cranberries
- ½ cup golden raisins
- ½ cup chopped pecans

1. In a saucepan, combine the juice, sugar, cinnamon, nutmeg and cloves. Cook over medium heat, stirring frequently, until sugar is dissolved. Add cranberries and raisins; bring to a boil. Reduce heat; simmer 3-4 minutes or until cranberries pop. Remove from the heat; stir in nuts. Chill for several hours.

Liberty Sauerkraut Salad

If you're planning to serve grilled items at your gathering, consider adding this tangy, easy-to-make salad to the party.

—LAURIE NEVERMAN DENMARK, WISCONSIN

PREP: 10 MIN. + CHILLING **MAKES:** 8 SERVINGS

- 1 can (14 ounces) sauerkraut, rinsed and drained
- 1 medium green pepper, diced
- 1 cup diced celery
- 1 medium onion, diced
- ¾ to 1 cup sugar
- ½ cup cider vinegar
- 1 jar (2 ounces) diced pimientos, drained

1. In a 1-qt. serving bowl, combine all of the ingredients. Cover and refrigerate overnight. Serve with a slotted spoon.

Fruit Slush

I mix up this sweet fruity slush using juices, berries and soft drink mix. Then I store it in the freezer for unexpected company. Simply pour a little citrus soda over scoops of the colorful mixture for frosty and refreshing beverages.

—DARLENE WHITE HOBSON, MONTANA

PREP: 10 MIN. + FREEZING **MAKES:** ABOUT 5 QUARTS

- 1 can (46 ounces) pineapple juice
- 8 cups water
- 1 can (12 ounces) frozen lemonade concentrate, thawed
- 1 can (12 ounces) frozen orange juice concentrate, thawed
- 4 cups sugar
- 2 cups fresh or frozen unsweetened raspberries
- 2 envelopes unsweetened cherry soft drink mix or other red flavor of your choice

ADDITIONAL INGREDIENT
  Grapefruit or citrus soda

1. In a 6-qt. container, combine the first seven ingredients. Cover and freeze for 12 hours, stirring every 2 hours. May be frozen for up to 3 months.

2. For each serving: Place ½ cup fruit slush in a glass. Add ½ cup soda.

◄● dishing about food

Cranberries are big in Wisconsin, which grows 60 percent of the nation's crop. The state has been the top producer of cranberries for more than 15 years. The little red berry that's loaded with antioxidants has caught the attention of other countries, too. The U.S. exports about 30 percent of its total production.

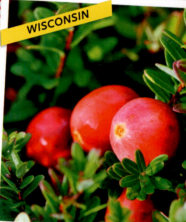

WISCONSIN

In central Wisconsin, where most of the state's crop grows, you can take a drive on "Cranberry Highway." You'll see cranberry marshes, berry-centric landmarks and exhibits along the way.

> **In the cold months, I like to put on a big pot of this comforting soup. It cooks away while I do other things, like baking bread, crafting or even cleaning the house.**

—GLENNA REIMER
GIG HARBOR, WASHINGTON

Italian Sausage Bean Soup

PREP: 20 MIN.   **COOK:** 1½ HOURS   **MAKES:** 8 SERVINGS (3 QUARTS)

1   **pound bulk Italian sausage**
1   **medium onion, finely chopped**
3   **garlic cloves, sliced**
4   **cans (14½ ounces each) reduced-sodium chicken broth**
2   **cans (15 ounces each) pinto beans, rinsed and drained**
1   **can (14½ ounces) diced tomatoes, undrained**
1   **cup medium pearl barley**
1   **large carrot, sliced**
1   **celery rib, sliced**
1   **teaspoon minced fresh sage**

½   **teaspoon minced fresh rosemary or ⅛ teaspoon dried rosemary, crushed**
6   **cups chopped fresh kale**

1. In a Dutch oven, cook sausage and onion over medium heat until meat is no longer pink. Add garlic; cook 1 minute longer. Drain.

2. Stir in the broth, beans, tomatoes, barley, carrot, celery, sage and rosemary. Bring to a boil. Reduce the heat; cover and simmer for 45 minutes.

3. Stir in kale; return to a boil. Reduce heat; cover and simmer for 25-30 minutes or until vegetables are tender and kale is wilted.

Swedish Cardamom Braids

Swedish people love their coffee—especially with this classic coffee cake. The recipe came from my father's aunt, and I remember my mother crushing cardamom seeds to make it. Back then, you couldn't buy cardamom already ground.

—**HARRIET MEOLA** MAULDIN, SOUTH CAROLINA

PREP: 45 MIN. + RISING **BAKE:** 20 MIN. + COOLING **MAKES:** 2 LOAVES (12 SLICES EACH)

- 1 package (¼ ounce) active dry yeast
- ¼ cup warm water (110° to 115°)
- 1¼ cups warm 2% milk (110° to 115°)
- ½ cup butter, softened
- ⅓ cup sugar
- 3 egg yolks
- 2½ teaspoons ground cardamom
- ⅛ teaspoon salt
- 5 to 5½ cups all-purpose flour

TOPPING

- 2 tablespoons butter, melted
- ¼ cup chopped pecans
- 2 tablespoons sugar
- 2 teaspoons ground cinnamon

1. In a large bowl, dissolve yeast in warm water. Add the milk, butter, sugar, egg yolks, cardamom, salt and 3 cups flour. Beat until smooth. Stir in enough remaining flour to form a soft dough.

2. Turn onto a floured surface; knead until smooth and elastic, about 6-8 minutes. Place in a greased bowl, turning once to the grease top. Cover and let rise in a warm place until doubled, about 1 hour.

3. Punch dough down; divide in half. Divide each half into three portions. On a lightly floured surface, shape each portion into a 16-in.-long rope. Place three ropes on a greased baking sheet and braid; pinch ends to seal and tuck under. Repeat with remaining dough. Cover and let rise until doubled, about 45 minutes.

4. Bake at 375° for 20-25 minutes or until golden brown. Remove from pans to wire racks. Brush the warm loaves with butter. Combine the pecans, sugar and cinnamon; sprinkle over the loaves.

Native Americans used every part of the pumpkin. They ate the blossoms and flesh, kept the seeds for medicines, then dried the rinds to make bowls and storage containers.

Spicy Pumpkin Seeds

We look forward to fall in anticipation of making these spicy pumpkin seeds. I often put some in a decorated jar to give as a gift.

—**CAROLYN HAYES** JOHNSTON CITY, ILLINOIS

PREP: 10 MIN. **BAKE:** 45 MIN. + COOLING
MAKES: 2 CUPS

    2 cups fresh pumpkin seeds
    2 tablespoons canola oil
    1 teaspoon Worcestershire sauce
  ⅛ to ¼ teaspoon hot pepper sauce
  ½ teaspoon salt
  ½ teaspoon paprika
  ¼ teaspoon ground cumin
  ¼ teaspoon cayenne pepper

1. In a small bowl, toss pumpkin seeds with oil, Worcestershire sauce and hot pepper sauce. Combine the salt, paprika, cumin and cayenne; sprinkle over seeds and toss to coat.

2. Line a 15x10x1-in. baking pan with foil; grease the foil. Spread pumpkin seeds in pan. Bake, uncovered, at 250° for 45-50 minutes or until lightly browned and dry, stirring occasionally. Cool completely. Store in an airtight container.

Chestnut Sausage Stuffing

I discovered this recipe in a four-generation family cookbook. I'm glad I gave it a try. It has become "the" stuffing at our holiday table.

—**JUDI OUDEKERK** BUFFALO, MINNESOTA

PREP: 30 MIN. **BAKE:** 40 MIN. **MAKES:** 8-10 SERVINGS

    1 pound bulk pork sausage
    2 cups finely chopped fresh mushrooms
  1½ cups finely chopped onion
    2 celery ribs, chopped
  ⅓ cup butter
  ¼ cup minced fresh parsley
    2 teaspoons dried thyme
  ¼ teaspoon pepper
    1 cup chicken broth
    4 cups day-old bread cubes
    1 package (8¾ ounces) whole chestnuts, chopped (about 2 cups)

1. In a large skillet, cook the sausage over medium heat until no longer pink; drain and set aside. In the same skillet, saute the mushrooms, onions and celery in butter until

tender. Stir in the sausage, parsley, thyme and pepper. Add broth; heat through. Remove from the heat. Add bread cubes and chestnuts; toss to coat.

2. Transfer to a greased shallow 2½-qt. baking dish. Cover and bake at 350° for 30 minutes. Uncover; bake 10-15 minutes longer or until heated through. Let stand for 5 minutes before serving.

Editor's Note: *These are sweet chestnuts, not water chestnuts.*

Roasted Root Veggies

Baking root vegetables in the oven instead of steaming them in the microwave makes them especially tender. Plus, they scent my house with a wonderful aroma.

—**REBECCA DORNFELD** GRASS LAKE, MICHIGAN

PREP: 15 MIN. **BAKE:** 1 HOUR **MAKES:** 15 SERVINGS

    3 large red potatoes, cut into 1-inch cubes
    1 large red onion, cut into wedges
    5 medium carrots, halved and quartered
    2 medium turnips, peeled and quartered
    2 medium parsnips, peeled and cut into ¼-inch strips
    1 small rutabaga, peeled and cut into ¾-inch cubes
    2 tablespoons canola oil
    1 teaspoon dried thyme
  ⅛ teaspoon pepper

1. Toss all of the ingredients in a large bowl. Transfer to a 15x10x1-in. baking pan coated with cooking spray.

2. Bake, uncovered, at 425° for 40-50 minutes or until the vegetables are tender, stirring occasionally.

Toasted Cheese Ravioli

Be sure to make enough of these crispy, coated ravioli. They're bound to be the hit of your party. The golden brown pillows are easy to pick up and dip in pasta sauce.

—**KATE DAMPIER** QUAIL VALLEY, CALIFORNIA

PREP: 15 MIN. **COOK:** 20 MIN. **MAKES:** 3-½ DOZEN.

- 1 package (9 ounces) refrigerated cheese ravioli
- 2 eggs
- 2 cups seasoned bread crumbs
- ½ cup shredded Parmesan cheese
- 3 teaspoons dried basil
- ½ cup canola oil, divided
  Additional shredded Parmesan cheese, optional
- 1 cup marinara sauce or meatless spaghetti sauce, warmed

1. Cook ravioli according to the package directions; drain and pat dry. In a shallow bowl, lightly beat the eggs. In another shallow bowl, combine the bread crumbs, cheese and basil. Dip the ravioli in eggs, then in bread crumb mixture.

2. In a large skillet or deep-fat fryer, heat ¼ cup oil over medium heat. Fry the ravioli in batches for 30-60 seconds on each side or until golden brown and crispy; drain on paper towels. Halfway through frying, replace the oil; wipe out skillet with paper towels if necessary.

3. Sprinkle with additional cheese if desired. Serve with marinara sauce.

Triple Mash with Horseradish Bread Crumbs

An English neighbor always referred to rutabagas as "swedes" because this is what they were called at home in England. There's a subtle sweetness hidden in these knobby root vegetables that makes them wonderful on their own, but they're even better mashed with sturdy Yukon Golds.

—**LILY JULOW** GAINESVILLE, FLORIDA

PREP: 15 MIN. **COOK:** 35 MIN.
MAKES: 12 SERVINGS (⅔ CUP)

- 4 medium Yukon Gold potatoes, peeled and cubed
- 4 medium parsnips, peeled and cubed
- 2-½ cups cubed peeled rutabaga
- 2 teaspoons salt
- ½ cup butter, divided
- 1 cup soft bread crumbs
- 2 tablespoons prepared horseradish
- 1 cup whole milk
- ¼ teaspoon pepper

1. Place vegetables and salt in a Dutch oven; add water to cover. Bring to a boil. Reduce heat; cook, uncovered, 15-20 minutes or until tender.

2. Meanwhile, in a skillet, melt 4 tablespoons butter. Stir in bread crumbs; toast over medium heat 3-5 minutes or until golden brown, stirring frequently. Stir in horseradish; remove from heat.

3. Drain vegetables; return to pan. Mash vegetables over low heat, gradually adding milk, pepper and remaining butter. Spoon into serving dish; top with bread crumb mixture.

Pumpkin patches can be found for miles upon miles around Peoria, Illinois. The many patches around the city help make Illinois the top pumpkin producer in the U.S. After harvest, the pumpkins travel to the nearby town of Morton, home of the Libby pumpkin processing plant, which cans about 85 percent of the world's pumpkins. No wonder Morton calls itself the Pumpkin Capital of the World!

Pumpkin Dinner Rolls

Serve these spicy-sweet pumpkin rolls for dinner—or any time of day—and get ready to hear a chorus of "yums" in your kitchen!

—**LINNEA REIN** TOPEKA, KANSAS

PREP: 20 MIN. + RISING **BAKE:** 20 MIN. **MAKES:** 20 ROLLS

¾ cup milk
⅓ cup packed brown sugar
5 tablespoons butter, divided
1 teaspoon salt
2 packages (¼ ounce each) active dry yeast
½ cup warm water (110° to 115°)
2 to 2½ cups all-purpose flour
1½ cups whole wheat flour
½ cup canned pumpkin
½ teaspoon ground cinnamon
¼ teaspoon ground ginger
¼ teaspoon ground nutmeg

1. In a small saucepan, heat milk, brown sugar, 4 tablespoons butter and salt to 110°-115°; set aside.

2. In a large bowl, dissolve yeast in warm water. Stir in milk mixture. Add 1½ cups all-purpose flour, wheat flour, pumpkin, cinnamon, ginger and nutmeg. Beat until smooth. Add enough remaining all-purpose flour to form a soft dough.

3. Turn onto a floured surface; knead until smooth and elastic, about 6-8 minutes.

Place in a greased bowl, turning once to grease top. Cover and let rise in a warm place until doubled, about 1 hour.

4. Punch dough down. Divide into 20 pieces; shape into balls. Place in a greased 13x9-in. baking pan. Cover and let rise for 30 minutes or until doubled.

5. Melt the remaining butter; brush over the dough. Bake at 375° for 20-25 minutes or until golden brown. Remove from pan to a wire rack. Serve warm.

Tabbouleh

This dish is so good, and good for you, that I have a special place in my flower garden for mint and parsley plants. It's best after it's chilled overnight.

—**MARION COSGROVE** KEARNEY, NEBRASKA

PREP: 35 MIN. + CHILLING **MAKES:** 10 SERVINGS

- 1¼ cups bulgur
- 1½ cups boiling water
- 2 medium tomatoes, diced
- 1 cup chopped peeled cucumber
- ¾ cup minced fresh flat-leaf parsley
- ½ cup thinly sliced green onions
- 3 tablespoons minced fresh mint
- 1¼ teaspoons salt
- ½ teaspoon dill weed
- ¼ teaspoon celery salt
- ⅓ cup lemon juice
- 2 tablespoons olive oil

1. Place the bulgur in a small bowl; cover with boiling water. Cover and let stand for 30 minutes or until water is absorbed.

2. In a large serving bowl, combine tomatoes, cucumber, parsley, onions, mint, salt, dill and celery salt. Combine lemon juice and oil; pour over vegetable mixture and toss to coat. Stir in bulgur. Cover and refrigerate for at least 4 hours before serving.

Holiday Fruit Soup

I remember eating this soup every Christmas while growing up. I considered it a real treat. My mother, who was born in Sweden, made it during holidays, and now I carry on the family tradition. I look forward to all of our Swedish Christmas traditions—especially eating this soup.

—**ENICE JACOBSON** WILDROSE, NORTH DAKOTA

PREP: 15 MIN. **COOK:** 1 HOUR **MAKES:** 8-10 SERVINGS

- 1 pound mixed dried fruit (about 4 cups)
- ¾ cup small pearl tapioca
- 6 cups water, divided
- 5 apples, peeled and cubed
- 1 cup sugar
  Ground cinnamon

1. In a large saucepan, combine the fruit, tapioca and 4 cups water. Cover and let stand overnight.

2. Stir in the apples, sugar and remaining water; bring to a boil. Reduce heat; cover and simmer for 1 hour or until tapioca is transparent. Add additional water if necessary. Serve warm or cold with a dash of cinnamon.

DEARBORN, MI

Learn about automobiles and all sorts of other American innovations inside the Henry Ford Museum. Then, step back in time at Greenfield Village, an interactive museum, also located on the grounds.

German-Style Pickled Eggs

I make these eggs and refrigerate them in a glass gallon jar for my husband to sell at his tavern, and the customers can't get enough of them. I found the recipe in an old cookbook years ago.

—MARJORIE HENNIG GREEN VALLEY, ARIZONA

PREP: 20 MIN. + CHILLING **MAKES:** 12 SERVINGS

- 2 cups cider vinegar
- 1 cup sugar
- ½ cup water
- 2 tablespoons prepared mustard
- 1 tablespoon salt
- 1 tablespoon celery seed
- 1 tablespoon mustard seed
- 6 whole cloves
- 2 medium onions, thinly sliced
- 12 hard-cooked eggs, peeled

1. In a large saucepan, combine the first eight ingredients. Bring to a boil. Reduce heat; cover and simmer for 10 minutes. Cool completely.

2. Place onions and eggs in a large jar; add enough vinegar mixture to completely cover. Cover and refrigerate for at least 8 hours or overnight. Use a clean spoon each time you remove eggs for serving. May be refrigerated for up to 1 week.

NAPPANEE, IN

This round barn at Amish Acres is just one of many that grace the rural Indiana landscape.

Creamed Corn with Bacon

My family is addicted to this yummy, crunchy side. I like to make it in the summer with farm-fresh corn!

—TINA REPAK MIRILOVICH JOHNSTOWN, PENNSYLVANIA

PREP/TOTAL TIME: 25 MIN. **MAKES:** 6 SERVINGS

- 1 small onion, finely chopped
- 1 tablespoon butter
- 4 cups fresh or frozen corn, thawed
- 1 cup heavy whipping cream
- ¼ cup chicken broth
- 4 bacon strips, cooked and crumbled
- ¼ teaspoon pepper
- ¼ cup grated Parmesan cheese
- 2 tablespoons minced fresh parsley

1. In a large skillet, saute onion in butter for 3 minutes. Add corn; saute 1-2 minutes longer or until onion and corn are tender.

2. Stir in the cream, broth, bacon and pepper. Cook and stir for 5-7 minutes or until slightly thickened. Stir in cheese and parsley.

Four-Grain Bread

My family usually gobbles up these loaves before I even have a chance to get them in the freezer. But I'm pleased they like this original recipe of mine.

—RITA REESE HUNTSBURG, OHIO

PREP: 25 MIN. + RISING
BAKE: 40 MIN. + COOLING
MAKES: 2 LOAVES (16 SLICES EACH)

- 1 cup quick-cooking oats
- 2 cups boiling water
- 2 tablespoons butter, softened
- 2 packages (¼ ounce each) active dry yeast
- ⅓ cup warm water (110° to 115°)
- ½ cup cornmeal
- ½ cup whole wheat flour
- ½ cup honey
- 2 teaspoons salt
- 5 to 6 cups all-purpose flour
  Additional butter, melted

1. In a large bowl, pour boiling water over oats. Add butter. Let stand until mixture cools to 110°-115°, stirring occasionally.

2. In a small bowl, dissolve yeast in warm water. Add to oat mixture. Add the cornmeal, whole wheat flour, honey, salt and 3 cups all-purpose flour. Beat until smooth. Stir in enough remaining all-purpose flour to form a soft dough.

3. Turn onto a floured surface; knead until smooth and elastic, about 6-8 minutes. Place in a greased bowl, turning once to grease the top. Cover and let rise in a warm place until doubled, about 1 hour.

4. Punch dough down. Turn onto a lightly floured surface; divide in half. Shape each portion into a loaf. Place in two greased 9x5-in. loaf pans. Cover and let rise until doubled, about 45 minutes.

5. Bake at 350° for 40-45 minutes or until golden brown. Remove from pans to wire racks. Brush with melted butter. Cool.

Hot Apple Cider

In this recipe, brown sugar and spices add extra flavor to already delicious apple cider.

—MARLYS BENNING ACKLEY, IOWA

PREP/TOTAL TIME: 15 MIN.   **MAKES:** 16-20 SERVINGS

- ⅔ cup packed brown sugar
- 1 teaspoon whole cloves
- 1 teaspoon ground allspice
- 3 cinnamon sticks (3 inches), broken
- 1 gallon apple cider

1. Fill the filter-lined basket of a large automatic percolator with the brown sugar, cloves, allspice and cinnamon sticks. Prepare as you would coffee according to manufacturer's directions, but substitute cider for water.

Editor's Note: *Do not use a drip-style coffee maker for this recipe.*

BLACK HILLS, SD

Farmland certainly does sweep across South Dakota, but in the southwest, the Black Hills take over. Here, you'll find the Mount Rushmore National Memorial, carved in the 1930s. Nearly 3 million people stop to see the majestic faces of George Washington, Thomas Jefferson, Theodore Roosevelt and Abraham Lincoln each year.

German Potato Salad

PREP: 30 MIN. + COOLING **COOK:** 20 MIN.
MAKES: 8 SERVINGS

- 3 pounds medium red potatoes
- 5 bacon strips, diced
- 1 medium onion, chopped
- ¼ cup all-purpose flour
- 2 teaspoons salt
- ¼ teaspoon celery seed
- ¼ teaspoon pepper
- 1¼ cups sugar
- 1 cup cider vinegar
- ¾ cup water
- 3 tablespoons minced fresh parsley

1. Place potatoes in a Dutch oven; cover with water. Bring to a boil. Reduce heat; cover and simmer for 25-30 minutes or until tender. Drain and cool.

2. In a large skillet, cook bacon over medium heat until crisp; using a slotted spoon, remove to paper towels. Drain, reserving 4 tablespoons drippings. In the drippings, saute onion until tender.

3. Stir in flour, salt, celery seed and pepper until blended. Gradually add sugar, vinegar and water. Bring to a boil over medium-high heat; cook and stir for 2 minutes or until thickened.

4. Cut potatoes into ¼-in. slices. Add potatoes and bacon to the skillet; cook and stir gently over low heat until heated through. Sprinkle with parsley. Serve warm.

Wild Rice Pilaf

I make this rice dish for almost every holiday and often take it to potlucks. Usually, I make the pilaf ahead to allow the flavors to blend and then reheat it in the microwave before serving. This also gives me more room in the oven and less chaos when I'm putting out a big meal.

—DIANNE BETTIN TRUMAN, MINNESOTA

PREP: 1 HOUR **BAKE:** 25 MIN. **MAKES:** 10 SERVINGS

- 2 cans (14½ ounces each) chicken broth
- ¾ cup uncooked wild rice
- 1 cup uncooked long grain rice
- 1 large onion, chopped
- 2 medium carrots, halved lengthwise and sliced
- ½ teaspoon dried rosemary, crushed
- ½ cup butter, cubed
- 1 garlic clove, minced
- 3 cups fresh broccoli florets
- ¼ teaspoon pepper

1. In a large saucepan, bring broth to a boil. Add the wild rice; reduce heat. Cover and cook for 30 minutes. Add the long grain rice; cook 20-25 minutes longer or until liquid is absorbed and rice is tender.

2. Meanwhile, in a large skillet, saute the onion, carrots and rosemary in butter until vegetables are tender. Add garlic; cook 1 minute longer. Stir in the rice, broccoli and pepper.

3. Transfer to a greased shallow 2-qt. baking dish. Cover and bake at 350° for 25-30 minutes or until broccoli is crisp-tender. Fluff with a fork before serving.

Hanky Pankies

The fact that these go from freezer to oven means there is less last-minute kitchen fuss—and more time to spend with guests!

—SHARON SKILDUM MAPLE GROVE, MINNESOTA

PREP: 30 MIN. **COOK:** 15 MIN. **MAKES:** ABOUT 4 DOZEN

- 1 pound ground beef
- 1 pound bulk pork sausage
- 1 medium onion, chopped
- 1 pound Mexican process cheese (Velveeta), cubed
- 1 tablespoon Worcestershire sauce
- 1 teaspoon dried oregano
  Salt and pepper to taste
- 1 loaf (1 pound) snack rye bread
  Minced fresh parsley, optional

1. In a large skillet, cook the beef, sausage and onion over medium heat until meat is no longer pink; drain. Stir in the cheese, Worcestershire sauce and seasonings.

2. Spread rye bread slices with 1 heaping tablespoon of mixture; place on baking sheets. Broil 4-6 in. from heat for 3 minutes or until bubbly. May be frozen and broiled without thawing. If desired, sprinkle with parsley before serving.

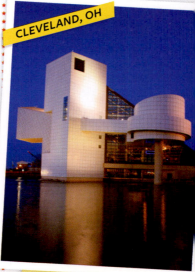

◀● dishing about food

This crowd-pleasing snack—not to be confused with the alcoholic beverage— is a Cleveland favorite, especially at tailgate parties and potlucks.

CLEVELAND, OH

Though rock music has been around for several decades, the Rock and Roll Hall of Fame and Museum was completed much more recently, in 1995.

> " I taste the berries or filling before adding to the pie crust just to make sure it's sweet enough. Slicing the berries helps them absorb more of the sugar and flavorings. It's delicious served warm. "

—ELAINE MOODY
CLEVER, MISSOURI

Ozark Mountain Berry Pie

PREP: 15 MIN. **BAKE:** 45 MIN. + COOLING **MAKES:** 8 SERVINGS

1 cup sugar
¼ cup cornstarch
½ teaspoon ground cinnamon, optional
    Dash salt
⅓ cup water
1 cup fresh blueberries
    Pastry for a double-crust pie (9 inches)
1 cup halved fresh strawberries
1 cup fresh raspberries
¾ cup fresh blackberries
1 tablespoon lemon juice
2 tablespoons butter

1. In a large saucepan, combine the sugar, cornstarch, cinnamon if desired, salt and water until smooth; add the blueberries. Bring to a boil; cook and stir for 2 minutes or until thickened. Set aside to cool slightly.

2. Line a 9-in. pie plate with bottom crust; trim pastry even with edge. Gently fold the strawberries, raspberries, blackberries and lemon juice into the blueberry mixture. Pour into pastry; dot with butter. Roll out remaining pastry; make a lattice crust. Trim, seal and flute edges.

3. Bake at 400° for 10 minutes. Reduce heat to 350°; bake for 45-50 minutes or until the crust is golden brown and filling is bubbly. Cool on a wire rack. Store in the refrigerator.

German Black Forest Cake

As far as I know, this cake recipe can be traced back to my German great-grandma. When I got married, my mother gave me my own copy.
—**STEPHANIE TRAVIS** FALLON, NEVADA

PREP: 45 MIN. + COOLING **BAKE:** 30 MIN. + COOLING
MAKES: 12 SERVINGS

- 1 **cup whole milk**
- 3 **eggs**
- ½ **cup canola oil**
- 3 **teaspoons vanilla extract**
- 2 **cups plus 2 tablespoons all-purpose flour**
- 2 **cups sugar**
- ¾ **cup baking cocoa**
- 1½ **teaspoons baking powder**
- ¾ **teaspoon baking soda**
- ¾ **teaspoon salt**

FILLING
- 2 **cans (14½ ounces each) pitted tart cherries**
- 1 **cup sugar**
- ¼ **cup cornstarch**
- 3 **tablespoons cherry brandy or 2 teaspoons vanilla extract**

WHIPPED CREAM
- 3 **cups heavy whipping cream**
- ⅓ **cup confectioners' sugar**

1. Preheat oven to 350°. Line bottoms of two greased 9-in. round baking pans; grease paper.

2. In a large bowl, beat milk, eggs, oil and vanilla until well blended. Whisk together flour, sugar, cocoa, baking powder, baking soda and salt; gradually beat into milk mixture.

3. Transfer to prepared pans. Bake 30-35 minutes or until a toothpick inserted near the center comes out clean. Cool in pans 10 minutes before removing to a wire rack; remove paper. Cool completely.

4. For filling, drain cherries, reserving ½ cup juice. In a small saucepan, whisk sugar, cornstarch and reserved juice; add cherries. Cook and stir over low heat 10-12 minutes or until thickened and bubbly. Remove from heat; stir in brandy. Cool completely.

5. In a large bowl, beat cream until it begins to thicken. Add sugar; beat until stiff peaks form.

6. Using a long serrated knife, cut each cake horizontally in half. Place one cake layer on a serving plate. Top with 1½ cups whipped cream. Spread ¾ cup filling to within 1 in. of edge. Repeat twice. Top with remaining cake layer. Frost top and sides of cake with remaining whipped cream, reserving some to pipe decorations, if desired. Spoon remaining filling onto top of cake. Refrigerate until serving.

BISMARCK, ND

The capital city of North Dakota isn't named for a doughnut, but rather for the German statesman Otto von Bismarck. This bison statue, honoring the important symbol of the Great Plains, stands on the capitol grounds.

WEST ALLIS, WI

The Wisconsin State Fair has been held in this Milwaukee area city since 1892. Nowadays, nearly 1 million folks of all ages come to enjoy the 11-day festival.

State Fair Cream Puffs

Here's a classic recipe for cream puffs. Be sure to try the three variations for fillings, too! You won't believe how easy it is to make this favorite treat.

—**RUTH JUNGBLUTH** DODGEVILLE, WISCONSIN

PREP: 25 MIN. **BAKE:** 35 MIN. + COOLING
MAKES: 10 SERVINGS

- 1 **cup water**
- ½ **cup butter**
- ¼ **teaspoon salt**
- 1 **cup all-purpose flour**
- 4 **eggs**
- 2 **tablespoons milk**
- 1 **egg yolk, lightly beaten**
- 2 **cups heavy whipping cream**
- ¼ **cup confectioners' sugar**
- ½ **teaspoon vanilla extract**
  Additional confectioners' sugar

1. In a large saucepan, bring the water, butter and salt to a boil over medium heat. Add flour all at once and stir until a smooth ball forms. Remove from the heat; let stand for 5 minutes. Add eggs, one at a time, beating well after each addition. Continue beating until mixture is smooth and shiny.

2. Drop by ¼ cupfuls 3 in. apart onto greased baking sheets. Combine milk and egg yolk; brush over puffs. Bake at 400° for 30-35 minutes or until golden brown. Remove to wire racks. Immediately cut a slit in each for steam to escape; cool.

3. In a large bowl, beat cream until it begins to thicken. Add sugar and vanilla; beat until almost stiff. Split cream puffs; discard soft dough from inside. Fill the cream puffs just before serving. Dust with confectioners' sugar. Refrigerate leftovers.

Strawberry Cream Puffs: *Omit whipped cream filling. In a small mixing bowl, beat 2 packages (8 ounces each) softened cream cheese and 1 cup sugar until fluffy. Fold in 4 cups whipped cream and 3 cups coarsely chopped strawberries.*

Vanilla Cream Puffs: *Omit whipped cream filling. In a bowl, whisk 1½ cups milk, 1 package (5.1 ounces) instant vanilla pudding mix and ½ teaspoon almond extract for 2 minutes. Let stand for 2 minutes or until soft-set. Fold in 4 cups whipped cream. Fill as directed.*

Chocolate Glaze for Cream Puffs: *In a heavy saucepan, melt 6 tablespoons semisweet chocolate chips, 1½ teaspoons shortening and ¾ teaspoon corn syrup over low heat, stirring until smooth. Drizzle over cream puffs.*

Hazelnut Apricot Strudel

Did you know that strudel is the German word for whirlpool? The swirling layers of this filled and rolled dessert likely led to its unusual name.

—TASTE OF HOME TEST KITCHEN

PREP: 30 MIN. + COOLING **BAKE:** 15 MIN. + COOLING
MAKES: 8 SERVINGS

- 1 package (6 ounces) dried apricots, chopped
- ¼ cup sugar
- 1 teaspoon orange peel
- ½ cup orange juice
- ¼ cup water
- ⅓ cup chopped hazelnuts
- 6 sheets phyllo dough (14x9-inches)
- 2 tablespoons butter, melted
- ⅓ cup graham cracker crumbs (about 5 squares)

1. In a small saucepan, combine the apricots, sugar and peel. Stir in orange juice and water. Bring to a boil. Reduce heat; simmer, uncovered, for 15 minutes or until juice is absorbed, stirring occasionally. Remove from the heat and cool to room temperature. Set aside 1 tablespoon nuts; toast remaining nuts. Stir into apricot mixture.

2. Place one sheet of phyllo dough on a work surface; brush with butter and sprinkle with 1 tablespoon of crumbs. Repeat with 5 more sheets of phyllo; brushing each layer with butter and sprinkling with crumbs. (Keep remaining phyllo covered with plastic wrap and a damp towel to prevent it from drying out.)

3. Carefully spread filling along one long edge to within 2 in. of edges. Fold the two short sides over filling. Roll up jelly-roll style, starting with a long side.

4. Place seam side down on a greased baking sheet. Brush the top with butter and score top lightly every 1½ in. Sprinkle with the reserved nuts.

5. Bake at 375° for 15 minutes or until golden brown. Cool the strudel on a wire rack. Slice at scored marks.

Golden Apple Snack Cake

This moist, old-fashioned cake is hard to beat, especially when warmed up and finished off with a dollop of whipped topping!

—CARRIE GRAVOT BELLEVILLE, ILLINOIS

PREP: 15 MIN. **BAKE:** 35 MIN. + COOLING
MAKES: 9 SERVINGS

- ½ cup butter, softened
- 1 cup sugar
- 1 egg
- 1 cup all-purpose flour
- ½ teaspoon baking soda
- ½ teaspoon ground cinnamon
- 2½ cups chopped peeled tart apples
- ½ cup chopped pecans

1. In a large bowl, cream butter and sugar until light and fluffy. Add egg. Combine the flour, baking soda and cinnamon; gradually beat into the creamed mixture. Fold in apples and pecans.

2. Transfer to a greased 9-in. square baking pan. Bake at 350° for 32-38 minutes or until a toothpick inserted near the center comes out clean. Cool on a wire rack.

Swedish Tea Rings

Although my family is of Polish and German descent, we sure enjoy this sweet bit of Sweden! Mom was always sure to make this for Easter breakfast.

—**MYRA PRATT** FAIRVIEW, PENNSYLVANIA

PREP: 25 MIN. + CHILLING **BAKE:** 20 MIN. + COOLING
MAKES: 2 PASTRY RINGS (12-16 SERVINGS EACH)

2¼ cups all-purpose flour
2 tablespoons plus 1 teaspoon sugar, divided
1 teaspoon salt
½ cup cold butter
1 package (¼ ounce) active dry yeast
¼ cup warm water (110° to 115°)
¼ cup warm evaporated milk (110° to 115°)
1 egg
¼ cup dried currants or raisins

FILLING
¼ cup butter, softened
½ cup packed brown sugar
½ cup chopped pecans

BROWNED BUTTER GLAZE
2 tablespoons butter
1 cup confectioners' sugar
½ teaspoon vanilla extract
3 to 4 teaspoons evaporated milk

1. In a bowl, combine flour, 2 tablespoons sugar and salt. Cut in butter until mixture resembles fine crumbs. In a large another large bowl, dissolve yeast and remaining sugar in warm water. Add milk, egg and crumb mixture; beat until well blended. Stir in currants. Cover and refrigerate overnight.

2. Line two baking sheets with foil and grease the foil; set aside. For filling, in a small bowl, cream butter and brown sugar until light and fluffy; stir in pecans.

3. Punch down dough. Turn onto a lightly floured surface; divide in half. Roll each portion into a 14x7-in. rectangle; spread filling to within ½ in. of edges. Roll up jelly-roll style, starting with a long side; pinch seams to seal.

4. Place loaves seam side down on prepared pans; pinch ends together to form a ring. With scissors, cut from outside edge two-thirds of the way toward center of ring at 1-in. intervals. Separate strips slightly; twist to allow filling to show. Cover and let rise in a warm place until doubled, about 45 minutes.

5. Bake at 350° for 18-22 minutes or until golden brown. Remove from pans to wire racks to cool.

6. For glaze, in a small saucepan, cook butter over medium heat until lightly browned, stirring constantly. Remove from the heat. Stir in confectioners' sugar, vanilla and enough milk to achieve desired consistency. Drizzle over pastry rings.

Crisp Sunflower Cookies

Kansas is the "Sunflower State," and these crisp cookies feature sunflower seeds.

—**KAREN ANN BLAND** GOVE, KANSAS

PREP: 10 MIN. **BAKE:** 15 MIN./BATCH **MAKES:** 5 DOZEN

¾ cup shortening
1 cup sugar
1 cup packed brown sugar
2 eggs
1 teaspoon vanilla extract
2 cups all-purpose flour
1 teaspoon baking soda
½ teaspoon baking powder
½ teaspoon salt
2 cups quick-cooking oats
1 cup flaked coconut
1 cup salted sunflower kernels

1. In a bowl, cream shortening and sugars until light and fluffy. Add eggs and vanilla; mix well. Combine flour, baking soda, baking powder and salt; add to creamed mixture and mix well. Stir in the oats, coconut and sunflower kernels.

2. Drop by teaspoonfuls onto greased baking sheets. Bake at 350° for 12-15 minutes or until golden brown.

Fruit Kuchen

This German recipe—passed down by my grandma—is one of the first desserts I made when I was young. I remember patting the crust into the pan many times. Now I work at a bakery and still make it often!

—CONNIE MEISELWITZ KIEL, WISCONSIN

PREP: 20 MIN. **BAKE:** 50 MIN. **MAKES:** 12-15 SERVINGS

CRUST
- 1½ cups all-purpose flour
- ½ teaspoon salt
- 1 tablespoon sugar
- ½ cup cold butter, cubed
- 1 egg, beaten
- 1 tablespoon milk

FILLING
- 4 to 6 cups fresh fruit (quartered apples, peaches, plums, etc.)
- 1 cup sugar
- 1 tablespoon all-purpose flour
- 2 eggs, beaten
- 1 cup heavy whipping cream
- ½ teaspoon vanilla extract

CRUMB TOPPING
- ½ cup sugar
- ½ cup all-purpose flour
- 2 tablespoons butter, softened

1. In a bowl, combine flour, salt and sugar; cut in butter until mixture resembles cornmeal. Mix egg and milk; add to flour mixture.

2. Press into a greased 13x9-in. baking dish. Arrange fruit on crust. Combine remaining filling ingredients; pour over fruit. For topping, combine ingredients until crumbly; sprinkle over filling. Bake at 350° for 50-60 minutes or until fruit is tender.

Fresh Cherry Pie

PREP: 25 MIN. **BAKE:** 55 MIN. + COOLING
MAKES: 8 SERVINGS

- 1¼ cups sugar
- ⅓ cup cornstarch
- 1 cup cherry juice blend
- 4 cups fresh tart cherries, pitted, or frozen pitted tart cherries, thawed
- ½ teaspoon ground cinnamon
- ¼ teaspoon ground nutmeg
- ¼ teaspoon almond extract

PASTRY
- 2 cups all-purpose flour
- ½ teaspoon salt
- ⅔ cup shortening
- 5 to 7 tablespoons cold water

1. In a large saucepan, combine sugar and cornstarch; gradually stir in the cherry juice until smooth. Bring to a boil; cook and stir for 2 minutes or until thickened. Remove from the heat. Add the cherries, cinnamon, nutmeg and extract; set aside.

2. In a large bowl, combine flour and salt; cut in shortening until crumbly. Gradually add cold water, tossing with a fork until a ball forms. Divide pastry in half so that one ball is slightly larger than the other.

3. On a lightly floured surface, roll out larger ball to fit a 9-in. pie plate. Transfer pastry to pie plate; trim ½ in. beyond edge of plate. Add filling. Roll out remaining pastry; make a lattice crust. Trim, seal and flute edges.

4. Bake at 425° for 10 minutes. Reduce heat to 375°; bake 45-50 minutes longer or until crust is golden brown. Cool on a wire rack.

> **"This ruby-red treat is just sweet enough, with a hint of almond flavor and a good level of cinnamon. The cherries peeking out of the lattice crust makes it so pretty, too!"**
>
> —JOSIE BOCHEK
> STURGEON BAY, WISCONSIN

Super Banana Splits

These yummy banana splits are topped with a velvety chocolate sauce that's scrumptious...and so easy to make!

—LIZZ (ELIZABETH) LODER
FOX POINT, WISCONSIN

PREP/TOTAL TIME: 20 MIN.   **MAKES:** 6 SERVINGS

- 2   cups (12 ounces) semisweet chocolate chips
- ⅔   cup heavy whipping cream
- ¾   teaspoon cherry extract
- 6   medium firm bananas, cut in half lengthwise
- 6   scoops each strawberry, vanilla and chocolate ice cream
      Whipped topping, chopped nuts and maraschino cherries with stems

1. In a small heavy saucepan, cook and stir chocolate chips and cream over low heat until smooth and blended. Remove from the heat. Stir in extract; keep warm.

2. Place two banana pieces in each of six shallow serving dishes. Top each with a scoop of strawberry, vanilla and chocolate ice cream. Drizzle with warm chocolate sauce. Garnish with whipped topping, nuts and a cherry.

Old-Time Custard Ice Cream

My family's custardy ice cream recipe is very creamy and tastes just like the good old-fashioned cranked type.

—MARTHA SELF MONTGOMERY, TEXAS

PREP: 55 MIN. + CHILLING
PROCESS: 55 MIN./BATCH + FREEZING
MAKES: 2¾ QUARTS

- 1½ cups sugar
- ¼   cup all-purpose flour
- ½   teaspoon salt
- 4   cups milk
- 4   eggs, lightly beaten
- 3   tablespoons vanilla extract
- 2   pints heavy whipping cream

1. In a heavy saucepan, combine sugar, flour and salt. Gradually add the milk until smooth. Bring to a boil over medium heat; cook and stir for 2 minutes or until thickened. Remove from the heat; cool slightly.

2. Whisk a small amount of hot milk mixture into the eggs; return all to the pan, whisking constantly. Cook and stir over low heat until mixture reaches at least 160° and coats the back of a metal spoon. Cool quickly by placing pan in a bowl of ice water; stir for 2 minutes. Stir in vanilla. Press plastic wrap onto the surface of custard. Refrigerate for several hours or overnight.

3. Stir cream into custard. Fill cylinder of ice cream freezer two-thirds full; freeze according to manufacturer's directions. Refrigerate remaining mixture until ready to freeze. Allow ice cream to ripen in ice cream freezer or firm up in the refrigerator freezer for 2-4 hours before serving.

Whipped Cream Krumkake

Our town of Decorah, in the northeast corner of Iowa, has a rich Norwegian heritage. That heritage is evident at holidays and during our annual "Nordic Fest," when krumkake is king! There are demonstrations of krumkake-making in many store windows, and this rich delicious pastry is served at most family dinners and many bake sales.

—**IMELDA NESTEBY** DECORAH, IOWA

PREP: 20 MIN. + CHILLING   **BAKE:** 20 MIN.   **MAKES:** ABOUT 3 DOZEN KRUMKAKES

- 3 **large eggs**
- 1 **cup sugar**
- ½ **cup sweet butter, melted**
- ½ **cup heavy whipping cream, whipped**
- ½ **teaspoon nutmeg**
- 1½ **cups all-purpose flour**
  Sweet butter for krumkake plates

1. Beat eggs in bowl until very light. Add sugar gradually, beating to blend. Slowly add melted butter, then whipped cream and nutmeg. Mix in flour. (Dough will be consistency of cookie dough.) Chill dough thoroughly.

2. Preheat krumkake plates over medium heat for about 10 minutes or until a drop of water "dances" when dropped on the plates. Brush plates with sweet butter; place 1 slightly rounded tablespoon of dough in center of lower plate; close iron and press handles together. If excess dough comes out the sides, remove with table knife.

3. Bake for about 30 seconds; flip iron and bake for about 30 seconds on other side. Remove krumkake and immediately roll over cone-shaped form. Place seam side down on parchment paper to cool; remove form.

4. Fill cooled cones with sweetened whipped cream if desired. Serve immediately.

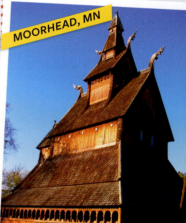

◀● dishing about food

Krumkake is a traditional Norwegian cookie, usually made at Christmastime using a hot iron. While the cookie is still warm, it's rolled into a cone, which can then be filled with whipped cream. Yum!

MOORHEAD, MN

The Hjemkomst Center in Moorhead—a city proud of its Norwegian heritage—is a community facility that houses the Chamber of Commerce, a Viking ship, cultural archives and the Stave Church, a full-scale replica of one in Vik, Norway.

ST. LOUIS, MO

German-Americans from the St. Louis area have had quite an impact on the culinary world, including the beer-brewing Busch family and famed cookbook author Irma Rombauer.

Lebkuchen

It's tradition for my family to get together on Thanksgiving weekend and bake these spice-filled treats. The recipe came from my great-grandmother.

—ESTHER KEMPKER JEFFERSON CITY, MISSOURI

PREP: 25 MIN. **BAKE:** 25 MIN. + COOLING
MAKES: 3 DOZEN

- ½ cup butter, softened
- ½ cup sugar
- ⅓ cup packed brown sugar
- 2 eggs
- 1 cup molasses
- ¼ cup buttermilk
- ½ teaspoon anise extract
- 4½ cups all-purpose flour
- 1½ teaspoons baking powder
- 1 teaspoon baking soda
- 1 teaspoon ground cinnamon
- ½ teaspoon salt
- ½ teaspoon each ground cloves, allspice and cardamom
- ½ cup ground walnuts
- ½ cup raisins
- ½ cup pitted dates
- ½ cup candied lemon peel
- ⅓ cup flaked coconut
- ¼ cup candied orange peel
- 3 tablespoons candied pineapple

GLAZE
- ½ cup sugar
- ¼ cup water
- 2 tablespoons confectioners' sugar

1. Line a 15x10x1-in. baking pan with foil; grease the foil and set aside.

2. In a large bowl, cream butter and sugars until light and fluffy. Add eggs, one at a time, beating well after each. Beat in the molasses, buttermilk and anise extract. Combine the flour, baking powder, baking soda, cinnamon, salt, cloves, allspice and cardamom; gradually add to creamed mixture and mix well. Stir in the walnuts.

3. In a food processor, combine the raisins, dates, lemon peel, coconut, orange peel and pineapple in batches; cover and process until chopped. Stir into batter. Press dough into prepared pan.

4. Bake at 350° for 25-28 minutes or until lightly browned. In a small saucepan, bring sugar and water to a boil. Boil for 1 minute. Whisk in confectioners' sugar. Spread over warm bars. Immediately cut into squares. Cool in pan on a wire rack.

Sunflower-Cherry Granola Bars

These chewy bars have plenty of oats and nuts, and the dried cherries add just the right amount of tang.

—**LAURA MCDOWELL** LAKE VILLA, ILLINOIS

PREP: 30 MIN. + COOLING **MAKES:** 2½ DOZEN

- 4 **cups old-fashioned oats**
- 1 **cup sliced almonds**
- 1 **cup flaked coconut**
- 1 **cup sugar**
- 1 **cup light corn syrup**
- 1 **cup creamy peanut butter**
- ½ **cup raisins**
- ½ **cup dried cherries**
- ½ **cup sunflower kernels**

1. Spread oats into an ungreased 15x10x1-in. baking pan. Bake at 400° for 15-20 minutes or until lightly browned. Meanwhile, spread almonds and coconut into another ungreased 15x10x1-in. baking pan. Bake for 8-10 minutes or until lightly toasted.

2. In a Dutch oven over medium heat, bring sugar and corn syrup to a boil. Cook and stir for 2-3 minutes or until sugar is dissolved. Remove from the heat; stir in peanut butter until combined. Add the raisins, cherries, sunflower kernels, and toasted oats, almonds and coconut.

3. Using a metal spatula, press mixture into an ungreased 15x10x1-in. baking pan. Cool to room temperature. Cut into bars.

Popcorn Delight

Whenever I take this sweet mix somewhere, I bring copies of the recipe because people always ask for it. Once you start munching, it's hard to stop!

—**CHERYL BULL** BLUE GRASS, IOWA

PREP: 15 MIN. + CHILLING **MAKES:** ABOUT 6 QUARTS

- 14 **cups popped popcorn**
- 2 **cups salted peanuts**
- 2 **cups crisp rice cereal**
- 2 **cups miniature marshmallows**
- 1 **pound white candy coating, coarsely chopped**
- 3 **tablespoons creamy peanut butter**

1. In a large bowl, combine the popcorn, peanuts, cereal and marshmallows. In a microwave, melt candy coating and peanut butter; stir until smooth. Pour over popcorn mixture; toss to coat.

2. Spread onto waxed paper-lined baking sheets; refrigerate for 15 minutes or until set. Break into pieces. Store in an airtight container in the refrigerator.

KANSAS

Kansas is nicknamed the Sunflower State. The wild variety of this native plant is so common there, it's actually considered a weed!

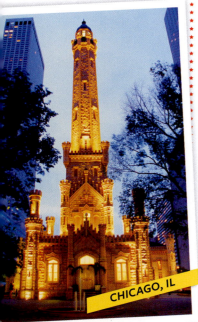

CHICAGO, IL

A reminder of Chicago's rich past, the Historic Water Tower stands beside bustling Michigan Avenue. Completed in 1869, it survived the Great Chicago Fire two years later. Now, local artists display their work inside.

Fruity Cereal Bars

With dried apple and cranberries, these crispy cereal bars are perfect for snacks or brown-bag lunches. Store the extras in plastic containers...that is, if you have any!

—GIOVANNA KRANENBERG
CAMBRIDGE, MINNESOTA

PREP/TOTAL TIME: 30 MIN. **MAKES:** 20 SERVINGS

- 3 tablespoons butter
- 1 package (10 ounces) large marshmallows
- 6 cups crisp rice cereal
- ½ cup chopped dried apples
- ½ cup dried cranberries

1. In a large saucepan, combine butter and marshmallows. Cook and stir over medium-low heat until melted. Remove from the heat; stir in the cereal, apples and cranberries.

2. Pat into a 13x9-in. pan coated with cooking spray; cool. Cut into squares.

Glazed Pfeffernuesse

This version of the classic German cookie is nice to have on hand throughout the holiday season. The cookies stay fresh—and actually become more intense in flavor when stored in an airtight container.

—TASTE OF HOME TEST KITCHEN

PREP: 1¼ HOURS + CHILLING **BAKE:** 10 MIN./BATCH
MAKES: ABOUT 10 DOZEN

- 1¼ cups butter, softened
- 1¼ cups packed brown sugar
- ¾ cup molasses
- ½ cup water
- 1 teaspoon anise extract
- 6 cups cake flour
- ½ teaspoon baking soda
- ½ teaspoon salt
- 1½ teaspoons ground cinnamon
- ½ teaspoon ground allspice
- ½ teaspoon ground cloves
- ¼ teaspoon ground nutmeg
- ¼ teaspoon ground mace
- ⅛ teaspoon pepper
- ⅛ teaspoon ground cardamom
- 2 cups finely chopped nuts

GLAZE
- 1 cup confectioners' sugar
- 3 tablespoons 2% milk
- ¼ teaspoon vanilla extract
  Additional confectioners' sugar

1. In a large bowl, cream butter and brown sugar until light and fluffy. Beat in the molasses, water and extract. Combine the flour, baking soda, salt and spices; gradually add to creamed mixture and mix well. Stir in nuts. Cover and refrigerate for 1 hour.

2. Roll dough into 1-in. balls. Place 2 in. apart on greased baking sheets. Bake at 375° for 10-12 minutes or until golden brown.

3. Meanwhile, in a shallow bowl, combine the confectioners' sugar, milk and vanilla. Place additional confectioners' sugar in another shallow bowl. Remove cookies to wire racks; cool 5 minutes. Dip tops of warm cookies in glaze, allow excess to drip off; dip in confectioners' sugar. Cool completely on wire racks. Store in an airtight container.

Editor's Note: *This recipe does not use eggs.*

Traditional Popcorn Balls

Kids of all ages enjoy these old-fashioned holiday treats. One batch goes a long way.

—CATHY KARGES HAZEN, NORTH DAKOTA

PREP/TOTAL TIME: 20 MIN. **MAKES:** 20 SERVINGS

- 7 quarts popped popcorn
- 1 cup sugar
- 1 cup light corn syrup
- ¼ cup water
- ¼ teaspoon salt
- 3 tablespoons butter
- 1 teaspoon vanilla extract
  Food coloring, optional

1. Place popcorn in a large baking pan; keep warm in a 200° oven.

2. In a heavy saucepan, combine the sugar, corn syrup, water and salt. Cook over medium heat until a candy thermometer reads 235° (soft-ball stage).

3. Remove from the heat. Add the butter, vanilla and food coloring if desired; stir until butter is melted. Immediately pour over popcorn and stir until evenly coated.

4. When mixture is cool enough to handle, quickly shape into 3-in. balls, dipping hands in cold water to prevent sticking.

Editor's Note: *We recommend that you test your candy thermometer before each use by bringing water to a boil; the thermometer should read 212°. Adjust your recipe temperature up or down based on your test.*

Sandbakkelse (Sand Tarts)

Translated from Norwegian, the name of these cookies is "sand tarts." They're most attractive if baked in authentic sandbakkelse molds, which can be purchased in Scandinavian import shops. The interesting shapes will make these tarts the focus of your cookie tray, although most any decorative cookie mold will do!

—KAREN HOYLO DULUTH, MINNESOTA

PREP: 15 MIN. + CHILLING **BAKE:** 10 MIN.
MAKES: ABOUT 8 DOZEN

- 1 cup plus 2 tablespoons butter, softened
- 1 cup sugar
- 1 egg
- 1 teaspoon almond extract
- ½ teaspoon vanilla extract
- 3 cups all-purpose flour

1. In a bowl, cream butter and sugar. Add egg and extracts. Blend in flour. Cover and chill for 1-2 hours or overnight. Using ungreased sandbakkelse molds, press about 1 tablespoon dough into each mold.

2. Bake at 375° for 10-12 minutes or until cookies appear set and just begin to brown around the edges. Cool for 2-3 minutes in molds. When cool to the touch, remove cookies from molds. To remove more easily, gently tap with a knife and carefully squeeze the mold.

SAC CITY, IA

About 250 people packed together the World's Largest Popcorn Ball at Noble Popcorn Farms. It's on display downtown.

This cardamom-spiced Christmas bread is like those made in Scandinavian countries. The yeast bread is studded with candied fruit and raisins, then topped with an icing.

Julekage

When we lived in California, a friend made these breads for us at Christmas. Once we moved here, I found myself missing those light, moist loaves dotted with candied fruit and blanketed with thick frosting. So I hunted up this recipe and started making them. The cardamom gives the bread a wonderfully distinctive flavor. Nice for gifts, too!

—**CAROL MEAD** LOS ALAMOS, NEW MEXICO

PREP: 25 MIN. + RISING **BAKE:** 35 MIN. **MAKES:** 2 LOAVES

- 2 packages (¼ ounce each) active dry yeast
- 1 teaspoon plus ½ cup sugar, divided
- ½ cup warm water (110° to 115°)
- ¾ cup warm milk (110° to 115°)
- ½ cup butter, softened
- 1 egg
- 1 teaspoon salt
- ½ teaspoon ground cardamom
- 5 to 5½ cups all-purpose flour
- 1½ cups chopped mixed candied fruit
- ½ cup golden raisins

FROSTING
- 1 cup confectioners' sugar
- 2 tablespoons butter, melted
- 1 tablespoon milk
  Red and green candied cherries

1. In a bowl, dissolve yeast and 1 teaspoon sugar in water; let stand for 5 minutes. Add milk, butter, egg, salt, cardamom, 2¼ cups flour and remaining sugar. Beat until smooth. Stir in the fruit, raisins and enough remaining flour to form a soft dough.

2. Turn onto a floured surface; knead until smooth and elastic, about 6-8 minutes. Place in a greased bowl, turning once to grease the top. Cover and let rise in a warm place until doubled, about 1½ hours.

3. Punch dough down; shape into two loaves; place in two greased 8x4-in. loaf pans. Cover and let rise until doubled, about 45 minutes. Bake at 350° for 35-40 minutes or until golden brown. Remove from pans ; cool on wire racks.

4. For frosting, combine confectioners' sugar, butter and milk until smooth; spread over the loaves. Decorate with cherries.

Sugar Cream Pie

I absolutely love sugar cream pie—especially this recipe that my grandma made for me. You can serve it warm, but I like it better cold so I refrigerate it for a couple of hours before eating.

—LAURA KIPPER WESTFIELD, INDIANA

PREP: 20 MIN. **BAKE:** 15 MIN. + CHILLING **MAKES:** 8 SERVINGS

Pastry for single-crust pie (9 inches)
- 1 **cup sugar**
- ¼ **cup cornstarch**
- 2 **cups 2% milk**
- ½ **cup butter, cubed**
- 1 **teaspoon vanilla extract**
- ¼ **teaspoon ground cinnamon**

1. Preheat oven to 450°. Roll out pastry to fit a 9-in. pie plate. Transfer pastry to pie plate. Trim pastry to ½ in. beyond rim of plate; flute edge. Line unpricked pastry with a double thickness of heavy-duty foil. Fill with pie weights, dried beans or uncooked rice.

2. Bake 8 minutes. Remove the foil and weights; bake 5-7 minutes longer or until light brown. Cool on a wire rack. Reduce oven setting to 375°.

3. Meanwhile, in a large saucepan, combine sugar and cornstarch; stir in milk until smooth. Bring to a boil. Reduce heat; cook and stir 2 minutes or until thickened and bubbly. Remove from heat; stir in butter and vanilla. Transfer to crust; sprinkle with cinnamon. Bake 15-20 minutes or until golden brown. Cool on a wire rack; refrigerate until chilled.

◄● dishing about food

Sugar Cream Pie goes by many names, including Hoosier Sugar Cream Pie, Indiana Cream Pie or Sugar Pie. It's an example of what's called a "desperation pie," one that uses ingredients readily available in most pantries. This basic vanilla version has a caramel flavor. The Amish, Quakers and Shakers also have versions of this recipe.

INDIANAPOLIS, IN

Step inside the Indianapolis Motor Speedway, and you'll be walking in the footsteps of some of the fastest drivers in history!

Sugar Plum Kringles

This recipe makes four kringles. That's too many for one family, so go ahead and share with your neighbors, relatives and co-workers!

—TASTE OF HOME TEST KITCHEN

PREP: 1 HOUR + CHILLING **BAKE:** 20 MIN. **MAKES:** 4 PASTRIES (6 SLICES EACH)

- 2 **cups all-purpose flour**
- 1 **cup cold butter**
- 1 **cup (8 ounces) sour cream**
- ¾ **cup plum jam, divided**
- 4 **teaspoons grated orange peel**
- 8 **teaspoons finely chopped walnuts or pecans, divided**
- 1¼ **cups confectioners' sugar**
- 2 **tablespoons 2% milk**
- 4 **teaspoons sugar**
- ½ **teaspoon ground cinnamon**

1. Place flour in a large bowl; cut in butter until crumbly. Stir in sour cream. Wrap in plastic wrap. Refrigerate for 1 to 1½ hours or until easy to handle.

2. Divide dough into four portions. On a lightly floured surface, roll one portion into a 12x6-in. rectangle. (Keep remaining dough refrigerated until ready to use.) Spread 3 tablespoons jam lengthwise down the center. Fold in sides of pastry to meet in the center; pinch seam to seal. Sprinkle with 1 teaspoon each orange peel and nuts. Repeat. Place on two ungreased baking sheets.

3. Bake at 375° for 18-22 minutes or until lightly browned. In a small bowl, combine confectioners' sugar and milk; drizzle over warm pastries. Combine sugar, cinnamon and remaining nuts; sprinkle over warm pastries.

Blueberry Slump

PREP/TOTAL TIME: 30 MIN.   **MAKES:** 6 SERVINGS

- 3   cups fresh or frozen blueberries
- ½   cup sugar
- 1¼ cups water
- 1   teaspoon finely grated lemon peel
- 1   tablespoon lemon juice
- 1   cup all-purpose flour
- 2   tablespoons sugar
- 2   teaspoons baking powder
- ½   teaspoon salt
- 1   tablespoon butter
- ½   cup milk
  Cream or whipped cream, optional

1. In a large heavy saucepan, combine the blueberries, sugar, water, lemon peel and juice; bring to a boil. Reduce heat and simmer, uncovered, for 5 minutes.

2. Meanwhile, in a large bowl, combine the flour, sugar, baking powder and salt; cut in butter until mixture resembles coarse crumbs. Add milk quickly; stir until moistened.

3. Drop dough by spoonfuls onto berries (makes six dumplings). Cover and cook over low heat for 10 minutes. Do not lift lid while simmering. Spoon dumplings into individual serving bowls; top with sauce. Serve warm with cream or whipped cream if desired.

❝My mother-in-law used to make slump with wild blueberries and serve it warm with a pitcher of cream on the table. My husband and I have been eating this for over 65 years, but the recipe is even older!❞

—ELEANORE EBELING
BREWSTER, MINNESOTA

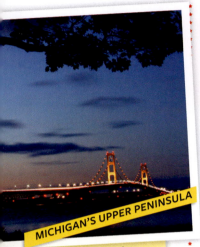

MICHIGAN'S UPPER PENINSULA

A large percentage of Upper Peninsula residents claim Scandinavian—especially Finnish—roots. The Mackinac Bridge, the world's third-longest suspension bridge, connects Michigan's two peninsulas.

Berliner Kranz Cookies

Use these cookies as a great Christmas gift. They also make a pretty presentation on a buffet table. Mother handed down the recipe to me, and I'm sure you'll get compliments!

—EDIE DESPAIN LOGAN, UTAH

PREP: 40 MIN. + CHILLING **BAKE:** 10 MIN./BATCH
MAKES: 4 DOZEN

    4   hard-cooked eggs
    1   cup butter-flavored shortening
    1   cup sugar
    4   uncooked egg yolks
    ½   teaspoon almond extract
    3¾ cups all-purpose flour
    ¼   teaspoon salt
    ½   cup half-and-half cream
    1   egg white, lightly beaten
        Red and green sugar
        Red-hot candies

1. Cut hard-cooked eggs in half lengthwise. Remove yolks; discard whites or save for another use. Press yolks through a potato ricer or strainer into a small bowl.

2. In a large bowl, cream shortening and sugar until light and fluffy. Beat in the uncooked egg yolks, hard-cooked egg yolks and extract. Combine flour and salt; add to the creamed mixture alternately with cream, beating well after each addition. Refrigerate for 1 hour or until easy to handle.

3. On a lightly floured surface, roll out dough to ⅛-in. thickness; cut with a floured 2½-in. doughnut cutter. Reroll scraps if desired.

4. Place 1 in. apart on ungreased baking sheets; brush with egg white. Sprinkle as desired with colored sugar. Bake at 350° for 6 minutes; carefully decorate as desired with candies. Bake 4-8 minutes longer or until edges are lightly browned. Remove to wire racks to cool.

Hot Milk Cake

When I think back on my mom's delicious meals, her milk cake always comes to mind as the perfect dessert. A simple, old-fashioned recipe, it tastes so good that I think you'll be pleasantly surprised!

—ROSEMARY PRYOR PASADENA, MARYLAND

PREP: 20 MIN. **BAKE:** 30 MIN. + COOLING
MAKES: 12-16 SERVINGS

    4   eggs
    2   cups sugar
    1   teaspoon vanilla extract
    2¼ cups all-purpose flour
    2¼ teaspoons baking powder
    1¼ cups 2% milk
    10 tablespoons butter, cubed

1. In a large bowl, beat eggs on high speed for 5 minutes or until thick and lemon-colored. Gradually add sugar, beating until mixture is light and fluffy. Beat in vanilla. Combine flour and baking powder; gradually add to batter; beat at low speed until smooth.

2. In a small saucepan, heat milk and butter just until butter is melted. Gradually add to batter; beat just until combined.

3. Pour into a greased 13x9-in. baking pan. Bake at 350° for 30-35 minutes or until a toothpick inserted near the center comes out clean. Cool on a wire rack.

Rhubarb Icebox Dessert

A light and fluffy marshmallow layer tops the rhubarb filling in this make-ahead recipe.
—**RENEE SCHWEBACH** DUMONT, MINNESOTA

PREP: 15 MIN. **BAKE:** 10 MIN. + COOLING
MAKES: 15 SERVINGS

- 1¾ cups graham cracker crumbs, divided
- 3 tablespoons butter, melted
- 1 cup sugar
- 2 tablespoons cornstarch
- 4 cups diced fresh or frozen rhubarb
- 1 package (3 ounces) raspberry or strawberry gelatin
- 1 carton (8 ounces) frozen whipped topping, thawed
- 1½ cups miniature marshmallows
- 2 cups cold milk
- 1 package (3.4 ounces) instant vanilla pudding mix

1. In a small bowl, combine 1½ cups cracker crumbs and butter. Press mixture into a greased 13x9-in. baking dish. Bake at 350° for 10 minutes or until lightly browned. Cool on a wire rack.

2. In a large saucepan, combine the sugar, cornstarch and rhubarb. Bring to a boil; cook and stir for 2-3 minutes or until thickened and rhubarb is tender. Remove from the heat; stir in gelatin until dissolved. Cover and refrigerate for 1 hour or until partially set.

3. Spoon rhubarb mixture over crust. Combine whipped topping and marshmallows; spread over rhubarb mixture.

4. In a large bowl, whisk milk and pudding mix for 2 minutes. Let stand for 2 minutes or until soft-set. Carefully spread over marshmallow topping (the dish will be full). Sprinkle with remaining cracker crumbs. Refrigerate for at least 2 hours before serving.

Rhubarb Custard Bars

Once I tried these rich gooey bars, I just had to have the recipe so I could make them for my family and friends. The shortbread-like crust and the rhubarb and custard layers inspire people to find some rhubarb just so they can fix a batch for themselves!
—**SHARI ROACH** SOUTH MILWAUKEE, WISCONSIN

PREP: 25 MIN. + CHILLING **BAKE:** 50 MIN. + CHILLING
MAKES: 3 DOZEN

- 2 cups all-purpose flour
- ¼ cup sugar
- 1 cup cold butter

FILLING
- 2 cups sugar
- 7 tablespoons all-purpose flour
- 1 cup heavy whipping cream
- 3 eggs, beaten
- 5 cups finely chopped fresh or frozen rhubarb, thawed and drained

TOPPING
- 2 packages (3 ounces each) cream cheese, softened
- ½ cup sugar
- ½ teaspoon vanilla extract
- 1 cup heavy whipping cream, whipped

1. In a bowl, combine the flour and sugar; cut in butter until the mixture resembles coarse crumbs. Press into a greased 13x9-in. baking pan. Bake at 350° for 10 minutes.

2. Meanwhile, for filling, combine sugar and flour in a bowl. Whisk in cream and eggs. Stir in the rhubarb. Pour over crust. Bake at 350° for 40-45 minutes or until custard is set. Cool.

3. For topping, beat cream cheese, sugar and vanilla until smooth; fold in whipped cream. Spread over top. Cover and chill. Cut into bars. Store in the refrigerator.

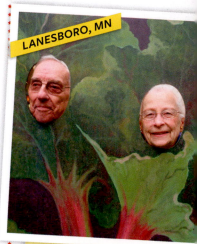
LANESBORO, MN

Not only is Lanesboro the Bed & Breakfast Capital of the World, it's also the Rhubarb Capital of Minnesota. Why not honor both by taking a weekend getaway during the annual Rhubarb Festival?

COLUMBUS, OH

Meet Brutus Buckeye, mascot of the Ohio State University. He's been pumping up fans in the stands since 1965.

Chocolate-Covered Buckeyes

These candies are always popular at my church's annual Christmas fund-raiser. Try them!

—**MERRY KAY OPITZ** ELKHORN, WISCONSIN

PREP: 15 MIN. + CHILLING **MAKES:** ABOUT 5½ DOZEN

5½ cups confectioners' sugar
1⅔ cups peanut butter
1   cup butter, melted
4   cups (24 ounces) semisweet chocolate chips
1   teaspoon shortening

1. In a large bowl, beat the sugar, peanut butter and butter until smooth. Shape into 1-in. balls; set aside.

2. In a microwave, melt chocolate chips and shortening; stir until smooth. Dip balls in chocolate, allowing excess to drip off. Place on a wire rack over waxed paper; refrigerate for 15 minutes or until firm. Cover and store in the refrigerator.

Vinegar Pie

For an adventure in taste, this pie is the way to go. It is very inexpensive and will surprise you with its unique flavor!

—**DORA WILLIAMS** LAINGSBURG, MICHIGAN

PREP: 10 MIN. **BAKE:** 45 MIN. **MAKES:** 8 SERVINGS

- 4 **eggs**
- 1½ **cups sugar**
- ¼ **cup butter, melted**
- 1-½ **tablespoons cider or white vinegar**
- 1 **teaspoon vanilla extract**
- 1 **unbaked pie shell (9 inches)**

1. In a large bowl, combine eggs, sugar, butter, vinegar and vanilla. Mix well. Pour into the pie shell. Bake at 350° for 45-50 minutes or until set. Cool on a wire rack.

Ginger-Pear Upside-Down Pie

Pears aren't featured nearly enough in pies. I wanted to showcase this wonderful fruit in my recipe—and put a bit of a twist on it.

—**MARCY KAMERY** BLASDELL, NEW YORK

PREP: 45 MIN. + CHILLING **BAKE:** 1 HOUR + COOLING **MAKES:** 8 SERVINGS

CRUST
- 1 **cup cake flour**
- 1 **cup all-purpose flour**
- 1½ **teaspoons salt**
- 1 **teaspoon sugar**
- ⅔ **cup cold butter, cubed**
- 1 **teaspoon white vinegar**
- ⅓ to ½ **cup ice water**

NUT MIXTURE
- ½ **cup chopped walnuts, toasted**
- ½ **cup chopped pecans, toasted**
- ½ **cup packed brown sugar**
- ¼ **cup butter, melted**

FILLING
- 6 **cups sliced peeled fresh pears**
- ½ **cup sugar**
- 3 **tablespoons all-purpose flour**
- ½ **teaspoon ground ginger**
- ¼ **teaspoon ground cinnamon**
- ⅛ **teaspoon ground nutmeg**

1. Line bottom and sides of a greased 9-in. deep-dish pie plate with parchment paper; coat with cooking spray. For crust, in a bowl, combine flours, salt and sugar. Cut in butter until crumbly. Add vinegar; gradually add water, tossing with a fork until dough forms a ball.

2. Divide dough in half so that one portion is slightly larger than the other; wrap each in plastic wrap. Refrigerate for 15 minutes or until easy to handle.

3. Combine nuts, brown sugar and butter. Spread in prepared pie plate.

4. On a lightly floured surface, roll out larger portion of dough to fit prepared pie plate. Place pastry over nut mixture. Trim pastry even with edge.

5. Place filling ingredients in a large bowl; toss. Transfer to pie pastry.

6. Roll out remaining pastry to fit top of pie. Place over filling. Trim, seal and flute edges. Cut slits in pastry.

7. Bake at 375° for 60-70 minutes or until crust is golden brown and filling is bubbly. Cool on a wire rack for 5 minutes.

8. Carefully loosen the parchment paper around edge of pie; invert pie onto a serving plate. Remove and discard paper. Cool for at least 15 minutes before serving. Serve warm.

◀◀ dishing about food

Vinegar pie is another "desperation pie" (also known as starvation pies) that farm women and pioneers created with what they had on hand—when fresh fruit wasn't available. This recipe is a stand-in for lemon pie.

CIRCLEVILLE, OH

It's been more than a century since this Central Ohio town put on the first Circleville Pumpkin Show, featuring entertainers, crafts and pumpkins big and small! Word has spread, and now more than 400,000 people come for the mid-October spectacle.

Streusel Pumpkin Pie

Basic pumpkin pie is good, but we think this dressed-up version is way better! Plenty of pecans add a nutty crunch to both the pastry and the streusel topping. It's a perfect dessert for Thanksgiving or any time you want to end a dinner with something really special.

—BERTHA JOHNSON INDIANAPOLIS, INDIANA

PREP: 20 MIN. **BAKE:** 40 MIN. + COOLING **MAKES:** 2 PIES (6-8 SERVINGS EACH)

- 2 **cups all-purpose flour**
- ¼ **cup finely chopped pecans**
- 1 **teaspoon salt**
- ⅔ **cup plus 1 tablespoon shortening**
- 4 **to 5 tablespoons water**

FILLING
- 1 **can (30 ounces) pumpkin pie filling**
- 1 **can (14 ounces) sweetened condensed milk**
- 1 **egg, lightly beaten**

STREUSEL TOPPING
- ½ **cup packed brown sugar**
- ¼ **cup all-purpose flour**
- ¼ **cup chopped pecans**
- ½ **teaspoon ground cinnamon**
- 3 **tablespoons cold butter**

1. In a bowl, combine flour, pecans and salt; cut in the shortening until crumbly. Gradually add water, tossing with a fork until a ball forms. Divide dough in half. Roll out each portion to fit a 9-in. pie plate; place pastry in pie plates. Flute edges and set aside.

2. Combine pie filling, milk and egg; pour into pastry shells. For topping, combine brown sugar, flour, pecans and cinnamon in a small bowl; cut in butter until crumbly. Sprinkle over filling. Cover edges of pastry loosely with foil.

3. Bake at 375° for 40-45 minutes or until a knife inserted near the center comes out clean. Cool on a wire rack for 2 hours. Refrigerate until serving.

Crispy Norwegian Bows

I've been fixing these cookies for so long, I don't even recall where the recipe came from. They're a "must" at our house!

—**JANIE NORWOOD** ALBANY, GEORGIA

PREP/TOTAL TIME: 30 MIN. **MAKES:** 4 DOZEN

- 3 egg yolks
- 3 tablespoons sugar
- 3 tablespoons heavy whipping cream
- ½ teaspoon ground cardamom
- 1 to 1¼ cups all-purpose flour
  Oil for deep-fat frying
  Confectioners' sugar

1. In a large bowl, beat egg yolks and sugar until light and lemon-colored. Add cream and cardamom; mix well. Gradually add flour until dough is firm enough to roll.

2. On a lightly floured surface, roll into a 15-in. square. Using a pastry wheel or knife, cut into 15x1½-in. strips; cut diagonally at 2½-in. intervals. In the center of each diamond, make a 1-in. slit, pull one end through slit.

3. In an electric skillet or deep-fat fryer, heat oil to 375°. Fry bows, a few at a time, for 20-40 seconds or until golden brown on both sides. Drain on paper towels. Dust with confectioners' sugar.

Cardamom Cookies

Cardamom, almond extract and walnuts enhance the flavor of these buttery cookies.

MARY STEINER WEST BEND, WISCONSIN

PREP: 20 MIN. **BAKE:** 15 MIN./BATCH
MAKES: 6 DOZEN

- 2 cups butter, softened
- 2½ cups confectioners' sugar, divided
- 1½ teaspoons almond extract
- 3¾ cups all-purpose flour
- 1 teaspoon ground cardamom
- ⅛ teaspoon salt
- 1 cup finely chopped walnuts

1. In a large bowl, cream butter and 1½ cups confectioners' sugar until smooth. Beat in extract. Combine the flour, cardamom and salt; gradually add to the creamed mixture. Stir in the walnuts.

2. Roll into 1-in. balls. Place 2 in. apart on ungreased baking sheets. Bake at 350° for 15-17 minutes or until edges are golden.

3. Roll warm cookies in the remaining confectioners' sugar. Cool on wire racks.

Gooseberry Meringue Pie

This pie has a creamy filling studded with tangy gooseberries. It's a dessert that draws compliments every time I serve it!

—**MARY HAND** CLEVELAND, MISSOURI

PREP/TOTAL TIME: 30 MIN. **MAKES:** 6-8 SERVINGS

- 2 cups canned, fresh or frozen gooseberries
- 2 tablespoons water
- 1½ cups sugar, divided
- 3 tablespoons cornstarch
- 1 cup milk
- 2 eggs, separated
- 1 pastry shell (9 inches), baked

1. In a covered saucepan over medium heat, cook gooseberries and water for 3-4 minutes or until tender. Stir in ¾ cup sugar; set aside.

2. In another saucepan, combine ½ cup sugar and cornstarch. Gradually add milk until smooth; bring to a boil. Cook and stir over medium-high heat until thickened. Reduce heat; cook and stir 2 minutes longer. Remove from the heat.

3. In a bowl, beat egg yolks. Gradually whisk a small amount of hot filling into yolks; return all to the pan. Bring to a gentle boil; cook and stir for 2 minutes. Remove from the heat; stir in gooseberry mixture. Pour into pastry shell.

4. In a small bowl, beat egg whites until soft peaks form. Gradually add remaining sugar, beating on high until stiff peaks form. Spread evenly over hot filling, sealing meringue to crust. Bake at 350° for 10-15 minutes or until golden. Store in the refrigerator.

Black Walnut Butter Cookies

My part of the Show-Me State has an abundance of black walnuts, so these cookies are really representative of my little region of the country. I created the recipe after a lot of experimentation...my family thinks these cookies are a hit!

—**PATSY BELL HOBSON** LIBERTY, MISSOURI

PREP: 20 MIN. **BAKE:** 20 MIN./BATCH + COOLING
MAKES: 6 DOZEN

   ¾ **cup butter, softened**
   1 **cup all-purpose flour**
   ½ **cup cornstarch**
   ½ **cup confectioners' sugar**
   ½ **cup chopped black walnuts or walnuts**
      Additional confectioners' sugar

1. In a bowl, cream butter. Combine the flour, cornstarch and confectioners' sugar; add to butter and mix well. Stir in walnuts.

2. Roll into ¾-in. balls. Place 1 in. apart on greased baking sheets.

3. Bake at 300° for 20-25 minutes or until set. Remove to wire racks to cool. Dust with additional confectioners' sugar.

Cranberry-Carrot Layer Cake

This moist cake is smothered with rich cream cheese frosting and makes any dinner festive. Every autumn, I go to a cranberry festival in Wisconsin and load up on fresh cranberries to freeze for year-round cooking.

—**NELLIE RUNNE** ROCKFORD, ILLINOIS

PREP: 20 MIN. **BAKE:** 25 MIN. + COOLING
MAKES: 14 SERVINGS

   4 **eggs**
   1½ **cups packed brown sugar**
   1¼ **cups canola oil**
   1 **teaspoon grated orange peel**
   2 **cups all-purpose flour**
   1 **teaspoon baking soda**
   1 **teaspoon ground cinnamon**
   ¾ **teaspoon baking powder**
   ½ **teaspoon salt**
   ¼ **teaspoon ground cloves**
   2 **cups shredded carrots**
   1 **cup dried cranberries**
CREAM CHEESE FROSTING
   2 **packages (8 ounces each) cream cheese, softened**
   ¾ **cup butter, softened**
   4 **cups confectioners' sugar**
   1 **tablespoon milk**
   ½ **teaspoon ground ginger**
   ½ **teaspoon grated orange peel, optional**

1. In a large bowl, combine the eggs, brown sugar, oil and orange peel. Combine the flour, baking soda, cinnamon, baking powder, salt and cloves; gradually add to egg mixture and mix well. Stir in carrots and cranberries.

2. Pour into two greased and floured 9-in. round baking pans. Bake at 350° for 25-30 minutes or until a toothpick inserted in center comes out clean. Cool for 10 minutes; remove from pans to wire racks to cool completely.

3. For frosting, in a large bowl, beat cream cheese and butter until fluffy. Gradually beat in confectioners' sugar, milk, ginger and orange peel if desired.

4. Cut each cake horizontally into two layers. Place bottom layer on a serving plate; spread frosting between layers and over the top and sides of cake.

Swedish Christmas Rice Pudding

Rice pudding is another old-fashioned dessert that is so comforting and delicious. Here's a recipe with a mild and creamy vanilla flavor.

—KARLA LARSON EAST MOLINE, ILLINOIS

PREP: 10 MIN. **COOK:** 50 MIN. + CHILLING
MAKES: 9 SERVINGS

- 1 **cup water**
- ½ **cup uncooked long grain rice**
  Dash salt
- 4 **cups milk**
- ⅔ **cup sugar, divided**
- 2 **eggs**
- 2 **tablespoons butter**
- 1 **teaspoon vanilla extract**
- ¼ **teaspoon ground cinnamon**

1. In a heavy saucepan, combine the water, rice and salt; bring to a boil over medium heat. Reduce heat; cover and simmer for 15 minutes or until water is absorbed. Add milk and ⅓ cup sugar; bring to a boil. Reduce heat; simmer, uncovered, for 30-40 minutes or until slightly thickened.

2. Whisk together the eggs and remaining sugar. Gradually stir 2 cups hot rice mixture into the egg mixture; return all to pan, stirring constantly. Cook and stir over low heat for 3-5 minutes until mixture reaches 160°. Remove from the heat; stir in butter and vanilla. Pour into a serving bowl.

3. Refrigerate for 2 hours or until chilled. Just before serving, sprinkle with cinnamon.

Swedish Butter Cookies

It's impossible to eat just one of these treats! Naturally, they're a favorite with my Swedish husband and children—but anyone with a sweet tooth will appreciate them. My recipe is "well-traveled" among our friends and neighbors.

—SUE SODERLAND ELGIN, ILLINOIS

PREP: 10 MIN. **BAKE:** 25 MIN./BATCH
MAKES: ABOUT 6 DOZEN

- 1 **cup butter, softened**
- 1 **cup sugar**
- 2 **teaspoons maple syrup**
- 2 **cups all-purpose flour**
- 1 **teaspoon baking soda**
  Confectioners' sugar

1. In a large bowl, cream the butter and sugar until light and fluffy. Add syrup. Combine flour and baking soda; gradually add to the creamed mixture and mix well.

2. Divide dough into eight portions. Roll each portion into a 9-in. log. Place 3 in. apart on ungreased baking sheets.

3. Bake at 300° for 25 minutes or until lightly browned. Cut into 1-in. slices. Remove to wire racks. Dust with confectioners' sugar.

> **My sister, Judith, brought this recipe with her when she came to the United States from Sweden in 1928.**

—LILLY DECKER
CLANCY, MONTANA

Swedish Spice Cutouts

PREP: 25 MIN. + CHILLING **BAKE:** 10 MIN./BATCH + COOLING **MAKES:** ABOUT 10 DOZEN

1½ cups butter, softened
1¾ cups packed dark brown sugar
1 egg
⅔ cup dark corn syrup
¼ cup molasses
4½ cups all-purpose flour
1¼ teaspoons ground cinnamon
1 teaspoon baking soda
¾ teaspoon ground cloves
Slivered almonds, optional
Frosting of your choice, optional

1. In a large bowl, cream butter and brown sugar until light and fluffy. Beat in the egg, corn syrup and molasses. Combine the flour, cinnamon, baking soda and cloves; gradually add to the creamed mixture and mix well. Cover and refrigerate for 4 hours or until easy to handle.

2. On a lightly floured surface, roll dough to ⅛-in. thickness. Cut with floured 2½-in. cookie cutters. Place 1 in. apart on ungreased baking sheets. Top with almonds if desired or leave plain.

3. Bake at 375° for 8-10 minutes or until edges are lightly browned. Remove to wire racks to cool. Frost plain cookies if desired.

Persimmon Pudding

Fall is a wonderful time of year in the Midwest, and this dessert is a Hoosier favorite. The old-fashioned pudding is moist, dense and firm—not at all like the packaged pudding mixes.

—JUDY THARP INDIANAPOLIS, INDIANA

PREP: 15 MIN. **BAKE:** 40 MIN. + COOLING
MAKES: 24 SERVINGS

- 1½ cups all-purpose flour
- 1 cup sugar
- 1 cup packed brown sugar
- 1 teaspoon baking powder
- 1 teaspoon baking soda
- ½ teaspoon ground cinnamon
- ⅛ teaspoon salt
- 2 cups mashed ripe hachiya persimmon pulp
- 1½ cups buttermilk
- 3 eggs
- ¼ cup butter, melted
- 1 teaspoon vanilla extract
- 1 teaspoon maple flavoring
  Sweetened whipped cream

1. In a large bowl, combine the first seven ingredients. In another large bowl, whisk the persimmon, buttermilk, eggs, butter, vanilla and maple flavoring. Stir into dry ingredients just until moistened.

2. Transfer to a greased 13x9-in. baking pan. Bake at 325° for 40-45 minutes or until pudding begins to pull away from sides of the pan and center is firm. Serve warm with whipped cream.

Traditional Stollen

This recipe came from my grandmother and was originally written in German. It is one of my favorite treats to share at the holidays.

—JESSIE BARNES ATCHISON, KANSAS

PREP: 30 MIN. + RISING **BAKE:** 25 MIN.
MAKES: 2 LOAVES

- 1 package (¼ ounce) active dry yeast
- 2 tablespoons warm water (110° to 115°)
- 1 cup warm 2% milk (110° to 115°)
- ¾ cup butter, softened
- ½ cup sugar
- 2 eggs, lightly beaten
- 1½ teaspoons grated lemon peel
- ½ teaspoon salt
- 4¾ to 5¼ cups all-purpose flour
- ¾ cup raisins
- ½ cup mixed candied fruit
- ½ cup chopped almonds
  GLAZE
- 1½ cups confectioners' sugar
- 2 to 3 tablespoons 2% milk

1. In a large bowl, dissolve yeast in warm water. Add the milk, butter, sugar, eggs, lemon peel, salt and 3 cups flour. Add the raisins, candied fruit and almonds. Add enough remaining flour to form a soft dough.

2. Turn onto a floured surface; knead until smooth and elastic, about 6-8 minutes. Place in a greased bowl, turning once to grease the top. Cover and let rise in a warm place until doubled, about 1½ hours.

3. Punch dough down and divide in half; cover and let rest for 10 minutes. Roll or press each half into a 12x7-in. oval. Fold a long side over to within 1 in. of opposite side; press edge lightly to seal. Place on greased baking sheets; curve ends slightly. Cover and let rise until nearly doubled, about 1 hour.

4. Bake at 375° for 25-30 minutes or until golden brown. Cool on wire racks. Combine the confectioners' sugar and enough milk to achieve desired consistency; spread over the stollen.

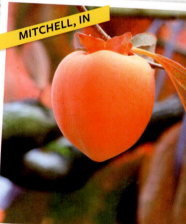

MITCHELL, IN

Citizens of Mitchell are big fans of this tart orange fruit—there's even one pictured on their water tower! Since 1946, volunteers have been putting on the annual Persimmon Festival, the biggest community event of the year.

MINNEAPOLIS, MN

At the Minneapolis Sculpture Garden, you'll find a variety of alluring 3-D artwork, including *Spoonbridge and Cherry*.

Grandma's Applesauce Cake

Here's a moist cake recipe that's a treasured heirloom passed down from my Grandma Stuit, who cooked for a family of 13 during the Depression. At reunions, it's always the first dessert gone...including the crumbs!

—**JOANIE JAGER** LYNDEN, WASHINGTON

PREP: 20 MIN. **BAKE:** 40 MIN. **MAKES:** 12-16 SERVINGS

- ¾ cup raisins
- 1 cup hot water
- ½ cup shortening
- 2 cups sugar
- 1 egg
- 2½ cups all-purpose flour
- 2 teaspoons baking soda
- ½ teaspoon salt
- ½ teaspoon each ground cinnamon, cloves and nutmeg
- 1½ cups applesauce
- ½ cup water
- ½ cup chopped walnuts
  Confectioners' sugar, optional

1. Place raisins and hot water in a small bowl; set aside.

2. In a large bowl, cream shortening and sugar until light and fluffy. Beat in egg. Combine the flour, baking soda, salt and spices; add to creamed mixture alternately with applesauce and water. Drain raisins; fold into batter with the walnuts.

3. Transfer to a greased 13x9-in. baking pan. Bake at 300° for 40 minutes or until a toothpick inserted in center comes out clean. Place pan on a wire rack. Dust with confectioners' sugar if desired. Serve warm or cold.

Poteca Nut Roll

You'll need a large surface to roll out the dough for this traditional Yugoslavian treat.

—**ANTHONY SETTA** SAEGERTOWN, PENNSYLVANIA

PREP: 30 MIN. + RISING **BAKE:** 35 MIN.
MAKES: 1 COFFEE CAKE

- 1 package (¼ ounce) active dry yeast
- ¼ cup warm water (110° to 115°)
- ¾ cup warm milk (110° to 115°)
- ¼ cup sugar
- 1 teaspoon salt
- 1 egg, lightly beaten
- ¼ cup shortening
- 3 to 3½ cups all-purpose flour
  FILLING
- ½ cup butter, softened
- 1 cup packed brown sugar
- 2 eggs, lightly beaten
- 1 teaspoon vanilla extract
- 1 teaspoon lemon extract, optional
- 4 cups ground or finely chopped walnuts
  2% milk
  Confectioners' sugar, optional

1. In a large bowl, dissolve yeast in warm water. Add the milk, sugar, salt, egg, shortening, and 1½ cups flour; beat until smooth. Add enough remaining flour to form a soft dough.

2. Turn onto a floured surface; knead until smooth and elastic, about 6-8 minutes. Place in a greased bowl, turning once to grease top. Cover and let rise in a warm place until doubled, about 1 hour.

3. Punch down. Turn onto a lightly floured surface; roll into a 30x20-in. rectangle. In a bowl, combine the butter, brown sugar, eggs, vanilla, lemon extract if desired and nuts. Add about ½ cup milk until mixture reaches spreading consistency. Spread over rectangle to within 1 in. of edges.

4. Roll up jelly-roll style, starting with a long side; pinch seams and ends to seal. Place on a greased baking sheet; shape into a tight spiral. Cover and let rise until nearly doubled, about 1 hour.

5. Bake at 350° for 35 minutes or until golden brown. Remove from pan to a wire rack to cool. If desired, combine the confectioners' sugar and enough milk to make a thin glaze; brush over roll.

Russian Krendl Bread

PREP: 45 MIN. + RISING **BAKE:** 45 MIN. + COOLING **MAKES:** 24 SERVINGS

- 1 package (¼ ounce) active dry yeast
- 3 tablespoons sugar
- ¾ cup warm half-and-half cream or milk (110° to 115°)
- ¼ cup butter, softened
- 2 egg yolks
- 1½ teaspoons vanilla extract
- ½ teaspoon salt
- 2¾ to 3¼ cups all-purpose flour

FILLING
- 1 cup apple juice
- 1 large apple, peeled and chopped
- ⅔ cup finely chopped dried apples
- ⅓ cup finely chopped dried apricots
- ⅓ cup chopped pitted dried plums
- 2 tablespoons plus ¼ cup butter, divided
- 4 tablespoons sugar, divided
- ½ teaspoon ground cinnamon
   Confectioners' sugar

1. In a small bowl, dissolve yeast and sugar in warm cream. In a large bowl, combine the softened butter, egg yolks, vanilla, salt, yeast mixture and 1½ cups flour; beat on medium speed until smooth. Stir in enough remaining flour to form a soft dough (dough will be sticky).

2. Turn onto a floured surface; knead until smooth and elastic, about 6-8 minutes. Place in a greased bowl, turning once to grease the top. Cover with plastic wrap and let rise in a warm place until doubled, about 1 hour.

3. In a large saucepan, combine the first five filling ingredients; add 2 tablespoons butter and 2 tablespoons sugar. Bring to a boil. Reduce heat; simmer for 30 minutes or until mixture reaches a jam-like consistency, stirring occasionally. Cool completely.

4. Punch down dough. Turn onto a lightly floured surface; roll into a 32x10-in. rectangle. Melt remaining butter; brush over dough. Sprinkle with remaining sugar and cinnamon. Spread fruit mixture to within 1 in. of edges. Roll up jelly-roll style, starting with a long side; pinch seam and ends to seal.

5. Place on a greased baking sheet, seam side down; form into a pretzel shape. Cover with a kitchen towel; let rise in a warm place until almost doubled, about 30 minutes.

6. Bake at 350° for 40-45 minutes or until golden brown. Remove from pan to a wire rack to cool. Just before serving, sprinkle with confectioners' sugar.

> "While dining with a Russian immigrant family, I jumped at the chance to add this wonderful bread they served to my recipe collection. Of course, I never turn down hugs from my grandchildren after I've prepared something special...and this recipe always works."

—ANN SODMAN
EVANS, COLORADO

Rosettes

Dipping the edges of these traditional favorites in icing defines their pretty lacy pattern.

—**IOLA EGLE** BELLA VISTA, ARKANSAS

PREP: 20 MIN. **COOK:** 30 MIN. **MAKES:** ABOUT 5 DOZEN

2	**eggs**
2	**teaspoons sugar**
1	**cup 2% milk**
3	**teaspoons vanilla extract**
1	**cup all-purpose flour**
¼	**teaspoon salt**
	Oil for deep-fat frying

ICING

2	**cups confectioners' sugar**
1	**teaspoon vanilla extract**
1	**to 3 tablespoons water**

1. In a small bowl, beat eggs and sugar; stir in milk and vanilla. Combine flour and salt; gradually add to batter until smooth.

2. Heat 2½ in. of oil to 375° in a deep-fat fryer or electric skillet. Place rosette iron in hot oil, then dip in batter, three-fourths up the sides of iron (do not let batter run over top of iron). Immediately place in hot oil; loosen rosette with fork and remove iron.

3. Fry rosettes 1-2 minutes on each side or until golden brown. Remove to paper towel-lined wire racks. Repeat with remaining batter.

4. For icing, combine the confectioners' sugar, vanilla and enough water to achieve a dipping consistency. Dip edges of rosettes into icing; let dry on wire racks.

Delightful Apple Pie

PREP: 25 MIN. **BAKE:** 45 MIN. + COOLING **MAKES:** 8 SERVINGS

1 sheet refrigerated pie pastry
6 cups thinly sliced peeled tart apples (about 5 medium)
¼ cup apple butter
3 tablespoons all-purpose flour
2 tablespoons plus 1½ teaspoons sugar
1½ teaspoons apple pie spice
1 teaspoon ground cinnamon

TOPPING
½ cup all-purpose flour
¼ cup sugar
¼ cup packed brown sugar
½ teaspoon apple pie spice
½ teaspoon ground cinnamon
3 tablespoons cold butter
½ cup chopped walnuts
 Vanilla ice cream, optional

1. Unroll pastry into a 9-in. pie plate; flute edges. In a large bowl, toss apples with apple butter. Combine the flour, sugar, pie spice and cinnamon; add to apple mixture and toss to coat. Transfer to crust.

2. In a small bowl, combine the flour, sugar, brown sugar, pie spice and cinnamon. Cut in butter until mixture resembles coarse crumbs. Add walnuts; sprinkle over filling.

3. Bake at 375° for 45-50 minutes or until filling is bubbly and topping is browned. Cover edges with foil during the last 15 minutes to prevent overbrowning if necessary. Cool on a wire rack. Serve with ice cream if desired.

Editor's Note: *This recipe was tested with commercially prepared apple butter.*

> "There aren't many things more American than hot-out-of-the-oven apple pie. This recipe is one you can hang your hat on."
>
> —AMY WOOD
>
> WICHITA, KANSAS

Southwest

Looking for a surefire way to spice up dinnertime at your house? Consider a specialty from the Southwest! Loaded with flavor as well as weeknight convenience, savory Mexican dishes, Tex-Mex standbys and other fiery favorites leave lasting imprints on this region. Now you can dig into the family-friendly tastes this area has to offer. Whether you're simmering up supper, rounding out a sizzling menu or simply looking for a change-of-pace dessert, you'll never go wrong by setting a touch of the Southwest on your table.

> My family likes garlic, so I dreamed up this delicious marinade for our summer fajita dinners. It needs only 8 hours to work its magic—but is even better left overnight. It's awesome on chicken breasts, too!

—KARYN "KIKI" POWER
ARLINGTON, TEXAS

Sizzling Tex-Mex Fajitas

PREP: 30 MIN. + MARINATING **GRILL:** 10 MIN. **MAKES:** 6 SERVINGS

⅓ cup beef broth
¼ cup lime juice
3 tablespoons olive oil, divided
4 garlic cloves, minced
2 teaspoons Worcestershire sauce
1 teaspoon salt
1 envelope savory herb with garlic soup mix, divided
1 teaspoon Dijon mustard
½ teaspoon pepper
½ teaspoon cayenne pepper
½ teaspoon Liquid Smoke, optional
2 pounds beef skirt steak, cut into 4- to 6-inch portions
2 large onions, sliced
1 medium green pepper, sliced
1 medium sweet yellow pepper, sliced
12 flour tortillas (8 inches)
   Salsa, shredded cheese, guacamole and sour cream, optional

1. In a large resealable plastic bag, combine the broth, lime juice, 1 tablespoon oil, garlic, Worcestershire sauce, salt, 1 teaspoon soup mix, mustard, pepper, cayenne and Liquid Smoke if desired. Add the steaks; seal bag and turn to coat. Refrigerate for 8 hours or overnight.

2. In a large bowl, combine onions, green pepper, yellow pepper and remaining oil and soup mix. Place half of mixture on each of two double thicknesses of heavy-duty foil (about 12 in. square). Fold foil around vegetables and seal tightly.

3. Drain beef and discard marinade. Grill steaks and vegetable packets, covered, over medium heat for 10-13 minutes or until meat reaches desired doneness (for medium-rare, a thermometer should read 145°; medium, 160°; well-done, 170°) and vegetables are tender, turning steaks once.

4. Open foil packets carefully to allow steam to escape. Thinly slice steaks; place beef and vegetables on tortillas. Serve with salsa, cheese, guacamole and sour cream if desired.

Arroz con Pollo

This authentic specialty gets its wonderful flavor from a robust blend of seasonings that includes garlic, Mexican oregano and chili powder.

—TASTE OF HOME TEST KITCHEN

PREP: 15 MIN. **COOK:** 50 MIN. **MAKES:** 5-6 SERVINGS

- 1 can (14½ ounces) diced tomatoes, drained
- ½ cup chopped onion
- 4 garlic cloves, peeled
- 1 teaspoon salt, divided
- ½ teaspoon dried Mexican oregano
- ½ teaspoon chili powder
- ½ teaspoon pepper, divided
- 1 broiler/fryer chicken (3 to 4 pounds), cut up
- 3 tablespoons canola oil, divided
- 1½ cups uncooked long grain rice
- 3 cups chicken broth
- 1 cup frozen peas

1. In a blender, combine the tomatoes, onion, garlic, ½ teaspoon salt, oregano, chili powder and ¼ teaspoon pepper; cover and process until smooth. Set aside.

2. Sprinkle chicken with remaining salt and pepper. In a large skillet over medium heat, cook the chicken in batches in 2 tablespoons oil for 10 minutes or until lightly browned. Remove and keep warm. In the same skillet, saute the rice for 2 minutes or until lightly browned. Stir in broth.

3. In a Dutch oven, heat the remaining oil; add tomato mixture. Bring to a boil; cook and stir for 4 minutes. Stir in the rice mixture; bring to a boil.

4. Arrange chicken in the pan. Reduce heat to medium; cover and cook for 25-30 minutes or until rice is tender and chicken juices run clear. Stir in peas; cover and let stand for 4 minutes or until peas are heated through.

Chili Rellenos Burgers

My husband loves hamburgers and Mexican food, so I combined the two to create this zesty sandwich. Garnish these dressed-up burgers with sliced avocados if you like.

—DARLENE WILKINSON QUILCENE, WASHINGTON

PREP/TOTAL TIME: 30 MIN. **MAKES:** 4 SERVINGS

- 1 pound ground beef
- 1 medium onion, thinly sliced
- 1 teaspoon chili powder
- 1 teaspoon ground cumin
- ½ teaspoon salt
- ⅛ teaspoon pepper
- 1 can (4 ounces) whole green chilies, drained and halved
- 4 slices Colby-Monterey Jack cheese
- ½ cup salsa
- 2 tablespoons ketchup
- 4 sandwich buns, split
  Sour cream

1. Shape beef into four patties. In a skillet over medium heat, brown patties on both sides. Top each with onion, chili powder, cumin, salt and pepper. Reduce heat; cover and simmer for 5 minutes or until meat is no longer pink.

2. Top each patty with the chilies and a slice of cheese. Cover and cook 3 minutes longer or until the cheese is melted. In a small bowl, combine salsa and ketchup. Place burgers on buns; serve with salsa mixture and sour cream.

COLORADO SPRINGS, CO

Spanish explorers took a cue from Colorado's ruddy sandstone rocks (like those at the Garden of the Gods) when naming the area. Colorado means "red."

Tucson, Arizona, has dubbed itself the Mexican Food Capital of the U.S. Restaurant chefs and home cooks alike are proud of their mouthwatering traditional favorites and their tasty innovations on the classics.

TUCSON, AZ

It's no wonder Mexican cuisine from this southern Arizona city is so revered: The city was part of Mexico until the end of 1853!

Chimichangas

Though still debated, Tucson is generally credited as the original home of the chimichanga (or fried "burro," as we call it), stuffed with meat, onions and chilies. I've combined several recipes into this one, and it's fairly authentic.

—LAURA TOWNS GLENDALE, ARIZONA

PREP/TOTAL TIME: 30 MIN. **MAKES:** 12 SERVINGS

- ¼ cup bacon grease
- 2 cups chopped or shredded cooked beef, pork or chicken
- 1 medium onion, diced
- 2 garlic cloves, minced
- 2 medium tomatoes, chopped
- 2 cans (4 ounces each) chopped green chilies
- 1 large peeled boiled potato, diced
- 1 teaspoon salt
- 1½ teaspoons dried oregano
- 1 to 2 teaspoons chili powder or to taste
- 2 tablespoons minced fresh cilantro
- 12 large flour tortillas, warmed
  Canola oil
  Shredded cheddar cheese
  Sour cream
  Guacamole
  Salsa
  Shredded lettuce
  Chopped tomatoes
  Sliced ripe olives

1. In a skillet, melt bacon grease over medium heat. Cook the meat, onion, garlic, tomatoes, chilies and potato until the onion softens. Add salt, oregano, chili powder and cilantro; simmer 2-3 minutes.

2. Place a scant ½ cup meat filling on each tortilla. Fold, envelope-style, like a burrito. Fry, seam side down, in ½ in. of hot oil (360°-375°) until crispy and brown. Turn and brown other side. Drain on a paper towel.

3. Place on a serving plate and top with shredded cheese, a dollop of sour cream, guacamole and salsa. Place shredded lettuce next to chimichanga and top with tomatoes and olives. Serve immediately.

Chorizo-Stuffed Turkey Breast with Mexican Grits

A heavenly combination of well-seasoned ingredients is featured in this recipe. It's also a simple but special dinner option for company.

—VERONICA GANTLEY NORFOLK, VIRGINIA

PREP: 30 MIN. **BAKE:** 1¼ HOURS + STANDING
MAKES: 6 SERVINGS

- 1 boneless skinless turkey breast half (2 pounds)
- ½ pound uncooked chorizo, crumbled
- 2 tablespoons olive oil
- 1 teaspoon salt, divided
- 1 teaspoon pepper, divided
- 2 cups water
- 1 cup milk
- 1 cup quick-cooking grits
- 1 can (4 ounces) chopped green chilies
- ½ cup shredded Mexican cheese blend
  Minced fresh parsley, optional

1. Cover turkey with plastic wrap; flatten to ½-in. thickness. Remove plastic. Spread the chorizo over turkey to within 1 in. of edges. Roll up jelly-roll style, starting with a short side; tie with kitchen string.

2. Rub with oil. Sprinkle with ½ teaspoon salt and ½ teaspoon pepper. In a large ovenproof skillet, brown turkey on all sides. Bake at 350° for 1¼ to 1½ hours or until a thermometer reads 165°. Cover and let stand for 10 minutes before slicing.

3. In a large saucepan, bring the water, milk and remaining salt to a boil. Slowly stir in grits. Reduce heat; cook and stir for 5-7 minutes or until thickened. Stir in the chilies, cheese and remaining pepper. Serve grits with turkey. Sprinkle with parsley if desired.

Chicken with Black Bean Salsa

There's nothing timid about the flavors in this Southwestern-style entree. Prepared on the grill or broiled, it's a fast, fun meal for a busy weeknight or a weekend get-together.

—TRISHA KRUSE EAGLE, IDAHO

PREP/TOTAL TIME: 25 MIN. **MAKES:** 4 SERVINGS

- 1 can (15 ounces) black beans, rinsed and drained
- 1 can (8 ounces) unsweetened crushed pineapple, drained
- 1 small red onion, chopped
- 1 plum tomato, chopped
- 1 garlic clove, minced
- 2 tablespoons lime juice
- ¼ teaspoon salt
- ¼ teaspoon coarsely ground pepper

RUB
- 1 tablespoon brown sugar
- 1 teaspoon hot pepper sauce
- ½ teaspoon garlic powder
- ½ teaspoon salt
- ½ teaspoon coarsely ground pepper
- 4 boneless skinless chicken breast halves (4 ounces each)

1. For salsa, in a large bowl, combine the first eight ingredients; refrigerate until serving. Combine the brown sugar, pepper sauce, garlic powder, salt and pepper; rub over both sides of chicken.

2. Moisten a paper towel with cooking oil; using long-handled tongs, lightly coat the grill rack. Grill chicken, covered, over medium heat or broil 4 in. from the heat for 4-7 minutes on each side or until a thermometer reads 165°. Serve with salsa.

Tacoritos

PREP: 40 MIN. **BAKE:** 20 MIN. **MAKES:** 8 SERVINGS

- ¼ cup butter, cubed
- ¼ cup all-purpose flour
- 4 cups water
- 3 tablespoons chili powder
- 1 teaspoon garlic salt
- 1 pound ground beef
- 1 pound bulk pork sausage
- ¼ cup chopped onion
- 1 cup refried beans
- 8 flour tortillas (8 inches), warmed
- 3 cups (12 ounces) shredded Monterey Jack cheese
  Optional toppings: shredded lettuce, chopped tomatoes, sliced ripe olives and sour cream

1. In a large saucepan, melt butter. Stir in the flour until smooth; gradually add water. Bring to a boil; cook and stir for 1 minute or until thickened. Stir in chili powder and garlic salt. Bring to a boil. Reduce heat; simmer, uncovered, for 10 minutes.

2. In a large skillet over medium heat, cook beef, sausage and onion until meat is no longer pink; drain. Stir in refried beans; heat through.

3. Spread ¼ cup sauce in a greased 13x9-in. baking dish. Spread 1 tablespoon sauce over each tortilla; place ⅔ cup meat mixture down the center of each. Top each with ¼ cup cheese. Roll up and place seam side down in prepared dish. Pour remaining sauce over top; sprinkle with remaining cheese.

4. Bake, uncovered, at 350° for 18-22 minutes or until bubbly and cheese is melted. Serve with optional toppings if desired.

> My mild and meaty Southwestern dish blends the delicious flavor of tacos with the heartiness of burritos. Your family's going to love this.

—MONICA FLATFORD
KNOXVILLE, TENNESSEE

SAN DIEGO, CA

Franciscan friars from Mexico's Baja California were sent north to form missions. They founded San Diego de Alcala in 1769; it's California's first mission.

Beef Flautas

One of my favorite dishes to make for my family is Mexican beef flautas. The spices and onion give the meat so much flavor!

—**MARIA GOCLAN** KATY, TEXAS

PREP: 1¼ HOURS **COOK:** 5 MIN./BATCH
MAKES: 20 FLAUTAS

2½ teaspoons canola oil
2 pounds fresh beef brisket
2 medium onions, chopped
2 medium green peppers, chopped
2 cups water
1 teaspoon salt
1 teaspoon dried oregano
1 teaspoon dried marjoram
1 teaspoon pepper
20 corn tortillas (6 inches), warmed
   Oil for deep-fat frying
   Optional toppings: guacamole, sour cream and salsa

1. In a Dutch oven, heat oil over medium heat. Brown brisket on all sides. Add onions, peppers, water and seasonings. Bring to a boil. Reduce heat; simmer, covered, 1 to 1½ hours or until meat is tender.

2. Remove meat; cool slightly. Shred meat with two forks. Drain onion mixture; add to meat. Spoon ¼ cup beef mixture down the center of each tortilla. Roll up and secure with toothpicks. In an electric skillet or deep fryer, heat oil to 375°. Fry flautas, a few at a time, for 1 minute on each side or until golden brown.

3. Drain on paper towels. Remove toothpicks. Serve with toppings of your choice.

Editor's Note: *This is a fresh beef brisket, not corned beef.*

Baja Chicken Taco Pizza

With cilantro, taco seasoning, chicken, avocado and lots of cheese, this flavorful pizza is filling and so refreshing.

—**JENNY FLAKE** NEWPORT BEACH, CALIFORNIA

PREP: 20 MIN. **BAKE:** 20 MIN. + STANDING
MAKES: 6 SERVINGS

1 cup ranch salad dressing
¼ cup salsa
1 tablespoon lime juice
3 tablespoons minced fresh cilantro
2 cups cubed cooked chicken breast
1 envelope taco seasoning
1 prebaked 12-inch thin pizza crust
½ cup chopped tomato
½ cup finely chopped red onion
2 cups (8 ounces) shredded part-skim mozzarella cheese
2 cups shredded lettuce
2 medium ripe avocados, peeled and thinly sliced

1. In a blender or food processor, combine the salad dressing, salsa, lime juice and cilantro. Cover and process on high for 1-2 minutes or until smooth; set aside. In a small bowl, combine chicken and taco seasoning; set aside.

2. Place crust on an ungreased 12-in. pizza pan. Spread salsa mixture over crust. Sprinkle with the chicken mixture, tomato, onion and cheese. Bake at 425° for 17-20 minutes or until crust is golden brown and cheese is melted. Let stand for 10 minutes before cutting. Sprinkle with lettuce; top with avocado slices. Serve immediately.

Corn Dogs

You can prepare corn dogs at home that taste just like those sold at the fair. Grown-ups and kids alike will enjoy this summer favorite.

—**RUBY WILLIAMS** BOGALUSA, LOUISIANA

PREP/TOTAL TIME: 25 MIN. **MAKES:** 10 SERVINGS

- ¾ cup yellow cornmeal
- ¾ cup self-rising flour
- 1 egg, lightly beaten
- ⅔ cup milk
- 10 Popsicle sticks
- 10 hot dogs
  Oil for deep-fat frying

1. In a large bowl, combine the cornmeal, flour and egg. Stir in milk to make a thick batter; let stand 4 minutes. Insert sticks into hot dogs; dip in batter.

2. In an electric skillet or deep-fat fryer, heat oil to 375°. Fry corn dogs, a few at a time, about 8-6 minutes or until golden brown, turning occasionally. Drain on paper towels.

Editor's Note: *As a substitute for self-rising flour, place 1 teaspoon baking powder and ¼ teaspoon salt in a measuring cup. Add all-purpose flour to measure ¾ cup.*

South-of-the-Border Meat Loaf

This zesty recipe uses black beans, chopped jalapeno, green peppers and crushed taco shells. It's a really tasty twist on a classic!

—**RUTH BOGDANSKI** GRANTS PASS, OREGON

PREP: 10 MIN. **BAKE:** 1 HOUR + COOLING
MAKES: 6-8 SERVINGS

- 1 can (15 ounces) black beans, rinsed and drained
- 4 taco shells, crushed
- ½ cup chopped onion
- ½ cup chopped green pepper
- ⅓ cup minced fresh cilantro
- 2 egg whites
- 2 tablespoons chopped jalapeno pepper
- 2 teaspoons ground cumin
- 2 teaspoons chili powder
- 3 garlic cloves, minced
- 1 teaspoon salt
- ½ teaspoon pepper
- 2 pounds lean ground beef (90% lean)
  Salsa, optional

1. In a large bowl, combine the first 12 ingredients. Crumble beef over mixture and mix well. Press into a 9x5-in. loaf pan coated with cooking spray. Bake, uncovered, at 375° for 1 hour or until meat is no longer pink and a thermometer reads 160°.

2. Cool for 10 minutes before removing from pan. Drizzle with salsa if desired.

Editor's Note: *Wear disposable gloves when cutting hot peppers; the oils can burn skin. Avoid touching your face.*

DALLAS, TX

SUPER MIDWAY

The State Fair of Texas has been an autumn highlight for locals and travelers alike since 1886.

A culinary necessity during pioneer times, the Dutch oven was dubbed Utah's official State Cooking Pot in 1997. Utah is also home to the International Dutch Oven Society, which hosts the annual World Championship Dutch Oven Cook-Off.

SANDY, UT

Competitors in this world championship cook-off use their Dutch ovens to make mouthwatering entrees and breads—even desserts!

Award-Winning Chuck Wagon Chili

For an extra-spicy kick, use even more chili powder, but make sure there's a cool drink close by!

—**EUGENE JARZAB JR.** PHOENIX, ARIZONA

PREP: 30 MIN.   **COOK:** 80 MIN.   **MAKES:** 6 SERVINGS

- 1 boneless beef chuck roast (3 pounds), cut into ½-inch cubes
- 1 pound pork stew meat, cut into ½-inch cubes
- ⅓ cup chili powder, divided
- 4 tablespoons canola oil, divided
- 1 large onion, finely chopped
- 1 celery rib, finely chopped
- 3 garlic cloves, minced
- 1 tablespoon chopped canned green chilies
- 1 carton (32 ounces) beef broth
- ¾ cup beer
- ¾ cup tomato sauce
- 2 tablespoons grated dark chocolate
- 3 teaspoons ground cumin
- 1 teaspoon dried oregano
- ½ teaspoon salt
- ½ teaspoon ground mustard
- ½ teaspoon cayenne pepper

1. Sprinkle beef and pork with half of the chili powder. In a Dutch oven, brown meat in batches in 2 tablespoons oil; drain and set aside. In the same pan, saute onion and celery in remaining oil until crisp-tender. Add the garlic, chilies and remaining chili powder; cook 1 minute longer.

2. Stir in the broth, beer, tomato sauce, chocolate, cumin, oregano, salt, mustard, cayenne and meat. Bring to a boil. Reduce heat; simmer, uncovered, for 1 to 1½ hours or until meat is tender.

Flank Steak Santa Fe

Here's a recipe that's truly representative of the flavors we enjoy in this region of the country. It's a favorite in my family for those special Saturday-night dinners.

—TANYA JOHNSON SAN DIEGO, CALIFORNIA

PREP: 15 MIN. **BAKE:** 1½ HOURS
MAKES: 6-8 SERVINGS

- ¾ **pound bulk spicy pork sausage or uncooked chorizo**
- 2 **eggs, lightly beaten**
- 1½ **cups unseasoned croutons**
- ⅓ **cup sliced green onions**
- ⅓ **cup minced fresh parsley**
- 1 **beef flank steak (1½ to 2 pounds)**
- 3 **tablespoons canola oil**
- 1 **jar (16 ounces) picante sauce or salsa verde**
   Additional picante sauce or salsa verde, optional

1. Crumble sausage into a large skillet; cook and stir for 6-8 minutes over medium heat until fully cooked. Drain. Cool to room temperature; stir in the eggs, croutons, onions and parsley.

2. Cut steak in half horizontally to within ½ in. of end; open steak and pound to 1½-in. thickness. Spread with sausage mixture. Roll up, jelly-roll style, beginning with a short side; tie with string.

3. In a large skillet, brown steak in oil. Place in a greased 13x9-in. baking dish. Spread picante sauce over steak.

4. Cover and bake at 350° for 1½ to 1¾ hours or until meat is tender. Garnish with additional picante sauce if desired.

Zesty Tacos

Jazz up everyday tacos in a snap! Black-eyed peas and a drizzle of Italian dressing are the surprise ingredients that perk up this recipe.

—SUSIE BONHAM FAIRVIEW, OKLAHOMA

PREP/TOTAL TIME: 30 MIN. **MAKES:** 8 SERVINGS

- 1 **pound ground beef**
- 1 **cup water**
- 1 **envelope taco seasoning**
- 8 **taco shells**
- 1 **can (15½ ounces) black-eyed peas, rinsed and drained**
- 1 **cup chopped tomatoes**
- 1 **cup shredded lettuce**
- 1 **cup (4 ounces) shredded cheddar cheese**
- ½ **cup zesty Italian salad dressing**

1. In a large skillet, cook beef over medium heat until no longer pink; drain. Stir in water and taco seasoning. Bring to a boil. Reduce heat; simmer, uncovered, for 4-5 minutes or until thickened.

2. Meanwhile, prepare taco shells according to package directions. Stir peas into skillet; heat through. Spoon ¼ cup beef mixture into each taco shell. Top with tomatoes, lettuce and cheese. Drizzle with salad dressing.

Whether the variation is called Chicken-Fried Steak, Country-Fried Steak or Pan-Fried Steak, this Texas classic boasts the flavor of the Lone Star State. Many stories chronicle its origins. One of our favorites? A cook who mixed up his orders for chicken and steak created the dish more than 100 years ago! But no matter its background, this recipe is always served up with mashed potatoes and cream gravy.

Chicken-Fried Steaks

These crispy steaks will earn raves when you serve them for dinner. My husband asks me to prepare this recipe regularly. I like it because it's just so easy to make.

—DENICE LOUK GARNETT, KANSAS

PREP/TOTAL TIME: 25 MIN.
MAKES: 4 SERVINGS (2 CUPS GRAVY)

- 2¼ cups all-purpose flour, divided
- 2 teaspoons baking powder
- ¾ teaspoon each salt, onion powder, garlic powder, chili powder and pepper
- 2 eggs, lightly beaten
- 1⅔ cups buttermilk, divided
- 4 beef cubed steaks (4 ounces each)
  Oil for frying
- 1½ cups 2% milk

1. In a shallow bowl, combine 2 cups flour, baking powder and seasonings. In another shallow bowl, combine the eggs and 1 cup of buttermilk. Dip each cubed steak in buttermilk mixture, then roll in flour mixture. Let stand for 5 minutes.

2. In a large skillet, heat ½ in. of oil on medium-high. Fry the steaks for 5-7 minutes. Turn carefully; cook 5 minutes longer or until coating is crisp and meat is no longer pink. Remove steaks and keep warm.

3. Drain, reserving ⅓ cup drippings; stir the remaining flour into drippings until smooth. Cook and stir over medium heat for 2 minutes. Gradually whisk in milk and the remaining buttermilk. Bring to a boil; cook and stir for 2 minutes or until thickened. Serve with steaks.

Barbecued Beef Short Ribs

For a real straight-from-the-chuckwagon beef meal, you can't rope a better main dish than this! It's the recipe I rely on when feeding a hungry group. The wonderfully tangy sauce is lip-smacking good.

—MILDRED SHERRER FORT WORTH, TEXAS

PREP: 20 MIN. **COOK:** 2½ HOURS
MAKES: 4-6 SERVINGS

- 3 to 4 pounds bone-in beef short ribs
- 1 tablespoon canola oil
- 2½ cups water, divided
- 1 can (6 ounces) tomato paste
- 1 cup ketchup
- 1 garlic clove, minced
- ¾ cup packed brown sugar
- ½ cup chopped onion
- ½ cup white vinegar
- 2 tablespoons prepared mustard
- 1½ teaspoons salt
  Hot cooked noodles

1. In Dutch oven, brown ribs in oil. Add 2 cups water; bring to a boil. Reduce heat. Cover and simmer for 1½ hours; drain.

2. Combine the tomato paste, ketchup, garlic, brown sugar, onion, vinegar, mustard, salt and remaining water. Pour over ribs; bring to a boil. Reduce heat; cover and simmer for 1 hour or until meat is tender. Serve with noodles.

Stuffed Breakfast Burritos

Soon after we moved to Arizona, I received this recipe. It's a big hit with everyone. For a fun variation, add part of a green pepper and some whole kernel corn. Or omit the potatoes and eggs and add your favorite canned beans and a little shredded cheddar cheese.

—**ANITA MEADOR** MESA, ARIZONA

PREP/TOTAL TIME: 20 MIN. **MAKES:** 2 SERVINGS

- ¼ **pound bulk pork sausage**
- ½ **cup cooked diced peeled potato**
- 2 **tablespoons chopped onion**
- 4 **teaspoons canned chopped green chilies**
  Dash pepper
- 2 **eggs, lightly beaten**
- ½ **cup shredded Mexican cheese blend**
- 2 **flour tortillas (8 inches), warmed**

1. Crumble sausage into a skillet; cook over medium heat until no longer pink. Remove sausage with a slotted spoon and set aside.

2. In the same skillet, fry potato and onion until onion is crisp-tender. Add the chilies and pepper. Return sausage to the pan. Add eggs; cook and stir until eggs are completely set.

3. Remove from the heat; stir in cheese. Spoon mixture off-center onto tortillas. Fold in bottom and sides of tortilla and roll up.

Scampi Adobo

PREP/TOTAL TIME: 30 MIN. **MAKES:** 4 SERVINGS

- 2 **plum tomatoes, seeded and chopped**
- 1 **poblano pepper, seeded and chopped**
- 1 **tablespoon minced chipotle pepper in adobo sauce**
- 3 **garlic cloves, minced**
- 1 **tablespoon olive oil**
- 1 **pound uncooked medium shrimp, peeled and deveined**
- ½ **cup white wine or reduced-sodium chicken broth**
- ⅓ **cup minced fresh cilantro**
- 3 **tablespoons lime juice**
- 2 **tablespoons reduced-fat butter**
- ½ **teaspoon salt**
- ¼ **cup shredded part-skim mozzarella cheese**
  Lime slices, optional

1. In a large nonstick skillet, saute tomatoes, peppers and garlic in oil for 2 minutes. Reduce heat to medium; stir in the shrimp, wine, cilantro, lime juice, butter and salt. Cook and stir for 3-4 minutes or until shrimp turn pink.

2. Remove from the heat; sprinkle with the cheese. Garnish with lime slices if desired.

Editor's Note: *This recipe was tested with Land O'Lakes light stick butter.*

" Being a homegrown Texan, I love spicy foods and the sweet flavor of cilantro. I created this unique Southwestern version of shrimp scampi in my own kitchen. "

—**LAURIE LACLAIR**

NORTH RICHLAND HILLS, TEXAS

> **Here's a simple recipe for a casual dinner with friends or family. Use any leftover filling as a topping for tomorrow's quick taco salad!**
>
> —TRACY GUNTER
> BOISE, IDAHO

Lime Chicken Tacos

PREP: 10 MIN. **COOK:** 5½ HOURS **MAKES:** 12 TACOS

- 1½ **pounds boneless skinless chicken breasts**
- 3 **tablespoons lime juice**
- 1 **tablespoon chili powder**
- 1 **cup frozen corn**
- 1 **cup chunky salsa**
- 12 **flour tortillas (6 inches), warmed**
  Sour cream, shredded cheddar cheese and shredded lettuce, optional

1. Place the chicken in a 3-qt. slow cooker. Combine lime juice and chili powder; pour over chicken. Cover and cook on low for 5-6 hours or until chicken is tender.

2. Remove chicken; cool slightly. Shred meat with two forks and return to the slow cooker; heat through. Stir in corn and salsa.

3. Cover and cook on low for 30 minutes or until heated through. Serve in tortillas with sour cream, cheese and lettuce if desired.

Green Chili Pork Stew

Green chilies are a big favorite here in the Southwest, and my family likes anything with them in it—especially this stew!

—**PAT HENDERSON** DEER PARK, TEXAS

PREP: 25 MIN. **COOK:** 1 HOUR **MAKES:** 8 SERVINGS

- 2 **pounds lean boneless pork, cut into 1½-inch cubes**
- 1 **tablespoon canola oil**
- 4 **cups chicken broth, divided**
- 3 **cans (11 ounces each) whole kernel corn, drained**
- 2 **celery ribs, diced**
- 2 **medium potatoes, peeled and diced**
- 2 **medium tomatoes, diced**
- 3 **cans (4 ounces each) chopped green chilies**
- 2 **teaspoons ground cumin**
- 1 **teaspoon dried oregano**
- 1 **teaspoon salt, optional**
- 3 **tablespoons all-purpose flour**
  Corn bread or warmed flour tortillas, optional

1. In a 5-qt. Dutch oven over medium-high heat, brown pork in oil. Add 3½ cups broth, corn, celery, potatoes, tomatoes, chilies, cumin, oregano and salt if desired; bring to a boil. Reduce heat; cover and simmer for 1 hour or until meat and vegetables are tender.

2. Combine flour and remaining broth; stir into stew. Bring to a boil; cook, stirring constantly, until thickened. Serve with corn bread or tortillas if desired.

Huevos Rancheros with Tomatillo Sauce

My husband and I visited Cuernavaca, Mexico, a year ago and had huevos rancheros for breakfast while there. My husband loved the dish so much, he asked me to cook it for him when got home. This is my version, which is suited to my family's preference for sunny-side-up eggs, but poached or scrambled eggs would also be good.

—CHERYL WOODSON LIBERTY, MISSOURI

PREP/TOTAL TIME: 25 MIN. **MAKES:** 8 SERVINGS

- 5 **tomatillos, husks removed and halved**
- 2 **tablespoons coarsely chopped onion**
- 1 **to 2 serrano peppers, halved**
- 3 **garlic cloves, peeled**
- 1 **teaspoon chicken bouillon granules**
- 1 **can (15 ounces) Southwestern black beans, undrained**
- 8 **eggs**
- 4 **ounces manchego cheese, shredded**
- 8 **tostada shells, warmed**
- ½ **cup sour cream**
  Chopped tomato, sliced avocado and minced fresh cilantro, optional

1. To make salsa verde, place the tomatillos, onion, peppers, garlic and bouillon in a food processor. Cover and process until finely chopped; set aside. In a small saucepan, mash beans. Cook on low until heated through, stirring occasionally.

2. Meanwhile, break eggs in batches into a large nonstick skillet coated with cooking spray. Cover and cook over low heat for 5-7 minutes or until eggs are set. Sprinkle with the cheese.

3. To serve, spread beans over tostada shells; top with eggs, salsa verde and sour cream. Garnish with tomato, avocado and cilantro if desired.

Editor's Note: *Wear disposable gloves when cutting hot peppers; the oils can burn skin. Avoid touching your face.*

Chimichurri is a parsley-based sauce that hails from Argentina. Besides the parsley, chimichurri should include oregano, garlic, vinegar and olive oil. This sauce goes well with most grilled meats, from seafood and poultry to beef and lamb.

CALIFORNIA COAST

About 300 fish and shellfish species—including shrimp—make up the California seafood industry's catch. Eureka's coastal waters are among the best for shrimping.

Chimichurri Shrimp Skillet

Fresh fruit adds sweetness to this bright Southwestern shrimp entree. The contrast of colors, flavors and textures in this dish is wonderful!

—**SUSAN RILEY** ALLEN, TEXAS

PREP/TOTAL TIME: 30 MIN. **MAKES:** 6 SERVINGS

- 2 **cups uncooked instant rice**
- 3 **cups packed fresh parsley sprigs**
- ½ **cup olive oil**
- 2 **tablespoons lime juice**
- 4 **garlic cloves, halved**
- 2 **teaspoons red wine vinegar**
- 1½ **teaspoons ground cumin**
- 1 **teaspoon salt**
- 1 **teaspoon dried oregano**
- ½ **teaspoon pepper**
- 1 **pound uncooked large shrimp, peeled and deveined**
- 1 **cup chopped sweet red pepper**
- 1 **medium onion, chopped**
- 1½ **cups seedless red grapes, halved**

1. Cook rice according to package directions. Meanwhile, in a food processor, combine the parsley, oil, lime juice, garlic, vinegar, cumin, salt, oregano and pepper; cover and process until blended.

2. In a large skillet, saute shrimp in ¼ cup parsley mixture for 3-4 minutes or until shrimp turn pink; remove and keep warm.

3. In the same skillet, saute red pepper and onion in ¼ cup parsley mixture until tender. Stir in the shrimp, rice, grapes and remaining parsley mixture; heat through.

Black Beans with Brown Rice

Your family will never miss the meat in my hearty, colorful and fresh-tasting main dish. Served over brown rice, these beans make a healthy, stick-to-the-ribs dinner.

—**SHEILA MEYER** NORTH CANTON, OHIO

PREP: 15 MIN. **COOK:** 20 MIN. **MAKES:** 5 SERVINGS

- 1 small green pepper, chopped
- ½ cup chopped sweet red pepper
- ½ cup chopped sweet yellow pepper
- ½ cup chopped red onion
- 2 tablespoons canola oil
- 2 cans (15 ounces each) black beans, rinsed and drained
- 1 can (14½ ounces) diced tomatoes, undrained
- 2 tablespoons cider vinegar
- ½ teaspoon garlic salt
- ⅛ teaspoon pepper
- ⅛ teaspoon cayenne pepper
- 2½ cups hot cooked brown rice

1. In a large saucepan, saute peppers and onion in oil until tender. Stir in the beans, tomatoes, vinegar, garlic salt, pepper and cayenne. Bring to a boil. Reduce heat; simmer, uncovered, for 12-15 minutes or until desired consistency, stirring occasionally. Serve with rice.

Mexican Pork Stew

PREP: 10 MIN. **COOK:** 55 MIN. **MAKES:** 5 SERVINGS

- 1 pound boneless pork loin roast, cut into ¾-inch cubes
- 3 teaspoons olive oil
- 1 large onion, chopped
- 2 celery ribs, chopped
- 1 jalapeno pepper, seeded and chopped
- 1 garlic clove, minced
- 1½ cups water
- 1 tablespoon chili powder
- 2 teaspoons brown sugar
- 1 teaspoon ground cumin
- ½ teaspoon salt
- ¼ teaspoon pepper
- 1 can (6 ounces) tomato paste
- 1 can (16 ounces) kidney beans, rinsed and drained
- 1 can (15 ounces) pinto beans, rinsed and drained
- 1 can (14½ ounces) diced tomatoes, undrained
- 2 teaspoons minced fresh cilantro

1. In a Dutch oven or large stockpot over medium-high heat, brown meat on all sides in 1 teaspoon oil; drain. Remove meat; keep warm.

2. In the same pan, saute the onion, celery, jalapeno and garlic in remaining oil until tender. Stir in the water, chili powder, brown sugar, cumin, salt and pepper. Return meat to pan. Bring to a boil. Reduce heat; cover and simmer for 30 minutes.

3. Stir in tomato paste, beans and tomatoes. Return to a boil. Reduce the heat; cover and simmer 20 minutes longer or until the meat is tender and beans are heated through. Sprinkle with cilantro.

Editor's Note: *Wear disposable gloves when cutting hot peppers; the oils can burn skin. Avoid touching your face.*

❝I heat up cold nights by serving this thick and zesty stew with corn bread. I also like to spoon leftovers into corn tortillas with a little salsa and reduced-fat sour cream for a filling snack.❞

—**MICKEY TERRY**
DEL VALLEY, TEXAS

For hundreds of years, various types of this comforting hominy stew have been simmering in kitchens across the Southwest and Mexico.

ALBUQUERQUE, NM

What's more enchanting than a sky speckled with colorful hot air balloons? For more than 40 years, people have visited the Albuquerque International Balloon Fiesta to marvel at that very sight.

Land of Enchantment Posole

We usually make this spicy soup over the holidays, when we have lots of family visiting. And we never have any leftovers.

—**SUZANNE CALDWELL** ARTESIA, NEW MEXICO

PREP: 30 MIN. **COOK:** 1 HOUR **MAKES:** 5 SERVINGS

- 1½ **pounds pork stew meat, cut into ¾-inch cubes**
- 1 **large onion, chopped**
- 2 **tablespoons canola oil**
- 2 **garlic cloves, minced**
- 3 **cups beef broth**
- 2 **cans (15½ ounces each) hominy, rinsed and drained**
- 2 **cans (4 ounces each) chopped green chilies**
- 1 **to 2 jalapeno peppers, seeded and chopped, optional**
- ½ **teaspoon salt**
- ½ **teaspoon ground cumin**
- ½ **teaspoon dried oregano**
- ¼ **teaspoon pepper**
- ¼ **teaspoon cayenne pepper**
- ½ **cup minced fresh cilantro**
  Tortilla strips, optional

1. In a Dutch oven, cook pork and onion in oil over medium heat until meat is no longer pink. Add garlic; cook 1 minute longer. Drain. Stir in the broth, hominy, chilies, jalapeno if desired, salt, cumin, oregano, pepper and cayenne.

2. Bring to a boil. Reduce heat; cover and simmer for 45-60 minutes or until meat is tender. Stir in cilantro. Serve with tortilla strips if desired.

Editor's Note: *Wear disposable gloves when cutting hot peppers; the oils can burn skin. Avoid touching your face.*

Chicken Tamales

I love making tamales. They're a little time-consuming but definitely worth the effort. I usually make them for a special Christmas treat, but my family demands them more often!

—**CINDY PRUITT** GROVE, OKLAHOMA

PREP: 2½ HOURS + SOAKING **COOK:** 45 MIN. **MAKES:** 20 TAMALES

- 20 **dried corn husks**
- 1 **broiler/fryer chicken (3 to 4 pounds), cut up**
- 3 **quarts water**
- 1 **medium onion, quartered**
- 2 **teaspoons salt**
- 1 **garlic clove, crushed**

DOUGH
- 1 **cup shortening**
- 3 **cups masa harina**

CHICKEN CHILI FILLING
- 6 **tablespoons canola oil**
- 6 **tablespoons all-purpose flour**
- ¾ **cup chili powder**
- ½ **teaspoon salt**
- ¼ **teaspoon garlic powder**
- ¼ **teaspoon pepper**
- 2 **cans (2¼ ounces each) sliced ripe olives, drained**

1. Place corn husks in a large bowl; cover with cold water and soak for at least 2 hours.

2. Meanwhile, in a Dutch oven, combine the chicken, water, onion, salt and garlic. Bring to a boil. Reduce heat; cover and simmer for 45-60 minutes or until meat is tender. Remove chicken from broth; set aside until cool enough to handle. Strain broth; skim fat. Finely chop or shred chicken.

3. For dough, in a large bowl, beat shortening until light and fluffy, about 1 minute. Add small amounts of the masa harina alternately with 2 cups of the reserved broth, beating until well blended.

4. Drop a small amount of dough into a cup of cold water; dough should float to the top. If dough does not float, continue beating until dough is light enough to float.

5. In a Dutch oven, heat oil over medium heat; stir in flour until blended. Cook and stir for 7-9 minutes or until lightly browned. Stir in the spices, chicken and 4 cups reserved broth. Bring to a boil. Reduce heat; simmer, uncovered, for 45 minutes or until filling is thickened, stirring occasionally.

6. Drain corn husks and pat dry. Place a corn husk on a work surface with the small end pointing away from you. On large end, spread 3 tablespoons dough to within 1 in. of edges. Top with 2 tablespoons chicken mixture and 2 teaspoons olives. Fold long sides of husk over filling, overlapping slightly. Fold over ends of husk; tie with string to secure. Repeat.

7. In a large steamer basket, position tamales upright. Place basket in a Dutch oven over 1 in. of water. Bring to a boil; cover and steam for 45-50 minutes or until dough peels away from husk, adding additional hot water to the pan as needed.

Editor's Note: *Look for dried corn husks and masa harina in the ethnic aisle.*

Spanish for "crumbs," migas has its roots in the Iberian Peninsula, Mexico and the Southwest. The Tex-Mex style, which includes eggs, is said to have been developed as a meatless dish for Lent. When meat is added, traditional chorizo gives it a spicy kick.

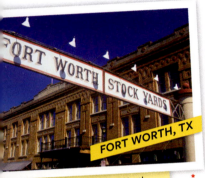

FORT WORTH, TX

Though the Fort Worth Stockyards now offer plenty of other attractions, you can still see steers in this historic district! There are daily cattle drives, plus other bovine-related events, including a rodeo.

Migas, My Way

We love migas for breakfast or a weekend dinner. It is quick, easy and delicious. My family loves any foods with a Southwestern flair so this recipe gets a big "thumbs up" from them. I have, on occasion, substituted fresh corn tortillas for the chips by cutting them into strips and sauteing them with the pepper and onion.

—**JOAN HALLFORD** FORT WORTH, TEXAS

PREP/TOTAL TIME: 25 MIN. **MAKES:** 2 SERVINGS

¼ **cup chopped onion**
¼ **cup chopped green pepper**
1 **tablespoon bacon drippings or canola oil**
4 **eggs**
1 **tablespoon water**
1 **tablespoon salsa**
½ **cup crushed tortilla chips**
½ **cup shredded cheddar cheese, divided**
  Chopped green onions, additional salsa and warm flour tortillas, optional

1. In a large skillet, saute onion and green pepper in drippings until tender. In a small bowl, whisk the eggs, water and salsa. Add to skillet; cook and stir until set. Stir in tortilla chips and ¼ cup cheese.

2. Sprinkle with remaining cheese. Top with green onions and additional salsa and serve with tortillas if desired.

Corn Bread with Black-Eyed Peas

Black-eyed peas are a good-luck tradition for New Year's Day...but my family is so fond of this recipe, I make it all year long!

—JEANNE SHINN BANDERA, TEXAS

PREP: 15 MIN. **BAKE:** 40 MIN. **MAKES:** 8-10 SERVINGS

- 1 pound ground beef, browned and drained
- 1 cup cornmeal
- ½ cup all-purpose flour
- ¾ cup cream-style corn
- 1 cup cooked or canned black-eyed peas, drained
- 1 medium onion, chopped
- ½ cup canola oil
- 1 cup buttermilk
- 2 eggs, beaten
- 2 cups (8 ounces) shredded cheddar cheese
- ½ teaspoon baking soda

1. In a bowl, combine all the ingredients. Pour into a greased 13x9-in. baking dish. Bake at 350°, uncovered, for 40-45 minutes or until the bread is golden.

Chicken Tortilla Bake

PREP: 25 MIN. **BAKE:** 25 MIN. **MAKES:** 6 SERVINGS

- 1 pound boneless skinless chicken breasts, cut into 1-inch cubes
- ½ teaspoon ground cumin
- ¼ teaspoon salt
- 1 tablespoon plus 1 teaspoon olive oil, divided
- 1 can (16 ounces) refried beans
- 1 can (14½ ounces) diced tomatoes with mild green chilies, drained
- 8 flour tortillas (8 inches), cut into 1-inch strips
- 1 can (11 ounces) Mexicorn, drained
- 2 cups (8 ounces) shredded cheddar cheese

1. In a large skillet, saute the chicken, cumin and salt in 1 tablespoon oil until chicken is no longer pink.

2. Combine the refried beans and tomatoes; spread 1 cup into a greased 11x7-in. baking dish. Top with 24 tortilla strips; layer with half of the corn, bean mixture, chicken and cheese. Repeat layers.

3. Using remaining tortilla strips, make a lattice crust over filling; brush with remaining oil. Bake, uncovered, at 350° for 25-30 minutes or until heated through and cheese is melted.

4. Serve immediately or before baking, cover and freeze casserole for up to 3 months.

To use frozen casserole: *Thaw in the refrigerator overnight. Remove from the refrigerator 30 minutes before baking. Bake according to directions.*

> "You get two for the price of one in this combo enchilada/lasagna casserole. Enjoy all the flavors of the Mexican staple, and all the ease of a layered lasagna."

—TASTE OF HOME
TEST KITCHEN

> **It was traditional for Native American girls in our village to learn to cook at an early age. I made fry bread many times for my father and seven brothers, and after I perfected the recipe, Father said it was the best he'd ever eaten!**
>
> **—SANDRA CAMERON**
> FLAGSTAFF, ARIZONA

Fry Bread Sandwiches

PREP: 15 MIN. + RESTING **COOK:** 20 MIN.
MAKES: 6 SERVINGS

- 3 cups all-purpose flour
- 1 teaspoon baking powder
- ½ teaspoon salt
- 1¼ cups milk
  Oil for deep-fat frying
- 12 lettuce leaves
- 12 slices deli ham
- 1 small onion, sliced and separated into rings
- 6 slices cheddar cheese
- 18 thin slices tomato
- 1 can (4 ounces) chopped green chilies

1. In a large bowl, combine the flour, baking powder and salt. Add milk and stir to form a soft dough. Cover and let rest for 1 hour.

2. Divide dough into six portions. On a lightly floured surface, roll each portion into an 8-in. circle.

3. In an electric skillet or deep-fat fryer, heat oil to 375°. Fry bread circles, one at a time, until golden, turning once; drain on paper towels. Keep warm.

4. Cut each circle in half. On six halves, layer the lettuce, ham, onion, cheese and tomato; sprinkle with the chilies. Top with the remaining bread.

Chipotle BBQ Pork Sandwiches

I first made these sandwiches for a summer barbecue with guests who love traditional BBQ pork sandwiches but wanted something lighter. They loved these and didn't miss the extra calories one bit. Crunchy coleslaw tames the heat!

—PRISCILLA YEE CONCORD, CALIFORNIA

PREP: 20 MIN. **GRILL:** 20 MIN. **MAKES:** 4 SERVINGS

- ½ cup barbecue sauce
- 1 tablespoon honey
- 2 chipotle peppers in adobo sauce, chopped
- 1 pork tenderloin (1 pound)
- 1½ cups coleslaw mix
- 2 tablespoons reduced-fat sour cream
- 2 tablespoons Miracle Whip Light
- 1 tablespoon Dijon mustard
- 4 hamburger buns, split

1. In a small bowl, combine barbecue sauce, honey and peppers. Set aside ¼ cup until serving.

2. Moisten a paper towel with cooking oil; using long-handled tongs, lightly coat grill rack. Prepare grill for indirect heat, using a drip pan.

3. Place pork over drip pan and grill, covered, over indirect medium-hot heat for 20-25 minutes or until a thermometer reads 145°, basting occasionally with remaining barbecue sauce. Let stand for 5 minutes before slicing.

4. Meanwhile, combine the coleslaw mix, sour cream, Miracle Whip Light and mustard. Brush cut sides of buns with reserved barbecue sauce. Cut pork into ¼-in. slices; place on bun bottoms. Top with coleslaw and bun tops.

Pork Ribs and Chilies

This recipe comes from my mother-in-law, but my husband—who has a knack for spicy creations—perfected the flavor. When we invite people for dinner, they always ask if this is on the menu!

—JAYNE YOUNT AURORA, COLORADO

PREP: 1¼ HOURS **BAKE:** 2¼ HOURS
MAKES: 8 SERVINGS

- 2½ to 3 pounds boneless country-style pork ribs
- 2 cans (14½ ounces each) diced tomatoes, undrained
- 2 cans (14½ ounces each) chicken broth
- 1 jar (16 ounces) salsa
- 1 can (4 ounces) chopped green chilies
- 2 to 3 garlic cloves, minced
- 2 teaspoons ground cumin
- 1 teaspoon crushed red pepper flakes
- ½ teaspoon ground coriander, optional
- ¼ teaspoon salt
- ⅛ teaspoon pepper
- 2 tablespoons cornstarch
- ¼ cup cold water
  Hot cooked rice
  Shredded cheddar or Monterey Jack cheese, optional
  Sour cream and guacamole, optional

1. Place ribs in a deep roasting pan. Cover and bake at 450° for 30 minutes; drain. Reduce temperature to 350° and bake, uncovered, 45 minutes longer; drain. Allow to cool; cut meat into 1-in. cubes and return to pan. Combine tomatoes, broth, salsa, chilies and seasonings; pour over ribs. Cover and bake for 2 hours.

2. Combine cornstarch in water until smooth; stir into the rib mixture. Bake, uncovered, 15 minutes longer. Serve over rice. Top with cheese, sour cream and guacamole if desired.

Chili Chicken Sandwiches

My husband tells me that these sandwiches are real "man food." I like that! We serve them when we have friends come over to watch a game on TV. They're also great for a quick family dinner.

—DENA PETERSON LAPORTE, TEXAS

PREP/TOTAL TIME: 20 MIN. **MAKES:** 4 SERVINGS

- 1 package (8 ounces) cream cheese, softened
- 2 cups cubed cooked chicken
- 1½ cups shredded cheddar cheese
- 1 can (4 ounces) chopped green chilies
- 3 tablespoons chopped green onions
- 1 teaspoon ground cumin
- ¼ teaspoon crushed red pepper flakes
- ¼ teaspoon chili powder
- 4 hard rolls
- 2 tablespoons minced fresh cilantro

1. In a small bowl, beat the cream cheese until fluffy. Stir in the chicken, cheddar cheese, chilies, onions and seasonings.

2. Cut top fourths off of rolls; carefully hollow out bottoms, leaving ¼-in. shells (discard removed bread or save for another use). Fill bottom portions with the chicken mixture; replace tops.

3. Place on a baking sheet. Bake at 375° for 5-7 minutes or until golden brown. Sprinkle with cilantro.

LAS CRUCES, NM

Meet Big Jim, a medium-spicy variety of New Mexican (or NuMex) chili. Sometimes measuring more than 12 inches, this is the *Guiness Book of World Records'* longest pepper.

AUSTIN, TX

As they say, "Everything's bigger in Texas." That applies to the state capitol, too. It's the largest in the country (only the U.S. Capitol takes up more space).

Grilled Chiles Rellenos

Here's a healthy version of one of my favorite Mexican dishes. The grilled peppers go great with Spanish rice, gazpacho or a refreshing salad with jicama and citrus.

—LORI NELSON AUSTIN, TEXAS

PREP: 45 MIN. **GRILL:** 10 MIN. **MAKES:** 4 SERVINGS

- 1 cup (8 ounces) sour cream
- 2 tablespoons lime juice
- ½ cup minced fresh cilantro, divided
- 1 small onion, finely chopped
- 1 tablespoon butter
- 1 large portobello mushroom cap, finely chopped
- 1 small yellow summer squash, finely chopped
- 1 small zucchini, finely chopped
- 1 jalapeno pepper, seeded and finely chopped
- 1 garlic clove, minced
- 1 can (15 ounces) black beans, rinsed and drained
- 2 cups (8 ounces) shredded Mexican cheese blend, divided
- 1 cup frozen corn, thawed
- 1 teaspoon ground cumin
- ½ teaspoon salt
- ¼ teaspoon pepper
- 4 large poblano peppers, halved and seeded

1. In a small bowl, combine the sour cream, lime juice and ¼ cup cilantro. Cover and refrigerate until serving.

2. In a large skillet, saute onion in butter until tender. Add mushroom, yellow squash, zucchini, jalapeno and garlic; saute 3-5 minutes longer or until the vegetables are crisp-tender.

3. Stir in the beans, 1½ cups cheese, corn, cumin, salt, pepper and remaining cilantro. Remove from the heat. Spoon into poblano halves; sprinkle with remaining cheese.

4. Grill peppers, covered, over indirect medium heat for 10-14 minutes or until tender. Serve with sour cream sauce.

Editor's Note: *Wear disposable gloves when cutting hot peppers; the oils can burn skin. Avoid touching your face.*

> "I don't recall my mom ever using a recipe for her tamale pie, but I came up with this version that tastes very much like hers did. The grits add a Southern accent."

—WALDINE GUILLOTT
DEQUINCY, LOUISIANA

Mom's Tamale Pie

PREP: 25 MIN. **BAKE:** 20 MIN. **MAKES:** 12 SERVINGS

- 2 **pounds ground beef**
- 1 **large onion, chopped**
- 1 **large green pepper, chopped**
- 1 **can (15¼ ounces) whole kernel corn, undrained**
- 1½ **cups chopped fresh tomatoes**
- 5 **tablespoons tomato paste**
- 1 **envelope chili seasoning**
- 1½ **teaspoons sugar**
- 1 **teaspoon garlic powder**
- 1 **teaspoon dried basil**
- 1 **teaspoon dried oregano**
- 6 **cups cooked grits (prepared with butter and salt)**
- 1½ **teaspoons chili powder, divided**
- 1½ **cups (6 ounces) shredded cheddar cheese**

1. In a large skillet, cook the beef, onion and green pepper over medium heat until meat is no longer pink; drain. Add the corn, tomatoes, tomato paste, chili seasoning, sugar, garlic powder, basil and oregano. Cook and stir until heated through; keep warm.

2. Spread half of the grits in a greased 3-qt. baking dish. Sprinkle with 1 teaspoon chili powder. Top with the beef mixture and cheese. Pipe the remaining grits around edge of dish; sprinkle with remaining chili powder.

3. Bake, uncovered, at 325° for 20-25 minutes or until cheese is melted. Let stand for 5 minutes before serving.

> **"** What better place to find a fantastic barbecue sauce than Texas—and that's where this one is from. It's my father-in-law's own recipe. We've served it at many family reunions and think it's the best! **"**
>
> **—BOBBIE MORGAN**
> WOODSTOCK, GEORGIA

Favorite Barbecued Chicken

PREP: 15 MIN. **GRILL:** 35 MIN. **MAKES:** 6 SERVINGS

- 1 broiler/fryer chicken (3 pounds), cut up
  Salt and pepper to taste

BARBECUE SAUCE
- 1 small onion, finely chopped
- 1 tablespoon canola oil
- 1 cup ketchup
- 2 tablespoons lemon juice
- 1 tablespoon brown sugar
- 1 tablespoon water
- ½ teaspoon ground mustard
- ¼ teaspoon garlic powder
- ⅛ teaspoon pepper
  Dash salt
  Dash hot pepper sauce

1. Sprinkle chicken with salt and pepper. Grill chicken, skin side down, uncovered, over medium heat for 20 minutes.

2. Meanwhile, in a small saucepan, saute the onion in oil until tender. Stir in the remaining sauce ingredients. Bring to a boil. Reduce heat; simmer, uncovered, for 10 minutes.

3. Turn chicken; grill 15-25 minutes longer or until juices run clear, brushing often with barbecue sauce.

Country-Style Grilled Ribs

A sweet and tangy barbecue sauce, sprinkled with celery seed, coats these tender ribs. Chili powder and hot pepper sauce punch up the heat and zesty flavor.

—MARILYN BEERMAN WORTHINGTON, OHIO

PREP: 5 MIN. **COOK:** 70 MIN. + STANDING
MAKES: 4 SERVINGS

- 3 pounds boneless country-style pork ribs
- 1 cup water
- 1 cup ketchup
- ¼ cup packed brown sugar
- ¼ cup cider vinegar
- ¼ cup Worcestershire sauce
- 1 tablespoon celery seed
- 1 teaspoon chili powder
- ⅛ teaspoon hot pepper sauce
  Dash pepper

1. Place ribs in a shallow roasting pan. Cover and bake at 325° for 1¼ hours or until a meat thermometer reads 160°.

2. Meanwhile, in a small saucepan, combine remaining ingredients. Bring to a boil. Reduce heat; simmer, uncovered, for 5 minutes, stirring occasionally. Pour 1 cup sauce over ribs, turn to coat. Let stand for 15 minutes.

3. Drain and discard marinade. Grill ribs, uncovered, over medium heat for 10-12 minutes, basting with 1 cup sauce and turning occasionally. Serve with remaining sauce.

King Ranch Casserole

Every time I serve this creamy casserole, it gets rave reviews. The recipe was passed down to me and is so good! It's really easy to make, freezes well and has just a touch of heat. If your family likes things spicy hot, add some jalapenos!

—**KENDRA DOSS** KANSAS CITY, MISSOURI

PREP: 25 MIN. **BAKE:** 30 MIN. **MAKES:** 8 SERVINGS

- 1 large onion, finely chopped
- 2 celery ribs, finely chopped
- 1 medium green pepper, finely chopped
- 1 medium sweet red pepper, finely chopped
- 1 tablespoon canola oil
- 1 garlic clove, minced
- 3 cups cubed cooked chicken breast
- 1 can (10¾ ounces) reduced-fat reduced-sodium condensed cream of celery soup, undiluted
- 1 can (10¾ ounces) reduced-fat reduced-sodium condensed cream of chicken soup, undiluted
- 1 can (10 ounces) diced tomatoes and green chilies, undrained
- 1 tablespoon chili powder
- 12 corn tortillas (6 inches), cut into 1-inch strips
- 2 cups (8 ounces) shredded reduced-fat cheddar cheese, divided

1. In a large nonstick skillet coated with cooking spray, saute the onion, celery and peppers in oil until crisp-tender. Add garlic; cook 1 minute longer. Stir in the chicken, soups, tomatoes and chili powder.

2. Line the bottom of a 3-qt. baking dish with half of the tortilla strips; top with half of the chicken mixture and 1 cup cheese. Repeat layers. Bake, uncovered, at 350° for 30-35 minutes or until bubbly.

Black Bean Veggie Enchiladas

I created this dish one night when we were in the mood for enchiladas, but didn't want all the fat and calories of the traditional ones. I used ingredients I had on hand that day, and now this recipe's a family favorite!

—**NICOLE BARNETT** CENTENNIAL, COLORADO

PREP: 30 MIN. **BAKE:** 25 MIN. **MAKES:** 6 ENCHILADAS

- 1 small onion, chopped
- 1 small green pepper, chopped
- ½ cup sliced fresh mushrooms
- 2 teaspoons olive oil
- 1 garlic clove, minced
- 1 can (15 ounces) black beans, rinsed and drained
- ¾ cup frozen corn, thawed
- 1 can (4 ounces) chopped green chilies
- 2 tablespoons reduced-sodium taco seasoning
- 1 teaspoon dried cilantro flakes
- 6 whole wheat tortillas (8 inches), warmed
- ½ cup enchilada sauce
- ¾ cup shredded reduced-fat Mexican cheese blend

1. In a large skillet, saute onion, green pepper and mushrooms in oil until crisp-tender. Add garlic; cook 1 minute longer. Add the beans, corn, chilies, taco seasoning and cilantro; cook for 2-3 minutes or until heated through.

2. Spoon ½ cup bean mixture down the center of each tortilla. Roll up and place seam side down in a greased 13x9-in. baking dish. Top with enchilada sauce and cheese.

3. Bake, uncovered, at 350° for 25-30 minutes or until heated through.

The classic tostada base is a corn tortilla that's been baked, toasted or fried until crispy. It is usually prepared flat, but can also be shaped into a bowl and layered with your choice of toppings.

Chicken Tostadas with Mango Salsa

Ginger adds a pleasant touch of flavor to this twist on a traditional tostada. It's so easy to eat healthful foods when good fresh salsa is around!

—**ERIN RENOUF MYLROIE** SANTA CLARA, UTAH

PREP: 30 MIN. + MARINATING **COOK:** 20 MIN. **MAKES:** 6 SERVINGS

- ⅓ cup orange juice
- 5 tablespoons lime juice, divided
- 1 teaspoon garlic powder
- 1 teaspoon ground cumin
- 1 pound boneless skinless chicken breast halves
- 2 medium mangoes, peeled and diced
- 1 small red onion, chopped
- ½ cup minced fresh cilantro
- 1 serrano pepper, seeded and minced
- 2 tablespoons finely chopped crystallized ginger
- 1 tablespoon brown sugar
- ¼ teaspoon salt
- 6 corn tortillas (6 inches)
- 3 cups coleslaw mix
- 6 tablespoons fat-free sour cream

1. In a large resealable plastic bag, combine the orange juice, 3 tablespoons lime juice, garlic powder and cumin; add the chicken. Seal bag and turn to coat; refrigerate for at least 20 minutes.

2. For salsa, in a small bowl, combine the mangoes, onion, cilantro, serrano pepper, ginger, brown sugar, salt and remaining lime juice. Cover and chill until serving.

3. Drain and discard marinade. Place chicken on a broiler pan coated with cooking spray. Broil 4-6 in. from the heat for 5-7 minutes on each side or until a thermometer reads 165°. Cut into thin strips.

4. In a nonstick skillet, cook tortillas over medium heat for 1-2 minutes on each side or until lightly browned. Top each with coleslaw mix, chicken, mango salsa and sour cream.

Editor's Note: *Wear disposable gloves when cutting hot peppers; the oils can burn skin. Avoid touching your face.*

Cobre Valley Casserole

We live in southeastern Arizona, in a part of the state known as Cobre Valley. "Cobre" is a Spanish word for copper, which is mined here. Variations of this recipe have been enjoyed in this area for many years.

—CAROLYN DEMING MIAMI, ARIZONA

PREP: 15 MIN. **BAKE:** 30 MIN. **MAKES:** 8 SERVINGS

- 1 **pound ground beef**
- 1 **medium onion, chopped**
- 1 **celery rib, chopped**
- 1 **envelope taco seasoning**
- ¼ **cup water**
- 2 **cans (16 ounces each) refried beans**
- 1 **can (4 ounces) chopped green chilies, optional**
- 1 **cup (4 ounces) shredded cheddar cheese**
- 2 **green onions, sliced**
- 1 **large tomato, peeled, seeded and chopped**
- ⅓ **cup sliced ripe olives**
- 1½ **cups crushed tortilla chips**

1. In a large skillet, cook the beef, onion and celery over medium heat until meat is no longer pink; drain. Stir in the taco seasoning, water, beans and green chilies if desired.

2. Transfer to a greased 11x7-in. baking dish. Bake, uncovered, at 350° for 30 minutes or until heated through. Top with cheese, green onions, tomato, olives and chips.

Pinto Bean Chili

PREP: 20 MIN. + SOAKING **COOK:** 1¾ HOURS
MAKES: 8 SERVINGS

- 1 **pound dried pinto beans**
- 2 **pounds ground beef**
- 1 **medium onion, chopped**
- 3 **celery ribs, chopped**
- 3 **tablespoons all-purpose flour**
- 4 **cups water**
- 2 **tablespoons chili powder**
- 2 **tablespoons ground cumin**
- ½ **teaspoon sugar**
- 1 **can (28 ounces) crushed tomatoes**
- 2 **teaspoons cider vinegar**
- 1½ **teaspoons salt**

CHILI CHEESE QUESADILLAS
- 2 **cans (4 ounces each) chopped green chilies**
- 12 **flour tortillas (6 inches)**
- 3 **cups (12 ounces) shredded cheddar cheese**
- 3 **teaspoons canola oil**

1. Place beans in a Dutch oven or stockpot; add water to cover by 2 in. Bring to a boil; boil for 2 minutes. Remove from the heat; cover and let stand for 1-4 hours. Drain and rinse beans, discarding liquid.

2. In a Dutch oven, cook the beef, onion and celery over medium heat until the meat is no longer pink; drain. Stir in the flour until blended. Gradually stir in the water. Add the beans, chili powder, cumin and sugar. Bring to a boil. Reduce heat; cover and simmer for 1½ hours or until the beans are tender. Stir in the tomatoes, vinegar and salt; heat through, stirring occasionally.

3. Meanwhile, for quesadillas, spread about 1 tablespoon of chilies on half of each tortilla. Sprinkle with ¼ cup of cheese; fold in half. In a large skillet, cook tortillas in 1 teaspoon of oil over medium heat until lightly browned on each side, adding more oil as needed. Cut each in half. Serve with chili.

> Plenty of cumin and chili powder season this chili, which is great with homemade quesadillas served on the side. It all makes a terrific Southwestern meal.

—SANDY DILATUSH
DENVER, COLORADO

"Barbecue" may refer to pork in the Deep South, but in Texas, it means beef—and more specifically, brisket. When brisket is roasted low and slow, the results are out of this world! The meat is so tender, it melts in your mouth, and so flavorful, you'll want seconds and thirds.

LOCKHART, TX

Named Barbecue Capital of Texas, Lockhart's four BBQ joints smoke meat to perfection. Altogether, they serve about 5,000 people per week!

Barbecued Beef Brisket

A guest at the RV park and marina my husband and I used to run gave me this flavorful brisket recipe. It's become the star of countless gatherings, from potlucks to holiday dinners. My family looks forward to it as much as our Christmas turkey!

—**BETTYE MILLER** OKLAHOMA CITY, OKLAHOMA

PREP: 20 MIN. **GRILL:** 2¼ HOURS **MAKES:** 6 SERVINGS

½ cup packed brown sugar
½ cup ketchup
¼ cup water
¼ cup cider vinegar
¼ cup canola oil
3 tablespoons dark corn syrup
2 tablespoons prepared mustard
1 tablespoon prepared horseradish
1 garlic clove, minced

BRISKET
2 tablespoons canola oil
1 fresh beef brisket (2 to 2½ pounds), trimmed

1. Combine the first nine ingredients in a saucepan. Cook and stir over medium heat 3-4 minutes or until brown sugar is dissolved. Transfer to a disposable aluminum pan.

2. Heat oil in a large skillet over medium heat. Brown brisket on all sides. Place in aluminum pan, turning to coat with sauce. Cover pan tightly with foil.

3. Grill, covered, over indirect medium heat 2 to 2¼ hours or until meat is fork-tender, adding additional briquettes as needed.

4. Remove brisket from pan; tent with foil. Let stand 10 minutes. Meanwhile, skim fat from sauce in pan. Cut brisket diagonally across the grain into thin slices; serve with sauce.

Editor's Note: *This is a fresh beef brisket, not corned beef.*

Steak Burritos

These meaty burritos team up tender steak slices with black beans and avocado. They're nicely seasoned with fresh cilantro, salsa and sour cream.

—REBECCA BAIRD SALT LAKE CITY, UTAH

PREP/TOTAL TIME: 30 MIN. **MAKES:** 2 SERVINGS

- 4 ounces beef flank steak
- ⅛ teaspoon salt
- ⅛ teaspoon pepper
- ½ teaspoon canola oil
- 2 flour tortillas (8 inches), warmed
- ½ cup cold cooked rice
- ½ medium ripe avocado, peeled and diced
- ½ cup canned black beans, rinsed and drained
- 2 tablespoons sour cream
- 1 tablespoon salsa
- 1 tablespoon finely chopped onion
- 1½ teaspoons minced fresh cilantro

1. Sprinkle steak with salt and pepper. In a small skillet coated with cooking spray, cook steak in oil over medium-high heat for 3-4 minutes on each side or until meat reaches desired doneness (for medium-rare, a thermometer should read 145°; medium, 160°; well-done, 170°).

2. Thinly slice steak across the grain; place down the center of each tortilla. Top with the rice, avocado, beans, sour cream, salsa, onion and cilantro. Roll up; serve immediately.

Fiesta Smothered Chicken

PREP/TOTAL TIME: 30 MIN. **MAKES:** 2 SERVINGS

- 3 tablespoons reduced-sodium soy sauce
- 1 tablespoon Worcestershire sauce
- ¼ teaspoon garlic powder
- 2 boneless skinless chicken breast halves (5 ounces each)
- ½ cup sliced fresh mushrooms
- ¼ cup chopped onion
- 4 teaspoons chopped seeded jalapeno pepper
- 6 teaspoons butter, divided
- ¼ cup shredded pepper jack cheese
- ¼ cup shredded cheddar cheese

1. In a large resealable plastic bag, combine the soy sauce, Worcestershire sauce and garlic powder; add the chicken. Seal bag and turn to coat; set aside.

2. In a large nonstick skillet coated with cooking spray, saute the mushrooms, onion and jalapeno in 2 teaspoons butter until tender. Remove and keep warm.

3. Drain and discard marinade. In the same skillet, cook chicken in remaining butter over medium heat for 4-5 minutes on each side or until a thermometer reads 165°. Spoon vegetable mixture over each chicken breast; sprinkle with cheeses. Cover and cook for 1-2 minutes or until cheese is melted.

Editor's Note: *Wear disposable gloves when cutting hot peppers; the oils can burn skin. Avoid touching your face.*

> "Topped with ooey-gooey shredded cheese, this tender skillet chicken looks great and tastes even better. You'll get a kick out of its jalapeno zip."
>
> —TERESA JONES
> ASHDOWN, ARKANSAS

Chuck Wagon Tortilla Stack

Piling on loads of hearty flavor at mealtime is a snap. I simply roll out this skillet specialty. Layers of meat mixture with tortillas simmer in a deep skillet. It's easy to cut and spoon out.

—BERNICE JANOWSKI STEVENS POINT, WISCONSIN

PREP: 15 MIN. COOK: 40 MIN. MAKES: 4-6 SERVINGS

- 1 pound ground beef
- 2 to 3 garlic cloves, minced
- 1 can (16 ounces) baked beans
- 1 can (14½ ounces) stewed tomatoes, undrained
- 1 can (11 ounces) whole kernel corn, drained
- 1 can (4 ounces) chopped green chilies
- ¼ cup barbecue sauce
- 4½ teaspoons chili powder
- 1½ teaspoons ground cumin
- 4 flour tortillas (10 inches)
- 1⅓ cups (about 5 ounces) shredded pepper jack cheese
  Shredded lettuce, chopped red onion, sour cream and/or chopped tomatoes, optional

1. In a large skillet, cook beef until the meat is no longer pink; drain. Add the garlic, beans, tomatoes, corn, chilies, barbecue sauce, chili powder and cumin. Bring to a boil. Reduce the heat; simmer, uncovered, for 10-12 minutes or until liquid is reduced.

2. Coat a large deep skillet with cooking spray. Place one tortilla in skillet; spread with 1½ cups meat mixture. Sprinkle with ⅓ cup cheese. Repeat layers three times. Cover and cook on low for 15 minutes or until cheese is melted and tortillas are heated through. Cut into wedges. Serve with toppings of your choice.

Citrus Chicken Fajitas

I've tried several variations of this recipe, choosing chicken for a lighter fare and just the perfect blend of spices. I'll have to say, everyone raves about these.

—DEBRA KAPITAN SACRAMENTO, CALIFORNIA

PREP: 20 MIN. + MARINATING COOK: 15 MIN.
MAKES: 4 SERVINGS

- 6 tablespoons lemon juice
- ¼ cup lime juice
- 2 tablespoons minced fresh cilantro
- 1 tablespoon olive oil
- 1 teaspoon sugar
- ½ teaspoon garlic powder
- ½ teaspoon ground cumin
- 1 pound boneless skinless chicken breasts, cut into strips
- 1 each medium green, sweet red and yellow peppers, julienned
- 1 large red onion, halved and thinly sliced
- 4 flour tortillas (8 inches), warmed
- ½ cup shredded lettuce
- ¼ cup sliced ripe olives
- ¼ cup shredded reduced-fat cheddar cheese

1. In a small bowl, combine the first seven ingredients. Divide marinade equally between two large resealable plastic bags; add the chicken to one bag. Add peppers and onion to remaining bag. Seal bags and turn to coat; refrigerate for several hours or overnight.

2. Drain chicken and vegetables; discard marinade. In a large nonstick skillet coated with cooking spray, cook and stir chicken over medium heat for 3 minutes. Add vegetables; cook 3-5 minutes longer or until chicken is no longer pink and vegetables are crisp-tender.

3. Spoon filling onto tortillas; top with lettuce, olives and cheese. Roll up.

Citrus Veggie Chicken Fajitas: *Add 1 each small julienned zucchini and yellow summer squash to the peppers. Marinate and cook as directed.*

Carne de Cerdo Sopes

I call this "dude food," as my husband and son would eat it weekly if I prepared it. The tender shredded pork is delicious.

—JOHNNA JOHNSON SCOTTSDALE, ARIZONA

PREP: 25 MIN. + MARINATING **COOK:** 2 HOURS
MAKES: 12 SERVINGS

- 3 cups chicken broth, divided
- ¾ cup chili powder
- 2 tablespoons red wine vinegar
- 1 tablespoon chopped fresh cilantro
- 1 tablespoon honey
- 2 teaspoons ground cumin
- 2 teaspoons dried oregano
- 1 teaspoon salt
- 1 teaspoon ground cinnamon
- 1 boneless pork shoulder butt roast (3 to 4 pounds), cut into ¾-inch cubes
- 5 tablespoons canola oil, divided
- 2 large onions, chopped
- 6 garlic cloves, minced
- 1 can (10 ounces) diced tomatoes and green chilies, undrained

SOPES

- 3 cups masa harina
- ½ teaspoon salt
- 2 cups water
- 3 tablespoons canola oil
  Optional toppings: hot refried beans, shredded lettuce, chopped tomatoes, shredded cheddar cheese, guacamole and/or sour cream

1. In a large resealable plastic bag, combine 1 cup broth, chili powder, vinegar, cilantro, honey and seasonings. Add the pork; seal bag and turn to coat. Refrigerate for 4 hours or overnight.

2. In an ovenproof Dutch oven, brown pork in 4 tablespoons oil in batches. Remove and keep warm. In the same pan, saute onions in remaining oil until tender. Add garlic; cook 2 minutes longer.

3. Return pork to pan; add remaining broth and tomatoes. Bring to a boil. Cover and bake at 350° for 1½ to 1¾ hours or until meat is tender. With a slotted spoon, remove meat to a large bowl. Skim fat from cooking liquid. Bring to a boil over high heat; cook until slightly thickened and reduced to about 2 cups, stirring occasionally. Return meat to pan; set aside and keep warm.

4. For sopes, in a large bowl, combine masa harina and salt; stir in water. Knead until smooth, adding additional water, 1 teaspoon at a time, if necessary. Divide into 12 portions, about ¼ cup each. Roll each to form a ball; flatten to 4-in. patty. Cover with plastic wrap.

5. Heat a large ungreased skillet over medium heat until hot. Cook the sopes in batches for 1 minute on each side or until lightly browned. Remove from pan. Immediately pinch edges to form a ½-in. rim; set aside.

6. To serve, in same skillet, cook the sopes in hot oil in batches over medium-high heat for 15-30 seconds on each side or until golden brown and slightly crisp. Drain on paper towels. Using a slotted spoon, place pork on sopes; serve with toppings of your choice.

Arizona Chicken

I have a large collection of recipes with a Southwest flavor. Served with either pasta or rice, this is one of my husband's favorites. The moist, flavorful chicken suits any occasion.

—CAROLYN DEMING MIAMI, ARIZONA

PREP: 20 MIN. **COOK:** 45 MIN. **MAKES:** 6 SERVINGS

- 6 boneless skinless chicken breast halves (4 ounces each)
- ¼ cup canola oil, divided
- 1 medium onion, sliced
- 4 cups chopped fresh tomatoes
- 2 celery ribs, sliced
- ¼ cup water
- ¼ cup sliced pimiento-stuffed olives
- 2 teaspoons garlic powder
- 2 teaspoons dried oregano
- 1 teaspoon salt, optional
- ¼ teaspoon pepper
- ½ pound fresh mushrooms, sliced

1. In a skillet, brown chicken on both sides in 2 tablespoons of oil. Remove and set aside. In the same skillet, saute onion in remaining oil until tender. Add the tomatoes, celery, water, olives, garlic powder, oregano, salt if desired and pepper; bring to a boil.

2. Cover and simmer for 15 minutes. Return chicken to pan. Simmer, uncovered, for 15 minutes. Add mushrooms; simmer 15 minutes longer or until a thermometer reads 170°.

dishing about food ●➜

Sopes are made with the same ingredients as tortillas, but are smaller in diameter, thicker and have a raised edge, like a tart shell.

PHOENIX, AZ

The Desert Botanical Garden offers solid proof that even in arid climates, beauty abounds. Winding trails offer a good look at five Arizona habitats, and special exhibits, events and spectacular sunset displays mean no visit is ever the same.

SANTA FE, NM

This distinctive adobe-style structure might look ancient, but it's only been around since 1975. A luxury hotel in historic Santa Fe, the Inn and Spa at Loretto is one of the state's most frequently photographed buildings.

Southwest Frito Pie

I got a real culture shock when we moved to New Mexico several years ago, but we grew to love the food. Now back in South Carolina, we still crave New Mexican dishes, and this is one of my go-to favorites.

—JANET SCOGGINS
NORTH AUGUSTA, SOUTH CAROLINA

PREP: 20 MIN.   **COOK:** 25 MIN.   **MAKES:** 6 SERVINGS

- 2 **pounds lean ground beef (90% lean)**
- 3 **tablespoons chili powder**
- 2 **tablespoons all-purpose flour**
- 1 **teaspoon salt**
- 1 **teaspoon garlic powder**
- 2 **cups water**
- 1 **can (15 ounces) pinto beans, rinsed and drained, optional**
- 4½ **cups corn chips**
- 2 **cups shredded lettuce**
- 1½ **cups (6 ounces) shredded cheddar cheese**
- ¾ **cup chopped tomatoes**
- 6 **tablespoons finely chopped onion**
  Sour cream and minced fresh cilantro, optional

1. In a Dutch oven, cook beef over medium heat until no longer pink; drain. Stir in the chili powder, flour, salt and garlic powder until blended; gradually stir in water.

2. Add beans, if desired. Bring to a boil. Reduce heat; simmer, uncovered, for 12-15 minutes or until thickened, stirring occasionally.

3. To serve, divide chips among six serving bowls. Top with beef mixture, lettuce, cheese, tomatoes and onion; garnish with sour cream and cilantro, if desired.

Ribeyes with Chili Butter

A couple spoonfuls of spicy butter instantly give these steaks a delicious Southwestern slant. Meat lovers will be delighted by the chili and mustard flavors.

—ALLAN STACKHOUSE JR., JENNINGS, LOUISIANA

PREP/TOTAL TIME: 20 MIN.   **MAKES:** 2 SERVINGS

- ¼ **cup butter, softened**
- 1 **teaspoon chili powder**
- ½ **teaspoon Dijon mustard**
  Dash cayenne pepper
- 2 **beef ribeye steaks (8 ounces each)**
- ½ **to 1 teaspoon coarsely ground pepper**
- ¼ **teaspoon sugar**

1. In a small bowl, beat the butter, chili powder, mustard and cayenne until smooth. Refrigerate until serving.

2. Rub the steaks with pepper and sugar. Grill, covered, over medium heat for 5-6 minutes on each side or until meat reaches desired doneness (for medium-rare, a thermometer should read 145°; medium, 160°; well-done, 170°). Spoon chili butter over steak.

Southwestern Potpie with Cornmeal Biscuits

PREP: 35 MIN. + SIMMERING **BAKE:** 15 MIN. + STANDING **MAKES:** 12 SERVINGS

¼ cup all-purpose flour
1½ pounds boneless pork loin roast, cut into ½-inch cubes
2 tablespoons butter
1 jalapeno pepper, seeded and chopped
2 garlic cloves, minced
2 cups beef broth
1 can (14½ ounces) diced tomatoes, undrained
1 teaspoon ground cumin
½ teaspoon chili powder
¼ to ½ teaspoon ground cinnamon
1 can (15¼ ounces) whole kernel corn, drained
1 can (15 ounces) pinto beans, rinsed and drained
1 can (4 ounces) chopped green chilies

BISCUITS
3 cups biscuit/baking mix
¾ cup cornmeal
½ cup shredded cheddar cheese
4½ teaspoons sugar
1 cup 2% milk

1. Place flour in a large resealable plastic bag. Add pork, a few pieces at a time, and shake to coat. In a Dutch oven, brown pork in butter in batches. Remove and set aside.

2. In the same pan, saute jalapeno and garlic in the drippings for 1 minute. Stir in the broth, tomatoes, cumin, chili powder, cinnamon and pork. Bring to a boil. Reduce heat; cover and simmer for 1 hour or until pork is tender.

3. Add corn, beans and chilies; heat through. Transfer to a greased 13x9-in. baking dish.

4. In a large bowl, combine the biscuit mix, cornmeal, cheese and sugar; stir in milk just until moistened. Turn onto a lightly floured surface; knead 8-10 times.

5. Pat or roll out to ½-in. thickness; cut with a floured 2½-in. biscuit cutter. Arrange over meat mixture. Bake at 400° for 15-18 minutes or until golden brown. Let stand for 10 minutes before serving.

Editor's Note: *Wear disposable gloves when cutting hot peppers; the oils can burn skin. Avoid touching your face.*

> "My Southwestern-inspired potpie is full of sweet and spicy pork, corn, beans and chilies. It's a surefire winner for any gathering! The cornmeal gives the biscuits a delightful little crunch."

—ANDREA BOLDEN
UNIONVILLE, TENNESSEE

> **Fresh herbs and Cajun seasoning enhance these delicious shrimp, paired with a spicy butter sauce. You can serve them as an entree or as appetizers. You'll love them either way!**
>
> **—DWAYNE VERETTO**
> ROSWELL, NEW MEXICO

Spicy Shrimp Skewers

PREP: 20 MIN. + MARINATING   **GRILL:** 5 MIN.   **MAKES:** 8 SERVINGS

¾ cup canola oil
1 medium onion, finely chopped
2 tablespoons Cajun seasoning
6 garlic cloves, minced
2 teaspoons ground cumin
1 teaspoon minced fresh rosemary
1 teaspoon minced fresh thyme
2 pounds uncooked large shrimp, peeled and deveined

SPICY BUTTER
1 cup butter, cubed
1 teaspoon minced fresh basil
1 teaspoon minced fresh tarragon
1 teaspoon Cajun seasoning
½ teaspoon garlic powder
3 drops hot pepper sauce

1. In a small bowl, combine the first seven ingredients. Place the shrimp in a large resealable plastic bag; add half of the marinade. Seal bag and turn to coat; refrigerate for 1-2 hours. Cover and refrigerate remaining marinade for basting.

2. In a small saucepan, combine the spicy butter ingredients; heat until butter is melted. Keep warm.

3. Drain and discard marinade. Thread shrimp onto eight metal or soaked wooden skewers. Grill, uncovered, over medium heat for 2-4 minutes on each side or until shrimp turn pink, basting once with reserved marinade. Serve with spicy butter.

Chicken Mole Ole

You'll get a kick out of this full-flavored Southwestern favorite that requires a bit of prep time, but is well worth it.

—JOHNNA JOHNSON SCOTTSDALE, ARIZONA

PREP: 40 MIN. **COOK:** 4 HOURS **MAKES:** 6 SERVINGS

- 2 dried ancho chilies
- 1½ pounds tomatillos, husks removed, halved
- 2 medium onions, sliced, divided
- 1 serrano pepper, halved and seeded
- 3 garlic cloves, peeled
- 3 pounds bone-in chicken breast halves, skin removed
- 1 tablespoon canola oil
- 2 teaspoons ground cumin, divided
- 1½ teaspoons chili powder
- 1 teaspoon pepper
- ¼ teaspoon ground cinnamon
- 2 whole cloves
- ½ cup almonds
- 1 ounce unsweetened chocolate, chopped
- 1 tablespoon lime juice
- 1 teaspoon salt
- 1½ cups (6 ounces) shredded cheddar-Monterey Jack cheese
- ½ cup minced fresh cilantro

1. Place chilies in a small bowl. Cover with boiling water; let stand for 20 minutes. Drain. Remove stems and seeds. Coarsely chop; set aside. Place the tomatillos, 1 onion, serrano pepper and garlic in a greased 15x10x1-in. baking pan. Bake, uncovered, at 400° for 10-15 minutes or until tender, stirring once.

2. In a large skillet, brown chicken in oil. Transfer to a 4-qt. slow cooker. In the same skillet, saute remaining onion until tender. Add 1 teaspoon cumin, chili powder, pepper, cinnamon, cloves and hydrated chilies; cook 1 minute longer. Discard cloves.

3. Place almonds in a food processor; cover and process until ground. Add spiced onion mixture and chocolate; cover and process until blended. Transfer to a small bowl.

4. Place the tomatillo mixture, lime juice, salt and remaining cumin in food processor; cover and process until chopped. Stir into almond mixture. Pour over chicken. Cover and cook on low for 4 to 5 hours or until chicken is tender. Sprinkle each serving with cheese and cilantro.

Editor's Note: *Wear disposable gloves when cutting hot peppers; the oils can burn skin. Avoid touching your face.*

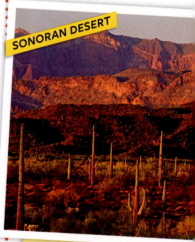

SONORAN DESERT

It shares its name with a Mexican state, but the Sonoran Desert stretches into Arizona and California, too. It is home to many unique plants and animals, including the Saguaro cactus and the greater roadrunner.

Tomatillos resemble green tomatoes with brown, papery husks. Their tangy, herbal flavor nicely complements many Southwestern and Mexican dishes. When shopping, look for firm, lime-green fruit wrapped snugly in dry husks.

Braised Pork with Tomatillos

Braised pork is a sure way to make people's mouths water. The tomatillos in this dish offer a bright hint of tangy flavor to the meat. For ultimate enjoyment, make the dish one day ahead and reheat.

—**MATTHEW LAWRENCE** VASHON, WASHINGTON

PREP: 25 MIN. **BAKE:** 3 HOURS **MAKES:** 6 SERVINGS

- 1 tablespoon coriander seeds
- 1 tablespoon cumin seeds
- 1 bone-in pork shoulder roast (3 to 4 pounds)
- ¼ teaspoon salt
- ¼ teaspoon pepper
- 1 tablespoon canola oil
- 15 tomatillos, husks removed, and chopped
- 1 medium onion, chopped
- 2 garlic cloves, peeled and halved
- 1 cup white wine
- 8 cups chicken broth

POLENTA
- 4 cups chicken broth
- 1 cup yellow cornmeal

1. In a small dry skillet over medium heat, toast coriander and cumin seeds until aromatic, about 1-2 minutes. Remove from skillet. Crush seeds using a spice grinder or mortar and pestle; set aside.

2. Sprinkle pork with salt and pepper. In a Dutch oven, brown roast in oil on all sides. Remove and set aside. Add tomatillos and onion to the pan; saute until tomatillos are tender and lightly charred. Add the garlic and crushed spices; cook 1 minute longer.

3. Add wine stirring to loosen browned bits from pan. Stir in broth and return roast to pan. Bring to a boil. Cover and bake at 350° for 3 to 3½ hours or until pork is tender.

4. Meanwhile, in a large heavy saucepan, bring broth to a boil. Reduce heat to a gentle boil; slowly whisk in cornmeal. Cook and stir with a wooden spoon for 15-20 minutes or until polenta is thickened and pulls away cleanly from the sides of the pan. Serve with pork.

Southwestern Beef Burritos

We became acquainted with Mexican food after moving here from the Midwest. I got this recipe from my brother-in-law, who used to run a Mexican restaurant.

—**JACQUELINE HERGERT** PAYSON, ARIZONA

PREP: 15 MIN. **COOK:** 2¼ HOURS **MAKES:** 8 SERVINGS

- 2 to 2½ pounds beef top round steak, cut into 1-inch cubes
- 2 tablespoons canola oil
- 2 large onions, chopped
- 2 garlic cloves, minced
- 1 can (15 ounces) enchilada sauce
- 1 can (14½ ounces) diced tomatoes, undrained
- 1 to 2 cans (4 ounces each) chopped green chilies
- 1 teaspoon salt
- ¼ teaspoon pepper
- 2 tablespoons all-purpose flour
- ¼ cup cold water
- 8 flour tortillas (10 inches)
     Diced tomatoes, sliced ripe olives, shredded cheddar cheese, sour cream, chopped green onions, shredded lettuce and/or guacamole, optional

1. In a large skillet over medium heat, brown meat in oil; drain. Add onions and garlic; cook and stir for 2 minutes. Add the enchilada sauce, tomatoes, chilies, salt and pepper; bring to a boil. Reduce heat; cover and simmer for 2 hours or until meat is tender.

2. Combine flour and water; add to beef mixture, stirring constantly. Bring to a boil; cook and stir for 1 minute or until thickened.

3. Warm tortillas; spoon ½ cup filling, off center, on each one. Fold sides and bottom of tortilla over filling, then roll up. Spoon a little more filling over top of burritos. Serve immediately. Garnish with tomatoes, olives, cheese, sour cream, onions, lettuce and/or guacamole if desired.

Tex-Mex Beef Sandwiches

Everyone loves these when I serve them. The cocoa is a surprise ingredient that adds real depth of flavor. It's hard to identify, so I'm often asked, "What's that interesting taste?"

—**BRENDA THEISEN** ADDISON, MICHIGAN

PREP: 25 MIN. **COOK:** 8 HOURS **MAKES:** 8 SERVINGS

- 1 boneless beef chuck roast (3 pounds)
- 1 envelope burrito seasoning
- 2 tablespoons baking cocoa
- 1 large green pepper, coarsely chopped
- 1 large sweet red pepper, coarsely chopped
- 1 large onion, chopped
- 1 cup beef broth
- ½ cup ketchup
- 8 hoagie buns, split

1. Cut the roast in half. Combine burrito seasoning and cocoa; rub over meat. Place peppers and onion in a 3- or 4-qt. slow cooker; top with meat. Combine broth and ketchup; pour over meat.

2. Cover and cook on low for 8-10 hours or until meat is tender. Skim fat. When cool enough to handle, shred meat with two forks and return to slow cooker; heat through. Using a slotted spoon, spoon ½ cup onto each bun.

Traditional carnitas are made with seasoned pork that's slow-roasted, braised and/or fried until it melts in your mouth! Once ready, it's used in all sorts of dishes, from tacos to tamales.

Mexican Carnitas

Ever hear of "carnitas?" They're easy-to-make pork crisps that are very popular in Mexico. The secret to this recipe is the citrus—and quick frying. Be sure the meat is well-drained before it's placed in oil, though, or it will splatter and pop.

—PATRICIA COLLINS IMBLER, OREGON

PREP: 10 MIN. **BAKE:** 2 HOURS 10 MIN. **MAKES:** 12-16 SERVINGS

1 boneless pork shoulder butt roast (3 to 4 pounds), cut into 1-inch cubes
6 large garlic cloves, minced
½ cup fresh cilantro leaves, chopped
1 teaspoon salt
   Pepper to taste
3 large oranges, divided
1 large lemon
   Oil for frying
12 to 16 flour tortillas (8 inches), warmed
   Optional toppings: shredded cheddar cheese, salsa and guacamole

1. Place meat in a medium-size roasting pan. Sprinkle with garlic and cilantro. Season with salt and pepper. Squeeze the juice from one orange and the lemon over the meat. Slice the remaining oranges and place over the meat.

2. Cover and bake at 350° for about 2 hours or until meat is tender. With a slotted spoon, remove meat and drain well on paper towels. Heat a small amount of oil in a skillet and fry meat, 1 lb. at a time, until brown and crispy.

3. Serve warm in tortillas with toppings of your choice.

Spicy Pork Tostadas

PREP: 20 MIN. **BAKE:** 2 HOURS **MAKES:** 8 SERVINGS

- 3 teaspoons dried oregano
- 1 teaspoon salt
- ½ teaspoon coarsely ground pepper
- ½ teaspoon cayenne pepper
- 1 bone-in pork loin roast (about 3 pounds)
- 3 large onions, chopped
- 4 tablespoons canola oil, divided
- 3 garlic cloves, minced
- 1 medium green pepper, chopped
- 1 cup salsa
- ½ cup frozen corn, thawed
- ½ cup canned black beans, rinsed and drained
- 1 teaspoon paprika
- ½ teaspoon crushed red pepper flakes
- ¼ teaspoon hot pepper sauce
- ¼ cup minced fresh cilantro
- 8 corn tortillas (6 inches)
- 1 cup (4 ounces) shredded Monterey Jack cheese

1. Combine the oregano, salt, pepper and cayenne; rub over roast. Place fat side up on a rack in a shallow roasting pan. Bake, uncovered, at 325° for 2 hours or until a thermometer reads 160°.

2. In a large skillet, saute the onions in 2 tablespoons oil until tender. Add garlic; cook 1 minute longer. Add the green pepper, salsa, corn, beans, paprika, pepper flakes and hot pepper sauce. Bring to a boil. Reduce heat; cover and simmer for 15-20 minutes, stirring occasionally. Stir in the cilantro; keep warm.

3. Shred pork with two forks; keep warm. In a large skillet, fry tortillas, one at a time, in remaining oil for 2 minutes on each side or until golden. Drain on paper towels.

4. Place tortillas on serving plates; top with shredded pork, onion mixture and cheese.

“I serve these flavorful tostadas as a casual meal for family or friends. My husband and I love the salsa topping so much that I often double that part of the recipe so we have some left over to serve with chicken, on burgers or as a dip.”

—KATHY SMITH
PITTSBURGH, PENNSYLVANIA

> "Even though this recipe has a long list of ingredients, it is acutally a snap to fix. Most of the ingredients are already in your pantry."
>
> —JAN PERI-WYRICK
> FORT WORTH, TEXAS

Tortilla-Vegetable Chicken Soup

PREP: 20 MIN. **COOK:** 15 MIN. **MAKES:** 6 SERVINGS

- 3 flour tortillas (6 inches), cut into 1-inch strips
- ¼ cup chicken drippings, optional
- 1 cup chopped celery
- ¾ cup finely chopped carrot
- ½ cup chopped red onion
- 2 tablespoons olive oil
- 3 cans (14½ ounces each) reduced-sodium chicken broth
- 1 can (15 ounces) black beans, rinsed and drained
- 1 can (14½ ounces) beef broth
- 1 can (10 ounces) diced tomatoes with mild green chilies
- 2 cups cubed cooked chicken breast
- 2 cups frozen corn
- 2 teaspoons dried parsley flakes
- 1 teaspoon garlic powder
- 1 teaspoon dried basil
- 1 teaspoon ground cumin
- 1 teaspoon ground coriander
   Shredded Monterey Jack cheese, optional

1. Place tortilla strips on a baking sheet coated with cooking spray; bake at 350° for 8-10 minutes or until lightly browned. Set aside.

2. Meanwhile, skim fat from drippings. In a Dutch oven, saute the celery, carrot and onion in oil until tender. Stir in the chicken broth, black beans, beef broth, tomatoes, chicken, corn, seasonings and drippings if desired. Bring to a boil. Reduce heat; simmer, uncovered, for 15 minutes.

3. Serve with the tortilla strips and cheese if desired.

Texas Jalapeno Jelly

Here's a great recipe for homemade holiday or hostess gifts, and a jar of this jelly is always warmly received. I like to add a Southwestern accent by trimming the lid with a bandanna.

—**LORI MCMULLEN** VICTORIA, TEXAS

PREP: 15 MIN. **PROCESS:** 10 MIN. **MAKES:** 7 HALF-PINTS

- 2 jalapeno peppers, seeded and chopped
- 3 medium green peppers, cut into 1-inch pieces, divided
- 1½ cups white vinegar, divided
- 6½ cups sugar
- ½ to 1 teaspoon cayenne pepper
- 2 pouches (3 ounces each) liquid fruit pectin
  About 6 drops green food coloring, optional
  Cream cheese and crackers, optional

1. In a blender or food processor, place the jalapenos, half of green peppers and ½ cup vinegar; cover and process until pureed. Transfer to a large Dutch oven.

2. Repeat with remaining green peppers and another ½ cup vinegar. Add the sugar, cayenne and remaining vinegar to pan. Bring to a rolling boil over high heat, stirring constantly.

Quickly stir in pectin. Return to a rolling boil; boil for 1 minute, stirring constantly.

3. Remove from the heat; skim off foam. Add food coloring if desired. Carefully ladle hot mixture into hot half-pint jars, leaving ¼-in. headspace. Remove air bubbles; wipe rims and adjust lids.

4. Process for 10 minutes in a boiling-water canner. Serve over cream cheese with crackers if desired.

Editor's Note: *When cutting hot peppers, disposable gloves are recommended. Avoid touching your face. The processing time listed is for altitudes of 1,000 feet or less. Add 1 minute to the processing time for each 1,000 feet of additional altitude.*

SAN ANTONIO, TX

Both days and nights are colorful on San Antonio's River Walk. The public park winds through the city's downtown on the banks of the San Antonio River.

Jicama Slaw with Peanuts

Peanuts add interest and crunch to my crisp coleslaw featuring jicama and tangerines. For a creamy dressing, I sometimes stir in two heaping tablespoons of mayonnaise or yogurt.

—**DONNA NOEL** GRAY, MAINE

PREP/TOTAL TIME: 20 MIN. **MAKES:** 6 SERVINGS

1 medium jicama, julienned
⅓ cup orange juice
½ teaspoon salt
⅛ to ¼ teaspoon cayenne pepper
⅛ teaspoon pepper
3 tangerines, peeled and sectioned

¼ cup minced fresh cilantro
½ cup salted peanuts

1. In a large bowl, combine the first five ingredients. Stir in tangerines and cilantro. Cover and refrigerate until serving. Just before serving, stir in peanuts.

Chili con Queso

I love to make this dip for parties because it is so easy and I usually have all the ingredients on hand. I double the recipe and prepare it in my slow cooker so it will not scorch. This makes it completely worry-free when entertaining!

—**MARIE STOUT** APO, AP

PREP/TOTAL TIME: 15 MIN. **MAKES:** 2¾ CUPS

- 1   **pound process cheese (Velveeta), cubed**
- ½   **cup chunky-style salsa**
- 1   **can (4 ounces) chopped green chilies**
- 1   **jar (4 ounces) diced pimientos, drained**
- ½   **teaspoon garlic powder**
- ¼   **teaspoon cayenne pepper**
- ⅛   **teaspoon ground cumin**
- ⅛   **teaspoon crushed red pepper flakes**
     Tortilla chips

1. In a microwave-safe bowl, combine the first eight ingredients. Cover and microwave on high for 6-7 minutes or until cheese is melted, stirring occasionally. Serve with tortilla chips.

Editor's Note: *This recipe was tested in a 1,100-watt microwave.*

Smoky Grilled Corn

A friend and I cooked up this corn one evening while getting ready to grill. The buttery corn, with its sweet-spicy seasoning, actually won top honors over our steaks!

—**LINDA LANDERS** KALISPELL, MONTANA

PREP: 25 MIN. **GRILL:** 10 MIN. **MAKES:** 6 SERVINGS

- 2   **tablespoons plus 1½ teaspoons butter**
- ½   **cup honey**
- 2   **large garlic cloves, minced**
- 2   **tablespoons hot pepper sauce**
- ½   **teaspoon salt**
- ¼   **teaspoon pepper**
- ¼   **teaspoon paprika**
- 6   **medium ears sweet corn, husks removed**

1. In a small saucepan, melt butter. Stir in the honey, garlic, pepper sauce and seasonings until blended; heat through. Brush over corn.

2. Moisten a paper towel with cooking oil; using long-handled tongs, lightly coat grill rack.

3. Grill corn, covered, over medium heat for 10-12 minutes or until the corn is tender, turning and basting occasionally with butter mixture. Serve the corn with any remaining butter mixture.

tasteofhome.com | **SOUTHWEST** *sides & more*

◄● dishing about food

Served in Tex-Mex restaurants for decades, chili con queso is a popular dip from coast to coast today. As with so many classic American foods, its actual moment of creation has been lost in history. But in Austin, Texas, for example, Matt's El Rancho Restaurant has been serving an old family recipe since 1952, and the menu at Mexico Chiquito in Little Rock, Arkansas, has featured this kickin' cheese dip since 1935!

AUSTIN, TX

There's always plenty for music-lovers to do in Texas' capital. Every night, there are more than 100 live acts performing.

Southwestern Watermelon Salad

Cilantro, jicama and lime punch up the Southwestern flavor in this fresh fruit salad.

—TASTE OF HOME TEST KITCHEN

PREP: 20 MIN. + CHILLING **MAKES:** 6 SERVINGS

- 4 cups cubed seedless watermelon
- 2 cups cubed peeled mangoes
- ½ cup diced peeled jicama
- 3 tablespoons chopped sweet onion
- 2 tablespoons minced fresh cilantro
- 2 tablespoons lime juice
- 1 tablespoon honey
- 1 teaspoon white balsamic vinegar
- 1 teaspoon grated lime peel
- ⅛ teaspoon salt
  Dash cayenne pepper

1. In a large bowl, combine the watermelon, mangoes, jicama, onion and cilantro. In a small bowl, whisk the lime juice, honey, vinegar, lime peel, salt and cayenne. Pour over fruit mixture; gently toss to coat.

2. Cover and chill for 20 minutes, stirring occasionally. Serve with a slotted spoon.

Fresh Lime Margaritas

This basic margarita recipe is easy to modify to your own tastes. Try it frozen (as shown) or with strawberries.

—TASTE OF HOME TEST KITCHEN

PREP/TOTAL TIME: 15 MIN. **MAKES:** 4 SERVINGS

- 4 lime wedges
- 1 tablespoon kosher salt
- ½ cup gold tequila
- ¼ cup Triple Sec
- ¼ cup lime juice
- ¼ cup lemon juice
- 2 tablespoons superfine sugar
- 1⅓ cups crushed ice

1. Using lime wedges, moisten rims of four glasses. Holding each glass upside down, dip rim into salt; set aside.

2. In a pitcher, combine the tequila, Triple Sec, lime juice, lemon juice and sugar; stir until sugar is dissolved. Serve in prepared glasses over crushed ice.

For Frozen Lime Margaritas: *Reduce lemon and lime juices to 2 tablespoons each. Increase the superfine sugar to ¼ cup and the crushed ice to 4 cups. Add ¾ cup limeade concentrate. Prepare glasses as directed. In a blender, combine the tequila, Triple Sec, lime juice, lemon juice, limeade concentrate, superfine sugar and crushed ice; cover and process until smooth. .*

For Frozen Strawberry Margaritas: *Follow directions for Frozen Lime Margaritas, except reduce crushed ice to 2 cups and add 2 cups frozen unsweetened strawberries.*

◄◆ dishing about food

Texas Caviar was made famous by transplanted New Yorker Helen Corbitt. Unfamiliar with black-eyed peas, she noticed how all Texans, rich and not so rich, enjoyed them. So she whipped up the dish for a New Year's Eve party at her country club. Eventually, her marinated black-eyed peas got the moniker Texas Caviar.

Texas Caviar

My neighbor gave me a container of this zippy, tangy salsa one Christmas, and I just had to have the recipe! Now I fix it regularly for potlucks and get-togethers and never have any leftovers. I take copies of the recipe with me whenever I take the salsa—because I'm always asked for it!

—KATHY FARIS LYTLE, TEXAS

PREP: 10 MIN. + CHILLING **MAKES:** 4 CUPS

- 1 **can (15½ ounces) black-eyed peas, rinsed and drained**
- ¾ **cup chopped sweet red pepper**
- ¾ **cup chopped green pepper**
- 1 **medium onion, chopped**
- 3 **green onions, chopped**
- ¼ **cup minced fresh parsley**
- 1 **jar (2 ounces) diced pimientos, drained**
- 1 **garlic clove, minced**
- 1 **bottle (8 ounces) fat-free Italian salad dressing**
  Tortilla chips

1. In a large bowl, combine the peas, peppers, onions, parsley, pimientos and garlic. Pour salad dressing over pea mixture; stir gently to coat. Cover and refrigerate for 24 hours. Serve with tortilla chips.

> " I have a very hearty tomatillo plant in my garden. To use up the abundant produce, I decided to make a relish. You can use it as a dip or as a condiment on hot dogs, meat loaf, burgers or eggs. It's addicting, it's so good! "

—DEB LABOSCO
FOLEY, MINNESOTA

Tomatillo Relish

PREP: 45 MIN. **PROCESS:** 20 MIN. + STANDING **MAKES:** 4 PINTS

- 1 **pound tomatillos, husks removed, quartered**
- 1 **pound plum tomatoes, quartered**
- 2 **medium green peppers, seeded and quartered**
- 1 **medium sweet red pepper, seeded and quartered**
- 4 **jalapeno peppers, seeded**
- 1 **large onion, quartered**
- 1 **whole garlic bulb, separated into cloves**
- ¼ **cup fresh cilantro leaves**
- ¼ **cup packed fresh parsley sprigs**
- ½ **cup olive oil**
- ½ **cup cider vinegar**
- 1 **can (2¼ ounces) sliced ripe olives, drained**
- 4 **teaspoons canning salt**
- 1½ **teaspoons pepper**
- ¼ **teaspoon crushed red pepper flakes**
- 4 **tablespoons bottled lemon juice**

1. In a food processor, process the tomatillos, tomatoes, peppers, onion, garlic, cilantro and parsley in batches until chopped.

2. Transfer to a large kettle; stir in the oil, vinegar, olives, salt, pepper and pepper flakes. Bring to a boil. Reduce heat; cover and simmer for 20 minutes or until vegetables are tender.

3. Add lemon juice to four hot pint jars, 1 tablespoon in each. Ladle hot mixture into jars, leaving ¼-in. headspace. Remove air bubbles; wipe rims and adjust lids. Process for 20 minutes in a boiling-water canner. Serve with grilled meats or your favorite snack chips.

Editor's Note: *Wear disposable gloves when cutting hot peppers; the oils can burn skin. Avoid touching your face. The processing time listed is for altitudes of 1,000 feet or less. For altitudes up to 3,000 feet, add 5 minutes; 6,000 feet, add 10 minutes; 8,000 feet, add 15 minutes; 10,000 feet, add 20 minutes.*

Chili 'n' Cheese Grits

Although I live in the city, I'm really a country cook at heart. Most of our friends laugh about eating grits, but they're pleasantly surprised when they try my recipe.

—ROSEMARY WEST LAS VEGAS, NEVADA

PREP: 20 MIN. **BAKE:** 30 MIN. **MAKES:** 6-8 SERVINGS

- 2 **cups water**
- 2 **cups milk**
- 1 **cup grits**
- 2 **egg yolks**
- 1 **cup (4 ounces) shredded cheddar cheese, divided**
- ¼ **cup butter, cubed**
- 1 **can (4 ounces) chopped green chilies, drained**
- 1 **teaspoon salt**

1. In a large saucepan, bring water and milk to a boil. Add grits; cook and stir over medium heat for 5 minutes or until thickened.

2. In a small bowl, beat egg yolks. Stir a small amount of hot grits into yolks; return all to the pan, stirring constantly.

3. Add ¾ cup cheese, butter, chilies and salt. Pour into a greased 1½-qt. baking dish. Sprinkle with remaining cheese. Bake, uncovered, at 350° for 30-35 minutes or until a thermometer reads 160°.

Tex-Mex Spinach Salad

I was new to jicama, a root vegetable that's popular in Mexican and Southwestern cooking. But it lends plenty of fresh crunch to this no-fuss salad and blends well with all the other zippy ingredients.

—DEB WILLIAMS PEORIA, ARIZONA

PREP/TOTAL TIME: 15 MIN. **MAKES:** 10 SERVINGS

- 1 **package (6 ounces) fresh baby spinach**
- 4 **medium tomatoes, chopped**
- 1½ **cups cubed peeled jicama**
- ¾ **cup shredded Mexican cheese blend**
- 1 **medium sweet red pepper, chopped**
- 1 **can (2¼ ounces) sliced ripe olives, drained**
- ⅔ **cup chipotle ranch salad dressing**

1. In a salad bowl, combine the first six ingredients. Serve with dressing.

◄● dishing about food

Southwest cuisine boasts Southern and Western influences, and dishes such as Chili 'n' Cheese Grits show off the best of both worlds. Here, green chilies lend their Western flair to grits, an undisputed cornerstone of Southern cooking.

LAS VEGAS, NV

Part of the Strip since 1959, this sign has become a Las Vegas icon. Gone are the days of running out into traffic to snap a photo nearby. Now a parking lot helps keep tourists and drivers safe.

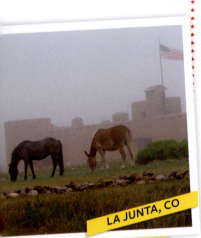

LA JUNTA, CO

With a prime spot on the Santa Fe Trail's mountain branch, Bent's Old Fort was a bustling trading post. It's now a National Historic Site where historians re-create day-to-day life.

Bacon-Wrapped Cajun Jalapenos

These peppers are so addictive that if I want any for myself, I either need to make a double batch or hide some! The jalapenos are not that spicy after they're baked (I take out the seeds and white membrane), but have a wonderful flavor.

—**LINDA FOREMAN** LOCUST GROVE, OKLAHOMA

PREP: 20 MIN. **BAKE:** 25 MIN. **MAKES:** 16 APPETIZERS

- 8 large jalapeno peppers
- 1 package (3 ounces) cream cheese, softened
- ½ cup finely shredded cheddar cheese
- 1 teaspoon Cajun seasoning
- 8 thick-sliced peppered bacon strips

1. Cut jalapenos in half lengthwise; remove seeds and center membranes. In a small bowl, combine the cream cheese, cheddar cheese and Cajun seasoning. Stuff about 1½ teaspoonfuls into each pepper half.

2. Cut bacon strips in half widthwise. In a large skillet, cook bacon until partially cooked. Wrap a bacon piece around each pepper; secure with a toothpick.

3. Place on a wire rack in a shallow baking pan. Bake, uncovered, at 350° for 25-30 minutes or until bacon is crisp. Discard toothpicks. Serve immediately.

Editor's Note: *Wear disposable gloves when cutting hot peppers; the oils can burn skin. Avoid touching your face.*

Cuban Chimichurri

Here's a fresh-tasting Cuban sauce that really complements steak, but just try pouring it over a burger, too. Awesome!

—**ELAINE SWEET** DALLAS, TEXAS

PREP/TOTAL TIME: 20 MIN. **MAKES:** 1 CUP

- 7 garlic cloves, peeled
- 1¼ cups packed fresh cilantro leaves
- ¾ cup packed fresh parsley sprigs
- 1 teaspoon crushed red pepper flakes
- 1 teaspoon coarsely ground pepper
- ¼ cup white balsamic vinegar
- 2 tablespoons lime juice
- 1 tablespoon soy sauce
- ½ teaspoon grated lime peel
- ⅓ cup olive oil
   Grilled steak

1. Place garlic in a small food processor; cover and chop. Add the cilantro, parsley, pepper flakes and pepper; cover and process until finely chopped.

2. Add the vinegar, lime juice, soy sauce and lime peel. While processing, gradually add oil in a steady stream. Serve with steak.

Calico Corn Bread Dressing

My mother first made this recipe after tasting her mother-in-law's corn bread dressing. Now it's become a tradition for us to make it every Thanksgiving—we make enough to enjoy on the holiday and still have plenty left over to freeze and enjoy throughout the whole year!

—COLLEEN RUPLE BEAUMONT, TEXAS

PREP: 45 MIN. + COOLING **BAKE:** 35 MIN.
MAKES: 58 SERVINGS (¾ CUP EACH)

- 4 **cups all-purpose flour**
- 4 **cups yellow cornmeal**
- 2 **tablespoons plus 2 teaspoons baking powder**
- 2 **teaspoons salt**
- 4 **eggs**
- 4 **cups milk**
- 1 **cup canola oil**

DRESSING
- 4 **pounds bulk pork sausage**
- 5 **cups water**
- 8 **cups sliced celery (about 1½ bunches)**
- 2 **medium green peppers, chopped**
- 2 **tablespoons plus 1½ teaspoons dried minced garlic**
- 2 **teaspoons pepper**
- ¼ **teaspoon cayenne pepper**
- 24 **slices white bread, cubed**
- 6 **cans (14½ ounces each) chicken broth**
- 2 **bunches green onions, sliced**
- ¼ **cup minced fresh parsley**

1. In a large bowl, combine flour, cornmeal, baking powder and salt. In another large bowl, whisk the eggs, milk and oil; stir into dry ingredients just until moistened.

2. Pour into two greased 13x9-in. baking dishes. Bake at 425° for 15-20 minutes or until a toothpick inserted in center comes out clean. Cool on wire racks.

3. In a two Dutch ovens, cook sausage over medium heat until no longer pink; drain. Stir in water, celery, green peppers, garlic, pepper and cayenne. Bring to a boil. Reduce heat; cover and simmer for 5-7 minutes or until vegetables are crisp-tender.

4. In several large bowls, crumble the corn bread into ½-in. pieces. Stir in white bread, broth, onions and parsley. Add the sausage mixture. Divide among four greased 13x9-in. baking dishes.

5. Cover and bake at 350° for 25 minutes. Uncover; bake 10-15 minutes longer or until lightly browned.

Prairie Fire Dip

PREP/TOTAL TIME: 10 MIN.   **MAKES:** 1¾ CUPS

- 1 **can (16 ounces) refried beans**
- ½ **cup shredded provolone cheese**
- 2 **tablespoons butter, optional**
- 1 **tablespoon finely chopped onion**
- 1 **garlic clove, minced**
- 2 **to 3 teaspoons chili powder**
  Dash hot pepper sauce
  Large corn chips

1. In a saucepan, combine the beans, cheese, butter if desired, onion, garlic, chili powder and hot pepper sauce. Cook over low heat until cheese is melted and dip is heated through. Serve with corn chips.

> "This flavorful dip for crunchy corn chips goes fast at get-togethers, so be sure to make enough. For a bit more zip, use a little more chili powder."
>
> **—JO JOHNSON**
> PARK CITY, MONTANA

Gazpacho, like many other recipes, has evolved over thousands of years. One tale says the original soup was made from stale bread, garlic, olive oil and water or vinegar—foods that Roman soldiers carried. Another tells of the Moors, who ruled Spain during medieval times, making a soup that used almonds and garlic. In either case, gazpacho became very popular in Spain's Andalusian region. When tomatoes were introduced there, they became the base for the cold soup we know and enjoy today.

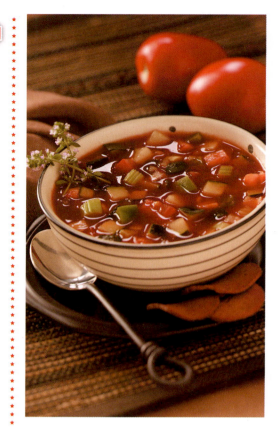

Easy Gazpacho

"Simple as can be" best describes this hearty cold soup. You just chop and combine the ingredients, then chill for a few hours. Serve with crunchy croutons or breadsticks.

—**CHRIS BROOKS** PRESCOTT, ARIZONA

PREP: 15 MIN. + CHILLING
MAKES: 12 SERVINGS (3 QUARTS)

- 1 can (46 ounces) vegetable juice
- 1 can (10½ ounces) condensed beef consomme, undiluted
- 2 cups chopped cucumber
- 2 cups chopped tomatoes
- 1 cup chopped green pepper
- ½ cup chopped onion
- ½ cup chopped celery
- ⅓ cup red wine vinegar
- 2 tablespoons lemon juice
- 2 garlic cloves, minced
- 3 to 4 drops hot pepper sauce

1. In a large bowl, combine all ingredients. Cover and chill for 2-3 hours before serving. Serve cold.

Mulled Dr Pepper

When neighbors or friends visit us on a chilly evening, I like to serve this warm beverage with ham sandwiches and deviled eggs.

—**BERNICE MORRIS** MARSHFIELD, MISSOURI

PREP: 10 MIN.   **COOK:** 2 HOURS
MAKES: 8-10 SERVINGS

- 8 cups Dr Pepper
- ¼ cup packed brown sugar
- ¼ cup lemon juice
- ½ teaspoon ground allspice
- ½ teaspoon whole cloves
- ¼ teaspoon salt
- ¼ teaspoon ground nutmeg
- 3 cinnamon sticks (3 inches)

1. In a 3-qt. slow cooker, combine all ingredients.

2. Cover and cook on low for 2 hours or until heated through. Discard cloves and cinnamon sticks.

Horchata

Bet you haven't yet had a sip of this ground rice-and-almond mix accented with a just hint of lime. Depending on your preference, use more or less water for a thinner or creamier beverage.

—TASTE OF HOME TEST KITCHEN

PREP: 5 MIN. + STANDING **PROCESS:** 10 MIN. **MAKES:** 6 SERVINGS

- ¾ cup uncooked long grain rice
- 2 cups blanched almonds
- 1 cinnamon stick (3 inches)
- 1½ teaspoons grated lime peel
- 4 cups hot water
- 1 cup sugar
- 1 cup cold water
  Ground cinnamon, optional
  Lime wedges, optional

1. Place rice in a blender; cover and process 2-3 minutes or until very fine. Transfer to a large bowl; add almonds, cinnamon stick, lime peel and hot water. Let stand, covered, at room temperature for 8 hours.

2. Discard cinnamon stick. Transfer rice mixture to a blender; cover and process for 3-4 minutes or until smooth. Add sugar; process until sugar is dissolved.

3. Place a strainer over a pitcher; line with double-layered cheesecloth. Pour rice mixture through strainer.

4. Stir in cold water. Serve over ice. If desired, sprinkle with cinnamon and serve with lime.

◀▶ dishing about food

Horchata is a refreshing, creamy-looking Mexican beverage that's made with rice and sometimes contains milk. Spanish folks drink a variation called *horchata de chufa*, made from chufa nuts, which are actually small tubers and have a sweet, nutty flavor.

Guacamole

Lemon or lime juice will keep this dip looking fresh and prevent discoloration until serving. Or, before chilling, place plastic wrap directly on the dip, eliminating any air between the dip and the wrap.

—**ANNE TIPPS** DUNCANVILLE, TEXAS

PREP/TOTAL TIME: 10 MIN. **MAKES:** ABOUT 1½ CUPS

 1 **medium ripe avocado, halved, seeded and peeled**
4½ **teaspoons lemon juice**
 1 **small tomato, seeded and finely chopped**
 ¼ **cup finely chopped onion**
 1 **tablespoon finely chopped green chilies**
 1 **garlic clove, minced**
 ¼ **teaspoon salt, optional**
    Tortilla chips

1. In a large bowl, mash avocado with lemon juice. Stir in the tomato, onion, chilies, garlic and salt if desired. Cover; chill. Serve with tortilla chips.

Nacho Mac 'n' Cheese

Your entire family will really go for the punched-up flavors of this Tex-Mex-inspired dish. And since most of the ingredients are mixed in one pot, cleanup is a breeze!

—**TASTE OF HOME TEST KITCHEN**

PREP/TOTAL TIME: 25 MIN. **MAKES:** 6 SERVINGS

 3 **cups uncooked gemelli or spiral pasta**
 1 **pound ground beef**
 2 **cups chopped sweet red peppers**
 ¼ **cup butter, cubed**
 ¼ **cup all-purpose flour**
 1 **envelope taco seasoning**
 ¼ **teaspoon pepper**
2¼ **cups 2% milk**
 2 **cups (8 ounces) shredded cheddar cheese**
 1 **cup frozen corn, thawed**
 1 **cup coarsely crushed tortilla chips**

1. Cook gemelli according to the package directions. Meanwhile, in a Dutch oven, cook beef and red peppers over medium heat until meat is no longer pink; drain.

2. Stir in the butter, flour, taco seasoning and pepper until blended. Gradually stir in milk. Bring to a boil; cook and stir for 2 minutes or until thickened. Remove from the heat. Stir in cheese and corn until cheese is melted.

3. Drain gemelli; add to beef mixture and stir to coat. Sprinkle with tortilla chips.

1. In a large bowl, combine the first six ingredients; set aside. In a saucepan, heat the sour cream, oil and onions to 120°-130°. Add to cornmeal mixture; beat until blended. Beat in eggs, cheese, corn and jalapenos. Stir in enough flour to form a stiff dough.

2. Turn onto a floured surface; knead until smooth and elastic, about 6-8 minutes. Place in a greased bowl, turning once to grease the top. Cover and let rise in a warm place until doubled, about 1 hour.

3. Punch dough down. Turn onto a lightly floured surface; divide in half. Shape into two loaves. Grease two 9x5-in. loaf pans; dust with additional cornmeal. Place loaves seam side down in prepared pans. Cover and let rise until doubled, about 30 minutes.

4. Brush butter over loaves. Bake at 375° for 30-35 minutes or until golden brown; cover loosely with foil if tops brown too quickly. Remove from pans to wire racks to cool.

Editor's Note: *Wear disposable gloves when cutting hot peppers; the oils can burn skin. Avoid touching your face.*

Arizona Corn Bread

Unlike other corn breads, this one uses yeast. Oil and sour cream make it so moist and tender, while peppers add a bit of zip!

—**MARGARET PACHE** MESA, ARIZONA

PREP: 20 MIN. + RISING **BAKE:** 30 MIN.
MAKES: 2 LOAVES (16 SLICES EACH)

- 1 cup cornmeal
- 2 tablespoons sugar
- 2 packages (¼ ounce each) active dry yeast
- 1 teaspoon salt
- ½ teaspoon baking soda
- ¼ teaspoon pepper
- 1 cup (8 ounces) sour cream
- ½ cup canola oil
- ½ cup chopped green onions
- 2 eggs
- 1¼ cups shredded pepper jack cheese
- 1 cup cream-style corn
- 2 jalapeno peppers, seeded and chopped
- 5 to 6 cups all-purpose flour
  Additional cornmeal
  Melted butter

Watermelon Salsa

PREP/TOTAL TIME: 25 MIN.
MAKES: 15 SERVINGS (⅓ CUP EACH)

- ¼ cup lime juice
- 3 tablespoons brown sugar
- 2 tablespoons cider vinegar
- 1 tablespoon honey
- ¼ teaspoon salt
- 3 cups seeded chopped watermelon
- 1 medium cucumber, seeded and chopped
- 1 small red onion, finely chopped
- 2 jalapeno peppers, seeded and finely chopped
- ¼ cup finely chopped sweet yellow pepper
- ¼ cup minced fresh cilantro
- 2 tablespoons minced fresh basil

1. Combine the first five ingredients in a large bowl. Add remaining ingredients; toss to combine. Refrigerate, covered, until serving. If necessary, drain before serving.

> "I threw this together after one overzealous trip to the farmers market! My family loved it from the first bite. You can serve it right away, but the flavor is best after letting the salsa chill for a few hours."
>
> —**ANDREA HEYART**
> AUBREY, TEXAS

Grilled Sweet Potato and Red Pepper Salad

PREP: 30 MIN. **GRILL:** 20 MIN. **MAKES:** 8 SERVINGS

¼ cup olive oil
2 tablespoons lime juice
1 garlic clove, minced
1 teaspoon chopped seeded jalapeno pepper, optional
1 teaspoon salt
½ teaspoon ground cumin
¼ teaspoon pepper
2 large sweet red peppers
1-½ pounds medium sweet potatoes, peeled and cut into ½-inch slices
2 celery ribs, thinly sliced
3 green onions, thinly sliced
⅓ cup minced fresh cilantro

1. For dressing, in a small bowl, whisk the first seven ingredients; set aside.

2. Using long-handled tongs, moisten a paper towel with cooking oil and lightly coat the grill rack. Grill red peppers over medium heat for 10-15 minutes or until the skins blister, turning frequently. Immediately place the peppers in a large bowl; cover and let stand for 15 minutes.

3. Meanwhile, in a shallow bowl, drizzle sweet potato slices with 2 tablespoons dressing; toss to coat. Set remaining dressing aside. Arrange potato slices on a grilling grid; place on a grill rack. Grill, covered, over medium heat for 5-6 minutes on each side or until tender. Cut into bite-size pieces.

4. Peel off and discard charred skin from peppers; seed and coarsely chop. In a large bowl, combine the potatoes, peppers, celery, onions and cilantro. Whisk the reserved dressing; pour over salad and toss to coat. Serve at room temperature.

Editor's Note: *If you do not have a grilling grid, use a disposable foil pan. Poke holes in the bottom of the pan with a meat fork to allow liquid to drain.*

Mexican Hot Chocolate

This delicious, not-too-sweet hot chocolate is richly flavored with cocoa and delicately seasoned with spices. The blend of cinnamon and chocolate flavors is wonderful!

—KATHY YOUNG WEATHERFORD, TEXAS

PREP/TOTAL TIME: 10 MIN. **MAKES:** 4 SERVINGS

- ¼ cup baking cocoa
- 2 tablespoons brown sugar
- 1 cup boiling water
  Dash ground cloves or nutmeg
- ¼ teaspoon ground cinnamon
- 3 cups milk
- 1 teaspoon vanilla extract
  Whipped cream
  Whole cinnamon sticks

1. Combine cocoa and sugar in small saucepan; stir in water. Bring to boil; reduce heat and cook 2 minutes, stirring constantly.

2. Add the cloves, cinnamon and milk. Simmer 5 minutes (do not boil). Whisk in vanilla. Pour hot chocolate into mugs; top with whipped cream. Use cinnamon sticks for stirrers.

Cheesy Beans and Rice

After my dad had heart trouble years ago, my mom adapted an old recipe to come up with this colorful all-in-one dish. It has been a dinnertime hit for a long time. Even our kids like it, and they can be quite picky!

—LINDA RINDELS LITTLETON, COLORADO

PREP: 15 MIN. **BAKE:** 35 MIN. **MAKES:** 6 SERVINGS

- 1 cup uncooked brown rice
- 1 can (16 ounces) kidney beans, rinsed and drained
- 1 large onion, chopped
- 1 tablespoon canola oil
- 1 can (14½ ounces) diced tomatoes and green chilies, undrained
- 2 teaspoons chili powder
- ¼ teaspoon salt
- 1¼ cups shredded reduced-fat cheddar cheese, divided

1. Cook rice according to package directions. Transfer to a large bowl; add the beans. In a nonstick skillet, saute onion in oil for 4-5 minutes. Stir in the tomatoes, chili powder and salt. Bring to a boil; remove from the heat.

2. In a 2-qt. baking dish coated with cooking spray, layer a third of the rice mixture, cheese and tomato mixture. Repeat layers. Layer with remaining rice mixture and tomato mixture.

3. Cover and bake at 350° for 30 minutes or until heated through. Uncover; sprinkle with remaining cheese. Bake 5-10 minutes longer or until cheese is melted.

Armadillo Eggs aren't eggs at all. Here, cheese-stuffed jalapeno peppers are encased in sausage and coated in a crispy shell. Yum!

TEXAS

The armadillo is the official small mammal of Texas.

Armadillo Eggs

The crust is crispy, and the peppers give these bites a nice zesty flavor.

—**PEGGY CAMPBELL** WELCH, TEXAS

PREP: 20 MIN. **BAKE:** 35 MIN.
MAKES: ABOUT 3 DOZEN

- 3 cans (12 ounces each) pickled jalapeno peppers
- 4 cups (16 ounces) shredded cheddar cheese, divided
- 1 pound bulk pork sausage
- 1½ cups biscuit/baking mix
- 3 eggs, lightly beaten
- 2 envelopes pork-flavored seasoned coating mix

1. Cut each jalapeno in half lengthwise; remove seeds and stems. Stuff each pepper half with about 1 tablespoon cheddar cheese. In a bowl, combine the uncooked sausage, biscuit mix and remaining cheese; mix well. Shape about 2 tablespoonfuls of sausage mixture around each pepper.

2. Dip into eggs, then roll in coating mix. Place on a baking sheet coated with cooking spray. Bake at 350° for 35-40 minutes or until golden brown.

Editor's Note: *Wear disposable gloves when cutting hot peppers; the oils can burn skin. Avoid touching your face.*

Microwave Texas Nachos

Ready in minutes, these easy nachos are perfect for a light luncheon or snack.

—**CARL DAHLGREN** FORT WORTH, TEXAS

PREP/TOTAL TIME: 25 MIN. **MAKES:** 2 SERVINGS

- 2 ounces uncooked chorizo or bulk spicy pork sausage
- 1 garlic clove, minced
- ¼ cup refried beans
- 2 cups tortilla chips
- ½ cup shredded Colby-Monterey Jack cheese
- ½ cup shredded lettuce
- 1 small tomato, seeded and diced
- 3 tablespoons chopped onion
- ¼ cup sour cream
- ¼ cup guacamole
- 2 tablespoons sliced jalapeno pepper

1. Crumble chorizo into a small skillet; add garlic. Cook over medium heat for 6-8 minutes or until fully cooked; drain. In a microwave-safe dish, combine chorizo mixture and beans. Cover and microwave on high for 1-2 minutes or until heated through; stir.

2. Place tortilla chips on a microwave-safe serving plate; sprinkle with the cheese. Heat, uncovered, on high for 1 minute or until the cheese is melted. Spoon the chorizo mixture over chips and cheese. Top with the lettuce, tomato, onion, sour cream, guacamole and jalapeno. Serve immediately.

Editor's Note: *When cutting hot peppers, disposable gloves are recommended. Avoid touching your face. This recipe was tested in a 1,100-watt microwave.*

Tortilla Dressing

PREP: 30 MIN. **BAKE:** 35 MIN. **MAKES:** 9 CUPS

- 8 corn tortillas (6 inches), cut into ¼-inch strips
- ¼ cup canola oil
- 8 flour tortillas (6 inches), cut into ¼-inch strips
- 1 cup crushed corn bread stuffing
- 1 small onion, finely chopped
- ⅓ cup finely chopped sweet red pepper
- 1 jalapeno pepper, seeded and chopped
- 1 tablespoon minced fresh cilantro
- 1 tablespoon chili powder
- 1 teaspoon minced fresh sage or ¼ teaspoon dried sage leaves
- ½ teaspoon ground coriander
- ½ teaspoon ground cumin
- ¼ teaspoon salt
- 1 egg, lightly beaten
- 1 cup chicken broth

1. In a large skillet, saute corn tortilla strips in oil in batches for 1 minute or until golden brown. Drain on paper towels.

2. In a large bowl, combine the corn tortilla strips, flour tortilla strips, stuffing, onion, red pepper, jalapeno, cilantro, chili powder, sage, coriander, cumin and salt. Stir in the egg and the broth.

3. Transfer to a greased 13x9-in. baking dish. Cover and bake at 325° for 35-45 minutes or until a thermometer reads 160°.

Editor's Note: *Wear disposable gloves when cutting hot peppers; the oils can burn skin. Avoid touching your face.*

> "This is not your typical stuffing. Tortillas, jalapenos, chili powder and cilantro kick up the Southwest flavors."
>
> —DOROTHY BRAY
>
> ADKINS, TEXAS

> "Sopes (pronounced "SOH-pehs") is a traditional Mexican dish. You can find the needed ingredients in the ethnic section of a larger local supermarket.

—TASTE OF HOME
TEST KITCHEN

Sopes

PREP: 15 MIN. **COOK:** 35 MIN. **MAKES:** 16 SERVINGS

- 2 cups masa harina
- 1 teaspoon salt
- 1-⅓ cups warm water
- 1-½ cups shredded cooked chicken breast
- 1 cup salsa, divided
- ¼ cup shortening
- 1 cup refried beans
- 1 cup shredded lettuce
- ½ cup crumbled queso fresco

1. In a small bowl, combine masa harina and salt; stir in water. Knead until mixture forms a ball. Divide dough into 16 portions; shape into balls and cover with plastic wrap.

2. Working between two sheets of plastic wrap, press four balls into 3½-in. circles. On an ungreased griddle, cook dough circles over medium-low heat for 1-2 minutes or until bottoms are lightly set. Turn and cook 2 minutes longer. Remove from the heat; quickly pinch edges of circles to form a ½-in. rim. Return to the griddle; cook 2 minutes longer or until bottoms are lightly browned. Remove to wire racks; cover. Repeat with remaining dough.

3. In a small saucepan, combine chicken and ½ cup salsa. Cook over medium-low heat until heated through, stirring occasionally. In a large skillet, melt shortening. Cook sopes over medium-high heat for 2 minutes on each side or until crisp and lightly browned. Remove to paper towels to drain.

4. To assemble, layer each sope with refried beans, chicken mixture and remaining salsa. Sprinkle with lettuce and queso fresco. Serve immediately.

Home-Style Refried Beans

Lime juice, cumin and cayenne pepper make these beans so tasty—especially when compared to the canned variety. I like to dress them up with reduced-fat cheese and salsa.

—MYRA INNES AUBURN, KANSAS

PREP/TOTAL TIME: 15 MIN. **MAKES:** 2⅔ CUPS

- ⅔ cup finely chopped onion
- 4 teaspoons canola oil
- 4 garlic cloves, minced
- 1 teaspoon ground cumin
- ½ teaspoon salt
- ¼ teaspoon cayenne pepper
- 2 cans (15 ounces each) pinto beans, rinsed and drained
- ½ cup water
- 4 teaspoons lime juice

1. In a large saucepan, saute the onion in oil until tender. Stir in the garlic, cumin, salt and cayenne; cook and stir for 1 minute. Add beans and mash. Add water; cook and stir until heated through and water is absorbed. Remove from the heat; stir in lime juice.

Homemade Tortillas

I usually have to double this recipe for tortillas because we go through them so quickly! They're tender, chewy and simple— and you'll never use store-bought again.

—KRISTIN VAN DYKEN W. RICHLAND, WASHINGTON

PREP/TOTAL TIME: 30 MIN. **MAKES:** 8 TORTILLAS

- 2 cups all-purpose flour
- ½ teaspoon salt
- ¾ cup water
- 3 tablespoons olive oil

1. In a large bowl, combine flour and salt. Stir in water and oil. Turn onto a floured surface; knead 10-12 times, adding a little flour or water if needed to achieve a smooth dough. Let rest for 10 minutes.

2. Divide dough into eight portions. On a lightly floured surface, roll each portion into a 7-in. circle.

3. In a large nonstick skillet coated with cooking spray, cook tortillas over medium heat for 1 minute on each side or until lightly browned. Keep warm.

Also called nopales, cactus pads are the prickly pear's succulent leaves. Native Americans used this cactus for food and water, and fashioned its spines into needles. The cactus pads and fruit sold in supermarkets are often harvested from spineless cultivated varieties of prickly pear.

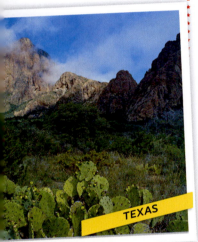

TEXAS

In Texas, where the prickly pear is the official state plant, and in other Southwestern states, this cactus often grows en masse. Ranchers burn off the spines so their cattle can graze on them

Fried Cactus Strips

This fun recipe makes a tasty, crunchy treat that uses a wild resource abundant here in the Southwest. Many people don't even know cactus is edible—and tasty! If it doesn't grow where you live, your grocery store may carry cactus pads in the produce section.

—NEMA LU PARKER EASTLAND, TEXAS

PREP/TOTAL TIME: 20 MIN. **MAKES:** 8 SERVINGS

- 4 to 6 large cactus pads (about 8x4 inches)
- 1 cup all-purpose flour
- 1½ teaspoons salt, divided
- ¼ teaspoon pepper
- 3 eggs
- ½ cup milk
- 1 cup soft bread crumbs
- ¾ cup saltine crumbs
- 1½ teaspoons chili powder
- 1½ teaspoons cayenne pepper
  Oil for frying
  Picante sauce

1. Remove all needles and spines from cactus pads. Slice into ½-in.-wide strips. Wash thoroughly; drain and pat dry. Set aside.

2. In a shallow bowl, combine the flour, ½ teaspoon salt and pepper. In another bowl, lightly beat the eggs and milk. Combine the bread and saltine crumbs, chili powder, cayenne pepper and remaining salt; set aside. Dredge cactus strips in flour mixture, shake off excess. Dip in egg mixture, then coat with crumb mixture.

3. In a deep-fat fryer, heat oil to 375°. Fry catus strips until golden brown, about 1-2 minutes. Drain on paper towels. Serve with the picante sauce.

Fire-Roasted Tomato Salsa

I've been making this salsa for a few years now. Chipotle pepper gives it a wonderful smoky kick. The recipe makes a big batch, but it doesn't last a day in our house!

—PAMELA PAULA SPRINGHILL, FLORIDA

PREP: 30 MIN. + CHILLING **MAKES:** 4 CUPS

- 2 pounds tomatoes (about 6 medium)
- 1 jalapeno pepper
- ½ cup fresh cilantro leaves
- 2 green onions, cut into 2-inch pieces
- 4 garlic cloves, peeled
- 1 chipotle pepper in adobo sauce
- 1 can (4 ounces) chopped green chilies
- 2 tablespoons lime juice
- 1 tablespoon olive oil
- ¼ teaspoon salt
  Tortilla chips

1. Grill tomatoes and jalapeno, covered, over medium-hot heat for 8-12 minutes or until skins are blistered and blackened, turning occasionally. Immediately place in a large bowl; cover and let stand for 20 minutes.

2. Peel off and discard charred skins. Discard stem and seeds from jalapeno; cut tomatoes into fourths. Set jalapeno and tomatoes aside.

3. Place the cilantro, onions and garlic in a food processor; cover and process until blended. Add the chipotle pepper, tomatoes and jalapeno; cover and pulse until blended.

4. Transfer to a large bowl; stir in the chilies, lime juice, oil and salt. Cover and refrigerate for at least 1 hour. Serve with chips.

Editor's Note: *Wear disposable gloves when cutting hot peppers; the oils can burn skin. Avoid touching your face.*

Mini Chicken Empanadas

Refrigerated pie pastry makes quick work of assembling these bite-size appetizers loaded with chicken and cheese..

—**BETTY FULKS** ONIA, ARKANSAS

PREP: 30 MIN. **BAKE:** 15 MIN./BATCH
MAKES: ABOUT 2½ DOZEN

- 1 **cup finely chopped cooked chicken**
- ⅔ **cup shredded Colby-Monterey Jack cheese**
- 3 **tablespoons cream cheese, softened**
- 4 **teaspoons chopped sweet red pepper**
- 2 **teaspoons chopped seeded jalapeno pepper**
- 1 **teaspoon ground cumin**
- ½ **teaspoon salt**
- ⅛ **teaspoon pepper**
- 1 **package (14.1 ounces) refrigerated pie pastry**

1. In a small bowl, combine the first eight ingredients. On a lightly floured surface, roll each pastry sheet into a 15-inch circle. Cut with a floured 3-in. round biscuit cutter.

2. Place about 1 teaspoon filling on one half of each circle. Moisten pastry edges with water. Fold pastry over the filling. Press edges with a fork to seal.

3. Transfer to greased baking sheets. Bake at 400° for 12-15 minutes or until golden brown. Remove to wire racks. Serve warm.

Editor's Note: *Wear disposable gloves when cutting hot peppers; the oils can burn skin. Avoid touching your face.*

Dr Pepper BBQ Sauce

My family is stationed in Italy with my husband, Lieutenant William Robert Blackman. He grew up in Memphis, Tennessee, and I'm from Texas, so the dish that spells "home" for us both is a good ol' barbecue. I have my own recipe for barbecue sauce that we like to pour over sliced brisket. Eating it reminds us of weekend barbecues with our families back home.

—**TINA BLACKMAN** NAPLES, ITALY

PREP: 5 MIN. **COOK:** 35 MIN. **MAKES:** 1 CUP

- 1 **can (12 ounces) Dr Pepper**
- 1 **cup crushed tomatoes**
- ¼ **cup packed brown sugar**
- 2 **tablespoons spicy brown mustard**
- 1 **tablespoon orange juice**
- 1 **tablespoon Worcestershire sauce**
- 1 **garlic clove, minced**
- ¼ **teaspoon salt**
- ⅛ **teaspoon pepper**

1. In a small saucepan, combine all ingredients; bring to a boil. Reduce heat; simmer, uncovered, 30-35 minutes or until slightly thickened, stirring occasionally. Refrigerate leftovers.

◀◆ dishing about food

Depending on their size and filling, empanadas can be eaten as appetizers, main dishes, snacks or desserts! Empanadas have their roots in Spanish and Portuguese cookery; however, many cuisines feature hand pies like these—such as Italian calzones.

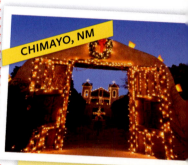

CHIMAYO, NM

The front gate of El Santuario de Chimayo showcases luminarias, or farolitos, a beloved Christmastime symbol in New Mexico. Making empanadas is another holiday tradition there.

Two claims have been made on the origin of this drink. One belongs to San Diego businessman Baron Long, who opened a resort at the Agua Caliente mineral springs in 1927. The Tijuana, Mexico, area adult playground featured drinks, entertainment and *more* drinks—and the Tequila Sunrise was served as a hangover cure. The other legend credits Gene Sulit, a bartender at the Arizona Biltmore, with creating the drink for a guest who liked tequila. Interestingly, both versions used creme de cassis but not orange juice, which is the standard today.

PHOENIX, AZ

The Arizona Biltmore has been an opulent oasis for many noteworthy guests since 1929.

Tequila Sunrise

Everyone loves the pretty layers in this refreshing cocktail classic. It's like a mini-vacation in a glass!

—TASTE OF HOME TEST KITCHEN

PREP/TOTAL TIME: 5 MIN.   **MAKES:** 1 SERVING

1 to 1¼ cups ice cubes
1½ ounces tequila
4½ ounces orange juice
1½ teaspoons grenadine syrup
GARNISH
   Orange slice and maraschino cherry

1. Place ice in a Collins or highball glass. Pour the tequila and orange juice into the glass. Slowly pour grenadine over a bar spoon into the center of the drink. Garnish as desired.

Corn Soup with Pico de Gallo

PREP: 50 MIN. **COOK:** 20 MIN. **MAKES:** 6 SERVINGS

- 3 **corn tortillas (6 inches), cut into 1-inch strips**
- 4 **medium ears sweet corn, husks removed**
- ½ **teaspoon canola oil**
- ½ **teaspoon each salt, pepper and paprika**
- 1 **medium red onion, chopped**
- 1 **bacon strip, chopped**
- 6 **garlic cloves, minced**
- ¼ **cup all-purpose flour**
- 3 **cups reduced-sodium chicken broth**
- 1 **cup fat-free milk**
- 1 **can (4 ounces) chopped green chilies**
- 1 **teaspoon ground cumin**
- 1 **teaspoon dried oregano**
- ½ **cup minced fresh cilantro**
- ¼ **cup lime juice**

PICO DE GALLO

- 2 **plum tomatoes, chopped**
- 1 **medium ripe avocado, peeled and chopped**
- 1 **small serrano pepper, seeded and chopped**
- 1 **garlic clove, minced**
- ¼ **teaspoon salt**
- ¼ **teaspoon pepper**

1. Place the tortilla strips on a baking sheet coated with cooking spray; bake at 350° for 8-10 minutes or until crisp.

2. Rub corn with canola oil; sprinkle with seasonings. Moisten a paper towel with cooking oil; using long-handled tongs, lightly coat the grill rack.

3. Grill corn, covered, over medium heat for 10-12 minutes or until tender, turning frequently. Cool slightly; cut corn from cobs and set aside.

4. In a large saucepan, saute onion and bacon for 5 minutes; add garlic, cook 1 minute longer. Stir in flour until blended; gradually add broth. Bring to a boil; cook and stir for 2 minutes or until thickened. Add corn, milk, chilies, cumin and oregano; heat through. Remove from heat; stir in cilantro and lime juice.

5. Combine pico de gallo ingredients. Serve with soup and tortilla strips.

Editor's Note: *Wear disposable gloves when cutting hot peppers; the oils can burn skin. Avoid touching your face.*

> "The wonderful aroma of this Southwestern soup always entices my family to the dinner table. The blend of seasonings and succulent pico de gallo add to its fabulous flavor."
>
> —ELAINE SWEET
>
> DALLAS, TEXAS

dishing about food ❖➤

Pepitas, or hulled pumpkin seeds, are used in many Latin American dishes. The tasty green kernels are sold raw, roasted and salted.

Cilantro-Pepita Pesto

Looking for ways to use up all the cilantro in my garden, I came up with this flavorful recipe. Serve it with pasta, tortilla chips for dipping, or in any dish that needs perking up!

—**AMI OKASINSKI** MEMPHIS, TENNESSEE

PREP/TOTAL TIME: 20 MIN. **MAKES:** 1½ CUPS

1	**package (6 ounces) fresh baby spinach**
2	**cups fresh cilantro leaves**
⅓	**cup grated Romano cheese**
⅓	**cup salted pumpkin seeds or pepitas, toasted**
3	**to 4 garlic cloves**
2	**tablespoons lime juice**
1	**tablespoon lemon juice**
⅛	**teaspoon salt**
3	**tablespoons olive oil**

1. Place the first five ingredients in a food processor; cover and pulse just until chopped. Add the lime and lemon juices and salt; cover and process until blended. While processing, gradually add oil in a steady stream. Store in an airtight container in the refrigerator.

Salsa Verde

This salsa is fresh and creamy! It's great as a dip for chips and raw veggies, or as a topper for tacos and other Mexican dishes. You can adjust the heat level to suit your tastes.

—NANETTE HILTON LAS VEGAS, NEVADA

PREP: 15 MIN. + CHILLING   **MAKES:** 2½ CUPS

- 8 **tomatillos, husks removed**
- 1 **medium ripe avocado, peeled and pitted**
- 1 **small onion, halved**
- 1 **jalapeno pepper, peeled and pitted**
- ⅓ **cup fresh cilantro leaves**
- ½ **teaspoon salt**
  Tortilla chips

1. In a large saucepan, bring 4 cups water to a boil. Add tomatillos. Reduce heat; simmer, uncovered, for 5 minutes. Drain.

2. Place the avocado, onion, jalapeno, cilantro, salt and tomatillos in a food processor. Cover and process until blended. Refrigerate until chilled. Serve with chips.

Editor's Note: *Wear disposable gloves when cutting hot peppers; the oils can burn skin. Avoid touching your face.*

Nuts and Seeds Trail Mix

Although a handful of this can't-stop-eatin'-it combo is packed with protein and fiber, the fat and calorie count can soon get out of hand. Take care to eat healthfully throughout the day to keep calories under control.

—KRISTIN RIMKUS SNOHOMISH, WASHINGTON

PREP/TOTAL TIME: 15 MIN.   **MAKES:** 5 CUPS

- 1 **cup salted pumpkin seeds or pepitas**
- 1 **cup unblanched almonds**
- 1 **cup unsalted sunflower kernels**
- 1 **cup shelled walnuts**
- 1 **cup chopped dried apricots**
- 1 **cup dark chocolate chips**

1. In a large bowl, combine all ingredients. Store in an airtight container.

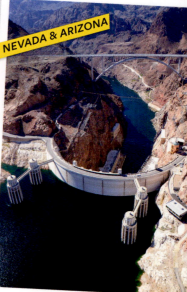

NEVADA & ARIZONA

Spanning the Nevada-Arizona border, the formidable Hoover Dam harnesses the power of the Colorado River, generating electricity for millions.

Authentic Spanish Rice

For a great side with any main dish, try this quick-and-easy rice dish. Bacon drippings add another layer of flavor and make it simply delectable!

—MARIA GOCLAN KATY, TEXAS

PREP: 10 MIN. **COOK:** 25 MIN. **MAKES:** 6 SERVINGS

- 1 tablespoon bacon drippings
- ¾ cup long-grain white rice
- ½ cup chopped onion
- 1 garlic clove, minced
- 3 small canned tomatoes, diced
- 2 tablespoons tomato juice
- 2 cups hot water
- ½ teaspoon salt

1. In a skillet, heat bacon drippings on medium-high. Add rice; cook and stir until rice is golden brown. Add onion and garlic; stir and cook 3 additional minutes. Add all remaining ingredients. Cook, uncovered, on medium heat for 20 minutes, stirring only once after 10 minutes. Check rice for doneness by tasting a few top grains. If rice is firm, add a little water; cover and cook 5 minutes more.

Mexican Fried Corn

When I was growing up, my mother used to serve fried corn for breakfast with scrambled eggs and tortillas. Here in Arizona, corn is widely used in many dishes. My husband and I both enjoy this recipe.

—SYLVIA KESSICK DEWEY, ARIZONA

PREP/TOTAL TIME: 15 MIN. **MAKES:** 4-6 SERVINGS

- 3 cups fresh corn
- ½ cup diced onion
- ¼ cup butter, cubed
- 1 can (4 ounces) chopped green chilies
  Salt and pepper to taste

1. In a skillet, cook corn and onion in butter until tender. Add chilies, salt and pepper; cook and stir over medium heat for about 5-7 minutes. Serve immediately.

Navajo Fry Bread

While taking a trip to the Grand Canyon, my family drove through the Navajo reservation and stopped at a little cafe for dinner. When I complimented the young Navajo waiter on the delicious bread, he gave me the recipe. It's very easy to make.

—MILDRED STEPHENSON HARTSELLE, ALABAMA

PREP: 5 MIN. + STANDING **COOK:** 5 MIN.
MAKES: 2 SERVINGS

- 1 cup all-purpose flour
- 1 teaspoon baking powder
- ⅛ teaspoon salt
- ⅓ cup hot water
  Oil for deep-fat frying

1. In a small bowl, combine the flour, baking powder and salt; stir in hot water to form a soft dough. Cover and let stand for 30 minutes.

2. Divide dough in half. On a lightly floured surface, roll each portion into a 6-in. circle.

3. In an electric skillet, heat 1 in. of oil to 375°. Fry bread in hot oil for 2-3 minutes on each side or until golden brown; drain on paper towels.

Chipotle Sliders

PREP/TOTAL TIME: 30 MIN. **MAKES:** 10 SLIDERS

- 1 **package (12 ounces) Hawaiian sweet rolls, divided**
- 1 **teaspoon salt**
- ½ **teaspoon pepper**
- 8 **teaspoons minced chipotle peppers in adobo sauce, divided**
- 1½ **pounds ground beef**
- 10 **slices pepper jack cheese**
- ½ **cup mayonnaise**

1. Place 2 rolls in a food processor; process until crumbly. Transfer to a large bowl; add the salt, pepper and 6 teaspoons chipotle peppers. Crumble beef over mixture and mix well. Shape into 10 patties.

2. Grill burgers, covered, over medium heat for 3-4 minutes on each side or until a thermometer reads 160° and juices run clear. Top with cheese. Grill 1 minute longer or until cheese is melted.

3. Split remaining rolls and grill, cut side down, over medium heat for 30-60 seconds or until toasted. Combine mayonnaise and remaining chipotle peppers; spread over roll bottoms. Top each with a burger. Replace the roll tops.

> *This recipe has to be the ultimate in a fast-fixing mini burger with simply fabulous flavor! Creamy mayo, cheese and sweet Hawaiian rolls help tame the heat of the chipotle peppers.*

—SHAWN SINGLETON
VIDOR, TEXAS

Though her name has long been forgotten, we can thank a Dallas homemaker for submitting her German chocolate cake recipe to a newspaper in 1957. The rich dessert used an old and rare variety of chocolate sold by Baker's Chocolate Company—German's Sweet Chocolate, named for its creator, Samuel German. As soon as Baker's started receiving letters asking where cooks could buy the star ingredient, they started a publicity campaign and sales of German's Sweet Chocolate took off.

German Chocolate Cake

This cake is my husband's absolute favorite! It's so special, most people ask for a second slice.

—JOYCE PLATFOOT WAPAKONETA, OHIO

PREP: 30 MIN. **BAKE:** 30 MIN. + COOLING **MAKES:** 12 SERVINGS

- 4 ounces German sweet chocolate, chopped
- ½ cup water
- 1 cup butter, softened
- 2 cups sugar
- 4 eggs, separated
- 1 teaspoon vanilla extract
- 2½ cups cake flour
- 1 teaspoon baking soda
- ½ teaspoon salt
- 1 cup buttermilk

FROSTING
- 1½ cups sugar
- 1½ cups evaporated milk
- ¾ cup butter
- 5 egg yolks, beaten
- 2 cups flaked coconut
- 1½ cups chopped pecans
- 1½ teaspoons vanilla extract

ICING
- 1 teaspoon shortening
- 2 ounces semisweet chocolate

1. Line three greased 9-in. round baking pans with waxed paper. Grease waxed paper and set aside. In small saucepan, melt chocolate with water over low heat; cool.

2. In a large bowl, cream butter and sugar until light and fluffy. Beat in 4 egg yolks, one at a time, beating well after each addition. Blend in melted chocolate and vanilla. Combine the flour, baking soda and salt; add to the creamed mixture alternately with buttermilk, beating well after each addition.

3. In a small bowl and with clean beaters, beat the 4 egg whites until stiff peaks form. Fold a fourth of the egg whites into the creamed mixture; fold in remaining whites.

4. Pour batter into prepared pans. Bake at 350° for 24-28 minutes or until a toothpick inserted near center comes out clean. Cool for 10 minutes before removing from pans to wire racks to cool completely.

5. For frosting, in a small saucepan, heat the sugar, milk, butter and egg yolks over medium-low heat until mixture is thickened and golden brown, stirring constantly. Remove from the heat. Stir in the coconut, pecans and vanilla extract. Cool until thick enough to spread. Spread a third of the frosting over each cake layer and stack the layers.

6. In a microwave, melt the chocolate and shortening; stir until smooth; drizzle over cake.

Oklahoma Coconut Poke Cake

Coconut is the star of this cake. You get a double dose, one in the mixture that soaks into the cake and second with the coconut sprinkled on top. Don't worry though, it's a nice flavor treat…it's not too much coconut.
—TASTE OF HOME TEST KITCHEN

PREP: 10 MIN. **BAKE:** 25 MIN. + COOLING
MAKES: 20 SERVINGS

- 1 package white cake mix (regular size)
- 1 can (15 ounces) cream of coconut
- 1 can (14 ounces) sweetened condensed milk
- 1 carton (16 ounces) frozen whipped topping, thawed
- 1 cup flaked coconut

1. Preheat oven to 350°. Prepare and bake cake mix according to package directions, using a 13x9-in. baking pan.

2. Meanwhile, in a small bowl, mix cream of coconut and milk. Remove cake from oven; place on a wire rack. Using a wooden skewer, pierce top of cake to within 1 inch of edge; twist skewer gently to make slightly larger holes. Spoon milk mixture evenly over cake, being careful to fill each hole. Cool completely.

3. Spread whipped topping over cake; sprinkle with coconut. Refrigerate until serving.

Espresso Cream Cake

PREP/TOTAL TIME: 25 MIN. **MAKES:** 8 SERVINGS

- 2 tablespoons instant espresso powder
- 2 tablespoons hot water
- 1 carton (8 ounces) mascarpone cheese
- 1 cup heavy whipping cream
- ⅓ cup confectioners' sugar
- 1 prepared angel food cake (8 to 10 ounces)
- ½ cup coffee liqueur
- 2 teaspoons baking cocoa

1. In a large bowl, dissolve espresso powder in water; cool. Stir in cheese.

2. In a small bowl, beat cream until it begins to thicken. Gradually add confectioners' sugar; beat until soft peaks form. Stir ½ cup cream into cheese mixture; fold in remaining cream.

3. Serve mascarpone cream with cake. Drizzle each serving with liqueur and dust with cocoa.

"After a satisfying meal, I like to go with something light for dessert. This recipe combines two of our favorite flavors, coffee and chocolate, in a delicious cream that's served alongside a slice of angel food cake. Yum!"
—NICOLE CLAYTON
PRESCOTT, ARIZONA

Classic Fruit Kolaches

We love making these melt-in-your-mouth goodies. For extra fun, use Christmas cookie cutters instead of a biscuit cutter.

—**GLEN & SUE ELLEN BORKHOLDER** STURGIS, MICHIGAN

PREP: 35 MIN. + RISING **BAKE:** 15 MIN./BATCH
MAKES: 2½ DOZEN

      6 to 7 cups all-purpose flour
     ¼ cup sugar
      2 packages (¼ ounce each) active dry yeast
      2 teaspoons salt
      2 cups 2% milk
     ½ cup butter, cubed
     ½ cup water
      6 egg yolks
     ¼ cup butter, melted
      1 can (12 ounces) raspberry and/or apricot cake and pastry filling
   ICING
      3 cups confectioners' sugar
     ¼ cup butter, softened
      2 teaspoons vanilla extract
     ½ teaspoon salt
      4 to 6 tablespoons 2% milk

1. In a large bowl, combine 3 cups flour, sugar, yeast and salt. In a large saucepan, heat the milk, butter and water to 120°-130°. Add to dry ingredients; beat just until moistened. Add egg yolks; beat until smooth. Stir in enough remaining flour to form a soft dough (dough will be sticky). Do not knead. Cover and let rise until doubled, about 45 minutes.

2. Turn the dough onto a floured surface; roll to ½-in. thickness. Cut with a floured 2½-in. biscuit cutter. Place 2 in. apart on lightly greased baking sheets. Brush with melted butter. Cover and let rise in a warm place until doubled, about 30 minutes.

3. Using the back of a spoon, make an indentation in the center of each roll. Spoon a heaping teaspoonful of raspberry and/or apricot filling into each indentation. Bake at 350° for 15-20 minutes or until golden brown. Remove from pans to wire racks to cool.

4. Combine the confectioners' sugar, butter, vanilla, salt and enough milk to achieve desired consistency. Drizzle over rolls.

Editor's Note: *This recipe was tested with Solo brand cake and pastry filling. Look for it in the baking aisle.*

Cherry Pie Chimis

In New Mexico, we love to make these yummy fried pies for dessert. Because they call for flour tortillas and convenient canned pie filling, they're a snap to put together when time is short!

—**TERRY DOMINGUEZ** SILVER CITY, NEW MEXICO

PREP/TOTAL TIME: 25 MIN. **MAKES:** 6 SERVINGS

      2 cans (21 ounces each) cherry pie filling
      6 flour tortillas (10 inches)
         Oil for deep-fat frying
         Confectioners' sugar

1. Spoon pie filling down the center of each tortilla; fold sides and ends over filling and roll up. Seal with toothpicks.

2. In an electric skillet or deep fryer, heat oil to 375°. Fry chimichangas, a few at a time, for 2 minutes on each side or until golden brown on both sides. Drain on paper towels. Dust with confectioners' sugar. Serve immediately.

Texas Pecan Pie

This ooey-gooey pie's luscious and creamy filling offers all the good old familiar flavor that so many have come to love!

—LAUREL LESLIE SONORA, CALIFORNIA

PREP: 20 MIN. **BAKE:** 1 HOUR + COOLING **MAKES:** 8 SERVINGS

½ cup sugar
3 tablespoons all-purpose flour
1 cup light corn syrup
1 cup dark corn syrup
3 eggs
1 teaspoon white vinegar
½ teaspoon vanilla extract
1 cup chopped pecans
Pastry for single-crust pie (9 inches)

1. In a large bowl, whisk the sugar, flour, corn syrups, eggs, vinegar and vanilla until smooth. Stir in pecans. Pour into pastry shell. Cover edges with foil.

2. Bake at 350° for 35 minutes. Remove foil; bake 25-30 minutes longer or until a knife inserted near the center comes out clean. Cool on a wire rack. Refrigerate leftovers.

◄● dishing about food

Since the pecan is their state's official tree, it's not surprising that Texans share a fondness for pecan pie with most other Southerners. Texas is second only to Georgia in pecan production.

GROVES, TX

The eastern Texas town of Groves has an appropriate name, thanks to its many pecan trees. It's only natural that the citizens host the annual Texas Pecan Festival there.

This cream-and-egg combo goes back to Roman times, when it was served as a savory dish. Over the centuries, however, flan has turned into the sweet, silky custard we know today. The Spanish added the rich caramel topping and brought the dessert to Mexico, where it remains popular.

SOUTHWEST

The Colorado River doesn't flow only in its namesake state; its waters pass through Utah, Arizona, Nevada and California, too. It's a favored destination for whitewater rafting.

Caramel Flan

To make my flan even more indulgent, I sometimes top it with whipped cream and toasted slivered almonds.

—ANELLE MACK MIDLAND, TEXAS

PREP: 20 MIN. + STANDING
BAKE: 55 MIN. + CHILLING **MAKES:** 8-10 SERVINGS

- ½ cup sugar
- 1⅔ cups sweetened condensed milk
- 1 cup milk
- 3 eggs
- 3 egg yolks
- 1 teaspoon vanilla extract

1. In a large skillet over medium heat, cook sugar until melted, about 12 minutes. Do not stir. When sugar is melted, reduce heat to low and continue to cook, stirring occasionally, until syrup is golden brown, about 2 minutes.

2. Quickly pour into an ungreased 2-qt. round souffle dish, tilting to coat the bottom; let stand for 10 minutes.

3. In a blender, combine the condensed milk, milk, eggs, yolks and vanilla. Cover and process for 15 seconds or until well blended. Slowly pour over syrup.

4. Place the souffle dish in a larger baking pan. Add 1 in. of boiling water to baking pan. Bake at 350° for 55-60 minutes or until center is just set (mixture will jiggle). Remove souffle dish from larger pan. Place on a wire rack; cool for 1 hour. Cover and refrigerate overnight.

5. To unmold, run a knife around edge and invert flan onto a large rimmed serving platter. Cut into wedges or spoon onto dessert plates; spoon sauce over each serving.

Candy Apple Pie

This is the only apple pie my husband will eat—but that's just fine, since he makes it as often as I do. Like a combination of apple and pecan pie, it's a sweet treat that usually tops off our holiday meals from New Year's all the way through to Christmas!

—CINDY KLEWENO BURLINGTON, COLORADO

PREP: 20 MIN. **BAKE:** 45 MIN. **MAKES:** 8 SERVINGS

- 6 cups sliced peeled tart apples
- 2 tablespoons lime juice
- ¾ cup sugar
- ¼ cup all-purpose flour
- ½ teaspoon ground cinnamon
- ¼ teaspoon salt
  Pastry for double-crust pie (9 inches)
- 2 tablespoons butter

TOPPING
- 2 tablespoons butter
- ¼ cup packed brown sugar
- 1 tablespoon heavy whipping cream
- ¼ cup chopped pecans

1. In a large bowl, toss apples with lime juice. Combine the sugar, flour, cinnamon and salt; add to apples and toss lightly.

2. Line a 9-in. pie plate with bottom crust and trim even with edge; fill with apple mixture. Dot with butter. Roll out remaining pastry to fit top of pie. Place over filling. Trim, seal and flute edges; cut slits in pastry.

3. Bake at 400° for 40-45 minutes or until golden brown and apples are tender.

4. For topping, melt butter in a small saucepan. Stir in brown sugar and cream; bring to a boil, stirring constantly. Remove from the heat and stir in pecans.

5. Pour over top crust. Bake 3-4 minutes longer or until bubbly. Place on a wire rack. Serve warm.

Strawberry Shortcake

Although I've tried a few other recipes for strawberry shortcake over the years, I always come back to this one.

—JANICE MITCHELL AURORA, COLORADO

PREP/TOTAL TIME: 30 MIN. **MAKES:** 2 SERVINGS

- 1½ cups sliced fresh strawberries
- ⅓ cup sugar

BISCUITS

- 1 cup all-purpose flour
- 7 teaspoons sugar, divided
- 2 teaspoons baking powder
- ¼ teaspoon salt
- ¼ teaspoon cream of tartar
- ⅛ teaspoon baking soda
- ¼ cup shortening
- ⅓ cup buttermilk
- ¼ teaspoon vanilla extract
- ½ cup heavy whipping cream

1. In a small bowl, mash the strawberries; stir in sugar. Cover and refrigerate until serving.

2. For biscuits, in a large bowl, combine the flour, 4½ teaspoons sugar, baking powder, salt, cream of tarter and baking soda. Cut in shortening until mixture resembles coarse crumbs. Stir in buttermilk and vanilla until moistened.

3. Turn dough onto a lightly floured surface; knead 8-10 times. Shape into two 4-in. circles. Place on an ungreased baking sheet. Bake at 450° for 12-14 minutes or until golden brown.

4. To assemble, split shortcakes in half. Place the cake bottoms on dessert plates. Top each with half of the strawberry mixture. Replace shortcake tops.

5. In a small bowl, beat the cream until it begins to thicken. Add remaining sugar; beat until stiff peaks form. Dollop onto shortcakes.

Croissant Pudding with Chocolate Kahlua Sauce

PREP: 25 MIN. **BAKE:** 40 MIN. **MAKES:** 9 SERVINGS

- 6 croissants, torn into pieces
- 4 egg yolks
- 2 eggs
- 3 cups heavy whipping cream
- 2¼ cups sugar
- 1½ cups half-and-half cream
- 4½ teaspoons vanilla extract
- 1½ teaspoons salt

SAUCE

- 2 ounces unsweetened chocolate, coarsely chopped
- 2 tablespoons butter
- 1 cup sugar
- ½ cup evaporated milk
  Dash salt
- 3 tablespoons Kahlua (coffee liqueur)

1. Divide croissant pieces among nine greased 10-oz. ramekins or custard cups. Place on baking sheets.

2. In a large bowl, combine the egg yolks, eggs, cream, sugar, half-and-half, vanilla and salt. Pour over croissant pieces; let stand for 15 minutes or until croissants are softened. Bake at 325° for 40-45 minutes or until a knife inserted near the center comes out clean.

3. For sauce, in a small saucepan, melt chocolate and butter over medium-low heat. Add the sugar, milk and salt; cook and stir for 3-4 minutes or until thickened. Remove from the heat; stir in Kahlua. Serve with warm pudding.

> "These custards puff up slightly while baking, creating beautiful, golden crowns. Kahlua brings a mild coffee flavor to the heavenly chocolate sauce."
>
> **—CHERYL TUCKER**
> HOUSTON, TEXAS

> **This refreshing no-bake cheesecake's delicate flavor and creamy texture are complemented by a nutty coconut crust.**
>
> **—INGE SCHERMERHORN**
>
> EAST KINGSTON, NEW HAMPSHIRE

Lime Coconut Cheesecake

PREP: 30 MIN. + CHILLING   **MAKES:** 10-12 SERVINGS

1½ **cups flaked coconut**
  3 **tablespoons ground macadamia nuts or almonds**
  3 **tablespoons butter, melted**
  1 **envelope unflavored gelatin**
  ¼ **cup cold water**
  ¾ **cup sugar**
  2 **packages (8 ounces each) cream cheese, softened**
  ¼ **cup lime juice**
  1 **tablespoon grated lime peel**
     Green food coloring
1½ **cups heavy whipping cream, whipped**
     Toasted coconut and additional whipped cream, optional

1. In a bowl, combine coconut and nuts; stir in butter. Press onto the bottom of a greased 9-in. springform pan. Bake at 350° for 10-15 minutes or until crust is golden brown around the edges. Cool on a wire rack.

2. In a saucepan, sprinkle gelatin over cold water; let stand for 1 minute. Stir in sugar; cook over low heat until sugar and gelatin are dissolved. Remove from the heat. In a bowl, beat cream cheese until smooth. Gradually beat in gelatin mixture. Add lime juice and peel; beat until blended. Tint pale green with food coloring. Fold in whipped cream. Pour over crust. Refrigerate for 5 hours or overnight.

3. Carefully run a knife around the edge of pan to loosen. Remove sides of pan. Garnish with coconut and additional whipped cream if desired.

Chocolate Texas Sheet Cake

My husband is from Texas, and we love this chocolate sheet cake. The recipe is simple but oh-so-good!

—KRISTI WELLS RALEIGH, NORTH CAROLINA

PREP: 25 MIN. **BAKE:** 20 MIN. + COOLING
MAKES: 20 SERVINGS

- 1 cup butter, cubed
- 1 cup water
- ¼ cup baking cocoa
- 2 cups all-purpose flour
- 2 cups sugar
- 1 teaspoon baking soda
- ½ teaspoon salt
- 2 eggs, lightly beaten
- ½ cup sour cream

FROSTING

- ½ cup butter, softened
- 3¾ cups confectioners' sugar
- ¼ cup baking cocoa
- 1 teaspoon vanilla extract
- 5 to 6 tablespoons milk

1. In a large saucepan, bring the butter, water and cocoa just to a boil. Immediately remove from the heat. Combine flour, sugar, baking soda and salt; stir into butter mixture. Combine the eggs and sour cream; stir into butter mixture until blended.

2. Pour into a greased 15x10x1-in. baking pan. Bake at 350° for 18-25 minutes or until a toothpick inserted near the center comes out clean. Cool on a wire rack.

3. For frosting, in a large bowl, cream the butter and confectioners' sugar. Add cocoa, vanilla and enough milk to achieve desired consistency. Spread over cake.

Mayan Chocolate Biscotti

Those who enjoy Mexican hot chocolate will go for the subtle sweetness and slight heat found in every bite of this perked-up biscotti.

—CHRIS MICHALOWSKI DALLAS, TEXAS

PREP: 35 MIN. **BAKE:** 40 MIN. + COOLING
MAKES: 2 DOZEN

- ½ cup butter, softened
- ¾ cup sugar
- 2 eggs
- 1½ teaspoons coffee liqueur
- 1½ teaspoons vanilla extract
- 2 cups all-purpose flour
- 1½ teaspoons ground ancho chili pepper
- ½ teaspoon baking soda
- ½ teaspoon baking powder
- ½ teaspoon ground cinnamon
- ⅛ teaspoon salt
- 1½ cups chopped pecans
- 1 cup (6 ounces) semisweet chocolate chips
- 1 ounce 53% cacao dark baking chocolate, grated

1. In a large bowl, cream the butter and sugar until light and fluffy. Add eggs, one at a time, beating well after each addition. Stir in coffee liqueur and vanilla. Combine the flour, chili pepper, baking soda, baking powder, cinnamon and salt; gradually add to creamed mixture and mix well. Stir in the pecans, chocolate chips and grated chocolate.

2. Divide dough in half. On an ungreased baking sheet, shape each half into a 10x2-in. rectangle. Bake at 350° for 20-25 minutes or until set and lightly browned.

3. Place pans on wire racks. When cool enough to handle, transfer to a cutting board; cut diagonally with a serrated knife into ¾-in. slices. Place cut side down on ungreased baking sheets.

4. Bake for 8-10 minutes on each side or until golden brown. Remove to wire racks to cool completely. Store in an airtight container.

This classic Spanish dessert is enjoyed in many Latin American countries—each with its own special take. Basic ingredients include rice and milk (hence, the name of the dish), plus a flavoring ingredient, such as cinnamon.

Arroz con Leche (Rice Pudding)

Sweet and simple, this creamy dessert is real comfort food in any language! You'll love the warm raisin and cinnamon flavors. It's great served cold, too.

—**MARINA CASTLE** CANYON COUNTRY, CALIFORNIA

PREP: 5 MIN. **COOK:** 30 MIN. **MAKES:** 4 SERVINGS

- 1½ cups water
- ½ cup uncooked long grain rice
- 1 cinnamon stick (3 inches)
- 1 cup sweetened condensed milk
- 3 tablespoons raisins

1. In a small saucepan, combine the water, rice and cinnamon. Bring to a boil. Reduce heat; simmer, uncovered, for 15-20 minutes or until water is absorbed.

2. Stir in milk and raisins. Bring to a boil. Reduce heat; simmer, uncovered, for 10-15 minutes or until thick and creamy, stirring frequently. Discard cinnamon. Serve warm or cold.

Tres Leches Cake

During our extensive travels to Central America, my husband and I have sampled many kinds of the popular tres leches (three milks) cake. We think this is the absolute best!

—**JOAN MEYERS** PALOS PARK, ILLINOIS

PREP: 45 MIN. + CHILLING
BAKE: 20 MIN. + STANDING **MAKES:** 15 SERVINGS

- 6 eggs
- 1½ cups sugar
- 1 teaspoon vanilla extract
- 2 cups all-purpose flour
- 2 teaspoons baking powder

MILK MIXTURE
- 1 can (14 ounces) sweetened condensed milk
- 1 can (12 ounces) evaporated milk
- 1 cup 2% milk
- 3 egg yolks, beaten
- ¼ cup rum, optional

FROSTING
- 1 cup sugar
- 3 egg whites
- ¼ cup water
- ¼ teaspoon cream of tartar

1. In a large bowl, beat the eggs for 3 minutes. Gradually add the sugar and vanilla; beat for 2 minutes or until mixture becomes thick and lemon-colored. Combine flour and baking powder; fold into the egg mixture. Spread batter into a greased 13x9-in. baking dish.

2. Bake at 350° for 20-25 minutes or until golden brown. Place on a wire rack. Poke holes in cake with a skewer, about ½ in. apart.

3. In a small saucepan, bring the three milks to a boil over medium-low heat. Remove from the heat; gradually stir a small amount of hot mixture into egg yolks. Return all to the pan, stirring constantly. Stir in rum if desired. Bring to a gentle boil; cook and stir for 2 minutes.

4. Slowly pour the milk mixture over cake, allowing mixture to absorb into cake. Let stand for 30 minutes. Cover and refrigerate for 8 hours or overnight.

5. In a large heavy saucepan, combine the frosting ingredients over low heat. With a hand mixer, beat on low speed for 1 minute. Continue beating on low over low heat until the frosting reaches 160°, about 14-18 minutes.

6. Pour into a large bowl; beat on high until stiff peaks form, about 7 minutes. Spread over cake. Store in the refrigerator.

Dr Pepper Cake

Here is my favorite "go-to" recipe any time I have to take food anywhere. Everyone loves it! When baked in two layers rather than in one, it makes an impressive presentation. This is one surefire crowd-pleaser!

—SHANNON PARUM VERNON, TEXAS

PREP: 30 MIN. **BAKE:** 20 MIN. + COOLING
MAKES: 12 SERVINGS

- 1 package German chocolate cake mix, regular size
- 1 package (3.4 ounces) instant chocolate pudding mix
- 4 eggs
- 1 can (12 ounces) Dr Pepper
- 1 teaspoon vanilla extract

FROSTING

- 1 container (12 ounces) whipped cream cheese, room temperature
- ⅓ cup butter, softened
- ⅓ cup baking cocoa
- 3½ cups confectioners' sugar
- 1½ teaspoons vanilla extract

1. Preheat oven to 350°. Line bottoms of three greased 9-in. round baking pans with parchment paper; grease paper.

2. In a large bowl, combine cake and pudding mixes. Add the eggs, one at a time, beating well after each addition. Gradually beat in the Dr Pepper and vanilla.

3. Transfer the batter to prepared pans. Bake 20-25 minutes or until the top springs back when lightly touched. Cool in pans 10 minutes before removing to wire racks; remove paper. Cool completely.

4. For frosting, in a large bowl, beat cream cheese and butter until smooth. Beat in the cocoa. Add confectioners' sugar and vanilla; beat until creamy.

5. Place one cake layer on a serving plate; spread with ½ cup frosting. Repeat layers. Top with remaining cake layer. Frost top and sides of cake with remaining frosting.

Anise Butter Cookies

In New Mexico, these cookies are known as "bizcochitos," which means "small biscuits." Many variations of the recipe have been passed down through the generations. The cookies are enjoyed during the Christmas holidays, at wedding receptions and for other special celebrations. They're good all by themselves or dunked in milk or coffee.

—MARI LYNN VAN GINKLE
SANDIA PARK, NEW MEXICO

PREP: 30 MIN. **BAKE:** 40 MIN. **MAKES:** 5 DOZEN

- 2 cups butter, softened
- 1¾ cups sugar, divided
- 2 eggs
- ¼ cup thawed orange juice concentrate
- 4 teaspoons aniseed, crushed
- 6 cups all-purpose flour
- 3 teaspoons baking powder
- ½ teaspoon salt
- 1 teaspoon ground cinnamon

1. In a large bowl, cream the butter and 1½ cups sugar until light and fluffy. Add eggs, one at a time, beating well after each addition. Beat in orange juice concentrate and aniseed. Combine the flour, baking powder and salt; gradually add to creamed mixture and mix well.

2. On a lightly floured surface, roll out the dough to ¼-in. thickness. Cut with a floured 2½-in. round cookie cutter. Place 1 in. apart on ungreased baking sheets.

3. Combine the cinnamon and remaining sugar; sprinkle over cookies. Bake at 350° for 12-15 minutes or until golden brown. Remove to wire racks.

WACO, TX

Find everything you ever wanted to know about this distinctive soft drink (and other soda pops, too) at the Dr Pepper Museum.

> " This creamy concoction is the result of several attempts to duplicate a dessert I enjoyed on vacation. It looks so beautiful on a buffet table that many folks are tempted to forgo the main course in favor of this chocolaty treat. "

—MOLLY SEIDEL
EDGEWOOD, NEW MEXICO

Chocolate Velvet Dessert

PREP: 20 MIN. **BAKE:** 45 MIN. + CHILLING **MAKES:** 16 SERVINGS

- 1½ **cups chocolate wafer crumbs**
- 2 **tablespoons sugar**
- ¼ **cup butter, melted**
- 2 **cups (12 ounces) semisweet chocolate chips**
- 6 **egg yolks**
- 1¾ **cups heavy whipping cream**
- 1 **teaspoon vanilla extract**

CHOCOLATE BUTTERCREAM FROSTING
- ½ **cup butter, softened**
- 3 **cups confectioners' sugar**
- 3 **tablespoons baking cocoa**
- 3 **to 4 tablespoons 2% milk**

1. In a small bowl, combine wafer crumbs and sugar; stir in butter. Press onto the bottom and 1½ in. up the sides of a greased 9-in. springform pan. Place on a baking sheet. Bake at 350° for 10 minutes. Cool on a wire rack.

2. In a large microwave-safe bowl, melt chocolate chips; stir until smooth. Cool. In a small bowl, combine the egg yolks, cream and vanilla. Gradually stir a small amount of egg yolk mixture into melted chocolate until blended; gradually stir in remaining mixture. Pour into crust.

3. Place pan on a baking sheet. Bake at 350° for 45-50 minutes or until center is almost set. Cool on a wire rack for 10 minutes. Carefully run a knife around edge of pan to loosen; cool 1 hour longer. Refrigerate overnight.

4. In a large bowl, combine the butter, confectioners' sugar, cocoa and enough milk to achieve a piping consistency. Using a large star tip, pipe frosting on dessert.

Chocolate Mexican Wedding Cakes

These spiced balls are a yummy twist on a traditional favorite. Sometimes I add mini chocolate chips to the dough and, after baking, dip the cooled cookies in melted almond bark.

—**JOANNE VALKEMA** FREEPORT, ILLINOIS

PREP: 20 MIN. **BAKE:** 15 MIN./BATCH **MAKES:** ABOUT 3½ DOZEN

- 1 cup butter, softened
- 1¾ cups confectioners' sugar, divided
- 1 teaspoon vanilla extract
- 1½ cups all-purpose flour
- ¼ cup cornstarch
- ¼ cup baking cocoa
- ½ teaspoon salt
- 1¼ cups finely chopped pecans or almonds
- ½ teaspoon ground cinnamon

1. In a large bowl, cream butter and 1 cup confectioners' sugar until light and fluffy. Beat in vanilla. Combine the flour, cornstarch, cocoa and salt; gradually add to creamed mixture and mix well. Stir in nuts.

2. Shape tablespoonfuls of dough into 1-in. balls. Place 2 in. apart on ungreased baking sheets. Bake at 325° for 12-14 minutes or until set.

3. In a small bowl, combine cinnamon and remaining confectioners' sugar. Roll warm cookies in sugar mixture; cool on wire racks. Store in an airtight container.

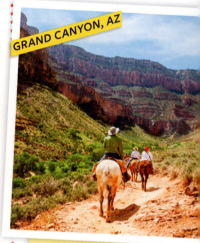

GRAND CANYON, AZ

If the views from the North or South Rim aren't enough for you, take a riding tour or hike down into the Grand Canyon!

Fried Mexican ice cream appears to be an American invention. It's a riff on Asian fried ice cream, which uses a tempura batter. For the "Mexican" recipe, scoops of ice cream are rolled in cornflakes or cookie crumbs before they're fried.

LOS ANGELES, CA

A classic Latin American treat, paletas have recently become popular in the States. These ice pops have long been sold from pushcarts in Latino areas, but are now available at grocery stores and gourmet shops. One of the first companies to make the jump was L.A.-based Palapa Azul.

Mexican Ice Cream

I made this ice cream for my grandma and her friends, and they said it was "so good." This simple, flavorful dessert is a perfect way to get kids involved in the kitchen.

—**BEN PHIPPS** LIMA, OHIO

PREP: 20 MIN. + FREEZING **MAKES:** 4 SERVINGS

    2 cups vanilla ice cream
    ½ cup frosted cornflakes, crushed
    ¼ cup sugar
    1 teaspoon ground cinnamon
    ¼ cup honey

1. Place four ½-cup scoops of ice cream on a waxed paper-lined baking sheet. Freeze for 1 hour or until firm.

2. In a shallow bowl, combine cornflake crumbs, sugar and cinnamon. Roll ice cream in crumb mixture to coat. Freeze until serving. Drizzle each serving with 1 tablespoon honey.

Coconut Chocolate Cake

Hope other families enjoy this cake as much as my family does. I've given out almost 100 copies of this recipe to others who have tried the cake and liked it.

—**DOROTHY WEST** NACOGDOCHES, TEXAS

PREP: 35 MIN. **BAKE:** 20 MIN. **MAKES:** 35 SERVINGS

    2 cups all-purpose flour
    2 cups sugar
    1 teaspoon baking soda

    ½ teaspoon salt
    1 cup butter, cubed
    1 cup water
    ¼ cup baking cocoa
    2 eggs
    ½ cup buttermilk
    1 teaspoon vanilla extract
TOPPING
    1 can (12 ounces) evaporated milk, divided
    1¼ cups sugar, divided
    20 large marshmallows
    1 package (14 ounces) coconut
    2 cups slivered almonds, toasted, divided
    ½ cup butter, cubed
    1 cup semisweet chocolate chips

1. In a large bowl, combine the flour, sugar, baking soda and salt. In a small saucepan, combine the butter, water and cocoa. Cook and stir until butter is melted; add to dry ingredients. Combine the eggs, buttermilk and vanilla; add to chocolate mixture and mix well.

2. Pour into a greased 15x10x1-in. baking pan. Bake at 350° for 20-25 minutes or until a toothpick inserted in center comes out clean.

3. Meanwhile, in a large saucepan, combine 1 cup evaporated milk, ¾ cup sugar and the marshmallows; cook and stir until the marshmallows are melted. Remove from heat; stir in coconut. Immediately sprinkle 1 cup almonds over cake. Spread the coconut mixture over top. Sprinkle with remaining almonds (pan will be full).

4. In a small saucepan, combine butter with remaining milk and sugar. Cook and stir until butter is melted. Remove from the heat; stir in chocolate chips until melted. Drizzle over almonds. Cool on a wire rack.

Sopaipillas

Light, crispy pastry puffs, sopaipillas are a sweet way to round out a spicy meal. They make a nice winter dessert served warm and topped with honey or sugar.

—MARY ANNE MCWHIRTER PEARLAND, TEXAS

PREP: 15 MIN. + STANDING **COOK:** 25 MIN. **MAKES:** 6-8 SERVINGS

- 1 **cup all-purpose flour**
- 1½ **teaspoons baking powder**
- ¼ **teaspoon salt**
- 1 **tablespoon shortening**
- ⅓ **cup warm water**
  Oil for deep-fat frying
  Honey, optional
  Confectioners' sugar, optional

1. In a large bowl, combine flour, baking powder and salt. Cut in shortening until mixture resembles fine crumbs. Gradually add water, tossing with a fork until a loose ball forms (dough will be crumbly).

2. On a lightly floured surface, knead the dough for 3 minutes or until smooth. Cover and let rest for 10 minutes. Roll out into a 12x10-in. rectangle. Cut into 12 squares with a knife or cut into 12 circles using a round biscuit cutter.

3. In a deep-fat fryer, heat 2 in. of oil to 375°. Fry the sopaipillas for 1-2 minutes on each side. Drain sopaipillas on paper towels; keep warm. Serve with honey and/or dust with confectioners' sugar if desired.

◆● dishing about food

One of Texas' official state pastries, the sopaipilla is thought to have been created in New Mexico. Cooks tuck sweet or savory filling inside the tender fried pillows. Sopaipillas are similar to other pastries of South and Central America, such as churros.

NEW MEXICO

HISTORIC
NEW MEXICO
U.S.
66
ROUTE

Take in the sights of the Land of Enchantment by cruising on Route 66. The historic highway stretches straight across the state, passing by must-see cities and retro, neon-lit attractions.

West

Out of all the regions in the U.S., the Western states quite possibly deliver the tastiest mix of flavors, ingredients and cooking influences. California, for instance, offers succulent specialties featuring wine and fresh produce, while the Mountain States rely on hearty beef entrees that meat-and-potato lovers crave! Families in the Pacific Northwest enjoy an abundance of seafood dinners and take advantage of locally grown apples and cherries for unforgettable desserts. And let's not forget Hawaii! Its home cooks add plenty of Polynesian flair to this colorful mix.

Talk about your multicultural cuisine! Hawaii's was influenced by Polynesians, Chinese, Koreans, Japanese, English, Portuguese, Puerto Ricans, Filipinos and mainlanders—all bringing their own favorite ingredients, recipes and traditions.

HANALEI VALLEY, HI

One of the main crops grown in this fertile Kauai valley is taro, or kalo. The plant's tuber is the main ingredient in poi, a traditional Hawaiian dish.

Aloha Burgers

I love hamburgers and pineapple, so it just seemed natural for me to combine them. My family frequently requests these unique sandwiches. They're a nice change of pace from the same old boring burgers.

—**JOI MCKIM-JONES** WAIKOLOA, HAWAII

PREP/TOTAL TIME: 30 MIN. **MAKES:** 4 SERVINGS

- 1 **can (8 ounces) sliced pineapple**
- ¾ **cup reduced-sodium teriyaki sauce**
- 1 **pound ground beef**
- 1 **large sweet onion, sliced**
- 1 **tablespoon butter**
- 4 **lettuce leaves**
- 4 **sesame seed or onion buns, split and toasted**
- 4 **slices Swiss cheese**
- 4 **bacon strips, cooked**

1. Drain pineapple juice into a small bowl; add teriyaki sauce. Place 3 tablespoons in a resealable plastic bag. Add pineapple; toss to coat and set aside.

2. Shape beef into four patties; place in an 8-in. square baking dish. Pour the remaining teriyaki sauce mixture over patties; marinate for 5-10 minutes, turning once.

3. Drain and discard teriyaki marinade. Grill, covered, over medium heat or broil 4 in. from the heat for 6-9 minutes on each side or until a thermometer reads 160° and juices run clear. Meanwhile, in a small skillet, saute onion in butter until tender, about 5 minutes; set aside.

4. Drain and discard pineapple marinade. Place pineapple on grill or under broiler to heat through. Layer with lettuce and onion on bottom of buns. Top with burgers, cheese, pineapple and bacon. Replace tops.

Rack of Lamb with Figs

Your dinner guests are sure to enjoy this special preparation. Roasted lamb is served with a full-bodied sauce made with port wine and figs, then sprinkled with walnuts.

—SYLVIA CASTANON LONG BEACH, CALIFORNIA

PREP: 30 MIN. **BAKE:** 45 MIN. **MAKES:** 6-8 SERVINGS

- 2 racks of lamb (2 pounds each)
- 1 teaspoon salt, divided
- 1 cup water
- 1 small onion, finely chopped
- 1 tablespoon canola oil
- 1 garlic clove, minced
- 2 tablespoons cornstarch
- 1 cup port wine or ½ cup grape juice plus
  ½ cup reduced-sodium beef broth
- 10 dried figs, halved
- ¼ teaspoon pepper
- ½ cup coarsely chopped walnuts, toasted

1. Rub lamb with ½ teaspoon salt. Place meat side up on a rack in a greased roasting pan. Bake, uncovered, at 375° for 45-60 minutes or until meat reaches desired doneness (for medium-rare, a thermometer should read 145°; medium, 160°; well-done, 170°).

2. Remove to a serving platter; cover loosely with foil. Add 1 cup water to roasting pan; stir to loosen browned bits from pan. Using a fine sieve, strain mixture; set drippings aside.

3. In a small saucepan, saute onion in oil until tender. Add the garlic; cook 1 minute longer. Stir in cornstarch until blended; gradually add the wine, drippings, figs, pepper and the remaining salt. Bring to a boil. Reduce heat to medium-low; cook, uncovered, until the figs are tender and the sauce is thickened, about 10 minutes, stirring occasionally.

4. Sprinkle the walnuts over lamb; serve with fig sauce.

Asparagus Salmon Pie

I received this recipe from a dear neighbor years ago, when we lived in the mountains near Yosemite National Park. We had four small children, and the whole family really loved this recipe. Now I make it for my husband, for guests, and for my children and grandchildren when they visit.

—SHIRLEY MARTIN FRESNO, CALIFORNIA

PREP: 30 MIN. **BAKE:** 30 MIN. **MAKES:** 6 SERVINGS

- 1 pound fresh asparagus
- ½ cup chopped onion
- 2 tablespoons butter
- 3 eggs, lightly beaten
- ½ cup milk
- 2 tablespoons minced fresh parsley
- ½ teaspoon dried basil
- ½ teaspoon salt
- 1 can (14¾ ounces) pink salmon, drained, boned and flaked
- 1 unbaked pastry shell (9 inches)

1. Place asparagus in a saucepan with enough water to cover; cook until crisp-tender. Drain well. Reserve six spears for garnish; cut the remaining spears into bite-size pieces. Set aside.

2. In a small saucepan, saute onion in butter until tender. Set aside.

3. In small bowl, mix eggs, milk, parsley, basil, salt and salmon. Add sauted onion. Place cut asparagus in pastry shell; top with salmon mixture. Arrange reserved asparagus spears, spoke fashion, on top. Cover edges of crust with foil to prevent over-browning.

4. Bake at 425° for 30-35 minutes or until filling is set.

> **We live in a farming community, and among our main crops are onions. When I competed in a cooking contest at the Idaho-Eastern Oregon Onion Festival, I was flabbergasted when I won the top three prizes. This was the first-place recipe.**
>
> **—NELL CRUSE**
> ONTARIO, OREGON

Caramelized-Onion Pork

PREP: 30 MIN. **BAKE:** 35 MIN. + STANDING
MAKES: 4 SERVINGS

- 1 **large sweet onion, thinly sliced**
- 1 **teaspoon sugar**
- 2 **teaspoons olive oil**
- 1 **pork tenderloin (1 pound)**
- ¼ **teaspoon salt**
- ⅛ **teaspoon pepper**

1. In a large skillet, cook onion and sugar in oil over medium-low heat until onion is tender and golden brown, about 30 minutes, stirring occasionally.

2. Place the pork in a 13x9-in. baking dish coated with cooking spray. Sprinkle with salt and pepper. Top with the onion mixture.

3. Bake, uncovered, at 350° for 35-40 minutes or until a thermometer reads 145°. Let stand for 5 minutes before slicing.

Saucy Chicken and Asparagus

You won't believe how delicious, yet how easy this dish is! We tasted it for the first time when our son's godparents made it for us.

—VICKI SCHLECHTER DAVIS, CALIFORNIA

PREP: 10 MIN. **BAKE:** 40 MIN. **MAKES:** 4 SERVINGS

- 1½ **pounds fresh asparagus spears, halved**
- 4 **boneless skinless chicken breast halves**
- 2 **tablespoons canola oil**
- ½ **teaspoon salt**
- ¼ **teaspoon pepper**
- 1 **can (10¾ ounces) condensed cream of chicken soup, undiluted**
- ½ **cup mayonnaise**
- 1 **teaspoon lemon juice**
- ½ **teaspoon curry powder**
- 1 **cup (4 ounces) shredded cheddar cheese**

1. If desired, partially cook asparagus; drain. Place the asparagus in a greased 9-in. square baking dish. In a skillet over medium heat, brown the chicken in oil on both sides. Season with the salt and pepper. Arrange the chicken over the asparagus.

2. In a bowl, mix soup, mayonnaise, lemon juice and curry powder; pour over chicken. Cover and bake at 375° for 40 minutes or until the chicken is tender and juices run clear. Sprinkle with cheese. Let stand for 5 minutes before serving.

Sweet Onion BBQ Burgers

Sometimes we don't even bother with a bun for these moist, flavorful burgers. Smoked cheese, grilled onions and a special sauce make them out-of-the-ordinary.

—**CHRISTIE GARDINER** PLEASANT GROVE, UTAH

PREP: 30 MIN. + MARINATING   **GRILL:** 15 MIN.
MAKES: 4 SERVINGS

- ½ cup dry bread crumbs
- 2 teaspoons onion salt
- 2 teaspoons brown sugar
- 1 egg, lightly beaten
- 1 pound ground beef
- 1¼ cups barbecue sauce

SAUCE
- ½ cup mayonnaise
- ½ cup barbecue sauce
- 1 teaspoon brown sugar

ONION TOPPING
- 2 tablespoons butter
- ¼ cup honey
- 2 large sweet onions, thinly sliced
- 4 slices smoked cheddar cheese
- 4 hamburger buns, split

1. In a large bowl, combine the bread crumbs, onion salt and brown sugar. Add egg. Crumble beef over mixture and mix well. Shape into four patties. Place in a shallow dish; pour barbecue sauce over patties. Cover and refrigerate for 2-4 hours.

2. In a small bowl, combine sauce ingredients; cover and refrigerate until serving. For topping, melt butter in a small skillet. Stir in honey until blended. Add onions; saute for 15-20 minutes or until tender and lightly browned. Remove from the heat and keep warm.

3. Drain and discard barbecue sauce. Grill patties, uncovered, over medium heat or broil 4 in from the heat for 5-7 minutes on each side or until a thermometer reads 160° and juices run clear. Top each with a cheese slice; cook 1 minute longer or until cheese is melted. Serve on buns with sauce and onion topping.

Artichoke Shrimp Linguine

With its hint of garlic and a delicate wine sauce, this seafood sensation will have artichoke lovers asking for seconds. Toss in some sliced olives for added flavor. We round out the menu with rolls and Key lime pie.

—**DANIEL SPENGLER** SEATTLE, WASHINGTON

PREP/TOTAL TIME: 20 MIN.   **MAKES:** 2 SERVINGS

- 4 ounces uncooked linguine
- ½ cup chopped sweet red pepper
- 1½ teaspoons minced garlic
- 1 green onion, chopped
- 2 tablespoons olive oil
- 4½ teaspoons butter
- 12 ounces uncooked medium shrimp, peeled and deveined
- 1 can (14 ounces) water-packed artichoke hearts, rinsed, drained and chopped
- ¼ cup white wine or chicken broth
- 1 tablespoon lemon juice
- ¼ teaspoon salt
- ¼ teaspoon Creole seasoning

1. Cook the linguine according to package directions.

2. Meanwhile, in a large saucepan, saute the red pepper, garlic and onion in oil and butter until vegetables are crisp-tender. Add the shrimp; saute until shrimp turn pink. Stir in the remaining ingredients; heat through. Drain linguine; serve with shrimp mixture.

Editor's Note: *The following spices may be substituted for 1 teaspoon Creole seasoning: ¼ teaspoon each salt, garlic powder and paprika; and a pinch each of dried thyme, ground cumin and cayenne pepper.*

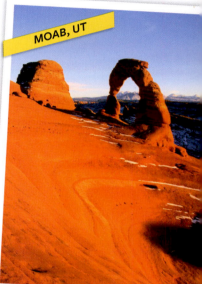

MOAB, UT

Utah's terrain is so spellbinding, the state boasts five national parks. One of them is Arches, where Delicate Arch is found.

Plum Chicken Wraps

Dinner's a wrap with this easy, nutritious recipe loaded with the fruity flavors of pineapple and plum! It makes a handheld sweet-and-sour chicken that's hard to beat.

—JENNIFER MICHALICEK PHOENIX, ARIZONA

PREP/TOTAL TIME: 20 MIN. **MAKES:** 4 SERVINGS

  1 **can (8 ounces) unsweetened crushed pineapple, drained**
 ⅓ **cup plum sauce**
  1 **tablespoon rice vinegar**
 ½ **teaspoon sesame oil**
  2 **cups cubed cooked chicken breast**
 ½ **cup chopped green onions**
 ¼ **cup salted cashews**
  2 **medium fresh plums, sliced**
 12 **Boston or Bibb lettuce leaves**

1. In a large saucepan, combine the pineapple, plum sauce, vinegar and oil. Cook and stir over medium heat for 5 minutes.

2. Stir in the chicken, green onions and cashews; heat through. Remove from the heat; stir in plums. Place ⅓ cup chicken mixture on each lettuce leaf. Fold lettuce over filling.

Cedar Plank Salmon with Blackberry Sauce

Here's my go-to entree for a cookout. The salmon has a rich, grilled taste that's enhanced by the savory blackberry sauce. It's a nice balance of sweet, smoky and spicy.

—**STEPHANIE MATTHEWS** TEMPE, ARIZONA

PREP: 20 MIN. + SOAKING **GRILL:** 15 MIN.
MAKES: 6 SERVINGS (¾ CUP SAUCE)

- 2 **cedar grilling planks**
- 2 **cups fresh blackberries**
- 2 **tablespoons white wine**
- 1 **tablespoon brown sugar**
- 1½ **teaspoons honey**
- 1½ **teaspoons chipotle hot pepper sauce**
- ¼ **teaspoon salt, divided**
- ¼ **teaspoon pepper, divided**
- ¼ **cup finely chopped shallots**
- 1 **garlic clove, minced**
- 6 **salmon fillets (5 ounces each)**

1. Soak the grilling planks in water for at least 1 hour.

2. In a food processor, combine blackberries, wine, brown sugar, honey, hot pepper sauce, ⅛ teaspoon salt and ⅛ teaspoon pepper; cover and process until blended. Strain and discard seeds. Stir the shallots and garlic into the sauce; set aside.

3. Place planks on grill over medium-high heat. Cover and heat until planks create a light to medium smoke and begin to crackle, about

3 minutes (this indicates planks are ready). Turn planks over.

4. Sprinkle salmon with remaining salt and pepper. Place on planks. Grill, covered, over medium heat for 12-15 minutes or until fish flakes easily with a fork. Serve with sauce.

Crab-Stuffed Avocados

We enjoy having this creamy and crunchy salad out on our deck on summer evenings. And it goes together in just minutes flat!

—**GAIL VANGUNDY** PARKER, COLORADO

PREP/TOTAL TIME: 20 MIN. **MAKES:** 2 SERVINGS

- 1 **can (6 ounces) crabmeat, drained, flaked and cartilage removed**
- ½ **cup sliced celery**
- ½ **cup shredded lettuce**
- 3 **tablespoons mayonnaise**
- 1 **teaspoon finely chopped onion**
- ½ **teaspoon lemon juice**
- ⅛ to ¼ **teaspoon seafood seasoning**
- ⅛ **teaspoon paprika**
- 1 **medium ripe avocado, halved and pitted**

1. In a large bowl, combine the first eight ingredients. Spoon onto the avocado halves. Serve immediately.

SEATTLE, WA

If you're at the Pike Place Fish Market, watch your head! Seafood goes flying as wader-clad fishmongers arrange the catch of the day. Be quick if you want to buy—the fresh fish goes fast.

> **" To the best of my knowledge, this recipe came from the early days in Colorado... or from the cattle trails leading into Colorado. It is a cowboy recipe and its ingredients can be varied, depending on what's available. "**
>
> **—ED JONES**
> BAKER CITY, OREGON

Chuck Wagon Chow

PREP: 20 MIN. **BAKE:** 55 MIN. **MAKES:** 6-8 SERVINGS

- ½ cup all-purpose flour
- 1 teaspoon salt
- ¼ teaspoon pepper
- 2 pounds beef top round steak (½ inch thick), cut into ½-inch cubes
- ¼ cup canola oil
- 1 medium onion, chopped
- 1 green pepper, chopped
- 1 garlic clove, minced
- 1 tablespoon chili powder
- 1 teaspoon dried oregano
- 1 can (16 ounces) kidney beans, juice drained and reserved
- 1 can (16 ounces) whole kernel corn, juice drained and reserved

1. Combine flour, salt and pepper in a large plastic bag. Place beef cubes in bag and shake to coat evenly.

2. In a Dutch oven or large skillet, brown beef in oil. Add the onion, green pepper and garlic; cook until peppers are crisp-tender. Stir in the chili powder, oregano and reserved vegetable liquid; bring to a boil. Reduce heat and simmer, covered, until the meat is tender, about 45-50 minutes. Stir in the beans and corn; simmer for 10 minutes or until heated through.

Chipotle-Sparked Mustard Salmon

This delicious salmon packs huge flavors— chipotle, stone-ground mustard and horseradish come together in a fantastic blend that's anything but boring.

—HELEN CONWELL PORTLAND, OREGON

PREP/TOTAL TIME: 25 MIN. **MAKES:** 6 SERVINGS

- 6 salmon fillets (4 ounces each)
- ¼ cup reduced-fat mayonnaise
- ¼ cup prepared horseradish
- ¼ cup stone-ground mustard
- ¼ teaspoon lemon-pepper seasoning
- 1 teaspoon minced chipotle pepper in adobo sauce
- 1 teaspoon snipped fresh dill

1. Place salmon in a foil-lined 15x10x1-in. baking pan. Combine the mayonnaise, horseradish, mustard, lemon-pepper and chipotle pepper; spread over fillets.

2. Bake at 350° for 15-20 minutes or until fish flakes easily with a fork. Sprinkle with dill.

Montana Wildfire Chili

Here's a thick and chunky chili with some real kick to it! I like to top it with shredded cheddar and then serve it with a side of corn bread.

—DONNA EVARO CASPER, WYOMING

PREP: 30 MIN. **COOK:** 5 HOURS
MAKES: 8 SERVINGS (2½ QUARTS)

- 2 **pounds ground beef**
- 1 **large sweet onion, chopped**
- 1 **medium sweet red pepper, finely chopped**
- 1 **medium sweet yellow pepper, finely chopped**
- 2 **cans (16 ounces each) chili beans, undrained**
- 2 **cans (14½ ounces each) stewed tomatoes, drained**
- ½ **cup tomato juice**
- 2 **jalapeno peppers, seeded and minced**
- 2 **garlic cloves, minced**
- 2 **teaspoons ground cumin**
- 2 **teaspoons chili powder**
- 1 **teaspoon salt**
- 1 **teaspoon cayenne pepper**

1. In a large skillet, cook the beef, onion and peppers over medium heat until the meat is no longer pink; drain.

2. Transfer to a 4- or 5-qt. slow cooker. Stir in the beans, tomatoes, tomato juice, jalapenos, garlic, cumin, chili powder, salt and cayenne. Cover and cook on low for 5-6 hours or until heated through.

Editor's Note: *Wear disposable gloves when cutting hot peppers; the oils can burn skin. Avoid touching your face.*

Herbed Artichoke Cheese Tortellini

Vegetarians, as well as meat-and-potato lovers, will enjoy this hearty meatless recipe featuring tomatoes, black olives and artichoke hearts tossed with tender cheese tortellini.

—KAREN ANZELC PEORIA, ARIZONA

PREP/TOTAL TIME: 30 MIN. **MAKES:** 8 SERVINGS

- 2 **cans (14½ ounces each) Italian diced tomatoes**
- 2 **jars (6½ ounces each) marinated quartered artichoke hearts**
- 2 **packages (9 ounces each) refrigerated cheese tortellini**
- 2 **cups chopped onions**
- ½ **cup minced fresh parsley**
- 2 **to 4 tablespoons minced fresh or 2 to 4 teaspoons dried basil**
- 2 **teaspoons minced garlic**
- ½ **teaspoon dried oregano**
- ⅛ **teaspoon crushed red pepper flakes**
- ½ **cup olive oil**
- 1 **can (2¼ ounces) sliced ripe olives, drained**
- ½ **teaspoon salt**
- ¼ **cup shredded Parmesan cheese**

1. Drain tomatoes, reserving ⅔ cup juice; set aside. Drain artichokes, reserving ¾ cup liquid; chop and set aside.

2. Cook tortellini according to the package directions. Meanwhile, in a large skillet, saute the onions, parsley, basil, garlic, oregano and pepper flakes in oil for 4-5 minutes or until onions are tender. Add the reserved tomatoes, tomato juice and artichoke liquid.

3. Bring to a boil. Reduce the heat; simmer, uncovered, for 10-12 minutes or until slightly thickened. Drain the tortellini; add to tomato mixture. Stir in the olives, salt and reserved artichokes; heat through. Sprinkle with the Parmesan cheese.

◀● dishing about food

It's been said that chili recipes became popular because beans and other ingredients helped turn a dish with just a little meat into a hearty, filling meal.

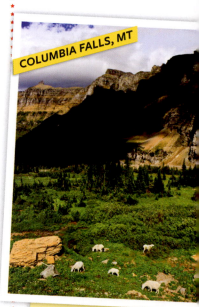

COLUMBIA FALLS, MT

Keep your eyes peeled for families of mountain goats while visiting majestic Glacier National Park. They graze freely!

> " Thai and Vietnamese restaurants serve curried shrimp, which I enjoy a lot. So I decided to try my hand at making it at home. What a success! Everyone who tries my version asks for the recipe. "
>
> **—NINETTE HOLBROOK**
> ORLANDO, FLORIDA

Thai Curry with Shrimp & Coconut

PREP: 30 MIN. **COOK:** 15 MIN. **MAKES:** 4 SERVINGS

- ¾ **cup coconut milk**
- ¾ **cup cream of coconut**
- ¼ **cup creamy peanut butter**
- 2 **tablespoons red curry paste**
- 1½ **teaspoons garlic salt**
- ½ **teaspoon crushed red pepper flakes**
- 2 **tablespoons olive oil, divided**
- 1 **medium onion, cut into ½-in. pieces**
- 1 **medium sweet red pepper, cut into ½-in. pieces**
- 3 **garlic cloves, thinly sliced**
- 1 **pound uncooked medium shrimp, peeled and deveined**
- ¼ **teaspoon salt**
- ¼ **teaspoon pepper**
  Hot cooked rice
- ¾ **cup salted peanuts**
- ⅓ **cup flaked coconut, toasted**

1. In a small saucepan, whisk the first six ingredients until blended. Bring to a boil over medium heat, stirring occasionally; remove from heat.

2. In a large skillet, heat 1 tablespoon oil over medium-high heat. Add onion and red pepper; cook and stir 4-5 minutes or until onion is golden brown. Add garlic; cook 1 minute longer. Remove from pan.

3. In the same skillet, heat remaining oil over medium-high heat. Add shrimp; stir-fry 3-4 minutes or until shrimp turn pink. Sprinkle with salt and pepper. Add onion and sauce mixtures; heat through, stirring occasionally. Serve with the rice; sprinkle with the peanuts and coconut.

Editor's Note: *To toast coconut, spread in a 15x10x1-in. baking pan. Bake at 350° for 5-10 minutes or until golden brown, stirring frequently.*

Rabanadas (Portuguese French Toast)

I find this dish a comforting reminder of my childhood. The creamy custard center contrasts so deliciously with the cinnamon sugar crust.

—**ANA PAULA CIOFFI** HAYWARD, CALIFORNIA

PREP: 15 MIN. **COOK:** 5 MIN./BATCH **MAKES:** 6 SERVINGS

- 1 **cup sugar**
- 2 **tablespoons ground cinnamon**
- 4 **eggs**
- 2 **cups 2% milk**
- 1 **loaf (8 ounces) French bread, cut into 1-inch slices**
- **Oil for frying**

1. In a small bowl, mix sugar and cinnamon until blended. In a large shallow dish, whisk eggs and milk. Dip bread in egg mixture, soaking lightly.

2. In an electric skillet, heat 1 in. of oil to 350°. Working with a few slices at a time, remove bread from egg mixture, allowing excess to drain, and fry 2-3 minutes on each side or until golden brown. Drain on paper towels.

3. Dip warm rabanadas in cinnamon-sugar to coat all sides. Serve warm or at room temperature.

OAKLAND, CA

Located across the Bay from San Francisco, Oakland has one of the largest Portuguese-American populations in the country. The City Center is enjoying a major revitalization.

> **" This lamb recipe would be perfect for Easter or any other festive gathering. I created it from a combination of several others. It's the only lamb recipe my daughter would eat when she was young. "**
>
> **—PATRICIA CRANDALL**
> INCHELIUM, WASHINGTON

Lemon-Herb Leg of Lamb

PREP: 10 MIN. + MARINATING
BAKE: 1¾ HOURS + STANDING **MAKES:** 12 SERVINGS

2	teaspoons lemon juice
1½	teaspoons grated lemon peel
1	teaspoon garlic salt
1	teaspoon dried oregano
1	teaspoon dried thyme
1	teaspoon dried rosemary, crushed
1	teaspoon ground mustard
1	boneless leg of lamb (4 pounds), rolled and tied

1. In a small bowl, combine the first seven ingredients. Rub over leg of lamb. Cover and refrigerate overnight.

2. Place lamb on a rack in a shallow roasting pan. Bake, uncovered, at 325° for 1¾ to 2¼ hours or until meat reaches desired doneness (for medium-rare, a thermometer should read 145°; medium, 160°; well-done, 170°). Let stand for 15 minutes before slicing.

Coconut Curry Chicken

My husband and I love this yummy dish! It's a breeze to prepare in the slow cooker, and it tastes just like a meal you'd have at your favorite Indian or Thai restaurant.

—ANDI KAUFFMAN BEAVERCREEK, OREGON

PREP: 20 MIN. **COOK:** 5 HOURS **MAKES:** 4 SERVINGS

2	medium potatoes, peeled and cubed
1	small onion, chopped
4	boneless skinless chicken breast halves (4 ounces each)
1	cup light coconut milk
4	teaspoons curry powder
1	garlic clove, minced
1	teaspoon reduced-sodium chicken bouillon granules
¼	teaspoon salt
¼	teaspoon pepper
2	cups hot cooked rice
¼	cup thinly sliced green onions
	Raisins, flaked coconut and chopped unsalted peanuts, optional

1. Place potatoes and onion in a 3- or 4-qt. slow cooker. In a large nonstick skillet coated with cooking spray, brown the chicken on both sides.

2. Transfer to slow cooker. In a small bowl, combine the coconut milk, curry, garlic, bouillon, salt and pepper; pour over chicken. Cover and cook on low for 5-6 hours or until meat is tender.

3. Serve chicken and sauce with rice; sprinkle with green onions. Garnish with raisins, coconut and peanuts if desired.

Buffalo Steak Salad

We raise buffalo on our ranch, so I cook plenty of buffalo steak as well as other cuts. During the warmer months, this cool salad is a refreshing change of pace from the heavier meals I feed my crew at other times of the year. The meat is tender, and the dressing is mouthwatering.

—**BURT GUENIN** CHAPPELL, NEBRASKA

PREP: 10 MIN. + CHILLING **GRILL:** 15 MIN.
MAKES: 4 SERVINGS

- ⅓ cup olive oil
- 2 tablespoons red wine vinegar
- 1 tablespoon lemon juice
- 1 garlic clove, minced
- ½ teaspoon salt
- ⅛ teaspoon pepper
  Dash Worcestershire sauce
- ½ cup crumbled blue cheese
- 2 buffalo sirloin or beef ribeye steaks (about 8 ounces each)
- 6 cups torn salad greens
- 1 medium tomato, thinly sliced
- 1 small carrot, thinly sliced
- ½ cup thinly sliced onion
- ¼ cup sliced pimiento-stuffed olives

1. In a small bowl, combine the first seven ingredients; mix well. Stir in the blue cheese. Cover and refrigerate.

2. Grill steaks, uncovered, over medium-hot heat for 6-10 minutes on each side or until meat reaches desired doneness (for medium-rare, a thermometer should read 145°; medium, 160°; well-done, 170°). Thinly slice meat.

3. On a serving platter or individual salad plates, arrange lettuce, tomato, carrot, onion and olives. Top with steak and dressing.

Chipotle Pomegranate Pulled Pork

Once I was making pulled pork and wanted to kick it up a bit. Pomegranate jelly made the perfect addition to this tender entree!

—**TATIANA KUSHNIR** MONTARA, CALIFORNIA

PREP: 10 MIN. **COOK:** 8½ HOURS
MAKES: 10 SERVINGS

- 1 boneless pork shoulder butt roast (3 pounds)
- 2 tablespoons steak seasoning
- ½ cup water
- 1 cup pomegranate or red currant jelly
- 3 tablespoons minced chipotle peppers in adobo sauce
- 10 kaiser rolls, split

1. Cut roast in half. Place in a 5-qt. slow cooker; sprinkle with steak seasoning. Add water. Cover and cook on low for 8-10 hours or until meat is tender.

2. In a small saucepan, combine jelly and peppers. Cook over medium heat for 5 minutes or until heated through. Remove the meat from slow cooker; discard cooking liquid. Shred pork with two forks.

3. Return to the slow cooker; top with jelly mixture. Cover and cook on low for 30 minutes or until heated through. Spoon about ⅔ cup of meat onto each roll.

Editor's Note: *This recipe was tested with McCormick's Montreal Steak Seasoning. Look for it in the spice aisle.*

WYOMING

Emblazoned on Wyoming's flag, the American bison is the state's official mammal. Herds once roamed the Great Plains, but due to overhunting, the best places to see them now are national parks such as Yellowstone and the Grand Tetons.

> Colorado sheep ranchers raise a great supply of lamb. In this recipe, I take our homegrown product and add a dash of Tex-Mex flair.

—KAREN GORMAN
GUNNISON, COLORADO

Colorado Lamb Chili

PREP: 20 MIN. **COOK:** 1½ HOURS **MAKES:** 6 SERVINGS (2¼ QUARTS)

- 1 **pound lamb stew meat, cut into 1-inch pieces**
- 2 **tablespoons canola oil, divided**
- 1 **large onion, chopped**
- 1 **large sweet yellow pepper, chopped**
- 4 **garlic cloves, minced**
- 1 **can (30 ounces) black beans, rinsed and drained**
- 1 **can (28 ounces) diced tomatoes, undrained**
- 1 **can (14½ ounces) reduced-sodium beef broth**
- 1 **tablespoon dried oregano**
- 1 **tablespoon chili powder**
- 1 **tablespoon brown sugar**
- 2 **teaspoons Worcestershire sauce**
- 1 **teaspoon ground cumin**
- ½ **teaspoon fennel seed, crushed**
  Sliced green onions, chopped tomatoes and corn chips, optional

1. In a Dutch oven, brown lamb in 1 tablespoon oil. Remove and set aside.

2. In the same pan, saute onion and pepper in remaining oil until tender. Add garlic; cook 1 minute longer. Add the beans, tomatoes, broth, oregano, chili powder, brown sugar, Worcestershire sauce, cumin and fennel. Return lamb to the pan.

3. Bring to a boil. Reduce heat; cover and simmer for 1¼ to 1½ hours or until lamb is tender. Garnish each serving with green onions, tomatoes and corn chips if desired.

Fish Tacos with Avocado Sauce

I grew up in Alaska, where halibut is readily available for recipes like this. A good friend who normally doesn't eat fish went back for a fourth helping of these tacos. They're that good!

—CORTNEY CLAESON SPOKANE, WASHINGTON

PREP: 30 MIN. + MARINATING **BROIL:** 10 MIN. **MAKES:** 4 SERVINGS

- ¼ cup lemon juice
- 1 tablespoon olive oil
- 3 garlic cloves, minced
- 1 pound halibut or tilapia fillets

SAUCE
- 2 medium ripe avocados, divided
- ¼ cup fat-free sour cream
- ¼ cup reduced-fat mayonnaise
- 1 tablespoon lime juice
- 1 garlic clove, minced
- 1 teaspoon dill weed
- ¼ teaspoon ground cumin
- ¼ teaspoon dried oregano
- ¼ teaspoon dried parsley flakes
  Dash cayenne pepper

SALSA
- 1 medium tomato, seeded and chopped
- 1 small red onion, chopped
- 4½ teaspoons chopped seeded jalapeno pepper
- 1 tablespoon minced fresh cilantro
- 1½ teaspoons lime juice
- 1 garlic clove, minced
- ⅛ teaspoon salt

TACOS
- 8 flour tortillas (6 inches)
- 2 cups shredded cabbage

1. In a large resealable plastic bag, combine lemon juice, oil and garlic. Add halibut; seal bag and turn to coat. Refrigerate for 30 minutes.

2. For sauce and salsa, peel and cube avocados. In a small bowl, mash ¼ cup avocado. Stir in the remaining sauce ingredients. Place remaining avocado in a small bowl; stir in the remaining salsa ingredients. Refrigerate sauce and salsa until serving.

3. Drain fish and discard marinade. Broil halibut 4-6 in. from the heat for 8-10 minutes or until fish flakes easily with a fork. Place fish on the center of each tortilla. Top each with ¼ cup cabbage, about 1 tablespoon sauce and ¼ cup salsa.

Editor's Note: *Wear disposable gloves when cutting hot peppers; the oils can burn skin. Avoid touching your face.*

◄► dishing about food

Fish tacos were first conceived in Baja California about 50 years ago. Deep-fried mild white fish served in a corn tortilla with shredded cabbage, sauce and a splash of lime was standard fare for surfers. As the dish traveled north and east, it was modified into many different recipes.

WAIKIKI, HI

Even though he was born more than a century ago, Duke Kahanamoku is still revered in Hawaii and beyond. In fact, a bronze statue of the swimming and surfing sensation stands on Waikiki Beach.

Company Swordfish

My fantastic entree is so easy to prepare! We're not big fish eaters in my family, but believe me, the plates are always scraped clean when this is on the table!

—**CALLIE BERGER** DIAMOND SPRINGS, CALIFORNIA

PREP: 10 MIN. **BAKE:** 25 MIN. **MAKES:** 4 SERVINGS

- 4 **swordfish or halibut steaks (7 ounces each)**
- 2 **jars (7½ ounces each) marinated artichoke hearts, drained and chopped**
- ½ **cup oil-packed sun-dried tomatoes, drained and chopped**
- 4 **shallots, chopped**
- 2 **tablespoons butter, melted**
- 1 **teaspoon lemon juice**

1. Place fish in a greased 13x9-in. baking dish. In a small bowl, combine the artichokes, tomatoes and shallots; spread over fish. Drizzle with butter and lemon juice.

2. Cover and bake at 425° for 15 minutes. Uncover; bake 6-8 minutes longer or until fish just turns opaque.

Cheese-Topped Swordfish: *Omit topping. Combine ¼ cup melted butter and 1 cup each shredded Parmesan cheese and mayonnaise. Spread a fourth of the mixture over each steak. Bake, uncovered, for 15-20 minutes.*

Pan-Fried Venison Steak

Growing up, this recipe was a family favorite whenever we had deer meat on hand. I loved it then, and now my children do, too!

—GAYLEEN GROTE BATTLEVIEW, NORTH DAKOTA

PREP/TOTAL TIME: 25 MIN. **MAKES:** 4 SERVINGS

- 1 pound venison or beef tenderloin, cut into ½-inch slices
- 2 cups crushed saltines
- 2 eggs
- ¾ cup milk
- 1 teaspoon salt
- ½ teaspoon pepper
- 5 tablespoons canola oil

1. Flatten venison to ¼-in. thickness. Place saltines in a shallow bowl. In another shallow bowl, whisk the eggs, milk, salt and pepper. Coat venison with saltines, then dip in egg mixture and coat a second time with saltines.

2. In a large skillet over medium heat, cook venison in oil in batches for 2-3 minutes on a side or until meat reaches desired doneness (for medium-rare, a thermometer should read 145°; medium, 160°; well-done, 170°).

Northwest Salmon Chowder

PREP: 10 MIN. **COOK:** 1 HOUR
MAKES: 8 SERVINGS (2 QUARTS)

- ½ cup each chopped celery, onion and green pepper
- 1 garlic clove, minced
- 3 tablespoons butter
- 1 can (14½ ounces) chicken broth
- 1 cup uncooked diced peeled potatoes
- 1 cup shredded carrots
- 1½ teaspoons salt
- ½ teaspoon pepper
- ¼ to ¾ teaspoon dill weed
- 1 can (14¾ ounces) cream-style corn
- 2 cups half-and-half cream
- 1¾ to 2 cups fully cooked salmon chunks or 1 can (14¾ ounces) salmon, drained, flaked, bones and skin removed

1. In a large saucepan, saute celery, onion, green pepper and garlic in butter until the vegetables are tender. Add broth, potatoes, carrots, salt, pepper and dill; bring to a boil.

2. Reduce heat; cover and simmer for 40 minutes or until vegetables are nearly tender. Stir in corn, cream and salmon. Simmer 15 minutes or until heated through.

> "I've lived on a farm in the Yakima Valley all my life. I have a big garden, and by the end of fall, my cellar shelves are filled with canned fruits and vegetables. This recipe uses some of the vegetables I grow...along with the delicious fresh salmon that is so plentiful here."

—JOSEPHINE PARTON
GRANGER, WASHINGTON

Vegetable Pad Thai

Classic flavors of Thailand abound in this fragrant and flavorful dish featuring peanuts, tofu and noodles. Tofu adds protein to this satisfying entree.

—**SARA LANDRY** BROOKLINE, MASSACHUSETTS

PREP: 25 MIN. **COOK:** 15 MIN. **MAKES:** 6 SERVINGS

- 1 **package (12 ounces) whole wheat fettuccine**
- ¼ **cup rice vinegar**
- 3 **tablespoons reduced-sodium soy sauce**
- 2 **tablespoons brown sugar**
- 2 **tablespoons fish sauce or additional reduced-sodium soy sauce**
- 1 **tablespoon lime juice**
  Dash Louisiana-style hot sauce
- 1 **package (12 ounces) extra-firm tofu, drained and cut into ½-inch cubes**
- 3 **teaspoons canola oil, divided**
- 2 **medium carrots, grated**
- 2 **cups fresh snow peas, halved**
- 3 **garlic cloves, minced**
- 2 **eggs, lightly beaten**
- 2 **cups bean sprouts**
- 3 **green onions, chopped**
- ½ **cup minced fresh cilantro**
- ¼ **cup unsalted peanuts, chopped**

1. Cook fettuccine according to package directions. Meanwhile, in a small bowl, combine the vinegar, soy sauce, brown sugar, fish sauce, lime juice and hot sauce until smooth; set aside.

2. In a large skillet or wok, stir-fry tofu in 2 teaspoons oil until golden brown. Remove and keep warm. Stir-fry carrots and snow peas in remaining oil for 1-2 minutes. Add garlic, cook 1 minute longer or until vegetables are crisp-tender. Add eggs; cook and stir until set.

3. Drain pasta; add to vegetable mixture. Stir vinegar mixture and add to the skillet. Bring to a boil. Add tofu, bean sprouts and onions; heat through. Sprinkle with cilantro and peanuts.

Dan's Peppery London Broil

I was bored making the usual London broil, so I got a little creative and sparked up the flavor.

—**DAN WRIGHT** SAN JOSE, CALIFORNIA

PREP: 5 MIN. + MARINATING **GRILL:** 10 MIN.
MAKES: 2 SERVINGS

- 1 **beef flank steak (about ¾ pound)**
- 1 **garlic clove, minced**
- ½ **teaspoon seasoned salt**
- ⅛ **teaspoon crushed red pepper flakes**
- ¼ **cup Worcestershire sauce**

1. With a meat fork, poke holes in both sides of meat. Make a paste of garlic, seasoned salt and red pepper flakes; rub over both sides of meat. Place steak in a resealable gallon-size plastic bag. Add Worcestershire sauce and seal bag. Refrigerate for at least 4 hours, turning once.

2. Drain and discard marinade. Grill, uncovered, over hot heat or broil 4 in. from the heat for 4-5 minutes on each side or until meat reaches desired doneness (for medium-rare a thermometer should read 145°; medium, 160°; well-done, 170°). To serve, thinly slice across the grain.

Crab Egg Foo Yung

Enjoy a classic Chinese takeout without leaving your home! This makes a quick dinner and is as delicious as what you would get in any restaurant.

—BEVERLY PRESTON FOND DU LAC, WISCONSIN

PREP/TOTAL TIME: 30 MIN. **MAKES:** 4 SERVINGS

- 4 teaspoons cornstarch
- 2 teaspoons sugar
- 1 can (14½ ounces) chicken broth
- 2 tablespoons soy sauce
- 1 tablespoon white vinegar

EGG FOO YONG

- 2 tablespoons all-purpose flour
- 4 eggs
- 1 can (14 ounces) bean sprouts, drained
- 2 cans (6 ounces each) lump crabmeat, drained
- ⅓ cup thinly sliced green onions
- ⅛ teaspoon garlic powder
- ⅛ teaspoon pepper
- 3 tablespoons canola oil

1. In a small saucepan, combine cornstarch and sugar. Stir in the broth, soy sauce and vinegar until smooth. Bring to a boil; cook and stir for 2 minutes or until thickened. Set aside and keep warm.

2. In a large bowl, whisk flour and eggs until smooth. Stir in the bean sprouts, crab, onions, garlic powder and pepper. In a large skillet, heat oil. Drop crab mixture by ⅓ cupfuls into oil. Cook until for 2 minutes on each side or until golden brown. Serve with sauce.

Garlicky Herbed Shrimp

I love shrimp. Love garlic. Love herbs. Cook 'em up in butter and what could be better?

—DAVE LEVIN VAN NUYS, CALIFORNIA

PREP/TOTAL TIME: 25 MIN. **MAKES:** ABOUT 3 DOZEN

- 2 pounds uncooked jumbo shrimp, peeled and deveined
- 5 garlic cloves, minced
- 2 green onions, chopped
- ½ teaspoon garlic powder
- ½ teaspoon ground mustard
- ¼ teaspoon seasoned salt
- ¼ teaspoon crushed red pepper flakes
- ⅛ teaspoon pepper
- ½ cup butter, divided
- ¼ cup lemon juice
- 2 tablespoons minced fresh parsley
- 1 tablespoon minced fresh tarragon

1. In a large bowl, combine the first eight ingredients; toss to combine. In a large skillet, heat ¼ cup butter over medium-high heat. Add half of the shrimp mixture; cook and stir for 4-5 minutes or until shrimp turns pink. Transfer to a clean bowl.

2. Repeat with remaining butter and shrimp mixture. Return cooked shrimp to pan. Stir in lemon juice; heat through. Stir in herbs.

◀◆ dishing about food

This dish is an Americanized version of a Shanghai egg white omelet called "foo yung egg slices." In St. Louis, you can order a St. Paul sandwich, which is deep-fried egg foo yung on white bread with mayonnaise, lettuce, tomato and a pickle.

SAN FRANCISCO, CA

America's first Chinatown, San Francisco's is also one of the largest. People converge here for daily living and sightseeing, whether they're at an open-air market, a festival or one of the famous dim sum restaurants.

SEATTLE, WA

Put your mind at peace in the Seattle Japanese Garden, part of the Washington Park Arboretum. The garden's caretakers use age-old methods to preserve the landscape's authenticity and beauty.

Tonkatsu

My dear friend Junie Obi shared the recipe for these breaded pork cutlets years ago. Her mom owned a food stand and served this traditional dish.

—**YUKO SHIBATA** MONTEREY PARK, CALIFORNIA

PREP: 20 MIN. **COOK:** 5 MIN. **MAKES:** 4 SERVINGS

- 4 boneless pork loin chops (6 ounces each)
- 3 tablespoons all-purpose flour
- 1 tablespoon garlic salt
- 2 eggs
- 2 cups panko (Japanese) bread crumbs
  Oil for deep-fat frying

SAUCE
- ¼ cup ketchup
- 2 tablespoons Worcestershire sauce
- 1 tablespoon sugar
- 1 tablespoon reduced-sodium soy sauce
- 2 teaspoons prepared hot mustard

1. Flatten pork chops to ¼-in. thickness. In a shallow bowl, combine flour and garlic salt. In a separate shallow bowl, whisk eggs. Place bread crumbs in a third bowl. Coat pork with flour mixture, then dip in eggs and coat in crumbs.

2. In an electric skillet, heat ¼ in. of oil to 375°. Fry pork chops for 2-3 minutes on each side or until crisp and juices run clear. Drain on paper towels.

3. Meanwhile, in a small bowl, combine the sauce ingredients; serve with pork.

Artichoke Chicken

This recipe has evolved through generations to satisfy my family's fondness for artichokes. I enjoy preparing it for casual suppers as well as special-occasion dinners.

—**ROBERTA GREEN** HEMET, CALIFORNIA

PREP: 10 MIN. **BAKE:** 30 MIN. **MAKES:** 8 SERVINGS

- 2 cans (14 ounces each) water-packed artichoke hearts, rinsed, drained and quartered
- 2 tablespoons olive oil
- 3 garlic cloves, minced
- 2⅔ cups cubed cooked chicken
- 2 cans (10¾ ounces each) condensed cream of chicken soup, undiluted
- 1 cup mayonnaise
- 1 teaspoon lemon juice
- ½ teaspoon curry powder
- 1½ cups (6 ounces) shredded cheddar cheese
- 1 cup seasoned bread crumbs
- ¼ cup grated Parmesan cheese
- 2 tablespoons butter, melted

1. In a small bowl, combine the artichokes, oil and garlic. Transfer to a greased 2½-qt. baking dish. Top with chicken. Combine the soup, mayonnaise, lemon juice and curry; pour over the chicken. Sprinkle with cheddar cheese. Combine the bread crumbs, cheese and butter; sprinkle over top.

2. Bake, uncovered, at 350° for 30-35 minutes or until bubbly.

◄ ◆ dishing about food

African immigration to the U.S. exploded after 1960. Most of these newcomers settled in California, New York, Texas and Virginia, bringing with them the cooking traditions and techniques of another continent.

West African Chicken Stew

I really love African flavors, but you don't really encounter them much in America. Here the combination of native African ingredients, all of which are readily accessible to Americans, really transports you to a new culinary place!

—MICHAEL COHEN LOS ANGELES, CALIFORNIA

PREP: 40 MIN. **COOK:** 15 MIN. **MAKES:** 8 SERVINGS (2½ QUARTS)

- 1 pound boneless skinless chicken breasts, cut into 1-inch cubes
- ½ teaspoon salt
- ¼ teaspoon pepper
- 3 teaspoons canola oil, divided
- 1 medium onion, thinly sliced
- 6 garlic cloves, minced
- 2 tablespoons minced fresh gingerroot
- 2 cans (15½ ounces each) black-eyed peas, rinsed and drained
- 1 can (28 ounces) crushed tomatoes
- 1 large sweet potato, peeled and cut into 1-inch cubes
- 1 cup reduced-sodium chicken broth
- ¼ cup creamy peanut butter
- 1½ teaspoons minced fresh thyme or ½ teaspoon dried thyme, divided
- ¼ teaspoon cayenne pepper
  Hot cooked brown rice, optional

1. Sprinkle chicken with salt and pepper. In a Dutch oven, cook chicken over medium heat in 2 teaspoons oil for 4-6 minutes or until no longer pink; remove and keep warm. In the same pan, saute the onion in remaining oil until tender. Add the garlic and ginger; cook 1 minute longer.

2. Stir in the peas, tomatoes, sweet potato, broth, peanut butter, 1¼ teaspoons thyme and cayenne. Bring to a boil. Reduce heat; cover and simmer for 15-20 minutes or until potato is tender. Add chicken; heat through. Serve with rice if desired. Sprinkle with remaining thyme.

> **Fennel adds to the flavor of this wonderful chicken dish, along with lemon, capers, wine, spices and a bit of bacon. Serve with a colorful salad or veggie for a special meal.**
>
> **—REBECCA HUNT**
> SANTA PAULA, CALIFORNIA

Aromatic Fennel Chicken

PREP: 35 MIN. **COOK:** 50 MIN. **MAKES:** 6 SERVINGS

- 4 bacon strips, chopped
- 1 broiler/fryer chicken (3½ to 4 pounds), cut up, skin removed
- ½ teaspoon salt
- ½ teaspoon pepper
- 2 fennel bulbs, sliced
- 2 medium onions, chopped
- 6 garlic cloves, minced
- ¾ cup white wine or reduced-sodium chicken broth
- ¼ cup lemon juice
- 1 tablespoon grated lemon peel
- 2 bay leaves
- 2 teaspoons dried thyme
  Pinch cayenne pepper
- 3 tablespoons capers, drained

1. In a large nonstick skillet, cook bacon over medium heat until crisp. Using a slotted spoon, remove bacon to paper towels; drain, reserving 1 tablespoon drippings.

2. Sprinkle the chicken with salt and pepper. Brown the chicken on all sides in reserved drippings; remove and keep warm. Add the fennel and onions to the pan; cook and stir for 3-4 minutes or until onions are tender. Add garlic; cook 1 minute longer.

3. Stir in the wine, lemon juice and peel, bay leaves, thyme and cayenne. Return chicken to the pan. Bring to a boil. Reduce heat; cover and simmer for 20-25 minutes or until the chicken juices run clear. Remove the chicken and keep warm.

4. Cook the fennel mixture, uncovered, for 8-10 minutes or until slightly thickened, stirring occasionally. Stir in the capers and reserved bacon. Discard bay leaves. Serve fennel mixture with chicken.

Sirloin Roast with Gravy

This recipe is perfect for my husband, who is a meat-and-potatoes kind of guy. The peppery, fork-tender roast combined with the rich gravy creates a tasty centerpiece for any meal.

—RITA CLARK MONUMENT, COLORADO

PREP: 15 MIN. **COOK:** 5½ HOURS **MAKES:** 10 SERVINGS

- 1 beef sirloin tip roast (3 pounds)
- 1 to 2 tablespoons coarsely ground pepper
- 1½ teaspoons minced garlic
- ¼ cup reduced-sodium soy sauce
- 3 tablespoons balsamic vinegar
- 1 tablespoon Worcestershire sauce
- 2 teaspoons ground mustard
- 2 tablespoons cornstarch
- ¼ cup cold water

1. Rub roast with pepper and garlic; cut in half and place in a 3-qt. slow cooker. Combine the soy sauce, vinegar, Worcestershire sauce and mustard; pour over beef. Cover and cook on low for 5½ to 6 hours or until the meat is tender.

2. Remove roast and keep warm. Strain cooking juices into a small saucepan; skim fat. Combine cornstarch and water until smooth; gradually stir into cooking juices. Bring to a boil; cook and stir for 2 minutes or until thickened. Serve with beef.

Baked Halibut

I got this easy, delicious recipe from Sandy Schroth of the Puffin Bed & Breakfast in Gustavus, Alaska.

—MRS. EDWARD MAHNKE HOUSTON, TEXAS

PREP: 5 MIN. **BAKE:** 30 MIN. **MAKES:** 6 SERVINGS

- 3 pounds halibut steaks (1 inch thick)
- 1 cup (8 ounces) sour cream
- ½ cup grated Parmesan cheese
- ¼ cup butter, softened
- ½ teaspoon dill weed
- ½ teaspoon salt
- ¼ teaspoon pepper
  Paprika

1. Place halibut in a greased 13x9-in. baking dish. Combine sour cream, Parmesan cheese, butter, dill, salt and pepper; spoon over halibut.

2. Cover and bake at 375° for 20 minutes. Uncover; sprinkle with paprika. Bake for 10-15 minutes or until fish flakes easily with a fork.

Spicy Sesame Shrimp & Noodle Salad

One of our favorite Korean dishes has always been the Cold Sesame Noodles that my Mom made. She served it at room temperature, but I like it warm. This shrimp-noodle salad recipe was a result of memories of my mom's Korean background, and my love of fresh vegetables.

—KAREN BOWLDEN BOISE, IDAHO

PREP: 20 MIN. **COOK:** 15 MIN. **MAKES:** 4 SERVINGS

- 6 ounces uncooked multigrain spaghetti

SAUCE
- 3 tablespoons sesame seeds, toasted
- 3 tablespoons sesame oil
- 3 tablespoons reduced-sodium soy sauce
- 6 garlic cloves, minced
- 2 tablespoons rice vinegar
- 2 tablespoons honey
- 1 tablespoon Sriracha Asian hot chili sauce or 1½ teaspoons hot pepper sauce
- ½ teaspoon salt
- ½ teaspoon pepper

SHRIMP & VEGETABLES
- 2 teaspoons canola oil
- ½ pound uncooked medium shrimp, peeled and deveined
- 1½ cups coleslaw mix
- ¾ cup julienned carrots
- 1 celery rib, thinly sliced
- 1 small sweet red pepper, julienned
- ½ cup sliced water chestnuts
- 2 green onions, chopped

1. Cook spaghetti according to the package directions. In a small bowl, mix the sauce ingredients.

2. In a large skillet, heat oil over medium-high heat. Add shrimp; stir-fry 2-3 minutes or until shrimp turn pink. Remove from pan. Add the sauce mixture to same pan; bring just to a boil. Reduce heat; simmer, uncovered, for 2 minutes.

3. Drain the spaghetti; add to pan. Toss to combine with sauce. Return the shrimp to pan and add vegetables; cook and toss over medium-low heat until vegetables begin to wilt, about 4 minutes.

Stuffed Mountain Trout

You can use any whole fish in this recipe, but I like it best when it's made with fresh-caught trout from our local mountain streams.

—LORETTA WALTERS OGDEN, UTAH

PREP: 15 MIN. **BAKE:** 25 MIN. **MAKES:** 4 SERVINGS

- 2 trout (10 to 11 ounces each)
- 4 tablespoons plus 1½ teaspoons lemon juice, divided
- 3 teaspoons dill weed, divided
- 2 teaspoons lemon-pepper seasoning, divided
- 1 small onion, chopped
- 1 tablespoon butter
- ½ cup minced fresh parsley
- 2 cups soft bread crumbs

1. Place the trout in a 13x9-in. baking dish coated with cooking spray. Sprinkle 3 tablespoons lemon juice, 1½ teaspoons dill and 1½ teaspoons lemon-pepper in the fish cavities and over outside of fish; set aside.

2. In a nonstick skillet, saute onion in butter until tender. Add the parsley and remaining dill and lemon-pepper. Stir in bread crumbs; heat through. Sprinkle with remaining lemon juice; stir gently until moistened. Stuff into the fish cavities.

3. Bake, uncovered, at 400° for 25-30 minutes or until fish flakes easily with a fork.

GUSTAVUS, AK

Sport fishing is a major draw at Glacier Bay National Park & Preserve, where visitors angle for Pacific halibut, salmon, trout and other sought-after fish.

Chicken Long Rice

Ginger gives this dish a great flavor. If you like more veggies in your meal, add chopped celery, chopped sweet peppers, julienned carrots and zucchini, or shredded bok choy.

—TASTE OF HOME TEST KITCHEN

PREP: 20 MIN. + MARINATING   **COOK:** 15 MIN.
MAKES: 4 SERVINGS

- 1 **tablespoon minced fresh gingerroot**
- 1 **teaspoon sesame oil**
- 1 **teaspoon sugar**
- 1 **garlic clove, minced**
- ¼ **teaspoon pepper**
- 4 **tablespoons reduced-sodium soy sauce, divided**
- 2 **pounds boneless skinless chicken thighs, cut into strips**
- 5 **ounces uncooked bean thread noodles or spaghetti**
- 1 **tablespoon canola oil**
- 1 **cup chicken broth**
- 2 **cups sliced fresh mushrooms**
- 1 **green onion, thinly sliced**

1. In a large resealable plastic bag, combine the first five ingredients and 2 tablespoons soy sauce. Add chicken; seal bag and turn to coat. Refrigerate 1 hour.

2. Meanwhile, place noodles in a large bowl; cover with water. Let stand 30 minutes or until noodles are translucent and softened. Drain noodles. Using scissors, cut noodles into 4-in. lengths. (If using spaghetti, cook according to package directions until al dente; drain.)

3. In a large skillet, heat canola oil over medium-high heat. Add half of the chicken mixture; stir-fry 4-6 minutes or until no longer pink. Remove from pan. Repeat with remaining chicken.

4. In same pan, combine broth, mushrooms and remaining soy sauce; bring to a boil. Add noodles and chicken; cook and stir until noodles are tender. Remove from heat; sprinkle with green onion.

Honey-Glazed Lamb Chops

What a lot of flavor for such little effort! We're always glad to find a recipe like this that is company-special but so fast to put together.

—DOLORES HURTT FLORENCE, MONTANA

PREP/TOTAL TIME: 20 MIN.   **MAKES:** 4 SERVINGS

- ⅓ **cup honey**
- ⅓ **cup prepared mustard**
- ⅛ **teaspoon onion salt**
- ⅛ **teaspoon pepper**
- 8 **lamb loin chops (1 inch thick and 3 ounces each)**

1. In a small saucepan, combine the honey, mustard, onion salt and pepper. Cook and stir over medium-low heat for 2-3 minutes or until heated through.

2. Brush sauce over both sides of lamb. Broil 4-6 in. from the heat for 5-7 minutes on each side or until meat reaches desired doneness (for medium-rare, a thermometer should read 145°; medium, 160°; well-done, 170°).

Asian Chicken Thighs

A thick tangy sauce coats the golden chicken pieces in this savory skillet recipe. I like to serve them over long grain rice or with a helping of ramen noodle slaw.

—DAVE FARRINGTON MIDWEST CITY, OKLAHOMA

PREP: 15 MIN. **COOK:** 50 MIN. **MAKES:** 5 SERVINGS

- 5 bone-in chicken thighs (about 1¾ pounds), skin removed
- 5 teaspoons olive oil
- ⅓ cup warm water
- ¼ cup packed brown sugar
- 2 tablespoons orange juice
- 2 tablespoons reduced-sodium soy sauce
- 2 tablespoons ketchup
- 1 tablespoon white vinegar
- 4 garlic cloves, minced
- ½ teaspoon crushed red pepper flakes
- ¼ teaspoon Chinese five-spice powder
- 2 teaspoons cornstarch
- 2 tablespoons cold water
  Hot cooked rice
  Sliced green onions

1. In a large skillet over medium heat, cook chicken in oil for 8-10 minutes on each side or until no longer pink. In a small bowl, whisk the warm water, brown sugar, orange juice, soy sauce, ketchup, vinegar, garlic, pepper flakes and five-spice powder.

2. Pour over chicken. Bring to a boil. Reduce heat; simmer, uncovered, for 30-35 minutes or until chicken is tender, turning occasionally.

3. Combine cornstarch and cold water until smooth; gradually stir into the pan. Bring to a boil; cook and stir for 2 minutes or until thickened. Serve with rice. Garnish with the green onions.

Mushroom Asparagus Quiche

PREP: 20 MIN. **BAKE:** 25 MIN. **MAKES:** 8 SERVINGS

- 1 tube (8 ounces) refrigerated crescent rolls
- 2 teaspoons prepared mustard
- 1½ pounds fresh asparagus, trimmed and cut into ½-inch pieces
- 1 medium onion, chopped
- ½ cup sliced fresh mushrooms
- ¼ cup butter, cubed
- 2 eggs, lightly beaten
- 2 cups (8 ounces) shredded part-skim mozzarella cheese
- ¼ cup minced fresh parsley
- ½ teaspoon salt
- ½ teaspoon pepper
- ¼ teaspoon garlic powder
- ¼ teaspoon each dried basil, oregano and rubbed sage

1. Separate the crescent dough into eight triangles; place in an ungreased 9-in. pie plate with points toward the center. Press onto the bottom and up the sides to form a crust; seal perforations. Spread with mustard; set aside.

2. In a large skillet, saute asparagus, onion and mushrooms in butter until asparagus is crisp-tender. In a large bowl, combine the remaining ingredients; stir in the asparagus mixture. Pour into crust.

3. Bake at 375° for 25-30 minutes or until a knife inserted near the center comes out clean. Let stand for 10 minutes before cutting.

> Loads of asparagus pieces add color and flavor to this hearty, creamy quiche. And its easy crescent-roll crust means you'll have dinner ready in a snap!

—SHARON FUJITA
FONTANA, CALIFORNIA

> When I lived in Cleveland, I used to dine at a really good Vietnamese restaurant that had a dish I just couldn't get enough of. Since I had it so frequently, I figured out the components and flavors and created my own easy-to-make version. Everyone who tastes it loves it!

—ERIN SCHILLO
SAGAMORE HILLS, OHIO

Vietnamese Crunchy Chicken Salad

PREP: 30 MIN. + MARINATING   **COOK:** 10 MIN.   **MAKES:** 4 SERVINGS

- 3 **tablespoons olive oil**
- 2 **tablespoons lime juice**
- 1 **tablespoon minced fresh cilantro**
- 1½ **teaspoons grated lime peel**
- ½ **teaspoon salt**
- ½ **teaspoon pepper**
- ¼ **teaspoon cayenne pepper**
- 1 **pound boneless skinless chicken breasts, cut into thin strips**

DRESSING
- ½ **cup olive oil**
- ¼ **cup lime juice**
- 2 **tablespoons rice vinegar**
- 2 **tablespoons sugar**
- 1 **tablespoon grated lime peel**
- ¾ **teaspoon salt**
- ½ **teaspoon crushed red pepper flakes**
- ¼ **teaspoon pepper**

SALAD
- 5 **cups thinly sliced cabbage (about 1 pound)**
- 1 **cup minced fresh cilantro**
- 1 **cup julienned carrots**
- 1 **cup salted peanuts, coarsely chopped**

1. In a large bowl, mix the first seven ingredients; add chicken and toss to coat. Refrigerate, covered, 30 minutes. In a small bowl, whisk dressing ingredients.

2. In a large skillet over medium-high heat, add half of the chicken mixture; stir-fry for 4-5 minutes or until no longer pink. Remove from the pan; repeat with the remaining chicken. Cool slightly.

3. In a large bowl, combine the cabbage, cilantro, carrots and chicken; toss to combine. Add the peanuts and dressing; toss to coat. Serve immediately.

Country-Style Pot Roast

My husband goes deer hunting, so I have quite a few recipes for venison. This is his favorite. Hope you enjoy it, too!

—JOAN BEST GARRISON, MONTANA

PREP: 10 MIN. + MARINATING   **COOK:** 3½ HOURS   **MAKES:** 6-8 SERVINGS

- 2 cups water
- 2 cups cider vinegar
- 2 teaspoons salt
- 1 teaspoon Worcestershire sauce
- ½ teaspoon garlic powder
- ½ teaspoon pepper
- 6 medium onions, thinly sliced, divided
- 12 whole peppercorns, divided
- 4 bay leaves, divided
- 4 whole cloves, divided
- 1 boneless beef or venison rump or chuck roast (3½ to 4 pounds)
- 2 tablespoons canola oil
- 10 medium carrots, cut into 1-inch chunks
- 5 to 7 tablespoons cornstarch
- ⅓ cup cold water

1. In a large bowl, combine the first six ingredients. Pour half of the marinade into a large resealable plastic bag. Evenly divide the onions, peppercorns, bay leaves and cloves between the mixture in the bowl and bag. Cover the bowl and refrigerate. Add the meat to the bag; seal bag and turn to coat. Refrigerate for 24 hours.

2. Drain and discard marinade from meat. In a Dutch oven, brown roast in oil; drain. Add the carrots and reserved marinade; bring to a rolling boil. Reduce heat; cover and simmer for 3½ to 4 hours or until meat is tender.

3. Remove roast and keep warm. Strain the cooking juices; discard vegetables and spices. Return juices to pan. Combine cornstarch and cold water until smooth; gradually add to pan juices. Bring to a boil; cook and stir for 2 minutes or until thickened. Slice roast; serve with gravy.

◄● dishing about food

West of the Rockies, the mule deer is the most common type of deer. East of the Rockies, it is the white-tailed deer.

MOUNT HOOD, OR

The dense temperate rainforest at the base of Mount Hood, Oregon's famous peak, is a refuge for many indigenous animals, including mule deer, whose numbers have been declining in recent years.

Tofu Manicotti

To create a light main course, I borrowed bits from different recipes—including my mom's lasagna. No one suspects that the creamy filling is made with tofu. It's so easy to prepare, and my kids love it!

—CAROLYN DIANA SCOTTSDALE, ARIZONA

PREP: 25 MIN. **BAKE:** 50 MIN. **MAKES:** 5 SERVINGS

- 2 cups meatless spaghetti sauce
- 1 can (14½ ounces) diced tomatoes, undrained
- ⅓ cup finely shredded zucchini
- ¼ cup finely shredded carrot
- ½ teaspoon Italian seasoning
- 1 package (12.3 ounces) silken firm tofu
- 1 cup (8 ounces) 1% cottage cheese
- 1 cup (4 ounces) shredded part-skim mozzarella cheese
- 1 tablespoon grated Parmesan cheese
- 10 uncooked manicotti shells

1. Combine the spaghetti sauce, tomatoes, zucchini, carrot and Italian seasoning; spread ¾ cup into a 13x9-in. baking dish coated with cooking spray.

2. Combine the tofu and cheeses; stuff into uncooked manicotti shells. Place over spaghetti sauce; top with remaining sauce.

3. Cover and bake at 375° for 50-55 minutes or until noodles are tender. Let stand for 5 minutes before serving.

Garlic-Roasted Chicken and Potatoes

This recipe has been in my "favorites" file for almost 20 years. My husband and I enjoyed it before we had kids, and now they love it, too. It's a real time-saver!

—BETH ERBERT LIVERMORE, CALIFORNIA

PREP: 20 MIN. **BAKE:** 1 HOUR **MAKES:** 6 SERVINGS

- 6 **bone-in chicken thighs (about 2¼ pounds)**
- 6 **chicken drumsticks**
- 6 **medium red potatoes (about 2 pounds), cut into 1-inch cubes**
- 24 **garlic cloves, peeled**
- ¼ **cup butter, melted**
- 1 **teaspoon salt, divided**
- ¼ **cup maple syrup**

1. Place the chicken, potatoes and garlic in a large roasting pan. Drizzle with butter; sprinkle with ¾ teaspoon salt. Toss to coat. Bake, uncovered, at 400° for 40 minutes.

2. Combine the syrup and remaining salt; drizzle over chicken. Spoon pan juices over potatoes and garlic. Bake 20 minutes longer or until a thermometer reads 180° and the potatoes are tender.

Campfire Trout Dinner for Two

PREP: 20 MIN. **GRILL:** 20 MIN. **MAKES:** 2 SERVINGS

- 4 **bacon strips**
- 2 **pan-dressed trout (1 pound each)**
- 4 **lemon slices**
- 1 **small onion, halved and sliced**
- ¼ **teaspoon salt**
- ⅛ **teaspoon pepper**

CARROTS
- 4 **medium carrots, thinly sliced**
- ⅛ **teaspoon salt**
  Dash pepper
- 1 **tablespoon butter**
  Lemon wedges

1. Cook bacon until partially cooked but not crisp; drain. Place each trout on a double thickness of heavy-duty foil (about 20x18 in.). Place lemon and onions in the trout cavities; sprinkle with salt and pepper. Wrap trout with bacon. Fold foil around trout and seal tightly.

2. Place carrots on a double thickness of heavy-duty foil (about 20x18 in.); sprinkle with salt and pepper. Dot with butter. Fold foil around carrots and seal tightly.

3. Grill carrots, covered, over medium heat for 10 minutes. Add trout packets to grill; cook 20-25 minutes longer or until fish flakes easily with a fork and carrots are tender. Serve with lemon wedges.

> **Your fresh catch will taste even better with this simple treatment that keeps the fish moist. Carrots are an excellent side; cook up in a separate foil packet.**

—WENDY MCGOWAN
FONTANA, CALIFORNIA

> **" My family loves this main dish summer and winter. We all go blackberry picking together, and I freeze some of the berries left over from our jams and pies so we can enjoy this chicken all year long. "**
>
> **—LAURA VAN NESS**
> CLEARLAKE OAKS, CALIFORNIA

Blackberry Chicken

PREP: 20 MIN.　**BAKE:** 20 MIN.　**MAKES:** 6 SERVINGS

- 2 tablespoons plus ½ cup fresh blackberries, divided
- ½ cup reduced-sodium chicken broth, divided
- 2 tablespoons brown sugar
- 2 tablespoons white wine vinegar
- 1 teaspoon olive oil
- 2 garlic cloves, minced
- ¾ teaspoon paprika, divided
- ¼ teaspoon ground cumin
- 6 boneless skinless chicken breast halves (5 ounces each)
- 4½ teaspoons minced fresh thyme
- ½ teaspoon salt
- ¼ teaspoon pepper
- 2 teaspoons cornstarch

1. In a small bowl, mash 2 tablespoons berries. Add ¼ cup broth, brown sugar, vinegar, oil, garlic, ¼ teaspoon paprika and cumin.

2. Place chicken in an 11x7-in. baking dish coated with cooking spray; pour broth mixture over the top. Sprinkle with thyme, salt, pepper and remaining paprika.

3. Bake, uncovered, at 375° for 20-25 minutes or until a thermometer reads 165°, basting occasionally with pan juices. Remove chicken and keep warm.

4. Skim the fat from pan drippings. In a small saucepan, combine cornstarch and remaining broth until smooth. Gradually stir in drippings. Bring to a boil; cook and stir for 1-2 minutes or until thickened. Serve with chicken; sprinkle with the remaining blackberries.

Curried Tofu with Rice

Tofu takes the place of meat in this bold dish with lots of curry and cilantro flavor.

—CRYSTAL BRUNS ILIFF, COLORADO

PREP: 15 MIN.　**COOK:** 20 MIN.　**MAKES:** 4 SERVINGS

- 1 package (12.3 ounces) extra-firm tofu, drained and cubed
- 1 teaspoon seasoned salt
- 1 tablespoon canola oil
- 1 small onion, chopped
- 3 garlic cloves, minced
- ½ cup light coconut milk
- ¼ cup minced fresh cilantro
- 1 teaspoon curry powder
- ¼ teaspoon salt
- ¼ teaspoon pepper
- 2 cups cooked brown rice

1. Sprinkle tofu with seasoned salt. In a large nonstick skillet coated with cooking spray, saute tofu in oil until lightly browned. Remove and keep warm.

2. In the same skillet, saute onion and garlic for 1-2 minutes or until crisp-tender. Stir in the coconut milk, cilantro, curry, salt and pepper. Bring to a boil. Reduce heat; simmer, uncovered, for 4-5 minutes or until sauce is slightly thickened. Stir in tofu; heat through. Serve with rice.

Cornish Pasties

On a vacation many years ago, my family stopped for lunch at a little cafe, the Game Keeper Cafe, in Butte, Montana. We ordered a Welsh dish—Cornish pasties—and it was absolutely delicious. We couldn't resist asking to meet the cook. We asked for the recipe, and he was happy to share it with us.

—NELLIE RADER EMMETT, IDAHO

PREP: 30 MIN. **BAKE:** 55 MIN. **MAKES:** 12 SERVINGS

- 1 **pound beef sirloin tip steak, diced**
- 3 **medium potatoes, peeled and diced (3 cups)**
- 3 **green onions with tops, thinly sliced**
- 1 **teaspoon salt**
- ¼ **teaspoon pepper**
  Dash nutmeg

PASTRY
- 4 **cups all-purpose flour**
- 2 **teaspoons salt**
  Pinch baking powder
- 1 **cup shortening**
- 2 **tablespoons butter**
- ⅔ **cup cold water**
- 1 **egg, lightly beaten**
- 1 **tablespoon heavy whipping cream**

1. In a large bowl, combine the beef, potatoes, onions and seasonings; set aside. For pastry, in a large bowl, combine the flour, salt and baking powder. Cut in shortening and butter. Gradually add water, tossing with a fork until dough forms a ball.

2. Turn onto a lightly floured surface. Divide dough into 12 pieces; roll each into a 6-in. circle. Moisten edges with water. Place about ½ cup filling on half of each circle. Fold other half over filling; press edges together with a fork to seal.

3. Cut several slits in top of each pastry. Place on a baking sheet. Combine egg and cream; brush over pastry tops. Bake at 400° for 15 minutes. Reduce heat to 350° and bake 40-45 minutes longer or until golden brown.

If Cooking for Two: *Freeze unbaked pasties on baking sheets until firm, then wrap and store in the freezer. When ready to bake, defrost and bake as directed above.*

Scrumptious California Salmon

California cuisine is all about balancing flavors. This recipe brings out the sweetness in orange juice and honey and balances it with the kick of ancho chili pepper and balsamic.

—DUSTIN ANDERSON FILLMORE, CALIFORNIA

PREP: 35 MIN. **BAKE:** 10 MIN. **MAKES:** 4 SERVINGS

- 3 **garlic cloves, minced**
- 1 **teaspoon minced shallot**
- 1 **cup orange juice**
- 1 **tablespoon balsamic vinegar**
- 3 **tablespoons honey**
- 1 **tablespoon ground ancho chili pepper**
- ¼ **teaspoon salt**
- ⅛ **teaspoon pepper**
- 1 **salmon fillet (1 pound)**
- 2 **teaspoons canola oil**
- 2 **tablespoons minced fresh cilantro**

1. In a small saucepan coated with cooking spray, saute garlic and shallot until tender. Add orange juice and vinegar. Bring to a boil. Reduce heat; simmer, uncovered, for 20-25 minutes or until reduced to ¼ cup. Stir in the honey, chili pepper, salt and pepper.

2. In a large ovenproof skillet, brown salmon in oil on both sides. Brush with ¼ cup sauce. Bake, uncovered, at 400° for 8-10 minutes or until fish flakes easily with a fork.

3. Brush with remaining sauce and sprinkle with cilantro.

◄◄ dishing about food

Cornish pasties, turnovers filled with meat and potatoes, were popular with copper miners in Montana and other mining communities because the men could eat them while still covered with dust from the mines. They would hold one tip of the pasty in their dirty hands, and when they reached that end, they would throw the last bit of the pasty away.

BUTTE, MT

The World Museum of Mining imparts the rich history of one of the West's oldest professions. Walk through the underground exhibit and explore Hell-Roarin' Gulch, a re-created mining town.

Asian Veggie Glass Noodles

I took my mom's version of this noodle dish and added my own touches to make it easier. Mom immigrated from the Philippines and often we would eat "pancit," one of the country's most famous noodle dishes. I've lightened up my version by removing the meat and adding more vegetables. I also took some shortcuts—such as using bagged tricolor slaw mix. You can substitute other vegetables you have on hand if desired.

—**JASMIN BARON** LIVONIA, NEW YORK

PREP: 30 MIN. + STANDING **COOK:** 15 MIN. **MAKES:** 4 SERVINGS

5	ounces uncooked bean thread noodles
2	tablespoons canola oil
⅓	cup finely chopped onion
2	garlic cloves, minced
1½	teaspoons minced fresh gingerroot
1½	cups thinly sliced fresh mushrooms
4	cups coleslaw mix
1	cup fresh snow peas, trimmed and halved diagonally
½	cup thinly sliced sweet red pepper
1¼	cups vegetable broth
3	tablespoons reduced-sodium soy sauce
¼	teaspoon pepper
3	green onions, thinly sliced
3	tablespoons minced fresh cilantro
3	hard-cooked eggs, sliced
	Lime or lemon wedges, optional

1. Place noodles in a large bowl; cover with water. Let stand 30 minutes or until noodles are translucent and softened.

2. In a large skillet, heat oil over medium-high heat. Add the onion, garlic and ginger; stir-fry 2 minutes. Add mushrooms; stir-fry 2 minutes. Add remaining vegetables; stir-fry 1-2 minutes or until crisp-tender. Remove from pan.

3. Drain noodles. Using scissors, cut noodles into 4-in. lengths. In same pan, combine broth, soy sauce and pepper; bring to a boil. Add the noodles; cook and stir until noodles are tender. Add vegetable mixture, green onions and cilantro; heat through, stirring occasionally.

4. Transfer to a serving plate. Top with eggs; if desired, serve with lime wedges.

Cobb Salad

Made on the fly by Hollywood restaurateur Bob Cobb in 1937, the Cobb salad now is a world-famous American dish. Here's a fresh take, with all the original appeal and an extra-special presentation.
—TASTE OF HOME TEST KITCHEN

PREP/TOTAL TIME: 40 MIN.
MAKES: 6 SERVINGS (1¼ CUPS DRESSING)

- ¼ cup red wine vinegar
- 2 teaspoons salt
- 1 teaspoon lemon juice
- 1 small garlic clove, minced
- ¾ teaspoon coarsely ground pepper
- ¾ teaspoon Worcestershire sauce
- ¼ teaspoon sugar
- ¼ teaspoon ground mustard
- ¾ cup canola oil
- ¼ cup olive oil

SALAD
- 6½ cups torn romaine
- 2½ cups torn curly endive
- 1 bunch watercress (4 ounces), trimmed, divided
- 2 cooked chicken breasts, chopped
- 2 medium tomatoes, seeded and chopped
- 1 medium ripe avocado, peeled and chopped
- 3 hard-cooked eggs, chopped
- ½ cup crumbled blue or Roquefort cheese
- 6 bacon strips, cooked and crumbled
- 2 tablespoons minced fresh chives

1. In a blender, combine the first eight ingredients. While processing, gradually add canola and olive oils in a steady stream.

2. In a large bowl, combine the romaine, endive and half of the watercress; toss lightly. Transfer to a serving platter. Arrange the chicken, tomatoes, avocado, eggs, cheese and bacon over the greens; sprinkle with chives. Top with remaining watercress. Cover and chill until serving.

3. To serve, drizzle 1 cup dressing over salad. Serve with remaining dressing if desired.

Pineapple Ham Casserole

Since I live in Hawaii, I wanted to share this delicious recipe that features pineapple, our most important fruit crop.
—MARSHA FLEMING KULA, HAWAII

PREP: 15 MIN. **BAKE:** 30 MIN. **MAKES:** 4 SERVINGS

- 2 cups uncooked wide egg noodles
- ½ cup chopped celery
- 2 tablespoons butter, divided
- 1 package (8 ounces) cream cheese, cubed
- ¾ cup milk
- 2 cups cubed fully cooked ham
- 2 cans (8 ounces each) crushed pineapple, drained
- 2 teaspoons Worcestershire sauce
- ½ teaspoon salt
  Dash pepper
- ¼ cup dry bread crumbs

1. Cook noodles according to the package directions; drain. In a large skillet, saute celery in 1 tablespoon butter until tender. Stir in the cream cheese and milk; cook and stir until cheese is melted. Add the noodles, ham, pineapple, Worcestershire sauce, salt and pepper.

2. Transfer to an ungreased 1½-qt. baking dish. Melt remaining butter; toss with bread crumbs. Sprinkle over the top. Bake, uncovered, at 350° for 30-35 minutes or until heated through.

HOLLYWOOD, CA

Now called the TCL Chinese Theatre, this historic cinema has been a hot spot for moviegoers and star-gazers since 1927.

> **" I came across this recipe in a local fundraising cookbook. We made some slight adjustments to it since then, but it is a great recipe to use when grilling—and a favorite summer meal. "**
>
> **—AMY SAUSER**
> OMAHA, NEBRASKA

Pacific Rim Salmon

PREP: 15 MIN. + MARINATING **GRILL:** 15 MIN.
MAKES: 8 SERVINGS

- ½ cup unsweetened pineapple juice
- ¼ cup reduced-sodium soy sauce
- 2 tablespoons prepared horseradish
- 2 tablespoons minced fresh parsley
- 5 teaspoons sesame oil, divided
- 2 teaspoons honey
- ½ teaspoon coarsely ground pepper
- 8 salmon fillets (6 ounces each)
- 5 green onions, coarsely chopped

1. In a small bowl, combine pineapple juice, soy sauce, horseradish, parsley, 3 teaspoons sesame oil, honey and pepper. Pour ⅔ cup marinade into a large resealable plastic bag; add salmon and green onions. Seal the bag and turn to coat; refrigerate for 1 to 1½ hours, turning occasionally. Add the remaining sesame oil to the remaining marinade. Cover and refrigerate for basting.

2. Drain and discard marinade. Using long-handled tongs, moisten a paper towel with cooking oil and lightly coat the grill rack.

3. Grill salmon, skin side down, covered, over medium heat or broil 4 in. from the heat for 8-12 minutes or until fish flakes easily with a fork, basting frequently with reserved marinade.

Grilled Huli Huli Chicken

I got this grilled chicken recipe from a friend while living in Hawaii. It sizzles with the flavors of brown sugar, ginger and soy sauce. Huli means "turn" in Hawaiian.

—SHARON BOLING CORONADO, CALIFORNIA

PREP: 15 MIN. + MARINATING **GRILL:** 15 MIN.
MAKES: 12 SERVINGS

- 1 cup packed brown sugar
- ¾ cup ketchup
- ¾ cup reduced-sodium soy sauce
- ⅓ cup sherry or chicken broth
- 2½ teaspoons minced fresh gingerroot
- 1½ teaspoons minced garlic
- 24 boneless skinless chicken thighs (about 5 pounds)

1. In a small bowl, mix first six ingredients. Reserve 1⅓ cups for basting; cover and refrigerate. Divide remaining marinade between two large resealable plastic bags. Add 12 chicken thighs to each; seal bags and turn to coat. Refrigerate for 8 hours or overnight.

2. Drain and discard marinade from chicken. Moisten a paper towel with cooking oil; using long-handled tongs, lightly coat the grill rack.

3. Grill chicken, covered, over medium heat for 6-8 minutes on each side or until no longer pink; baste occasionally with reserved marinade during the last 5 minutes.

Rosemary-Garlic Roast Beef

This tender and juicy roast looks so beautiful when I serve it to guests! It also fills the house with a wonderful aroma as it cooks. I usually serve it with warm French bread and a salad topped with buttermilk dressing.

—**BRENDA HLIVYAK** LA CENTER, WASHINGTON

PREP: 15 MIN. **BAKE:** 40 MIN. **MAKES:** 6 SERVINGS

- 4   garlic cloves, minced
- 1   tablespoon dried rosemary, crushed
- 1   teaspoon salt
- ½   teaspoon pepper
- 1   beef tri-tip roast (2 to 3 pounds)
- 4½   teaspoons olive oil
- 12   small red potatoes, quartered
- 2   medium sweet yellow peppers, cut into 1-inch pieces
- 1   large sweet onion, cut into 1-inch slices

1. Combine the garlic, rosemary, salt and pepper; set aside 4 teaspoons. Rub the remaining mixture over roast; place in a greased shallow roasting pan.

2. In a small bowl, whisk reserved herb mixture with oil. In a large resealable plastic bag, combine the potatoes, yellow peppers and onion; add oil mixture. Seal bag and toss to coat. Arrange vegetables around roast.

3. Bake, uncovered, at 425° for 30-60 minutes or until meat reaches desired doneness (for medium-rare, a thermometer should read 145°; medium, 160°; well-done, 170°).

4. Transfer roast and peppers to a warm serving platter. Let stand for 10-15 minutes before slicing. Meanwhile, return potatoes and onion to the oven; bake 10 minutes longer or until potatoes are tender.

Pineapple Chicken Salad

Although I love to cook, I appreciate recipes that have me out of the kitchen fast so I can spend more time with my family. We love this main-dish salad.

—**STEPHANIE MOON** BOISE, IDAHO

PREP/TOTAL TIME: 30 MIN. **MAKES:** 4 SERVINGS

- 4   boneless skinless chicken breast halves (4 ounces each)
- ¼   teaspoon lemon-pepper seasoning
- 1   can (8 ounces) unsweetened sliced pineapple
- 3   tablespoons canola oil
- 2   tablespoons soy sauce
- 1   tablespoon white vinegar
- 1   tablespoon honey
- ¼   teaspoon ground ginger
- 8   cups assorted vegetables (lettuce, red onion, carrots, sweet red pepper and broccoli)
      Salted peanuts, optional

1. Sprinkle chicken with lemon-pepper. Grill over medium-hot heat or broil 4-6 in. from the heat for 15-18 minutes or until juices run clear, turning once. Set aside and keep warm.

2. Drain pineapple, reserving 2 tablespoons juice (discard the remaining juice or save for another use); set pineapple aside. In a jar with a tight-fitting lid, combine oil, soy sauce, vinegar, honey, ginger and reserved pineapple juice; shake well. Brush some of the dressing over pineapple; grill or broil for 2 minutes.

3. Cut chicken into strips. Arrange vegetables on serving plates; top with the pineapple and chicken. Sprinkle with peanuts if desired. Serve with remaining dressing.

Cioppino is a distinctive San Francisco dish. Created by immigrants who worked on the fishing boats and wharfs, the fish stew incorporated whatever was caught that day, along with a few staples. The stew would change as the catch would vary.

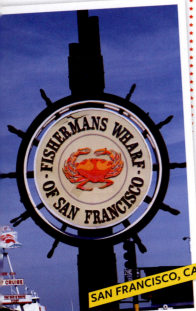

A wide variety of seafood is caught by the fleet at Fisherman's Wharf, but perhaps the most notable is the Dungeness crab, depicted on the iconic sign.

Fresh and Spicy Cioppino

Using prepared pasta sauce makes this hearty and hot one-pot dinner a cinch.

—DORIS MANCINI PORT ORCHARD, WASHINGTON

PREP: 25 MIN. **COOK:** 25 MIN.
MAKES: 8 SERVINGS (3 QUARTS)

- 5 garlic cloves, minced
- 2 tablespoons olive oil
- 1 jar (24 ounces) tomato basil pasta sauce
- 1 bottle (8 ounces) clam juice
- 1 cup dry white wine or chicken broth
- ¼ cup water
- 1 teaspoon salt
- 1 teaspoon sugar
- 1 teaspoon crushed red pepper flakes
- 1 teaspoon minced fresh basil
- 1 teaspoon minced fresh thyme
- 1 pound fresh littleneck clams
- 1 pound fresh mussels, scrubbed and beards removed
- 1 pound uncooked medium shrimp, peeled and deveined
- 1 pound bay scallops
- 1 package (6 ounces) fresh baby spinach

1. In a Dutch oven, saute garlic in oil until tender. Add the pasta sauce, clam juice, wine, water and seasonings. Bring to a boil. Reduce heat; simmer, uncovered, for 10 minutes.

2. Add the clams, mussels and shrimp. Bring to a boil. Reduce heat; simmer, uncovered, for 10 minutes, stirring occasionally.

3. Stir in the scallops and spinach; cook 5-7 minutes longer or until the clams and mussels open, shrimp turn pink and scallops are opaque. Discard any unopened clams or mussels.

Teriyaki Meatballs

This one-time appetizer recipe was changed many times because of my family's insistence that it eventually became a main course. I think it's the homemade sauce that sets these meatballs apart.

—EVETTE NOWICKI OAK HARBOR, WASHINGTON

PREP: 20 MIN. **BAKE:** 20 MIN. **MAKES:** 42 MEATBALLS

- 2 cans (8 ounces each) pineapple chunks
- 1 medium onion, finely chopped
- ¼ cup finely chopped sweet yellow pepper
- ¼ cup finely chopped sweet red pepper
- ½ cup dry bread crumbs
- ½ teaspoon ground ginger
- ¼ teaspoon salt
- 1 pound lean ground beef

SAUCE
- ¼ cup canola oil
- ¼ cup soy sauce
- 3 tablespoons honey
- 2 tablespoons white vinegar
- ¾ teaspoon garlic powder
- ½ teaspoon ground ginger

1. Drain pineapple, reserving ¼ cup juice; set pineapple aside. In a bowl, combine the onion, peppers, bread crumbs, ginger, salt and reserved pineapple juice. Crumble beef over mixture and mix well. Shape into 1-in. balls.

2. Place sauce ingredients in a blender; cover and process for 1 minute. Place 2 tablespoons of sauce in a greased 13x9-in. baking dish. Add the meatballs. Pour the remaining sauce over meatballs. Bake, uncovered, at 400° for 20 minutes or until meat is no longer pink. Place one pineapple chunk on each meatball; secure with a toothpick.

Editor's Note: *To serve the meatballs as an appetizer, place the cooked meatballs in a chafing dish.*

Mango-Chutney Chicken Salad

I often make this recipe and take it to school for lunch. It makes me feel like I've ordered out from a fancy restaurant! It's equally wonderful as a salad or gourmet lunch wrap.

—MICHELLE SICHAK MERIDIAN, IDAHO

PREP: 15 MIN. + CHILLING **MAKES:** 6 SERVINGS

- 1 carton (6 ounces) plain yogurt
- ¼ cup light coconut milk
- 1½ teaspoons curry powder
- 2 cups cubed cooked chicken
- 2 cups green grapes, halved
- 6 green onions, chopped
- ½ cup dried cranberries
- ⅓ cup mango chutney
- ¼ cup slivered almonds, toasted

1. In a small bowl, whisk the yogurt, milk and curry until smooth.

2. In a large bowl, combine chicken, grapes, onions and cranberries. Drizzle with yogurt dressing and toss to coat. Fold in mango chutney. Refrigerate for at least 1 hour. Just before serving, sprinkle with almonds.

Tropical Turkey Meat Loaf

PREP: 10 MIN. **BAKE:** 1 HOUR
MAKES: 8 SERVINGS (⅔ CUP SAUCE)

- ½ cup egg substitute
- 1 can (8 ounces) unsweetened crushed pineapple, undrained, divided
- 3 tablespoons reduced-sodium soy sauce
- 1 teaspoon sugar
- ¾ teaspoon ground ginger
- ½ teaspoon ground mustard
- ¼ teaspoon garlic powder
- 1 cup dry bread crumbs
- 1½ pounds lean ground turkey
- 1 tablespoon finely chopped onion
- 1 green onion, finely chopped
- 2 teaspoons finely chopped jalapeno pepper
- 1 teaspoon honey
- 1 teaspoon lime juice
  Pinch pepper

1. In a bowl, combine egg substitute, ⅓ cup pineapple and seasonings. Add bread crumbs; mix well. Crumble meat over mixture; mix well. Press into an 8x4-in. loaf pan coated with cooking spray. Top with 1 tablespoon of pineapple.

2. Bake at 350° for 1 to 1¼ hours or until a thermometer reads 165°. Let stand 5 minutes before serving. Meanwhile, in a bowl, combine onion, jalapeno, honey, lime juice, pepper and remaining pineapple. Serve with the meat loaf.

Editor's Note: *Wear disposable gloves when cutting hot peppers; the oils can burn skin. Avoid touching your face.*

> "After modifying another recipe, I came up with this wonderful moist and tender meat loaf. The pineapple-jalapeno picante makes a sweet and tangy topping."
>
> **—FRANCES PAGE**
> ONTARIO, CALIFORNIA

> 66 **This mouthwatering casserole makes an excellent potluck dish. It's creamy and just bursting with flavor. A golden topping made of cornflakes and almonds offers the perfect amount of crunch!** 99

—MICHELLE KRZMARCZICK
REDONDO BEACH, CALIFORNIA

Almond Chicken Casserole

PREP: 15 MIN. **BAKE:** 25 MIN. **MAKES:** 6-8 SERVINGS

2 cups cubed cooked chicken
1 can (10¾ ounces) condensed cream of chicken soup, undiluted
1 cup (8 ounces) sour cream
¾ cup mayonnaise
2 celery ribs, chopped
3 hard-cooked eggs, chopped
1 can (4 ounces) mushroom stems and pieces, drained
1 can (8 ounces) water chestnuts, drained and chopped
1 tablespoon finely chopped onion
2 teaspoons lemon juice
½ teaspoon salt
¼ teaspoon pepper
1 cup (4 ounces) shredded cheddar cheese
½ cup crushed cornflakes
2 tablespoons butter, melted
¼ cup sliced almonds

1. In a large bowl, combine the first 12 ingredients. Transfer to a greased 13x9-in. baking dish; sprinkle with cheese.

2. Toss cornflakes with butter; sprinkle over cheese. Top with almonds. Bake, uncovered, at 350° for 25-30 minutes or until heated through.

Cashew Chicken Casserole: *Substitute shredded Swiss cheese for the cheddar, crushed butter-flavored crackers for the cornflakes and coarsely chopped cashews for the almonds.*

Macadamia-Crusted Mahi Mahi

Turn mahi mahi fillets into fancy company fare with a crunchy coating of macadamia nuts and panko, then drizzle with a gingery sauce. Your family and friends will rave about the flavor!

—IDANA MOONEY CORONA, CALIFORNIA

PREP/TOTAL TIME: 30 MIN.   **MAKES:** 4 SERVINGS

- 1 cup panko (Japanese) bread crumbs
- ¾ cup macadamia nuts
- ¼ teaspoon salt
- ¼ teaspoon white pepper
- 1 egg
- 2 teaspoons water
- ⅓ cup all-purpose flour
- 4 mahi mahi fillets (4 ounces each)
- ¼ cup canola oil
- 2 tablespoons brown sugar
- 2 tablespoons reduced-sodium soy sauce
- 2 teaspoons minced fresh gingerroot

1. Place the bread crumbs, nuts, salt and pepper in a food processor; cover and pulse until nuts are finely chopped.

2. In a shallow bowl, whisk egg and water. Place flour and nut mixture in separate shallow bowls. Coat fillets with flour, then dip in egg mixture and coat with nut mixture.

3. In a large skillet, heat oil over medium heat; cook fillets for 3-4 minutes on each side or until golden brown.

4. Meanwhile, in a small microwave-safe bowl, combine the brown sugar, soy sauce and ginger. Microwave, uncovered, on high for 30-60 seconds or until the sugar is dissolved. Drizzle over fish.

BIG ISLAND, HI

Almost all macadamia nuts on the market are grown on the Big Island, but that isn't its main claim to fame. That title goes to Kilauea, one of the most active volcanoes on Earth.

Between May and October, several species of salmon swim furiously upstream to spawn. The daily catch skyrockets—for humans and bears. If you want to try your hand, the Kenai River is a prime locale.

Northwest Salmon Salad

I love that I can use my favorite Northwest ingredients—fresh salmon, blueberries and hazelnuts—all in one colorful recipe. And the salmon and sour cream dressing is just as scrumptious in a sandwich.

—ELDA CLEVENGER DEXTER, OREGON

PREP: 45 MIN. **MAKES:** 4 SERVINGS

- 1 **salmon fillet (1 pound)**
- ½ **teaspoon salt**
- ½ **teaspoon plus ⅛ teaspoon coarsely ground pepper, divided**
- 2 **tablespoons lemon juice, divided**
- 4 **fresh dill sprigs**
- 1 **cup chopped peeled cucumber**
- ½ **cup reduced-fat sour cream**
- ¼ **cup finely chopped sweet red pepper**
- ¼ **cup snipped fresh dill**
- 3 **tablespoons capers, drained**
- 8 **cups torn Bibb lettuce**
- 1 **medium peach, peeled and sliced**
- ¼ **cup chopped hazelnuts**
- ¼ **cup fresh blueberries**
- 4 **thin slices red onion, separated into rings**

1. Place salmon on a greased baking sheet; sprinkle with salt and ½ teaspoon pepper. Drizzle with 1 tablespoon lemon juice; top with dill sprigs.

2. Bake, uncovered, at 425° for 15-18 minutes or until fish flakes easily with a fork. Flake salmon into large pieces.

3. In a small bowl, combine the cucumber, sour cream, red pepper, snipped dill, capers and remaining pepper and lemon juice.

4. Divide lettuce among four plates. Top with peach, hazelnuts, blueberries, onion and salmon. Serve with dressing.

Warm 'n' Fruity Breakfast Cereal

Overnight guests will love the heartiness of this nutritious cooked cereal that is seasoned with cinnamon and loaded with chopped fruit and nuts. We enjoy it with plain yogurt and blueberries or sliced bananas.

—**JOHN VALE** HARDIN, MONTANA

PREP: 10 MIN. **COOK:** 6 HOURS **MAKES:** 10 CUPS

- 5 **cups water**
- 2 **cups seven-grain cereal**
- 1 **medium apple, peeled and chopped**
- 1 **cup unsweetened apple juice**
- ¼ **cup dried apricots, chopped**
- ¼ **cup dried cranberries**
- ¼ **cup raisins**
- ¼ **cup chopped dates**
- ¼ **cup maple syrup**
- 1 **teaspoon ground cinnamon**
- ½ **teaspoon salt**
  Chopped walnuts, optional

1. In a 5-qt. slow cooker, combine the first 11 ingredients. Cover and cook on low for 6-7 hours or until fruits are softened. Sprinkle individual servings with walnuts if desired.

Balsamic-Glazed Pork Chops

The tangy sauce and restaurant-quality flavor of this entree prompted one of my guests to say, "I wish my mom made chops like this when I was growing up!"

—**SANDY SHERMAN** CHESTER, VIRGINIA

PREP/TOTAL TIME: 30 MIN. **MAKES:** 4 SERVINGS

- 4 **boneless pork loin chops (6 ounces each)**
- ¾ **teaspoon salt, divided**
- ½ **teaspoon pepper**
- 3 **tablespoons butter, divided**
- 1 **large red onion, halved and thinly sliced**
- ⅔ **cup balsamic vinegar**
- 2 **teaspoons brown sugar**
- ½ **teaspoon dried rosemary, crushed**

1. Sprinkle pork chops with ½ teaspoon salt and pepper. In a large skillet, brown chops in 1 tablespoon butter. Remove and keep warm.

2. In the same skillet, saute the onion in 1 tablespoon butter until tender. Stir in the vinegar, brown sugar, rosemary and the remaining salt. Bring to a boil; cook until liquid is reduced by half.

3. Return chops to the pan; cook, uncovered, over medium heat for 4-6 minutes on each side or until a thermometer reads 145°. Remove the chops to a serving plate and let stand for 5 minutes before serving. Stir the remaining butter into skillet until melted. Serve with the pork chops.

> " Casual, flavorful and low in carbohydrates, Vietnamese Pork Lettuce Wraps are a perfect and low-fuss way to feed a group. Place the ingredients in separate dishes and let your guests assemble their own wraps, personalized to suit their tastes. "

—GRETCHEN BARNES

FAIRFAX, VIRGINIA

Vietnamese Pork Lettuce Wraps

PREP: 25 MIN. + STANDING   **COOK:** 10 MIN.   **MAKES:** 8 SERVINGS

- ½ cup white vinegar
- ¼ cup sugar
- ⅛ teaspoon salt
- 2 medium carrots, julienned
- ½ medium onion, cut into thin slices

FILLING
- 1 pound ground pork
- 1 tablespoon minced fresh gingerroot
- 1 garlic clove, minced
- 2 tablespoons reduced-sodium soy sauce
- 1 tablespoon mirin (sweet rice wine)
- ¼ teaspoon salt
- ¼ teaspoon pepper
- 1 teaspoon fish sauce, optional

ASSEMBLY
- 8 Bibb lettuce leaves
- ½ English cucumber, finely chopped
- 1 small sweet red pepper, finely chopped
- 3 green onions, chopped
- ½ cup each coarsely chopped fresh basil, cilantro and mint

- 1 jalapeno pepper, seeded and finely chopped
- ¼ cup salted peanuts, chopped
  Hoisin sauce
  Lime wedges

1. In a small bowl, mix vinegar, sugar and salt until blended. Stir in carrots and onion; let stand at room temperature 30 minutes.

2. In a large skillet, cook the pork, ginger and garlic over medium heat 6-8 minutes or until pork is no longer pink, breaking up pork into crumbles; drain. Stir in soy sauce, mirin, salt, pepper and, if desired, fish sauce.

3. To serve, drain carrot mixture. Place pork mixture in lettuce leaves; top with cucumber, red pepper, green onions, carrot mixture and herbs. Sprinkle with jalapeno and peanuts; drizzle with hoisin sauce. Squeeze lime juice over tops. Fold lettuce over filling.

Chicken Pesto Pizza

This is the only pizza I make now. We love it! Keeping the spices simple helps the flavor of the chicken and vegetables to come through. The pizza tastes great and is good for you, too.

—HEATHER THOMPSON WOODLAND HILLS, CALIFORNIA

PREP: 35 MIN. + RISING **BAKE:** 20 MIN. **MAKES:** 8 SLICES

- 2 teaspoons active dry yeast
- 1 cup warm water (110° to 115°)
- 2¾ cups bread flour, divided
- 1 tablespoon plus 2 teaspoons olive oil, divided
- 1 tablespoon sugar
- 1½ teaspoons salt, divided
- ½ pound boneless skinless chicken breasts, cut into ½-inch pieces
- 1 small onion, halved and thinly sliced
- ½ each small green, sweet red and yellow peppers, julienned
- ½ cup sliced fresh mushrooms
- 3 tablespoons prepared pesto
- 1½ cups (6 ounces) shredded part-skim mozzarella cheese
- ¼ teaspoon pepper

1. In a large bowl, dissolve yeast in warm water. Beat in 1 cup flour, 1 tablespoon oil, sugar and 1 teaspoon salt. Add the remaining flour; beat until combined.

2. Turn onto a lightly floured surface; knead until smooth and elastic, about 6-8 minutes. Place in a bowl coated with cooking spray, turning once to coat top. Cover and let rise in a warm place until doubled, about 1 hour.

3. In a large nonstick skillet over medium heat, cook the chicken, onion, peppers and mushrooms in remaining oil until chicken is no longer pink and vegetables are tender. Remove from the heat; set aside.

4. Punch dough down; roll into a 15-in. circle. Transfer to a 14-in. pizza pan. Build up edges slightly. Spread with pesto. Top with chicken mixture and cheese. Sprinkle with pepper and remaining salt.

5. Bake at 400° for 18-20 minutes or until crust and cheese are lightly browned.

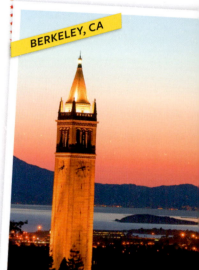

BERKELEY, CA

Berkeley is a small city with a big hunger for the arts, culture and cuisine, including Chez Panisse, one of the eateries credited with inventing California-style pizza.

" My husband, daughter and I raise hazelnuts in the Willamette Valley—so this salad is a family favorite. Since pears and cherries are also in abundance in our area, I included them in this recipe. **"**

—KAREN KIRSCH
ST. PAUL, OREGON

Hazelnut and Pear Salad

PREP/TOTAL TIME: 25 MIN. **MAKES:** 6 SERVINGS

⅓ **cup plus ½ cup chopped hazelnuts, toasted, divided**
2 **tablespoons plus ½ cup chopped red onion, divided**
2 **tablespoons water**
4½ **teaspoons balsamic vinegar**
4½ **teaspoons sugar**
½ **teaspoon salt**
1 **garlic clove, halved**
⅛ **teaspoon paprika**
¼ **cup olive oil**
1 **package (5 ounces) spring mix salad greens**
1 **medium pear, thinly sliced**
½ **cup crumbled Gorgonzola cheese**
¼ **cup dried cherries**

1. For dressing, place ⅓ cup hazelnuts, 2 tablespoons onion, water, vinegar, sugar, salt, garlic and paprika in a food processor; cover and process until blended. While processing, gradually add oil in a steady stream.

2. In a large bowl, combine salad greens and remaining onion; add ½ cup dressing and toss to coat. Divide among six salad plates.

3. Top each salad with pear, cheese, cherries and remaining hazelnuts; drizzle with the remaining dressing.

Elegant Artichokes

Artichokes lend an elegant touch to any meal. This recipe adds a tangy lemon dressing for an extra-special touch.

—**PAT STEVENS** GRANBURY, TEXAS

PREP: 10 MIN. **COOK:** 35 MIN. + CHILLING **MAKES:** 5 SERVINGS (1¾ CUPS DIP)

- 5 **medium artichokes**
- 4 **teaspoons lemon juice**
- 2 **medium lemons, sliced**
- 2 **garlic cloves, minced**

LEMON-PEPPER DIP
- 1 **cup canola oil**
- ¼ **cup lemon juice**
- ¼ **cup red wine vinegar**
- 2 **tablespoons spicy brown mustard**
- 3 **garlic cloves, minced**
- 1 **teaspoon salt**
- ¾ **teaspoon pepper**
- ½ **cup diced green pepper**
- 2 **tablespoons sliced green onion**

1. Cut off stem at base of artichoke. Cut 1 in. from the top. With scissors, snip the tip end of each leaf. Remove outer leaves. Rub cut ends of leaves with lemon juice.

2. Place artichokes in a Dutch oven; add lemon slices and garlic. Cover with water. Bring to a boil. Reduce heat; cover and simmer for 30-45 minutes or until artichoke leaves near the center pull out easily. Drain; arrange on a serving platter. Refrigerate for 1 hour.

3. For dip, in a bowl, whisk the oil, lemon juice, vinegar, mustard, garlic, salt and pepper. Stir in green pepper and onion. Serve with artichokes.

Microwaved Elegant Artichokes: *Place prepared artichokes in a microwave-safe dish, omitting the lemon slices and garlic; add 1 in. of water. Cover and microwave on high for 10-15 minutes or until leaves near the center pull out easily. Chill and serve as directed.*

◆─◆ dishing about food

Most of California's artichoke production is in Monterey County. The bulk of the crop is harvested between March and May.

CASTROVILLE, CA

Artie the Artichoke presides over festivities at the Castroville Artichoke Festival. For two days in May, visitors will find these spiky treats whipped up in recipes and fashioned into agro-art—ever see an artichoke armadillo? Here's your chance!

Idaho supplies us with more potatoes than any other state, about one-fifth of the nation's crop. Idaho growers proudly claim their mashed russets are fluffier and more flavorful than those from other states.

IDAHO

Potato fields and irrigation systems stretch across southern Idaho's landscape, from Driggs in the east to Caldwell in the west.

Baked Potato Cheddar Soup

A few simple kitchen staples make for an impressive soup. Use a better-quality yellow cheddar cheese; it adds greater depth of color and flavor to this dish.

—**KRISTIN REYNOLDS** VAN BUREN, ARKANSAS

PREP/TOTAL TIME: 30 MIN. **MAKES:** 4 SERVINGS

- ⅓ **cup all-purpose flour**
- 3 **cups milk**
- 2 **large potatoes, baked, peeled and coarsely mashed (1½ pounds)**
- ⅓ **cup plus 2 tablespoons shredded cheddar cheese, divided**
- ½ **teaspoon salt**
- ¼ **teaspoon pepper**
- ½ **cup sour cream**
- ½ **cup thinly sliced green onions, divided**
   Crumbled cooked bacon, optional

1. In a large saucepan, whisk flour and milk until smooth. Bring to a boil; cook and stir for 2 minutes or until thickened. Stir in the

potatoes, ⅓ cup cheese, salt and pepper. Cook over medium heat for 2-3 minutes or until the cheese is melted.

2. Remove from the heat. Stir in sour cream and ¼ cup onions until blended. Cover; cook over medium heat for 10-12 minutes or until soup is heated through (do not boil). Garnish with the remaining cheese, onions and, if desired, bacon.

Chili Artichoke Dip

It's not tricky to prepare this warm, tempting dip. Cheesy and satisfying, it gets a bit of zip from the chilies and marinated artichokes.

—**LEANNE MUELLER** STOCKTON, CALIFORNIA

PREP/TOTAL TIME: 25 MIN. **MAKES:** ABOUT 3½ CUPS

- 1 **can (14 ounces) water-packed artichoke hearts, rinsed, drained and chopped**
- 1 **jar (6½ ounces) marinated artichoke hearts, drained and chopped**
- 1 **can (4 ounces) chopped green chilies**
- 3 **cups (12 ounces) shredded cheddar cheese**
- ¼ **cup mayonnaise**
   Assorted crackers or tortilla chips

1. In a large bowl, combine the artichokes, chilies, cheese and mayonnaise. Transfer to a greased 8-in. square baking dish.

2. Bake, uncovered, at 350° for 20-25 minutes or until cheese is melted. Serve warm with crackers or tortilla chips.

Avocado Malibu Salad

One of the first things I learned when I moved here from Oregon was to make light salads like this. They're practical, easy and delicious.

—**BRENDA BRINKLEY** WATSONVILLE, CALIFORNIA

PREP: 10 MIN. + CHILLING **MAKES:** 4 SERVINGS

- ¼ **cup sour cream**
- ¼ **teaspoon curry powder**
- ⅛ **teaspoon salt**
- 1 **cup diced cooked chicken**
- 1 **can (8 ounces) pineapple chunks, drained**
- ¼ **cup chopped green pepper**
- ¼ **cup frozen or canned crabmeat, drained, flaked and cartilage removed**
- 1 **tablespoon diced pimientos**
- 2 **large avocados, peeled and sliced**
- 2 **tablespoons lemon juice**
  Lettuce leaves
  Red grapes, optional

1. In a large bowl, combine sour cream, curry powder and salt. Add the chicken, pineapple, green pepper, crab and pimientos. Cover and refrigerate for 1-2 hours. Just before serving, toss avocados with lemon juice. Place avocados and crab mixture on lettuce. Garnish with grapes if desired.

Cowboy Baked Beans

Baked beans are a perennial favorite at barbecues. My meaty recipe uses a variety of beans and has a great smoky taste.

—**JOE SHERWOOD** TRYON, NEBRASKA

PREP: 25 MIN. **BAKE:** 50 MIN.
MAKES: 12 SERVINGS (¾ CUP EACH)

- 1 **pound ground beef**
- 1 **pound bacon, cooked and crumbled**
- 2 **cups barbecue sauce**
- 1 **can (16 ounces) butter beans, rinsed and drained**
- 1 **can (15¾ ounces) pork and beans**
- 1 **can (15½ ounces) navy beans, rinsed and drained**
- 1 **can (15 ounces) black beans, rinsed and drained**
- 2 **medium onions, chopped**
- ¼ **cup packed brown sugar**
- ¼ **cup molasses**
- 2 **tablespoons balsamic vinegar**
- 2 **teaspoons ground mustard**
- 2 **teaspoons Worcestershire sauce**
- 1 **teaspoon salt**
- 1 **teaspoon garlic powder**
- 1 **teaspoon pepper**

1. In a Dutch oven, cook beef over medium heat until no longer pink; drain. Stir in the remaining ingredients.

2. Transfer to a greased 13x9-in. baking dish. Bake, uncovered, at 350° for 50-60 minutes or until heated through.

Summer Kimchi

Ginger enhances these spicy Korean-style pickled veggies. Spoon some on hot dogs for a real treat!

—**STEPHEN EXEL** DES MOINES, IOWA

PREP: 30 MIN. + CHILLING **MAKES:** 10 CUPS

- 1 head Chinese or napa cabbage, chopped
- ⅓ cup plus 1 tablespoon kosher salt, divided
- 1 large cucumber, peeled and thinly sliced
- 12 radishes, thinly sliced
- 4 green onions, chopped
- 3 large garlic cloves, thinly sliced
- 1 piece peeled fresh gingerroot (1 inch), sliced
- 3 quarts water
- ¼ cup rice vinegar
- 1 tablespoon Asian red chili paste

1. Place cabbage in a colander over a plate; sprinkle with ⅓ cup salt and toss. Let stand for 30 minutes. Rinse and drain well. In a very large container, combine the cabbage, cucumber, radishes, onions, garlic and ginger.

2. In a large bowl, combine water, vinegar, chili paste and remaining salt; pour over vegetable mixture. Cover and refrigerate for at least 2 days before serving, stirring occasionally. May be transferred to small airtight containers and stored in the refrigerator for up to 3 weeks. Serve with a slotted spoon.

Sourdough Starter

Some 25 years ago, I received this recipe and some starter from a good friend who is now a neighbor. I've used it to make many loaves.

—**DELILA GEORGE** JUNCTION CITY, OREGON

PREP: 10 MIN. + STANDING **MAKES:** ABOUT 3 CUPS

- 1 package (¼ ounce) active dry yeast
- 2 cups warm water (110° to 115°)
- 2 cups all-purpose flour

1. In a 4-qt. nonmetallic bowl, dissolve yeast in warm water; let stand for 5 minutes. Add flour; stir until smooth. Cover loosely with a clean towel. Let stand in a warm place (80°-90°) to ferment for 48 hours; stir several times daily (the mixture will become bubbly and rise, have "yeasty" sour aroma and a transparent yellow liquid will form on the top).

2. Use the starter for your favorite sourdough recipes. It will keep in the refrigerator for up to 2 weeks. Use and replenish at least every 2 weeks. Replenish with equal amounts of flour and water to restore the volume; stir.

Sourdough French Bread

These loaves rival any found in stores and can be made with relative ease.

—**DELILA GEORGE** JUNCTION CITY, OREGON

PREP: 15 MIN. + RISING **BAKE:** 20 MIN. + COOLING
MAKES: 2 LOAVES (10 SLICES EACH)

- 1 package (¼ ounce) active dry yeast
- 1¾ cups warm water (110° to 115°)
- ¼ cup Sourdough Starter (recipe at left)
- 2 tablespoons canola oil
- 2 tablespoons sugar
- 2 teaspoons salt
- 4¼ cups all-purpose flour

CORNSTARCH WASH
- ½ cup water
- 1½ teaspoons cornstarch

1. In a large bowl, dissolve yeast in warm water. Add the Sourdough Starter, oil, sugar, salt and 3 cups flour. Beat until smooth. Stir in enough additional flour to form a soft ball.

2. Turn onto a floured surface; gently knead 20-30 times (dough will be slightly sticky). Place in a greased bowl, turning once to grease the top. Cover and let rise in a warm place until doubled, about 1 to 1½ hours.

3. Punch dough down. Turn onto a lightly floured surface; divide in half. Roll each into a 12x8-in. rectangle. Roll up, jelly-roll style, starting with a long side; pinch ends to seal. Place, seam side down, on two greased baking sheets; tuck ends under. Cover and let rise until doubled, about 30 minutes.

4. With a sharp knife, make four shallow diagonal slashes across top of each of the loaves. In a small saucepan, combine water and cornstarch. Cook and stir over medium heat until thickened. Brush some over loaves.

5. Bake at 400° for 15 minutes. Brush loaves with the remaining cornstarch wash. Bake 5-10 minutes longer or until lightly browned. Remove from pans to wire racks to cool.

All-Day Apple Butter

I make several batches of this simple and delicious apple butter to freeze in jars. You can adjust the sugar to taste, depending on the sweetness of the apples used.

—**BETTY RUENHOLL** SYRACUSE, NEBRASKA

PREP: 20 MIN.   **COOK:** 11 HOURS   **MAKES:** 4 PINTS

- 5½ pounds apples, peeled and finely chopped
- 4 cups sugar
- 2 to 3 teaspoons ground cinnamon
- ¼ teaspoon ground cloves
- ¼ teaspoon salt

1. Place apples in a 3-qt. slow cooker. Combine sugar, cinnamon, cloves and salt; pour over apples and mix well. Cover and cook on high for 1 hour.

2. Reduce heat to low; cover and cook for 9-11 hours or until thickened and dark brown, stirring occasionally (stir more frequently as it thickens to prevent sticking).

3. Uncover and cook on low 1 hour longer. If desired, stir with a wire whisk until smooth. Spoon into freezer containers, leaving ½-in. headspace. Cover and refrigerate or freeze.

Miso Soup with Tofu and Enoki

Here's a traditional Japanese soup recipe that has a mild flavor but is so comforting. Sliced green onions provide a bit of color.

—**BRIDGET KLUSMAN** OTSEGO, MICHIGAN

PREP/TOTAL TIME: 30 MIN.   **MAKES:** 5 SERVINGS

- 2 packages (3½ ounces each) fresh enoki mushrooms or ½ pound sliced fresh mushrooms
- 1 medium onion, chopped
- 2 garlic cloves, minced
- 1 teaspoon minced fresh gingerroot
- 1 tablespoon canola oil
- 4 cups water
- ¼ cup miso paste
- 1 package (16 ounces) firm tofu, drained and cut into ¾-inch cubes
  Thinly sliced green onions

1. In a Dutch oven, saute the mushrooms, onion, garlic and ginger in oil until tender. Add the water and miso paste. Bring to a boil. Reduce heat; simmer, uncovered, for 15 minutes. Add the tofu; heat through. Ladle into bowls; garnish with green onions.

Editor's Note: *Look for miso paste in natural food or Asian markets.*

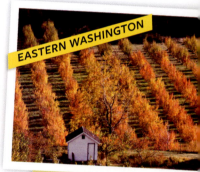

EASTERN WASHINGTON

On the land east of the Cascade Mountains, you'll find more than 175,000 acres of apple orchards.

When most of us hear the word "scones," the Utah variety don't usually come to mind. These scones are fried bread—but sweeter than the typical Navajo fry bread. Since Utah is the Beehive State, there's no better accompaniment for these scones than honey butter.

Utah Buttermilk Scones

Buttermilk makes these classic Utah scones so delightful that you'll most likely eat too many. Their texture is light and airy, and their taste, delightful! This recipe is a family favorite that we enjoy often. Don't forget the honey butter—it's the perfect addition to the perfect scone!

—NICHOLE JONES PLEASANT GROVE, UTAH

PREP: 30 MIN. + RISING   **COOK:** 5 MIN./BATCH   **MAKES:** 2 DOZEN

- 1 **tablespoon active dry yeast**
- ½ **cup warm water (110° to 115°)**
- 1 **cup warm buttermilk, (110° to 115°)**
- 1 **egg**
- 3 **tablespoons canola oil**
- 1½ **teaspoons sugar**
- ½ **teaspoon salt**
- ¼ **teaspoon baking soda**
- 4 **to 4½ cups all-purpose flour**
  Oil for deep-fat frying

HONEY BUTTER
- ½ **cup butter, softened**
- ¼ **cup honey**
- ¼ **cup confectioners' sugar**
- ¼ **teaspoon vanilla extract**

1. In a large bowl, dissolve yeast in warm water. In another large bowl, combine the buttermilk, egg, oil, sugar, salt, baking soda, yeast mixture and 2 cups flour; beat on medium until smooth. Stir in enough remaining flour to form a stiff dough.

2. Turn onto a floured surface; knead until smooth and elastic, about 6-8 minutes. Place in a greased bowl, turning once to grease the top. Cover with plastic wrap and let rise in a warm place until doubled, about 1 hour.

3. Punch dough down. Turn onto a lightly floured surface; roll dough into a 16x8-in. rectangle. Cut into 24 rectangles. Cover with a clean kitchen towel and let rest for 1 hour.

4. In an electric skillet or deep fryer, heat oil to 375°. Fry scones, a few at a time, until golden brown on both sides. Drain on paper towels.

5. For honey butter, in a large bowl, combine butter, honey, confectioners' sugar and vanilla; beat until smooth. Spread on scones.

Pineapple Lime Gelatin

This recipe was passed down by my mother. We serve it often, but especially at Christmas and Thanksgiving. Of course, the green color makes it nice for St. Patrick's Day, too. With the marshmallows, pecans and whipped cream, the sweet salad can even be served as a light dessert. I like to cook for both small groups and large crowds. And when our entire family gets together for thanks and feasting, it's a wonderful time!

—WANDA WEATHERMON COMANCHE, TEXAS

PREP: 15 MIN. + CHILLING **MAKES:** 12 SERVINGS

- 1 **package (3 ounces) lime gelatin**
- 2 **cups boiling water, divided**
- 16 **large marshmallows**
- 1 **package (3 ounces) cream cheese, softened**
- 1 **can (8 ounces) unsweetened crushed pineapple, undrained**
- 1 **cup heavy whipping cream, whipped**
- 1 **cup chopped pecans**
- 2 **to 3 drops green food coloring, optional**

1. In a large bowl, dissolve gelatin in 1 cup boiling water; set aside. In a small saucepan, combine marshmallows and remaining water.

Cook over low heat until marshmallows are melted, stirring occasionally. Stir into gelatin. Refrigerate until partially set.

2. In a large bowl, beat cream cheese until smooth. Beat in pineapple. Fold in the gelatin mixture, whipped cream, pecans and food coloring if desired. Pour into a 6-cup mold coated with cooking spray. Refrigerate until set. Unmold onto a serving plate.

Teriyaki Beef Jerky

Jerky is a portable, chewy snack—and now you can make your own with our easy recipe. The meat has a savory flavor and a bit of heat.

—TASTE OF HOME TEST KITCHEN

PREP: 40 MIN. + MARINATING **BAKE:** 4 HOURS
MAKES: 8 SERVINGS

- 1 **beef flank steak (1½ to 2 pounds)**
- ⅔ **cup reduced-sodium soy sauce**
- ⅔ **cup Worcestershire sauce**
- ¼ **cup honey**
- 3 **teaspoons coarsely ground pepper**
- 2 **teaspoons onion powder**
- 2 **teaspoons garlic powder**
- 1½ **teaspoons crushed red pepper flakes**
- 1 **teaspoon liquid smoke**

1. Trim all visible fat from steak. Freeze, covered, 30 minutes or until firm. Slice steak along the grain into long ⅛-in. thick strips.

2. Transfer to a large resealable plastic bag. In a small bowl, whisk remaining ingredients; add to the beef. Seal the bag and turn to coat. Refrigerate 2 hours or overnight, turning occasionally.

3. Preheat oven to 170°. Transfer beef and marinade to a large saucepan; bring to a boil. Reduce heat; simmer 5 minutes. Using tongs, remove beef from marinade; drain on paper towels. Discard marinade.

4. Arrange beef strips in single layer on wire racks placed on 15x10x1-in. baking pans. Dry in oven 4-5 hours or until beef becomes dry and leathery, rotating pans occasionally. (Or use a commercial dehydrator, following manufacturer's directions.)

5. Remove from oven; cool completely. Using paper towels, blot any beads of oil on jerky. For best quality and longer storage, store jerky, covered, in refrigerator or freezer.

California produces the most garlic of any state in the union. The Christopher Ranch in Gilroy is one of the largest garlic shippers in the world. Gilroy has been hosting a garlic festival every year since 1979, raising money for community organizations.

GILROY, CA

Who knew that garlic could draw a crowd? The Gilroy Garlic Festival is one of America's largest food-centric celebrations! Each year, it's held on the last full weekend in July.

Creamy Garlic Dressing

This zippy dressing punches up the flavor of any refreshing warm-weather salad. The wonderful garlic taste comes through and the creamy mix coats the lettuce beautifully.

—**SALLY HOLBROOK** PASADENA, CALIFORNIA

PREP/TOTAL TIME: 5 MIN. **MAKES:** 1⅔ CUPS

- 1   cup canola oil
- ½   cup sour cream
- ¼   cup heavy whipping cream
- ¼   cup cider vinegar
- 1   teaspoon salt
- 1   large garlic clove, minced
      Salad greens

1. In a jar with a tight-fitting lid, combine the oil, sour cream, cream, vinegar, salt and garlic; shake well. Chill. Serve with salad greens. Refrigerate leftovers.

Finnish Bread

Here's a recipe brought over from Finland by pioneers who settled the area. We make this bread for a local festival that features foods from different countries.

—**ARTHUR LUAMA** RED LODGE, MONTANA

PREP: 20 MIN. + RISING **BAKE:** 40 MIN.
MAKES: 2 LOAVES (12 SLICES EACH)

- 1   package (¼ ounce) active dry yeast
- 2   cups warm water (110° to 115°)
- 1   cup whole wheat flour
- ¼   cup butter, melted, divided
- 1   tablespoon brown sugar
- 2   teaspoons salt
- 4½ to 5 cups all-purpose flour

1. In a large bowl, dissolve yeast in water. Add the whole wheat flour, 2 tablespoons of butter, brown sugar, salt and 2 cups of flour; beat until smooth. Add enough remaining flour to form a soft dough.

2. Turn onto a floured surface; knead until smooth and elastic, about 6-8 minutes. Place in a greased bowl, turning once to grease top. Cover and let rise in a warm place until doubled, about 1 hour.

3. Punch the dough down. Shape into two 6-in. rounds; place on a greased baking sheet. Cut slashes in tops with a knife. Cover and let rise in warm place until doubled, about 40 minutes.

4. Bake at 400° for 40-45 minutes or until golden brown. Brush with remaining butter.

Hawaiian Sweet Bread

Pineapple juice enhances the slightly sweet flavor of this delicious bread. My recipe makes three loaves, so you can keep one for yourself and offer the others as gifts.

—**RUTHIE BANKS** PRESCOTT, ARIZONA

PREP: 20 MIN. + RISING **BAKE:** 20 MIN. + COOLING
MAKES: 3 LOAVES (12 WEDGES EACH)

- 7 to 7½ cups all-purpose flour
- ¾ cup mashed potato flakes
- ⅔ cup sugar
- 2 packages (¼ ounce each) active dry yeast
- 1 teaspoon salt
- ½ teaspoon ground ginger
- 1 cup milk
- ½ cup water
- ½ cup butter, softened
- 1 cup pineapple juice
- 3 eggs
- 2 teaspoons vanilla extract

1. In a large bowl, combine 3 cups flour, potato flakes, sugar, yeast, salt and ginger. In a small saucepan, heat the milk, water, butter and pineapple juice to 120°-130°. Add to dry ingredients; beat just until moistened. Add the eggs; beat until smooth. Beat in vanilla. Stir in enough remaining flour to form a soft dough.

2. Turn onto a floured surface; knead until smooth and elastic, about 6-8 minutes. Place in a greased bowl, turning once to grease the top. Cover and let rise in a warm place until doubled, about 1¼ hours.

3. Punch dough down. Turn onto a lightly floured surface; divide into thirds. Shape each into a ball. Place in three greased 9-in. round baking pans. Cover and let rise until doubled, about 45 minutes.

4. Bake at 375° for 20-25 minutes or until golden brown. Cover loosely with foil if top browns too quickly. Remove from pans to wire racks to cool.

Lentil-Tomato Soup

Double the recipe and share this hearty soup with neighbors and loved ones on cold winter nights. I serve it with corn bread for dunking.

—**MICHELLE CURTIS** BAKER CITY, OREGON

PREP: 15 MIN. **COOK:** 30 MIN. **MAKES:** 6 SERVINGS

- 4½ cups water
- 4 medium carrots, sliced
- 1 medium onion, chopped
- ⅔ cup dried lentils, rinsed
- 1 can (6 ounces) tomato paste
- 2 tablespoons minced fresh parsley
- 1 tablespoon brown sugar
- 1 tablespoon white vinegar
- 1 teaspoon garlic salt
- ½ teaspoon dried thyme
- ¼ teaspoon dill weed
- ¼ teaspoon dried tarragon
- ¼ teaspoon pepper

1. In a large saucepan, combine the water, carrots, onion and lentils; bring to a boil. Reduce heat; cover and simmer for 20-25 minutes or until vegetables and lentils are tender.

2. Stir in the remaining ingredients; return to a boil. Reduce heat; simmer, uncovered, for 5 minutes to allow flavors to blend.

dishing about food

Portuguese settlers came to Hawaii in the 1870s to work the sugarcane fields. Their recipe for sweet bread was so popular that it became known as Hawaiian sweet bread.

> **Here is my twist on the popular tomato-mozzarella salad. Go ahead and splurge on the fresh mozzarella, the rest of the salad is so light!**
>
> —**TARI AMBLER**
> SHOREWOOD, ILLINOIS

Colorful Tomato 'n' Mozzarella Salad

PREP: 20 MIN. + STANDING   **MAKES:** 4 SERVINGS

- 1 **cup fresh baby spinach**
- 2 **medium yellow tomatoes, sliced**
- 2 **medium red tomatoes, sliced**
- 4 **ounces fresh mozzarella cheese, sliced**
- 2 **tablespoons thinly sliced fresh basil leaves**
- ¼ **teaspoon salt**
- ¼ **teaspoon pepper**
- 1 **tablespoon balsamic vinegar**
- 2 **teaspoons olive oil**

1. Arrange spinach on a platter; top with tomato and cheese slices. Sprinkle with basil, salt and pepper. Drizzle with vinegar and oil. Let stand for 15 minutes before serving.

California Sushi Rolls

This tastes as good as any restaurant California roll. For best results, be sure to use sushi rice.

—TASTE OF HOME TEST KITCHEN

PREP: 1 HOUR + STANDING **MAKES:** 64 PIECES

- 2 **cups sushi rice, rinsed and drained**
- 2 **cups water**
- ¼ **cup rice vinegar**
- 2 **tablespoons sugar**
- ½ **teaspoon salt**
- 2 **tablespoons sesame seeds, toasted**
- 2 **tablespoons black sesame seeds**
  Bamboo sushi mat
- 8 **nori sheets**
- 1 **small cucumber, seeded and julienned**
- 3 **ounces imitation crabmeat, julienned**
- 1 **medium ripe avocado, peeled and julienned**
  Reduced-sodium soy sauce, prepared
  wasabi and pickled ginger slices, optional

1. In a large saucepan, combine the rice and water; let stand for 30 minutes. Bring to a boil. Reduce heat to low; cover and simmer for 15-20 minutes or until water is absorbed and rice is tender. Remove from heat. Let stand, covered, for 10 minutes.

2. Meanwhile, in small bowl, combine vinegar, sugar and salt, stirring until sugar is dissolved.

3. Transfer the rice to a large shallow bowl; drizzle with vinegar mixture. With a wooden paddle or spoon, stir rice with a slicing motion to cool slightly. Cover with a damp cloth to keep moist. (Rice mixture may be made up to 2 hours ahead and stored at room temperature, covered with a damp towel. Do not refrigerate.)

4. Sprinkle toasted and black sesame seeds onto a plate; set aside. Place sushi mat on a work surface so mat rolls away from you; line with plastic wrap. Place ¾ cup rice on plastic. With moistened fingers, press rice into an 8-in. square. Top with one nori sheet.

5. Arrange a small amount of cucumber, crab and avocado about 1½ in. from bottom edge of nori sheet. Roll up rice mixture over filling, using the bamboo mat to lift and compress the mixture as you roll; remove plastic wrap as you roll.

6. Remove mat; roll sushi rolls in sesame seeds. Cover with plastic wrap. Repeat with remaining ingredients to make eight rolls. Cut each into eight pieces. Serve with soy sauce, wasabi and ginger slices if desired.

The mai tai, which means "the very best" in Tahitian, may bring to mind gentle ocean breezes and tropical white sand beaches, but it was created in Oakland. Victor Bergeron served the first one at his Trader Vic's restaurant in 1944. In the 1950s, he introduced it in Hawaii; it's now considered that state's signature cocktail.

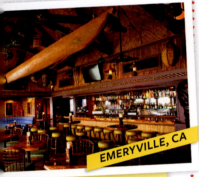

EMERYVILLE, CA

Trader Vic's is synonymous with classic tiki cocktails. In fact, bartenders still turn to Victor's 1946 book, *Trader Vic's Book of Food and Drink*. The tropical flavors became so popular, the restaurant is now an international chain, with its flagship in Emeryville.

Mai Tai

This party favorite has been around for quite some time. It's not overly fruity and features a good blend of sweet and sour. For a splash of color, garnish with strawberries and lime.

—TASTE OF HOME TEST KITCHEN

PREP/TOTAL TIME: 5 MIN. **MAKES:** 1 SERVING

- 1½ to 2 cups ice cubes
- 2 ounces light rum
- ¾ ounce Triple Sec
- ½ ounce lemon juice
- 1½ teaspoons lime juice
- 1½ teaspoons amaretto

GARNISH

Lime slice and twist

1. Fill a shaker three-fourths full with ice. Place remaining ice in a rocks glass; set aside.

2. Add rum, Triple Sec, juices and amaretto to shaker; cover and shake for 10-15 seconds or until condensation forms on outside of shaker. Strain into prepared glass. Garnish as desired.

Stir-Fried Asparagus

Asparagus is one of my favorite veggies—but then, I grew up in Stockton, California, where there's an annual festival to celebrate it! I like it best stir-fried.

—CAROLYN SUTTER ORANGEVALE, CALIFORNIA

PREP/TOTAL TIME: 20 MIN. **MAKES:** 4 SERVINGS

- 1½ pounds fresh asparagus, trimmed and cut into 2-inch pieces (about 4 cups)
- 2 tablespoons butter
- 1 tablespoon canola oil
- 3 tablespoons chicken broth
- 1 teaspoon lemon juice
- 1 teaspoon soy sauce
- ¼ teaspoon pepper
- 2 tablespoons slivered almonds, toasted

1. In a large skillet or wok, stir-fry asparagus in butter and oil for 2 minutes. Stir in the broth, lemon juice, soy sauce and pepper. Cover and cook for 2-3 minutes or until asparagus is tender. Sprinkle with almonds.

Holiday Almonds

These sweet and flavorful nuts are downright addictive! They're simple to make, and I love serving them at parties or as a quick snack.

—TRISHA KRUSE EAGLE, IDAHO

PREP/TOTAL TIME: 30 MIN. **MAKES:** 2 CUPS

- ½ cup packed brown sugar
- 1 teaspoon apple pie spice or pumpkin pie spice
- ½ teaspoon curry powder
- ¼ teaspoon salt
- 1 tablespoon egg white
- 2 cups blanched almonds

1. In a small bowl, combine brown sugar and seasonings; set aside. In another bowl, whisk egg white until foamy. Add almonds; toss to coat. Add spice mixture; toss to coat.

2. Spread the almonds on a greased foil-lined baking sheet. Bake at 325° for 20-25 minutes or until lightly browned, stirring occasionally. Cool completely. Store in an airtight container.

Lick-the-Bowl-Clean Hummus

Everyone loves hummus, but I enjoy the garlic and onion flavors so much that I decided to let them shine in this homemade version. I get so many compliments on it!

—SARAH GILBERT HARTWELL BEAVERTON, OREGON

PREP: 10 MIN. **COOK:** 35 MIN. **MAKES:** 2½ CUPS

- 2 large sweet onions, thinly sliced
- ¼ cup plus ⅓ cup olive oil, **divided**
- 1 can (15 ounces) garbanzo beans or chickpeas, rinsed and drained
- ¼ cup plus 2 tablespoons lemon juice
- ¼ cup tahini
- 4 garlic cloves, minced
- ⅛ teaspoon salt
- ⅛ teaspoon pepper
  Baked pita chips or assorted fresh vegetables

1. In a large skillet, saute onions in ¼ cup oil until softened. Reduce heat to medium-low; cook, stirring occasionally, for 30 minutes or until deep golden brown.

2. Transfer to a food processor; add beans, lemon juice, tahini, garlic, salt, pepper and remaining oil. Cover and process for 30 seconds or until smooth. Serve with chips.

Wine coolers, once a homemade concoction, became big business in the early 1980s. California Wine Coolers were the first to hit the market, followed by products from Bartles & Jaymes, Seagram's and Gallo. Consumers lost interest in wine coolers in the late '80s, and when Congress increased the federal excise tax on wine in 1991, the wine in coolers was replaced with malt-based alcohol.

CALIFORNIA'S NORTH COAST

The North Coast includes wine hot spots like Napa Valley and Sonoma County. Vineyards in this region make up more than half of those in all of California.

Peach Wine Coolers

The fantastic flavors of honey, wine and brandy come through to make this special and summery drink for a party. It's like sunshine in a glass!

—ANNIE HENDRICKS BURBANK, CALIFORNIA

PREP: 15 MIN. + CHILLING **MAKES:** 9 SERVINGS

- 2 **cups frozen unsweetened sliced peaches, thawed**
- ½ **cup brandy**
- ⅓ **cup honey**
- ½ **lemon, very thinly sliced**
- 1 **bottle (750 milliliters) dry white wine**
- 1½ **cups carbonated water, chilled**
  Ice cubes

1. In a 2-qt. pitcher, combine the peach slices, brandy, honey and lemon slices; stir in wine. Refrigerate for 2-4 hours or until chilled.

2. Just before serving, stir in sparkling water. Serve over ice.

Lentil Vegetable Soup

Here is one good-for-you dish that our kids really enjoy. You can serve this tasty soup as a hearty meatless entree or pair it with a favorite sandwich.

—**JOY MAYNARD** ST. IGNATIUS, MONTANA

PREP: 10 MIN. **COOK:** 65 MIN. **MAKES:** 6 SERVINGS

- 3 cans (14½ ounces each) vegetable broth
- 1 medium onion, chopped
- ½ cup dried lentils, rinsed
- ½ cup uncooked long grain brown rice
- ½ cup tomato juice
- 1 can (5½ ounces) spicy hot V8 juice
- 1 tablespoon reduced-sodium soy sauce
- 1 tablespoon canola oil
- 1 medium potato, peeled and cubed
- 1 medium tomato, cubed
- 1 medium carrot, sliced
- 1 celery rib, sliced

1. In a large saucepan, combine the first eight ingredients. Bring to a boil. Reduce heat; cover and simmer for 30 minutes.

2. Add the potato, tomato, carrot and celery; cover and simmer 30 minutes longer or until rice and vegetables are tender.

PULLMAN, WA

If you visit the National Lentil Festival, keep an eye out for Tase T. Lentil! This annual August event is held in the Palouse region of Washington and Idaho, where about 25 percent of the nation's lentils are cultivated.

Viva Panzanella

Add some white beans, and suddenly this traditional Italian bread and tomato salad is filling enough to stand on its own. It's also a delicious way to use up those fresh tomatoes from the garden or farmers market.

—**PATRICIA LEVENSON** SANTA ANA, CALIFORNIA

PREP: 40 MIN. **MAKES:** 6 SERVINGS

- ¾ **pound sourdough bread, cubed (about 8 cups)**
- 2 **tablespoons olive oil**
- 2½ **pounds tomatoes (about 8 medium), chopped**
- 1 **can (15 ounces) white kidney or cannellini beans, rinsed and drained**
- 1 **can (14 ounces) water-packed artichoke hearts, rinsed, drained and quartered**
- 1 **cup thinly sliced roasted sweet red peppers**
- ½ **cup fresh basil leaves, thinly sliced**
- ⅓ **cup thinly sliced red onion**
- ¼ **cup Greek olives, quartered**
- 3 **tablespoons capers, drained**

DRESSING
- ¼ **cup balsamic vinegar**
- 3 **tablespoons minced fresh parsley**
- 3 **tablespoons olive oil**
- 3 **tablespoons lemon juice**
- 2 **tablespoons white wine vinegar**
- 3 **teaspoons minced fresh thyme or 1 teaspoon dried thyme**
- 1½ **teaspoons minced fresh marjoram or ½ teaspoon dried marjoram**
- 1½ **teaspoons minced fresh oregano or ½ teaspoon dried oregano**
- 1 **garlic clove, minced**

1. In a large bowl, toss the bread with oil and transfer to a baking sheet. Bake at 450° for 8-10 minutes or until golden brown. Cool to room temperature.

2. In a large bowl, combine tomatoes, beans, artichokes, peppers, basil, onion, olives, capers and bread.

3. In a small bowl, whisk dressing ingredients. Drizzle over the salad and toss to coat. Serve immediately.

Irish Coffee

Creme de menthe adds a festive and colorful touch to the cream floating atop these yummy drinks. If you prefer, simply top the coffee with a dollop of canned whipped cream. The drink would also be delicious with a little Irish cream liqueur stirred in.

—TASTE OF HOME TEST KITCHEN

PREP/TOTAL TIME: 10 MIN. **MAKES:** 2 SERVINGS

- 2 teaspoons sugar
- 2 ounces Irish whiskey
- 2 cups hot strong brewed coffee (French or other dark roast)
- ¼ cup heavy whipping cream
- 1 teaspoon green creme de menthe

1. Divide the sugar and whiskey between two mugs; stir in coffee. In a small bowl, beat cream and creme de menthe until thickened. Gently spoon onto tops of drinks, allowing cream to float. Serve immediately.

Editor's Note: *You may also use a portable mixer with whisk attachment to thicken the cream mixture in a 1-cup measuring cup.*

Artichoke Stuffing

This is so fabulous with turkey! I also halve the recipe and use it when I bake a chicken.

—**LORIE VERKUYL** RIDGECREST, CALIFORNIA

PREP: 30 MIN. **BAKE:** 35 MIN. **MAKES:** 14 CUPS

- 1 loaf (1 pound) sourdough bread, cut into 1-inch cubes
- ½ pound sliced fresh mushrooms
- 2 celery ribs, chopped
- 1 medium onion, chopped
- 2 tablespoons butter
- 3 to 4 garlic cloves, minced
- 2 jars (6½ ounces each) marinated artichoke hearts, drained and chopped
- ½ cup grated Parmesan cheese
- 1 teaspoon poultry seasoning
- 1 egg
- 1 can (14½ ounces) chicken broth

1. Place bread cubes in two ungreased 15x10x1-in. baking pans. Bake at 350° for 15 minutes or until lightly browned.

2. In a large skillet, saute the mushrooms, celery and onion in butter until tender. Add garlic; cook 1 minute longer. Stir in the artichokes, cheese and poultry seasoning. Transfer to a large bowl; stir in bread cubes.

3. In a small bowl, whisk egg and broth until blended. Pour over bread mixture; mix well.

4. Transfer to a greased 3-qt. baking dish (dish will be full). Cover and bake at 350° for 30 minutes. Uncover; bake 5-15 minutes longer or until a thermometer reads 165°.

SAN FRANCISCO, CA

Find the Buena Vista cafe on the corner of Hyde and Beach Streets in San Francisco's Russian Hill area.

Classic Pesto

This versatile pesto boasts a perfect basil flavor. Pair it with pasta, and you've got a quick and classic Italian dinner.

—IOLA EGLE BELLA VISTA, ARKANSAS

PREP/TOTAL TIME: 10 MIN. **MAKES:** 1 CUP

- 4 cups loosely packed basil leaves
- ½ cup grated Parmesan cheese
- 2 garlic cloves, halved
- ¼ teaspoon salt
- ½ cup pine nuts, toasted
- ½ cup olive oil

1. Place the basil, cheese, garlic and salt in a food processor; cover and pulse until chopped. Add nuts; cover and process until blended. While processing, gradually add oil in a steady stream.

Bistro Mac & Cheese

I like to serve this classic comfort food with a salad and crusty bread. It's a satisfying meal that feels upscale, but will fit into just about any grocery budget.

—CHARLOTTE GILTNER MESA, ARIZONA

PREP/TOTAL TIME: 30 MIN. **MAKES:** 8 SERVINGS

- 1 package (16 ounces) uncooked elbow macaroni
- 3 tablespoons butter
- 3 tablespoons all-purpose flour
- 2½ cups 2% milk
- 1 teaspoon salt
- ½ teaspoon onion powder
- ½ teaspoon pepper
- ¼ teaspoon garlic powder
- 1 cup (4 ounces) shredded part-skim mozzarella cheese
- 1 cup (4 ounces) shredded cheddar cheese
- 1 package (3 ounces) cream cheese, softened
- ½ cup crumbled Gorgonzola cheese
- ½ cup sour cream

1. Cook macaroni according to the package directions. Meanwhile, in a Dutch oven, melt butter. Stir in flour until smooth. Gradually stir in milk and seasonings. Bring to a boil; cook and stir for 2 minutes or until thickened.

2. Reduce heat; add the cheeses and stir until melted. Stir in sour cream. Drain macaroni; stir into sauce.

Crumb-Topped Bistro Mac: *Place prepared macaroni in a greased 3-qt. baking dish. Combine ⅓ cup seasoned bread crumbs and 2 tablespoons melted butter; sprinkle over the macaroni. Bake, uncovered, at 350° for 20-25 minutes or until casserole is bubbly.*

Fry Sauce

Want a change of pace from dipping your French fries into ketchup? Try a favorite condiment from Utah...Fry Sauce. It's a spiced-up blend of ketchup and mayo.

—TASTE OF HOME TEST KITCHEN

PREP/TOTAL TIME: 5 MIN. **MAKES:** 1½ CUPS

- 1 cup mayonnaise
- ½ cup ketchup
- 4 teaspoons sweet pickle juice
- ½ teaspoon hot pepper sauce
- ½ teaspoon onion powder
- ¼ teaspoon pepper
- ⅛ teaspoon salt
- 1 tablespoon sweet pickle relish, optional
  Hot prepared French-fried potatoes

1. In a small bowl, whisk the first seven ingredients; if desired, add pickle relish. Serve with fries. Refrigerate leftovers.

Herbed Fennel and Onion

PREP/TOTAL TIME: 30 MIN.   **MAKES:** 3 SERVINGS

- 1 large sweet onion, halved and sliced
- 1 medium fennel bulb, halved and cut into ½-inch slices
- 1 tablespoon olive oil
- 1 cup reduced-sodium chicken broth
- 1 tablespoon minced fresh sage or 1 teaspoon dried sage leaves
- 2 teaspoons minced fresh rosemary or ½ teaspoon dried rosemary, crushed
- 2 teaspoons balsamic vinegar
- ¼ teaspoon salt
- ¼ teaspoon pepper

1. In a large skillet, saute the onion and fennel in oil until crisp-tender. Add the broth, sage and rosemary. Bring to a boil; cook until broth is evaporated.

2. Remove from the heat; stir in the vinegar, salt and pepper.

> "Thinking about what to do with those fennel bulbs you brought home from the market? Try them in this aromatic and savory side dish that's so rich, no one will ever guess it's healthy. Vinegar adds just a slight tang."
>
> **—MEGHANN MINTON**
> PORTLAND, OREGON

Pomegranate Jelly

For as long as I can remember, my mom has been preparing pomegranate jelly and sending us all home with a few jars. For an even tangier jelly, substitute cranberry juice for pomegranate juice.

—**TATIANA KUSHNIR** MONTARA, CALIFORNIA

PREP: 15 MIN. **PROCESS:** 5 MIN. **MAKES:** 6 HALF-PINTS

- **3½ cups pomegranate juice**
- **1 package (1¾ ounces) powdered fruit pectin**
- **5 cups sugar**

1. In a Dutch oven, combine pomegranate juice and pectin. Bring to a full rolling boil over high heat, stirring constantly. Stir in sugar; return to a full rolling boil. Boil for 2 minutes, stirring constantly.

2. Remove from the heat; skim off foam. Pour hot liquid into hot sterilized half-pint jars, leaving ¼-in. headspace. Wipe rims and adjust lids. Process for 5 minutes in a boiling-water canner.

Editor's Note: *The processing time listed is for altitudes of 1,000 feet or less. Add 1 minute to the processing time for each 1,000 feet of additional altitude.*

Guava Coconut Rum Cocktail

My beverage is so sensational, it's like a taste of the tropics in a glass! The guava adds a touch of sweetness to the coconut drink.

—**MELANIE MILHORAT** NEW YORK, NEW YORK

PREP/TOTAL TIME: 5 MIN. **MAKES:** 1 SERVING

　　Ice cubes
2　**ounces coconut rum**
2　**ounces guava nectar**
2　**teaspoons lemon juice**
3　**to 4 dashes bitters**
1　**teaspoon simple syrup**
2　**ounces coconut water**
GARNISH
　　Fresh pineapple wedge

1. Fill a mixing glass or tumbler three-fourths full with ice. Add rum, guava nectar, lemon juice, bitters and simple syrup; stir until condensation forms on outside of glass. Strain into a chilled cocktail glass. Add ice and top with coconut water. Garnish as desired.

For nonalcoholic version: *Increase the coconut water and guava nectar to 3 ounces each. Eliminate the bitters and add ⅛ teaspoon coconut extract.*

Nutty Berry Trail Mix

This recipe, my son's favorite, earned me an A in my early childhood nutrition course. I like the fact that it gives you some control over what your children snack on!

—**CHERI MAJORS** CLAREMONT, CALIFORNIA

PREP/TOTAL TIME: 5 MIN. **MAKES:** 10 CUPS

1　**can (15 ounces) mixed nuts**
2　**cups (12 ounces) semisweet chocolate chips**
1　**package (9 ounces) raisins**
1　**package (6 ounces) chopped dried pineapple**
1　**jar (5.85 ounces) sunflower kernels**
1　**package (5 ounces) dried cranberries**

1. In a large bowl, combine all ingredients; mix well. Store in an airtight container.

KILAUEA, HI

This Kauai town (not to be confused with the volcano), has been dubbed Guava Capital of the World.

Buffalo Burger Topping

Blue cheese lovers will come out of the woodwork for this spicy, full-flavored sauce, paired perfectly with grilled burgers.

—**MICHAEL COHEN** LOS ANGELES, CALIFORNIA

PREP/TOTAL TIME: 10 MIN.   **MAKES:** 6 SERVINGS

- 2 **tablespoons butter, softened**
- 2 **tablespoons brown sugar**
- ¾ **cup mayonnaise**
- ¼ **cup Louisiana-style hot sauce**
- 1 **celery rib, finely chopped**
- 6 **tablespoons crumbled blue cheese**

1. In a small bowl, beat the butter and brown sugar until light and fluffy. Beat in mayonnaise and hot sauce until smooth. Cover and refrigerate until serving.

2. Spoon onto your favorite burger; top with celery and cheese.

Fruity Rum Punch

Four different fruit juices are used to make this sweet punch. Feel free to omit the rum for a kid-friendly option.

—**TASTE OF HOME TEST KITCHEN**

PREP: 10 MIN. + CHILLING
MAKES: 10 SERVINGS (2½ QUARTS)

- 2 **cups unsweetened apple juice**
- 1½ **cups unsweetened pineapple juice**
- 1 **can (12 ounces) frozen cranberry juice concentrate, thawed**
- 1 **can (6 ounces) frozen orange juice concentrate, thawed**
- 1 **cup golden or light rum**
- 1 **bottle (1 liter) club soda, chilled**
  Ice cubes

GARNISH
   Pineapple wedges and orange twists

1. In a large pitcher or punch bowl, combine the apple juice, pineapple juice, cranberry juice concentrate, orange juice concentrate and rum. Refrigerate until chilled.

2. Just before serving, add club soda. Serve over ice in hurricane or highball glasses. Garnish as desired.

Editor's Note: *This recipe was tested with Bacardi Gold rum.*

Potato Casserole Bread

PREP: 25 MIN. + RISING **BAKE:** 40 MIN. **MAKES:** 2 LOAVES (16 SLICES EACH)

- 2 packages (¼ ounce each) active dry yeast
- ½ cup warm water (110° to 115°)
- 1 can (12 ounces) evaporated milk
- 2 cups mashed potatoes (without added milk and butter)
- 8 bacon strips, cooked and crumbled
- ¼ cup butter, softened
- 2 eggs
- 3 tablespoons sugar
- 2 tablespoons dried minced onion
- 1 tablespoon caraway seeds
- 1 teaspoon garlic salt
- 1 teaspoon salt
- 6¼ to 6¾ cups all-purpose flour

1. In a large bowl, dissolve yeast in warm water. Add the milk, potatoes, bacon, butter, eggs, sugar, onion, caraway seeds, garlic salt, salt and 3 cups flour. Beat until smooth. Stir in enough remaining flour to form a soft dough.

2. Turn onto a floured surface; knead until smooth and elastic, about 6-8 minutes. Place in a greased bowl, turning once to grease the top. Cover and let rise in a warm place until doubled, about 1 hour.

3. Punch dough down. Turn onto a lightly floured surface; divide in half. Shape each into a round loaf. Place in two greased 2-qt. round baking dishes with straight sides. Cover and let rise in a warm place until doubled, about 40 minutes.

4. Bake at 350° for 40-50 minutes or until golden brown. Remove from baking dishes to wire racks to cool.

SEATTLE, WA

Established in 1907, this well-known Seattle site began as a farmers market. These days, more than 200 small businesses are based there, and shoppers can find anything from fish and flowers to doughnuts and art.

Iced Coffee Latte

Here is a great alternative to regular hot coffee—and it's much more economical than store-bought coffee drinks. Sweetened condensed milk and a hint of chocolate lend a delicious touch.

—**HEATHER NANDELL** JOHNSTON, IOWA

PREP/TOTAL TIME: 10 MIN. **MAKES:** 8 SERVINGS

- ½ **cup instant coffee granules**
- ½ **cup boiling water**
- 4 **cups chocolate milk**
- 2 **cups cold water**
- 1 **can (14 ounces) sweetened condensed milk**
  Ice cubes

1. In a large bowl, dissolve coffee in boiling water. Stir in the chocolate milk, cold water and condensed milk. Serve over ice.

Wheat Yeast Rolls

These wonderful, golden rolls are light and have a delicate flavor. They're also versatile—it seems I can pair them with just about any main dish and end up with a great meal. It's nice to have a simple and inexpensive recipe that adds homemade appeal to menus.

—**PEGGY STARKWEATHER** GARDINER, MONTANA

PREP: 20 MIN. + RISING **BAKE:** 15 MIN.
MAKES: 1 DOZEN

- 1 **package (¼ ounce) active dry yeast**
- 1 **cup warm water (110° to 115°)**
- ⅓ **cup canola oil**
- 3 **tablespoons sugar**
- 1 **teaspoon salt**
- 1½ **cups whole wheat flour**
- 1½ to 2 **cups all-purpose flour**

1. In a large bowl, dissolve yeast in warm water. Add the oil, sugar, salt and whole wheat flour. Beat until smooth. Add enough of the all-purpose flour to form a soft dough.

2. Turn onto a floured surface; knead until smooth and elastic, about 6-8 minutes. Place in a greased bowl; turn once to grease the top. Cover and let rise in a warm place until doubled, about 1 hour.

3. Punch down; divide into 12 pieces. Shape into rolls; place 3 in. apart on greased baking sheets. Cover; let rise until doubled, about 30 minutes.

4. Bake at 375° for 15-20 minutes or until golden. Cool on wire racks.

Champagne Cocktail

PREP/TOTAL TIME: 5 MIN. **MAKES:** 1 SERVING

- 1 sugar cube or ½ teaspoon sugar
- 6 dashes bitters
- ½ ounce brandy
- ½ cup Champagne, chilled

GARNISH

- Maraschino cherry and lemon slice

1. Place sugar in a champagne flute or cocktail glass; sprinkle with bitters. Pour the brandy into the glass. Top with Champagne. Garnish as desired.

Blueberry-Orange Onion Salad

Blueberries combine nicely with oranges, onion and a tangy dressing to make this green salad something special. I like to take it when we go on family picnics. My grandson always wants a second helping.

—ELLEN IRENE SMITH WOODLAND, WASHINGTON

PREP/TOTAL TIME: 15 MIN. **MAKES:** 4 SERVINGS

- 3 cups torn salad greens
- 2 medium navel oranges, peeled and sliced
- 4 slices sweet onion, separated into rings
- 2 cups fresh blueberries

BLUEBERRY SOUR CREAM DRESSING

- ½ cup sour cream
- 1 tablespoon white wine vinegar
- 1 tablespoon crushed blueberries
- 1½ teaspoons sugar
- 1½ teaspoons lemon juice
- ¼ teaspoon salt

1. Arrange greens on four salad plates. Top with the orange slices and onion rings. Sprinkle with blueberries.

2. In a small bowl, combine the dressing ingredients; stir until blended. Drizzle over salads. Serve immediately.

> "This pretty amber drink is a champagne twist on the traditional Old-Fashioned. Try it with extra-dry Champagne."
>
> —TASTE OF HOME TEST KITCHEN

> **Mango adds an interesting twist to this healthy and colorful fruit salsa.**

—MALA UDAYAMURTHY

SAN JOSE, CALIFORNIA

Mango Salsa

PREP/TOTAL TIME: 15 MIN. **MAKES:** 2¼ CUPS

- 2 medium mangoes, peeled and finely chopped
- ¼ cup finely chopped red onion
- ¼ cup finely chopped green pepper
- ¼ cup finely chopped sweet red pepper
- 1 jalapeno pepper, chopped
- 3 tablespoons minced fresh cilantro
- 2 tablespoons cider vinegar
- 1 tablespoon sugar
- 1 tablespoon olive oil
- ½ teaspoon salt
- ½ teaspoon pepper
   Baked potato chips

1. In a large bowl, combine first 11 ingredients. Chill until serving. Serve with chips.

Editor's Note: *Wear disposable gloves when cutting hot peppers; the oils can burn skin. Avoid touching your face.*

Zesty Lemon Curd

There are lemon trees in our backyard, so I'm always on the prowl for new ways to use the fruit. When we shared some of our homegrown citrus with neighbors—Canadians who were spending the winter here—the wife repaid us by giving us this recipe!

—**JEAN GAINES** BULLHEAD CITY, ARIZONA

PREP/TOTAL TIME: 25 MIN. **MAKES:** 3 CUPS

- 3 **egg, lightly beaten**
- 2 **cups sugar**
- ¾ **cup lemon juice**
- 2 **teaspoons grated lemon peel**
- 1 **cup butter, cubed**

1. In a large heavy saucepan over medium heat, whisk the eggs, sugar, lemon juice and peel until blended. Add butter; cook, whisking constantly, until mixture is thickened and coats the back of a metal spoon. Transfer to a small bowl; cool for 10 minutes. Cover and refrigerate until chilled.

2. Spread on muffins or rolls, or serve over waffles or ice cream.

◀●▶ **dishing about food**

Lemon curd, also called lemon cheese, is a classic English recipe. This flavorful custard-like spread is smeared on scones and toast, or used as fillings for cakes and pies. Curd is thicker and more tart than regular cake filling.

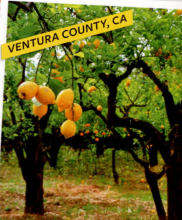

VENTURA COUNTY, CA

Lemons are a huge crop in this super-fertile area north of Los Angeles. Groves cover some 16,000 acres, which means that in an average year, it would take 87 million Americans to consume the whole supply!

FRESNO, CA

Food, wine and figs abound at the annual Fig Fest. All of the commercially grown dried figs in the U.S. come from Fresno and the San Joaquin Valley.

Gorgonzola Figs with Balsamic Glaze

For an elegant, eye-catching appetizer, try these delightful stuffed figs wrapped with prosciutto.

—**SARAH VASQUES** MILFORD, NEW HAMPSHIRE

PREP: 30 MIN. **BAKE:** 10 MIN. **MAKES:** 16 APPETIZERS

- 1 **cup balsamic vinegar**
- 16 **dried figs**
- ½ **cup crumbled Gorgonzola cheese**
- 8 **thin slices prosciutto, halved widthwise**
- 2 **teaspoons minced fresh rosemary**
- ¼ **teaspoon pepper**

1. For glaze, in a small saucepan, bring vinegar to a boil over medium heat; cook until reduced to about ¼ cup.

2. Cut a lengthwise slit down the center of each fig; fill with 1½ teaspoons cheese.

Wrap each fig with a piece of prosciutto; place on a baking sheet. Sprinkle with the rosemary and pepper.

3. Bake at 425° for 10-12 minutes or until prosciutto is crisp. Serve warm with glaze.

Editor's Note: *Amber-colored dried figs (labeled Turkish or Calimyrna) are recommended for this recipe. Mission figs, which are black, are smaller and hold less cheese. If large stems are present, remove them before stuffing figs.*

Ranch Dressing and Dip Mix

Give this versatile mix in a decorative jar with instructions for making dip or dressing. Then tuck it into a gift basket along with a pretty serving bowl and snack crackers or chips!

—**JOAN HALLFORD** NORTH RICHLAND HILLS, TEXAS

PREP: 10 MIN. **MAKES:** 2 CUPS

- 4½ teaspoons dried parsley flakes
- 1 tablespoon minced chives
- 1 tablespoon garlic powder
- 2 teaspoons lemon-pepper seasoning
- 1½ teaspoons dried tarragon
- 1½ teaspoons dried oregano
- 1 teaspoon salt

RANCH SALAD DRESSING
- ½ cup mayonnaise
- ½ cup buttermilk

RANCH DIP
- 1 cup mayonnaise
- 1 cup (8 ounces) sour cream

1. In a small bowl, combine the first seven ingredients. Transfer to a 4-ounce jar. Shake well before using.

For salad dressing: *In a small bowl, whisk the mayonnaise, buttermilk and 1 tablespoon mix. Refrigerate for at least 1 hour.*

For dip: *In a small bowl, combine the mayonnaise, sour cream and 2 tablespoons mix. Refrigerate for at least 2 hours. Serve with assorted crackers and fresh veggies or as a topping for baked potatoes.*

Apple & Blue Cheese on Endive

This fresh, fancy appetizer features a creamy blue cheese and apple spread on crunchy endive leaves. You can also use pears instead of apples or spread it on top of crackers.

—**KATIE FLEMING** EDMONDS, WASHINGTON

PREP/TOTAL TIME: 30 MIN. **MAKES:** 32 APPETIZERS

- 1 tablespoon lemon juice
- 1 tablespoon water
- 1 large red apple, finely chopped
- 2 celery ribs, finely chopped
- ¾ cup crumbled blue cheese
- 3 tablespoons mayonnaise
- 4 heads Belgian endive, separated into leaves
- ½ cup chopped hazelnuts, toasted

1. In a small bowl, combine the lemon juice and water; add apple and toss to coat. Drain and pat dry.

2. Combine the apple, celery, blue cheese and mayonnaise; spoon 1 tablespoonful onto each endive leaf. Sprinkle with hazelnuts.

2. In a salad bowl, combine the romaine, Parmesan cheese and croutons. Drizzle with dressing; toss to coat. Serve immediately.

Chicken Caesar Salad: *Grill or broil 8 chicken breast halves seasoned with salt and pepper. Cut each chicken breast half into strips. Top each individual salad with a cooked chicken breast half.*

Cranberry Honey Butter

If you are traveling to a friend's or loved one's for the holidays, why not bring them something even better than a bottle of wine—this easy-to-whip-up treat!

—ARISA CUPP WARREN, OREGON

PREP/TOTAL TIME: 10 MIN. **MAKES:** 24 SERVINGS

- 1 cup butter, softened
- ⅓ cup finely chopped dried cranberries
- ¼ cup honey
- 2 teaspoons grated orange peel
- ⅛ teaspoon kosher salt

1. In a small bowl, beat all ingredients until blended. Store, covered, in the refrigerator for up to 2 weeks.

Green Goddess Salad Dressing

It's no trick to fix this time-honored dressing at home with this quick recipe. Made with fresh ingredients, it's excellent—and a real treat compared to store-bought versions.

—PAGE ALEXANDER BALDWIN CITY, KANSAS

PREP/TOTAL TIME: 10 MIN. **MAKES:** 2 CUPS

- 1 cup mayonnaise
- ½ cup sour cream
- ¼ cup chopped green pepper
- ¼ cup packed fresh parsley sprigs
- 3 anchovy fillets
- 2 tablespoons lemon juice
- 2 green onion tops, coarsely chopped
- 1 garlic clove, peeled
- ¼ teaspoon pepper
- ⅛ teaspoon Worcestershire sauce

1. Place all ingredients in a blender; cover and process until smooth. Transfer to a bowl or jar; cover and store in the refrigerator.

Romaine Caesar Salad

After tasting this terrific salad my daughter made, I was very eager to get the recipe and try it myself. The dressing, which includes hard-cooked egg yolks, is easy to mix up in the blender.

—MARIE HATTRUP SPARKS, NEVADA

PREP: 10 MIN. + CHILLING **MAKES:** 8 SERVINGS

- 2 hard-cooked eggs
- ¼ cup lemon juice
- 2 tablespoons balsamic vinegar
- 1 anchovy fillet
- 1 tablespoon Dijon mustard
- 2 garlic cloves, peeled
- 1 teaspoon Worcestershire sauce
- 1 teaspoon pepper
- ¾ teaspoon salt
- ½ cup olive oil
- 1 bunch romaine, torn
- 1 cup (4 ounces) shredded Parmesan cheese
- 1 cup Caesar salad croutons

1. Slice eggs in half; remove yolks. Refrigerate whites for another use. In a blender or food processor, combine the lemon juice, vinegar, anchovy, mustard, garlic, Worcestershire sauce, pepper, salt and egg yolks; cover and process until blended. While processing, gradually add oil in a steady stream. Cover and refrigerate for 1 hour.

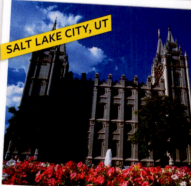

SALT LAKE CITY, UT

Brigham Young broke ground for the Salt Lake Temple in 1853, but the ornate structure wasn't completed for 40 years. To this day, it's the largest temple in the Latter Day Saints church.

Shredded Potato Casserole

This potato dish is perfect with prime rib and many other entrees. Make it ahead and have it ready to pop into the oven for a party. The topping of cornflake crumbs and Parmesan cheese adds a nice crunch.

—PAULA ZSIRAY LOGAN, UTAH

PREP: 10 MIN. **BAKE:** 45 MIN. **MAKES:** 6-8 SERVINGS

- 1 **can (10¾ ounces) condensed cream of mushroom soup, undiluted**
- 1 **cup (8 ounces) sour cream**
- ½ **cup 2% milk**
- 1 **cup (4 ounces) shredded cheddar cheese**
- ½ **cup butter, melted, divided**
- 1 **package (30 ounces) frozen shredded hash brown potatoes, thawed**
- 1 **cup cornflake crumbs**
- ¼ **cup grated Parmesan cheese**

1. In a large bowl, combine soup, sour cream, milk, cheddar cheese and ¼ cup butter. Stir in hash browns. Transfer to a greased 13x9-in. baking dish.

2. In a small bowl, combine the cornflake crumbs, Parmesan cheese and remaining butter; sprinkle over the top. Bake, uncovered, at 325° for 45-50 minutes or until casserole is heated through.

The Walla Walla sweet onion is Washington's official state vegetable. Walla Wallas were introduced to the area in the late 1880s and started from seeds from Corsica, Italy. The onions were first sold in 1900. Over time, area farmers produced an even larger, sweeter onion. To be called a Walla Walla sweet, an onion must be grown in Washington or Oregon and harvested between June and August.

Company Onion Soup

The onions in this part of the country are superb, and this soup is proof. Try it and see if your family enjoys this recipe as much as mine does.

—ROSE MARIE MOORE WALLA WALLA, WASHINGTON

PREP: 20 MIN. COOK: 65 MIN. MAKES: 4 SERVINGS

- 4 tablespoons unsalted butter
- 4 large sweet or Walla Walla onions, sliced
- 1 tablespoon sugar
- 6 cups beef broth, divided
- 2 tablespoons Worcestershire sauce
  Salt and pepper to taste
- 4 thick slices French bread
  Additional unsalted butter
  Garlic salt or 1 garlic clove, halved
- 1 cup (4 ounces) shredded Gruyere or Swiss cheese

1. In a Dutch oven, melt butter over medium heat. Saute onions until tender. Sprinkle sugar over onions. Reduce heat and cook, stirring occasionally, until onions are caramelized, about 20 minutes. Add 3 cups broth; simmer 15 minutes. Add remaining broth, Worcestershire sauce, salt and pepper. Cover and simmer for 30-40 minutes.

2. Meanwhile, spread both sides of the bread with additional butter; sprinkle with garlic salt or rub with the cut-side of the garlic clove. Broil bread until golden brown, then turn and brown other side. Ladle soup into individual ovenproof soup bowls. Float a slice of bread in each bowl and sprinkle with cheese. Broil until the cheese is melted and bubbly. Serve immediately.

Pineapple Salsa

This mouthwatering salsa features fresh pineapple and a handful of seasonings. Serve it with tortilla chips or with grilled chicken or fish for a jazzed-up meal.

—SUZI LAPAR WAHIAWA, HAWAII

PREP/TOTAL TIME: 20 MIN. **MAKES:** 3½ CUPS

- 2 **cups diced fresh pineapple**
- 2 **medium tomatoes, seeded and chopped**
- ¾ **cup chopped sweet onion**
- ¼ **cup minced fresh cilantro**
- 1 **jalapeno pepper, seeded and chopped**
- 1 **tablespoon olive oil**
- 1 **teaspoon ground coriander**
- ¾ **teaspoon ground cumin**
- ½ **teaspoon salt**
- ½ **teaspoon minced garlic**
  Tortilla chips

1. In a large bowl, combine the first 10 ingredients. Cover and refrigerate until serving. Serve with tortilla chips.

Editor's Note: *Wear disposable gloves when cutting hot peppers; the oils can burn skin. Avoid touching your face.*

Southwestern Barley Salad

Cilantro punches up the flavor of this colorful side that's zesty but not too spicy. It makes a great luncheon dish when served with sesame breadsticks, sherbet and sugar cookies. And it's sure to satisfy!

—TOMMI ROYLANCE CHARLO, MONTANA

PREP/TOTAL TIME: 20 MIN. **MAKES:** 8 SERVINGS

- 3 **cups cooked medium pearl barley**
- 1 **can (15 ounces) black beans, rinsed and drained**
- 1½ **cups frozen corn, thawed**
- 1½ **cups chopped seeded tomatoes**
- 1 **cup frozen peas, thawed**
- ¼ **cup minced fresh cilantro**
- 1 **teaspoon salt**
- ¼ **teaspoon pepper**
- ½ **cup water**
- 3 **tablespoons lemon juice**
- 1 **tablespoon finely chopped onion**
- 1 **tablespoon canola oil**
- 2 **garlic cloves, minced**
- 8 **lettuce leaves**
- 1 **ripe avocado, peeled and sliced**
- 2 **medium tomatoes, cut into wedges**

1. In a bowl, combine the first eight ingredients. In a jar with a tight-fitting lid, combine the water, lemon juice, onion, oil and garlic; shake well. Pour over barley mixture and toss to coat. Serve on lettuce-lined plates. Garnish with avocado and tomatoes.

WAHIAWA, HI

There's more than one type of pineapple! Learn all about them (including red ones) at the Dole Plantation, which has been bringing this sweet, succulent fruit to the world since 1901.

MOUNT RAINIER, WA

With its summit towering 14,410 feet above sea level, it's easy to see Mount Rainier from Seattle on a clear day. This mountain is the namesake for blushing golden Rainier cherries.

Cherry-Cream Crumble Pie

I created this yummy recipe for a cherry pie contest at the San Diego County Fair when I was first married in 1984. It won the blue ribbon! I love entering contests and I have won many of them.

—**MARIAN HOLLINGSWORTH** LA MESA, CALIFORNIA

PREP: 20 MIN. **BAKE:** 45 MIN. + COOLING **MAKES:** 8 SERVINGS

- ½ cup sugar
- 3 tablespoons all-purpose flour
- 2 cans (15 ounces each) pitted tart cherries, drained
- 1 cup (8 ounces) sour cream
- 1 egg, lightly beaten
- ¼ teaspoon almond extract
- 1 unbaked pastry shell (9 inches)

TOPPING
- ½ cup quick-cooking oats
- ⅓ cup all-purpose flour
- ⅓ cup packed brown sugar
- ¼ teaspoon ground cinnamon
- ¼ cup cold butter
- ½ cup chopped pecans

1. In a large bowl, combine the sugar, flour, cherries, sour cream, egg and extract. Spoon the filling into the pastry shell. Bake at 400° for 20 minutes.

2. For topping, combine the oats, flour, brown sugar and cinnamon in a small bowl; cut in the butter until mixture resembles coarse crumbs. Stir in pecans. Sprinkle over filling. Cover the edges of crust to prevent overbrowning.

3. Bake for 25-30 minutes or until topping is lightly browned. Cool on a wire rack for 1 hour. Store in the refrigerator.

Apricot Bars

These moist bars have such a great flavor. My family loves them, and I get lots of requests for the recipe.

—KIM GILLILAND SIMI VALLEY, CALIFORNIA

PREP: 15 MIN. **BAKE:** 50 MIN. **MAKES:** 16 BARS

- ⅔ cup dried apricots
- ½ cup water
- ½ cup butter, softened
- ¼ cup confectioners' sugar
- 1⅓ cups all-purpose flour, divided
- 2 eggs
- 1 cup packed brown sugar
- ½ teaspoon baking powder
- ¼ teaspoon salt
- ½ teaspoon vanilla extract
- ½ cup chopped walnuts
  Additional confectioners' sugar

1. In a small saucepan, cook apricots in water over medium heat for 10 minutes or until softened. Drain, cool and chop; set aside. In a large bowl, cream butter and confectioners' sugar until light and fluffy. Gradually add 1 cup flour until well blended.

2. Press into a greased 8-in. square baking dish. Bake at 350° for 20 minutes or until lightly browned.

3. Meanwhile, in a small bowl, beat eggs and brown sugar until blended. Beat in the vanilla. In a small bowl, combine the baking powder, salt, and remaining flour; gradually add to egg mixture. Stir in apricots and nuts. Pour over the crust.

4. Bake at 350° for 30 minutes or until set. Cool on wire rack. Dust with confectioners' sugar; cut into bars.

Very Berry Crisp

I love this recipe because it's easy, low-fat, versatile and delicious! The crispy topping is flavored with graham cracker crumbs, cinnamon and almonds and doesn't taste light at all. Great with frozen yogurt or whipped topping.

—SCARLETT ELROD NEWNAN, GEORGIA

PREP: 20 MIN. **BAKE:** 25 MIN. **MAKES:** 8 SERVINGS

- 2 cups fresh raspberries
- 2 cups sliced fresh strawberries
- 2 cups fresh blueberries
- ⅓ cup sugar
- 2 tablespoons plus ¼ cup all-purpose flour, divided
- ⅓ cup graham cracker crumbs
- ⅓ cup quick-cooking oats
- ¼ cup packed brown sugar
- 2 tablespoons sliced almonds
- ½ teaspoon ground cinnamon
- 1 tablespoon canola oil
- 1 tablespoon butter, melted
- 1 tablespoon water

1. In a large bowl, combine the berries, sugar and 2 tablespoons flour; transfer to an 11x7-in. baking dish coated with cooking spray.

2. In a small bowl, combine cracker crumbs, oats, brown sugar, almonds, cinnamon and remaining flour. Stir in the oil, butter and water until moistened. Sprinkle over berries.

3. Bake at 375° for 25-30 minutes or until filling is bubbly and topping is golden brown.

Marionberries, a cross between Chehalem and Olallieberry blackberries, are named for Marion County, Oregon, where they were developed. The berries are medium to large, with colors ranging from dark red to black. Their flavor is described as rich, earthy, and tart with a hint of sweetness. They are grown exclusively in Oregon.

PORTLAND, OR

You'll find berries galore (including Marionberries, shown here in the foreground) at the Oregon Berry Festival.

Oregon's Best Marionberry Pie

I believe Oregon Marionberries make about the best berry pie in the world!

—FRANCES BENTHIN SCIO, OREGON

PREP: 30 MIN. **BAKE:** 65 MIN. + COOLING
MAKES: 8 SERVINGS

- 2 **cups all-purpose flour**
- 1 **tablespoon sugar**
- 1 **teaspoon salt**
- ½ **cup cold butter, cubed**
- 5 **tablespoons shortening**
- 4 **tablespoons ice water**
- 2 **tablespoons lemon juice**

FILLING

- 1 **cup plus 1 teaspoon sugar, divided**
- 2 **tablespoons plus 2 teaspoons quick-cooking tapioca**
- 1 **tablespoon lemon juice**
- 4 **cups fresh Marionberries or blackberries**
- 1 **package (8 ounces) cream cheese, softened**
- ½ **cup confectioners' sugar**
- ½ **teaspoon almond extract**
- ½ **teaspoon vanilla extract**
- 1 **tablespoon heavy whipping cream**

1. In a large bowl, mix flour, sugar and salt; cut in butter and shortening until crumbly. Gradually add the ice water and lemon juice, tossing with a fork until dough holds together when pressed. Divide dough in half. Shape each into a disk; wrap in plastic wrap. Chill 10 minutes.

2. Meanwhile, in a large bowl, mix 1 cup sugar, tapioca and lemon juice. Add the berries; toss to coat. Let stand 15 minutes. Preheat oven to 425°. On a lightly floured surface, roll one half of dough to a ⅛-in.-thick circle; transfer to a 9-in. pie plate. Trim pastry to ½ in. beyond rim of plate.

3. In a small bowl, beat the cream cheese, confectioners' sugar and extracts; spread over prepared crust. Top with berry mixture.

4. Roll out remaining dough to a ⅛-in.-thick circle; cut into ½-in.-wide strips. Arrange over filling in a lattice pattern. Trim and seal strips to edge of bottom pastry; flute edge. Brush lattice strips with cream; sprinkle with remaining sugar.

5. Bake 15 minutes. Reduce oven setting to 350°; bake 50-60 minutes longer or until crust is golden brown and filling is bubbly. (Cover edges with foil during last 15 minutes to prevent overbrowning if necessary.) Cool on a wire rack.

Chocolate Hazelnut Gateau

Gateau (pronounces ga-tow) is the French word for any rich and fancy cake. I think you'll agree this dense chocolate dessert has just the right amount of sweetness.

—MICHELLE KRZMARZICK TORRANCE, CALIFORNIA

PREP: 20 MIN. **BAKE:** 30 MIN. + COOLING **MAKES:** 12 SERVINGS

- ⅔ cup butter, softened
- ¾ cup sugar
- 3 eggs, separated
- 1 cup (6 ounces) semisweet chocolate chips, melted and cooled
- 1 teaspoon vanilla extract
- ¾ cup all-purpose flour
- ½ teaspoon salt
- ¼ cup milk
- ⅔ cup ground hazelnuts, toasted

GLAZE
- 3 tablespoons butter
- 2 tablespoons light corn syrup
- 1 tablespoon water
- 1 cup (6 ounces) semisweet chocolate chips
  Toasted slivered almonds and fresh mint leaves

1. In a large bowl, cream butter and sugar until light and fluffy. Beat in egg yolks, melted chocolate and vanilla. Combine the flour and salt; gradually add to creamed mixture alternately with milk, beating well after each addition. Stir in the hazelnuts.

2. In a small bowl, beat egg whites until stiff peaks form; carefully fold into batter. Spread into a greased 9-in. springform pan. Place pan on a baking sheet.

3. Bake at 350° for 30-35 minutes or until a toothpick inserted near the center comes out clean. Cool on wire rack for 10 minutes. Carefully run a knife around edge of pan to loosen; remove sides of pan. Cool completely.

4. In a saucepan, bring the butter, corn syrup and water to a boil; stirring constantly. Remove from the heat. Add the chocolate chips; stir until smooth. Cool to room temperature. Spread over top and sides of gateau. Garnish with almonds and mint.

George Whitney created these treats—oatmeal cookie ice cream sandwiches dipped in chocolate—in 1928 and sold them at Playland, his San Francisco amusement park, for decades. Once Playland closed in the 1970s, the treat disappeared. It made a comeback in 1974, when a local business began making the ice cream sandwiches to distribute to small stores. Distribution has since expanded into more than a dozen states, and the treat known as It's It has been declared the official food of San Francisco!

It's It Ice Cream Sandwiches

It's easy to see why this treat is so popular in San Francisco. It's snack heaven...ice cream, delicious oatmeal cookies and a touch of chocolate. Swap out the vanilla for your own favorite flavor, such as chocolate, caramel or pumpkin!

—TASTE OF HOME TEST KITCHEN

PREP: 40 MIN. + FREEZING   **BAKE:** 15 MIN./BATCH + COOLING   **MAKES:** 7 SERVINGS

- ½ cup butter, softened
- ¾ cup packed brown sugar
- ¼ cup sugar
- 1 egg
- ½ teaspoon vanilla extract
- ¾ cup all-purpose flour
- ½ teaspoon baking soda
- ½ teaspoon ground cinnamon
- ¼ teaspoon baking powder
- ¼ teaspoon salt
- 1½ cups quick-cooking oats
- ¼ cup chopped raisins, optional

ASSEMBLY
- 3 cups vanilla ice cream
- 1 bottle (7¼ ounces) chocolate hard-shell ice cream topping

1. Preheat oven to 350°. In a large bowl, cream butter and sugars until light and fluffy. Beat in egg and vanilla. In another bowl, whisk flour, baking soda, cinnamon, baking powder and salt; gradually beat into creamed mixture. Stir in oats and, if desired, raisins.

2. Shape into fourteen 1¼-in. balls; place 2½ in. apart on ungreased baking sheets. Bake 11-13 minutes or until golden brown. Cool on pans for 3 minutes. Remove to wire racks to cool completely.

3. To assemble, place about ⅓ cup ice cream on bottom of a cookie. Top with a second cookie, pressing gently to flatten ice cream. Place on a baking sheet; freeze until firm. Repeat with remaining cookies and ice cream.

4. Remove ice cream sandwiches from the freezer. Working over a small bowl, drizzle chocolate topping over half of each sandwich, allowing excess to drip off.

5. Place on a waxed paper-lined baking sheet; freeze until serving. Wrap individually for longer storage.

Peach and Raspberry Clafouti

Clafouti is a dessert like a custard, made with fresh fruit and batter in a baking dish. It is so wonderful to serve during the summer when the fruit is ripe.

—ANNE CASTLE ELLEN GRINSFELDER LOGAN, OHIO

PREP: 20 MIN. **BAKE:** 30 MIN. + COOLING
MAKES: 4 SERVINGS

- 4 **cups thickly sliced peeled peaches (about 2½ pounds)**
- ½ **cup fresh raspberries**
- 2 **tablespoons cold butter, cut into small pieces**
- ¼ **cup blanched almonds**
- 2 **tablespoons all-purpose flour**
- ¾ **cup heavy whipping cream or half-and-half cream or milk**
- ⅓ **cup plus 2 tablespoons sugar**
- 2 **eggs**
- 1 **tablespoon tawny red port or sherry, optional**
- ¼ **teaspoon salt**
- 1 **cup whipped cream**
  Raspberries, mint leaves to garnish

1. Layer peaches and raspberries in a shallow greased 5-cup baking dish; dot with butter.

2. In a food processor, cover and process the almonds with flour until ground. Add the cream, ⅓ cup sugar, eggs, port, salt; blend, scraping sides as necessary.

3. Pour custard slowly over fruit. Sprinkle with 2 tablespoons sugar. Bake at 400° for 30-40 minutes until top is golden and custard set. Cool on a wire rack for 20 minutes. Serve warm with whipped cream. Garnish with raspberries and mint.

Wyoming Cowboy Cookies

These cookies are very popular here in Wyoming. They're great for lunch boxes or for munching anytime.

—PATSY STEENBOCK SHOSHONI, WYOMING

PREP: 25 MIN. **BAKE:** 15 MIN. **MAKES:** 6 DOZEN

- 1 **cup flaked coconut**
- ¾ **cup chopped pecans**
- 1 **cup butter, softened**
- 1½ **cups packed brown sugar**
- ½ **cup sugar**
- 2 **eggs**
- 1½ **teaspoons vanilla extract**
- 2 **cups all-purpose flour**
- 1 **teaspoon baking soda**
- ½ **teaspoon salt**
- 2 **cups old-fashioned oats**
- 2 **cups (12 ounces) chocolate chips**

1. Place coconut and pecans on a 15x10x1-in. baking pan. Bake at 350° for 6 to 8 minutes or until toasted, stirring every 2 minutes. Set aside to cool.

2. In a large bowl, cream butter and sugars until light and fluffy. Add eggs and vanilla; beat well. Combine the flour, baking soda and salt. Add to the creamed mixture; beat well. Stir in the oats, chocolate chips and toasted coconut and pecans.

3. Drop by rounded teaspoonfuls onto greased baking sheets. Bake at 350° for about 12 minutes or until browned. Remove to wire racks to cool.

◀● dishing about food

Clafouti is a French dessert that is usually made with sweet cherries. The batter is poured over the fruit and puffs up around it. Using peaches and raspberries gives this classic an American twist. The French call a clafouti made with other fruit a *flaugnarde*.

WYOMING

Many Wyomingites celebrate the state's cowboy culture. The University of Wyoming's teams are even called the Cowboys and Cowgirls.

COEUR D'ALENE MOUNTAINS, ID

From June until October, wild huckleberries are a big draw to the picturesque Coeur d'Alene Mountains in northern Idaho. The berries star in the Wallace Huckleberry Festival, which is held every August.

Huckleberry Cheese Pie

To us Idahoans, huckleberries are a treasure! We like to serve this pie as a special treat when we have out-of-state guests.

—**PAT KUPER** MCCALL, IDAHO

PREP: 30 MIN. **BAKE:** 20 MIN. + CHILLING
MAKES: 8-10 SERVINGS

BUTTER CRUNCH CRUST
- 1 **cup all-purpose flour**
- ¼ **cup packed brown sugar**
- ½ **cup finely chopped nuts**
- ½ **cup cold butter**

CHEESE FILLING
- 1 **package (8 ounces) cream cheese, softened**
- ¾ **cup confectioners' sugar**
- 1 **teaspoon vanilla extract**
- 1 **cup whipped cream or 1 cup whipped topping**

FRUIT TOPPING
- ½ **cup sugar**
- 4½ **teaspoons cornstarch**
-    **Dash salt**
- ½ **cup water**
- 2 **cups fresh huckleberries or blueberries, divided**
- 1½ **teaspoons butter**

1. In a bowl, combine the flour, brown sugar and nuts. Cut in butter until mixture resembles coarse crumbs. Spread on baking sheet; bake at 400° for 20 minutes, stirring occasionally.

2. Remove from oven. While mixture is still hot, press into a 9-in. pie plate forming a pie shell. Cool completely.

3. For cheese filling, beat cream cheese, sugar and vanilla until smooth; gently fold in whipped cream. Pour or spoon filling into cooled crust; refrigerate.

4. For topping, combine the sugar, cornstarch and salt in saucepan. Stir in water until smooth; add 1 cup berries. Bring to a boil. Cook and stir for 1-2 minutes or until thickened. Add butter and remaining berries. Cool; pour over filling. Top with additional whipped cream if desired.

Apple Jelly Candy

Soft and fruity, these old-fashioned squares get a bit of crunch from chopped walnuts. Rolling the candy in sugar gives it a pretty look for the holidays.

—**HELEN ORESTAD** POWDERVILLE, MONTANA

PREP: 20 MIN. **COOK:** 20 MIN. + CHILLING
MAKES: ABOUT 6 DOZEN

- 2 **cups sugar**
- 1¾ **cups unsweetened applesauce**
- 2 **envelopes unflavored gelatin**
- 1 **package (3 ounces) lemon gelatin**
- ½ **cup chopped walnuts**
- 1 **teaspoon vanilla extract**
     Superfine, confectioners' and/or granulated sugar

1. In a large saucepan, combine the sugar, applesauce and gelatins; let stand for 1 minute. Bring to a boil over medium heat, stirring constantly. Boil for 15 minutes. Remove from the heat; stir in walnuts and vanilla.

2. Immediately pour into a greased 11x7-in. baking dish. Cover and refrigerate overnight. Cut into 1-in. pieces; roll in sugar. Store in an airtight container in the refrigerator.

Caramel-Frosted Potato Cake

I have been baking this cake every Christmas for decades. My sister-in-law gave me the recipe in 1941, and it has been in demand ever since. My grandchildren have never been able to figure out why it's called a potato cake, since it doesn't taste at all like potatoes!

—**PHYLLIS SCHMIDT** MANITOWOC, WISCONSIN

PREP: 20 MIN. **BAKE:** 55 MIN. + COOLING
MAKES: 12-16 SERVINGS

- ¾ cup butter, softened
- 2 cups sugar
- 4 eggs, separated
- 1 cup mashed potatoes (without added milk and butter)
- 2 ounces German sweet chocolate, melted
- 2 cups all-purpose flour
- 2 teaspoons baking soda
- 1 teaspoon ground nutmeg
- 1 teaspoon ground cloves
- ½ cup whole milk
- 1 cup chopped walnuts

FROSTING

- ¼ cup butter
- ½ cup packed brown sugar
- 1¼ cups confectioners' sugar
- ¼ teaspoon vanilla extract
- 2 to 4 tablespoons whole milk

1. In a large bowl, cream butter and sugar until light and fluffy. Beat in the egg yolks, potatoes and chocolate. Combine the flour, baking soda, nutmeg and cloves; gradually add to creamed mixture alternately with milk, beating well after each addition. Stir in walnuts.

2. In a small bowl, beat egg whites until stiff peaks form; fold into batter. Pour into a greased and floured 10-in. fluted tube pan.

3. Bake at 350° for 55-60 minutes or until cake springs back when lightly touched. Cool for 10 minutes before removing from pan to a wire rack to cool completely.

4. For frosting, in a small saucepan, melt the butter. Add brown sugar; cook and stir over low heat for 2 minutes. Remove from the heat; cool for 3 minutes. Stir in the confectioners' sugar, vanilla and enough milk to achieve a thick pouring consistency. Pour over cake.

Oregon's Hazelnut Chocolate Chip Cookie

These nutty cookies are a hit with the ladies at my craft club. I grew up during the Depression, and my mother taught me to use what was available—like the plentiful nuts here in Oregon. She'd say, "It doesn't have to be expensive to be good." And she was right!

—**SELMER LOONEY** EUGENE, OREGON

PREP/TOTAL TIME: 25 MIN. **MAKES:** 3 DOZEN

- 1 cup butter, softened
- ½ cup sugar
- 1 cup packed brown sugar
- 2 eggs
- 1 teaspoon vanilla extract
- 2⅓ cups all-purpose flour
- 1 teaspoon baking soda
- ½ teaspoon salt
- 1 cup (6 ounces) semisweet chocolate chips
- ¾ cup chopped hazelnuts

1. In a large bowl, cream butter and sugars on medium speed for 3 minutes. Add eggs, one at a time, beating well after each addition. Add vanilla. Combine flour, baking soda and salt; gradually add to batter. Fold in chocolate chips and nuts.

2. Drop by heaping tablespoonfuls 3 in. apart onto lightly greased baking sheets. Flatten lightly with a fork. Bake at 350° for 10-12 minutes or until light brown. Remove to a wire rack to cool.

◄● dishing about food

The Comstock Lode in Virginia City brought people to Nevada seeking riches in the silver mines. The women who cooked for the miners made them sourdough biscuits, Cornish pasties and, according to local lore, potato caramel cake. Using leftover mashed potatoes not only saved flour but also made the cake moist and tender.

> **❝ You'll get many compliments when you serve this layered banana beauty. It's a snap to prepare because the filling starts with instant pudding mix.❞**
>
> **—ISABEL FOWLER**
> ANCHORAGE, ALASKA

Creamy Banana Pecan Pie

PREP: 20 MIN. **BAKE:** 25 MIN. + COOLING **MAKES:** 6-8 SERVINGS

- 1 **cup all-purpose flour**
- 1 **cup finely chopped pecans**
- ½ **cup butter, softened**
- 1 **package (8 ounces) cream cheese, softened**
- 1 **cup confectioners' sugar**
- 1 **carton (8 ounces) frozen whipped topping, thawed, divided**
- 3 **large firm bananas, sliced**
- 1⅓ **cups cold milk**
- 1 **package (3.4 ounces) instant vanilla pudding mix**
    Additional chopped pecans, optional

1. In a small bowl, combine the flour, pecans and butter. Press onto the bottom and up the sides of a greased 9-in. pie plate. Bake at 350° for 25 minutes. Cool completely on a wire rack.

2. In a small bowl, beat cream cheese and sugar. Fold in 1 cup of whipped topping. Spread over the crust. Arrange bananas on top. In another bowl, whisk milk and pudding mix for 2 minutes. Immediately pour over bananas. Top with remaining whipped topping. Garnish with pecans if desired. Refrigerate for at least 3 hours before serving. Refrigerate leftovers.

Double Nut Baklava

It may take some time to make this rich, buttery treat, but it's well worth the effort! The blend of coconut, pecans and macadamia nuts is irresistible.

—**KARI CAVEN** POST FALLS, IDAHO

PREP: 25 MIN. **BAKE:** 30 MIN. + STANDING **MAKES:** 3 DOZEN

- 1¼ cups flaked coconut, toasted
- ½ cup finely chopped macadamia nuts
- ½ cup finely chopped pecans
- ½ cup packed brown sugar
- 1 teaspoon ground allspice
- 1¼ cups butter, melted
- 1 package phyllo dough (16 ounces, 14x9-inch sheet size), thawed
- 1 cup sugar
- ½ cup water
- ¼ cup honey

1. In a large bowl, combine the first five ingredients; set aside. Brush a 13x9-in. baking pan with some of the butter. Unroll the sheets of phyllo dough; trim to fit into pan.

2. Layer 10 sheets of phyllo in prepared pan, brushing each with butter. (Keep remaining dough covered with plastic wrap and a damp towel to prevent it from drying out.) Sprinkle with a third of the nut mixture. Repeat layers twice. Top with five phyllo sheets, brushing each with the butter. Brush top sheet of phyllo with butter.

3. Using a sharp knife, cut into 36 diamond shapes. Bake at 350° for 30-35 minutes or until golden brown. Cool completely on a wire rack.

4. In a small saucepan, bring the sugar, water and honey to a boil. Reduce heat; simmer for 5 minutes. Pour hot syrup over baklava. Cover and let stand overnight.

Plum Crisp

Made with fresh plums and a crunchy oat topping, this crisp is a lighter alternative to classic fruit pie. It goes over well with the women in my church group.

—DEIDRE KOBEL BOULDER, COLORADO

PREP: 25 MIN. + STANDING **BAKE:** 40 MIN.
MAKES: 8 SERVINGS

- ¾ cup old-fashioned oats
- ⅓ cup all-purpose flour
- ¼ cup plus 2 tablespoons sugar, divided
- ¼ cup packed brown sugar
- ¼ teaspoon salt
- ¼ teaspoon ground cinnamon
- ¼ teaspoon ground nutmeg
- 3 tablespoons butter, softened
- ¼ cup chopped walnuts
- 5 cups sliced fresh plums (about 2 pounds)
- 1 tablespoon quick-cooking tapioca
- 2 teaspoons lemon juice

1. In a small bowl, combine the oats, flour, ¼ cup sugar, brown sugar, salt, cinnamon and nutmeg. With clean hands, work butter into sugar mixture until well combined. Add nuts; toss to combine. Refrigerate for 15 minutes.

2. Meanwhile, in a large bowl, combine the plums, tapioca, lemon juice and remaining sugar. Transfer to a greased 9-in. pie plate. Let stand for 15 minutes. Sprinkle topping over plum mixture.

3. Bake at 375° for 40-45 minutes or until topping is golden brown and plums are tender. Serve warm.

Coconut Pineapple Cake

This cake is incredibly tender and dense, which makes it ideal for chilling and cutting up ahead of time to serve as bars at social events. It's always very popular.

—KRISTA KLIEBENSTEIN
HIGHLANDS RANCH, COLORADO

PREP: 25 MIN. **BAKE:** 35 MIN. + COOLING
MAKES: 12 SERVINGS

- 2 eggs
- 2 cups sugar
- 1 teaspoon vanilla extract
- 2 cups all-purpose flour
- ½ teaspoon baking soda
- ½ teaspoon baking powder
- ½ teaspoon salt
- 1 can (20 ounces) crushed pineapple, undrained
- ½ cup chopped walnuts

FROSTING
- 1 package (8 ounces) cream cheese, softened
- ½ cup butter, softened
- 2 cups confectioners' sugar
- ½ cup flaked coconut

1. In a large bowl, beat the eggs, sugar and vanilla until fluffy. Combine the flour, baking soda, baking powder and salt; add to the egg mixture alternately with pineapple. Stir in the walnuts.

2. Pour into a greased 13x9-in. baking pan. Bake at 350° for 35-40 minutes or until a toothpick inserted near the center comes out clean. Cool on a wire rack.

3. In a small bowl, beat cream cheese, butter and confectioners' sugar until smooth. Frost cake. Sprinkle with the coconut. Store in the refrigerator.

Portland Cream Doughnuts

If you don't live near Portland, Oregon, you can create your own version of that city's famous doughnut at home. The fresh homemade doughnuts with a touch of nutmeg, creamy filling and a smooth-as-silk chocolate frosting will disappear in minutes.
—TASTE OF HOME TEST KITCHEN

PREP: 50 MIN. + RISING **COOK:** 5 MIN./BATCH
MAKES: 1 DOZEN

- 3 **packages (¼ ounce each) active dry yeast**
- ¾ **cup warm water (110° to 115°)**
- ¾ **cup 2% milk**
- 1 **egg**
- 1 **egg yolk**
- 6 **tablespoons butter, softened**
- ½ **cup sugar**
- 1½ **teaspoons salt**
- ¾ **teaspoon ground nutmeg**
- 4¾ **to 5¼ cups all-purpose flour**

FILLING
- 1 **package (3 ounces) cook-and-serve vanilla pudding mix**
- ¼ **cup heavy whipping cream**

ASSEMBLY
- **Oil for deep-fat frying**
- ⅔ **cup semisweet chocolate chips**
- 2 **tablespoons butter**
- 1¼ **cups confectioners' sugar**
- 3 **tablespoons hot water**
- **Vanilla frosting of your choice, optional**

1. In a small bowl, dissolve yeast in warm water. In a large bowl, combine milk, egg, egg yolk, butter, sugar, salt, nutmeg, yeast mixture and 2 cups flour; beat on medium speed until smooth. Stir in enough remaining flour to form a soft dough (dough will be sticky).

2. Turn dough onto a floured surface; knead until smooth and elastic, about 6-8 minutes. Place in a greased bowl, turning once to grease the top. Cover with plastic wrap and let rise in a warm place until doubled, about 1 hour.

3. Meanwhile, for filling, prepare pudding mix according to the package directions. Press plastic wrap onto surface of pudding; refrigerate until cold.

4. Punch down dough. Turn onto a lightly floured surface; roll to ¾-in. thickness. Cut with a floured 3-in. biscuit cutter. Place 2 in. apart on greased baking sheets. Cover with plastic wrap; let rise in a warm place until nearly doubled, about 25 minutes.

5. In a small bowl, beat cream until stiff peaks form. Fold into pudding. Refrigerate, covered, while frying doughnuts.

6. In an electric skillet or deep fryer, heat oil to 350°. Fry doughnuts, a few at a time, for 1-2 minutes on each side or until golden brown. Drain on paper towels. Cool slightly.

7. Cut a small hole in the tip of a pastry bag or in a corner of a food-safe plastic bag; insert a small tip. Fill bag with filling. With a small knife, pierce a hole into the side of each doughnut; pipe filling into hole, allowing some of filling to spill out for a tongue.

8. In a microwave, melt chocolate chips and butter; stir until smooth. Whisk in confectioners' sugar and hot water.

9. Spread tops of doughnuts with glaze; let stand until set. If desired, pipe two small dots of vanilla frosting near the tongue for eyes. Refrigerate leftovers.

Pistachio Cranberry Bark

This bark makes a lovely holiday gift from the kitchen. Fill a plate or cup with the candy, then gather up clear cellophane around it and tie with red and green ribbons.
—SUSAN WACEK PLEASANTON, CALIFORNIA

PREP: 20 MIN. + CHILLING **MAKES:** ABOUT 1 POUND

- 2 **cups (12 ounces) semisweet chocolate chips**
- 5 **ounces white candy coating, chopped**
- 1 **cup chopped pistachios, toasted, divided**
- ¾ **cup dried cranberries, divided**

1. In a microwave-safe bowl, melt semisweet chips; stir until smooth. Repeat with white candy coating.

2. Stir ¾ cup pistachios and half of the cranberries into semisweet chocolate. Thinly spread onto a waxed paper-lined baking sheet. Drizzle with candy coating.

3. Cut through with a knife to swirl. Sprinkle with remaining pistachios and cranberries. Chill until firm. Break into pieces. Store in an airtight container in the refrigerator.

PORTLAND, OR

VOODOO DOUGHNUT

GOOD THINGS COME IN PINK BOXES

Portlanders and Oregonians have gone nuts for Voodoo Doughnut. Couples even serve these unique treats to their wedding guests! The company has expanded into three locations: two in Portland and one in Eugene.

CALIFORNIA

People have known that the Golden State's fertile soil was a valuable resource since missionaries began working the land in the 1500s. Today, California produces more than 400 commodities, and almost half of the fruits, vegetables and nuts grown in the U.S.!

Best Date Bars

These wholesome bar cookies freeze well. Simply cool them in the pan, cut into squares, and then store them in freezer containers or wrap in plastic wrap.

—**DOROTHY DELESKE** SCOTTSDALE, ARIZONA

PREP: 25 MIN. **BAKE:** 35 MIN. **MAKES:** 40 BARS

- 2½ **cups pitted dates, cut up**
- ¼ **cup sugar**
- 1½ **cups water**
- ⅓ **cup coarsely chopped walnuts, optional**
- 1¼ **cups all-purpose flour**
- 1 **teaspoon salt**
- ½ **teaspoon baking soda**
- 1½ **cups quick-cooking oats**
- 1 **cup packed brown sugar**
- ½ **cup butter, softened**
- 1 **tablespoon water**

1. In a saucepan, combine dates, sugar and water. Cook, stirring frequently, until very thick. Stir in walnuts; cool.

2. Sift the flour, salt and baking soda together in a large bowl; add oats and brown sugar. Cut in butter until mixture is crumbly. Sprinkle water over mixture; stir lightly.

3. Pat half into a greased 13x9-in. baking pan. Spread with date mixture; cover with remaining oat mixture and pat lightly.

4. Bake at 350° for 35-40 minutes or until lightly browned. Cool in pan on a wire rack. Cut into bars.

Oatmeal Raisin Cookies

A friend gave me this recipe years ago, and the cookies are just as delicious as the ones Mom used to make. The secret is to measure the ingredients exactly (no guessing on the amounts!) and to not overbake.

—**WENDY COALWELL** ABBEVILLE, GEORGIA

PREP/TOTAL TIME: 30 MIN. **MAKES:** ABOUT 3½ DOZEN

- 1 **cup shortening**
- 1 **cup sugar**
- 1 **cup packed light brown sugar**
- 3 **eggs**
- 1 **teaspoon vanilla extract**
- 2½ **cups all-purpose flour**
- 2 **teaspoons baking soda**
- 1 **teaspoon salt**
- 1 **teaspoon ground cinnamon**
- 2 **cups old-fashioned oats**
- 1 **cup raisins**
- 1 **cup coarsely chopped pecans, optional**

1. In a large bowl, cream the shortening and sugars until light and fluffy. Beat in eggs, one at a time, beating well after each addition. Beat in vanilla. Combine the flour, baking soda, salt and cinnamon. Add to creamed mixture, just until combined. Stir in the oats, raisins and pecans if desired.

2. Shape into 1-in. balls. Place 2 in. apart on ungreased baking sheets. Flatten with a greased glass bottom.

3. Bake at 350° for 10-11 minutes or until golden brown. Do not overbake. Remove to a wire rack to cool.

◄◆ dishing about food

Oatmeal cookies date back to 1,000 B.C., when the Scots used their oat harvest to make oat cakes. The first published recipe for oatmeal cookies may have been the one that appeared in The Fannie Farmer Cookbook in 1896. Quaker Oats soon began printing a recipe on its package, but we don't know who gets the credit for adding raisins. America's production of raisins, combined with Turkey's, accounts for about 80 percent of the world's supply.

SAN JOAQUIN VALLEY, CA

The California raisin industry is centered in San Joaquin Valley, where Scottish farmer William Thompson began cultivating seedless grapes in 1876.

> **"**This recipe is an interesting way to use apples. I usually make them on Fridays, so when family and friends drop in on the weekend, I have a nice dessert to serve. They bake up flaky and golden brown outside and moist inside.**"**

—LILA ELLER
EVERETT, WASHINGTON

Golden Apple Bundles

PREP: 20 MIN. **BAKE:** 25 MIN. **MAKES:** 10-12 SERVINGS

- 2 **cups chopped peeled apples**
- ⅓ **cup chopped walnuts**
- ¼ **cup packed brown sugar**
- ¼ **cup raisins**
- 1 **tablespoon all-purpose flour**
- ½ **teaspoon lemon peel**
- ½ **teaspoon ground cinnamon**
  Pastry for double-crust pie
  Milk
  Sugar

1. In a large bowl, combine apples, walnuts, brown sugar, raisins, flour, lemon peel and cinnamon; set aside.

2. Roll pastry to ⅛-in. thickness. Cut into 5-in. circles. Spoon about ¼ cup apple mixture into center of each circle. Moisten edges of the pastry with water. Fold over and seal edges with a fork.

3. Place on a greased baking sheet. Bake at 450° for 10 minutes. Reduce heat to 400°; bake 10 minutes longer. Brush each with milk and sprinkle with the sugar. Return to oven; bake 5 minutes longer.

Date Shake

Here's a cooling shake with a mild hint of dates. Use Medjool dates for the best flavor.

—TASTE OF HOME TEST KITCHEN

PREP/TOTAL TIME: 10 MIN. **MAKES:** 4 SERVINGS

- ⅔ **cup chopped dates**
- ¼ **cup water**
- 3 **cups vanilla ice cream**
- 1 **cup 2% milk**

1. In a microwave-safe dish, combine dates and water; microwave, covered, on high for 30-45 seconds or until dates are softened. Cool completely.

2. Place date mixture in a blender; cover and pulse until pureed. Add ice cream and milk; cover and process until blended. Serve immediately.

Danish Puff

I still remember Mom making this cream puff variation for special occasions.

—SUSAN GAROUTTE GEORGETOWN, TEXAS

PREP: 25 MIN. **BAKE:** 1 HOUR + COOLING
MAKES: 16 SERVINGS

- ½ **cup cold butter, cubed**
- 1 **cup all-purpose flour**
- 1 **to 2 tablespoons cold water**

FILLING
- 1 **cup water**
- ½ **cup butter**
- 1 **cup all-purpose flour**
- ¼ **teaspoon salt**
- 3 **eggs**
- ½ **teaspoon almond extract**

TOPPING
- 1½ **cups confectioners' sugar**
- 2 **tablespoons butter, softened**
- 1 **to 2 tablespoons water**
- 1½ **teaspoons vanilla extract**
- ½ **cup sliced almonds, toasted**

1. In a small bowl, cut butter into the flour until crumbly. Sprinkle with water; toss with a fork until moist enough to shape into a ball. Divide in half. On a floured surface, roll each portion into a 12x3-in. rectangle. Place on greased baking sheets.

2. In a large saucepan, bring water and butter to a boil. Add flour and salt all at once; stir until a smooth ball forms. Remove from the heat; let stand 5 minutes. Add the eggs, one at a time, beating well after each. Add extract; beat until smooth. Spread over dough.

3. Bake at 350° for 1 hour or until puffed and golden brown. Cool on pans for 10 minutes. Combine the sugar, butter, water and vanilla until smooth; spread over the warm puffs. Sprinkle with almonds. Refrigerate leftovers.

Caramel-Pecan Apple Pie

You'll love the aroma in your kitchen—and the smiles on everybody's faces—when you make this scrumptious pie that's drizzled with caramel sauce! It always takes me back home to Virginia and being at my granny's table.

—JEAN CASTRO SANTA ROSA, CALIFORNIA

PREP: 45 MIN. **BAKE:** 55 MIN. + COOLING **MAKES:** 8 SERVINGS

- 7 **cups sliced peeled tart apples**
- 1 **teaspoon lemon juice**
- 1 **teaspoon vanilla extract**
- ¾ **cup chopped pecans**
- ⅓ **cup packed brown sugar**
- 3 **tablespoons sugar**
- 4½ **teaspoons ground cinnamon**
- 1 **tablespoon cornstarch**
- ¼ **cup caramel ice cream topping, room temperature**
- 1 **unbaked pastry shell (9 inches)**
- 3 **tablespoons butter, melted**

STREUSEL TOPPING
- ¾ **cup all-purpose flour**
- ⅔ **cup chopped pecans**
- ¼ **cup sugar**
- 6 **tablespoons cold butter**

- ¼ **cup caramel ice cream topping, room temperature**

1. In a large bowl, toss apples with lemon juice and vanilla. Combine the pecans, sugars, cinnamon and cornstarch; add to the apple mixture and toss to coat. Pour caramel topping over bottom of pastry shell; top with the apple mixture (shell will be full). Drizzle with butter.

2. In a small bowl, combine the flour, pecans and sugar. Cut in the butter until mixture resembles coarse crumbs. Sprinkle over filling.

3. Bake at 350° for 55-65 minutes or until filling is bubbly and topping is browned. Immediately drizzle with caramel topping. Cool on a wire rack.

Cherry Chocolate Cake

Heads will turn when you bring this divine cake to the table. A luscious almond-cherry filling is sandwiched between four layers of rich, tender chocolate cake. The finishing touch is a creamy chocolate frosting. There won't be a crumb left on anyone's plate!

—VICTORIA FAULLING METHUEN, MASSACHUSETTS

PREP: 35 MIN. **BAKE:** 25 MIN. + COOLING
MAKES: 12 SERVINGS

- 1 cup butter, softened
- 1¼ cups sugar
- ¾ cup packed brown sugar
- 3 eggs
- 2 teaspoons vanilla extract
- 2 cups all-purpose flour
- 1 cup baking cocoa
- 1½ teaspoons baking soda
- ½ teaspoon baking powder
- ¼ teaspoon salt
- 1½ cups buttermilk

FILLING

- 1 package (8 ounces) cream cheese, softened
- 6 tablespoons butter, softened
- 1 teaspoon almond extract
- 3 cups confectioners' sugar
- 1 tablespoon maraschino cherry juice
- ⅔ cup finely chopped pecans
- ⅔ cup chopped maraschino cherries

FROSTING

- 3 cups confectioners' sugar
- ½ cup baking cocoa
- ½ cup butter, softened
- ⅓ cup half-and-half cream
- 1 teaspoon vanilla extract
  Chocolate curls and maraschino cherry, optional

1. In a large bowl, cream the butter, sugar and brown sugar until light and fluffy. Add eggs, one at a time, beating well after each addition. Beat in vanilla. Combine the flour, cocoa, baking soda, baking powder and salt; add to the creamed mixture alternately with buttermilk, beating well after each addition.

2. Transfer to two greased and floured 9-in. round baking pans. Bake at 350° for 25-30 minutes or until a toothpick inserted near center comes out clean. Cool for 10 minutes before removing from pans to wire racks to cool completely.

3. In a large bowl, beat the cream cheese, butter and extract until smooth. Add the confectioners' sugar and cherry juice; beat until smooth. Stir in the pecans and cherries. In another bowl, combine frosting ingredients; beat until smooth.

4. Cut each cake horizontally into two layers. Place one cake layer on a serving plate; spread with 1 cup filling. Repeat layers twice. Top with remaining cake layer. Spread the frosting over top and sides of cake. Garnish with chocolate curls and a maraschino cherry if desired. Store in the refrigerator.

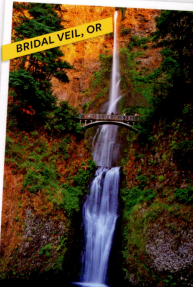

BRIDAL VEIL, OR

One of the country's tallest waterfalls that flows year-round, Multnomah Falls is a whopping 620 feet high.

When Portuguese from Madeira came to Hawaii to work on plantations, they brought with them their tradition of making doughnuts the day before Ash Wednesday. Like other cultures' Fat Tuesday treats, this practice was designed to use up the household stores of butter and sugar before Lent.

Portuguese Doughnuts

Fresh warm doughnuts—*felozes* (fell-o-ses)—are a Portuguese tradition, especially during the Easter season. Some people like to roll these doughnuts without holes in sugar. Others prefer eating them with maple syrup. Either way, they're wonderful! My mother and father came from Portugal and brought some old family recipes with them. When I was growing up, we'd always invite friends and relatives over the night we made felozes. Mother would have the dough rising and then drop pieces into hot oil to fry. We'd eat them as fast as she could make them!

—ISABELLA CASTRO GUSTINE, CALIFORNIA

PREP: 25 MIN. + RISING **COOK:** 30 MIN. **MAKES:** ABOUT 4½ DOZEN

> 2 packages (¼ ounce each) active dry yeast
> ½ cup warm water (110° to 115°)
> 1½ cups warm milk (110° to 115°)
> 5 eggs, lightly beaten
> 5 tablespoons sugar
> ¼ cup butter, softened
> ½ teaspoon salt
> 5 to 5½ cups all-purpose flour
>   Oil for deep-fat frying
>   Granulated sugar or maple syrup

1. In a large bowl, dissolve yeast in warm water. Add the milk, eggs, sugar, butter and salt; beat until smooth. Stir in enough flour to form a soft dough (do not knead). Place in a greased bowl turning once to grease the top. Cover and let rise in a warm place until doubled, about 1 hour.

2. In an electric skillet, heat oil to 375°. Drop tablespoonfuls of dough, a few at a time, into hot oil. Fry for 1½ to 2 minutes on each side or until deep golden brown. Drain on paper towels. Roll warm doughnuts in sugar or serve with syrup.

Surfer Split

Try a California take on the banana split. We predict it will become a favorite at your house—even if you're not a surfer!

—TASTE OF HOME TEST KITCHEN

PREP/TOTAL TIME: 10 MIN. **MAKES:** 1 SERVING

- ½ cup blueberry preserves
- 1 tablespoon water
- ½ cup whipped cream
- 1 medium banana, halved lengthwise
- 1½ cups chocolate ice cream
- 2 tablespoons flaked coconut
- 3 maraschino cherries

1. In a small bowl, mix preserves and water until blended. Spoon whipped cream onto bottom of a dessert dish. Arrange banana halves and three scoops of ice cream over whipped cream. Sprinkle with coconut; drizzle with blueberry mixture. Top with cherries; serve immediately.

Monster Caramel Apples

I dressed up this delicious recipe for caramel apples to create special Halloween treats.

—KAREN ANN BLAND GOVE, KANSAS

PREP: 40 MIN. **COOK:** 30 MIN. + COOLING
MAKES: 8-10 SERVINGS

- 8 to 10 medium apples
- 8 to 10 wooden sticks
- 32 Oreo cookies, coarsely chopped
- 1 cup butter, cubed
- 2 cups packed brown sugar
- 1 can (14 ounces) sweetened condensed milk
- 1 cup light corn syrup
- 1 teaspoon vanilla extract
- 8 squares (1 ounce each) white candy coating, coarsely chopped
- ½ cup orange and brown sprinkles

1. Wash and thoroughly dry apples; insert a wooden stick into each. Place on a waxed paper-lined baking sheet; chill. Place cookie crumbs in a shallow dish; set aside.

2. In a heavy 3-qt. saucepan, combine butter, brown sugar, milk and corn syrup; bring to a boil over medium-high heat. Cook and stir until mixture reaches 248° (firm-ball stage) on a candy thermometer, about 30-40 minutes. Remove from the heat; stir in vanilla.

3. Dip each apple into hot caramel mixture to completely coat, then dip the bottom in cookie crumbs, pressing lightly to adhere. Return to baking sheet to cool.

4. In a microwave, melt candy coating; stir until smooth. Transfer to a small plastic bag; cut a small hole in a corner of bag. Drizzle coating over apples. Decorate with sprinkles.

Monster Caramel Pears: *Substitute pears for the apples.*

Editor's Note: *We recommend that you test your candy thermometer before each use by bringing water to a boil; the thermometer should read 212°. Adjust your recipe temperature up or down based on your test.*

◀◆ dishing about food

The California Milk Advisory Board created this sundae to celebrate National Ice Cream Month and Southern California's surfing heritage. The blueberry jam represents the ocean, the whipped cream peaks are the whitecaps, and the bananas, of course, are the surfboards.

SANTA CRUZ, CA

Nearly smack-dab in the center of California's coast, Santa Cruz is named among the world's best surfing spots time and again.

MEDFORD, OR

Botanists believe the world's tallest pine tree grows in the Rogue River-Siskiyou National Forest. Discovered in 2011, the ponderosa pine measures 268.35 feet tall.

Pine Nut Caramel Shortbread

I simply love pine nuts and decided to use them in place of pecans in a friend's caramel bar recipe. I hope you'll like the end result as well as my family does!

—DARA MICHALSKI SANDY, UTAH

PREP: 30 MIN. **BAKE:** 20 MIN. + COOLING
MAKES: 4 DOZEN

- 1 cup plus 2 tablespoons butter, softened
- ¾ cup packed brown sugar
- 3 cups all-purpose flour
- ½ teaspoon salt

FILLING
- ¾ cup butter, cubed
- ¾ cup packed brown sugar
- ½ cup honey
- ¼ cup sugar
- 3 tablespoons heavy whipping cream
- ½ teaspoon salt
- 2 cups pine nuts
- ¾ teaspoon vanilla extract
    Coarse salt, optional

1. In a large bowl, cream the butter and sugar until light and fluffy. Combine the flour and salt; gradually add to the creamed mixture and mix well. Pat onto the bottom of a greased 15x10x1-in. baking pan. Prick dough thoroughly with a fork.

2. Bake at 375° for 15-18 minutes or until golden brown. Cool on a wire rack. Reduce temperature to 325°.

3. In a large saucepan, combine the butter, brown sugar, honey, sugar, cream and salt. Cook, stirring occasionally, until a candy thermometer reads 234° (soft-ball stage). Remove from the heat; stir in pine nuts and vanilla. Spread evenly over crust.

4. Bake for 20-25 minutes or until bubbly. Place pan on a wire rack. Sprinkle the top with coarse salt if desired. Cool completely. Cut into bars. Store in an airtight container.

Editor's Note: *We recommend that you test your candy thermometer before each use by bringing water to a boil; the thermometer should read 212°. Adjust your recipe temperature up or down based on your test.*

Simple Apricot Tart

Apricots and pumpkin pie spices really complement each other in this truly special tart. Cold vanilla ice cream makes a perfect finishing touch to the soft, warm apricots.

—TASTE OF HOME TEST KITCHEN

PREP: 15 MIN. **BAKE:** 35 MIN. + COOLING
MAKES: 6 SERVINGS

- ¼ cup plus 1 teaspoon sugar, divided
- 2 tablespoons cornstarch
- ½ teaspoon pumpkin pie spice
- 3 cans (15 ounces each) reduced-sugar apricot halves, drained
    Pastry for single-crust pie (9 inches)
- 1 egg white, beaten
- 2 tablespoons sliced almonds
- 1 tablespoon fat-free milk

1. In a large bowl, mix ¼ cup sugar, cornstarch and pumpkin pie spice. Add the apricots and toss to coat.

2. Place pastry on a parchment paper-lined 12-in. pizza pan. Brush with egg white to within 1½ in. of edges. Spoon apricot mixture over egg white; sprinkle with almonds. Fold up edges of pastry over filling, leaving center uncovered. Brush folded pastry with milk; sprinkle with remaining sugar.

3. Bake at 375° for 35-40 minutes or until crust is golden and filling is bubbly. Use parchment paper to slide tart onto a wire rack to cool.

Glazed Blackberry Pie

Every year, I use the first ripe berries of the season to make this wonderful pie.

—**MONICA GROSS** DOWNEY, CALIFORNIA

PREP: 25 MIN. + CHILLING **MAKES:** 6-8 SERVINGS

- 5 **cups fresh blackberries, divided**
- 1 **pastry shell (9 inches), baked**
- 1 **cup water, divided**
- ¾ **cup sugar**
- 3 **tablespoons cornstarch**
  Red food coloring, optional
  Whipped topping

1. Place 2 cups blackberries in pastry shell; set aside. In a saucepan, crush 1 cup berries. Add ¾ cup water. Bring to a boil over medium heat, stirring constantly. Cook and stir for 2 minutes. Press berries through a sieve. Set juice aside and discard pulp.

2. In a saucepan, combine the sugar and cornstarch. Stir in remaining water and reserved juice until smooth. Bring to a boil; cook and stir for 2 minutes or until thickened. Remove from the heat; stir in food coloring if desired. Pour half of the glaze over berries in pastry shell. Stir remaining berries into remaining glaze; carefully spoon over filling.

3. Refrigerate for 3 hours or until set. Garnish with whipped topping. Refrigerate leftovers.

Test Kitchen Tip: *Wild blackberries (bramble berries) work nicely as a substitution.*

General Indexes

Grilled Clam Bake, 38
Grilled Huli Huli Chicken, 416
Grilled Lobster Tail, 15
Grilled Sweet Potato and Red Pepper Salad, 354
Jersey-Style Hot Dogs, 10
Kentucky Grilled Chicken, 130
Lamb Kabobs with Bulgur Pilaf, 32
Marinated Ribeyes, 212
Molasses-Glazed Baby Back Ribs, 137
Pacific Rim Salmon, 416
Pineapple Chicken Salad, 417
Portobello Lamb Chops, 232
Ribeyes with Chili Butter, 332
Sizzling Tex-Mex Fajitas, 302
Smoky Grilled Corn, 343
South Carolina-Style Ribs, 140
Southern Barbecued Chicken, 110
Spicy Shrimp Skewers, 334
Spiedis, 26
Sweet 'n' Smoky Kansas City Ribs, 223
Sweet Onion BBQ Burgers, 387

GRITS
Cheese 'n' Grits Casserole, 156
Chili 'n' Cheese Grits, 347
Chorizo-Stuffed Turkey Breast
 with Mexican Grits, 304
Mom's Tamale Pie, 323
Shredded Barbecue Chicken over Grits, 131
Southern Pan-Fried Quail with
 Cream Cheese Grits, 115
Southern Shrimp & Grits, 126

GROUND BEEF
Aloha Burgers, 384
Bacon-Wrapped Meat Loaf, 212
Cajun Beef Burgers, 140
Chili Rellenos Burgers, 303
Chipotle Sliders, 367
Chuck Wagon Tortilla Stack, 330
Church Supper Hot Dish, 235
Cincinnati Chili, 218
Cobre Valley Casserole, 327
Cool-Kitchen Meat Loaf, 121
Corn Bread with Black-Eyed Peas, 319
Cowboy Baked Beans, 429
Easy Cuban Picadillo, 122
German Meatballs and Gravy, 225
Hanky Pankies, 269
Homemade Pizza, 31
Lakes Burgoo, 123
Lori's Marzetti Bake, 227
Mom's Dynamite Sandwiches, 46
Mom's Tamale Pie, 323
Montana Wildfire Chili, 391
Nacho Mac 'n' Cheese, 352

Onion Loose Meat Sandwiches, 226
Pizza Tot Casserole, 209
Prosciutto-Stuffed Meat Loaf, 14
Runza, 239
Salisbury Steak with Gravy, 211
Salisbury Steak with Onion Gravy, 25
South-of-the-Border Meat Loaf, 307
Southwest Frito Pie, 332
Swedish Meatballs, 215
Sweet Onion BBQ Burgers, 387
Tacoritos, 305
Teriyaki Meatballs, 418
Tourtieres, 35
Zesty Tacos, 309

GUAVA
Guava Coconut Rum Cocktail, 447

HAM & PROSCIUTTO
Baked Oysters with Tasso Cream, 155
Bourbon Baked Ham, 111
Breakfast Mess, 241
Country Ham Sandwiches, 115
Creole Jambalaya, 120
Fry Bread Sandwiches, 320
Gorgonzola Figs with Balsamic Glaze, 454
Ham 'n' Noodle Hot Dish, 229
Ham on Biscuits, 125
Horseshoe Sandwiches, 220
Pineapple Ham Casserole, 415
Prosciutto-Stuffed Meat Loaf, 14
Toasty Deli Hoagie, 34
U.S. Senate Bean Soup, 51

HAZELNUTS
Apple & Blue Cheese on Endive, 455
Chocolate Hazelnut Gateau, 463
Chocolate Hazelnut Tassies, 176
Hazelnut and Pear Salad, 446
Hazelnut Apricot Strudel, 273
Oregon's Hazelnut Chocolate Chip Cookie, 467

HOMINY
South Coast Hominy, 154

HONEY
Cranberry Honey Butter, 456
Four-Grain Bread, 267
Honey-Fried Walleye, 236
Honey-Glazed Lamb Chops, 406
Honey Whole Wheat Bread, 245
Peach Wine Coolers, 440
Persimmon Salad with Honey
 Spiced Vinaigrette, 171
Teriyaki Meatballs, 418
Utah Buttermilk Scones, 432

ICE CREAM & FROZEN DESSERTS
Date Shake, 475
Georgia Peach Ice Cream, 181
It's It Ice Cream Sandwiches, 464
Mexican Ice Cream, 380
Old-Time Custard Ice Cream, 276
Raspberry Ice Cream, 104
Super Banana Splits, 276
Surfer Split, 479

JAMS & JELLIES
Cinnamon Blueberry Jam, 74
Mixed Citrus Marmalade, 149
Over-the-Top Cherry Jam, 258
Pomegranate Jelly, 446
Texas Jalapeno Jelly, 341

JICAMA
Jicama Slaw with Peanuts, 342
Southwestern Watermelon Salad, 344
Tex-Mex Spinach Salad, 347

LAMB
Burgundy Lamb Shanks, 9
Colorado Lamb Chili, 396
Honey-Glazed Lamb Chops, 406
Irish Stew, 16
Lamb Kabobs with Bulgur Pilaf, 32
Lemon-Herb Leg of Lamb, 394
Portobello Lamb Chops, 232
Rack of Lamb with Figs, 385
Schreiner's Baked Lamb Shanks, 215
Scotch Broth, 50

LEMON
Citrus Chicken Fajitas, 330
Citrus Veggie Chicken Fajitas, 330
Lemon Chess Pie, 178
Lemon-Filled Coconut Cake, 194
Lemon-Herb Leg of Lamb, 394
Lemonade Icebox Pie, 202
Mai Tai, 438
Mexican Carnitas, 338
Mixed Citrus Marmalade, 149
Shortbread Lemon Tart, 183
Zesty Lemon Curd, 453

LENTILS
Lentil-Tomato Soup, 435
Lentil Vegetable Soup, 441

LIMES
Beer Margaritas, 251
Citrus Chicken Fajitas, 330
Citrus Veggie Chicken Fajitas, 330

OKRA

Chicken and Okra Gumbo, 108
Southern Fried Okra, 157

OLIVES

Antipasto Sub, 10
Black-and-Blue Pizzas, 114
Chicken Tamales, 317
Deluxe Muffuletta, 111
Easy Cuban Picadillo, 122
Herbed Artichoke Cheese Tortellini, 391
Tomatillo Relish, 346

ONIONS

Blueberry-Orange Onion Salad, 451
Caramelized-Onion Pork, 386
Company Onion Soup, 458
Fried Onion Rings, 171
Herbed Fennel and Onion, 445
Sweet Onion BBQ Burgers, 387
Vidalia Onion Bake, 171

ORANGE

Blueberry-Orange Onion Salad, 451
Cuban Pork Roast, 110
Fruity Rum Punch, 448
Mexican Carnitas, 338
Mixed Citrus Marmalade, 149
Orange-Glazed Crullers, 90
Orange Julius, 53
Orange Meringue Pie, 199
Orange Natilla Custard Pie, 190
Orange-Pecan Hot Wings, 161
Tequila Sunrise, 362

OYSTERS

Baked Oysters with Tasso Cream, 155
Crispy Oven-Fried Oysters, 67
Oyster Stuffing, 162

PANCAKES

Flaxseed Oatmeal Pancakes, 214
Latkes with Lox, 46
Maple Pancakes, 17
Swedish Pancakes, 240
Sweet Potato Pancakes with Caramel Sauce, 119

PARSNIPS

Roasted Root Veggies, 262
Triple Mash with Horseradish
　Bread Crumbs, 263

PASTA *(also see Noodles)*

Appetizer

　Toasted Cheese Ravioli, 263

Main Dishes

　Artichoke Shrimp Linguine, 387
　Cajun Shrimp Lasagna Roll-Ups, 129
　Crawfish Fettuccine, 120
　Fiddlehead Shrimp Salad, 41
　Hearty Chili Mac, 248
　Herbed Artichoke Cheese Tortellini, 391
　Morel Mushroom Ravioli, 228
　Penne alla Vodka Sauce, 17
　Pesto Scallops Vermicelli, 13
　Sausage and Pumpkin Pasta, 213
　Spicy Sesame Shrimp & Noodle Salad, 405
　Tofu Manicotti, 410
　Vegetable Pad Thai, 400

Side Dishes

　Bistro Mac & Cheese, 444
　Crumb-Topped Bistro Mac, 444
　Four-Cheese Macaroni, 246
　Homey Mac & Cheese, 149
　Lamb Kabobs with Bulgur Pilaf, 32
　Mushroom-Swiss Mac & Cheese, 76
　Nacho Mac 'n' Cheese, 352

PEACHES

Baked Blueberry & Peach Oatmeal, 33
Butterscotch Peach Pie, 191
Georgia Peach Ice Cream, 181
Peach and Raspberry Clafouti, 465
Peach Chutney, 152
Peach Wine Coolers, 440
South Carolina Cobbler, 175

PEANUT BUTTER

Chocolate-Covered Buckeyes, 288
Chocolate Fluffernutter Sandwiches, 14
Grandma's Tandy Kake, 85
Popcorn Delight, 279
Spicy Peanut Soup, 243
Sunflower-Cherry Granola Bars, 279
Toasted PB & Banana Sandwiches, 109

PEANUTS

Georgia Peanut Salsa, 148
Jicama Slaw with Peanuts, 342
Peanutty Chicken, 128
Popcorn Delight, 279
Spicy Peanut Soup, 243

PEARS

Apple Pear Pie, 179
Ginger-Pear Upside-Down Pie, 289
Hazelnut and Pear Salad, 446
Monster Caramel Pears, 479

PEAS *see Black-Eyed Peas; Split Peas*

PECANS

Bourbon Chocolate Pecan Pie, 174
Bourbon Pecan Pralines, 183
Candied Pecans, 189
Caramel-Pecan Apple Pie, 476
Chocolate Mexican Wedding Cakes, 379
Chocolate Pecan Torte, 172
Creamy Banana Pecan Pie, 468
Double Nut Baklava, 469
German Chocolate Cake, 368
Lady Baltimore Cake, 182
Mayan Chocolate Biscotti, 375
Nutty Oven-Fried Chicken, 124
Old-Fashioned Jam Cake, 187
Orange-Pecan Hot Wings, 161
Pecan Chicken with Blue Cheese Sauce, 226
Pineapple Lime Gelatin, 433
Sad Cake, 191
Southern Lane Cake, 185
Texas Pecan Pie, 371

PEPPERS, SWEET *(also see Chili Peppers)*

Antipasto Sub, 10
Black Beans with Brown Rice, 315
Chicken Pesto Pizza, 425
Citrus Chicken Fajitas, 330
Citrus Veggie Chicken Fajitas, 330
Country Captain Chicken, 117
Easy Gazpacho, 350
Grilled Sweet Potato and Red Pepper Salad, 354
Hoppin' John, 152
Jersey-Style Hot Dogs, 10
Montana Wildfire Chili, 391
Nacho Mac 'n' Cheese, 352
Pat's King of Steaks Philly Cheese Steak, 12
Rosemary-Garlic Roast Beef, 417
Teriyaki Meatballs, 418
Texas Caviar, 345
Tomatillo Relish, 346
Viva Panzanella, 442

PERSIMMONS

Persimmon Pudding, 295
Persimmon Salad with Honey
　Spiced Vinaigrette, 171

PICKLES & PICKLED

Fried Pickle Coins, 166
German-Style Pickled Eggs, 266

Cranberry Pork Medallions, 28
Curried Tofu with Rice, 412
Spicy Sesame Shrimp & Noodle Salad, 405
Stir-Fried Asparagus, 438
Thai Curry with Shrimp & Coconut, 392
Vegetable Pad Thai, 400

STRAWBERRIES
Five-Fruit Pie, 80
Frozen Strawberry Margaritas, 344
Ozark Mountain Berry Pie, 270
Strawberry Biscuit Shortcake, 177
Strawberry Cream Puffs, 272
Strawberry Rhubarb Pie, 187
Strawberry Shortcake, 373
Very Berry Crisp, 461

SUNFLOWER KERNELS
Crisp Sunflower Cookies, 274
Nuts and Seeds Trail Mix, 365
Nutty Berry Trail Mix, 447
Sunflower-Cherry Granola Bars, 279

SWEET POTATOES
Candied Sweet Potatoes, 166
Grilled Sweet Potato and Red Pepper Salad, 354
Southern Sweet Potato Pie, 195
Spicy Peanut Soup, 243
Sweet Potato Fries, 146
Sweet Potato Muffins, 168
Sweet Potato Pancakes with Caramel Sauce, 119
West African Chicken Stew, 403

SWEET ROLLS *see Yeast Breads*

TACOS
Fish Tacos with Avocado Sauce, 397
Lime Chicken Tacos, 312
Tacoritos, 305
Zesty Tacos, 309

TAMALE
Chicken Tamales, 317

TEA
Sweet Tea Concentrate, 151

TEQUILA
Fresh Lime Margaritas, 344
Frozen Lime Margaritas, 344
Frozen Strawberry Margaritas, 344
Long Island Iced Tea, 48
Tequila Sunrise, 362
Texas Tea, 154

TOFU
Curried Tofu with Rice, 412
Miso Soup with Tofu and Enoki, 431
Tofu Manicotti, 410
Vegetable Pad Thai, 400

TOMATILLOS
Braised Pork with Tomatillos, 336
Chicken Mole Ole, 335
Huevos Rancheros with Tomatillo Sauce, 313
Salsa Verde, 365
Tomatillo Relish, 346

TOMATOES
Arizona Chicken, 331
Authentic Spanish Rice, 366
Black-and-Blue Pizzas, 114
Bloody Mary, 71
Brunswick Stew, 142
Chicago Deep-Dish Pizza, 210
Cobb Salad, 415
Colorful Tomato 'n' Mozzarella Salad, 436
Company Swordfish, 398
Country Captain Chicken, 117
Creole Chicken, 139
Creole Jambalaya, 120
Creole Steaks, 143
Easy Gazpacho, 350
Fire-Roasted Tomato Salsa, 360
Fried Green Tomatoes, 160
Guacamole, 352
Herbed Artichoke Cheese Tortellini, 391
Lentil-Tomato Soup, 435
Lori's Marzetti Bake, 227
Louisiana Red Beans and Rice, 135
Manhattan Clam Chowder, 72
Marinated Tomatoes, 159
Penne alla Vodka Sauce, 17
Pineapple Salsa, 459
Southwestern Barley Salad, 459
Tomato Sandwiches, 129
Viva Panzanella, 442

TORTILLAS & TORTILLA CHIPS
Beef Flautas, 306
Black Bean Veggie Enchiladas, 325
Cherry Pie Chimis, 370
Chicken Tortilla Bake, 319
Chicken Tostadas with Mango Salsa, 326
Chimichangas, 304
Chuck Wagon Tortilla Stack, 330
Citrus Chicken Fajitas, 330
Citrus Veggie Chicken Fajtas, 330
Cobre Valley Casserole, 327
Corn Soup with Pico de Gallo, 363

Fish Tacos with Avocado Sauce, 397
Green Chili Pork Stew, 312
King Ranch Casserole, 325
Land of Enchantment Posole, 316
Lime Chicken Tacos, 312
Mexican Carnitas, 338
Microwave Texas Nachos, 356
Migas, My Way, 318
Nacho Mac 'n' Cheese, 352
Pinto Bean Chili, 327
Sizzling Tex-Mex Fajitas, 302
Southwestern Beef Burritos, 337
Spicy Pork Tostadas, 339
Steak Burritos, 329
Stuffed Breakfast Burritos, 311
Tacoritos, 305
Tortilla Dressing, 357
Tortilla-Vegetable Chicken Soup, 340

TOSTADA
Spicy Pork Tostadas, 339

TURKEY
Black Bean 'n' Pumpkin Chili, 234
Blue Cheese Clubs, 231
Chorizo-Stuffed Turkey Breast
   with Mexican Grits, 304
Herb-Roasted Turkey, 216
Hot Brown Sandwiches, 113
Toasty Deli Hoagie, 34
Tropical Turkey Meat Loaf, 419

TURNIPS
New England Boiled Dinner, 22
Roasted Root Veggies, 262
Turnip Casserole, 69

VEAL
Bacon-Wrapped Meat Loaf, 212
Mock Chicken Legs, 24

VEGETABLES *(also see specific kinds)*
Beef Stew with Sesame Seed Biscuits, 11
Brunswick Stew, 142
Chicken and Okra Gumbo, 108
Chuck Wagon Tortilla Stack, 330
Church Supper Hot Dish, 235
Corn Bread Layered Salad, 165
Creamy Succotash, 151
Georgia Peanut Salsa, 148
Irish Stew, 16
Korean Wontons, 60
Lakes Burgoo, 123
Lentil Vegetable Soup, 441

Alphabetical Indexes

Photo Credits

Pat's King Of Steaks, 12
Old Sturbridge Village, 19
DiscoverLancasterPA.com, 20, 65
DiscoverLancasterPA.com / Terry Ross, 42
Jim Bush / Visit Buffalo Niagara, 59
Waldorf Astoria, 62
Delmonico's NYC, 64
Brand X Pictures / Punchstock, 70
Mushroom Festival, 76
D.G. Yuengling & Son, Inc., 89
Elvis image used by permission, Elvis
    Presley Enterprises, Inc., 109
Myrtle Beach Area Chamber of Commerce, 117
Jack Daniel Distillery, 137
North Carolina Sweet Potato Commission, 146
Arkansas Department of Parks
    & Tourism, 147, 166, 177
Florida Department of Citrus, 149
Mississippi Development Authority, 154, 197
Tamika Moore, 155
Kentucky Derby Museum, 161
Brennan's Restaurant, 175
Corbis / Punchstock, 181
National Quilt Museum, 187
Bell Buckle Chamber of Commerce, 199
Garrison Convention & Visitors Bureau, 207
Kelly Weber, 208
Pizzeria Uno Corporation, 210
Johnsonville Sausage, 221
Hormel Foods, 241
Corbis / Punchstock, 245, 279
Wisconsin State Fair, 272
Noble Popcorn Farms, 281
Lanesboro Area Chamber of Commerce, 287
Brand X Pictures / Punchstock, 290
State Fair of Texas, 307
Robert Love, 308
Chile Pepper Institute, NMSU, 321
National Park Service, 348
Arizona Biltmore, 362
Dr Pepper Museum, Waco, TX, 377
TCL Chinese Theatre, 415
Kathy Stefani / Artichoke Festival, 427
Trader Vic's, 438
National Lentil Festival, 441
Buena Vista Cafe, 443
California Fig Advisory Board, Fresno, CA, 454
Oregon Raspberry & Blackberry
    Commission, 462, 481
Rocko Billy, 471

Shutterstock.com Photos

June Marie Sobrito, 10
Teresa Levite, 41
Kuttelvaserova Stuchelova, 47
David Hughes, 50
David W. Leindecker, 52
rSnapshotPhotos, 53
Liviu Toader, 66
littleny, 81
Douglas Litchfield, 93
Brittany Courville, 94
Dennis Donohue, 98
Dave Newman, 100
Rudy Balasko, 102
Lone Wolf Photos, 118
Wendy Kaveney Photography, 120
Matty Symons, 124
Wildnerdpix, 128
Zack Frank, 138
Anne Power, 139
Brandon Alms, 141
Michelle Donahue Hillison, 142
Lawrence Roberg, 145
Dana Ward, 153
Phil Anthony, 157
Jason Patrick Ross, 160
spirit of america, 171, 179
Dave Newman, 172
Jason Tench, 182
Svetlana Larina, 189
Joyfnp, 192
Noam Wind, 196
zhuda, 198
Chicago, Andrey Bayda, 204
Rudy Balasko, 211
Stephane Bidouze, 214
nikitsin.smugmug.com, 215
Tom Reichner, 225
unverdorben jr, 228
cappi thompson, 236
Henryk Sadura, 239
Phantom Photos, 242
miker, 243
Action Sports Photography, 252
Stefanie Mohr Photography, 255

Lijuan Guo, 259
Snehit, 265
Tammy Venable, 266
Robert J. Daveant, 269
spirit of america, 271
MBoe, 277
Bryan Busovicki, 283
lphoto, 286
aceshot1, 288
QueSeraSera, 295
Photo Image, 296
John Hoffman, 303
pmphoto, 314
gary yim, 316
spirit of america, 318
Brandon Seidel, 322
Tricia Daniel, 328
Daniel Gratton, 331
GSPhotography, 343
nito, 347
Arto Hakola, 356
Sumikophoto, 361
Timothy OLeary, 365
Viktoriya Field, 371
Galyna Andrushko, 379
littlesam, 380
Don Fink, 391
Lynn Watson, 393
Andrey Bayda, 401
Liem Bahneman, 402
tusharkoley, 409
Radoslaw Lecyk, 413
bierchen, 422
Rafael Ramirez Lee, 425
Denton Rumsey, 428
JoLin, 434
Apollofoto, 447
Kostiantyn Ablazov, 453
guynamedjames, 459
Jeffrey T. Kreulen, 460
spirit of america, 465
Wollertz, 466
Christian Roberts-Olsen, 477
Rick Lord, 480

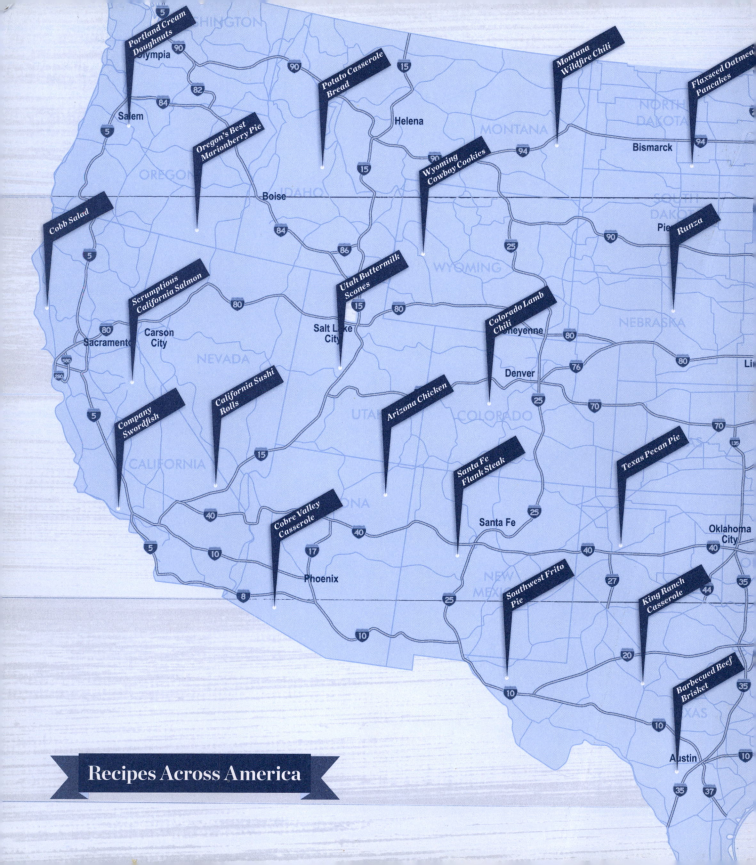

Recipes Across America